W9-CON-808

DOMINION OF THE NORTH

S

J

M

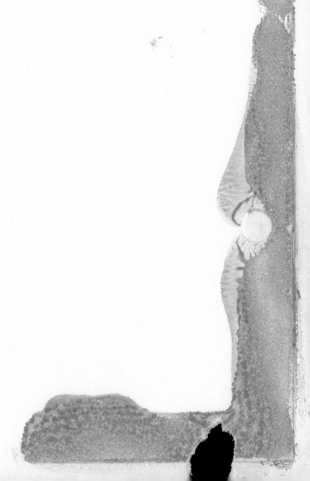

Also by Donald Creighton

DOMINION OF THE NORTH

A HISTORY OF CANADA

New Edition

BY DONALD CREIGHTON

THE MACMILLAN COMPANY OF CANADA LIMITED
TORONTO

Preface to the New Edition

THE FIRST EDITION of *Dominion of the North,* which was published in 1944, ended with the Canadian declaration of war against Germany on September 10, 1939. In this new edition, I have brought the account down to contemporary times by the addition of a chapter on Canada during and after the Second World War; and I have taken the opportunity of making a few corrections of fact or interpretation in the original text.

I should like to record my thanks to my colleagues, Professor J. M. S. Careless, who has given me the benefit of his advice on the revision and enlargement of the book, and Professor R. A. Spencer, who kindly permitted me to make use of the manuscript of his forthcoming volume in the series *Canada in World Affairs.*

D. G. CREIGHTON

Toronto, May, 1957

Contents

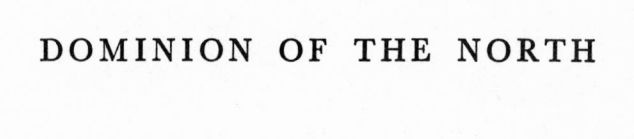

DOMINION OF THE NORTH

CHAPTER ONE

THE FOUNDING OF
NEW FRANCE

[*I*]

IT WAS the Norsemen who first discovered the giant stepping-stones which link northern Europe with northern North America. In the ninth and tenth centuries, these dynamic Scandinavian peoples were driven outward from their homeland by repeated explosive bursts of energy; and their savage raids and restless migrations carried them to places so scattered and remote as Russia, northern France, Sicily, and the British Isles. Somewhere about the middle of the ninth century they colonized Iceland; they found and occupied Greenland a little over a hundred years later; and it was apparently in the year 1000, on a long, troubled voyage from Norway to Greenland, that Leif Eriksson was blown far out of his course by storms and found for the first time the unknown countries of the west. After that first amazing discovery, the Norsemen from Greenland must have made many voyages to the strange lands which the *Saga of Eric the Red* called Markland and Vinland, and which could only have lain in North America. Almost certainly the Greenland Vikings must have ventured south along the Atlantic coastline at least as far as the Gulf of St. Lawrence. They may even have found that other great northern gateway to the continent, Hudson Bay; but though it is conceivable that a body of Norsemen may have struck out on an expedition south-westward from James Bay or Hudson Bay, the evidence so far produced in support of such an overland journey has either been rejected or has yet to have its authenticity satisfactorily established. At intervals for over three centuries these Norse voyages to the new continent may have continued. But no permanent settlements were ever made; and sometime in the fourteenth century the Greenland colony itself mysteriously vanished. All that remained of these half-fabulous exploits was an unsubstantial legend of the wondrous islands of the west.

Once the discovery of Columbus had awakened a general interest in western exploration, there was more than one reason why men should return to the northern route which the Vikings had discovered so long before. John Cabot, who, like Columbus, expected to sail direct to the far east, seems to have realized that the shortest route to Asia would lie along the high latitudes; and his successors in North Atlantic exploration, the Portuguese Corte Reals and his own son Sebastian Cabot, were already looking for a quick northwest passage around the great land mass which people were beginning to realize must lie between Europe and Asia. These navigators from England and Portugal discovered the shadowy lost empire of the Norsemen — Greenland, Labrador, Newfoundland, perhaps even Hudson Bay itself. And it was their discoveries which brought to light the major economic interest which was to draw the great nations of Europe in rivalry towards the North Atlantic for centuries to come. In 1497, when John Cabot sailed home from the discovery of Newfoundland, reports began to circulate that 'the sea there is swarming with fish'; and, in fact, a combination of circumstances had made the region perhaps the greatest fishing ground in the world. Once, in the remote geological past, the northern Appalachian Highlands and the Atlantic Coastal Plain of North America had extended out past Nova Scotia and Newfoundland; but ages later great masses of the low-lying plain had sunk below the sea.

Newfoundland, Nova Scotia, and the islands of the Gulf, the highest plateaus of this great continental shelf, still remained above the water. But below the ocean were other plateaus which came to be called banks; and these shallow areas, from Georges Bank to the Grand Bank south of Newfoundland, were favourite breeding-places of the prolific cod. In the very first years of the sixteenth century, the French and Portuguese were already established in the new fishing grounds. In France there was a steady market for cod, the 'beef of the ocean,' for fast days made salt fish a regular necessity and the rapid deterioration of fresh meat gave it a frequent preference. The French had ample supplies of solar salt, produced by the evaporation of sea water, which was needed in large quantities when the fish were stored away without drying; and, during the first half of the sixteenth century, French fishermen from Brittany, the Bay of Biscay, and the Channel ports outstripped all their competitors in the new Newfoundland fishing grounds. Before ever Jacques Cartier set sail on the King's mission, their little fishing ships had crept up the north shore of Newfoundland and into the Straits of Belle Isle.

Francis I, King of France, whose reign nearly paralleled that of Henry VIII in England, showed a far more active interest in America than either his royal English contemporary or his own descendants. In 1523 he commissioned Giovanni da Verazzano, who next year sailed up the coast of North America and claimed the land as Nova Francia for the French King. Francis I's first choice had thus fallen upon an Italian; but when he again enjoyed an interval of peace in his long struggle with Charles V, King of Spain and Holy Roman Emperor, he sought and found an official explorer among his own subjects, the hardy fishing population of Northern France. Jacques Cartier, the Breton of St. Malo, was an experienced navigator who, in all probability, had already made several fishing expeditions to Newfoundland; and the crew he took with him in his first voyage of

1534 was made up of fishermen. All along the north-east
coast of Newfoundland and into the Straits of Belle Isle,
the route was a familiar one, with stops at places already
well known to the French; but Cartier sailed past the 'stones
and horrible rugged rocks' of Labrador, and through the
fog and storm of the barren west coast of Newfoundland and
into the Gulf of St. Lawrence. It was midsummer, late June
and early July. The sun was hot, there were blue skies, and
the islands and the coastline of the Gulf were rich with the
luxuriant growth of northern summer. The French ships
passed the Magdalen Islands, skirted a part of Prince Edward
Island, followed the north shore of New Brunswick up to
Cape Gaspé, and then struck across the Gulf to the island of
Anticosti. They found strawberries, raspberries, gooseberry
bushes, and 'Provins Roses'; and there were fine meadows full
of wild wheat and oats and dense forests of trees which were
'wonderfully beautiful and very fragrant.' To the great
bay which now separates New Brunswick from Quebec, they
gave the name of Bay of Chaleur because of the heat which
they encountered; and on July 24, 1534, they formally
laid claim to the whole of this great new land by erecting a
huge cross, thirty feet high, at the mouth of Gaspé harbour.
Below the cross-bar they fixed a shield, with three fleurs-de-
lys in relief, and above it a board with the words 'Vive le
Roy de France' in gothic characters. And then they all
knelt down, with hands joined in prayer, and worshipped
the cross in the presence of the Indians.

The next summer, when Cartier returned on his second
voyage of exploration, he found the river which he had
missed in 1534. It was the route to Canada, the 'River of
Canada,' as they came to call it; and Cartier's Indian guides
assured him gravely that 'one could make one's way so far
up the river that they had never heard of anyone reaching
the head of it.' It flowed from mysterious dominions to the
west and south-west, from the Kingdom of Canada, the Kingdom of Hochelaga, and the Kingdom of the Saguenay. The

very grandeur of the titles may have helped to fill the French with expectations of refined and wealthy monarchies. During September, when the whole river valley was rich with the fruits of early autumn, they crept cautiously up the stream towards these countries whose wealth might rival that of Mexico. They passed the black chasm between sheer, sombre cliffs, from which issued the Saguenay River, leaving unexplored this kingdom of the north-west. But when they reached Stadacona, the capital of the Kingdom or Province of Canada, which stood on part of the site now occupied by the City of Quebec, they found only a poor, primitive Indian village; and Hochelaga, built on the island where now stands the City of Montreal, was almost equally dismal and disappointing. In all probability these were Iroquoian villages. Stadacona may have been a Mohawk town, Hochelaga an Onondaga stronghold; and, if the French had only known it, these tribes, with their skill in agriculture and their talent for political organization, had advanced far beyond the other native societies of north-eastern North America in the development of their culture. But, for the moment, the naïve and credulous French were profoundly disappointed. There was nothing here to satisfy cupidity or to excite the imagination. And then Cartier climbed the high hill back of Hochelaga, which he named Mount Royal, and surveyed the landscape for more than thirty leagues around. He could see the St. Lawrence, 'grand, large, et spacieulx' — the waterway to the rich Laurentian Lowlands, to the Great Lakes, to the heart of the entire continent — flowing from the remote horizon of the south-west, flowing in white violence through the rapids at Lachine and onwards towards the ocean. To the north he could see a range of low, blue mountains, the sombre Laurentian hills, the beginnings of the vast geological system of the Precambrian Shield, which was the ancient, battered core of the entire continent, and which surrounded Hudson Bay in an enormous lop-sided triangle of gnarled, rocky upland nearly two million square

miles in extent. Along the edge of these uplands, so the
Indians told him, ran another river from the west, a river
which in the seventeenth century the French would learn to
call the Ottawa.

Cartier was by all accounts a sober, cautious, and practical
man. He had just been profoundly disappointed in his
hopes. But he could hardly fail to be roused by such a
prospect. The very completeness of his disillusionment in
the provinces of Canada and Hochelaga compelled him to fix
all his remaining hopes upon the one shadowy kingdom
that remained. 'We thought,' writes the chronicler, 'this
river [Ottawa] must be the one that flows past the kingdom
and province of the Saguenay'; and the Indians, both at
Hochelaga and back in Canada, did nothing to discourage
this belief. The boundaries of the Kingdom of the Saguenay were pushed out until it became a kind of vast fabulous
island, encircled by rivers, of which the Saguenay, the St.
Lawrence, and the Ottawa were three. As the Indians
warmed to their loving task of description, the magnificence
of the kingdom increased and its store of copper and gold
and rubies accumulated; and in the end it seemed to combine all the accustomed comforts of the old world of Europe,
and all the imagined riches of Mexico and the Indies. The
picture of the Saguenay must have comforted Cartier in the
ordeals that followed in the next few months. He knew
the gorgeous summer of the Gulf of St. Lawrence and the
rich autumn of the river valley; but he had never spent a
winter at Quebec. During that winter of 1535-36, there
was more than four feet of snow on the ground. The ships
lay frozen up from November 15 to April 15; and twenty-
five of Cartier's men died of scurvy. As soon as spring came,
on May 6, 1536, the French set sail, taking with them Chief
Donnacona, 'Lord of the Canadians,' and other Indians, in
order that they might retell the marvels of the Saguenay to
those in authority at home.

The French did not come again until 1541. There **is**

little doubt that Francis I was interested; but his long contest, both diplomatic and military, with Charles V closed in upon him again, and it was not until some years after Cartier's return that he could devote much time or money to North America. The settlement of Canada and the discovery of the Saguenay were thus delayed; but the expedition, when eventually it was dispatched, was far more ambitious than anything which the French were to attempt again for nearly a hundred years. A court favourite, Jean François de la Rocque, Sieur de Roberval, was appointed commander of the enterprise with full political authority as lieutenant-general of the King; and Cartier was commissioned captain-general and master pilot of the fleet. Several hundred soldiers, sailors, skilled tradesmen, and colonists were entrusted to the care of the leaders. They were provided with ten ships, provisions supposedly sufficient for two years, quantities of *matériel*, and a numerous herd of domestic animals. They were expected, with this imposing and well-equipped expedition, to establish a solid colony in Canada, and from it as a base to search for a passage to the Orient and to discover and conquer the riches of the Kingdom of the Saguenay.

The whole scheme seemed full of promise; but, almost from the beginning, everything began to go wrong. At the last moment, Roberval was not ready to go in the spring of 1541, and Cartier sailed away alone, taking five of the ships. He wintered in Canada at Cap Rouge, about nine miles above Quebec, at a place which he called Charlesbourg-Royal. The previous autumn he had ventured up the river as far at least as the mouth of the Ottawa and he may at last have become a little sceptical of the Indian tales about the Saguenay. He was, at any rate, extremely worried about the Indians themselves, for he quarrelled with them during the winter and he feared their hostility. By the spring of 1542 he was ready to return to France. All the previous autumn he had waited in vain in Canada for Roberval; but

now he met the Lieutenant-General when he least expected
or desired to do so, in the harbour of St. John's, Newfoundland, when he was well on his way home. The tardy Roberval, at length en route to Canada, was in command of three
ships and a large company, including soldiers. He was prepared to meet any presumptuous Indians and he promptly
ordered Cartier to go back with him to Canada. But for
some reason Cartier's interest in the enterprise had completely evaporated. He was certainly apprehensive of the
Indians. He may very well have considered that two winters
on the St. Lawrence were enough, if not more than enough,
for one man. At all events, he 'stole privily away the next
night' with his ships, and continued on his way to France.
Roberval, in his turn, went on alone to Canada. He did
little more than repeat Cartier's experiment of the previous
winter and by the autumn of 1543 he too was back in France
again.

It is probable that neither Cartier nor Roberval got much
beyond the mouth of the Ottawa in their explorations. They
never found the passage to China or the fabulous wealth of
the Kingdom of the Saguenay. Even the barrels of Laurentian rock which Cartier carried home under the fond delusion that it contained 'diamants' and 'leaves of fine gold
as thicke as a man's nayle' turned out, not unnaturally, to
be highly disappointing. There is gold in the Precambrian
Shield, but it was not until the twentieth century that the
process of chemical extraction was developed. And the
'faire, pollished and excellently cut' stones that 'glister as it
were sparkles of fire' did little more than enrich the French
language with a proverb for the false and fraudulent: 'Voilà
un diamant de Canada!' The curtain dropped on these ambitious official enterprises, with their fleets of ships and
troops of soldiers and colonists. They had failed of their
ostensible objectives; their consequences seemed negligible.
And yet for the fishermen, the real makers of French power
in north-eastern North America, they had important results.

Cartier may have been subject to occasional delusions of grandeur; but he was an experienced fisherman and sober navigator. He found the two gateways to the Gulf of St. Lawrence through the Straits of Belle Isle and Cabot Strait, he systematically explored the Gulf and the lower St. Lawrence River, and he discovered new and valuable fishing grounds. In the wake of his pioneering vessels, the fishing ships of the French and Bretons ventured westward through Cabot Strait towards the gulf, and Cape Breton Island received the name which it bears to this day. The fishery increased its area; and, as it crept closer to the shores of North America, its character began significantly to alter.

The key to these changes is to be found in the homely but essential ingredient of salt. The French, with plentiful supplies of cheap solar salt, could afford to be lavish in their use of an article which the fog-bound English were forced largely to procure from abroad and to employ with strict economy. While the French at first seem to have relied mainly on the 'green' fishery and to have salted down their wet fresh cod as soon as caught, the English developed the 'dry' fishery and exposed their fish to the sun and wind upon the shore. The first method required quantities of salt, relatively few men, and little equipment, and yielded a commodity suited to trade in near-by home markets. The second method produced a dry, hard cure adapted to foreign trade in distant southern markets, and required much less salt but considerably more men and equipment on shore. The dry fishery enabled the English to force their way into the Spanish market in the latter part of the sixteenth century, when the defeat of the Armada had marked the beginning of the decline of Spain's imperial and maritime power. It was this commercial success which helped to persuade the French to diversify their own methods and to adopt the successful practices of their adroit rivals. They had been first in the field. Their fishing ships were to be found in great numbers upon the banks, and along the

shores of Newfoundland, Labrador, and Cape Breton. But
the English had already occupied the east coast of the Avalon
peninsula in Newfoundland as a region suitable for the dry
fishery; and the French were driven on towards the outlying
areas of the fishing grounds in search of harbours and
beaches suitable for the drying of fish. In part they were
compelled by the ever-increasing demands of their own
domestic market, and in part by the attractions of the Mediterranean and Spanish trade which the English had already
opened up. They found suitable areas for the dry fishery on
the shores of Cape Breton, Nova Scotia, Gaspé, and the Gulf
of St. Lawrence. They had discovered the continent; and at
once they came in touch with its native inhabitants, the
Indians.

From the beginning the fishery had involved occasional
brief meetings with the aborigines of the North American
coastline. These contacts, with the development of the dry-
fishing industry, simply became more frequent and more
prolonged. In the dry fishery, suitable harbours and
beaches were chosen with care, for a lengthy stay. A good
deal of durable equipment had to be erected, such as lodg-
ings for the fishermen, platforms for the stowage of fresh-
caught fish, and 'flakes' or stages for drying them where
good wind-swept rocks or beaches were not available. These
favoured places, so carefully selected and prepared, were
occupied by European fishermen for weeks and even for
months at regularly repeated intervals. Inevitably there
followed contact with the Indians and barter for the one
thing of value which they possessed, their furs. The origins
of this exchange must lie far back at the beginning of the
North Atlantic fishing industry; but the first recorded instance of it in Canadian history was supplied by the chronicler of Jacques Cartier's voyage of discovery in 1534. On
July 6 of that year, so runs the record, 'we caught sight of
two fleets of Indian canoes that were crossing from one side
[of Chaleur Bay] to the other, which numbered in all some

forty or fifty canoes. Upon one of the fleets reaching this
point, there sprang out and landed a large number of Indians, who set up a great clamour and made frequent signs
to us to come on shore, holding up to us some furs on sticks.'
The first sight of the Indians in such numbers apparently
intimidated Cartier's Frenchmen; and there was no trading
until they were visited by a much smaller group of the savages on the following day. The Indians 'held up some furs
of small value, with which they clothe themselves. We likewise made signs to them that we wished them no harm, and
sent two men on shore, to offer them some knives and other
iron goods, and a red cap to give to their chief. Seeing this,
they sent on shore part of their people with some of their
furs; and the two parties traded together. The savages
showed a marvellously great pleasure in possessing and obtaining these iron wares and other commodities, dancing and
going through many ceremonies, and throwing salt water
over their heads with their hands. They bartered all they
had to such an extent that all went back naked without anything on them; and they made signs that they would return
on the morrow with more furs.'

Evidently this was far from the first time that such a trans-
action had occurred. Each party knew too well what the
other required. The experienced Indians immediately advertised their furs from a distance, and Cartier had thought-
fully brought from France the most acceptable kind of trade
goods. At this early stage the fur trade was still unimportant, it was still incidental to the fishery; and for a long
time to come the barter for furs must have occurred normally at those points on the coastline of Cape Breton, Nova
Scotia, and Gaspé which the French fishermen had selected
for the drying of their fish. It was probably the Basques
and Biscayans who pushed furthest into the Gulf and up the
St. Lawrence River. They came to dry fish, to catch whales,
to kill walrus, and to trade with the Indians; and gradually
they established Tadoussac, at the mouth of the Saguenay

River, as the western rendezvous for the fur trade. From Tadoussac the precious tools and weapons of the French were carried up the Saguenay and down the St. Maurice, the Gatineau, and the upper Ottawa, to the Montagnais, Algonkin, and other migratory hunting bands belonging to the great Algonkian family of Indians, as well as to their more distant allies, the agricultural Huron-Iroquois of the Georgian Bay district. This was the vast shadowy land which Cartier had hoped to discover. Thus, in the end, the French did find the Kingdom of the Saguenay; but it was a kingdom peopled not by white men in woollen clothing, but by hunting savages in beaver skins; and its wealth lay not in gold and jewels but in furs. Gradually this wealth began to seem more desirable, more worthy of an undivided effort. During the last half of the sixteenth century the fur trade ceased to be an unimportant, casual adjunct of the fishery and began to assume an independent status of its own. Almost without realizing it, the French had crossed the frontier, of fundamental importance in Canadian history, which divided the maritime world of islands and peninsulas from the main mass of the continent. Some of them had almost ceased to be fishermen and were becoming fur traders. They had fallen, almost by accident, upon the trade which was to dominate the history of their empire in North America for the next hundred and fifty years.

[*II*]

The first furs which the French carried home to Europe were probably left on the pelt and were sold for warmth or ornament. It was the discovery and increasingly widespread use of the felting process in the manufacture of hats which completely changed the character of the fur trade and magnified its importance. The demand for fur felt provided a steadier, less capricious market; and it led the fur traders to concentrate on the beaver, which became the main staple product of the trade during the entire period of its greatness. The beaver has long and fittingly been a prominent symbol in Canadian heraldry; but this position was won through sober domestic industry rather than by romantic, martial valour. The beaver was a monogamist, it was not inclined to travel far or fast, and it developed great ingenuity in the trade of masonry and the profession of engineering. An amphibious animal, with a rich, luxuriant coat of fur, the beaver innocently advertised its presence to the hunter by the dams and lodges it constructed. The Indians, made more expert by the white man's tools and hatchets, trapped the beavers or broke into their lodges to destroy them. The fur on the pelts which they secured consisted of two layers — an outer layer of guard hairs, sparse and coarse, which could be loosened so as to drop off, and an inner layer of soft downy fur, less than an inch long, and pointed with microscopic barbs which made it extremely suitable for the felting process. If these pelts had been captured during the winter when the fur was most luxuriant and if they had been worn long enough by the Indians to make them pliable and greasy, they were rated 'castor gras d'hiver,' which was the highest grade known to the fur trade. From Canada the pelts were shipped to France, where the fur was sheered off close to the skin, felted, and in due course made into beaver hats by various companies of hat makers. Beaver fur was a light, highly valuable luxury staple which could support the heavy overhead costs involved in long sea voyages. It took its place, along with spices, sugar, and tobacco, as one of the favoured commodities in the early stages of Europe's commercial expansion overseas.

The demand seemed steady in Europe: in America it soon became voracious. The Indians revealed an insatiable and cumulative desire for European manufactured goods. Up to the coming of the white man, the tools, arms, clothing, and equipment of the hunting Indians of north-eastern North America were all made of stone, wood and bark, or bones, skins, and furs. They had no iron and only a rare copper tool. For them the French, who possessed these marvellous iron wares, were above all the 'gens de fer.' They innocently conceived the grades of the French social hierarchy in terms of skill in the fabrication of iron tools. 'The Hurons think that the greatest rulers of France are endowed with the greatest powers and having such great powers they can make the most difficult things such as hatchets, knives, kettles. They infer from this that the King makes the largest kettles.' The coming of this wondrous European equipment, these awls and knives of iron, these iron kettles, hatchets, and muskets, began immediately to alter age-old cultural traits and to set in motion a series of social and political disturbances which travelled westward across the continent with the progress of the white man. The beaver was a mild, defenceless animal, but he left his mark on all who trafficked in his fur. The fur trade profoundly affected both the declining Indian culture and the new French civilization in North America. For generations it remained the chief basis of that close relationship between the two races which was one of the distinctive peculiarities of the French Empire in the new world.

The first serious consequence of the fur trade appeared almost immediately. It concerned the commercial organization to which the French had so far been accustomed in their journeys to North America. They had scarcely begun the fur trade as a serious business before they were made unpleasantly aware of the fact that it could not be prosecuted in the same free fashion as the fishery. From the first the fishery had been a dispersed, individualistic, and highly competitive industry; but the fur trade seemed to necessitate centralization, company organization, and monopoly. The sea was wide, the coastline almost endless, and the supply of fish apparently inexhaustible; but in the fur trade, at least during its first stages, the supply consisted simply of what a few tribes of Indians happened to bring down to a small number of increasingly well-known places on the long coast-line between Nova Scotia and Tadoussac. If too many ships appeared, with too large a quantity of trade goods, which it would be uneconomic to carry back, then the barter turned rapidly into a seller's market, to the immediate disadvantage of the French. The Indians were shrewd enough to see the advantages of their position at a fairly early date. They preferred, wrote Champlain in 1611, 'to wait until several ships had arrived in order to get our wares more cheaply. Thus, those people are mistaken who think that by coming first, they can do better business; for these Indians are now too sharp and crafty.' Once the fur trade had become a serious business, in which a number of merchants were ready to venture whole ships and cargoes, it began to seem almost certain that competition would ruin the trade and that some form of monopoly alone could save it. But monopolies, enforceable at law, could be got from only one source — the state. Ever since the days of Jacques Cartier, the fishermen and fur traders had kept an independent initiative in North American expansion; but now, at the close of the sixteenth century, they began humbly to solicit the monarchy for some of the valuable favours which it had at its disposal. And the monarchy took the first step which was to lead it, slowly but inexorably, into the direct support of the fur-trading empire in North America.

At first it had no intention of assuming a leading rôle: it merely wished to regulate the actions of others for its own political profit. There was even some doubt as to whether it ought to do this. Sully, the new king's Controller-General of Finances, argued persistently that there was no wealth to be found in the new world north of the fortieth parallel and that settlements on the St. Lawrence were bound to end in dismal failure. Henry IV himself evidently took a less pessimistic view; but there was little possibility of his indulging in ambitious colonial ventures, even if he had wanted to do so. The civil and foreign war which had exploded on his advent to the throne in 1589 had largely wrecked France itself and wholly ruined the royal treasury. The King, whom Marc Lescarbot, the Paris advocate who wintered in Acadia, described simply as 'le Roy qui ne veut rien débourser,' had certainly no money to spend on colonies; but, in an age when everybody of any pretensions was going in for an overseas empire, he naturally nursed a few territorial ambitions of his own. Since the fishermen and fur traders wanted favours in the new world, he was disposed shrewdly to use them as agents in an inexpensive colonial policy. They desired monopolies and Sully was totally opposed to monopolies; but he might grant them these commercial privileges if they undertook the tasks of settlement for France. In short, Henry IV hoped to obtain a hold on the north-eastern coast of North America at the charge of the fur traders. He loaded the fur trade with an obligation which was in conflict with its basic character.

Like everybody else who tried to found colonies in America, the fur traders had to travel the hard road of trial and error. It was decades before their settlements developed any solidity: it was years before they could even decide upon suitable locations. As far back as 1588, two nephews of Jacques Cartier had petitioned for the monopoly of the fur trade; but the first tentative establishments on the American coast were not made until ten years later, at the very end of the century. The time seemed propitious. In France the civil war had petered out and the foreign war with Spain had been concluded by a peace in 1598. In the autumn of that year, Philip II, King of Spain and the Indies, who had hoped to be the monopolist of the new world and the arbiter of the old, went off in agony and ecstasy to meet his God; and there followed a period of free enterprise in North America of which France was the first, by a few years, to take advantage. In that hopeful year 1598 the Breton nobleman, Troilus de Mesgouez, Marquis de la Roche, sought to protect the monopoly which the King had granted him by establishing a semi-military colony on that long, narrow, desolate stretch of land, nearly a hundred miles east of Nova Scotia, known as Sable Island. La Roche planted about fifty colonists on this Atlantic sandbar, and it was not until 1603 that the last eleven miserable survivors of the absurd enterprise were mercifully taken back to France. In the meantime Henry IV had somewhat unthinkingly granted a second monopoly, applicable, it is true, only to the Gulf of St. Lawrence, to a Huguenot merchant of Honfleur, Pierre Chauvin. The monopoly was to run for ten years; but this time the condition was plainly stated and Chauvin was committed to take out fifty colonists a year.

Chauvin was an old fur trader, and from then on the monopoly remained in experienced business hands. The first results, however, were not particularly impressive. No permanent post was established at Tadoussac, for Chauvin brought out only a handful of settlers; and by the end of 1603 both he and his first successor in the monopoly were dead. These failures and disasters might have prejudiced the entire enterprise; but in actual fact they did not even interrupt its continuity. In 1604 the monopoly was granted for a fresh period of ten years to a new company. Among its members were several of the servants and associates of the old concern, and its leader was Pierre du Gua, Sieur de Monts, who had already visited the Gulf of St. Lawrence at least once and who had acquired some knowledge of the trade. He was a Huguenot, like Chauvin, and like him also, he had been governor of Honfleur for the King. During the next few years, while he made the most earnest efforts to found a settlement, he gathered around him a varied, interesting, and talented group of associates. There were distinguished and ornamental people like Marc Lescarbot, the erudite and romantic Parisian lawyer, and Poutrincourt, the nobleman of influence at court, who desired to settle himself and his family in the uncorrupted simplicity of the new world. There were experienced mariners and traders like François Gravé, Sieur du Pont, known to his companions as Pont-Gravé, and his far more famous associate, Samuel de Champlain.

Plain Samuel Champlain, as he was at the beginning, was born at Brouage, a port in the old province of Saintonge, close to the great Huguenot stronghold of La Rochelle. Champlain had fought for King Henry IV against the Spaniards; and when the peace left him without an employment he departed on what was a somewhat unusual adventure for a Frenchman, a visit to the Spanish settlements in the Americas. The book he wrote on his experiences gained him the favour of the King. He was made geographer royal and raised to the 'petite noblesse' as Sieur de Champlain of Saintonge. He was ready for his life work; and in 1603, when he first visited the St. Lawrence in the company of Pont-Gravé, he found it. The descendants of the Frenchmen whom he helped settle on the banks of the St. Lawrence look back upon him as the father of New France. He deserves the title. He was simple, straightforward, and devout. He had the immense curiosity, the tenacity, and the endurance of the born explorer and colonizer; and from the first he showed a quick imaginative understanding of the whole politico-economic problem involved in the founding of French power in the valley of the St. Lawrence.

In the spring of 1604, de Monts, Poutrincourt, and Champlain, soldiers, skilled workmen, and colonists, numbering all told about one hundred and twenty-five people, set out for the new world. They wintered the first year on St. Croix Island, a small island at the mouth of the river of that name which now divides the State of Maine from the Province of New Brunswick. It was a poor, inappropriate choice in every way; and next year the whole colony was moved across to the Nova Scotia side of the Bay of Fundy. In a protected inlet of the sea, known now as Annapolis Basin, they founded the first settlement of Port Royal. Port Royal, like Quebec a few years later, was a company establishment and in no sense a collection of individual settlers' cottages. It was a single large *habitation* as Champlain called it, built around a central court like many of the French châteaux of the period, with separate chambers for the gentlemen, a chapel, a dining-room, kitchens, and trading quarters. It was here, in the great dining-hall, that the 'Order of Good Cheer' held the nightly banquets that Lescarbot claimed were as good as anything Paris could offer; and it was here that Lescarbot composed the verses for 'Les Muses de la Nouvelle France' and planned the drama 'Neptune's Theatre' for the expected return of Poutrincourt from an exploring expedition. When spring came the colonists planted vegetable gardens in true prudent French fashion and began to sow wheat and rye in the wide fertile meadows of the Annapolis valley.

De Monts had taken his duties as a colonizer far more seriously than any of his predecessors; but he was head of a commercial company and the company was travelling rapidly through difficulties to eventual disaster. The independent traders, who had been excluded from the de Monts concern, were clamouring for free trade; and in 1607 Sully, who had apparently been opposed to de Monts and his venture from the beginning, suddenly cancelled the monopoly when it had still seven years to run. The court, in its usual arbitrary fashion, had abruptly reversed its policy at the expense of the merchants; but, even during the period when it honoured its engagement, the worries of de Monts had already begun. It was impossible for him to enforce his monopoly in this maritime world of obstreperous individualism and keen competition. He could not patrol the endless coastline of peninsula, bay, and island; and interlopers cut into his trade, carried away quantities of the best furs, and ruined the profits by which alone such expensive ventures as Port Royal could be maintained. Long before the spring of 1607, de Monts may very well have had enough of his doubtful privileges. As soon as he received word of the cancellation of the monopoly, he decided to abandon the project and he removed the whole colony back to France.

If it had not been for Champlain, de Monts might never again have ventured in the North American trade. But Champlain had been to the St. Lawrence in 1603. He must have seen immediately that the St. Lawrence region was something very different from the Atlantic seaboard. He may have become convinced that it looked far more promising for the fur trade. Whatever his arguments, he persuaded de Monts to make one final attempt in this new direction. Despite the protests of the independents and the opposition of Sully, de Monts applied for a renewal of his cancelled monopoly and unaccountably he got it. The renewal, it was true, was only good for one year; but, in recompense, the monopoly this time was burdened by no requirement of settlement. In the spring of 1608, Champlain and Pont-Gravé, with a small company of men, set out directly for the St. Lawrence. Poutrincourt, his son de Biencourt, and the group associated with them persevered in their trading and colonizing efforts in the Bay of Fundy region; and fishermen in hundreds and casual fur traders continued to visit the long shorelines of the maritime world. But the future of French dominion in North America lay in the organized fur trade, and the organized fur trade had shifted to the valley of the St. Lawrence. It was a strategic move of great importance for the future. It was also an admission of failure in the past. The fur traders had been forced to recognize the ominous fact that it was difficult to combine Acadia and the St. Lawrence in one organization and that the methods appropriate to the fur trade seemed completely ineffectual in the Maritimes. But they had yet to try the St. Lawrence seriously, and Champlain probably felt certain that they would have better luck. While Pont-Gravé stayed at Tadoussac to barter with the Indians, he pushed up the river to the 'narrows.' Here, on what the savages called the 'point of Quebec,' with the great rock of the future citadel behind him, he superintended the construction of the third *habitation* which the de Monts company had built on American soil.

[*III*]

The move to the St. Lawrence was decisive for the history of French power in North America. The outpost at Quebec put the French in early secure possession of the one great river system which led to the Atlantic seaboard from the heart of the continent. Ahead of them lay an imperial domain, the extent of which would have staggered them had they known it. To the south-west were the fertile lowlands of the St. Lawrence, crowded a little by the rival system of the Mississippi; and to the north and north-west lay the solemn, rocky uplands of the Precambrian Shield. The river unified this whole region. It provided a natural focus which was totally lacking among the raggedly scattered land areas of the Maritimes. Inevitably the river came to seem the natural basis of a great commercial empire stretching far into the distant west; and the achievement of this empire became the common objective of successive generations of Canadians, though their methods altered and the staple products of their trade were sometimes changed. The first staple of the St. Lawrence commercial system was beaver fur. This northern region, with its elaborate network of lakes and rivers, its immense forests and its scattered tribes of mainly hunting Indians, was territory designed by Nature for the prosecution of the fur trade.

From the first the French seem to have understood the meaning of the region they had occupied. They were prepared to accept the dictates of the river; they set themselves to realize its promises. In this process of adjustment Champlain provided a quick, intuitive leadership, and it was he who set the main style of French expansion in the new world. From the beginning the French were aggressive.

The Dutch on the Hudson River and, even more so, the English and Scots who later came to trade on Hudson Bay, preferred, in the main, to adopt a waiting attitude and to avoid too direct contacts with their Indian customers; but the French were ready to use the most vigorous methods in drumming up trade. They began systematically to explore the St. Lawrence-Great Lakes system and to use the river and its tributaries to establish contacts with the more distant tribes. Champlain, of course, was a professional explorer who was intensely interested in the geographical puzzle of the Great Lakes and who always cherished the hope of discovering a water route to the China seas. He had other than purely material motives back of his passion for discovery; but he was a man who promoted, served, and supervised fur-trade companies, and he was impatiently eager to push the trade further into the interior of the continent. In 1609, he travelled up the Richelieu or 'River of the Iroquois,' as he called it, and gave his name to Lake Champlain. In 1611, he was at the 'Great Rapid' (the Lachine Rapids), marvelling at the swiftness and ferocity of the waters and planning a further inland settlement on Montreal Island. He and his subordinates, 'Champlain's young men,' were to press much further west in the near future. The founding of Quebec simply foreshadowed that restless penetration of the continent in search of the retreating beaver which was to form the main theme of the fur trade during its entire history.

The French not only tried to establish contacts with the distant tribes; they also sought to win their confidence and friendship, and therefore their trade. The fur traders soon showed that they were prepared to live with the Indians, to accept the routine of their lives, and to share its triumphs and privations; and Champlain immediately laid the basis for these social and cultural relations of the future by contracting a number of political alliances with the tribes of the St. Lawrence region. When he arrived in 1608, he discovered that the river valley had evidently been the central battleground of a long warfare waged, on the one hand, by the northern, hunting Indians with whom the French had been in contact for decades and, on the other, by the Iroquoian tribes to the south. At one time the great Iroquois empire very probably extended so far north-east as to include the key, strategic centres of the future Quebec and Montreal. The sedentary, agricultural Indians whom Cartier met at Stadacona and Hochelaga were almost certainly Iroquoian bands. But in the long interval which followed his final departure, the sovereignty of the lower St. Lawrence was probably shifted by a major political upheaval which seems to have occurred among the tribes of north-eastern North America. When Champlain first arrived at Tadoussac, he found a band of Montagnais who were celebrating a victory over the Iroquois which they had won in the Richelieu River region; and when he ascended the St. Lawrence to Lachine, he discovered that the villages of Stadacona and Hochelaga had disappeared. What happened can never be known with any certainty; but it is at least probable that the metal tools and weapons which the French fur traders bartered at Tadoussac had enabled the northern Indians to overcome the Iroquois of the St. Lawrence and to drive them south to their historic habitat in northern New York State. By the time Champlain arrived, the Montagnais and Algonkins had almost cleared the river valley, with the help of French iron manufactures; and it was perhaps for this very reason that they so instinctively and persistently begged Champlain for his assistance. Apparently without pause or serious question, he agreed to grant it. When in turn he met the Montagnais, the Algonkins, and the Hurons, he promised each tribe his help in battle; and, as early as 1609, he was off up the Richelieu on a raiding expedition and met the Iroquois on the shores of Lake Champlain. 'When I saw them make a move to draw their bows upon us,' he wrote, 'I took aim with my arquebus and shot straight at one of the three chiefs, and with this shot two fell to the ground. ... The Iroquois were much astonished that two men should have been killed so quickly ... they lost courage and took to flight, abandoning the field and their fort, and fleeing into the depth of the forest, whither I pursued them and laid low still more of them.' That evening the Iroquois prisoner selected for torture sang his 'very sad song' of defiance; and Champlain saw his tormentors perform their ingenious cruelties until in the end they permitted him to fire one more shot from his arquebus and end the suffering.

Champlain has been censured for wantonly provoking the irreconcilable hatred of the Iroquois by this open assistance of their enemies. It is hard to see how his intervention in 1609 and his exploits in the following year could have had the enormous consequences attributed to them, and still more difficult to understand how he could have avoided the course he took. Champlain did not create the rivalry between those who lived in the valleys of the St. Lawrence and the Ottawa and those who lived in the valley of the Hudson. It arose long before he arrived in North America and it has lasted centuries after his death. It grew naturally and inevitably out of the rival ambitions which these two great regions inspired in the minds of those who lived in them. It had its roots in the very divisions of the geography of North America itself. In grandeur, the St. Lawrence-Great Lakes system was second to none upon the continent; but it had weaknesses which ominously contradicted its apparent strength; and one of these was its vulnerability before the danger inherent in the Hudson River, the only other river of the seaboard which overcame the mountain barrier and led into the west. The Hudson thrust itself into the inner defences of the St. Lawrence system. It became the pathway of both military aggression and commercial rivalry. The quarrel between the hunting and the agricultural Indians was simply the first phase of that long, unequal struggle between the northern and southern routes, between Montreal and New York, for the control of the Great Lakes system and the command of the western trade. French, Dutch, Scots, and English were to follow the Indians; lumber and wheat were to succeed furs. Rivers would be improved and portages eliminated by the construction of canals; and canoes would yield place to barges, steamboats, and railways. But, through all its various phases and manifestations, the conflict was to remain essentially the same and its vital importance for Canadians was to continue unaltered.

Thus the French, under Champlain's leadership, were quick to appreciate the implications of fur trading in the St. Lawrence valley. They could and did frame a policy; but it was far harder to carry it out. Obviously the fur trade was an expensive business, with a high overhead. There were heavy charges for explorations, for Indian wars, for the payment of the company's servants, and the upkeep of the posts. Such expenses could best be borne by a unified concern, just as a unified concern could best plan the policies, both political and economic, which the fur trade demanded. But the de Monts monopoly ran out in January of 1609, and this time it was not renewed. For the next four years the traders crowded into the St. Lawrence, taking advantage of the capital expenditures which de Monts and his partners had made and of the goodwill with the Indians which Champlain had laboriously created. There was little profit for anybody; there was certainly nothing to sustain such costly establishments as the *habitation* at Quebec. De Monts' partners soon came to the conclusion that it was stupid to pay the charges of monopoly in a régime of free trade; and de Monts, in order to keep the concern going, had to buy them out. He and Champlain were apparently the only people who stood between the enterprise and disaster.

In fact, the years 1610-1613 were ominous for the whole future of French power in North America. The tiny, unpopulated French settlements in Acadia and on the St. Lawrence led a perilous existence which could be ended at a touch by the first resolute aggressor. In 1613 Captain Samuel Argall appeared off the coast of Acadia, on a semi-official raid from Virginia; and, with the coolly impudent claim that French settlements which had been established prior to the founding of the London Company were an in-fringement of its charter, he systematically plundered and destroyed the Acadian posts and carried some of the colonists in triumph back to Jamestown. Quebec might very well have suffered the same abrupt fate, for it was equally de-fenceless; and, in any case, its existence was threatened just as effectively by the dwindling profits of the de Monts firm. Champlain's whole life was in the success of the settlement and in the exploration of the new world; and in this ex-tremity he made one of his greatest efforts to save the enter-prise from ruin. With a simple mixture of public spirit and self-interest, he sought a comprehensive solution which would raise the political prestige of the colony, ensure its financial stability, and provide for his own continued em-ployment in the new world. He had what seemed to be unusually complete success. A powerful and influential nobleman was appointed as lieutenant-general or viceroy of New France and entrusted with political power, land-granting authority, and the monopoly of the fur trade. The principal fur-trading merchants of the St. Lawrence region were organized in an association, sometimes called Cham-plain's Company; and this company was permitted to exploit the monopoly, on condition that it paid the Viceroy a con-sideration and agreed to take out six families of colonists a year. As for Champlain, he won a partly independent posi-tion, for the Viceroy made him his agent at Quebec and the company agreed to pay his salary. It was obvious that he could lobby as effectively at the French court as he could with the Indians; and, as has been said, he deserves the credit of organizing the first trust in North America.

Champlain's success must have excited him. The next few years are among the most vigorously active of his career.

He pressed up the Ottawa River in 1613 as far as Allumette Lake, in the Algonkian country; and in 1615 he followed the canoe route of the Ottawa westward through its infinity of portages and difficulties to the Sweetwater Sea, Lake Huron, and wintered with the Huron Indians of Georgian Bay. The Hurons were agricultural Indians, Iroquoian in origin, the descendants of one section of the great division of the Iroquois imperialist army which had crossed the Detroit River in its drive north-eastward and had occupied the region north of the Lower Lakes. Father Sagard-Théodat called the Hurons the nobility, the Algonkins the burghers, and the Montagnais the rabble of the Indian tribes; and it was inevitably the Hurons who became the principal members of the great fur-trading network of Indian nations with which Champlain and his associates proceeded to form the closest relations, commercial, cultural, and political. Already Champlain's young men, the reckless junior servants of the companies, had wintered with the Indians, learned their ways and languages, and founded the race of *coureurs-de-bois* and *voyageurs* who were to push French trade into the recesses of the continent. The four Récollet missionaries, members of a reformed Franciscan order, who somewhat apprehensively agreed to go to Canada in 1615, immediately began to rival the *coureurs-de-bois* in both daring and endurance; and one of them, Father Le Caron, scarcely stopping at Quebec in his whirlwind journey west, reached the Huron villages in the summer of his arrival in America, and actually before Champlain himself. These men had begun to realize the destiny which the St. Lawrence seemed to promise to the French: pressing impetuously westward along the waterways, they had linked red men and white in that strange blending of European and North American ways which was to constitute the commercial, ecclesiastical, and military French Empire in North America.

It was a brave beginning, after the reorganization of 1612-1613. But the fur trade, as experience had already revealed,

was full of reorganizations and fresh starts. And in an inexplicable and sinister fashion, each rearrangement appeared
merely to involve the fur traders more deeply, without materially strengthening their colony. Champlain and his partner had committed themselves to the use of the St. Lawrence-
Ottawa route as a main highway for the trade in furs. The
Algonkins and the Hurons were cast for the rôle of middlemen. They were expected to extend the market for the
French trade goods among the tribes of the remote north
and west, and to bring down the furs themselves to the rendezvous on the lower St. Lawrence. This monopoly of the
north-western fur trade, which Quebec hoped and intended
to win for itself, was now threatened seriously by the Iroquois. The Iroquois lay strategically close to the main
French route to the interior. They were populous, aggressive,
and politically well organized; and back of them, since 1609,
were the Dutch on the lower Hudson, who had begun to
increase the military strength of the Five Iroquois Nations
by supplying them with guns and ammunition. The Dutch
assumed a position analogous to that of the French on the
lower St. Lawrence; and the Iroquois intended to take the
place of the Hurons as middlemen for the trade of the western tribes. This Iroquois competition put the French and
their Indian allies in an impossibly difficult situation. The
only methods which they could devise to defeat the Iroquois
seemed inevitably to involve either a serious danger to the
colony or a considerable sacrifice to the trade. If, on the one
hand, they did nothing to end the existing quarrel, then the
Iroquois would continue to raid and harass both the French
outposts and the Huron villages. If, on the other hand, they
patched up an Indian peace, the Iroquois could freely vend
the manufactures of the Dutch and divert a substantial part
of the trade to New Netherland. This was a dreadful alternative. 'I had hoped,' wrote the Récollet Father Sagard-
Théodat naïvely, 'to promote a peace between the Hurons
and the Iroquois, so that Christianity could be spread among

them, and to open the roads to trade with many nations
which were not accessible, but some of the members of the
Company advised me that it was not expedient since if the
Hurons were at peace with the Iroquois, the same Iroquois
would lead the Hurons to trade with the Dutch and divert
them from Quebec which is more distant.'

The determination to use the St. Lawrence-Ottawa as the
main route for a monopoly trade in the best northern furs
almost inevitably implied a conflict with the Iroquois. From
the first Champlain had accepted this quarrel and tried to
win it for his Indians. His journey westward to Georgian
Bay in 1615 was undertaken partly in response to the incessant demands of the Hurons that he aid them in their conflict with the Iroquois. That summer he and his Indian
allies planned to break the heart of Iroquois aggression by
delivering a smashing attack on the main fortress of the
Onondaga, geographically the central tribe of the Five
Nations of Iroquois. But the grand strategy of the campaign
miscarried, for the Andastes, with whom the Hurons had
contracted a temporary offensive alliance, failed to appear in
time at the rendezvous. Despite all that Champlain and his
Frenchmen could do, the Hurons bungled the tactical plan,
delivered only spasmodic and unco-ordinated attacks upon
the fortress, and in the end trailed north-westward in defeat,
bearing the wounded Champlain with them. Up to this
time, from the moment when the French had first arrived on
the St. Lawrence, the northern Indians had, in the main,
carried the offensive victoriously into the lands of their
enemies. This whole phase of the war was now nearly over;
and from then on a sense of insecurity, of mounting peril,
began gradually to infect the northern Indians and even
their French allies as well. In 1620 Champlain superintended the construction of the first fort on the rock of
Quebec. A fort was one more heavy item in the overhead
costs of the fur trade; but even a fort could not prevent the
swift, secret Iroquois raiding parties from ambushing the

fleets of Huron canoes as they carried the precious cargoes of furs down the Ottawa to Lachine. In 1624 the worried Champlain actually succeeded in concluding a peace with the Iroquois. It was of short duration. It could not help but be. And if it had not been ended by some Montagnais warriors, in all probability it would have been broken by the Iroquois themselves. The war went on; and the French were committed to the giant risk of maintaining their monopolistic trading empire by a conflict which became increasingly more doubtful and more sanguinary.

The dangers from without accumulated; but there was no real increase of strength within. The establishment at Quebec was a commercial outpost. It was financed and supplied from old France and it had no real roots in North America. Every fur-trading company which had been granted a monopoly had had imposed upon it the obligation of promoting colonization; every company had tried to escape from its obligations, and Champlain's company was no exception to the rule. The truth was that settlement and the fur trade were in fundamental and irreconcilable opposition. The fur trade assumed a northern, forested region sparsely populated by roving, hunting Indians; but settlement meant naturally the growth of agriculture, the extinction of the beaver, and the westward flight of the Indian tribes. In a fur-trading colony the accepted, the desired 'settlers' were not immigrants from Europe, but natives of North America; and this emphasis on the Indians, this acceptance of Indian culture, was just as characteristic of the newly arrived clergy as it was of the fur traders themselves. The Récollets who came out with Champlain in 1615 and the Jesuits who followed ten years later had as their main purpose the christianizing of the Indians. The coming of these religious orders, whose members so frequently personified the exalted piety of the seventeenth-century French Roman Catholic revival, certainly portended changes for the future. Their presence meant the gradual disappearance of the hitherto numerous Huguenot fur traders, the systematic suppression of the Reformed Religion in New France, and the imposition of a puritanical régime which was just as harsh, inhuman, and inquisitorial as anything in seventeenth-century England or Massachusetts. The clericals were to busy themselves with many things; but unquestionably their great object was the soul of the native North American. Their one organized religious enterprise was the mission; and the mission, like the fur trade itself, assumed the central importance of the Indian tribes.

Thus there were only a few dozen factors, clerks, interpreters, skilled tradesmen, missionaries, and servants who made up the population of Quebec in the early days. Real colonists were unneeded and unwanted. When in 1617 Louis Hébert, a Parisian chemist who had already been out once to Acadia, imprudently offered himself and his family as prospective settlers, the company viewed him and his purposes with the deepest suspicion. He was forced to accept conditions limiting his freedom of action in the new world, as though the pursuit of agriculture on the St. Lawrence were certainly a misdemeanour and a colonist to all intents and purposes a criminal. All this was clearly contrary to the terms of the contract between the Viceroy and the company; and Champlain, who, with the Récollet missionaries, was one of the few people at Quebec occupying an independent position, laboured to convince the King, the Viceroy, and the Viceroy's agents of the faithlessness of the merchants and the miserable state of the colony. In 1620 came another of the now familiar reorganizations. The monopoly of the fur trade was withdrawn from the old company and transferred, under even more minutely detailed conditions, to a new concern headed by the brothers de Caën. The results might have been expected. As early as 1622 the new concern had united with the members of the old company and adopted all the old company's devious and dilatory ways. There were few, if any, new settlers and practically no agriculture. It was not until the spring of 1628 that oxen drew the first plough through the soil at Quebec; and Champlain repeatedly complained that, during his absences in France, the factors neglected to cultivate the vegetable gardens. Quebec remained almost wholly dependent upon supplies from the mother country, and by spring the inhabitants were often badly in want of food.

Even after a quarter-century of effort, the hold of the French upon the continent was feeble and precarious. Quebec was a weak and vulnerable place: the posts in Acadia had virtually ceased to exist. Every year hundreds of French fishing ships visited the banks and the long coastline of the North Atlantic; but, so far as occupation was concerned, the tiny French settlements in Acadia never recovered from the calamitous effects of the Argall raid. The noble promoters Poutrincourt and his son de Biencourt were dead, the Jesuit priests had vanished, the *habitation* at Port Royal was deserted; and Charles de la Tour, in his small post at Cape Sable, at the south-west tip of Nova Scotia, was apparently the principal resident representative of French interests in the maritime region. Settlements such as these, which in effect were little more than stakes to claims which had never been actively occupied, invited official interference from Europe, as well as casual raids from New Netherland or Virginia in America. In 1621, James I of Great Britain proceeded to disregard the prior claims of the French to Acadia with as little ceremony as the pirate Argall had done. He granted the entire maritime area from Cape Gaspé to the St. Croix River to a friend and a fellow Scotsman, Sir William Alexander, later Earl of Stirling. The name Nova Scotia, which came eventually to be the title of the province beyond the Isthmus of Chignecto, was the chief permanent result of Sir William's attempt to found a New Scotland in America; but he was active and enterprising in his first preparations, and it looked at the time as if the French would soon be expelled from their last foothold in Acadia.

In Quebec, Champlain found it difficult to obtain men to complete the rebuilding of the fort. 'Although the Sieur de Caën and all his partners signed an agreement to do so,' wrote Champlain, 'and although His Majesty and the Viceroy desired it, still they are opposed to it, and hinder it to the utmost of their power.' The partners left the place badly defended and inadequately provisioned. They cared nothing, Champlain declared angrily, for the welfare of the colony or the wishes of the Viceroy 'so long as they got forty per cent interest on their money.'

At this point, the state intervened again. Up to that time the French monarchy had exercised only a general and somewhat negligent supervision over the French outposts in the new world. The companies entrusted with a monopoly of trade had been required to promote the growth of New France, and a lieutenant-general or viceroy had been appointed to watch over its general welfare. The crown had used the company as an instrument of state policy; but initiative in the development of trade and the forming of companies had lain, on the whole, with the merchants themselves. Now this initiative was abruptly wrenched from the fur traders by the man who typified the new order in France, Cardinal Richelieu. Richelieu was to win his reputation chiefly in Europe as the restorer of French unity and the author of French aggrandizement; but in the realm of trade and colonies he at least anticipated some of the mercantilist views and methods which were to be practised so much more efficiently and completely by Colbert at a later time. He decided to make a complete break with the uninspiring past in New France by abolishing the office of viceroy and cancelling the monopoly of the united company. He proposed to establish, under his own patronage, a new company, more numerous, wealthy, and powerful than any of its predecessors, which would be really capable of promoting the growth of New France as the terms of its charter would require. The new company, with a capital of three hundred thousand

livres, divided among one hundred shareholders or associates, was called the Company of New France.

It was set up in the year 1627. By an odd, and unfortunate, coincidence, 1627 was also the year in which war
broke out between England and France. The war brought
Charles I of England little military prestige and considerable
financial embarrassment. The major expedition to the Isle
of Rhé, off the French coast from La Rochelle, was scarcely
carried out in the grand Elizabethan manner; and it was
only out in remote America that a real flash of the old buc-
caneering spirit appeared. David, Lewis, and Thomas Kirke
were an enterprising trio of sailor brothers, who were supposed to be half French themselves, and who certainly knew
a good deal about the French colonies and the French plans
concerning them. Since the war had happily legitimized
privateering, the brothers obtained letters of marque from
the English government which authorized them to seize
French ships and to capture French posts in Canada and
Acadia. They set out for the new world in the spring of
1628, in three ships and with the financial backing of a
group of London merchants. By another unfortunate concurrence of events, which this time had been anticipated
by the Kirke brothers, the Company of New France dispatched its first big colonizing expedition to the St. Lawrence about a month later. While David and Thomas
waited at Tadoussac for the French fleet, Lewis ascended
the St. Lawrence to demand the surrender of Quebec.
Champlain refused firmly and the Kirke brothers did not
press the issue, for they realized that by stopping his supplies they could easily starve Champlain out in time. The
fleet of the Company of New France, led by the unsuspecting de Roquemont, at length appeared in the Gulf. It was
encumbered with hundreds of non-combatant colonists and
masses of stores and *matériel*. The Kirke brothers attacked
and captured it with brisk efficiency and with little loss of
life. Having thus completely ruined the major effort of the

Company of New France, they sailed for England, leaving Champlain to eke out another winter at Quebec without supplies.

The exploit of the Kirke brothers, which produced a great sensation in both France and England, naturally revived the interests of Sir William Alexander and caused him to reassert his claims to the American dominions of the French. The Kirkes and their backers, realizing Sir William's favour at court, prudently came to an agreement with the baronet; and together they formed the Anglo-Scotch Company to exploit the territories of Acadia and Canada. The formidable squadron which David Kirke led out to America in the spring of 1629 to complete the work of conquest and occupation was thus composed of two divisions, one intended for Acadia and one for the St. Lawrence. Sir William's eldest son, Sir William the Younger, headed the party of Scots colonists bound for his father's province of Nova Scotia. In this maritime region, the Anglo-Scotch Company had only partial success, for although Sir William occupied the abandoned Port Royal, the Scots were expelled from Cape Breton and failed to take Charles de la Tour's post at Cape Sable. In the St. Lawrence, on the other hand, the Kirke brothers rounded off their victory with ease. The ships which the unfortunate Company of New France sent out were either captured or diverted back to France. Champlain, who had no provisions and no hope of assistance, surrendered; and Lewis Kirke, who combined a pleasant courtesy of manners with efficiency in privateering, occupied Quebec on July 21. 'The following day,' wrote Champlain of Kirke, 'he had the English flag hoisted on one of the bastions, ordered the drums to beat to assemble the soldiers, whom he placed in order on the ramparts; he then had a salute fired from the ships as well as with the five brass guns at the fort, the two small falconets at the factory, and some iron mortar-pieces; after which he made all his soldiers fire volleys of musketry — the whole in sign of rejoicing.

[*IV*]

Actually England held New France for only three years. The Kirkes had won Quebec by daring and Charles I let it go through financial necessity. He had become engaged with his Parliament in a quarrel over political principle which was evidently more to his liking than the wars with Spain and France. He could rout Parliament easily by dissolving it, but to keep it dissolved he had to have some substitutes for the taxes which Parliament alone could vote; and in these circumstances, he thought of the half-paid dowry of his wife, Henrietta Maria of France. Louis XIII and Richelieu wanted the return of New France; Charles I was anxious for the payment of his wife's dowry. This was the basis of a bargain which was finally concluded at St. Germain-en-Laye in 1632. That summer the Scots pulled out of Port Royal and Lewis and Thomas Kirke departed from Quebec; and by the spring of 1633 Champlain was back on the St. Lawrence again as governor.

This transitory conquest seemed outwardly to have altered nothing. But in actual fact it had an important effect which vitally influenced subsequent history: it nearly ruined the Company of New France. The company had promised to do great things. It had been built on an imposing scale and given large privileges. The seigniorial ownership of the whole of New France, together with a perpetual monopoly of the fur trade, and a monopoly for fifteen years of all other trade except the cod and whale fisheries, were the chief rights which the crown had granted. In return, the company agreed to take out three hundred colonists in 1628, the first year of its contract, and such further annual numbers as would be necessary to raise the total to four thousand in 1643, at the expiration of its general monopoly of trade. The salaries of the governor and his assistants, the pay of the garrisons, the allowance to the clergy, and the maintenance of the posts were all to be defrayed by the company. The company, in short, consented to people the colony, to provide for its defence and government, and to support its social institutions in return for the monopoly of trade. This whole ambitious programme had been vitiated, before it ever really began, by the privateering Kirke brothers. The Company of New France lost virtually its entire capital in the disasters of 1628 and 1629. Apparently it was unable to secure fresh funds; and it determined to lease its trade monopoly for a period of five years to a group of its own associates, a sub-company, in return for an annual payment of ten thousand livres, which represented the administrative costs of the colony, and a share in the sub-company's profits. The whole basis of the enterprise had been weakened. The development of New France, its defence, and the support of its institutions were once more left in doubt. The crown, having bestowed a gift of empire upon a trading company, was unwilling, and frequently unable, to give more direct assistance; and, during this period, it was the Society of Jesus that gave the colony its most effective support. The Jesuits were wealthy, influential, and powerful, and it was their propaganda, through the Jesuit *Relations*, that kept the plight of Quebec before the wealthy benefactors of France.

These two institutions, the Company of New France and the Society of Jesus, moulded the life of the colony and infused it with their spirit. They were both monopolies — double monopolies, in fact. So far as commerce was concerned, the Company of New France had excluded all other traders and the fur trade itself was virtually the colony's exclusive commercial concern. In the realm of religion, the Récollets and all other competing Romanist orders had been denied the right to enter, and the Huguenots, of course, were now rigidly shut out as well. The variety of economic occupation and commercial interest which was such a characteristic feature of the English colonies on the Atlantic seaboard was impossible at Quebec because of the undivided concentration on the fur trade. The old freedom of debate and dispute, which had marked even New France in the early days when Huguenot fur traders had visited the St. Lawrence, died away in a silent uniformity of belief. Each monopolist, commercial or religious, was supreme in his own sphere. The Company of New France nominated the governor, who at first exercised alone both political and judicial authority over the colonists. There were no secular clergy and no other religious order to compete with the Jesuits: and Father Le Jeune, the superior, and his successors were responsible only to the general of the society at Rome.

These two authoritarian monopolies combined to give New France its peculiar character. An air of piety and militarism, of mysticism and approaching conflict, seems to pervade the place in these early years. The very governors themselves suggest it. Champlain was an explorer and man of action; but, at the same time, he was an extremely pious and even ascetic Christian. His successor, Montmagny, who governed the colony from 1636 to 1648, was a Knight of Malta; and the simple inhabitants of New France must have been astonished when they saw him first, in the black robes of his order, with the white cross of eight points on his breast. The fur traders, of sheer necessity, had been obliged to organize their trade in expectation of a struggle with the Iroquois. The Society of Jesus was a crusading order planned long ago in military terms to give battle to paganism and error. Both organized religion and organized trade expected hazard and danger in the new world, for both, despite their enormous differences, looked upon New France in essentially the same fashion. Quebec, for them, was not simply, or even mainly, a community of transplanted Frenchmen. The company had contracted to bring out settlers and the Jesuits begged and prayed the crown to assist in colonization; and yet, at the same time, the gaze of both was really focussed on the Indians. If one group wanted to buy furs and the other to win souls, it meant, in both cases, an advance into the forested interior, contact with savage and often degraded people, and a prospect of discomfort, danger, and atrocious death. This combination of aggressive trade and militant Christianity, set against a background of wild nature and Indian wars, gives to this early period in the history of New France a quality of intensity and a pattern of drama in which the appropriate climaxes are the miracles of Montreal, the martyrdoms of Huronia, and the defence of Dollard des Ormeaux and his comrades at the Long Sault.

The Company of New France had agreed to promote the growth of the colony in ways which would be regarded as normal by general North American standards. Actually, the nature of the fur trade and the limited resources of the company dictated a very different type of growth; and a militaristic defensive system was built up to protect missionary enterprise and the fur trade from the assaults of the Iroquois. The company had neither the will nor the ability to fulfil its obligations with respect to settlers. The best it could do was to borrow a device which the crown itself had employed. As feudal overlord of New France, the company granted large tracts of land, *en seigneurie,* to persons of some substance, on condition that they agreed to settle their property with colonists. Despite or perhaps because of these efforts, the colony grew extremely slowly; and in 1643, by which time the Company of New France had promised to land at least four thousand settlers, there were probably not more than three hundred people in Quebec. There was no semblance of a freely and vigorously advancing agricultural frontier. Fortified posts were built at strategic intervals along the St. Lawrence; and settlement advanced up the river in well-marked stages and in close relationship to the defensive system. In 1634, Champlain had constructed a strong post at Three Rivers, at the mouth of the St. Maurice; and in 1642 the palisaded stronghold of Montreal — on Montreal Island, below the confluence of the Ottawa and St. Lawrence Rivers — was founded by an association of priests and devout laymen whose work from the first seemed blest by miraculous providences.

The work of the Jesuits was based upon this defensive system; but, like the commerce of the fur traders, it extended far beyond the protective limits of the posts. The Jesuits were not entirely alone in their labours, for representatives of two orders of nuns, the Hospitalières and the Ursulines, the latter led by Mother Marie de l'Incarnation, crossed the ocean to assist in evangelization. But it was the Jesuits who supplied the inspiration, the leadership, and the directing control for everything that concerned the spiritual and cultural life of New France. These missionaries, Fathers Le Jeune, Vimont, Jogues, Brébeuf, Lalemant, and others, acted as the historians, the apologists, and propagandists of the colony. Wealthy and powerful in their own right, the Jesuits tried to rouse the court of France to a sense of its religious and political obligations in Quebec, and to awaken the nobility and rich bourgeois to a realization of the opportunity for pious benefactions and personal self-sacrifices in the new world. The schools and hospitals at Quebec and Montreal, the Indian villages at Sillery and Three Rivers — all the chief foundations of the period — can be traced, either directly or indirectly, to the work of the Jesuits. But charitable and educational enterprises were secondary, of course, to the main work of the Christian mission. Since only a fraction of the tribes could be reached at the settlements on the St. Lawrence, the Jesuits, like the fur traders, decided to seek the Indians in their own homeland. Sometimes they visited nomadic groups of savages such as the band of wandering and primitive Montagnais whom Father Le Jeune followed through a winter of privations: but the most famous work of the society was the establishment of the mission among the Huron villages in the stretch of land between Lake Simcoe and Georgian Bay. In this missionary work, there were both heroic and pathetic elements, for the frontier of two such utterly contrasted cultures was a centre of friction and disturbance; and while the Indians misunderstood and mocked the message of the French, the French were continually disappointed in the religious and moral progress of the Indians.

The fur trade, which remained the almost exclusive economic interest of the inhabitants, developed along the lines which had already been laid down. The posts on the St. Lawrence gave protection against the Iroquois. In the upper country, the relatively advanced Hurons, with their settlements and their agriculture, replaced other tribes as the most important middlemen. Annual returns of pelts, which in the late 1620's had averaged twelve thousand to fifteen thousand, rose by 1645 to twenty thousand. There was no constant growth, however, but a series of violent oscillations which were reflected in the fortunes and misfortunes of the parent Company of New France and its various subsidiaries. The first sub-company, which lasted five years, realized a handsome profit of three hundred thousand livres; but the second sub-company, which held the monopoly from 1638 to 1641, suffered losses which were even heavier than the first sub-company's gains. In 1642, for the first time since France had received her American colonies from the English, the fur trade was once more in the hands of the parent Company of New France. It began to make profits. But they were modest profits, profits not sufficient to settle the confusion of its accounts or to wipe out the staggering total of its indebtedness. It became gradually but unmistakably clear that a great state-organized company, with headquarters at Paris, and a directorate drawn chiefly from noble, official, and financial circles in the capital, was scarcely capable of coping with the difficulties of trade on the remote St. Lawrence. In 1645, a small group of the more important colonists, organized as the *Compagnie des Habitants*, sought and secured the trading monopoly from a somewhat reluctant Company of New France. The Parisians carefully kept all their seigniorial rights and all their power of appointment;

but, so far as it went, the change was a first recognition of the importance of residence on the spot, experience in the trade, and knowledge of the Indians. The *habitants* had won a partial freedom from remote control. Almost immediately they began to agitate for an equal independence of monopoly. The *Compagnie des Habitants,* in the first year of its operations, made the astounding profit of three hundred and twenty thousand livres. These unexpected riches not only stirred up quarrels within the company itself, but also aroused the envy of those *habitants* who had remained without; and in the end the King had to step in to settle the dispute. In 1647, trade was made free for the first time — 'le commerce est libre' — and all citizens were permitted to traffic in furs with the Indians. They were permitted to trade freely on one important condition, which was that all their furs must be brought to the company's stores and sold at prices which the colony's government would determine.

Government, which was based upon the monopoly, naturally tended to reflect changes in the organization and in the fortunes of the fur trade. The pioneer Champlain, who died in 1635, and his successor Montmagny were absolute rulers, responsible only to the Company of New France which had appointed them: and when deputies were nominated, such as Duplessis-Bochart at Three Rivers and Maisonneuve at Montreal, they were subordinate to the governor at Quebec. So long as the Company of New France or its own subsidiaries exploited the monopoly, this régime continued. It was only when the trading privileges fell into the hands of the *Compagnie des Habitants* that an important change occurred. By an edict of 1647 the crown gave to a council of three the powers which the governor had previously exercised alone. By a second edict, issued in the following year and in response to renewed complaints on the part of the inhabitants, this council was further enlarged and slightly democratized. At first it was to have included only the governor, the superior of the Jesuits — or the bishop, when there should be one — and the governor of Montreal. The edict of 1648 substituted the ex-governor of the province for the governor of Montreal; and — what was much more important — it added two or three more members, who were to be elected for a period of three years in a special electoral session of the council; and this electoral session was to be attended not only by the nominated councillors, but also by the officers called the syndics — the popularly elected representatives of Quebec, Three Rivers, and Montreal — who were to appear for the express purpose of taking part in the election. This modest instalment of representative government was accompanied by a very large increase in the colony's budget for administrative expenses and for defence against the now aggressive Iroquois. The local *Compagnie des Habitants,* which thus found itself obligated to pay out nearly four times as much as the previous subsidiary companies for the support of the menaced colony, was permitted to unload a good part of this burden upon the colonists. The colonists had been granted free trade, and they could thus very reasonably be asked to pay taxes. The edict of 1647 ordained that half of the furs brought by private individuals to the company's stores became the company's property without payment. The *habitants* had paid pretty dearly in increased administrative charges and general taxation for their taste of local autonomy and representative government.

When the settlements on the St. Lawrence are compared with those of Acadia, these characteristic features of Quebec, economic, religious, and political, appear even more striking and peculiar. Monopolies, feudal land tenure, crusading religious orders, and centralized absolute government were all established European institutions; but while they were adapted with ease to the situation on the St. Lawrence, they never seemed to develop much vitality in the more primitive colonial society of Acadia. At the very beginning of settlement, it had become clear that monopoly was difficult to enforce in the peninsula of Nova Scotia — which was, in fact, the main reason why the organized fur trade had moved to the St. Lawrence. It also became evident, when the peninsula was restored to the French in 1632, that centralized government would be equally difficult to establish. The French began in their accustomed fashion by appointing Isaac de Razilly as lieutenant-general for the whole of Acadia; but Razilly died in 1635, and first two and then three men appeared to claim a share in the maritime succession. Charles de la Tour, who had been given the peninsula of Nova Scotia, and Charles de Menou, Sieur d'Aulnay-Charnisay, who was established in the mainland north of the Bay of Fundy, were the two principal contenders for Razilly's domain; but Nicolas Denys, who held a long strip of land on the south shore of the Gulf of St. Lawrence from the Company of New France, was really a maritime proprietor also and inevitably became involved in the rivalry for trade and jurisdiction in Acadia. The quarrel was kept up with immense gusto through a long series of sudden turns and dramatic surprises for over ten years. All the principals, including the wives of both la Tour and d'Aulnay, had excellent parts to play; but the irrepressible la Tour, who showed a daring, an ingratiating address, and an unfailing ingenuity throughout the whole complicated business, stands out as a really picturesque character even in that adventurous age. He was imprisoned and released, he lost his first wife and married his rival's widow, he fought valiantly for France and ended his days as a loyal subject of Great Britain.

Obviously, Acadia was a land of individualism, of rivalry, and divided jurisdiction. No centralized authoritarian government arose to supervise growth and no elaborate defences were made to ensure protection. The isolated and disconnected settlements developed, where they developed at all, in a natural and haphazard fashion. The posts on the Atlantic side of Nova Scotia were really fishing stations; Cape Sable and Fort St. John were mainly depots for Indian trade. The only considerable settlement was at Port Royal, where the settlers early began to improve the meadows of the Annapolis Basin with the dykes for which Acadia later became famous. De Razilly had brought out a small number of colonists, d'Aulnay a few more; and this little group of settlers, perhaps not more than two hundred and fifty in all, were the founders of the Acadian people. From the first they seem to have been a sober, practical, and self-sufficient lot. Far above them roared the storm of personal and national rivalries in Acadia. Governments were transitory and official supervision brief. There was no powerful Jesuit order to supply schools and hospitals. And though seigniories were granted, the seigniorial system never took root as it did in the St. Lawrence valley. The institutions of an authoritarian, paternal, and centralized régime were worn away in the divisions and distractions of Acadian life.

Of the two areas of French power in North America, Quebec seemed outwardly the better defended place. In the maritime region, where centrifugal tendencies ruled, enterprises were scattered and strength was frittered away in internal rivalries. On the St. Lawrence, where the river and the fur trade exerted a strong centripetal influence, effort was focussed and strength was absorbed in the preparation of a planned system of defence. The fortifications of the colony of the St. Lawrence, which stretched from Quebec to Ste. Marie, deep in the Huron country, supplied far more organized and systematic protection than anything in Acadia; but, for all that, Quebec was a vulnerable place, as only a fur-trade colony could be. The Company of New France, which would not and could not perform an obligation which contradicted the whole purpose of its existence, had not populated the colony any more effectively than its predecessors had done. The St. Lawrence region had never been occupied by a mass of people; the colony had not the native, inherent strength of deep-rooted settlement. In large measure, the defences were artificial, they had been imposed from above, and they were borne with difficulty by both the companies and the colonists. And yet protection was absolutely necessary. The life of the colony depended upon the fur trade and the fur trade depended upon the relative security of a long, difficult trade route into the remote interior. Even in peace, the route would have been hazardous enough; but it was now surrounded with all the perils of Iroquois warfare.

The Five Nations were poised on the edge of what was to be the greatest known imperialist offensive in the history of the northern American tribes. The Iroquois confederacy, the Mohawks, Oneidas, Onondagas, Cayugas, and Senecas, had reached maturity in politics and warfare. They stood at the height of their powers. They had won the strength of union without the sacrifice of their tribal individuality. They combined a talent for long-range strategy, which was unusual among the Indians, with a more normal use of swiftness and secrecy in tactics. Though their numbers were not particularly great, even collectively, the five tribes had thus a very considerable strength of their own; and this strength was now heavily supplemented by the muskets and ammunition which the Iroquois obtained from the Dutch. The Dutch West India Company was a huge corporation, more powerful and more varied in its interests than the Company of New France. Its agents were instructed not to participate in Indian quarrels; but the company was slow to impose restrictions upon the sale of brandy and firearms to the Indians, and private traders knew no limitations at all. By 1642, the Mohawks were reported to possess four hundred muskets. The day was past when the northern Indians could win battles with imported knives and hatchets. The Iroquois had won a definite superiority in the new armament. The Mohawks, who acted as middlemen for the Dutch and who were running short of furs, looked with hatred on the French and with jealousy on their abundant supply of northern pelts. And the whole confederacy hoped to annihilate the Huron nation.

The strategy of the Iroquois, though it may not have been at all times deliberately concerted in advance, was, almost by instinct, extraordinarily mature and effective. When their last great offensive began about 1640, they contented themselves, for a while, with raiding the flotillas of Huron canoes on their way down to Montreal and with harassing the French settlements on the St. Lawrence. The French reply to this was the building of Montreal in 1642 and the construction of a small fort at the mouth of the Richelieu River. They could protect the centre, but not the extremities, of the enormous fur-trading system; and the Iroquois then turned to an indirect attack, which was sudden and completely devastating. Far in the west, the Huron villages were clustered in a relatively small area between Lake Simcoe and Georgian Bay. In the summer of 1648, the Iroquois stormed and captured the outpost village of St. Joseph and murdered its priest, Father Daniel. In the early spring of the following year, when the snow was still on the ground, they returned, with equal suddenness and violence, to complete the wreck of Huronia. They destroyed the villages of St. Ignace and St. Louis, tortured the Jesuits Brébeuf and Lalemant to death, massacred the Indians, and completed the ruin and dispersal of the Huron nation.

Then they turned back again to the St. Lawrence. They were not afraid to attack even Montreal and Three Rivers directly; but it was more in their habit to ambush small parties, to cut off solitary workers, and to mock the isolated defenders of outposts with their taunts. At all times they tried to keep up the fur blockade. The northern Indians got through it by devious routes, for they had to do so to keep up their supplies of iron tools; but while the trade in furs never completely stopped, it dwindled to a pitiably small remnant. 'Never were there more Beavers in our lakes and rivers,' wrote the chronicler of the Jesuit *Relation* for 1652-53, 'but never have there been fewer seen in the warehouses of the country. Before the devastation of the

Hurons, a hundred canoes used to come to trade, all laden with Beaver-skins; and each year we had two or three hundred thousand livres' worth. That was a fine revenue with which to satisfy all the people and to defray the heavy expenses of the country. . . . The Iroquois war dried up all these springs. The Beavers are left in peace and in the place of their repose; the Huron fleets no longer come down to trade; the Algonquins are depopulated; and the more distant Nations are withdrawing still farther, fearing the fire of the Iroquois.' This systematic fur blockade was undermining the whole economic basis of the colony; and it was impossible for the French to break through it with the limited resources at their disposal. It was not that they lacked physical or moral courage; they had plenty of both. The Jesuits actually undertook a mission to the Onondaga. In the spring of 1660, Adam Dollard, Sieur des Ormeaux, and sixteen other Frenchmen, together with a small number of Algonkin and Huron warriors, defended a weak palisaded fort near the Long Sault on the Ottawa River for five days against the attack of two hundred Iroquois; and it was only when the defence had been weakened by the desertion of most of the Hurons, and the attackers strengthened by the arrival of five hundred new braves, that the Iroquois succeeded in storming the flimsy palisade and overwhelming its defenders.

The French showed courage, but they were forced to act upon the defensive. The economic existence of the colony depended upon the reopening of the St. Lawrence-Ottawa route for the trade in furs; but this involved the defeat of the Iroquois, and the French were not strong enough to effect it. They could not take the offensive, but even defensive measures were a heavy burden; and the costs had to be met out of an uncertain and declining revenue. The whole régime which had been built upon the monopolistic trading company was breaking down under this continuous pressure. The problem set the colonists against the *Compagnie des*

Habitants, and the *Compagnie des Habitants* against the Company of New France; and the authorities tried desperately to keep the machine going by cuts, concessions, and evasions all round. In 1653, the beaver duty paid by the colonists was reduced from one half to one quarter, and at the same time the *Compagnie des Habitants* was released from its principal annual payment to the Company of New France. It was only a question of how long the *Compagnie des Habitants* could keep going, and in 1660 it was compelled by debt to cede the trade of the whole country for a pittance to the Company of Normandy.

In Quebec, French power tottered ominously; but in Acadia, during this period, it was swept almost completely away. Quebec, it was true, was attacked only by the Iroquois confederacy, and Acadia by the first naval power in the world; but, even so, there was a hard core of resistance on the St. Lawrence which seemed lacking in the maritime region. Acadia had fallen once to the Scots and English, and it was now about to fall to the English and the Bostonians; and the minor part played by New England in this adventure was the first faint indication of a major interest in Acadia which it was to develop in the near future. In the spring of 1654 a little fleet of warships lay in Boston harbour. The Puritan Commonwealth of England was at war with Holland and the fleet was under orders to attack the Dutch post at Manhattan. It never sailed for Manhattan, however, for at this point there arrived from England the depressing information that Oliver Cromwell, the new Protector, had just made peace with the sister Protestant Commonwealth of the Netherlands. This dashed everybody's hopes until the Bostonians made the ingenious suggestion that the little fleet could be used to good account against the French settlement in Acadia. England was just as much at peace with France as she was with Holland by the new treaty; but this did not deter Robert Sedgwick, the leader of the expedition, any more than it had deterred Samuel

Argall back in 1613. He captured Port Royal without much difficulty, and Fort St. John surrendered without firing a shot. La Tour, who was at St. John, achieved his last and most surprising metamorphosis. He resurrected the Scottish title which at one time he had secured from Sir William Alexander, and unblushingly presented himself as a British subject. For a time he was even one of the three people to whom the Puritan Protectorate gave the proprietorship of Nova Scotia; and he died peacefully at St. John under the rule of Sir Thomas Temple, who soon became the sole proprietor. The Acadian farmers, who seemed equally unaffected by the conquest, continued to tend their cattle in the Annapolis valley. Only on the south shore of the Gulf of St. Lawrence, where Nicolas Denys had established himself, did French power continue in the Maritimes; and this survival served as a reminder of the fact that Acadia was a divided country which it was difficult to rule, and also difficult to capture, in its entirety.

The maritime part of the French Empire in North America had fallen, and the future of the St. Lawrence region was doubtful. Obviously the régime of adventurers and trading companies had failed. And on all sides a demand arose that the French crown should intervene directly and decisively to save the colonies which it had neglected from complete extinction.

CHAPTER TWO

FUR   TRADE   AND   EMPIRE

[*I*]

O N A MARCH DAY in 1661 Cardinal Mazarin lay dying in his palace at Vincennes. It was the end of a whole era in the history of the French monarchy. Richelieu's wars of conquest had been triumphantly concluded by the Treaty of Westphalia and the Peace of the Pyrenees. The religious divisions within the country had been ended, the last baronial revolts had been crushed; and a united nation accepted the absolute and centralized rule of the Bourbon monarchy. The young King, Louis XIV, who was not yet twenty-three years old, looked confidently forward to a long future of achievement. He was to hold ambitions far more grandiose than those of Richelieu and Mazarin. He was to drive, and harry, and exhaust the French people in his frantic efforts to reach these unattainable objectives. But the gift of the dying Mazarin was peace. There was an interval, brief and evanescent, which separated the wars of Richelieu and Mazarin from the wars of Louis XIV. For a moment the rulers of France could survey the whole position of the monarchy in the world at large. They looked abroad, towards the east and across the Atlantic, and they discovered their neglected colonial empire.

The man who typified this first constructive period in the reign of Louis XIV was Jean Baptiste Colbert. He never occupied the place or held the power of the two cardinals, for the real successor of Mazarin was Louis XIV himself. 'I have summoned you with my Ministers and Secretaries of State,' the King told the Chancellor on the day after Mazarin's death, 'to tell you that hitherto I have been willing to let my affairs be managed by the late Cardinal. It is time I looked after them myself.' From that day the ministers were never allowed to forget that they were subordinates; but a few of them came to yield enormous influence, and of these perhaps the most important was the man who first rose to prominence as an officer in Mazarin's household. 'Sire,' Mazarin is reported to have said to Louis XIV on one occasion, 'I owe you everything, but I believe I am acquitting myself of some of that debt to Your Majesty in giving you Colbert.' Colbert may stand for all time as the perfect pattern of the servant of the state. He was economical and incredibly hard-working. He possessed an immense resourcefulness and a tireless, impassive efficiency. His object was to exalt the wealth and power of France at the expense of the commercial greatness of its chief rivals, Holland and England. And, as an essential part of that programme, he set out to restore and reorganize the French colonial empire.

As things stood in 1661, it was obvious that the most drastic remedies were needed. In the far east, where Colbert hoped to compete with the Dutch and English, the French had not a foothold of territory. In the Atlantic world, Acadia had fallen to the English, Canada was menaced by the Iroquois, and the trade of Martinique, Guadeloupe, and the other French West India islands had almost become the monopoly of the Dutch. It was hardly an encouraging record. But Colbert was convinced that failure was due, not to any inherent weakness of French enterprise, but to mistakes which could be rectified and to unfortunate circumstances which could be overcome. In his opinion, the companies and colonies of the past had been inexcusably neglected by the home authorities; and from the first it was his policy to supply regular government supervision and consistent government support. He had all the bureaucrat's unquestioning faith in the wisdom of state intervention in economic and colonial development. In the better colonial world of the future he intended either to establish direct royal governments or to set up great corporations which would be the acknowledged instruments of state policy with all the financial and military backing of France behind them.

During the next few years, the French Empire was rapidly pulled together in the light of these ideas. All the little, weak, and half-bankrupt trading companies were swept away; and the era of military support, mercantilist policy, and paternal government began. In 1662, a small settlement, with a resident governor, was established at Plaisance (Placentia) on the south coast of Newfoundland, as a basis for the dry fishery. In 1663, the Company of New France at length surrendered its charter, and royal government was set up at Quebec. In 1664, Colbert founded two enormous corporations, the Company of the East Indies and the Company of the West Indies; and to the latter was given the monopoly of all trade to West Africa, South America, the West Indies, and New France. It was in this year, 1664, that the reorganization of the French Atlantic Empire entered upon an even more active stage. In February the new lieutenant-general of all the French possessions in North America, the tall old soldier, Alexandre de Prouville, Marquis de Tracy, sailed with warships and soldiers for the West Indies. In the islands the grand tour of reconquest and reorganization opened as favourably as could have been hoped. De Tracy recaptured Guiana, restored order in Martinique and Guadeloupe; and, after having remained about a year in the Indies, he headed north for New France. It was the last day of June, 1665, when he landed at Quebec. The shouts of the crowd followed him as he climbed up Mountain Street towards the upper town, the bells were ringing in the cathedral and the Jesuits' church. De Tracy knelt in

gratitude on the stone flooring of the cathedral, while the
Te Deum was chanted. Then he arose and told the popu-
lace of his mission and of the King's plans for New France.

The capital of Canada had never seen a summer like that
of 1665. During the first half-century of its history, Quebec
had barely clung to existence; and in 1665 there were not
more than seventy houses and five hundred and fifty people
in both the upper and lower town. The summer of 1665
was the first that brought to the inhabitants a definite reas-
surance in the might of France and a real belief in the
promise of the future. The rule of Jesuits and fur traders
seemed over. For the first time it was gloriously certain that
the King was going to defend the colony, to watch over it
politically, and to encourage its economic and social growth.
From June to September of that year the ships from the
homeland kept crowding up the river to Quebec. They
brought the new governor, Sieur Daniel Rémy de Courcelle,
and the first intendant, plain Jean Talon. They brought
bachelors and young girls, settlers with their families, great
piles of stores and equipment. The officials and the colonists were all welcome; but, in the eyes of the old inhabitants
of Quebec at least, everything was eclipsed in importance by
the coming of the soldiers. The Carignan-Salières regiment,
which had already distinguished itself in Switzerland and in
the wars against the Turks, arrived in Quebec that summer,
with over a thousand men and a hundred officers. The long,
reassuring lines of musketeers, pikemen, and grenadiers
paraded through the streets in their grey uniforms, wide-
brimmed black hats, and bright mauve stockings. The flag
of the regiment, with its wide white cross on a black ground,
fluttered in the air. The inhabitants of Quebec had scarcely
believed that such security could exist; and they saw the
future through a pink glow of confidence. ' ... His Majesty
is about to make a Kingdom of our Barbarous land, and
change our forests into towns, and our deserts into Provinces.
... Never will New France cease to bless our great Monarch

for undertaking to restore her to life and to rescue her from the fires of the Iroquois.'

The first task, in fact, was to smash the power of the Iroquois. It was the terror of the Iroquois that checked every impulse, inhibited every action, and paralyzed every will in the colony; and it was to lift this everlasting menace that the Carignan-Salières regiment had been sent to Canada. That very summer the soldiers were put to work at the construction of three forts on the Richelieu River. The prudent and mature de Tracy was content to wait until the summer of 1666 for the main offensive against the savages; but the new governor, the impetuous de Courcelle, whom they described in Quebec as 'breathing nothing but war,' dashed off in January for a raid against the Mohawks and returned with nothing but some bitter memories of winter campaigning in the Adirondack country. It was not until late in September of 1666 that the French returned by the Richelieu River-Lake Champlain route to deliver their main attack. In the army which the aged de Tracy now commanded in person there were some six hundred soldiers of the Carignan-Salières regiment, another six hundred *habitant* volunteers, and perhaps a hundred Huron and Algonkian warriors. In a great fleet of three hundred small boats and canoes they paddled across the still lakes in brilliant autumn weather. The woods were yellow with falling leaves when they marched off, from the head of Lake George, towards the Mohawk villages. The frightened Iroquois spies had watched the great flotilla of canoes as it moved across the empty lakes. They had heard the beating drums and glimpsed the brilliant uniforms as one of the crack regiments of Europe in full panoply of war trudged through the tangled forest. As the French neared the first of the Mohawk villages, the weather broke; and de Tracy marched his men all night through blinding wind and rain in the vain hope of surprising the savages. The village was empty. All the villages were empty. In the distance the soldiers could sometimes see the Indians — could hear them firing stray shots, and hooting far off in fearful derision. They marched on. The last village was the real Mohawk fortress, with four bastions and triple palisades, twenty feet high. But the Indians were fleeing as the advance guard approached in the obscurity of evening; and once again the grasp of the French closed on the empty air. They destroyed the villages, burnt the huge piles of corn and provisions, and systematically wrecked the Mohawk countryside. And then they toiled back through wild autumnal rains to Quebec. The next summer the envoys of the Iroquois came in humility to Quebec; and a peace was concluded, which, so far as the French were concerned, was to last for nearly twenty years.

The first part of Colbert's programme was virtually finished. In 1670 a long series of negotiations ended in the return of Acadia to France; and thus the work of reconquest and reoccupation by war and diplomacy was definitely over. Long before this Colbert had begun the second part of his task. He never saw French America; but he had throughout a perfectly clear, precise, and detailed picture of what it should become. It must, literally, be a New France overseas. The normal institutions of French civil life were to be set up in the colonies. So far as government was concerned, the rule of proprietors, Jesuits, and native fur traders was to go for ever; and the King's government must be established — centralized, authoritarian, paternalistic — with Quebec as the administrative centre of the French Empire in the new world.

The hard lines of this system began to appear as early as 1663. A sovereign council was set up at Quebec, composed of the governor, the intendant, the bishop, five councillors, an attorney-general, and a secretary. The few, small democratic elements, which had been introduced into the old council of New France in 1648, disappeared completely with the establishment of royal rule. The King, of course, now nominated all the officials; he soon resumed the right to nominate the councillors also, after a period when this was done jointly by the governor and the bishop; and there were no popularly elected members at all. The council, whose name, at Louis XIV's request, was later significantly altered to superior council, was at once an administrative, a legislative, and a judicial body. In theory its authority was supreme; but in actual fact the effective government of the colony was carried on by the administrators sent from France, and chiefly, of course, by the governor and the intendant. These were simply the normal chief officials of any French province; and their position and powers can best be explained in terms of the administrative history of the motherland.

Traditionally the French governor was one of the great nobles of his district, with powerful local influence and prestige: the intendant was almost invariably a trained middle-class bureaucrat and the special representative of the centralized government of the king. In France the governor had come to retain almost purely ceremonial authority, while the intendant had acquired real control. But in New France the powers of the two officials were never quite so unequal. The governor was the titular head of the colony and the commander of its armed forces: the intendant was the dispenser of justice, the financial expert, the economic planner. This system of dual control almost invited trouble, and the quarrels of the future were to be notorious. But, at the moment, everybody, including apparently the Governor, de Courcelle, was content to accept the leadership of the first Intendant, Jean Talon. Talon fittingly represented the new order which Colbert was trying to introduce. His rather handsome face, with its dapper little moustache of the period, is that of an urbane, shrewd, and highly intelligent man of the world. He was one of Colbert's best young administrators, for he had generations of public service behind him and for ten years he had been **intendant of the frontier province of Hainault.**

The other great institution of French civil life was, of course, the Roman Catholic Church. Canada at first had been simply an Indian mission; and the appointment of a bishop, the first representative of a secular clergy, was another indication that the colony had now been accepted as a normal settlement of Frenchmen. François de Laval-Montmorency, the first bishop, who arrived in the colony in 1659, a few years before the establishment of royal rule, was a typical product of the seventeenth century religious revival. He was a man of burning religious zeal, of mystical piety, of almost superhuman austerity. He was accustomed freely to practise those unpleasant acts of self-mortification which adorn the pious biographies of seventeenth-century ascetics. He slept, by choice, between thin blankets well filled with fleas; and the frigid atmosphere of his unheated church in the early winter morning seemed to inspire him to interminable supplications. He had been the selection of the Jesuits. His big nose, his firm pursed lips, and his cold protruding eye reveal the assertive ecclesiastic determined to preserve and increase the authority of the church. For him New France was not so much a temporal possession of His Majesty Louis XIV as it was an evangelizing outpost of the Roman Catholic faith. He respected the Jesuits; he admired the rigorous control which they had exercised; he hoped to continue their puritanical regimentation. The pretensions of the state irked him profoundly; he saw — and provoked — the Gallican in even the most pious and good-tempered civil administrators. There had been three governors of Quebec since his own arrival in the colony. He had quarrelled with all of them! It was a remarkable record — remarkable and, from Colbert's point of view, highly annoying. Colbert believed that these insinuating churchmen had gone beyond their proper sphere of action and had imposed far too strict a standard of conduct upon the community. The new royal colony was to be secular and Gallican in spirit; and Talon was told repeatedly that he must maintain a just balance of church and state.

Colbert had given protection to the colony, he had provided it with new institutions. His third objective was to guide its economic and social growth. He had no doubt about the goal towards which it should strive. Canada, he thought, must approximate, as far as possible in the circumstances, to the populous, thickly settled village communities of rural France. The fur trade, of course, had discouraged settlement; but for Colbert the first requisite of progress was a substantial increase in the population. He had the mercantilist's conviction that an abundance of goods could come only from an abundance of men; and he declared solemnly that 'the increase of the colony should be the rule and end of all the conduct of the intendant.' For a few years he gave state support, on a relatively substantial scale, to immigration from France to Canada. In this, as in everything else, Acadia tended to be neglected in favour of New France. Only some sixty settlers were sent out to Acadia during the governorship of Grandfontaine, who took over the colony in 1670: but probably nearly two thousand state-aided colonists reached Canada during the period of mass immigration from 1665 to 1672. Mechanics and labourers, settlers with their wives and families, were assisted over; soldiers of the Carignan-Salières regiment were persuaded to stay in the colony; and every year — the most picturesque episode in the migration — the King's ships brought a few score orphan girls and daughters of poor families who were known as the 'filles du roi.'

The destination of the latter was, of course, matrimony. Colbert had all the mercantilist's calculating enthusiasm for early marriages, continual child-bearing, and enormous families. He solemnly begged Talon to impress upon the people of New France 'that their prosperity, their subsistence and all that is dear to them, depend on a general resolution, never to be departed from, to marry youths at eighteen **or**

nineteen years and girls at fourteen or fifteen.' The atmosphere of New France was oppressively matrimonial in character. There were state rewards for early marriages and
state penalties for bachelordom; and in the spring, when the
King's ships arrived in port, the Quebec marriage market
developed a distinctly unsentimental briskness. ' . . . Several
Ships were sent hither from France,' wrote the irreverent
soldier Lahontan a little later, 'with a Cargoe of Women of
an ordinary Reputation, under the direction of some old
stale Nuns, who rang'd 'em in three Classes. The Vestal
Virgins were heap'd up, (if I may so speak) one above
another, in three different Apartments, where the Bride-
grooms singled out their Brides, just as a Butcher do's an
Ewe from amongst a Flock of Sheep. In these three Sera-
glios, there was such variety and change of Diet, as could
satisfie the most whimsical Appetites; for here were some big
some little, some fair some brown, some fat and some meagre.
In fine, there was such Accommodation, that every one might
be fitted to his Mind: And indeed the Market had such a
run, that in fifteen days time, they were all dispos'd of. . . . '
Even here the paternal interest of the state did not cease. Its
ultimate objective was not early marriages, but quantities of
children; and it held out modest rewards for those who were
willing to take the occupation of parenthood with real seriousness.

In the minds of Colbert and his colonial officials, the destiny of all these new colonists was simple. They were to
play their part in developing a colonial society which bore
the closest possible resemblance to that of rural France. The
first settlers were too scattered, isolated, dependent on their
own resources. They had formed the deplorable habit of
running in the woods for furs. All this must be changed.
In future, settlement throughout the colony must as far as
possible be contiguous and in the form of parishes, villages,
and towns. In these neat, compact, easily defended settlements, the main business of the colonists must, of course, be

agriculture. Colbert was unshakably convinced that it was 'much more advantageous to the colony that the inhabitants devote themselves to cultivating and clearing the land, rather than to hunting, which can never be of any use to the colony.' Talon never ceased to emphasize the importance of agriculture. But, at the same time, both he and Colbert agreed that even in a colony, industry should be diversified to a certain extent; and energetic efforts were made to promote mining, lumbering, shipbuilding, and even manufactures. If it developed in this fashion, New France would be able to ship flour, and provisions, and lumber to the French West Indies. And it could thus take its part in a great union of the Atlantic possessions which would make for the advantage of each and the grandeur of all.

[*II*]

This was a statesmanlike conception. It might be realized. But it could be realized only by the use of stubbornly difficult materials. Colbert had the West India islands, the North Atlantic region, and the St. Lawrence colony to work with. But everywhere there were forces of great potency working against him. The chief pursuits of the St. Lawrence and Acadia were the fur trade and the fishery. Essentially these pursuits were hostile to settlement. They could make little contribution to a real union of the French Atlantic Empire. They almost encouraged, rather than resisted, the rivalry which came from the English possessions in New England, New York, and Hudson Bay.

In the period after 1663, the French fishery developed in a fashion almost exactly the opposite of the English. There had always been differences; they now became even more conspicuous and acute. The whole tendency of the English fishery was to drift away from England and towards the new world of Newfoundland and New England. The fixed habit of the French fishery was to remain firmly anchored to the continent of Europe. England sought foreign trade and spawned overseas possessions; France approached self-sufficiency and was largely content with the home market. Every spring the great French fishing ships sailed westward from a score of different ports along the coastline; and every autumn the great majority of them returned direct to France. For Frenchmen, the bank fishery, the earliest form of the North Atlantic fishery, was still of prime importance. They had copied the English device of fishing off-shore and drying the product on the beach; but they had never developed this method as much as their competitors. Their dry-fishing areas were not concentrated, as the English were from Cape Race to Bonavista in Newfoundland, but scattered at intervals along the south shore of Newfoundland and along the coast of Gaspé, Nova Scotia, and Cape Breton Island. They were inferior areas also — restricted, barren, inhospitable. The best regions for colonization in Acadia were the tide-water flats of the Bay of Fundy; but these were inconveniently remote from the North Atlantic fishery.

All this discouraged settlement The French established a colony at Placentia on the south shore of Newfoundland as a base for the dry fishery. It was supplied with a governor and protected by a garrison; but it scarcely grew at all and it was not followed by other fishing settlements along the Gaspé and Acadian coasts. Actually, the French fishing industry expanded vigorously during this period, and often at the expense of the English. It even reached a high point of prosperity; but this prosperity left no permanent marks on the coast of North America. The success of the French fishery was the monopoly of continental France; the strength of the English fishery lay in the growth and spread of Empire. Whereas the French fishermen quarrelled among themselves and never with settlers, for there were no settlers to quarrel with, the disputes in the English fishery were between the West Country fishing interests on the one hand and the colonists of Newfoundland and New England on the other.

The great fact in the North Atlantic world was the rise of the New England colonies. Newfoundland was handicapped by position, and climate, and a rocky infertility; but New England had all the essentials requisite for the first great synthesis of industry and trade in North America. She advanced because of the navigation laws — and in despite of them. She prospered with the growth of settlement along the Atlantic seaboard and in Newfoundland, and with the rise of the sugar plantations of the West Indies and the slave trade of Africa. Her fisheries were linked with lumbering, shipbuilding, agriculture, distilling, and the provision trade in an economy which had strength and elasticity and great expansive powers. England, as she watched Massachusetts sell the goods and provide the shipping which should have come from the motherland, came to regard New England as 'the most prejudicial plantation to this kingdom.' But if New England competed within the Empire, she was ready also to join old England in the struggle against the French. She began to extend her influence over the whole world of the North Atlantic fisheries, pushing up the coast into Acadia, profiting by every weakness of the French. Her ships sold goods to the Acadian settlers in the Bay of Fundy. Her small fifteen- to forty-ton ketches, which swarmed into Nova Scotian waters, advanced the technique of the dry fishery at the expense of her rivals. While the great fishing ships of the French lay anchored in harbour and their small fishing boats were not able to venture more than a short distance from shore, the New England vessels could roam at will and fish as far out as the off-shore banks.

This conflict between official plans and natural tendencies in the fishing region was ominously suggestive of the difficulties which Colbert and his subordinates faced in other parts of the American Empire of Louis XIV. In Acadia the French fishery did not encourage colonization; in Canada the fur trade was positively hostile to settlement. Colbert had hoped to promote agriculture and diversified industry;

but the odd, ironical result of his efforts was a vast expansion of the fur trade. The coming of the Carignan-Salières regiment certainly brought peace to the lower St. Lawrence valley; but the defeat of the Iroquois also broke down the barrier to the west. The strongest ambitions and impulses in New France, which for nearly twenty years had been held back in frustration, were free now to seek their objectives in the interior. At once the French took advantage of this new freedom for expansion. And, within a short time, they became more deeply committed than ever before to the design of western empire.

This imperialist drive, which was to characterize the entire period that followed, was determined, in large measure, by the strange and novel conditions which now existed in the interior. When, in the 1660's the first Frenchmen ventured timidly into the west, they discovered that the Iroquois wars had changed the entire distribution of the Indian tribes. Fresh from their victories over the Hurons, the Iroquois had swept on, across Georgian Bay and across the peninsula between Lake Huron and Lake Michigan, driving the Hurons, Neutrals, Ottawas, and Saulteurs before them in a great, confused, panic mass. When at length their offensive finally ebbed away, it left a refugee mob of Indians behind it, like the detritus of some great avalanche, in the stretch of territory west of Lake Michigan and south of Lake Superior. In this remote haven, the fugitives from the east came in contact with those primitive and unspoiled western tribes, the Potawatomi, Sauks, Foxes, Illinois, Sioux, and Crees. These Indians had never seen European manufactures; they looked upon the ironware which the beaten and breathless refugees had brought with them with a childish and envious humility. 'They entreated the strangers to have pity on them and to share with them that iron, which they regarded as a divinity. . . .' They were ready and eager to give their best beaver robes for the 'old knives, blunted awls, wretched nets and kettles used until they were past service'

which the fleeing Hurons and Ottawas had managed to bring
with them in their headlong journey west. The desire for
manufactures had been quickened among the westerners.
With the fugitives from the east, it had already become an
insatiable appetite. But while the Iroquois terrorized the
lower St. Lawrence they could never get enough supplies;
and when at length the blockade was broken in 1666, they
were avidly awaiting the arrival of the French.

Thus the Iroquois wars had two consequences of immense
importance to the French. The Iroquois had annihilated
the Huron middlemen, through whom the French had previously done their western trading; and, at the same time,
they had helped to create a new and potentially vast fur-
trading market in the remote west. It was the combination
of these two facts which forced the French to go into the
interior themselves. No group of Indians ever really succeeded to the rôle of the Hurons, nor did the French desire
it so. They wanted now to break through this screen of
Indian middlemen and to grasp the riches offered so naïvely
by these unspoilt, primitive westerners. As Nicolas Perrot
said, the new west 'was a Peru for them.' As early as 1654, in
the first lull of the Iroquois war, Pierre Esprit Radisson and
Médard Chouart, Sieur des Groseilliers, had gone off to this
fur-trading Eldorado; and they were simply the first of that
new generation of western Frenchmen which was to become
a veritable company in the free, spacious days which followed 1665. As in the past, it included both the 'black
robes' and the fur traders. There were Jesuit missionaries
like Fathers Allouez, Marquette, and Dablon. There were
fur traders, explorers, and promoters like Perrot, Beaudry,
Jolliet, Dulhut, and La Salle, and with them a crowd of
obscure and unremembered *coureurs-de-bois,* who never
wrote their memoirs and never had their names flatteringly
recorded in government dispatches home. The urge towards
the west became an irresistible compulsion which troubled
a whole society and drove its strongest along the waterways

and into the remote interior. Missions and trading centres were established at Chequamegon Bay on Lake Superior, at Green Bay on Lake Michigan, at Sault Ste. Marie, at Michilimackinac, and other points at which it became customary for the Indians to assemble. As early as 1670, when the Sulpician priest Galinée visited the Jesuit mission at Sault Ste. Marie, he reported that there were often as many as twenty-five French fur traders in that vicinity alone. The whole focus of the trade was moving west. Less and less frequently did the great groups of Indians descend the Ottawa to the settlements; and the annual fur fairs at Montreal and Three Rivers gradually died away.

It was not only the annihilation of the Huron middlemen and the discovery of the new western riches, but also the revival of competition, that forced the French to go into the interior themselves. The competition came now from both north and south, across those low heights of land, those perfunctory defences, which separated the drainage basin of the St. Lawrence from those of Hudson Bay and the Hudson River. The punishment of the Iroquois had not ended their commercial competition, for it could not. By now their culture was adjusted to the constant use of iron implements; they were completely dependent upon regular supplies of European manufactures. But, at the same time, the beaver fields in their own territory south of Lake Ontario had long ago been exhausted. It was their own desperate necessity which drove the Iroquois westward to seek the business of the tribes around Lake Erie and the southern shores of Lake Michigan. They had always been effective in the fur trade; and their commercial and military strength was vastly increased in 1664, when the English captured New Netherland from the Dutch. The trade goods which the Iroquois now got from the Dutch and English in New York were often better, and almost invariably cheaper, than those which the French could offer. Their guns and ammunition, their clothing, blankets, and West India rum, were particularly prized by the western tribes. The Iroquois were formidable competitors. And back of them were the English, who sold them goods and were soon to claim them as subjects.

The conflict with the Iroquois was an old one, which even antedated Champlain's arrival in the new world; but competition from Hudson Bay was novel and completely unexpected. Henry Hudson had discovered the bay in 1610; but he had been looking for a north-west passage to Asia, and not for a new entry to the North American continent. Appropriately enough, it was those two picturesque prototypes of all *coureurs-de-bois*, Médard Chouart, Sieur des Groseilliers, and Pierre Esprit Radisson, who revealed the real significance of Hudson's entry by inventing an excellent North American use for it. It may be that Groseilliers and Radisson actually reached Hudson Bay or James Bay during their wanderings in the Lake Superior country in 1658-1660. At all events they came back down the Ottawa with a load of superb northern furs, and with the conviction that they could easily get more of the same without the trouble and expense of the endless overland journey. They proposed to trade with Hudson Bay direct by sea. It was the summer of 1660 when they reached the settlements. The Iroquois war was at its height and no doubt Radisson and Groseilliers expected to be received with cheers and admiration. But Governor Argenson remained unsympathetically bureaucratic in his attitude to their departure two years before without a licence. He fined them heavily. 'The Bougre,' said Radisson sourly, 'did grease his Chopps' with the profits. The two fur traders flung out of the colony in a rage, determined to reveal their idea concerning Hudson Bay to a more appreciative audience; and some time later they turned up in England. The Dutch war was on, the plague was raging in London. But Charles II affably gave them an allowance and put them up in Oxford and Windsor. And Prince Rupert, the colonial experts, and the London merchants listened with flattering attention to what they had to say about Hudson Bay.

At length, in 1668, Radisson and Groseilliers set out for the bay in ships provided by the English. Storms drove Radisson back, but Groseilliers reached the mouth of the Rupert River in James Bay. The bargain cargo of magnificent furs which he brought home convinced the London merchants and the aristocratic capitalists; and in 1670 they formed that long-lived trading enterprise which is known to this day as 'The Governor and Company of the Adventurers of England trading into Hudson's Bay.' Prince Rupert, the cousin of the King, the Royalist leader of cavalry in the far-off battles of Marston Moor and Naseby, was made first governor of the company; but there were other advantages besides distinguished royal patronage which promised the concern a real chance of success. From the beginning the Hudson's Bay Company had the solid benefit of cheap English goods and of low ocean freights which were as nothing compared to the huge costs of the long inland journey from Montreal. At the bay, which was a vast inlet cutting into the best beaver country in the world, the English traders came into direct contact with the Crees, Assiniboines, and other northern tribes who had been most remote from the French. They were avid for the magical iron goods, they were rich in supplies of downy *castor gras;* and it was not difficult to entice them down the Rupert, the Abitibi, the Moose, and the Albany Rivers in search of those more favourable rates of exchange which the Hudson's Bay Company could afford. 'The savages greatly praise their liberality,' a Jesuit wrote gloomily of the newcomers to the Governor at Quebec. The monopoly of the French had been broken; and from then on the Hudson's Bay Company remained a disturbing factor in the north-west.

Inexorably, for reasons both political and commercial, the state was drawn into this far-off conflict in the interior. Talon began it. No doubt he had gone out to Canada with his head full of neat, orderly Colbertian assumptions about the future of New France. His first term was almost exemplary. He planned some model villages at Charlesbourg. He built a brewery. He was busy encouraging shipbuilding, hemp production, and manufacture. And yet, almost from the beginning, something began to happen to him. He started writing the oddest letters back to Colbert. He dilated upon the vast extent of the country. He urged the capture of New York. He assured the King that 'nothing can prevent us from carrying the name and arms of his Majesty as far as Florida. . . .' These curious effusions, with their hints of suppressed excitement and their sudden vistas of gigantic empires, surprised and perplexed the minister at home. Talon, Colbert believed, was an excellent administrator — young, certainly, but experienced and reliable. And yet he was writing letters like these! It was all very unaccountable and disturbing. Colbert made the prudent comment 'Wait' on the margin of one of Talon's most intemperate suggestions. 'It is much better,' he replied with damping practicality, 'to restrict yourself to an extent of territory which the colony itself will be able to maintain than to embrace so much land that eventually a part may have to be abandoned, with some consequent discredit to His Majesty's Crown.' It was highly sensible advice, and Talon ought to have been impressed by it. But he was scarcely aware of the rebuke. He had suddenly become conscious of the river and of the enormous continent into which it led. He had yielded to that instinct for grandeur, that vertigo of ambition, that was part of the enchantment of the St. Lawrence. He waited for a while. He made his first, tentative moves before he left the colony for France in 1668; and in France, his passionate arguments may very well have succeeded where his letters failed to convince, for when eventually he returned in 1670, he had obviously secured a freer hand in the west. For the last two years of his tenure of office, he almost forgot the little affairs of the seigniories and gave his ardent ambition

and his cold intelligence to the aggrandizement of New
France. 'I am no courtier,' he wrote, 'and it is not merely
to please the king with unreasonable predictions that I say
this portion of the French monarchy will become something
great.'

In this game of western empire, Talon's agents were fur
traders, missionaries, soldiers, and gentlemen adventurers
from France. His methods — the methods by which the fur-
trading colony was to extend and hold its influence over the
native tribes of the interior — were an astute mixture of
diplomacy and force, of cajolery and intimidation, in which
presents, and pageants, and sermons were just as necessary
as soldiers and fortified posts. Talon's objectives were three.
He planned to strike north-west against Hudson Bay, south-
west against the Iroquois and the English towards the Spanish possessions, and due west towards the central crossroads
of the continent. It was in this last area that the French
made their first formal imperialist move. At Sault Ste.
Marie, which was one of the chief centres of the new western
fur-trading region, they held a solemn and brilliant pageant
of annexation by which they laid claim to the whole west in
the name of Louis XIV, King of France and of Navarre.
Delegates from fourteen Indian tribes assembled; and around
Saint-Lusson, the King's formal representative, were gathered Perrot, and Jolliet, and their *coureurs-de-bois*, and
Father Allouez and the Jesuits from the mission. It was a
June day, in the first flush of northern summer. They raised
a great cross against the sky, and broke out the fleur-de-lys
above it. Three times Saint-Lusson shouted aloud the claims
of the French King, and three times he took symbolic possession of the land by raising a sod of turf with his sword.
There was a long roll of musket fire and shouts of 'Vive le
Roy'; and then Father Allouez began to tell the watching
Indians of the grandeur of the monarch who had now become their king. 'When he attacks,' he solemnly assured
them, 'he is more terrible than the thunder; the earth

trembles, the air and sea are set on fire by the discharge of his cannon. . . . From all parts of the world people go to listen to his words and to admire him, and he alone decides all the affairs of the world. . . . He has towns of his own, more in number than you have people in all these countries five hundred leagues around; while in each town there are warehouses containing enough hatchets to cut down all your forests, kettles to cook all your moose, and glass beads to fill all your cabins.'

Saint-Lusson's task had been formal and relatively simple, for the Jesuits and *coureurs-de-bois* had already won the alle-giance of the western tribes. In the north, where the Hudson's Bay Company was beginning to divert the Indians by fine trade goods and excellent prices, the problem was much more difficult. In August, 1671, a small party led by Paul Denis, Sieur de Saint-Simon, and the Jesuit Father Albanel set out to make the incredible overland journey from the St. Lawrence to Hudson Bay. They pushed up the Saguenay River, across Lake Mistassini, and down the Rupert River to James Bay. 'Even the Savages dread this journey, as one full of fatigues and peril,' wrote Father Albanel in his journal. The good man was both awed and delighted by the strange, rugged, majestic country through which they passed. He found wild roses on the shores of James Bay in June of 1672 'as beautiful and fragrant as those at Quebec'; but it was strange to watch the immense, empty tidal reaches of the northern sea and to see the dawn coming up when the last light of sunset had not died out in the west. Saint-Simon claimed the land for France and they tried to renew their friendly relations with the natives. 'And, to that end,' said Father Albanel to the Mistassini Indians, 'abandon the plan of carrying on commerce with the Europeans who are trading toward the North Sea, among whom prayer is not offered to God; and resume your old route to Lake St. John, where you will always find some black gown to instruct and baptize you.'

The third direction was to the south-west. Here the plans were Talon's; but the accomplishment came, in the main, under his successor, Frontenac. Talon had conceived the idea of building a fort on Lake Ontario to overawe the Iroquois and to check their trading activities north of the lake. In 1671, Governor de Courcelle led an official military expedition into Lake Ontario; and the Iroquois were much impressed by this sudden advance towards their western flank and by the solemn words of warning which the Governor addressed to them. But the fortification of Lake Ontario was simply the first step towards the discovery and annexation of the great south-central mass of the continent. Talon hoped to hem in the English, to compete for the riches of Mexico, and to discover a passage to the California sea; and obviously the pathway to this southern dominion was the 'great river named Messipi' of which Father Claude Allouez had spoken and towards which the missionaries and *coureurs-de-bois* were drawing closer every year. Talon selected Robert René Cavalier, later Sieur de la Salle, as his official emissary for the exploration of the south-west. But La Salle, who had arrived in the colony in 1666 and whose mind was already full of ambitious schemes for exploration and for the development of a large-scale fur trade on the Great Lakes, was a moody and difficult man, who may actually have tried to avoid the Intendant. By 1672 the impatient Talon had found a substitute explorer of the Mississippi in the Canadian-born *coureur-de-bois* Louis Jolliet. Jolliet picked up Father Jacques Marquette at his new mission on the Straits of Michilimackinac; and in May of 1673 they were off on the first stage of their journey to Green Bay. It was all relatively easy. A short portage from the Fox River to the Wisconsin brought them into the Mississippi system. They drifted down 'this so renowned river' past friendly Indians until they had nearly reached the mouth of the Arkansas. And by the middle of September — travelling this time by the Illinois

River and the Chicago Portage — Father Marquette and Jolliet were back in Green Bay.

Long before this, Talon had returned to France. His departure in the late autumn of 1672 and the arrival of the new governor, Count Frontenac, serves to mark the end of an era in the history of both old and new France under Louis XIV. On the continent of Europe, the year 1672 saw the opening of the conflict with Holland, the first in that long series of wars of aggrandizement which was to close dismally a generation later in the Treaty of Utrecht. In North America, it meant the end of those active efforts to people and strengthen the colony which Louis XIV had begun in 1663. For nearly ten years, Colbert and his associates had tried to direct the growth of New France along traditional ways. But even while they were still willing to spend time and money on the colony, the forces of North America were working against them. Once their attention was diverted to Europe, these native tendencies simply strengthened. Colbert had not been able to impose his vast systematic design upon the new world. He had established new interests but he had not been able to obliterate the old.

Colbert's basic objectives had been increased population and concentrated settlement. In 1672, the year in which Talon returned to France, there were less than five hundred people in Acadia and less than seven thousand in Quebec. Undoubtedly these totals were an improvement on the past of New France; but, judged from the contemporary standards of English America, they were a pitiful failure. Despite all that Colbert and his agents had tried to do, these few settlers were still scattered far and wide by the geography and the pursuits of North America. Chedabucto (Canso), Chebucto (Halifax), La Hève, and Cape Sable — the infinitesimal French settlements on the Atlantic coast of Nova Scotia — were little more than fishing stations. The settlements on the shores of New Brunswick and Maine — the forts on the Saint John River and the post at Pentagoet on

Penobscot Bay — were largely centres for Indian trade. In 1672, the principal agricultural settlement was still at Port Royal, in the Annapolis valley; but before the turn of the century, the bulk of the Acadian farmers had moved further up the Bay of Fundy and settled on the shores of the Basin of Minas and the Isthmus of Chignecto. ' In Canada, settlement was far less scattered; but even in Canada, such concentration as existed was not the kind desired by Colbert but the kind suggested by the St. Lawrence River. Settlement followed the river, was not to be diverted from the river. Of the sixty seigniories which Talon granted in 1672, just before his term of office expired, a few fronted on the Richelieu and the vast majority on the St. Lawrence between Quebec and Montreal. The *habitant* farms, into which these seigniories were gradually divided, were narrow strips all fronting on the river, in exactly the same way as the seigniories. Colbert had hoped to organize the colony in terms of concentrated towns and villages. But New France was like a single, endless village, meandering disconnectedly along the banks of the river system.

Agriculture flourished, as it had never flourished before; but it still had to grow in a setting which was uncongenial and distracting. On the St. Lawrence, the *habitants* began to chop down trees and sow field crops: along the Bay of Fundy, the Acadians dyked the marsh lands, grew hay, and fattened their cattle. It was monotonous, back-breaking work which had to compete with other pursuits far more lucrative, varied, and exciting. The fishery withheld colonists from New France; the fur trade — and this was even more important — took actual settlers away from the settlements and into the remote interior. In 1672, before Jolliet and La Salle had opened the south-west trade, there were already several hundred *coureurs-de-bois,* who got their living by trading with the Indians; and this defection of the youngest, the most energetic and enterprising men in the community was to have the most drastic effect upon the economy of New

France. It limited its agriculture, its industry, and its export trade. In the main, the seigniories on the lower St. Lawrence produced not for export but for subsistence; and, as the future was to show only too convincingly, there were more than a few times when they could not live upon what they had produced. The brewery which Talon had established ceased to operate soon after his departure; the lumbering and shipbuilding industries made no great progress. Skilled workmen were even more scarce and expensive than village labourers; and, like agriculture, the traditional trades and occupations were scarcely able to compete with the rewards and excitements of fur trading.

In these circumstances, a varied and vigorous external trade was practically impossible. The capital, the enterprise, and the very commodities themselves were lacking. The aggressive energy which was so manifest in the interior, in the stretch of territory west and south of Lake Michigan, was balanced by a curious, supine inactivity at the seaboard and on the Atlantic Ocean. The imperialist planners had expected to promote the co-ordinated growth of the French American possessions by encouraging trade between New France, the West Indies, and Acadia. As they saw it, a ship would leave New France loaded with flour, provisions, and lumber; it would exchange part of its cargo at Cape Breton or Placentia for fish and then proceed to the West India islands; there it would trade its lumber and foodstuffs for sugar; and finally it would sail for France and pick up a cargo of manufactures in the homeland for the return voyage to Canada. This type of three-cornered trade, which Massachusetts was to develop so successfully, seemed beyond the capacity of the French colonies. Empire builders were never presented with such stubborn materials as the American possessions of the French. In July, August, and September, when the commercial season was at its height on the St. Lawrence, the hurricanes were thought to make trading dangerous in the West Indies; and in the late winter, when cargoes of sugar were again available in the islands, the St. Lawrence was sealed with ice. New France did develop a small direct trade to the fishing settlements and the West Indies; but it was relatively unimportant. The great trade route of New France was the single undeviating line along which the ships sailed from the homeland loaded with supplies and manufactures, and along which they returned to France carrying their light and valuable cargoes of furs.

[*III*]

This instinctive effort to create a true France overseas was just as obvious in the cultural sphere as in the political and economic order. Up until 1663, fishermen, fur traders, and missionaries had largely made up New France. It was only a misshapen fragment of French society: but the great colonizing movement with which Louis XIV's reign opened seemed at last to involve the transplantation of the major part of French culture to the new world. Instinctively the leaders of the colonial community tried to preserve the social organization, the standards of social welfare, the cultural and moral values, which made up the French variant of European civilization. All too frequently they forgot that these social classes and standards had developed in an environment which differed radically from that which they had come to occupy. It was true, of course, that they hoped in part to change the new environment, to make the economy of New France resemble that of the mother country, to increase settlement, encourage agriculture, and promote diversified production and trade. But, as has been seen, these efforts were only partial successes; and the inconclusive result in the economic order naturally prejudiced the outcome in the social sphere. The fur trade, which paradoxically expanded rather than contracted with the establishment of royal government, was not only an economic enterprise, but also a way of life — a strange, half-alien way of life which was to warp and weaken the organization and standards of the agricultural community on the lower St. Lawrence.

The first changes in the structure of French society were made on the initiative, or with the approval, of French officialdom itself. The feudal system, which was the basis of social organization in the mother country, was naturally transferred to New France as the seigniorial system. But it was considerably changed, and liberalized, in the process. Feudalism had been the product of an age of self-sufficient agriculture and minutely divided political authority. Even in France, where a commercial middle class had begun to rise, and where the crown had taken over political and judicial power from the nobles, the old institution was already changing. There was all the more reason, as the French colonial authorities sensibly realized, why it should be still more radically changed to conform to the demands of the American environment. Even with the best will in the world, the difficult process of adjustment was sometimes fatal. In Acadia, feudalism did not 'adapt' itself: it simply disappeared. But in Canada, where the texture of settlement was thicker and more durable, the seigniory survived in a not unskilfully modified form. It was given important functions, but granted few special privileges. It was supposed to act as a means of protection, of colonization, of social solidarity; but it was never intended to become the basis of inequity and favouritism.

The position of any individual or group in a feudal hierarchy must be described in terms of his relations both with his feudal superior and his feudal subordinate. In Canada, the seigneur's obligations to his formal superior, the King, were certainly not onerous. He was required to render fealty and homage to the sovereign of whom all land was held; and if he sold his seigniory he was obliged to pay the *Quint*, a fifth of the sale price. But his most important duties were of a different order: he owed them not so much to the King as to the colonial community. He had to live on his seigniory, or, as the phrase had it, keep 'feu et lieu'; he was expected to divide his property into farms and people it with settlers. To a large degree he had become a government agent for settlement. The royal Arrêts of Marly of 1711, which echoed previous administrative orders, compelled the seigneur to offer his land to all prospective settlers at the usual ground rent, without attempting to exact any bonus. And over his head was the threat — which, it should be remembered, largely remained a threat — that if he disobeyed too flagrantly, his seigniory would be forfeit to the King.

In Canada, the *censitaire*, so called because he paid *cens* or rent to his lord, bore no such crushing burden as was imposed upon the peasant in old France. His duties were similar in name to those of his European counterpart, but they were very different in character. His payments and services were of two chief kinds, annual and casual. The casual dues, or *lods et ventes*, were relatively unimportant, for they were paid only when the property changed hands, and on most seigniories payment was not demanded when a direct heir succeeded to a deceased holder. The annual dues, the *cens et rentes*, which were paid every year on Saint Martin's Day, November 11, constituted the major financial return which the landlord obtained from his seigniory. The *cens* was usually calculated on the river frontage of the *censitaire's* property, the *rentes* on the number of square arpents which it contained. Normally, the *habitant's* holding was a long, narrow strip, with a frontage of three to four arpents on the St. Lawrence or one of its tributaries, and a depth of about forty arpents. For such an average-sized farm the annual dues amounted to a sum of about six livres, which was sometimes paid in money, sometimes in kind, and sometimes in both. The *corvée* was a regularly recurring service which might be ranked with the annual dues: it obliged the *censitaire* to labour on his lord's home farm without payment for a day or two at ploughing, seeding, and harvest time. Finally, there was the *droit de banalité,* which permitted the seigneur to profit from the monopoly of certain essential community services. In old France the peasants had been obliged to pay toll for the use of their lord's wine-press, bake-oven, and flour-mill; but in Canada, for obvious reasons of climate and distance, only the flour-mill became of prime importance. The toll, which was one-fourteenth of the grain ground, was not likely to bring in much revenue until the seigniory became fairly populous: and at the beginning most seigneurs were inclined to look at their monopoly as an obligation rather than a privilege. Yet here again the state, by an Arrêt of 1686, stepped in to declare that the landlord must erect the mill or forfeit his *droit de banalité.*

Thus an attempt had been made to adapt feudalism for its reception in North America. The institution was still confining and paternalistic in character; but much of its formalism and inequity had been removed. Life on the seigniories was a hard, drab, monotonous affair, with simple pleasures and few diversions; but, at any rate, it was not likely to be embittered by serious quarrels between master and man. If the Canadian seigneur was permitted by a lax government to escape some of the obligations which were laid down so carefully in the Arrêts of Marly and elsewhere, he was never allowed to impose unusual burdens upon his tenants. Unlike the peasant of old France, the Canadian *habitant* was never impoverished by feudal demands and brutalized by seigniorial toil. The difficulty lay, not in the relation of the rural classes with each other, but in the position of the agricultural community as a whole in the society of New France — in a society which was still economically supported by the fur trade and permeated by its cultural influences. The fur trade limited the relative importance of agriculture; and, as a natural consequence, it tended to depress the social standing of those classes who depended upon it.

The fate of the seigneurs was characteristic. They repre-

sented the rural community, they might have been expected
to provide leadership in the colony; but their career as a
class was one of embarrassment from the beginning. It was
not that they were expected to rival the brilliant splendour
of high society in France. Very few of them came from the
titled nobility: they were members of the untitled *noblesse*,
bureaucrats, merchants, soldiers of good family like Saurel,
St. Ours, Berthier, Verchères, Contrecoeur, and other officers
of the Carignan-Salières regiment to whom Talon granted
seigniories. It was not in their nature to show the arrogance
of the French nobility and they had no chance of getting
the French nobility's fantastic favours and privileges. But,
at the same time, they were supposed to merit general respect
and they were accorded public honours. The Canadian
seigneur had his special pew in church, with his arms above
it, and special prayers were offered for him. He was first to
receive the Sacraments and first in procession after the priest.
The villagers doffed their hats in his presence; and, on New
Year's morning, they came early to the manor house and
begged his blessing. Theoretically, he was a distinguished
superior among admiring vassals; but, in fact, the prestige of
his feudal status was continually contradicted by his very
real insecurity and embarrassment. He had no important
functions, and — what was far worse — very little income. In
Canada, as in old France, the state had taken over the political and judicial duties which the nobility had once exercised.
The Canadian seigneur was simply a landlord — a landlord
in a country where agriculture was inferior to fur trading,
where property could simply not support a gentleman in the
life to which he was accustomed.

Desperately the seigneurs struggled to hold their position;
but the efforts which they made to increase their incomes did
not particularly improve their status in society. Some — perhaps a good many — abandoned the difficult career of gentility, and became hard-working, substantial farmers, slaving
away with their 'vassals' in the fields. A few took to shop-

keeping on a small scale: a few were given jobs in the badly paid civil service by an indulgent government. There were still others — more enterprising or reckless than the rest — who came to terms with the very forest which had mastered them, took to the woods themselves, captained brigades of *coureurs-de-bois* into the interior, and, later on, led Indians and fur traders in raids against the English settlements. But the successful, whether they stayed with the land or in effect abandoned it, were probably a minority. 'The nobility of this new country,' wrote the Governor, Denonville, a little later on, 'is everything which is most beggarly.' Crippled with debts, haunted by poverty, and yet unwilling to surrender all their social pretensions, the seigneurs were sometimes compelled to abandon normal standards of life in order to keep up a draggled show of gentility, or to send their children into the woods to trade with the Indians in order to eke out the miserable means of livelihood.

Just as the comparative failure of agriculture depressed the rural groups in general and the seigneurs in particular, so the expansion of the fur trade elevated the *coureurs-de-bois*. The *coureurs-de-bois* were the most distinctive social creation of New France, the personification of its dynamic vitality and its curious primitive weakness. People deprecated the existence of the *coureurs-de-bois* and deplored their activities; but they could not be suppressed. They sought the only real wealth which the colony had discovered and the only rich and varied experience which it could afford. When the last whitewashed stone house of the last seigniory disappeared behind them down the river, they slipped at once into a wilderness of rock and lake and forest, a vast fickle and unfriendly empire of perils and fatigues and privations. A sense of the treachery and violence of Nature in the new world was in their blood. They were inured to hardship, callused to danger. 'It is a strange thing,' wrote Radisson in his odd Frenchman's English, 'when victualls are wanting, worke whole nights & dayes, lye downe on the bare

ground, & not allwayes that hap, the breech in the water, the
feare in yᵉ buttocks, to have the belly empty, the wearinesse
in the bones, and drowsinesse of yᵉ body by the bad weather
that you are to suffer, having nothing to keepe you from
such calamity.'

But there were freedom and novelty as well as danger in
the forest. Here the King's writ could not run, here the
censorious eye of the parish priest could never penetrate.
'We weare Cesars,' said Radisson grandly, 'being nobody to
contradict us.' In the forest there was freedom from the
stuffy conventions and odious taboos of seigniorial society —
there was freedom to learn the strange, wild dissolute ways of
an alien culture. The fur trade in the west was an ambiguous frontier between two vastly different societies — an
equivocal, debased borderland between the ways of Europe
and the ways of native America. The canoe, the toboggan,
the sledge, the snowshoe, the *mocassin* or *botte sauvage,*
were all examples of the useful tools and devices which the
French borrowed from the Indians. But they learnt other
things as well, modes of behaviour, traits of character, attitudes to life. Uneasily and with an exciting sense of degradation, they took part in the gluttonous feasts, the drunken
orgies, the sexual promiscuity of the tribes. They acquired
something of the Indian's stoical fatalism, his superstition,
his secrecy and savagery in battle. When the triumphant
war-parties returned, dragging with them their helpless
prisoners, the *coureurs-de-bois* saw and heard the unbelievable extreme horrors of cruelty. Some of them bore the scars
of it on their own bodies. 'They bourned the soales of my
feet and leggs,' said Radisson of the Iroquois. 'A souldier
[warrior] run through my foot a sword red out of the fire, and
plucked severall of my nailes. . . . That very time there came
a litle boy to gnaw with his teeth the end of my fingers.'

If relatively few *coureurs-de-bois* bore back these physical
scars to the seigniories, they all returned with the deep marks
of their experience upon them. They had seen too much

and done too many things. Irreverent, impatient of authority, extravagantly friendly and violently quarrelsome by
turns, they were spendthrifts who squandered their money in
the taverns along the river bank and among the white and
Indian prostitutes who were beginning to creep into Montreal. The fur trade, said Governor Denonville sorrowfully
a little later, 'makes them undocile, debauched, and incapable of discipline, and turns them into pretended nobles, wearing the sword and decked out with lace. . . . ' Their jaunty
airs and ephemeral riches were far more impressive than the
drab, penurious gentility of the seigniories; and, as they
swaggered about the settlements in their gaudy finery, they
became the acknowledged heroes of the community, the real
nobility of New France, quickening the beat of its existence
with their violence and their vagaries, subtly infecting it with
their easy-going standards of conduct. 'You would be
amaz'd,' Lahontan wrote of the fur traders, 'if you saw how
lewd these Pedlars are when they return; how they Feast
and Game, and how prodigal they are, not only in their
Cloaths, but upon Women. Some of 'em as are married, have
the wisdom to retire to their own Houses; but the Batchelors
act just as our *East-India-Men,* and Pirates are wont to do;
for they Lavish, Eat, Drink and Play all away as long as the
Goods hold out; and when these are gone, they e'en sell
their Embroidery, their Lace, and their Cloaths. This done,
they are forc'd to go upon a new Voyage for Subsistence.'

As before, New France was a country of extremes. The
great traditional classes of French civil life existed in only
a rudimentary fashion in the colony; there was no splendid
court, no high nobility, no well-educated bureaucracy, no
wealthy commercial class. In Canada, society was dominated at one extreme by the reckless, slightly disreputable
personality of the *coureur-de-bois* and at the other by the
sober, austerely virtuous figure of the cleric. It had been
one of Colbert's original objectives — a characteristic objective of a seventeenth-century anti-clerical bureaucrat — to

change the whole character, position, and influence of organized religion in the colony. New France had begun its religious life as a mission — a Jesuit mission, connected, not with the French Church, but with the Papacy. It was impossible, even if it had been desirable, to get rid of the Jesuits: but their power, Colbert believed, should be limited by the state, and their influence could be balanced by that of other religious bodies. Colbert authorized the return of the Récollets to Canada in 1670, and the encouragement of the priests of Saint-Sulpice at Montreal. Even more important, he hoped to establish a secular clergy organized in a regular parish system as in France — a little colonial church, which would adopt the same attitude to Rome and the same relations with the state as the great Gallican Church of France. It was a scheme which broke down for years against the opposition of Laval and the inert resistance of the socially immature colony. The seigniories, for some time, could no more afford a resident clergy than they could a landed aristocracy. Tithes were established, but in 1667 the rate was reduced to one twenty-sixth of field crops; and the needs of the settlements were met, not by parish priests, but by missionary curés who travelled out from Laval's seminary at Quebec. The economies were probably necessary; but they had an important result. They left Laval in power — Laval the fervent ultramontane, the nominee of the Jesuits. And under Laval the assertiveness of the church, its evangelical spirit, and its missionary organization were all maintained.

So also was the puritanical rule which the Jesuits had first exercised. In a colony which lacked urbanity and civilization as much as it exhibited crudity and violence, the clergy were very conscious of their rôle as guardians of faith and morals. As the fur trade expanded, as the *coureurs-de-bois* increased in numbers and deepened in depravity, they became alarmed at the demoralization of New France. Bishop Laval launched *mandement* after long *mandement* against drunkenness, impiety, luxurious and carnal living, vain and immodest dress. Comedies were rejected as 'evil and criminal.' Mixed dancing was vehemently condemned; and even the Governor's daughter, because of 'her age and vivacity,' was merely permitted some 'modest and moderate dances . . . with persons of her own sex only and in the presence of her mother.' 'Here,' said the irreverent Lahontan, with some exaggeration perhaps, 'we cannot enjoy ourselves, either at Play, or in visiting the Ladies, but 'tis presently carried to the Curate's ears, who takes publick notice of it in the Pulpit. . . . You cannot imagine to what a pitch these Ecclesiastical Lords have screw'd their Authority.'

The clergy and the *coureurs-de-bois* personified the two chief interests in the colony. The *coureurs-de-bois*, of course, stood simply and solely for the fur trade, for the wild, reckless philosophy of the *pays d'en haut*. The clergy, far more effectively than the feeble and embarrassed seigneurs, represented settlement, the rural community, traditional cultural values. It was true, of course, that the clergy had interests of their own in the west. But the existence of their Indian missions, far from inclining them to support western expansion in general, simply increased their horror and detestation of it. Their great purpose in the west was the winning of Indian souls. They were convinced that the fur traders, who corrupted the Indian's morals with brandy and prostitution, were the one great impediment to successful evangelization. The fur trade, in fact, was their enemy in both east and west. It was responsible, not only for the demoralization of the Indians, but also for the corruption that seemed to be slowly infecting the seigniories. Stubbornly they tried to confine a trade which the *coureurs-de-bois* sought continually to expand. This quarrel between *coureurs-de-bois* and clergy, fur trade and settlement, expansion and stability, wormed its way, like everything else in the colony, into the affairs of government. The dispute at the council board ended in the triumph of expansion; and the triumph of expansion led to the outbreak of frontier war.

[*IV*]

This train of events reached its appointed climax under the new governor, Louis de Buade, Comte de Frontenac et de Palluau. He was already over fifty when he came to Canada in the autumn of 1672. The pattern of his life had been woven in the grand fashion of the seventeenth-century nobility. His birth was excellent, his connections distinguished, his whole career had been spent between the intrigues of the court and the excitements of campaigning. He brought back memories of old, half-forgotten battles and sieges in the Thirty Years' War, of the last efforts of ruined Venice to repel the Turks from Crete. He had roamed across Europe, squandered his small fortune, quarrelled with his wife. His vanity, his extravagance, his boastful choleric vigour were notorious. Outwardly he was now an aging aristocrat, a half broken-down army veteran, who might have frittered away his time at Quebec in sullen inactivity, brooding over a disappointing career and insolently insisting on every little deference which was due his rank and station. But he did nothing of the kind. The country seemed to rouse him, to inspire him, in the odd way in which it had inspired Talon. He was arrogant, quick-tempered, and quarrelsome; but now, in this last episode of his life, these qualities seemed curiously to suggest wilful youth and not irritable old age. In his governor's château, perched high on the rock of Quebec, overlooking the River of Canada and the great country which it drained, he showed an enthusiasm, an adaptability, and a furious efficient energy which was like a reawakening of his early manhood.

From the first, he seemed to have all Talon's interest in the west. The year 1672 meant many changes — the outbreak of the war in Europe, the decline of French interest in colonization, the return of Talon to the old country; but it did not interrupt the westward expansion of New France. Frontenac arrived in time to join with Talon in dispatching

the Jolliet expedition to the Mississippi. Next year he realized Talon's project of a fort to protect French interests
on Lake Ontario. The spot chosen was Cataraqui, the
present Kingston, near the outlet of Lake Ontario; and there
in the summer of 1673 La Salle gathered a great company
of Iroquois braves. Frontenac made the journey in a birch-
bark canoe. A superb showman who never missed a theatrical effect, he planned the whole affair in advance. He approached Cataraqui with a great flotilla of canoes, deployed
as in battle formation. He held audience next day withdrawn in his tent, guarded by files of French regulars, surrounded by officers in an array of blue-and-puce uniforms
and a profusion of lace and feathers and gold braid. He was
both majestic and simple. He threatened and cajoled. He
made long, condescending speeches to the chiefs; but he also
gave presents to their wives and played with their children.
And all the while the fort was being built with frantic speed.
La Salle was placed in charge of it. A little later, with Frontenac's full support, he was granted Cataraqui *en seigneurie*.
He was a capitalist — a promoter — who began to build sailing ships and to apply large-scale methods to the fur trade.
Under Frontenac and his lieutenant, La Salle, westward expansion was in full career.

At this point, when the race for furs and empire was at
its height, there appeared at Quebec two ardent champions
of settlement and stability. For the first three years of his
tenure of office, Frontenac had ruled in freedom, for he had
ruled alone. But in 1675 Laval returned in triumph to the
colony, and with him came the new intendant — the first
since Talon — Jacques Duchesneau. Almost immediately
the three men began to quarrel. Their quarrels ranged over
a great number of topics and reached an extreme low of pettiness; but the disputes over the brandy question and the
problem of fur-trade regulation were of central importance;
and in these Laval and Duchesneau called in question once
more the whole policy of westward expansion. Laval, who

was concerned for the progress of evangelism and morality
among the tribes, hoped to prohibit the sale of brandy to the
Indians. Duchesneau, who was interested in the growth of
agriculture and diversified trade in the colony, wished to
limit the number of *coureurs-de-bois* in the interior. Back
of Laval were the Archbishop of Paris, the doctors of the
Sorbonne, and the King's confessor, Père Lachaise, who condemned the sale of brandy to the Indians with the voice of
outraged piety. Back of Duchesneau were Colbert and the
mercantilists, who had always insisted that New France
should be based on a variety of interests and not dependent
on a single luxury specialty like fur. The two views were
roughly complementary. Laval and Duchesneau supported
each other, partly because their common enemy was Frontenac and largely because, at bottom, they represented the
two aspects of the same colonial policy. Fundamentally they
both opposed the expansionist programme which Frontenac
had adopted. Under the wrangling rule of these three men,
the conflict between fur trade and settlement, which had
been implicit in New France ever since 1663, broke violently
into the open.

By an odd coincidence, circumstances came to the support
of Laval and Duchesneau. They attacked the fur trade,
when the fur trade itself began to show serious signs of weakness. They criticized expansion, when the evil effects of
expansion began to appear even in the fur trade itself. The
work of the explorers and *coureurs-de-bois*, the movement
to the Upper Lakes and the Mississippi, had naturally and
vastly increased the supply of furs. The increase might have
been expected to raise the income of the colony and the
revenue of its government. But it did not; not, at least,
materially, for there were severely modifying consequences
of expansion. The first of these was an enormous increase
in costs — costs of transport, explorations, Indian presents,
fortified posts, military expeditions — the burden of the
whole elaborate system by which the French held down the

Iroquois and kept the trade and friendship of the western tribes. It would have been hard enough to bear these increased costs alone; but it was the misfortune of New France that they were accompanied by a fall in prices. This fall, of course, was partly due to the enlarged fur supply itself, partly to the deterioration of quality as the poorer grades of *castor sec* came flooding in from the south-west, and partly to the vagaries of fashion in France which now dictated smaller hats and permitted substitute materials for beaver fur. In 1674, the great West India Company, which Colbert had founded ten years before, disappeared in failure. The fur trade became a state monopoly, and in 1675 it was 'farmed' by the crown to Nicolas Oudiette, who consented to accept all furs at a fixed price. When this, as might have been expected, produced a further flood of poor grades of beaver, New France was urged to take a second step — the logical consequence of the first. It had begun by fixing prices. Surely it must now go on to regulate supply.

Laval and Duchesneau pressed their advantage. Now they could find justification for their policy not only in the problem of Indian morality and the state of seigniorial agriculture, but also in the very condition of the fur trade itself. When Talon left the colony in 1672 there had been free trade in furs and brandy; but in the next few years — and even under the rule of the expansionist Frontenac — the controls were gradually increased and strengthened. A system of licences, which permitted twenty-five canoes, with three men each, to go to the interior for trade, was established; and severe penalties were imposed upon unlicensed traders. It was harder, of course, to stop the brandy trade, for even Colbert was opposed to its prohibition, and the principal inhabitants of New France, when they were called together in the so-called 'Brandy Parliament' of 1678 to discuss the question, voted by a majority of fifteen to five against any restriction at all. Prohibition, they prophesied, would have only a single and terrible result: it would hand the fur trade over to the English. The morality of the Indians would not be improved, for the English would continue to sell them spirits. The faith of the Indians would certainly be corrupted, for the English would try to win them to the Protestant religion. Prohibition would simply substitute rum and Protestantism for brandy and the Roman Catholic faith. This was a dreadful prospect; but one which Louis XIV, if not the fur traders, found it possible to face. In 1679 he went so far as to prohibit the sale of brandy to the Indians in their native villages. This was the climax of the movement for regulation and control. It looked as if the interests of settlement, agriculture, and Christian morality were in the ascendant. It looked as if Laval and Duchesneau had really won.

But had they? The regulations and controls had behind them all the authority of provincial ordinances and all the majesty of the royal will. But how could they be enforced? The deepest impulses of the fur-trading colony burst through restrictions even when they were supposedly imposed in the interests of the fur trade itself. The licences permitted seventy-five men to go into the interior; but in 1679 Duchesneau estimated that there were perhaps five or six hundred *coureurs-de-bois* in the woods. 'I have done all in my power,' he wailed, 'to prevent this evil which may cause the ruin of the colony. I have made ordinances against the *coureurs-de-bois*, against the merchants who furnish them with supplies, against the *gentilshommes* and others who give them shelter and even against those who know of their whereabouts and do not inform the local judges. . . .' It was all useless. The controls broke down every time: ' . . . everyone agrees that there is almost general disobedience in the country.' The governor, the councillors, the bureaucrats, the soldiers, the seigneurs, and the clergy — everybody — was directly or indirectly bound up in the prosecution of the fur trade; and the unchangeable instinct of all who concerned themselves in the fur trade was towards expansion for increased supply. It was true — or so events had seemed to prove — that increased supply might mean falling prices, declining income for the colony, and straitened finances for its government. But the restrictions as a remedy defeated themselves, for they encouraged the Indians to trade with the English and the *coureurs-de-bois* to smuggle their furs through New York. Besides — and this was, perhaps, the main reason — the policy of maintaining prices by restricting output was simply too heroic a course for the colony to pursue for long. The individual trader struggled blindly to increase his falling income by a larger turnover. The failure of all these attempts at control drove the colony inexorably back to the alternative of expansion.

The pause had been only momentary — scarcely a pause at all; and it was followed by a new advance into the interior which led almost immediately to war. In 1678 Daniel Greysolon Dulhut left the colony for the country beyond Lake Superior, where he was to pacify the intertribal warfare and annex the Sioux territories to the French crown. In 1678 also, La Salle returned to New France, armed with royal concessions for the settlement and commercial development of the Mississippi valley. His plans were imperial in scope. He built the *Griffon*, the first sailing vessel on the upper lakes, established forts and trading posts on the Illinois River, started the construction of another sailing vessel for trade on the Mississippi, and in 1682 explored the Mississippi to its mouth. It was probably La Salle's restless energy in the south-west trade, the threat of his large-scale operations in a region where the Iroquois had always been keen competitors, that ended the Indian peace which de Tracy had imposed back in 1666. The peace had lasted fourteen years; but in 1680 a large Iroquois raiding-party descended upon the Illinois Indians. The raid was followed by others, against the Illinois and their neighbours, the Miamis; and the raids were succeeded in turn by other disturbances which began to break out at crucial points along

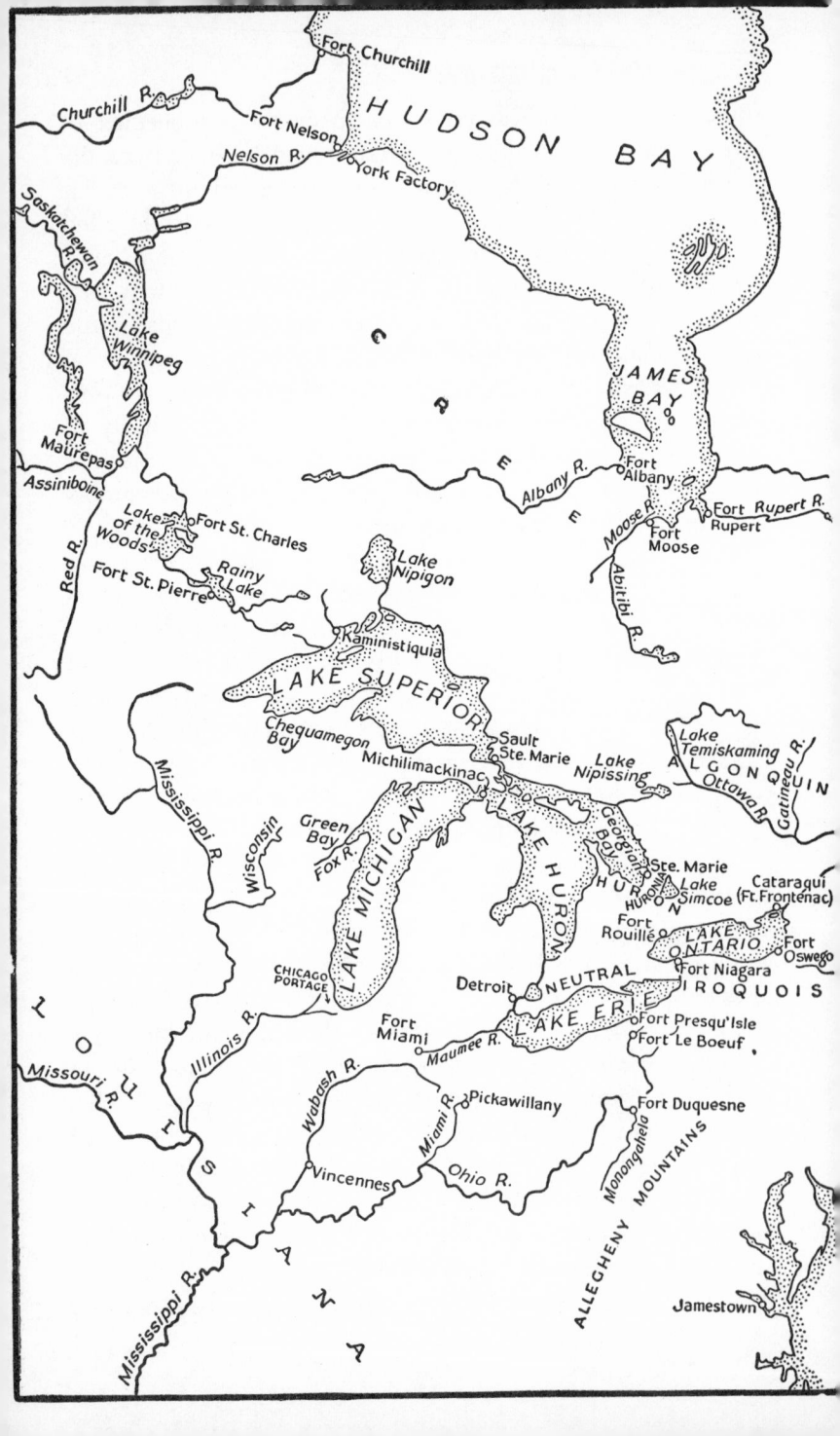

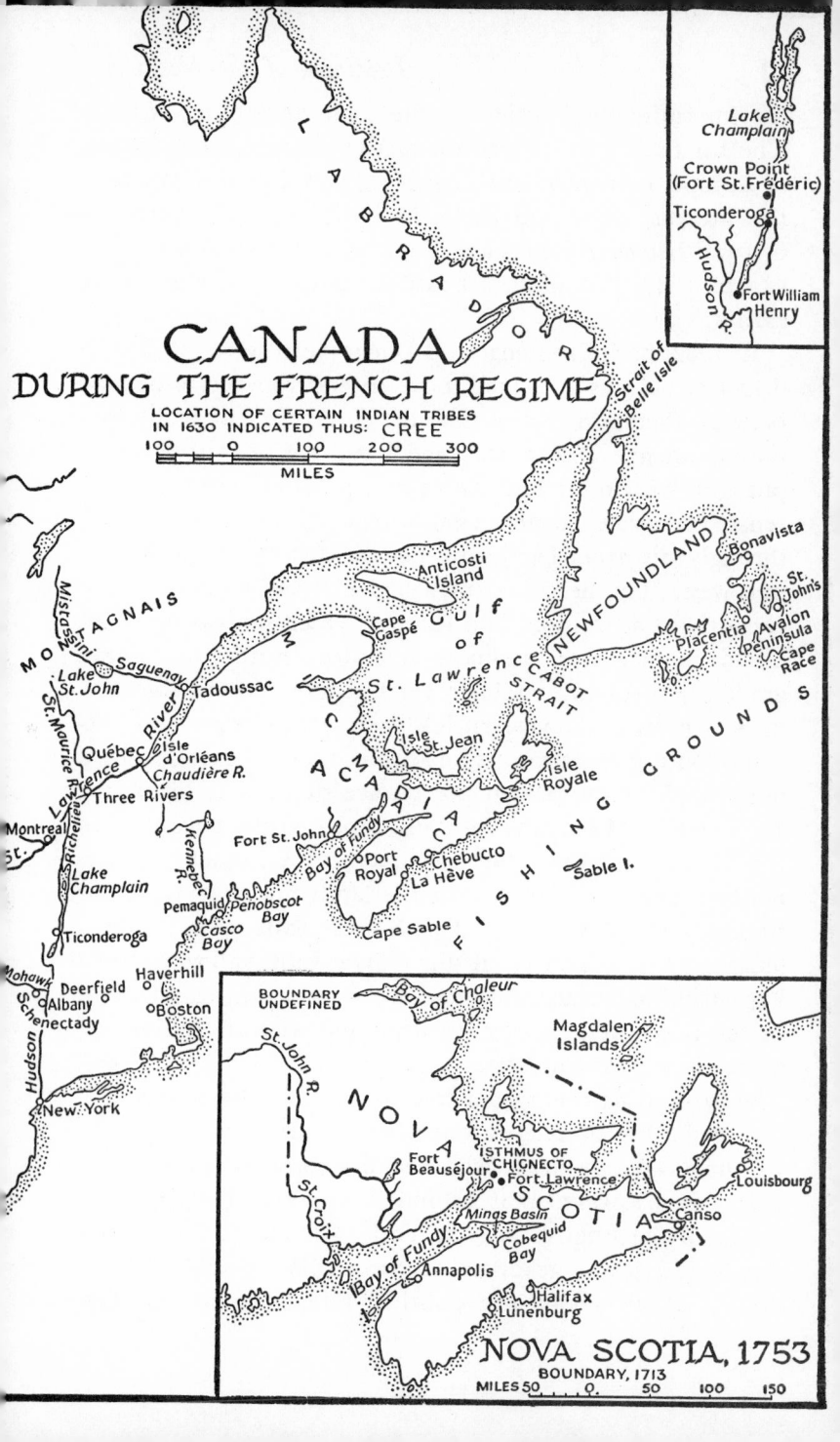

CANADA
DURING THE FRENCH REGIME

LOCATION OF CERTAIN INDIAN TRIBES
IN 1630 INDICATED THUS: CREE

100   0   100   200   300
MILES

Inset (upper right):

Lake Champlain
Crown Point (Fort St.Frédéric)
Ticonderoga
Fort William Henry
Hudson R.

Main map labels:

LABRADOR

Strait of Belle Isle

NEWFOUNDLAND

Bonavista
St. John's
Placentia
Avalon Peninsula
Cape Race

GULF of St. Lawrence
Anticosti Island
Cape Gaspé
CABOT STRAIT
Isle St. Jean
Isle Royale
Sable I.

FISHING GROUNDS

MONTAGNAIS
MISTASSINI
Lake St. John
Saguenay
Tadoussac
St. Maurice R.
St. Lawrence River
Québec
Isle d'Orléans
Chaudière R.
Three Rivers
Montreal
Richelieu
Lake Champlain
Ticonderoga
MOHAWK
Schenectady
Albany
Deerfield
Haverhill
Boston
Hudson
New York

St. John R.
MICMAC
ACADIA
Fort St. John
Bay of Fundy
Port Royal
Chebucto
La Hève
Cape Sable
Pemaquid
Penobscot Bay
Casco Bay
Kennebec R.

Inset (lower right):

NOVA SCOTIA, 1753
BOUNDARY, 1713

MILES 50   0   50   100   150

BOUNDARY UNDEFINED
Bay of Chaleur
Magdalen Islands
St. John R.
NOVA
St. Croix
SCOTIA
Fort Beauséjour
ISTHMUS OF CHIGNECTO
Fort Lawrence
Louisbourg
Canso
Mings Basin
Cobequid Bay
Bay of Fundy
Annapolis
Halifax
Lunenburg

the interminable frontiers of the rival fur-trading systems.
The fur trade had its own distinctive rhythm, independent
of Europe, native to North America, and, like the dances of
the Indians, rapid and hectic in movement. Officially the
first war between France and England in North America began in 1689; but in actual fact it started nearly a decade
earlier.

In 1682, both Frontenac and Duchesneau were recalled in
disgrace. It was a belated move to end the savage dispute
between them, for by this time the Governor had really won
the argument. Duchesneau and Laval had seen their views
put into provincial ordinances and royal edicts; but Frontenac had watched the vital forces of the colony break
through this paper barrier in their instinctive search for the
free west. The fierce old man had planned expansion and
encouraged aggression; and the war which he had not been
afraid to face was gradually spreading north and south,
gradually involving larger forces and more formidable enemies. In 1682, the veteran Radisson, who changed his allegiance with greater ease as he acquired more practice, sailed
north to Hudson Bay in the service of France, burnt the
Hudson's Bay Company fort, and captured the governor. In
the autumn of 1683, three companies of French regulars
reached Quebec from the motherland; and out west, fur
traders and government officials — La Salle and his lieutenant, Henry Tonty, in the Mississippi valley, Nicolas
Perrot and la Durantaye in the Michigan region, and Dulhut
in the north-west — began to draw the western Indians together in a great confederacy pledged to the French alliance.
The fur-trading colony gathered its natural allies and sought
out its natural objectives; but when it turned to punish the
Iroquois — the Iroquois who had first broken the peace of
1666 — it discovered that behind them loomed the military
power of the English in New York. Colonel Thomas Dongan, who became governor of New York in 1683, had no
doubts at all about the political allegiance of the Five

Nations. 'Those Indyans are under this Government, . . .' he curtly declared. 'His Royal Highness [the Duke of York's] territories reaches as far as the River of Canada.' When the French governor, in long, elaborate, and excessively polite dispatches, reminded him that Iroquois territory was French by right of prior discovery, military conquest, and Christian evangelization, he remained unimpressed and voluble. He irreverently suggested that France might as well put in a claim to the sovereignty of China because there were Jesuit missions there. ' 'Tis a hard thing,' he wrote, 'that all Countryes a Frenchman walks over in America must belong to Canada.'

It was the fight for which the French had been waiting and spoiling. But they began it badly. The new governor, Joseph Antoine Lefebvre de la Barre, planned an offensive against the Iroquois in 1684: he was to lead the French regulars and the Canadians up the St. Lawrence, and a war party of some four hundred western Indians started on the long journey down to Lake Ontario. It never reached the rendezvous. At Fort Frontenac, at Cataraqui, La Barre was in tragic difficulties. With many of his men ill of malaria, he did not dare to go forward; and the force which had started out bravely as an avenging army was somewhat hastily and unskilfully transformed into an embassy of peace. Only the Onondagas turned up for the parley, at a meeting-place which they themselves had selected; and when La Barre tried to imitate Frontenac's paternal sternness, the Onondagas' spokesman, who — appropriately enough — was called Grangula or Big Mouth, turned on him suddenly, and with threatening insolence. He ridiculed La Barre's transparent excuse that he had come on a mission of peace. 'Grangula knows better. He sees plainly that Onontio meant to knock them on the head if the French arms had not been so much weakened. . . .' He made no apologies for the past and many defiant threats for the future. La Barre stormed and blustered. But he renewed the peace. The western Indians, who had got no further than Niagara, were betrayed; and French influence in the interior was in complete eclipse.

The inevitable result of La Barre's failure was his recall. Jacques René de Brisay, Marquis de Denonville, who succeeded as governor in 1685, was a soldier aristocrat, who — oddly enough — represented in his own person the two antagonistic and clashing interests of New France. He was a respectful admirer of the clergy and a severe critic of the *coureurs-de-bois* and all they stood for. But he was also a soldier of real courage and considerable energy who came immediately to the conclusion that the peace of 1684 could not be kept. And he committed New France irrevocably to war. It was a war in which, after the first few years, the mother country could give little help — a Canadian war, which might serve as a lurid miniature of the entire personality of New France, as a melodramatic epitome of the whole history of the fur-trading colony of the St. Lawrence. It was fought against fantastic odds, with perhaps ten thousand Acadians and Canadians facing two hundred thousand British Americans. It was fought in poverty and by inflation, for as early as 1685, the new intendant, de Meulles, finding himself short of funds to pay the troops, cut playing cards in four, wrote his name and a denomination upon them, and issued a proclamation enforcing their acceptance. The skills of the forest, the expertness in Indian warfare, the fantastic ability to travel immense distances with speed and in complete secrecy — all the gifts which were the natural inheritance of the fur-trading colony — could be combined into a terrible instrument of warfare. The explorers, fur traders, discharged officers, and restless seigneurs — the amazing generation of resolute men who led New France from 1663 to 1713 — could put the accumulated wisdom of a quarter-century into the defence of French power in North America. New France was strong in its centralization, in its sense of continental strategy which was a product of the river system and the fur trade. A little colony of ten thousand people, with a few thousand Indian allies, was strong enough to plant the fleur-de-lys on Hudson Bay and the Gulf of Mexico, to terrorize the most populous settlements of the Atlantic seaboard, and to repel every attempt at invasion and reprisal.

Denonville intended to attack both north and south. But at the moment, after La Barre's virtual surrender in 1684, the region of the Lower Lakes was dominated by the commercial and military machine of the Iroquois and the English; and in 1685 and 1686, expeditions of Dutch and English traders from New York actually reached Michilimackinac and returned with great cargoes of furs. In these circumstances, the French made a sudden strategic shift away from the St. Lawrence and towards the other drainage basins of the continent, the Mississippi and Hudson Bay. Radisson had thought of this first over two decades before; he had put it into practice so far as Hudson Bay was concerned when he persuaded the English to support him; and now the French began to imitate him by making direct approaches to northern and southern gateways to the continent. In 1684, La Salle sailed from France to found a post on Matagorda Bay in the Gulf of Mexico; and in the spring of 1686, a war party of about a hundred, of whom two-thirds were Canadians, started overland for Hudson Bay by the Ottawa River-Lake Temiskaming-Abitibi River traverse. The titular head of the expedition was the Chevalier de Troyes, an old officer in the Carignan-Salières regiment; but its most picturesque personalities were the three Le Moyne brothers, Jacques, Sieur de Sainte-Hélène, Paul, Sieur de Maricourt, and Pierre, Sieur d'Iberville. Pierre, who was to fight the English by land and sea, in Hudson Bay, Newfoundland, Canada, Acadia, Louisiana, and the West Indies, may stand as the very personification of Canadian resistance and aggression. In 1686, he was just twenty-five — tall, an immense man, hardened and enduring, capable of anything, ready for anything. He and his companions toiled through the north woods on snowshoes, built themselves canoes, and raced down towards the bay on the spring freshets. Fort Moose was captured in complete surprise. In the stillness of a northern summer night, Iberville, Sainte-Hélène, and a few followers scaled the palisades and opened the gate; then the French fired at will into the blockhouse; and de Troyes 'could scarcely curb the impetuosity of the Canadians who uttered loud cries in the fashion of the savages. . . .' Fort Rupert and Fort Albany were captured with almost equal facility. English power had been annihilated on James Bay. And when Iberville, who had been left in command in the north, sailed for Quebec in a captured English ship in the summer of 1687, only Fort Nelson, on the west coast of Hudson Bay, remained in the hands of the English company. In the north success; in the south, murder and disaster. In 1687, the sombre, overbearing La Salle had started north to Canada to get help for his own colony, when a maddened group of his own men shot him and left his stripped body by a Texan river thicket.

In the meantime, the French had returned to the St. Lawrence front. There the course of events passed through dubious success towards final disaster. Denonville and Dongan continued, with diplomatic insolence, the old debate over the political allegiance of the Five Nations; but, at whatever risk of a break with New York, Denonville was determined to punish the Senecas and to re-establish French power on the Lower Lakes. Reinforcements arrived from France in 1686; Tonty, Dulhut, and Perrot once more led a vast company of western Indians down to Lake Ontario. In the summer of 1687 an army of perhaps three thousand men was trailing cumbrously about in the forest south of Lake Ontario, burning the empty Seneca strongholds and the fields of standing corn. It was de Tracy's work all over again — and twenty years too late. The shock of novelty had gone. The Iroquois were not humbled, nor particularly impressed;

and the peace negotiations were broken off by charges of duplicity. The Iroquois redoubled their raids on the settlements; they harried the fur-trade routes to the west. And at daybreak on August 5, 1689, some fifteen hundred of them fell upon the little village of Lachine, close to Montreal, and massacred about three score of the inhabitants. It was the greatest single disaster in the entire history of the colony.

This was in 1689. It was the year of the English Revolution, of the beginning of the long-delayed conflict between England and France. The European war, which was, of course, immediately extended to North America, altered the nature of the struggle between New France and the English colonies far less than might have been expected. It was true that it multiplied and magnified the dangers which threatened Canada; but it did not greatly strengthen the resources of the colony or change its methods of defence. A great plan for a naval and military attack on New York miscarried in the autumn of 1689 in a series of delays; and its only important result was that it brought back Frontenac as governor of New France. The old man was nearly seventy now — as fierce, as impetuous, as indomitable as ever. He brought no reinforcements: he had nothing but his unshakable confidence, his instinct for combat and his knowledge of the people. For the great miscarried formal invasion, he substituted a truly fur-trade offensive. That winter of 1690 he sent out three raiding parties — one for Schenectady in New York, one for the frontier villages on the border of New Hampshire and Maine, and one for the New England settlements on Casco Bay. The swift, secret passage through the woods, the sudden, violent attack on the bewildered settlement, the unrestrained massacre and flaming destruction, the straggling retreat through the snow punctuated occasionally by the torture of the prisoners — these were the common elements of the frontier raids on New England and New York. It was the instinctive way of New France, the way of a colony half-savage and half-civilized, the inevitable result of fur-trading primitiveness, religious fanaticism, and never-ending fear of the Iroquois. The horrors of two worlds — the persecution of the Huguenots and the massacres of the Indians — combined to inspire these raiders and drive them on. They looked upon their English enemies as rebels and heretics whose worst crime it had been to strengthen the power of the Iroquois. They were moved by a savage desire for retaliation and a fanatic zeal to do the will of God.

The successful raids of 1690 had two important consequences: they raised the prestige of the French with the Indians and they goaded the English to reprisals. That summer the fur-trade routes to the west were opened, the alliance with the western Indians was confirmed. That autumn the English descended upon Quebec. In population and real resources, New England and New York were vastly superior to New France; but the divisions which still existed in New York and the lamentable lack of co-operation between the different colonies prevented the full realization of their strength. The English colonists devised the plan which, after several tries, eventually led to the downfall of New France. They saw that a naval attack on Quebec and an overland attack by the Lake Champlain-Richelieu River route would bring the whole colony to its knees; but they failed to act in concert and they failed to push their scheme through. Major Peter Schuyler's brief raid was the only effort made by the large army which was assembled at the head of Lake Champlain. The real peril came from the naval expedition headed by Sir William Phips. In May, 1690, Phips captured Port Royal in Acadia; and this fairly easy success inspired Massachusetts to the greatest offensive effort in her history up to that time. In October, Phips sailed up the St. Lawrence with thirty ships. He hoped somewhat naïvely to surprise Quebec; and he sent off an officer under a flag of truce to demand the surrender of the fortress. The old Count gave him a theatrical reception. 'No,' he roared at the intimidated envoy, 'I will answer your general only with the mouths of my cannon and the shots of my muskets, that he may learn that a man like me is not to be summoned in this fashion.' Since the fortress did not surrender immediately, Phips planned to attack it by land and from the river. But the soldiers landed on the tidal flats of Beauport made little progress against the French troops, the *coureurs-de-bois,* and the Indians; and Phips's tremendous cannonade of the upper town was relatively futile. Within a week of his arrival, he had exchanged prisoners and sailed off down the river again to Boston.

It had been close enough. If the colonies had co-operated more fully, if they had combined effectively with England, there is no doubt that New France could have been ruined. Even as it was her condition was desperate enough. The colony lived under the endless terror of Iroquois raids. Its weak agriculture was continuously interrupted by the wars; there were years when food had to be imported from France and years when the long winters almost ended in famine. The fur trade fluctuated more violently than ever, its crazy rhythm accentuated by the very successes of the French in Hudson Bay. Seasons when not a pelt reached Montreal alternated sharply with other seasons when the market was swamped by the pent-up accumulations of the west and the vast loot from the captured Hudson's Bay Company posts. The problem of controlling supply seemed insoluble, prices broke sharply downwards, the capitalists who 'farmed' the royal fur monopoly failed in rapid succession; and in 1696 the home government took the extreme step of cancelling all licenses and virtually closing the west to the *coureurs-de-bois.* The colony, which was dependent for its revenue upon the fur trade, had to meet greatly increased expenditures from falling income. Inflation by card money continued unchecked. And, at the council board, the new anti-imperialists, Bishop Saint-Vallier, and the Intendant, Champigny, fought the old fight against expansion which Laval and Duchesneau had waged twenty years before.

And yet Frontenac kept his stand. He even took the offensive, using the human resources of the fur-trading colony, its Indians and hardened, forest-wise settlers, in a series of spasmodic, violent efforts for which New France became notorious. Out west, his lieutenants, Henry Tonty, the veteran Nicolas Perrot, and de la Mothe Cadillac, urged the Indians to united resistance and attack against the Iroquois. Down in Acadia, the Governor, de Villebon, from his post on the Saint John River, and the few French priests and settlers in the district led the Abenaki in their raids against the frontier settlements of New England. But the central figure was the paladin Iberville, the immense man with the mop of blond hair, whose fabulous career reads like a record of the defence, and who, in one breathless adventure, captured Pemaquid on the coast of Maine, ravaged the English settlements in Newfoundland, and, up in Hudson Bay, met and defeated three armed English merchantmen in his single ship, the *Pelican*. Frontenac, who planned so many of the campaigns on these dispersed battlefronts, himself led the fight against the Iroquois and the English of New York. The old man — he was getting on for eighty now — captained the army of two thousand which sacked the strongholds of the Oneidas and Onondagas in 1696.

By 1701 New France had flung free of its enemies and grasped the focal points of the continent. The Treaty of Ryswick ended the war between France and England in 1697. In 1700-01, after interminable negotiations and floods of solemn Indian oratory, the Iroquois on the one hand, and the French and their Indian allies on the other, finally exchanged belts and planted the tree of peace. Ryswick was a treaty made in Europe, in comparative disregard of American conditions; but its terms, on the whole, were no mean reward for the efforts of Frontenac and his Canadians. New France regained the whole of Nova Scotia, and, with the exception of the post at the Albany River, she retained all the forts on Hudson Bay. On the southern front, both before and after the peace with the Iroquois, the French were tightening their hold on the St. Lawrence and the Mississippi River systems. In 1701 Cadillac added Detroit to a string of forts which stretched from Cataraqui to the Illinois country; and in 1699, Iberville — the amazing, omnipresent North American — explored the lower Mississippi and founded a post at Biloxi on the Gulf. By that time Frontenac was gone. The violent, irreverent old man, half grandee and half savage, who had aped the majesty of Louis XIV and had danced shouting round an Indian campfire, waving a hatchet above his head, died at Quebec in the late autumn of 1698. He left nothing, though his enemies had always known that he was getting rich by illicit trade. But his last hours were highly edifying. And perhaps, after all, he had reason to be satisfied with his work.

If Louis XIV had only been content to stop . . . But he was not. And the struggle for the Spanish dominions in Europe wrecked his chances for a great empire in North America. The new war, the War of the Spanish Succession, differed radically from the conflict which New France had just concluded. The peace with the Iroquois was not broken, the fighting on Hudson Bay was not resumed, the whole problem of western dominion was never directly involved. It was the region of the fisheries, the debatable land of Acadia, New England, and Newfoundland, that became the chief theatre of war. Though Iberville was full of grandiose schemes for direct attacks on the cities of English America, France was soon far too impoverished and exhausted by the war in Europe to make any such attempts; and the new governor at Quebec, Philippe de Rigaud, Marquis de Vaudreuil, and the other French authorities in America were forced to mask an essentially defensive policy with border forays and spasmodic offensive operations. The privateers of Port Royal preyed on English commerce, the garrison of Placentia sacked St. John's, Newfoundland, the Abenaki Indians harried the frontier villages of Maine; and from Montreal war-parties of French and Indians set out to destroy the New England towns of Deerfield and Haverhill and massacre their inhabitants. When New England tried retaliation herself in Acadia, she was none too successful. When she sought the aid of her sister colonies and of England, co-operation seemed to break down every time. In 1709, Colonel Nicholson's colonial army waited the whole summer near Lake Champlain; and then at last it was learnt that the British fleet, which was to co-operate by attacking Quebec, had been diverted to the defence of Portugal. Again, in the summer of 1711, Nicholson waited in the same place and with the same patience; and this time the great British invasion fleet lost eight transports and two supply ships on the rocky islands in the Gulf of St. Lawrence and sailed away, leaving nearly a thousand bloated corpses behind it. . . . Only Port Royal — an easy conquest — was wrested from the French.

In Europe, however, the war and the reign were ending in disaster. The future of French America was to be decided in Europe and, in large measure, the work of the explorers, adventurers, and *coureurs-de-bois* was in vain. The men of this amazing generation of Canadians were dead now — La Salle by the distant Texan river, Iberville in Havana of yellow fever, and the old renegade Radisson in England. They had staked out an imperial domain for the French crown in North America; and by ingenuity and luck and courage, they had held it to the end.

CHAPTER THREE

THE CRISIS OF A CULTURE

[*1*]

FRANCE had fought the war against a great coalition of European powers; but she made the peace with England. This, in part at least, is the explanation of the large concessions she was forced to make in North America. For years the Tories in England had denounced the war. Once they obtained power in 1710 they ended it as rapidly as possible. Their methods of peace-making were a little unusual; but their very unorthodoxy helped to ensure English success. Instead of negotiating the peace with their allies and imposing it on the enemy, the Tories negotiated the peace with the enemy and imposed it on their allies. This method of 'bargaining for yourselves apart, and leaving your friends to shift at a general treaty,' as the Duke of Shrewsbury called it, proved highly successful. France naturally tried to buy off England with concessions which otherwise might have been shared among the allies; and Henry St. John, Viscount Bolingbroke, the principal Tory negotiator, proved to have just as shrewd an appreciation of England's commercial and colonial interests as the money-grubbing Whigs whom he affected to despise.

Urged on by the Board of Trade and commercial opinion generally, St. John fought to gain Acadia, Newfoundland, and the forts and territories of the Hudson's Bay Company.

The French had had the better of the fighting in all these areas, with the exception of the peninsula of Nova Scotia proper; and the Marquis de Torcy, the principal French negotiator, tried desperately to keep at least a foothold in the coasts and islands of the North Atlantic. So far as Newfoundland was concerned, he was only able to obtain the right for French fishermen to dry their fish on the northern and western shores; but in the vast area vaguely described as Acadia he did rather better. He compelled the English to make two concessions of real importance. In the first place, Acadia was surrendered, not with exactly described limits, but in accordance with 'its ancient boundaries' — a vague phrase which enabled the French to claim later that only the peninsula of Nova Scotia was involved. In the second place, France kept the islands in the gulf, including not only Cape Breton, or Isle Royale, but also Isle St. Jean. In the interior of the continent, it was France that made concessions — concessions without qualification or recompense. She abandoned her claim to the sovereignty of the Iroquois and she surrendered the forts and territories of the Hudson's Bay Company.

The Treaty of Utrecht settled the lines on which the last struggle for supremacy in North America was to be fought. It appointed the battlefields and, in large measure, determined the strategy. But it postponed the issue. Undeniably the position of the French had been worsened; but they still held great stakes in the new world. With the establishment of Louisiana, they had become possessed of a vast empire based upon the two great continental river systems, which formed an almost continuous waterway from Louisbourg to New Orleans. It was a superficial, tenuous empire, held together by isolated forts, trading posts and fishing stations — by dispersed and wandering fishermen, fur traders and Indians. The Treaty of Utrecht had left it even less defensible than it had been. In the maritime region, the French had been flung back upon an inner ring of defences. In the central part of the continent, they had been forced to accept the presence of two rivals, strategically located on their right and left flank. But in each of the three great battle-fronts — the north-western, the south-western, and the Acadian — the outcome had not yet been decided. The Treaty of Utrecht, with its evasions and half-measures, invited a renewal of the conflict and provoked the French to prepare for it. The balance of power in North America was moving, tilting — but had it tilted irrevocably against them? They could not believe it. Everything might yet be recovered. A little planning, a little expenditure, a little reorganization and ingenuity and vigour, and the English might be confined to a narrow strip of the coastline or driven from North America entirely.

In Acadia, which the French had neglected and which they had been forced partly to surrender, a new policy would obviously have to be devised. Cape Breton Island, or Isle Royale, as it was now called, was chosen as the centre of an ambitious scheme of reorganization. Close to the south-east corner of the island, there was a splendid harbour, almost enclosed by a long arm of the land. It was a sombre region, of moorland and marsh and forest, of rock and fog and wind and floating ice. Here, at a cost of four to five million livres for the fortifications alone, the French built Louisbourg, supposedly the strongest fortress in North America. Louisbourg was a totally artificial creation, a grandiose monument to French military pride and engineering genius, transported literally overseas, for the very brick and stone were brought in ships from France, and planted arbitrarily on this desolate and incongruous shoreline. The town lay near the point of the south-west arm of the harbour, protected by an elaborate system of bastions, curtain walls, and batteries in the approved fashion perfected by the French engineer Vauban. Inside the walls, the public buildings, the hospital, and the governor's residence, with its four storeys and tall, graceful tower, proclaimed the political grandeur of France and the dignity of its civilization. There were often great ships of the French fleet in port; and the garrison, in its uniform of white with blue facings, in the end numbered about fourteen hundred men. Louisbourg was an imposing effort — far more imposing than the French had ever made in the past at Placentia or Port Royal. The new fortress was intended to be the protecting centre of French fisheries, settlement, and commerce in the North Atlantic world.

Yet, even in this restricted area to which the French had now retreated, colonization seemed to lag and falter in an inexplicable fashion. The misfortune which had followed the French while they neglected Acadia, seemed still to haunt them while they lavished money and attention upon Louisbourg. It had been assumed, all too complacently, that the new colony could be peopled with settlers from surrendered Nova Scotia and Placentia; and in the Treaty of Utrecht a clause had been carefully inserted which permitted the Acadians 'to remove themselves within a year to any other place, as they shall think fit, together with all their moveable effects.' It was easy enough for the French to ship their few score colonists from Newfoundland and dump them on the rocky coast close to Louisbourg; but when they turned to the Acadians, they suddenly and unexpectedly bumped into difficulties. The Acadians, unnoticed and neglected for generations, had developed a peculiar and baffling collective personality. When the French officially invited them to migrate to Isle Royale, only a small number departed, and among these were a few who went with the prudent purpose of spying out the land. The great majority remained stoically in Nova Scotia. And next year they still remained. And they continued to stay precisely where they were.

It was true that the English authorities now began to put obstacles in the way of their departure, for the year allowed by the Treaty of Utrecht had certainly elapsed. It was also true that the Louisbourg officials might have offered them more real assistance than they did. But the unhelpfulness of the French and the opposition of the English would not have amounted to much if the Acadians had been really determined. In the end, they were the decisive factor in the situation. They did not want to go. They shrewdly suspected that they were far better off where they were. They were simple-minded local patriots whose affection for the ease and plenty of the Bay of Fundy was greater than their love for France or their hatred of England. Politics meant trouble. All that they wanted was to be left alone. They would not go to Isle Royale and only a few went later to Isle St. Jean.

The decision of the Acadians — there were nearly twenty-four hundred of them — was of decisive importance for the future. It meant that the reorganization of the French maritime empire was not to be nearly so thorough as had been expected. It meant that Isle Royale and Isle St. Jean were not going to develop into prosperous farming communities over night. Cape Breton had always been a French fishery; it now became a resident fishery, larger certainly than Placentia had been, but on somewhat the same complex lines. And as such there was no particular reason for it to grow spectacularly. The French fishery was still distributed over a number of different regions, of which Isle Royale was only one; and it was still carried on in large measure by the great fishing ships, which came and returned annually to France, often without visiting Louisbourg, even if they touched at an American port at all. Settlement increased in Newfoundland in the face of English efforts to restrict it; but settlement languished in Isle Royale, in spite of the lavish encouragement it got from the French.

Inevitably therefore, though Louisbourg was a strong competitor in the fishery, it was dependent and vulnerable in everything else. Its own base was narrow and precarious; and it could get little support from the other regions of the French empire — the tropical, maritime, and north-temperate regions, which nobody had ever been able to link effectively together. Provisions from fur-trading Canada were far too uncertain and expensive to be relied on; and Isle St. Jean, which might have become a base for the food supply of Isle Royale, developed with agonizing slowness. Louisbourg, the citadel of the North Atlantic, was forced to depend upon the cattle which the Acadians drove across the isthmus from the Bay of Fundy and on the flour, provisions, and lumber which the New Englanders exchanged for sugar and molasses. France and her colonies could not use all the sugar of the French West Indies, nor provide them with fish. But New England could do both, for she supplied more fish than the British West Indies could consume, and required more sugar than the British West Indies could produce. Isle Royale, like Martinique and Guadeloupe, became a place where surplus French sugar was traded for flour and provisions from Massachusetts. New England, which exploited every weakness and thrived on every limitation of the French, was building a great commercial system out of the ill-assorted parts of her rival's empire.

If the French were still weak in Acadia, however, they were not alone in their feebleness. The English had captured and held Nova Scotia; but it was odd how embarrassed they were by it, how little they could make out of it, how apt they were to avoid it or neglect it altogether. Neither English nor New Englanders showed the faintest desire of making homes in the new province; and virtually the only English settlements in the conquered territory — except purely temporary fishing stations — were at Canso and Annapolis Royal. At Annapolis, which was the seat of government, there was a neglected and decaying fort, a handful of officials and traders, and a small garrison of ill-disciplined soldiers, who, for sheer lack of practice, tended inevitably to become civilians. At Canso, during the height of the summer season, there could be as many as two hundred and fifty schooners and fifteen hundred to two thousand men engaged in the fishery. But Canso, important as it was, was still only a fishing station; and there were perhaps not more than a dozen people who lived there all the year around.

The fact was that the Acadians formed the real population of Nova Scotia in exactly the same way as they had before the conquest. It was vital that they should become good citizens; and the British officials blandly assumed at first that this was an almost automatic process. After all, the Acadians, for one reason or another, had not taken advantage of their treaty rights and 'removed themselves' from Nova Scotia in time. Obviously therefore they should now take the oath of allegiance at once and become loyal subjects of his Britannic Majesty. The conclusion seemed logical; but the Acadians had become particularly dense in the subject of political theory. They had never had much reason to be bothered by Port Royal; they had a certain amount of shrewd contempt for its weak successor, the English Annapolis Royal. They wanted to be left alone — they wanted to be neutral. They were, moreover, encouraged in this instinctive attitude by their priests, and also by the authorities at Louisbourg who were anxious to get whatever political capital they could from the strange situation. The upshot was that the Acadians either refused to take the oath of allegiance or agreed to take it only with qualifications, of which the most important was exemption from military service in any war against France and its allies.

The astounded British discovered that they did not know what to do with a few hundred obstinate and incomprehensible farmers. They kept pressing the matter — at the accession of George I, at the accession of George II, on the rare visits of Nova Scotia's absentee governor. But these eminently suitable occasions for oath-taking came and went, entirely without results. All that Governor Richard Philipps was ever able to extract from the Acadians was an oath which they stubbornly claimed afterwards had been accompanied by a verbal promise of exemption from military service. For years, for decades, the status of the Acadians remained ambiguous and their future unsettled; and their position was typical of the whole state of affairs in the region. The Indians — the Micmac and Abenaki — had not been persuaded to move to Isle Royale; but they kept their old alliance with the French and their old hatred of the English. Acadia was a land of disputed boundaries, of doubtful loyalties, of unsettled conflicts. At Utrecht, the balance of power in the region had wavered, had tilted ominously against the French. And then it seemed slowly to recover itself. Despite all that had happened, the future of Acadia was still uncertain.

It was the same in the interior of the continent. In the *pays d'en haut*, as in Acadia, the Treaty of Utrecht simply encouraged the continuance of the old struggles in new and even more acrimonious forms. On the north was the re-established Hudson's Bay Company. To the south was the rival trading organization of the Hudson River, and behind it the English settlements expanding slowly and inexorably into the interior. During the seventeenth century the Iroquois had been the chief southern enemy of New France; but now the danger from the Indians was yielding place to a new and far more sinister peril. In 1700 the weakened and defeated Iroquois had been forced to make peace. In 1713 they accepted the rule of a power which was certain to continue their old fight far more effectively in the future. By the Treaty of Utrecht they became subjects of Great Britain. The frontier native state had been absorbed in an empire which was even more fundamentally opposed to New France. The society of the Atlantic seaboard stood for a cultural and political heritage which was very different from that of the French, and for interests in North America which were basically antagonistic to fur-trading. The seaboard meant settlement; and ultimately settlement meant the wreckage of the forests, the disappearance of the beaver, and the westward flight of the Indian tribes. The whole long line of the French Empire — the disconnected, tenuous line that stretched from Quebec to New Orleans — was threat-ened without chance of escape by the advance of the English settlements.

All this, though it was slowly approaching, lay still in the future. For a while yet the rivalry from the south still kept the old form of fur-trading competition. Pennsylvania and Virginia were soon to have a hand in this competition; but in the early years after the Treaty of Utrecht it was still based largely on the Hudson-Mohawk River system as a gate-way to the west. In the struggle for the trade of the western Indians, which was now resumed with greater vigour than ever, the English and Dutch traders of New York pressed the advantages they derived from the industrial superiority of England and New England. From England they got coarse, cheap cloth, dyed scarlet and blue to the satisfaction of their Indian customers, which the French tried in vain to imitate successfully. From New England they got rum, often distilled, ironically enough, from French West Indies molasses, and so cheap that French brandy could not possibly rival it. Their competition became keener. In 1722 New York founded a fortified outpost for trade at Oswego, on Lake Ontario. 'The news of this establishment on territory which has been considered from all time to belong to France' alarmed the Governor, de Vaudreuil. It was a striking sign of the new expansionist urge of New York.

Certainly this imperialist drive existed; but its edge was still blunted a little. Just as, in Acadia, the New Englanders were not yet able to overcome the French fishery, so the New Yorkers were not yet ready to try final conclusions with the fur-trading organization of New France. There were many Dutch and English merchants who preferred to get their furs from the French rather than to struggle for them them-selves in the interior. Albany traded surreptitiously with Montreal for the best northern beavers just as Boston smug-gled French West India sugar and molasses from Louisbourg.

The trade to Albany was carried on *via* the Christianized or 'Praying' Indians who lived near Montreal and whose acceptance of Christian principles seemed to put no inhibition on smuggling; and by it the Montrealers got luxuries for themselves and indispensable English woollen cloth for trade with the Indians. To the *Compagnie des Indes*, which held the fur-trade monopoly from 1717, and even to the government of New France itself, smuggling was almost as objectionable as direct trade rivalry with the English, with all that that implied. Both cut down the turnover of the company and, as a natural consequence, reduced the revenue of a government which was financially dependent upon the fur trade. In the St. Lawrence region, as in Acadia, the traders of the English colonies were eating their way into the French colonial system, exploring its fissures systematically, preying upon its every weakness.

To meet this rivalry, which was still chiefly for the Indian trade but was soon to involve far larger stakes, the French defences in the west were curiously weak. There was little of the solid, enduring stuff of settlement in the unsubstantial fabric of their western empire. It was true that the fur trade could not be carried on without some agricultural bases, even though its spirit was hostile to settlement. There were usually a few settlers at least at the majority of the forts and trading posts; and at Detroit a little farming community developed with at least a few hundred colonists. On the whole, however, these tiny oases of settlement were tributary to the fur trade, which dominated their existence in the same way as the forest surrounded and engulfed them. Probably the most important farming community which the French ever established in the west lay not in Canada proper at all, but in northern Louisiana, in the so-called 'Illinois Country' where a group of five villages, clustered along the Mississippi, held about a thousand French and perhaps half as many negroes. Even as late as 1746, the total non-Indian population of Louisiana numbered only about nine thousand, of whom more than half were negro slaves, and the Canadians who lived in the upper country were even fewer in number. It was a shadowy empire, supported by animals which would die off, by forests which could be cut down, by Indian tribes which would inevitably dwindle away.

But so long as the old, untouched North America lasted, the French were still strong in the west. Theirs was a peculiar strength, a strength rooted in the trades, and skills, and loyalties, and savageries which were native to the new continent, a strength which was characteristic of the fur trade alone and which would die with it. Half military and half commercial in character, their power was based essentially on a system of trading posts, many of which were fortified, and an elaborate network of Indian alliances. Fort Frontenac and Fort Detroit were the first establishments built to defend the southern front of the fur-trading colony. In the period after the Treaty of Utrecht, this defensive system was rapidly extended with the idea of blocking any kind of English advance. Fort St. Frédéric (Crown Point), at the head of Lake Champlain, was intended to protect the Richelieu route and to check the smuggling between Albany and Montreal. Fort Niagara and Fort Rouillé, on Lake Ontario, were built to stop the flow of furs to the English post at Oswego; and in that debatable land south and east of Lake Michigan, which the Iroquois still tried to dominate and where Pennsylvania traders were soon to come, the French built Fort Miami, on the Maumee River, and Vincennes on the Wabash. Around these focal points of southern defence were grouped the Indian allies, whose trade, and loyalty, and affection the French still managed to keep by those personal and political methods for which they were famous. Economically they were beaten; but they still relied — and relied successfully — upon the effects of missionary enterprise, friendly treatment, cameraderie, pageantry, display, and military prestige.

On the north-western front, where for a long time to come

the threat was to remain purely commercial in character, this strange power of the French — this authority which was so transient, so precarious, and yet, for the moment, so irresistible — achieved one of its last and greatest successes. In 1713 the Hudson's Bay Company regained by diplomacy the territories which it had not been able to defend in war. In the north-west, as in the south-west, and in Acadia, the Treaty of Utrecht simply invited a renewal of the old commercial rivalry between the English and the French. From the first days of its existence, the Hudson's Bay Company had possessed two great advantages, one industrial and one geographic; it enjoyed a cheap supply of durable trade goods from English manufactories and an inexpensive, ocean transport into the heart of the beaver country. These were formidable advantages; and the Hudson's Bay Company was satisfied that it had merely to wait and the Indians would inevitably be attracted down the rivers to the Bay. Only one inland post was established. Only at long intervals was an exploring trader sent into the interior to drum up trade with the Indians.

It was this distant, slightly superior attitude which gave the French their chance. From Lake Temiskaming and Lake Nipigon they put up a stiff competition against Fort Moose and Fort Albany. But these English posts were on James Bay; and already the company was getting its best returns from the west coast of Hudson Bay — from York Factory, at the mouth of the Nelson River, and from Prince of Wales Fort (Fort Churchill), at the mouth of the Churchill River, which was even more northerly and more unapproachable. The trade of the Crees, of the Assiniboines, and of the Plains Indians behind them could be monopolized from the vantage point of these western posts. Almost without effort on its own part, and without molestation from others, the Hudson's Bay Company was coming to dominate the drainage basin of Lake Winnipeg and the Saskatchewan River valley. This was the last, untampered reserve of the downy *castor gras*. It was a prize for which the fur-trading colony was bound to fight. And it was won by the last great trader-explorer of the French régime, Pierre Gaultier de Varennes, Sieur de La Vérendrye.

There were three possible routes to Lake Winnipeg. One, by the Nelson River, was the exclusive monopoly of the Hudson's Bay Company; one, by the upper reaches of the Mississippi system, was blocked by the wars of the Fox Indians and by the hostility of the Sioux. There was a third way, westward from Kaministiquia, on the north shore of Lake Superior, where the French had already established a post and where the city of Fort William now stands. It was a tortuous route of many portages, of incredible difficulties, which led *via* Rainy Lake and Lake of the Woods across the height of land and into the Winnipeg drainage basin. La Vérendrye, his sons, and his nephew, Sieur de la Jemeraye, moved westward along this route by stages, systematically exploiting the fur-trade monopoly which had been granted them. In 1731, they built Fort St. Pierre on Rainy Lake. In 1732 La Vérendrye himself pushed on to Lake of the Woods, where a large post was erected, named Fort St. Charles; and in 1734 his sons completed the last stage of the advance by building Fort Maurepas a few miles up the Red River from Lake Winnipeg. In the years that followed La Vérendrye, his sons and their successors, laid down a protective line of forts and trading posts around Lake Winnipeg and up the rivers, the Assiniboine and the Saskatchewan, which drained into it from the west.

La Vérendrye has often been regarded as an explorer who simply financed his expeditions by fur trading; but it would probably be more accurate to see him as a fur trader who tried to justify his commercial monopolies by occasional explorations. He made one long and financially unprofitable expedition which took him at least as far as the Black Hills of South Dakota; and before he died it was realized that the Saskatchewan was the best route to pursue the search for the

'Western Sea.' But his great work lay in breaking the monopoly of the Hudson's Bay Company and in opening the vast Canadian north-west to exploitation by the fur-trading colony. 'When you deal with them [the English],' he told the Indians at Fort St. Charles in 1734, 'you have to do it as if they were your enemies; they give you no credit; they do not allow you inside their fort; you cannot choose the merchandise you want, but are obliged to take what they give you through a window good or bad; they reject some of your skins, which become a dead loss to you after you have had great trouble in carrying them to their post. It is true that our traders sell some things a little dearer — but they take all you have, they reject nothing, you run no risk, and you have not the trouble of carrying your stuff a long distance.' These old inducements, these old cunning devices, conquered in the north-west as they had in a hundred trade fights in the past. When in 1754-1755, on the eve of the Seven Years' War, the Hudson's Bay Company servant Anthony Henday made his long journey into the western plains, he found everywhere the miraculous effects of French competition. 'The French,' he wrote, 'talk several [Indian] languages to perfection; they have the advantage of us in every shape; and if they had Brazile tobacco which they have not would entirely cut off our trade.'

With this expansion to the prairies, the fur-trading colony of the St. Lawrence had reached its appointed limits. It stood at the height of its power and prosperity. The great fur-bearing resources of the north-west enriched the whole economic life of the colony and brought ample compensation for the decline which had already been noticed in the south. Production of furs remained relatively constant in the decades which followed the Treaty of Utrecht; prices grew better; and despite violent oscillations, such as those occasioned by the wars of the Fox Indians, there was far more stability in the fur trade than there had ever been in the seventeenth century. The long years of peace which followed the Treaty of 1713 had their culmination in a brief period of ease and well-being such as New France had never known before. It was a delusive prosperity, brief, for the conditions out of which it grew were inherently precarious and temporary. On all three frontiers of expansion — the Acadian, the south-western, and the north-western — the French were meeting ever-increasing opposition. Their successes had been won with great expense and difficulty, and were maintained only by a military system which threatened to collapse of its own weight.

[*II*]

On the eve of the War of the Austrian Succession, the French Empire in North America had been in existence for one hundred and forty years. There were perhaps fifty thousand Frenchmen in the two provinces of New France and Louisiana. It was a small society to hold a vast and showy empire; but it had lived a long time in the new world and it had formed and developed a distinctive character which could not easily be changed or subdued. By this time the adaptation of French institutions and French civilization to the northern latitudes of North America had gone a long, and a successful, distance. New France had almost developed a nationality of its own. It had created certain institutions, certain patterns of action, certain cultural values, which were adjusted to the new environment and which were to show enormous powers of endurance. The whole future of North America was still doubtful. Perhaps New France was too small to win victory. But she was big enough, and old enough, to survive defeat.

The two great principles of French imperial theory were centralized, authoritarian rule within the colonies and the strict subordination of the colonies to the control of the mother country. These principles were typical of France in the age of Louis XV; but, on the whole, they thrived rather than languished in the regions which the French occupied in North America. It was, of course, geographically impossible to keep up the full measure of centralization which the imperial planners over in Versailles thought desirable. In theory, the governor-general and the intendant at Quebec had jurisdiction over all the French possessions in North America from Newfoundland to the Gulf of Mexico; but in actual fact, Isle Royale and Louisiana were separate governments in direct communication with France. A few such important concessions had to be made to North American geography; but in other ways the environment did not seem to be unfriendly to orthodox French colonial theories. Acadia, to be sure, had never proved very tolerant of centralization; but Acadia was divided anyway, by the Treaty of Utrecht, between the French and the English. Isle Royale and Isle St. Jean, the two French maritime possessions, were far too weak and too primitive to merit or desire anything more than the centralized rule of Louisbourg and the paternal supervision of the Department of Marine over in France. In Louisbourg, as at Quebec, the two principal officers of government were the governor, who represented the important military function of the settlement, and the *commissaire-ordonnateur*, who stood for justice, finance, and commissariat, in much the same way as the intendant did in Canada. In Isle St. Jean, which was a dependency of Isle Royale, two subordinate officials maintained a similar system of dual control. A small nominated council, in which the official element predominated, sat in Louisbourg, performing chiefly judicial functions; but in Isle St. Jean, where the settlements were isolated and infinitesimal, the rule of the two officials went without guidance or check.

In Canada, where institutions of government were far more developed and mature than they ever became in Acadia, the St. Lawrence River and the fur trade still seemed to strengthen the centralized, paternal rule which had been imposed by France. In the west the French empire was spread out across enormous distances; but the far-flung, fan-shaped range of missions and trading posts was gradually narrowed and focussed by the overwhelming power of the St. Lawrence. The whole life of the colony poured along the lower reaches of the river as through a funnel. And beyond the gulf the lines of trade did not radiate outward in a complex network but continued across the ocean in one great trunk-line connection. The colony depended upon France for virtually everything — for protection, markets, financial support, spiritual and intellectual nourishment. There were no strange contacts, few remote interests, to distract its attention from the motherland or to weaken its instinctive attitude of subordination and loyalty.

The twin institutions which France had fixed in Canada — monopoly of trade and monopoly of political control — seemed to thrive under such conditions. In the eighteenth century the *Compagnie des Indes* held the fur-trade monopoly for a longer period and more successfully than any of its predecessors had done in the seventeenth. In government, even more obviously than in trade, the control of affairs became ever increasingly the business of a few key individuals appointed in France. The sovereign (later superior) council, which had been set up in 1663 in part as a check upon the hasty actions of governors, lost power from the beginning and kept on losing it in the eighteenth century. It acted as a high court for the province, though an appeal, increasingly used, lay with the King at home; and it continued to register royal edicts and ordinances, thus giving them legal effect in the colony, in somewhat the same way as the *Parlements* did in France. But the council had never had much administrative authority; and it steadily lost legislative and even judicial power to the governor and the intendant. These two men governed New France. Each had his subordinates, for there were separate governors for the districts of Three Rivers and Montreal, and commandants for important places like Detroit, while the intendant, on his part, usually had a number of sub-delegates, to whom he entrusted special and temporary authority for particular tasks. But these and the other few functionaries in the province possessed only very limited power. The greatest check on the vast authority of the governor and intendant was the scrutinizing eye of the Ministry of the Marine in France.

Yet, even though paternalism seemed so solidly established and so efficient, there were certain concessions which it had to make, certain limitations which it was forced to acknowledge. At its focus, the organization of Canada seemed to foster submission to authority; but in the hinterland, west and south and north, it encouraged initiative, independence, and a reckless and undisciplined valour. There were times when the state seemed everything in Canada; but the state could not have succeeded in the trade rivalries of the west or in the border forays against New York and New England if it had not been able to rely upon the skill and adaptability of the individual Canadian. In the main, these qualities of initiative and independence, which flourished in the hard world of western empire and border war, expressed themselves negatively rather than positively so far as political institutions were concerned. It was a hard job to rule the men who had ransacked the continent with Iberville and La Vérendrye; and although the state had tried to limit the sale of brandy and to regulate the fur trade in the approved mercantilist fashion, it could only do so within narrow limits. In addition, this urge towards independence and self-determination had helped the growth of a half-democratic institution in the very heart of the seigniories themselves. This was the office of the captain of militia (*capitaine de milice, capitaine de côté*) who technically received his nomination from the governor but who, in actual fact, seems to have been the approved choice of his fellow militiamen of the parish. In origin — and this itself was characteristic of the colony — the office had been a military one; but in the eighteenth century the captain of militia had come to be a general, all-purpose officer of local government.

Strangely enough, even Nova Scotia, though it had become a colony of Great Britain, still corresponded roughly with New France in the practice of government. By rights, the province had now inherited a different, and far more liberal, tradition of colonial government; but it was odd how the mere presence of the Acadians seemed to twist and alter the normal shape of English rule. Theoretically, Nova Scotia was supposed to be a royal colony, with a constitution modelled on that of Virginia. Its governor was expected to make laws with the advice and consent of a legislative assembly. This institution was definitely required in the royal instructions to the governor; but, as the baffled soldiers who ruled Nova Scotia soon discovered, it simply could not be provided. There were only two groups of people in the province by which a legislative assembly could be elected — the Acadians and the fishermen at Canso; and both groups, for different but equally valid reasons, would not do at all. The fishermen were only temporary residents, and although a form of local government was improvised for their benefit during the fishing season, they simply could not be regarded as a permanent source of assemblymen. Then there were the Acadians. But the Acadians, without exception, were Roman Catholics; and, by the Test and Corporation Acts of England, it was impossible for Roman Catholics to take part in government, central or local. Here, at the very beginning of its conquests in North America, England ran itself into an impasse in colonial government.

And there, in complete bafflement, it remained for a long time. The Board of Trade, in the brief and infrequent moments when it considered Nova Scotia at all, could think of no way of adapting the constitution to the Acadians or the Acadians to the constitution. This complete failure to bring the first group of conquered French Roman Catholics into the established routine of English colonial government had peculiar and important consequences. The harassed administrators of Nova Scotia were asked to govern a colony for which they could not legislate properly because they had no assembly. In their dilemma, they fell back on their military authority and on the assistance of a small executive council, which made land grants, issued proclamations, and acted as a court of justice. It was a make-shift system at best and of doubtful legality. But its great defect was its almost complete divorce from the real inhabitants of the colony, the Acadians.

Since legal contacts had not been provided, the men on the spot proceeded to improvise them. From the first the Acadians had preferred to deal with the English, not in a body, but through their elected deputies. This informal representative system was accepted and regularized by the authorities in Nova Scotia. These deputies, elected annually under the supervision of the English, were in reality the chief officers of local government in the province. The Acadians accepted, apparently without question, the centralized, semi-military rule of Annapolis, which was what they had been accustomed to anyway; but they took advantage of their peculiar situation to create local institutions which expressed and strengthened their sense of independence and their feeling of separateness. In effect, the Acadians, like the Canadians, were ruled locally by people of their own choice. And if at times their deputies looked like ordinary local administrators, at other times they acted as if they were the ambassadors of an independent and sovereign people.

The second great institution of New France was the Roman Catholic Church. In the future, the church was to help immensely in the defence of French civilization in America; and already its roots had clutched deeply into the soil of the new world. Canada had first challenged French Roman Catholics as a native mission field of almost unparalleled hardship and horror; and naturally enough the religious orders which had sent out their first missionary representatives in the early days still played an important part in the religious life of the colony. There were the priests of Saint-Sulpice, who had been associated with the district of Montreal ever since the founding of the town in 1642. There were Récollets, or Begging Friars, reformed Franciscans of the strict rule, with their coarse black gowns, their bag-like hoods, their sashes of hemp rope, their bare legs and wooden shoes, who went around from house to house begging their bread. Then there were the Jesuits, with their long, black, tight-fitting coats, their charming courtesy, their learning, and their air of elegant distinction. But perhaps the most important feature of organized religion in New France in the eighteenth century was the growth of the secular clergy, the development of the system of parish priests. In 1659, when Laval became the first bishop, there was not a single organized parish with its resident priest in the entire colony; but in 1740, on the eve of the War of the Austrian Succession, there were probably about seventy-five curés in Canada alone. As the church worked its way deeper into the life of the French communities in Acadia and on the St. Lawrence, it began to rely more and more upon the colony's native sons. The Jesuits and the Sulpicians were almost exclusively Frenchmen, born in the mother country. The Récollets were largely of the same origin. But, as the eighteenth century wore on, the great majority of the parish priests were natives of Canada, trained in the seminary at Quebec.

Under the Bishop of Quebec, the parish priests served the needs of the established settlements. The Jesuits had by this time confined themselves almost entirely to Indian missions. The priests of Saint-Sulpice did some missionary work and frequently acted as curés in the district of Montreal; and the Récollets seemed ready to take up any clerical job that wanted doing. Often they served as chaplains in the forts and trading posts of the interior, often they took charge of a parish when for any reason it was left vacant; and they had recently founded a monastery at Louisbourg from which their brothers were dispatched to the outlying settlements of Isle Royale and Isle St. Jean. Between them these two religious groups — the regular and secular clergy — reached nearly all Frenchmen in North America and many of their Indian allies. Even in Nova Scotia, where the English ruled, the Treaty of Utrecht had granted to the Acadians 'the free exercise of their religion according to the usage of the Church of Rome, as far as the laws of Great Britain do allow the same.' Actually, if the laws of Great Britain had been strictly enforced, they would have stopped the free exercise of the Roman Catholic religion completely. But in England, though certainly not in Ireland, custom permitted a toleration which the law still forbade. In the light of this example, the authorities in Nova Scotia accepted the work of the priests with a benevolence which was generous in view of the local circumstances.

Even more than the state, the church in New France had taken on a distinct and definitely Canadian quality. This had been so almost from the beginning, for the first missions to Canada had represented the fervour of the seventeenth-century French religious revival in a particularly pure and passionate form. These early religious ardours and endurances were over now; but, if the inward radiance of its early pioneering zeal had faded a little, the Church of New France had lost none of its other basic characteristics. Fundamentally, it was ultramontane, for it was tied directly to Rome and had no immediate connection with the Church of France and its Gallican Liberties. Its orthodoxy was irreproachable. Misguided people who arrived in New France with religious views which differed from those of the overwhelming majority were almost always subjected to a pitiless evangelistic propaganda. Since the earliest days the colony had never accepted Protestants. It was scarcely even affected by those less serious differences of opinion which sometimes appeared in the bosom of the Roman Church itself, or by that secular spirit which was sweeping over Europe in the eighteenth century. In Canada there was scarcely the smallest echo of the great controversy between the Jesuits and the Jansenists in France. In the inhospitable atmosphere of the St. Lawrence, there could be little of that spirit of philosophic doubt, of urbane scepticism, of cultivated worldliness which had affected the Protestant and Roman Catholic churches alike in the eighteenth century.

In the seventeenth century, and particularly at certain periods, the church had wielded great authority in the politics and society of New France. It still had enormous influence in affairs; but this influence was used now within narrower limits and more often in support of the state than in opposition to it. The church had lost its great fight to stop the brandy trade and curb the activities of the *coureurs-de-bois*. In the eighteenth century it took up no public questions of such magnitude; and, after the death of Bishop Saint-Vallier, it never had a leader who could rival the imperious, crusading spirit of Laval. The priests who became famous — and, indeed, notorious — for their political activities were to be found among the Indians and along the frontiers rather than in the settlements. Acadia, where the French hoped to keep the loyalty of the Acadians as well as the alliance of the Micmac and Abenaki Indians, was a great field for priests who considered that they could serve God best by advancing the cause of the French Empire. There were Indian missionaries like the notorious Abbé Le Loutre who frankly did everything in their power to bind the tribes to the French and poison their relations with the English. On the whole, the curés who ministered to the Acadians acted more circumspectly, either out of real conviction or mere expediency. But sometimes they were tempted to use their great influence against the new rulers of Nova Scotia. It was the existence, or the fear, of these political activities which caused most of the trouble between the authorities in Nova Scotia and the Roman Catholic Church.

Perhaps the church had lost a little of its authority. Perhaps even its standards of conduct, its rather puritanical human values, were not accepted so unquestioningly as they had been in the past. During the long peace and the growing prosperity of the eighteenth century, the structure of colonial society had been changing, though very slowly. As the fur trade advanced westward, as many fur traders took up permanent residence at places like Detroit, the direct impact of the Indian frontier declined in weight, and colonial society lost a little of its primitive simplicity. As population increased, as the economic life of the province became more varied and more stable, there appeared the beginnings of a colonial leading class with civilized tastes and interests. There were now a number of bureaucrats, army officers, and merchants who looked at life rather differently from the simple fashion in which it was viewed by *coureurs-de-bois* and clergy. And, at the end of the French régime, when wartime inflation brought a novel recklessness, a raffish set of gay people at Quebec aped quite cleverly the graces and vices of Versailles. If this class had continued to develop, it might have taken over the social leadership of the colony in a way that *coureurs-de-bois* and seigneurs had never been able to do. In the meantime the clergy kept its old position. As a class, it was a little less prominent, a little less aggressive; but it had not been displaced.

In its intellectual, as well as in its spiritual, life New France had already developed certain distinctive tendencies which were certain to be of real importance in the survival of its culture. In Europe the eighteenth century saw the final triumph of that secular spirit which the Renaissance had first awakened in art and science and scholarship. In France learning celebrated its emancipation from clerical control by a prolonged revel in every department of thought; and even the sources of religious faith and political obligation were attacked with a gay confidence in the sovereign power of human reason. The immense curiosity of the

French people, the excited, uninhibited pursuit of evasive truth, which was evident everywhere — in the provincial academies, the literary societies, the salons, the clubs, and the endless spate of books and pamphlets and erudite journals — was, of course, the product of a complex, mature, and highly civilized society. It was not to be expected that a colony — even a colony of this leader of the enlightenment — could imitate, or perhaps even understand, the brilliance and daring of European thought. Naturally New France fell short of her mother country. But did she not fall even shorter than might have been expected? She never seemed to be able to escape completely from the grim frown of clerical control. It was perhaps during the spiritually exalted seventeenth century that Canada had been closest to old France. In the eighteenth century the intellectual gulf between them seemed to widen. And with the French Revolution it was to become impassable.

In its system of formal education, New France did not, as yet, differ very greatly from the motherland. So far as primary education at least was concerned, the Canadians, if not the Acadians, were probably as well educated as contemporary Frenchmen, and by much the same methods. In France, as almost everywhere in Europe, primary education was still in the hands of the church. In Canada, the church maintained a strict supervision over the teaching personnel, the teaching methods, and the subjects taught. It looked with no great favour on lay instructors, and the great majority of the primary teachers were parish priests, or members of the religious orders. Religious instruction was naturally regarded as the essential basis of all education. In Acadia, the overburdened priests could probably do little more than teach the *habitant* children their catechism and alphabet; but in Canada religious instruction was simply one part of a general programme which included reading, writing, and arithmetic. In the rural communities of the St. Lawrence and particularly in the district of Three Rivers,

the slow growth of schools dissatisfied the governing officials
of the colony, who were kept at arm's length from education
by the church. But by about the middle of the eighteenth
century the greater number of the important parishes in the
colony were probably provided with a schoolhouse and a
resident schoolmaster.

In secondary and higher education, the cultural limitations of New France were a good deal more evident. In the
primitive, pioneer settlements of Nova Scotia, Isle Royale
and Isle St. Jean, there was no provision for advanced work
at all. Even in Canada there was only one completely organized secondary school during the entire period of the
French régime. This was the Jesuit College at Quebec,
which taught the traditional classical course in grammar,
the humanities, and rhetoric, along much the same lines as
in France; and apparently it maintained as high a standard
and enjoyed as good a reputation as the Jesuit institutions
in Europe. It was possible to get some vocational training
in the colony in the useful trades, and in navigation and
pilotage; but higher education was confined almost exclusively to theology. Most of the surgeons and physicians
came from France. Lawyers did not require formal training;
and when two crown attorneys opened private law schools,
they attracted few students. But, on the other hand, the
colony began to turn out accredited theologians with the
most amazing promptitude. In connection with their college, the Jesuits established a small faculty of theology,
which taught a five-year course along traditional scholastic
lines with heavy emphasis on Thomas Aquinas; and the first
native Canadian graduates were ordained as early as the
1670's.

As New France increased in population, as it began to develop at least the nucleus of a middle class with wealth and
leisure, the colony showed some signs of breaking through
those narrow intellectual limits which had been imposed by
frontier toil, and ignorance, and clerical control. It was

true that the Jesuit library at Quebec was the biggest in the province and that the best private collections were still very frequently in the hands of the clergy. But civil servants, magistrates, seigneurs, merchants, and soldiers had books as well; and the libraries of the magistrates Cugnet and Verrier reached the remarkable total of three thousand and four thousand volumes respectively. Works of piety and edification, the Latin classics, and practical and professional manuals were evidently the three most popular categories with readers in Canada. But a fairly good assortment of recent and contemporary literature and scholarship reached Quebec; and, in a few of the better libraries at least, there were representative works of Montaigne, Buffon, Fontenelle, Bayle, Locke, Voltaire, and Rousseau. 'I found,' wrote the Swedish scientist Kalm, who visited New France in his travels, 'that the people of distinction had here in general a much greater taste for natural history and other learning than in the English colonies, where it was everybody's sole care and employment to scrape a fortune together, and where the sciences were held in universal contempt.'

Despite all this, there were not many signs of a genuinely native intellectual awakening. It was La Galissonnière, the governor sent from France, who so delighted Peter Kalm with his learning in botany. It was Dupuy, the intendant sent from France, who probably possessed the largest private library ever seen in the colony. Canada and Acadia had already inspired a considerable number of histories, chronicles, and travellers' accounts; but, in the main, these were written, not by Canadians, but by Frenchmen. Almost certainly there was no printing press in Canada during the French régime; and there were no recorded theatrical performances after Bishop Saint-Vallier's famous quarrel with Frontenac over the production of Molière's *Tartuffe*. The number of colonials who kept thoroughly abreast of intellectual movements on the Continent was probably pretty small; and, small as it was, the clergy were characteristically

fearful of its increase. Bishop Saint-Vallier had tried nobly
to counteract the vice of reading by constantly emphasizing
the need of 'good books.' He went so far as to draw up a
helpful list of unexceptionable volumes. But his successor,
Bishop Pontbriand, did even better. He was able, through
the aid of the court, to purchase several thousand highly
edifying books, and he distributed this intellectual manna
gratis throughout the seigniories.

[*III*]

From the moment that England went to war with Spain in
1739 over Captain Jenkins's amputated ear, the French began to realize that the crisis in North America was at last at
hand. On all three fronts, eastern, south-western, north-
western, the opposing lines were drawing ominously closer.
The two empires in North America confronted each other,
crowded each other, jostled each other. Even more than
England, the English colonies were ready to push on towards
the final collision. Already they were dimly aware of their
imperial destiny in the new world, and for some of them
there was no more reason for delay or compromise. New
York and Virginia were to play a large part in the final struggle; but when the crisis first broke it was New England who
took the lead in the offensive against French power. By now
her leadership in the affairs of the Atlantic world was as
vigorous as it was instinctive. As her commercial system
expanded across the ocean, as her interests became more
truly imperial in scope, Massachusetts grew more than ever
conscious of the importance of Acadia in the whole Atlantic
system. From Nova Scotia, which had become an outpost
of her fishing and commercial organization, she surveyed
the competition of Isle Royale with rising indignation. Her
new governor, William Shirley, began to build a whole programme of colonial development around the destruction of
Louisbourg. He was an Englishman who understood Ameri-

can interests and appreciated American qualities better than most of his countrymen. And the war between France and England, which everybody had expected, gave him his chance at last in 1744.

The War of the Austrian Succession did not end the struggle in North America, but it virtually determined what its outcome would be. From the outset, Acadia, Nova Scotia, and the North Atlantic became the main theatre of the conflict. From the outset also the war began to go well for the English and badly for the French. It was true that Louisbourg, which got the first tidings that the war had opened, surprised its opponents by capturing the blockhouse at Canso and sending an expedition overland against Annapolis. But these first incidents simply served to popularize Shirley's warlike campaign; and by the early spring of 1745 about four thousand amateur soldiers from New England were off for Louisbourg. Bad co-operation between England and her colonies almost rose to the level of a sacred imperial tradition during the wars with the French in North America; but for once everything seemed to go like a charm. The two commanders, William Pepperrell, the New England merchant, and Peter Warren, the commodore of the British naval squadron, were capable men who got on well enough together. Warren had married a New Yorker and was doubtless prejudiced; but he was one of the first Englishmen to have a dim inkling of the fact that colonists could fight when they wanted to do so. The Puritan crusaders, inspired by George Whitefield's pious motto, *Nil Desperandum Christo Duce,* and refreshed by interminable prayers and hymn-singing, displayed a surprising zeal for plundering non-combatant property and an inexhaustible capacity for rum. But in the actual conduct of the siege they showed real resourcefulness and dash and endurance. Without aid — for the one effort to break Warren's blockade failed miserably — Louisbourg was in no condition to resist for long. The garrison had mutinied the previous autumn, the defences were neglected and dilapidated; and on June 17, 1745, Du Chambon surrendered the fortress with all the honours of war.

In the next year, when the French made their great effort at reprisal, it was a failure even more complete and over-whelming than the English effort had been a success. Like England and New England, France and her colonies planned a great joint enterprise, an attack by land and sea, with a home fleet and a colonial army, which would take Annapolis, recapture Louisbourg, and harry the New England coast. But the great fleet which de Roye de la Rochefoucauld, Mar-quis d'Anville, led out from France in June, 1746, sailed away on a voyage of unrelieved disaster. Perhaps nearly half the French navy was in that array; but plague infected the ships, and the long voyage brought famine, and the sea wrecked and scattered the armada. In the spacious, deserted harbour of Chebucto, where the battered remnant of the fleet took refuge, and where the soldiers and sailors died by hundreds with the pestilence, d'Anville died too, perhaps at his own hand. And his successor committed suicide, and La Jonquière, who was later to be governor of Canada, led what remained of the 'grand armament' back to France. By the next year it had even become difficult for the French to send supplies and reinforcements to Canada. The English were gaining sea mastery in the very waters where Iberville had once won his victories. England and New England, an island and its sea-going dependencies, a people who lived in terms of ships and far markets and ocean trade routes, were proving too strong for the naval power of continental France. In such circumstances, in a maritime region where sea power was ultimately decisive, the army of six hundred Canadians which de Ramezay led down from Quebec could do little. They could prove, of course, that there was still punishing power in the old, half-savage warfare; and in February, 1747, the Canadians and Le Loutre's Micmacs made their way on snowshoes across country blind with winter drifts and fell upon the English at Grand-Pré in the midst of a wild snowstorm. But, without naval support, they could not take Annapolis. Still less could they recapture Louisbourg. And in this indecisive fashion the war came to an end in 1748.

They made a peace at Aix-la-Chapelle in Europe which nobody ever accepted in America. In the English colonies it seemed an incomprehensible settlement, for the 'people's darling conquest,' Louisbourg, was restored to France. The colonials conveniently forgot, if they had ever realized, that France had done extremely well in Europe, though she had failed in North America; and they adopted the oversimplified explanation that an ungrateful England had swapped Louisbourg for a trumpery factory at Madras. The restitution of Louisbourg could simply not be accepted as permanent. In America the peace was scarcely even a truce. Each side began feverishly to prepare for renewed conflict and each side naturally chose the region in which it was strongest for its first efforts. England and New England attacked the long-neglected Acadian situation. France drove further into the far west.

In the summer of 1749, in that very harbour of Chebucto where d'Anville had died nearly two years before, the old régime in Nova Scotia came to an unnoticed end amid the brilliant opening promise of the new order. In their faded uniforms, the little group of officers who had tried to rule an alien people from the neglected fort at Annapolis presented themselves to Edward Cornwallis, the aristocratic new governor of Nova Scotia who had come out full of youthful hope to begin a new policy of defence and colonization in the province. For thirty-five years, the feeble Annapolis Royal, with its crumbling defences and aging soldiers, had been the only guardian of British interests in Acadia; but now, in the harbour which Cornwallis pronounced 'the finest perhaps in the world,' Great Britain proposed to erect a splendid fortress, Halifax, which could fearlessly confront its rival Louisbourg in Isle Royale. Halifax was to be the new capital of a completely revolutionized Nova Scotia. Nearly twenty-five hundred settlers who had followed Cornwallis out from England in the summer of 1749 were to be distributed in various strategic parts of the province. As for the Acadians, they were to be told plainly that the time for shilly-shallying was past. They were to take the oath of allegiance immediately; and — this was mainly the contribution of that naturalized New Englander, William Shirley — they were to be anglicized gently but efficiently and, if possible, converted to Protestantism.

All this looked very formidable. But Acadia was the borderland of two empires, the frontier of both New England and New France. The French had not finished with it yet. Over in Europe, when the powers once again took up the inexhaustible subject of the boundaries of Nova Scotia, the French envoys argued learnedly that only the peninsula had been ceded to Great Britain in 1713 and that all the mainland still belonged to France. In the meantime, while the diplomats debated without result, the French proceeded to occupy and fortify the northern limit of the Isthmus of Chignecto. Their two posts, Fort Beauséjour and Fort Gaspereau, faced the English Fort Lawrence across a little stream which became the unofficial international boundary. From these bases the French did everything in their power to thwart the new British plans. The Micmacs, under the influence of the fanatical Abbé Le Loutre, attacked isolated British settlers. Some of the Acadians, influenced by French threats and cajolery, moved north of the international boundary; and those who stayed in Nova Scotia still obstinately refused to take the unqualified oath. It looked as if Nova Scotia was relapsing into the old intolerable state from which it had just been rescued. But this time England and New England were aroused. And they were soon to find a quick answer to their old perplexities in Acadia.

In the centre of the continent, where, on its southern front, New France faced the English colonies, there was the same atmosphere of rising tension. More tentatively than

Massachusetts, but with rapidly growing purpose, the English colonies — New York, Pennsylvania and Virginia — began to shoulder their way into the western preserves of the French. During the War of the Austrian Succession, they had done little damage to New France on their own account; but they reaped an undeserved advantage from the victories which had been won by others. The French naval disasters interrupted the flow of trade goods into the far west and exasperated Indians who were completely dependent upon European manufactures. The shock of the downfall of d'Anville's great fleet was felt in tremors throughout the interior — in Indian restlessness and Indian risings which extended from Michilimackinac far into Louisiana. For the French, this Indian disaffection was particularly dangerous in the region south of Lake Erie and south-east from Lake Michigan, where competition from Oswego had always been strong and where traders from Pennsylvania and Virginia had recently appeared. The English did not start the Indian rebellion of 1747, nor could they give it much assistance; but it enabled them to strengthen their position in the Ohio. Elsewhere the French smothered the riots and restored their prestige. But in the Indian village of Pickawillany, the Miami chief whom the French called La Demoiselle became the centre of a pro-English intrigue which threatened to turn the trade and loyalty of all the tribes in the region against the French.

For a time the French hesitated. They did not want to undertake the expense of building new posts in the interior and they tried in vain to get their Indian allies to move against La Demoiselle. In 1749, when the veteran trader, Joseph Céloron, Sieur de Bienville, led a military expedition down the Ohio, he was surprised by the extent of English trade, disturbed by the apathy or hostility of the Indians, and totally unsuccessful in his efforts to regain the friendship of La Demoiselle. The French were checkmated. But, in the fur trade, war was the final solution of all difficulties; and the French were dragged onward by a fatal method which brought them temporary success and threatened the ultimate ruin of their entire empire. Inspired and led by Charles Langlade, a raiding party of Ottawa Indians fell upon Pickawillany, captured the English traders, and murdered the Miami chief. English influence in the region suddenly collapsed; and the French proceeded to make sure of the approaches to the Ohio by building the two forts Presqu'Isle and Le Bœuf.

But if the western empire of the French could crush fur-trading rivalry, it was powerless in the end against settlement. There is a curious appropriateness in the fact that first skirmishes in the war which broke New France should have come about at the instance of a land company. The Ohio Company, composed of a few Englishmen and a number of Virginians, was in 1749 granted a tract of five hundred thousand acres on the Ohio for settlement; and in the autumn of 1753 George Washington was sent out to Fort Le Bœuf to inform the French that they must remove themselves from territory which Virginia had decided to annex. When Washington toiled back with an emphatic French refusal, the Governor, Dinwiddie, had no thought of drawing back. The mere fact that the French were established on the ground seemed no reason why Virginia gentlemen should not get what they wanted when they wanted it; and in 1754 Washington led a scratch force of colonials westward to oust the objectionable squatters from the Ohio. The French, on their part, were moving down the river in force to extend their defensive system. The two little armies met first where the Allegheny and the Monongahela Rivers unite to form the Ohio, and where the French soon built Fort Duquesne. In a skirmish, the main body of Washington's forces overcame a small advance detachment of French; but, in the end, the Virginians were surrounded and capitulated under promise to leave the Ohio immediately.

The year 1755 was the year of crisis. There was a sudden explosion of impatience; and though war had not been declared in Europe, in America a fourfold attack was planned on New France — a more ambitious enterprise than had ever been attempted. It was true that only the attempt against Fort Beauséjour in Acadia succeeded — that in the central part of the continent, if not in the maritime region, the fur-trading colony was still able to beat back its foes. Baron Dieskau delayed Johnson's advance by the Lake Champlain route. Shirley never got anywhere in his attack on Niagara. Even Braddock, the professional, with his professional British army, marched into annihilation as his soldiers hacked their way through the forest towards Fort Duquesne. Huddled in disorder on the improvised roadway, firing blindly and ineffectively into the trees and underbrush which surrounded them, the red-coat battalions were shot to pieces by that intangible and murderous foe, a typical western Canadian army. And yet, though the fur-trading colony had won these smashing successes, there was something very ominous about the campaign of 1755 — something very frightening about the whole attitude of the English. They seemed so terribly in earnest. They struck so hard, where they had compromised and temporized so long. Everybody, including the Acadians, had come to believe that the impasse in Nova Scotia was permanent. But it was not, for a soldier, Charles Lawrence, ended it abruptly in 1755. He gave the Acadians one more chance to take the unqualified oath of allegiance; and when for the last time they refused, he collected the astounded and bewildered people and shipped them off to the other English possessions.

In 1756 France made her last serious effort for her doomed colony. She sent over considerable reinforcements and with them a new general officer, Louis Joseph, Marquis de Montcalm. Montcalm was a soldier of great experience, an aristocrat of distinguished lineage who enjoyed the tranquil pleasures of his country estate, a scholar who spent his spare time reading Mirabeau's *L'Ami des Hommes* and the latest volume of Diderot's encyclopedia. He was as typical of the civilized dignity of the eighteenth century as Frontenac had been of the intemperate violence of the seventeenth; and it was highly significant that whereas Frontenac had fitted admirably into the life of New France, Montcalm, almost from the start, was a little irritable and ill-at-ease. He came to believe that his command was a hopeless one. But — even more important — he began to look at the colony which he had been called to save with amazement and disapproval.

New France was an unusual colony, with characteristics which war seemed to exaggerate and distort into the grotesque and horrible. On a larger scale than ever before, the Seven Years' War brought inflation, profiteering, poverty, and famine. It mingled the military science of Europe with the savagery of native North America. New France became a country of ever more violent contrasts, where a dissipated corrupt coterie of provincial courtiers faced a mass of half-starving peasants, where exquisite *toilettes* and civilized licence confronted the plumed scalplocks, the greasy buffalo robes, and the barbarous codes of the Indians. As he drew back in disgust from native allies who murdered their prisoners and smart Quebec people who plundered the provincial treasury, Montcalm must have thought that the colony was rank with the vices of both savagery and civilization — that it presented an unnatural combination of the rottenness of the old world and the primitiveness of the new.

It was Montcalm's misfortune and the tragedy of New France that he had to work with men who stood for the very things he most despised and hated in the colony. Once again, as in the old days of Frontenac, the triumvirate which governed New France was split by incessant wrangling; and the newcomer, Montcalm, faced the opposition of two astute veterans, the Intendant, François Bigot, and the Governor, Pierre de Rigaud, Marquis de Vaudreuil-Cavagnal. Bigot was a little, fat, red-haired Frenchman, with wit and charming manners, who had been an efficient commissary at Louisbourg before he had come on to Canada. Vaudreuil was an empty and self-important Canadian aristocrat, born in New France, the son of the Marquis de Vaudreuil who had governed Canada in the early eighteenth century. Bigot was simply a light-hearted swindler who was interested in nothing but his own amusement, the pleasure of Major Péan's charming wife, and the plate, pictures, and *objets d'art* he was storing up for his estate in France. But Vaudreuil, for all his malice and incompetence, represented something positive — the slowly maturing Canadianism of his native country — the awakening sense of nationality which was already aware of French neglect and resentful of French patronage.

Even if it had been possible to save New France, these men could scarcely have done it. In this last extremity, the trained soldier was the only hope; but each in his own way, the amusing rogue and the pompous fool did everything in their power to undermine Montcalm's work. Bigot and the corrupt gang of Canadian officials who surrounded him practised every conceivable kind of fraud at the expense of the bankrupt colony and its distressed people. Vaudreuil and his tribe of jealous relatives actually succeeded in splitting the high command and in dividing the very army itself into hostile factions. By virtue of his office of governor, he was commander-in-chief of all the forces in Canada, with the power, as well as the malice, to block Montcalm. He tried to revise the general's strategy, to embarrass his plans, and belittle his achievements. He flattered the vanity and magnified the exploits of the Canadian militia and the permanent Colonial Regulars, or *Troupes de la Marine,* who had been a long time in New France. He did his best to set them and the Canadian people against the Regulars who had crossed to fight in the Seven Years' War — the battalions chosen from the seven splendid regiments of La Reine, Guienne, Béarn, La Sarre, Languedoc, Royal Roussillon, and Berry.

Though his command was torn with strife and riddled with corruption, though he usually faced superior numbers on the whole American front and even greater odds in terms of total population and resources, Montcalm was the ablest commander in America until the arrival of Wolfe and for the first two years he was able to take the offensive. In 1756 he captured that 'insolent' outpost, Oswego, and in 1757 he took Fort William Henry at the head of Lake George. It was the last time that New France showed so confident a front. In the autumn of 1756 an unconventional and per-emptory organizing genius named William Pitt became head of the war effort in England; and from that moment there was a new vigour and a new sense of direction in the American offensive. The British, it was true, made a few last fumbles. In 1757, by an odd fluke which was not repeated, the French actually had naval superiority in American waters; and in 1758, behind the piled logs in front of Fort Ticonderoga, Montcalm's army coolly shot down the assault-ing masses of red-coats that the imbecile commander Aber-cromby flung at their position. It was a butchery worse than Braddock's defeat. But, as a success, it stood in complete isolation. Everywhere else the ring was steadily closing in. Fort Oswego, Fort Duquesne, even Fort Frontenac, they had all been surrendered to the enemy. Worst of all, Louisbourg was captured in that same summer of 1758. At length the British had completed their mastery of Acadia and the North Atlantic. The sea approaches to New France lay open and unguarded. In June of the next year, 1759, a great invading force under General James Wolfe and Admiral Sir Charles Saunders sailed up the St. Lawrence. And Montcalm hurried down the river to make a last stand for the colony on the rock of Quebec.

On paper at least, Montcalm's army was bigger than Wolfe's. But Wolfe had a larger contingent of regulars than his opponent; and the total British naval and military forces vastly outnumbered the French. Montcalm's position was inevitably a defensive one; but the 'old fox,' as Wolfe called him, had no intention of waiting tamely within the weak defences of the fortress while the enemy closed in around him. Though he lost Point Lévy opposite Quebec, he tried to keep his hold on the whole north shore of the river for some distance on each side of the capital. Above Quebec, the high, abrupt cliffs gave a natural protection for at least a few miles. But further up the river beyond Cap Rouge the terrain was more open; and immediately below Quebec the low Beauport flats invited invasion. Montcalm systematically entrenched the whole Beauport shore as far as the Montmorency River. Here he placed the bulk of his army, and here, on July 31, he beat back a bungled British attack headed by the Grenadiers. This victory and the slow passage of the summer ought to have cheered him; but he was full of a consuming anxiety which strengthened as August drifted at last into September.

On September 3, Wolfe broke his camp on the north shore just below the Montmorency. From then on, the actions of the British became more than ever bewildering and mysterious. There was great activity far up the river. It seemed almost certain that the enemy was planning a break-through at Pointe au Trembles and a march down on Quebec. Yet Montcalm, who saw dangers everywhere, was not even satisfied about the heights immediately above the town. On September 5, he sent the Guienne battalion up to the Plains of Abraham, the high plateau just beyond Quebec, to guard the heights. On September 7, Vaudreuil ordered the battalion back to the Beauport lines. Three days later somebody at one of the defence posts on the cliffs close to the cove called the Anse au Foulon, saw a half-dozen British officers on the opposite shore, carefully surveying the heights around him. Montcalm made a last effort. He ordered La Guienne up to the heights at once. And, to his face, Vaudreuil countermanded the order. Tomorrow he would see about the defences of Anse au Foulon. Tomorrow: tomorrow was September 13.

At about four in the morning of that day, a French sentry

at the post near Point Sillery, a little above the Anse au Foulon, heard a strange sound from the river below.

'Qui vive?' he sang out.

'France.' The reply was low but reassuring.

'A quel régiment?' snapped the sentry.

'De la Reine.'

The sentry hesitated. Was there something odd about the accent, or was it merely that the tone of the voice was low?

'Pourquoi est-ce que vous ne parlez pas plus haut?'

The reply was peremptory and crushing.

'Tais-toi! Nous serions entendus.'

The sentry hesitated. The convoys by which Quebec was fed often came secretly down the river to discharge at Anse au Foulon. Another convoy was expected that very night. Who was to know that the British might take the place of the awaited French? And even if a night attack had been suspected, who could have imagined that a Highland officer named Simon Fraser, who spoke excellent French, would have taken his place in the leading boat? The sentry subsided. Down below in the darkness the boats moved silently on. A few moments later they grounded on the shore of Anse au Foulon, and the tall, lanky figure of the commander was the first on shore.

'I don't think,' Wolfe said deprecatingly as he led the officers to the spot he had chosen, 'we can by any possible means get up here, but however we must use our best endeavour.'

The first British soldiers began to clamber carefully up the heights in the obscurity.

It was late — far too late — in the morning before Montcalm was fully aware of what had happened. While the last of Wolfe's attacking force moved unopposed up the gully of the Anse au Foulon, Vaudreuil still kept issuing absurd and hampering orders; and it was not until a little after eight o'clock that Montcalm collected his men on the high plateau to the west of the town. Opposed to him, on a ridge about a mile from the city gates, deployed in two long, red lines, Wolfe's army was drawn up ready for battle. The tall, gawky commander, in a brand-new uniform, moved with rapt enthusiasm up and down the lines, encouraging his men. Montcalm's best green, gold-embroidered coat was open in front and his polished steel cuirass glittered brightly. He called his staff and principal officers together for a hurried council. Everybody favoured an immediate attack and it was the commander's own desire. The army began to deploy. On the flanks were the Canadian and Indian sharpshooters. The main body was made up of the Colonial Regulars in their grey uniforms, the French Regulars in white, the crack Royal Roussillon in its distinctive blue. It was ten o'clock.

On that flat tableland, the battle was an almost flawless exercise in eighteenth-century warfare. There was a little skirmishing, then Montcalm raised his sword and the whole French line began to advance. The men started with a shout; but once they came within range of the enemy the complete, uncanny silence of the British muskets was more than ever unnerving. The five battalions had already lost their order, they began to lose their resolution. They faltered, halted, moved on; and then, at the forty paces Wolfe had specified, they were stopped dead by a crashing volley from the unmoving red-coats. The charge collapsed. For a while the white- and blue-clad veterans held their ground, firing uncertainly; and then, as the British pressed forward, as the timed volleys succeeded like cannon strokes, the whole French army began to dissolve into a formless, fluid mass that streamed back into the city and over towards the St. Charles River bridge. Wolfe, in his moment of triumph, was shot and dying. Montcalm, while he tried desperately to rally his men, was fatally wounded. His black horse walked him slowly into the city by the St. Louis gate, while its rider tried to hold himself erect in his saddle. That evening Vaudreuil retreated with what remained of the French army by the

St. Charles River. Quebec was left virtually defenceless, and on September 17, de Ramezay capitulated. Long before that Montcalm was dead. 'I shall not see the surrender of Quebec.'

This was really the end. It was true that the French still had an army in being and that Canada had not accepted defeat. During the next winter Murray's garrison in Quebec suffered severely; and in the early spring, when the French under Lévis came up from Montreal to besiege their own capital, they almost avenged the defeat of the previous autumn. Then spring broke in earnest and the ice cleared in the river. The first British warships sailed up to Quebec. Soon, from all sides, the great armies began laboriously to converge on Montreal. On September 8, nearly a year after the defeat of the Plains of Abraham, Vaudreuil signed the Articles of Capitulation. It was all over. For better or worse, the rule of France in northern North America was done and ended.

And yet had it really ended after all? Even if the court of Louis XV had acknowledged defeat, even if the great machine at Versailles had ceased to govern its remote American dependencies, was there not a chance that an older, simpler, more devout France, the France of the seventeenth, not of the eighteenth, century, would maintain its footing and even increase its influence in North America? It was true that the society of the lower St. Lawrence now faced a future which was ominous and might be catastrophic. New France must accept the humiliation of defeat. Its laws and institutions were in jeopardy of the foreigner. Its entire culture might, sooner or later, be extinguished by mass British migrations to northern North America. The ordeals of the future were likely to be terrible. But the society of French Canada had grown stronger under the shocks of the past hundred and fifty years. Rooted in the soil of the new world, sustained by a distinctive faith and language from the old, it had shown a great tenacity, a great strength of endurance; and in its simple, healthy way, it was moved by an unconquerable will to live. No doubt the future struggle for survival would be crushing and narrowing in its exactions. No doubt nearly the whole spiritual resources of the society would have to be concentrated on the one fundamental necessity of self-defence. The welfare of the individual might have to yield to the continuance of the race; the expression of personality might be forced to subordinate itself to the maintenance of a common culture. Yet, at whatever cost to itself, the French-Canadian way of life might survive. And if it did survive, its continuance, in the midst of a predominantly British population, would create the central spiritual dichotomy, the fundamental social and cultural division, in British North American life.

CHAPTER FOUR

THE SURVIVAL OF BRITISH
NORTH AMERICA

[*I*]

IN 1763, by the Peace of Paris, France irrevocably ceded
Canada to Great Britain. All the French possessions in
North America, with the exception of Louisiana west of the
Mississippi, had now become part of a single British American Empire which stretched unbrokenly from Labrador to
the Floridas. It was an enormous empire, full of contradictions and difficulties, bristling with formidable problems of
government, defence, finance, commercial policy, and settlement. The very number and the obvious magnitude of
these problems compelled attention; and the British embarked upon a belated, a clumsy, and a fatal attempt to reorganize their American dominions. Their plan, which
was almost continental in scope, included the conquered, as
well as the original, English provinces. All colonies were to
subordinate their interests to the common welfare of the
Empire as a whole; and all colonies were to conform at least
roughly to the standard English type. It seemed almost to
be taken for granted that Nova Scotia and Quebec would
soon become typical members of the happy British American
community of provinces. Nobody appeared to realize very
clearly that Quebec and Nova Scotia were unusual colonies,
colonies which would show a stubborn tendency to preserve
their individuality and their separateness in North America.

Nobody foresaw that the meeting would be followed so soon by the parting of the ways.

For about twenty years the British held to a fairly consistent policy for the colonies which they had conquered from the French. This policy was described in the commissions and instructions of the governors of Nova Scotia and Quebec; and it was set forth openly in the famous Royal Proclamation of October, 1763, which in addition to the clauses relating to Quebec and the Floridas, contained several provisions of immense importance for the original English settlements on the Atlantic seaboard. The inland expansion of all the colonies, new and old, was halted at least temporarily by the Proclamation of 1763. The permanent western boundary of the Province of Quebec was to run north-west to Lake Nipissing from the point at which the forty-fifth parallel of latitude crossed the St. Lawrence River. The temporary western limit of the seaboard provinces was drawn along the watershed of the Allegheny Mountains from north to south. West of this so-called Proclamation Line, imperial officials were expected to seek a solution of the Indian problem, which had suddenly and violently been forced upon their attention by Pontiac's Rising. For a while, at least, settlement was not to be permitted in the Indian reserve; but, in recompense, it was to be encouraged to expand north and north-east into the conquered territories of Quebec and Nova Scotia. These colonies, which in the past had seemed mere outposts of the fisheries and the fur trade, were now regarded as places 'where Planting, perpetual Settlement and Cultivation ought to be encouraged.' With an odd echo of Colbert's bland confidence, the British Board of Trade assumed that Canada and Nova Scotia must now shed their old peculiarities and become normal and healthy. Obviously they needed British settlers; and obviously British settlers must be attracted by familiar British methods and institutions. Nova Scotia had won its legislative assembly in 1758, the year of the final downfall of

Louisbourg. The Proclamation of 1763 promised an assembly and 'the benefit of our Lawes of England' to the newly conquered colony of the St. Lawrence, which the British had renamed the Province of Quebec.

Whatever chances of success this programme had in Quebec, it looked at first as if it could not possibly fail in Nova Scotia. It was true that Nova Scotia was a rather strange colony, which for some mysterious reason had never profited from the British conquest of 1713, and which had shown a regrettable tendency to lapse back into its old state of anarchy even after England had taken it seriously in hand in 1749. All this, however, must surely have happened because of the Acadians; and the Acadians — rather harshly, it might be admitted, but, on the whole, providentially — had been removed *en masse* from their farms in 1755. This left the whole province open and waiting for occupation by New England, which had always been interested in the region anyway and whose citizens were already on the move in the very direction which the imperial planners desired. So far as Nova Scotia at least was concerned, the attempt to direct settlement laterally along the seaboard could scarcely have been better timed. To a large extent, the migrations which followed immediately after the conquest of New France instinctively travelled north and north-east rather than west; and Nova Scotia was settled in the 1760's by the same northward movement which peopled Maine, New Hampshire, and Vermont.

In 1760, when the New England immigration was just beginning, the province was nearly as empty as it had been at any time in the past. Apart from the small settlements of English and New Englanders at Halifax and Annapolis, and the small German colony at Lunenburg, Nova Scotia was almost a deserted country of untouched forest, broken dykes, and abandoned farms. Within fifteen years the New Englanders, together with a much smaller number of immigrants from the British Isles, had transformed this picture of desolation and remade the province. Largely avoiding the north-east of the peninsula, the Yankee newcomers naturally occupied those regions which were best known to them and most accessible from the south-west. Pioneer New England farmers gradually reclaimed the old lands of the Acadians in the Annapolis Valley, the Basin of Minas, Cobequid Bay, and the Isthmus of Chignecto. Adventurous New England fishermen and lumberers founded settlements in the superb harbours of that rocky coast which ran westward from Halifax and curved around by the Cape Sable shore to the Bay of Fundy. The population, which had totalled only a little over two thousand in 1763, increased to seventeen thousand in 1775, on the eve of the American Revolution. It was still only a tiny community; but there were now nearly twice as many people as there had been at any one time in the previous hundred and fifty years of the history of the province.

Despite the Germans at Lunenburg, the Irish on Cobequid Bay, and the Yorkshiremen at the Isthmus of Chignecto, the New Englanders remained the dominating group. 'The old stock comes from New England,' wrote Haliburton over half a century later, 'and the breed is tolerable pure yet, near about one half applesarce, and tother half molasses. . . . ' In 1775, the New Englanders easily formed two-thirds of the population and they stamped their mark on the province for all time. It was natural and easy for these newcomers, who often came in groups and had to travel such a short distance, to bring with them intact their forms of social organization, their religious and political institutions. To a large extent they had joined together to settle Nova Scotia by townships in the traditional New England fashion. The Congregational Church and the close village community helped to maintain New England cultural values and patterns of conduct. The town meeting served to foster the New England spirit of local independence. On the whole, it seemed that the tradition of Massachusetts had merely moved one stage further east. Nova Scotia, in the heart of what had once been French Acadia, had almost become a new New England.

Almost, but not quite. For if the New Englanders changed Nova Scotia, Nova Scotia changed the New Englanders as well. There were hard facts which even immigrants from Massachusetts could not alter; and among these was the important matter of the geographical position of the province. It was a peninsula, almost an island, a frontier of rival economic interests, an outpost of great strategic importance in the North Atlantic world. It faced New England, and the Atlantic, and the Gulf of St. Lawrence. It lay just within the grasp of several rival political systems; and yet it was remote from all of them. Inevitably, its isolation bred a certain insularity, a certain peculiar local point of view; but the difficulty of communications within the province and the pull of rival interests from without seemed to prevent this local outlook from rising to the level of a united provincial feeling. The New Englanders were certainly the largest group in Nova Scotia; but — in the peculiar situation of the province — this by no means meant that they wielded the dominating influence in it.

In the eastern part of the province generally, and in the city of Halifax in particular, Great Britain kept a hold which was as strong as that of New England in the west. Halifax was an important British military and naval base, upon which money had been lavished ever since 1749. 'Good God,' cried Edmund Burke in amazed indignation, 'what sums the nursing of that all-thriven hard visaged ill-favoured brat has cost this wittol nation. Sir, this colony Nova Scotia has stood us in a sum not less than seven hundred thousand pounds.' Isolated from the rest of the province, with a splendid harbour but no agricultural hinterland, Halifax depended on British parliamentary grants, bought British manufactures, and profited from British wars. A little group of merchants, war-contractors, and officials, whose business connections lay chiefly in England and whose boss and patron, Joshua Mauger, had retired to London, managed to run the capital and the province pretty much as they liked from their strategic positions on both sides of the Atlantic. While Mauger succeeded in getting himself accepted at the Colonial Office in London as the principal 'impartial' adviser on Nova Scotia, his friends and debtors out in Halifax continued to control the governor's council and to dominate the assembly at crucial moments.

It was hard to break the rule of this powerful Halifax-London combination. In a province with an isolated capital and virtually no roads, the distant country members found it very difficult to attend the assembly. Unacquainted with each other, ignorant of the public affairs of the province, they fell all too easily under the influence of the Halifax oligarchy; and though they inherited a strong democratic tradition from New England, they were never quite able to unite and impose their scheme of things by law. Their failure to insist upon the New England form of local self-government was the most complete revelation of their curious weakness in the new environment. Actually the Yankees of Nova Scotia were much attached to the town meeting and they kept going back to it surreptitiously for years. But, for some unaccountable reason, they never got it on the statute books. By the Township Act of 1765, the justices of the Court of Quarter Sessions were to appoint the local officers from lists drawn up by the grand jury of each county. In local as well as central government 'the new New England' had followed the practices of the 'royal colony' of Virginia rather than of the old 'republic' of Massachusetts Bay.

If something of the old Nova Scotia had survived despite the onslaught of the New Englanders, there was even greater likelihood that Canada would maintain its old individuality. In Nova Scotia, the British programme was launched under the most favourable circumstances, for the Acadians had already been removed and the New Englanders were ready to take their places. But there were few people who responded to the invitation to emigrate to the Province of Quebec; and the overwhelming majority of the sixty-five thousand Canadians stayed behind in the conquered colony. In the main, the officials and the officers left for France, but the majority of these were natives of the mother country anyway; and probably the English-speaking immigrants were even fewer in number than the departing French. In the 1760's, settlement had not yet advanced far enough up the Connecticut and Hudson valleys to bridge the gap into Canada easily; and the British who came to the Province of Quebec following the conquest were not farmers at all but soldiers, civil servants, and merchants. A tiny minority, without the power or the wish to alter the economic and social organization of the colony, these newcomers simply occupied jobs which the French had vacated and continued trades which the French had laid down. As they took over the traditional methods of the St. Lawrence and acquired its historic ambitions, they began, in their different ways, to identify themselves with the old Province of New France which their coming had altered so little. The two British groups — the soldiers and bureaucrats on the one hand and the merchants on the other — quarrelled by instinct. But they agreed fervently on one highly important point. For different but equally strong reasons they both came to dislike the whole programme of standardization which had been laid out for Quebec in the Royal Proclamation of 1763.

The position of the English, Scots, and colonial merchants who arrived in Quebec after the conquest was simple. They came first as army contractors; but they remained to take over the fur trade. In co-operation with the French Canadians as employees and minor partners, they began to work the commercial system of the St. Lawrence; and with it they inherited the traditional French alliance with the western Indians and the historic French rivalries with the Thirteen Colonies and the Hudson's Bay Company. In the end it mattered little that the Indians under Pontiac had at first been violently hostile. It mattered even less that the New York traders and the Hudson's Bay Company factors were fellow subjects of the same king and fellow members of a united British America. The fur trade soon ended these uncommercial feelings; and the fur-trading colony stood forth in its old position, with all its old ambitions, its old friendships, and its old antagonisms. Like the French before them, these new British traders wanted to monopolize the west, not to share it with others. They hoped to impose their own control in the hinterland, not to accept imperial supervision. They hated the Proclamation of 1763, which had cut off the Province of Quebec by a line drawn to Lake Nipissing and which had made an Indian reserve out of Canada's rightful inheritance in the west.

The task of the new Canadian merchants was to break through this absurd western boundary and to annex as much of the Indian reserve as they could to the Province of Quebec. Like the colonies of the Atlantic seaboard, Quebec struggled, in its own fashion, against the British scheme of imperial organization; and under this joint attack the whole plan began to break in pieces. Great Britain could not spare the money to maintain her expensive Indian reserve. She could not compel the colonies to grant it to her by imperial taxation. And in 1768 she decided to give up a part of her ambitious western scheme and to restore the control of the Indian trade to the provinces which were most interested in it. New York, Pennsylvania, and Quebec might have come together in friendly fashion to regulate the fur trade which concerned them all; but Quebec hated the thought of co-operation for the simple reason that she was intent upon monopoly. Could not the great western country be admin-istered most cheaply and efficiently by the colony to which it was geographically and historically linked? 'And here,' declared a committee of the Quebec council in 1769, 'we think we do not speak the Language of persons improperly devoted to our own Province, when we say that this has much better pretensions to give the Law upon this head to those Countries, than any other Government upon the Continent.' Years before the Quebec Act of 1774, the westward extension of the boundaries of Quebec began to seem the natural, the logical solution of the problem of the Indians and the fur trade.

While British merchants were earnestly trying to alter Quebec's boundaries, British bureaucrats were finding equally strong objections to other parts of the Proclamation of 1763. James Murray, Guy Carleton, and Frederick Haldimand, the first three governors of Quebec after the conquest, were all military men. Guy Carleton, whose long career and enormous influence in British North America were to make him a veritable proconsul, was more important than his fellows but fairly representative of them. A member of a good Anglo-Irish family, a professional soldier who had been quartermaster-general with Wolfe's army at Quebec, Carleton possessed a rather formal manner, a temper inclined to be vindictive, and a superb confidence in his own judgment — a confidence which was only weakened slowly with the passage of time. Like Murray and Haldimand, he was a political Tory and a social conservative, with a complacent belief in his own importance and an ingrained relish for authority. One after another these first three British governors fought to protect the interests and defend the customs of the French Canadians. This crusade was a great credit to their tender hearts. It was also strong evidence of their class and professional prejudices. They became convinced that Quebec would never change — for had not the immigration policy almost completely failed to attract settlers? Perhaps even more important, they discovered that they liked it better as it was. With its fine military history, its tradition of absolute government, its accepted landed gentry, and its docile and respectful peasants, Quebec seemed like a delightful bit of Europe transplanted to the forests of the new continent — a refreshing oasis of the old régime in the howling wilderness of democratic America. It was such a comfort to know that a place like Quebec could exist in this equalitarian new world. It was such a pity to disturb this last refuge of the good old order in America. The governors showed a consistent dislike for the whole programme of anglicization and standardization which had been marked out for Quebec. James Murray started the reaction against the Proclamation of 1763. Guy Carleton completed it.

In the social and political, as well as in the economic, sphere, the conquest seemed to have strangely little effect on the old colony of the St. Lawrence. The Proclamation of 1763 had promised English laws; but from the beginning, the Court of Common Pleas began to settle French-Canadian disputes according to the rules of the Custom of Paris. The Proclamation had also promised English freehold tenures; but as early as 1771, in anticipation of the Quebec Act, the authorities decided that future grants of land in the colony were to be made *en fief et seigneurie*. Even the Roman Catholic Church was permitted by these supposedly bigoted Protestant rulers to retain something of its old pre-eminence in the colony. The Treaty of Paris had merely repeated the promise made long ago in favour of the Acadians, that the Roman Catholic religion would be tolerated so far as the laws of Great Britain did permit. This, if taken literally, was very nearly a contradiction in terms; but, as the event proved, the British were willing to show, not merely a negative tolerance, but even a little positive benevolence to the Roman Church.

It was true that the Jesuit estates were confiscated, and, although the remaining brothers were to enjoy the revenues until death, no new appointments could be made. But the secular clergy, which had always been the most distinctively Canadian part of the church, was permitted to escape from a difficulty in which the British might very well have left it. At the conquest, the Canadian church was without a head, for Bishop Pontbriand had died just before the capitulation

of Montreal. Here was a dreadful calamity! The French
Canadians were accustomed to get along without a good
many things; but they could not conceivably do without a
bishop. The British authorities might wink at the presence
of a few unoffending priests, but they trembled to see a
'popish hierarchy' set up in one of their dominions. It was
all very difficult. Even if Great Britain swallowed its objections to a hierarchy in Canada, it still could not possibly
accept a bishop nominated by the French king or the Roman
Papacy. And on the other hand, the church was naturally
a little reluctant to welcome a bishop nominated by the Protestant monarch of England. In this curious dilemma, the
cathedral chapter of Quebec elected one of its own members,
Jean Olivier Briand. The Papacy reluctantly accepted the
Canadian choice; and the British authorities let it be known
that Briand might get himself consecrated and return unopposed to Quebec. When he arrived in the summer of 1766,
the new bishop was greeted by vast, palpitating crowds and
floods of faithful tears. A Frenchman born in the mother
country, Briand had done much for the land of his adoption.
The future of the church in Quebec was assured; its Canadian
character had been strengthened. And the clergy, with the
departure of the French officials and officers, became once
again the authoritative leading group in French-Canadian
society.

In politics, as in other spheres, the old institutions of New
France survived the conquest and threatened a revision of
the programme laid down in the Proclamation of 1763. The
Proclamation and the governors' commissions and instructions all required a legislative assembly; but no assembly
was ever called by Murray or Carleton. In England, of
course, the Test Act still prevented Roman Catholics from
sitting in Parliament; but, so far as Quebec was concerned,
many people were quite prepared to change this law for the
benefit of the French Canadians. What defeated the assembly was not Protestant prejudice, but fear and dislike of

representative government itself. The only group in the colony which was actively interested in a legislative assembly was made up almost entirely of the newly arrived British merchants. The British governors, and the Francophil bureaucracy which surrounded them, had a gentlemanly aversion to shopkeepers and a military dislike for democrats; and the fact that these merchants — these 'ignorant, licentious, factious men' — had advocated an assembly made the scheme all the more suspect in their eyes. With one voice the authorities at Quebec advised the British government against an assembly. The British government began itself to doubt the wisdom of a provincial parliament in the disturbed and uncertain state of America. As early as 1771, the scheme for an assembly was probably given up.

Thus, for a decade after the conquest, the Province of Quebec had stubbornly maintained its individuality and separateness, despite a great scheme for imperial unity and standardization. In 1774, the British Parliament recognized and completed by statute this victory of the old régime on the St. Lawrence. The Quebec Act, though it was passed in the gathering storm of the American Revolution and undoubtedly hastened its explosion, was simply the last formal step in the long retreat away from the Proclamation of 1763 and back to the old institutions of the French Empire. By the Quebec Act, the vast territory between the Ohio and the Mississippi was restored to the colony which had explored it, occupied it, and still monopolized its trade. The pledge of an assembly was repudiated; government by an appointed legislative council was re-established; and a special oath for Roman Catholics enabled the French Canadians to take part in their own government. The Act confirmed the feudal landholding system, specified that the 'Laws of Canada' were to be the rule in the settlement of civil suits, and gave the church statutory authority to collect the tithes. It was true that the framers of the Act intended that this French and feudal constitution should be qualified at least by a few institutions which were English in origin and liberal in spirit. In the instructions given to Carleton, the new Quebec legislature was advised to introduce the right of habeas corpus, and to establish English law in commercial suits. But by a fatal decision these amendments were left out of the statute and reserved for the instructions. They did not have to be obeyed. And a legislature now made up of soldiers, bureaucrats, and French-Canadian landowners showed no desire to take up the optional reform of their reactionary constitution.

By 1774, it was evident that, so far as Quebec and Nova Scotia were concerned, the great effort of Great Britain to unify and standardize her American empire had failed. Through nearly fifteen difficult and confusing years, the northern colonies had maintained their curious individuality and insisted on their aloof separateness. They had helped to defeat the British attempt to impose a unified system upon the continent. It was their first victory over continentalism — over the political programme against which they were to struggle from that time forward. But it was an incomplete and inconclusive victory; and already, just as the Quebec Act was imposing its peace upon the first campaign, the whole future grew suddenly darker with the certainty of a fresh struggle. The American Revolution was the second episode in the movement for continental unity. It was a more significant, a more crucial episode, for it brought into conflict the two great English-speaking programmes of continentalism. On the one hand was the British Parliament, with its design of a united empire; and on the other was the Philadelphia Congress, with its hope of a 'continental' resistance.

Wedged between these two formidable antagonists, what were the diminutive northern provinces to do? They had rejected one plan of continentalism. But might not a second, a truly North American variant of the same design, prove more acceptable? Despite the geographical remoteness of

Quebec and Nova Scotia, despite the peculiarities of their character, they did hold political grievances which were comparable to those of the Thirteen Colonies, and they did voice protests which might conceivably have become attuned to the rising clamour in the Empire as a whole. As the Revolution approached, the local struggle in Nova Scotia between the ruling oligarchy and the reforming governor, Francis Legge, neared its crisis. In Quebec, the denial of an assembly in the new constitution aroused the merchants to fury, and the statutory enforcement of the tithe had possibly awakened a secret grudge in the *habitants.* Certainly the northern provinces had their local grievances. But could they be incorporated in a general North American discontent?

Nobody could be very certain. In these isolated northern provinces, where people were dispersed by geography and divided by race, and class, and interest, a strong communal feeling on any subject was very difficult to rouse. The French-Canadian *habitants,* who had never joined the local campaign for an assembly, could scarcely be expected to thrill at the gospel of the American Revolution. The farmers and fishermen of Nova Scotia, who had failed to keep their democratic New England heritage, were incapable of uniting to break the military power and leadership of Halifax. In both provinces, the official class was stoutly loyal; and the clergy and seigneurs of Quebec, grateful for the lavish concessions of the Quebec Act, set their faces sternly against the revolutionary contagion. Everything depended on the merchants. And the merchants showed little sign of copying their brothers in the Thirteen Colonies and stirring up the rabble against imperial authority. The fact was that in both Halifax and Montreal the commercial group was as independent of the Atlantic seaboard as it was dependent upon England. Montreal was tied submissively to London by a group of fur traders who had to have European manufactures to hold their western commercial empire against the competition of the Thirteen Colonies and Hudson Bay. Halifax was almost identified with the imperial capital by a gang of bureaucrats and financiers who operated harmoniously in each other's interests on both sides of the Atlantic. In both provinces, the merchants had done well, and hoped to do better, out of the crisis in imperial affairs. The Montrealers rejoiced that the non-importation agreements in the Thirteen Colonies were slowly killing the fur-trade competition from Albany. The Haligonians, who had made their money out of the Seven Years' War, lived in hopes of bigger and better wars in the future; and if loyalism would bring the British fleets and armies back to Nova Scotia, then there was singularly little reason for them to turn revolutionary.

For all these reasons, the northern colonies were never completely diverted from their separate course. They had their own grievances; they made isolated and spasmodic replies to the American appeal; but they were never swept away wholly into the current of the Revolution. On the day the Stamp Act went into effect, the Quebec *Gazette* simply suspended publication. The Halifax *Gazette* carried on a mild campaign against the Act, and there was much 'carousing' in Liverpool and probably in other places when it was repealed; but even in Nova Scotia there were no open and organized protests, and scarcely a breath of criticism in Quebec. In both provinces, the merchants made no attempt to join the non-importation agreements against England, and there was no boycott against the East India Company's tea. In October, 1774, a month after it had assembled at Philadelphia, the Continental Congress openly invited the people of Quebec to elect a provincial convention and to send delegates to represent them at Philadelphia. And, in the spring of 1775, Doctor John Brown from Massachusetts arrived to make a personal appeal. Even in a province which was peopled by sullen French and disappointed British merchants, these various invitations awakened no united response. 'There is no prospect,' John Brown wrote bluntly to Boston, 'of Canada sending Delegates to the Continental Congress.' Evidently there was to be no fraternization, no touching concord of sentiments, no gallant comradeship of arms.

Instead of behaving like normal British provinces, Nova Scotia and Quebec seemed to be taking on a more and more disquieting resemblance to vanished Acadia and New France. In the War of the American Revolution, as in every previous conflict in the new continent, Nova Scotia remained a divided and disintegrated country, a borderland of uncertain loyalties, a battleground of rival imperial interests. While the provincial assembly voted loyal addresses to Great Britain, illegal town meetings gave secret support to New England. One set of merchants sold supplies to the British garrisons, while another group continued to deal with the New England towns. The British garrison held down Halifax and British warships patrolled Nova Scotian waters; but nearly every important outpost in the province suffered from American privateers. This seemed the inescapable fate of Nova Scotia — the fate which the Acadians had tried for over forty years to escape by insisting upon their neutrality. Neutrality was a typical Nova Scotian device which had revolted the New Englanders — so long as they lived in New England. Once they had moved to Nova Scotia they began to regard it as a principle of ineffable wisdom. 'We do all of us profess to be true Friends & Loyal Subjects to George our King,' declared the inhabitants of Yarmouth plaintively in their petition of 1775. 'We were almost all of us born in New England, we have Fathers, Brothers, & Sisters in that Country, divided betwixt natural affection to our nearest relations, and good Faith and Friendship to our King and Country, we want to know, if we may be permitted at this time to live in a peaceable State, as we look on that to be the only situation in which we with our Wives and Children, can be in any tolerable degree safe.'

The Americans, of course, were even less inclined to

tolerate this 'neutrality' in their blood-brothers than they had been to accept it of the Acadians. In 1776, they tried in vain to take Fort Cumberland on the Isthmus of Chignecto; and during the rest of the war repeated and valiant attempts were made to persuade Congress or the Massachusetts General Court to support an armed attack on Nova Scotia. But there was a sharp difference between this and every other struggle which had been fought over Acadia; and Washington put his finger on it when he rejected the project of an attack on Windsor in the Bay of Fundy. 'It might, perhaps, be easy,' he wrote, 'with the Force proposed to make an Incursion into the Province . . . but the same Force must Continue to produce any lasting Effects. As to furnishing Vessels of Force, you, Gent^n, will anticipate me, in pointing out our Weakness and the Enemy's Strength at Sea. There would be great Danger that, with the best preparation we could make, they would fall an easy prey either to the Men of War on that Station, or some who would be detach'd from Boston. . . .' This naval weakness was the fatal flaw in any plan for the conquest of Nova Scotia. It was also the chief defect in the Americans' defence of their own northeastern frontier. By 1779 the British had pretty well cleared the Bay of Fundy of American raiders and had established themselves as far west as the mouth of the Penobscot.

In the meantime, while Nova Scotia continued to play its indecisive rôle, Quebec had dramatically re-entered its spectacular career of aggression and warfare. In 1775 — to the disordered imaginations of the American patriots — the northern province loomed up suddenly like a spectre from some barbaric and vanished past. The Quebec Act was an honest attempt, matured over a period of ten years, to solve the peculiar problems of the colony; but it appeared in the evil company of the 'Intolerable Acts' of 1774 and its own aspect was sinister beyond belief to the Americans. Surely the Quebec Act denied democracy, condoned popery, defied frontiersmen to cross the Ohio! Once again, even despite the conquest which should have made it British, this strange, alien, northern world shouted its old menace to the rest of the continent. And it was not so much the desire to spread the new doctrine of revolution as it was the instinct to crush the military power of Quebec which sent the Americans northward into that province. The year 1775 did not bring the fraternization of two friendly peoples, but the invasion of one society by its neighbour. The Americans had simply renewed the traditional struggle between the St. Lawrence valley and the Atlantic seaboard.

The war which followed was full of the echoes of old battles and the memories of past mistakes. As the Americans had suspected, the ancient road to Canada was virtually open, for Governor Carleton's few hundred soldiers were widely distributed in the various garrisons of his enormous province. In May, 1775, less than two weeks after the odious Quebec Act went into force, the Green Mountain Boys captured the old French forts of Ticonderoga and Crown Point. In November, a larger American force under General Montgomery took St. Johns, on the Richelieu, and shortly after the defenceless Montreal capitulated. If at this point Benedict Arnold's famished and tattered army had not reached Quebec after its incredible journey up the Kennebec and down the Chaudière, Montgomery might have remained in Montreal, or even retired to Albany, satisfied with the work of the campaign. But Arnold's presence before Quebec committed him to join in a siege of the capital for which the combined American armies were not in the slightest degree prepared. Without cannon, and with insufficient numbers, a bombardment was impossible and a blockade hopeless. Their only real chance was a swift surprise; but the attack launched on the lower town on the night of December 31, 1775, in the teeth of a wild blizzard from the north-west, ended in the death of Montgomery and a hundred other colonials and in the capture of four hundred American prisoners.

The Americans could not effect the capture of Quebec. They could not even make a moral conquest in Montreal. At the beginning, when the invaders seemed to be sweeping everything before them, a few British-Canadian merchants and a much larger number of French-Canadian *habitants* gave the Americans assistance in various ways. On the whole, this support was inspired rather by the local grievances of the Canadians and by their awe at the bigness of the American forces than by any sympathetic understanding of the American cause. When the American forces dwindled, when the Americans added new grievances to those which already aggravated the Canadians, this naïve and accidental friendliness speedily changed to dislike. The British merchants were alienated when the Americans completely stopped their western trade. The *habitants* were estranged when the invaders mocked their religion and paid them in worthless paper money. The Americans, who had confidently seen themselves in the rôle of open-hearted liberators, discovered, to their astonishment, that they were regarded as pitiless tyrants. Obviously the invasion had been a military and a moral fiasco. The American soldiers hung on until the spring of 1776; and then, when the British fleet sailed up the St. Lawrence, they tumbled over themselves to get away from Quebec in time.

The British efforts to use the Richelieu River-Lake Champlain route were equally lamentable. Carleton's failure to profit by the large army which was sent to him in 1776 may have been deliberate, for he seems to have been anxious to grasp the last chance of conciliating the Americans; but Burgoyne's surrender in the following year was an unqualified military disaster. After 1777, the great campaigns were over in the north; and the war dwindled away into a series of raids and border forays, in which British regulars, Loyalists, and Indians revived the swift type of fighting for which New France had once been famous. There might have been another formal invasion of Quebec, if the Revolutionaries could have agreed with their French allies; but each partner wanted Canada himself and each disliked the thought of the other's getting it. And thus, by luck and staying power, the northern colony had preserved its separateness once again. It had survived another armed attempt to incorporate it in a continental union. The United States won its independence from Great Britain; but Quebec and Nova Scotia kept their independence of the United States.

[*II*]

The American War of Independence was a civil war of the English-speaking peoples. In the struggle, the West Indies, Newfoundland, Nova Scotia, and Quebec, as well as a large proportion of the population of the Thirteen Colonies, had remained loyal to the British cause. The war could not be ended by a simple recognition of the independence of the Thirteen Colonies: it could only be concluded by a formal division of the territories and assets of the British peoples in the new world. This settlement was embodied in the Peace of Paris of 1783; and the negotiations leading up to this treaty form one of the most curious episodes in the entire history of British diplomacy. Outwardly it was a record of weakness which seems almost incomprehensible in the light of the actual strength of the British bargaining position. Surely Great Britain had saved enough out of the wreck of the first Empire to assure the colonies which remained to her a really great future in the North American world. When the conflict ended on the Atlantic coast, the British were in control of the seaboard at least as far west as the Penobscot River; and in the central part of the continent they had kept possession of the forts and posts which dominated the entire region of the Great Lakes and the greater part of the territory between the Ohio and the Mississippi. This vast western region, which was linked geographically and historically with the colony of the St. Lawrence, had never come into the possession of any of the Thirteen Colonies at any time during the entire history of the continent. In both east and west, the British had a good historic case, amply confirmed by the clinching argument of possession. Yet in both regions they made concessions which virtually destroyed the natural development of British North America for ever.

The explanation of this surrender may be found partly in the character of the British diplomatists. Richard Oswald, the principal British agent in the negotiations with the Americans Adams, Jay, and Franklin, was just as pliant as he was naïve and uninformed; and the Prime Minister, Lord Shelburne, 'probably knew less about Canada than about any other portion of the British Empire.' But the indifference with which the British negotiators went through the motions of diplomatic bargaining was not so much a proof of their own incapacity as it was an expression of the attitude of the whole country to the war. Great Britain was sick to death of the war. She was soured by the defection of her eldest colonies, disillusioned about colonies in general, and largely indifferent to the fate of those which remained to her. In these circumstances it was not very difficult for the Americans to take and keep the initiative in the negotiations. They began by proposing that there should be no northern boundary at all, and that the whole of Canada should be ceded to the United States as a pledge of reconciliation. Oswald was impressed by this benevolent suggestion; but it was a little too much for even the British cabinet; and in the end, after a certain amount of rather perfunctory haggling, the American negotiators proposed two alternative boundaries from which Great Britain could choose. Both proposals were alike in the east, for both began with the St. Croix River, followed the height of land between the St. Lawrence system and the rivers draining into the Atlantic Ocean, and then continued along the forty-fifth parallel until it struck the St. Lawrence River. From that point westward the two proposed lines differed profoundly. By the first alternative the boundary was to continue straight west along the forty-fifth parallel to the Mississippi River; by the second, it was to follow the line of the Great Lakes and their connecting rivers to the Lake of the Woods, from whence it was to run due west until it struck the Mississippi. In the end the British chose the second alternative, not apparently because of any interest in the enormous issues involved, but simply because the water boundary looked more definite. Thus, with a few casual strokes of the pen, Great Britain ceded an empire which the colony of the St. Lawrence had built by over a century of effort. The western Indians, whose territory the British had guaranteed by solemn treaty, were betrayed; and the fur traders, who plied the one business which had sustained Canada from the beginning, were forgotten. A line, which at that time was completely arbitrary and meaningless, was drawn through the centre of the drainage basin of the Great Lakes; and the first unity of the St. Lawrence, based upon the fur trade, was suddenly partitioned at a moment when it still stood intact and unaltered. This, for British North America, was the first great consequence of the Treaty of 1783.

In the east, the British made another, and an almost equally important, concession which concerned, not the boundary of Nova Scotia, but the liberty of its coasts and territorial waters. The boundary had been settled at the St. Croix; but though the Americans had pushed the line thus far east it by no means represented all that they wanted in north-eastern North America. By the territorial settlement, Cape Breton, the Gulf of St. Lawrence, the Labrador coast, and the island of Newfoundland had all remained in the British Empire; and it was important for the United States, and vital for New England, to gain some access into these historic centres of the North Atlantic fishery. At Paris, the American diplomatists demanded not merely the right to fish on the Newfoundland Banks and in the Gulf of St.

Lawrence — which could hardly be denied to them — but also the liberty to take fish within the three-mile limit of British territorial waters and to dry and cure fish on British North American shores.   From the first, Franklin insisted that the fisheries were a *sine qua non;* and John Adams supported him vigorously with copious expert evidence, a good deal of moral indignation, and some remarkably plain threats.   'If,' he declared indignantly, 'we were forced off, at three leagues distance, we should smuggle eternally, that their men-of-war might have the glory of sinking now and then a fishing schooner, but this would not prevent a repetition of the crime, it would only inflame, and irritate, and enkindle a new war, that in seven years we should break through all restraints and conquer from them the Island of Newfoundland itself, and Nova Scotia too.'   Under this heavy attack, the British resistance, which had always been conditioned by a desire to weaken the Franco-American alliance and to win the friendship of the United States, at length gave way.   The Americans won nearly, but not quite, all they wanted in the fishery.   They were given both the liberty to take fish in British-American territorial waters and the liberty to dry and cure their catch on the unsettled bays, coasts, and harbours of British-American territory.   As the history of the French shore in Newfoundland had shown already, any treaty division of the fisheries would likely cause trouble; and the arrangement of 1783 was to affect the whole future of Nova Scotia and to bedevil its relations with the United States.

The third great consequence of the Revolution and the Peace of 1783 was the coming of the Loyalists.   The American War of Independence left an amount of bitterness which was unusual in the civil wars of English-speaking peoples; and in its final effects on the upholders of the lost cause it differed markedly from the English Civil War of the seventeenth century and the American Civil War of the nineteenth.   It is extremely unlikely that the Loyalists, had they been victorious, would have treated the revolutionaries any more generously; but at all events it was scarcely possible for them to have administered worse treatment than the revolutionaries meted out to them. If a Loyalist left his home to fight for the British cause, his private property was normally confiscated. If he took no part in the fight but refused to take the patriotic test which was imposed in most of the states, he was subjected to every kind of civil disability, to a constant surveillance reminiscent of that imposed on Roman Catholics in England two hundred years before, and to indignities, plunder, and injury by the mob. In these circumstances, the Revolution was accompanied by the flight of an unusually large proportion of the population who, though their property and all their attachment lay in the colonies, could not endure the new, and to them intolerable, state of affairs. As the war went on, some left the colonies, others collected at the British garrison towns or followed the British armies, and still others joined Butler's Rangers, Sir John Johnson's Battalions, de Lancey's regiments, the Queen's Rangers, and the rest of the over fifty units which were organized during the Revolution to fight for the Loyalist cause.

When the war was over, the British negotiators tried to get justice, if not mercy, for the Loyalists at the peace conference. But they ran into two difficulties, one of which was the limited power of Congress, and the other of which was the unrelenting attitude of the American people. Under the terms of the Articles of Confederation, the various states which had suspended the rights of the Loyalists and confiscated their property stood in a happy position of complete irresponsibility. They had given Congress enough power to bind Great Britain, but not enough power to bind themselves. All the American commissioners could do was to promise that Congress would 'earnestly recommend' to the different states that they should restore the confiscated rights and property both of residents of the British Isles and also of residents of the American colonies who had never fought against the United States, though they might have remained within the British lines. As for those people who had taken up arms to maintain a united empire, it was agreed that they might return to the United States for a year and use their best efforts to recover their property. Finally, it was stipulated that there were to be no more prosecutions or confiscations arising out of the war.

In due course, Congress sent out its 'earnest recommendations'; but, as most people expected, they were almost completely ignored by the states. Except in South Carolina, there were few generous acts of restitution. On the contrary, there was renewed and vigorous confiscation; and when Loyalists returned, as they had a right to do by the treaty, to recover their property, they were in many cases only too glad to get away again with their lives. For the great majority of these refugees, the peace terms and their subsequent dishonour by the states completed the breach between them and the new Republic. They sought compensation for losses from the new Commission on Loyalist Claims which the British set up in London; and, facing the enormous difficulties of adjustment, they set out to make new homes for themselves in loyal portions of the Empire. Of the total of perhaps one hundred thousand Loyalists, nearly a third, including many of the wealthy and cultivated, returned to England; but the majority remained in the new world either through poverty or through affection for the American environment. A good many went to the West Indies and the Floridas; and between thirty-five thousand and forty thousand followed the natural migration routes north into Quebec and north-east into Nova Scotia.

The mass migration to Nova Scotia was probably the most dramatic episode in the whole story of Loyalist wanderings in the new world. As the war drew to a close, thousands of Loyalist civilians and disbanded soldiers began to throng to New York, which was the last great port in British hands.

Here, under the care of Sir Guy Carleton, the veteran who had seen both the beginning and the end of the struggle, the refugees gradually overflowed the accommodation of the city and filled the camps which were established on Long Island, Staten Island, and the adjacent shores of New Jersey. In those last hectic days of preparation and departure that followed the peace, it seemed that 'everybody, all the world, moves on to Nova Scotia.' Already a few groups had left in the autumn of 1782; the great migration was due to begin the following spring; and Colonels Winslow, Allen, and de Lancey, of the colonial service, went on ahead to secure lands for the disbanded troops. Carleton said good-bye to them. 'Your task,' he said, 'is arduous; execute it as men of honour. The season for fighting is over; bury your animosities and persecute no man. Your ship is ready, and God bless you.'

The great fleets that sailed from New York during the season of 1783 bore most of the nearly thirty thousand Loyalists who went to Nova Scotia. A few sought homes in Cape Breton and Prince Edward Island (Isle St. Jean). A number settled on the Bay of Fundy, in the good, unoccupied lands east and west of the old town of Annapolis; and a still larger number congregated in that odd, artificial city of Shelburne, on the Atlantic shore, where the quality built handsome houses, and lounged in the parade, and intrigued and quarrelled with each other as long as the government rations held out. Perhaps the largest of all the Loyalist contingents sailed for the mouth of the Saint John River on the north shore of the Bay of Fundy. Here, in a river valley which seemed one dense and unending mass of green, the whole long adventure of their flight — the perils, hardships, and dissipation that had filled their days with excitement — ended at last in the terrible reality of pioneering. In the main these were people who had lived in the long-settled parts of North America; and among them were many who had been well educated, who had known ease and comfort, and who had given up positions of importance and distinction. Their old lives had unfitted them for the ordeal which they now confronted; and the casual existence of camp and exile had bred idleness in even the humblest. The process of adjustment was terrible for many. 'It is, I think, the roughest land I ever saw, . . .' wrote one woman who reached the Saint John valley in June of 1783. 'Indeed, I think there is nothing in comparison. . . .' But there was no alternative now; they landed — many without shelter — and watched the ships sail away to the west. 'I climbed to the top of Chipman's hill,' the grandmother of Sir Leonard Tilley told one of her descendants, 'and watched the sails disappearing in the distance, and such a feeling of loneliness came over me that, although I had not shed a tear all through the war, I sat down on the damp moss with my baby in my lap and cried.'

The Loyalist migration to Quebec differed in several important respects from that to Nova Scotia. The total number of Canadian refugees was probably not more than six thousand; and they came, not in a great mass movement, but singly and by small groups as the war progressed. In a great number of cases, the men, about half of whom were native Americans, had fought in Sir John Johnson's Battalions, Jessup's Corps, and Butler's Rangers. For the most part they were simple farmers who came from the frontier regions of New York, Pennsylvania, and Vermont; and by and large they had little property and less education. When they took the oath of allegiance, a large proportion of them signed with a cross and others wrote their names with shaky unfamiliarity. When they came to testify to the losses they had suffered during the war, most of them could claim nothing more substantial than a leased fifty- or hundred-acre farm, of which perhaps ten or twenty acres were improved. The authorities at Quebec were so convinced that the Canadian Loyalists' claims for compensation 'cannot singly be considerable' that they even wondered whether it was necessary for the British Commissioners on Loyalist Claims to take the trouble to travel up the St. Lawrence. In the end, when the commissioners did come, one of them reported that those he had interviewed were 'mostly farmers from the back parts of New York Province,' whose claims individually were quite trifling. In contrast with the Nova Scotia Loyalists, many of whom were quite unusual migrants, the Canadian refugees were typical frontiersmen, not unready for the next move and capable of making it efficiently.

Though a number of the Quebec Loyalists were shipped to Gaspé, and some remained in the old seigniory of Sorel, the great majority travelled west beyond the Ottawa River to occupy what was soon to become the Province of Upper Canada. A few went to Detroit. A number joined the disbanded veterans of Butler's Rangers at Niagara, which had been the headquarters of the corps during the war. But by far the largest group drew lots for lands in the two long rows of new townships which stretched up the St. Lawrence from the seigniory of Longueuil and westward beyond the old fur-trading post of Cataraqui on Lake Ontario. In the summer of 1784, one year after the main body of Loyalists had landed in Nova Scotia, the Canadian refugees who had been living on government bounty along the river near Montreal journeyed in companies up to Lachine, took to the French-Canadian flat-bottomed *bateaux* with their few goods, and began the long fight up the river and past the tumbling rapids towards their new homes in the forest.

The migration of nearly forty thousand people to British North America was the last of the immediate consequences of the Peace of 1783. Now the dismemberment of the first British Empire was complete. The assets were divided, the peoples had separated; and a bewildered and disillusioned Great Britain was left to reorganize the remaining fragments of her western dominion. How was the growth of the second Empire to be regulated? Was the Old Colonial System to be retained, or was some new system to be devised to meet the changed circumstances? What institutions were to be given to British North America, and what were to be its relations with the mother country and the new United States? These were terribly serious questions, which might have aroused a reforming spirit; but within a few years they had all been answered, and mainly in the traditional fashion. It soon became clear that Great Britain intended to make few important changes in her ancient colonial policies. It soon became clear also that her North American colonies, so far as they had any formed opinions at all, were pleased rather than displeased by this conservatism. The empire which Great Britain had colonized had rejected the Old Colonial System; but the empire which she had conquered accepted it. The rock which had wrecked the first American dominion was to become the cornerstone of the second.

So far as the regulation of trade was concerned, Great Britain looked hesitatingly for a moment in the direction of change and then fell comfortably back on tradition. For a while it seemed as if the British authorities would accept the principle of mutual free trade between the British Empire and the United States and mutual free navigation of British and American waters; but this precipitate revolt against the Old Colonial System, this premature attempt to reinstate the United States economically in the British Empire, met stubborn forces of resistance on both sides of the Atlantic. British North America opposed the scheme, for it would have been disastrous to her interests. From the French Empire, the merchants of these northern provinces had inherited a long tradition of reliance on imperial markets and an equally long tradition of competition with the Thirteen Colonies. For them the American Revolution was simply an opportunity to profit at the expense of their old rivals. Naturally they hoped to monopolize all the economic privileges of loyalty and to saddle the United States with all the economic disadvantages of independence. Naturally they looked to the British trade laws to exclude the Americans from imperial markets which they now hoped to monopolize themselves.

If the merchants of British North America had been obliged to rely simply on their own influence, they might not have got very far; but, after the first shock of post-war discouragement, the British mercantilists, led by Lord Sheffield, joined their British American brothers in the defence of the old shipping monopoly and the old colonial preferences. The vision of free trade within the English-speaking world was gradually replaced by the far older design of a self-sufficient British Empire in competition with other foreign powers, including the United States; and the regulations for the trade of the West Indies, which formed the most important of the coveted imperial markets, indicated clearly how the old mercantilist principles were to be applied for the benefit of the surviving colonies. Great Britain, of course, could not abruptly stop all American trade with the islands, for they had been too long dependent upon American products and shipping. But now the United States was permitted to export only a few products to the West Indies and these had to be carried in British ships. This privilege, moreover, was supposed to be temporary only, until the British North American provinces could undertake full supply.

In government, as well as in trade, Great Britain faced a major job of post-war reconstruction. And here again, with a conservatism which was partly the result of policy and partly the legacy of routine, the authorities eventually fell back upon the relatively unaltered methods of the Old Colonial System. What were the lessons of the American Revolution? How could they be applied? It was all very confusing and mysterious to the men who, after 1783, pondered over the wreck of the Empire, and tried to analyze the nature of the imperial tragedy. There were a number of people — American Loyalists like Edward Winslow and William Smith, the ex-Chief Justice of New York, as well as Britishers like Guy Carleton and William Knox, the Permanent Under-Secretary for Colonial Affairs — who came to the simple conclusion that the chief defect of the first Empire had been too much, not too little, democracy. The moral seemed sound enough; but it could be applied only within limits and it was never followed up with complete conviction. People argued that, in order to strengthen the principle of authority, the surviving colonies ought to be broken up into a number of small governments and the powers of their governors increased. But, on the other hand, nobody ever seriously planned to abandon the old system of representative institutions, and in 1786 the governor at Quebec was given commissions which made it possible, though difficult, for him to wield some of the powers of a governor-general for all British North America. Policies were contradictory; but, on the whole, the general drift was towards political division and oligarchic control. In drastic and almost unqualified contrast, British North America was being broken up into a number of small, immature, and feeble provinces, in the very years when the Thirteen Colonies were being brought together in a united and potentially imposing state.

In Nova Scotia, which had long ago become a royal province with a constitution modelled on that of Virginia, the main result of the post-revolutionary reorganization was the partition of the colony. Here North American geography and conservative policy seemed to point to the same conclusion. Incurably divided in character, inevitably impatient of centralization, Nova Scotia had proved difficult to conquer and to govern as a whole; and the Loyalists had barely arrived in the Saint John valley and Passamaquoddy Bay when they became violently discontented with the far-off government at Halifax, which neglected their interests, bungled their land grants, and denied them proper representation in the assembly. They soon discovered that, in addition to the remoteness and inefficiency of Halifax, there were a good many other features of the government and society of old Nova Scotia which were even more objectionable to social and political conservatives like themselves. Two thirds of the population of the province, so Edward Winslow believed, 'had been well-wishers in the late rebellion.' Its political leaders were principally persons 'of a republican turn of mind'; and its solicitor-general was 'a great, lubberly Irish rebel.' It would be wrong, Winslow argued, to unite such a people with the Loyalists, for the two groups were essentially distinct; and he and his friends conceived the idea of a new, Loyalist province, 'the most gentlemanlike on earth,' which would be created out of British territory north of the Isthmus of Chignecto. Over in London, their ideas were running on much the same lines. William Knox had formulated his principle of divide and rule, and a separate Loyalist province on the mainland had already been projected as a citadel of conservatism and imperial loyalty. As early as 1769 Prince Edward Island (Isle St. Jean) had been made a separate province; and in 1784 the partition of the old Province of Nova Scotia was completed. In that year, Cape Breton Island became an independent government; and the territory north-west of the Isthmus of Chignecto was created the Province of New Brunswick.

In Quebec, it was a question not only of boundaries, but also of representative government itself. Under the Quebec Act, the old feudal and authoritarian institutions of New France were still maintained. Even British reactionaries and American Loyalists in their wildest Tory imaginings could not hope to improve on the conservatism of this system; and the only question was how soon and how thoroughly it would be liberalized. In the first months after the war when the Loyalists were settling on the upper St. Lawrence, it seemed certain that the old seventeenth-century Province of Quebec could no longer escape the changes which it had avoided so long. The British merchants in Quebec and Montreal recommenced their old agitation for an assembly; and the Loyalists themselves, who represented the simple frontier spirit of America, began at once to petition for a reform of the antiquated and alien customs which they discovered to their surprise existed in the province of their adoption. Even Guy Carleton, who returned as Lord Dorchester in 1786 to govern the colony again, was no longer the cocksure reactionary who had planned and applied the Quebec Act. And with him, as his new chief justice, came the New York Loyalist William Smith, who was a moderate liberal with no great affection for the old order on the St. Lawrence.

The auspices looked excellent. Reform appeared inevitable. And yet, in fact, it was so difficult to achieve. Against the opposition of the British bureaucrats and the French-Canadian seigneurs, Dorchester and Smith found it impossible to carry anything in the council at Quebec; and it soon became obvious that if Great Britain wished to change the old order on the St. Lawrence, she must do so by statute of the Imperial Parliament. Dorchester had been sent out to recommend a plan upon which Parliament might act; but, instead of finding a solution, he seemed merely to deepen the mystery. Where before he had been so confident, so voluble, so emphatic, he now hesitated and qualified and demurred with a most unexpected and lamentable indecision. And, in truth, the problem seemed almost insoluble. Undoubtedly representative institutions would have to be granted sooner or later; but the political framework in which these institutions would be placed was the subject of a most prolonged and anxious debate. Should the old Province of Quebec be divided, or should it be kept intact? In 1791, the total population of the province was approximately one hundred and thirty thousand, of whom a little over twenty-one thousand were English-speaking, two-thirds of them living in the Loyalist settlements above the Ottawa. Unquestionably the inhabitants were divided into two main groups by nationality, language, and custom; but they were united geographically by the St. Lawrence River and economically by the commercial system based upon it. And to divide the province on the line of the Ottawa was simply a rough-and-ready solution which would respect the ethnic differences of the people but would almost certainly prejudice their common material interests. It was all very baffling. Dorchester had little to propose; and eventually the authorities in London got tired of waiting for him to discover a solution. George Grenville took the matter into his own hands; and, against the opposition of the Canadian merchants, who hoped to preserve the unity of the province, he imposed the easy and obvious settlement of division.

Actually the Constitutional Act of 1791 did not divide the old Province of Quebec, for this was done subsequently by special Order-in-Council; but it assumed the creation of the two new provinces of Upper and Lower Canada and provided institutions for both of them. On the whole, the Act altered relatively little; and in both what it did and what it failed to do, it tended to strengthen the inherited conservatism of politics and society in Canada. There was no reform of the antiquated Custom of Paris. Land had to be granted in freehold tenure in Upper Canada, and could be so granted in Lower Canada if desired; but the existing seigniorial system was left untouched. The privileges which had been given to the Roman Catholic Church by the Quebec Act were not revoked; and an earnest attempt was made to build up the Church of England, as another bulwark of royal authority and the established order, by reserving a portion of the crown lands in each province for the support of a Protestant clergy, and by empowering the governors to endow Church of England parsonages with these reserves. The two new legislatures were carefully planned to avoid the unfortunate precedents of the Thirteen Colonies and to copy the venerable traditions of the British Mother of Parliaments. In each there was a new house, which resembled nothing in British-American constitutional history and looked suspiciously like a half-hearted, second-best colonial substitute for the House of Lords. This was the legislative council, a body entirely distinct from the executive council, which was intended to act as a check upon the assembly and to share the power of law-making with it. In effect, the Constitutional Act had strengthened the principle of authority in government and the principle of hierarchy in society. It tended to preserve the old régime of France in Lower Canada, and it sought to establish the old régime of England in Upper Canada.

[*III*]

The new settlements had been founded, the new colonies established, the new constitutions set up. And under such governors as Thomas Carleton of New Brunswick and the vigorous, aggressive John Graves Simcoe of Upper Canada, the new colonial communities began to feel their way laboriously towards some measure of security and well-being. The Peace of 1783 and the coming of the Loyalists started a revolution in the whole life of the north. The settlers who fought their way, clearing by clearing, through the bush were destroying the old way of existence in British North America, as well as founding a new, with every stroke of the axe. Their presence meant the rise of agriculture, fishing, lumbering, and oceanic commerce; but it meant also the slow decline and fall of the ancient industry of the fur trade. For generations the fur trade had helped to maintain Indian society and to embarrass white settlement; but the new boundary of 1783 robbed some of the Indians of their old political support, and the onward march of the frontiersmen weakened the whole economic basis of their culture. The fur trade of Montreal travelled westward across the continent towards its extinction, leaving behind it a strange, youthful British North America, which was developing new economic interests, seeking new markets, trying to find a new basis for its prosperity within the British Empire.

Yet in the last few decades of its existence, the Canadian

fur trade performed some of the most spectacular acts of its entire career. As always in the past, it had to do battle on two fronts — south-west against the new United States and north-west against its traditional enemy the Hudson's Bay Company. In the end, the Canadians had to surrender in both regions; but whereas defeat came rather swiftly in the south-west, in the north-west it followed as the final anticlimax to a long and brilliant series of victories. North-west of Lake Winnipeg, it was a straight commercial struggle, uncomplicated by political advantages, between the Hudson's Bay Company and the new North West Company — a loose co-partnership of Canadian traders which had emerged definitely towards the end of the American Revolution. Organized as a last, desperate expedient by traders who could no longer support individually the enormous cost of transcontinental traffic, the North West Company summed up and embodied the entire experience of fur-trading Montreal. It produced organizers like Simon McTavish and Joseph Frobisher, who bettered the Frenchmen who had preceded them. It developed trader-explorers like Peter Pond, Alexander Mackenzie, and Simon Fraser, who rivalled the far-off exploits of La Salle and La Vérendrye. It was served by tough, thickset French Canadians, the descendants of generations of *coureurs-de-bois* — men who could bear the terrible fatigues of the trade, who loved its romances and respected its traditions. The last of a long line of fur-trading organizations which stretched back to the days of Champlain, the North West Company inherited the furious driving energy of its predecessors, and all the tricks and devices which they had accumulated in two centuries of trade.

The Nor'Westers were the real gentlemen adventurers of the north. They were the traders of fortune whose traffic was at once a gamble, an adventure, and an ordeal. 'Fortitude in Danger' was the motto of the Beaver Club, to which only the true westerners, the real aristocrats of the trade, were admitted; and this reckless courage, this spendthrift energy, which alone made commercial success possible, seemed to touch their whole lives with the colours of extravagance. The dinners of the Beaver Club, with their endless toasts and their long tale of broken glasses, made Dillon's Tavern famous in the history of Montreal. The annual gatherings at Grand Portage and Fort William, where the bourgeois, traders, clerks, interpreters, and canoemen assembled in full array for solemn conclaves, were like the grand muster of a clan for battle or the meeting of a feudal host. In their great houses in Montreal, the Nor'Westers were the expert hosts of lavish entertainments; they were travelled cosmopolitans who knew London as well as they knew the fur-trading west. And often, after all the chances, riches, and reversals of the trade were done and ended, they crept back, as did Peter Pond and David Thompson, to die in poverty and in obscure neglect. Perhaps Simon McTavish, though he was apparently never west of Grand Portage, may stand for the company he did so much to establish. It was he who built the great house at the foot of the mountain in Montreal which stood so long after his death in untenanted splendour. It was he who purchased the estate of Dunardarie, the ancient seat of the clan Tavish, far back in Argyllshire, and tried to ensure in his will that it would be held always by someone who bore the McTavish arms. With his sentimentalism, his cheerful cynicism, his driving, organizing energy, and the overbearing pride which earned him the title of the 'Marquis,' he seemed to sum up the exuberant spirit of this company of reckless and resolute men.

Though the North West Company summed up the past, it also anticipated the future. It set the style for Canadian business in the nineteenth and twentieth centuries; and, like the great corporations which followed it, its destiny was to cross the continent. While in the east the pioneers had scarcely even occupied the fringes of Upper Canada, the servants of the North West Company were staking out the western boundaries of the future Dominion of Canada. On the Pacific coast, they were anticipated — though only slightly anticipated — by British traders and explorers who came by the far easier sea route to grasp their share of the riches of Alaska seal and sea otter which the Russians had discovered on the northern coast. Captain Cook, on his last and fatal voyage, touched and traded at Nootka Sound in 1778. British traders followed him to barter with the Indians for the valuable sea-otter skins; and when, in a last effort to enforce her exclusive claims to the north-west coast, Spain seized their ships and property, she was forced, by the Nootka Convention, to surrender her monopoly. In 1791 Captain George Vancouver sailed to receive officially the restored British property and to complete Cook's explorations; and from 1792 to 1794 he systematically surveyed and charted the coast north from the Strait of Juan de Fuca.

He was scarcely ahead of the Nor'Westers. Their main purpose was to capture the trade of the great fur-bearing region beyond the North Branch of the Saskatchewan River from the Hudson's Bay Company; but they were also interested in the successes of the Russian fur traders on the north Pacific coast. The illiterate, violent Peter Pond, who began his lifetime of adventure far back in the town of Milford, Connecticut, pushed the trade north to Lake Athabaska and perhaps as far as Great Slave Lake. His successor at the lonely Athabaska outpost, the young Scotsman Alexander Mackenzie, completed the journeys Pond had hoped to make and solved the last great geographical puzzles of the northwest. With four French Canadians, a German, and a handful of Indians, Mackenzie found the great river which bears his name and travelled down it in frail bark canoes to the Arctic Ocean. It was an heroic exploit; but it left Mackenzie restless and dissatisfied, for his object was the Pacific and not the Arctic Ocean. In 1793 he returned to seek it by Pond's other river, the Peace. With only a few men, some of whom were veterans of the Mackenzie River expedition, he fought his way up the wild waters and over the great cliffs of Peace River canyon through the mountains; and then struck out overland to reach the Pacific at Dean Channel by the middle of the summer. He was the first man, by a dozen years, to cross the continent. And beside a flat face of rock in Dean Channel he 'mixed up some vermilion in melted grease, and inscribed, in large characters . . . this brief memorial: Alexander Mackenzie, from Canada, by land, the twenty-second of July, one thousand seven hundred and ninety-three.'

In the south-west, where there was no hope now of any such expansion as Pond and Mackenzie had begun in the north, the Canadians merely tried to hang on to a trading territory which was obviously threatened by the new boundary. For a few short years after 1783, it looked as if they had succeeded beyond their most extravagant hopes. Abruptly reversing the accommodating stand she had taken at Paris, Great Britain now refused to surrender the posts she had cheerfully signed away by treaty. When the Americans protested, they were told that the western posts would be handed over when the United States had done justice to the Loyalists and had provided properly for the recovery of pre-Revolutionary British debts. These American breaches of the treaty were so open that even John Adams and John Jay frankly admitted that they justified the British retention of the western territory. 'Under the circumstances,' wrote Jay in a secret report to Congress, 'it is not a matter of surprise to your secretary that the posts are detained; nor in his opinion would Britain be to blame in continuing to hold them until America shall cease to impede her enjoying every essential right secured to her, and her people and adherents, by the treaty.' There was no doubt that the United States had violated the terms of peace, as Great Britain claimed; but this British reply to the American demand for the posts, while partly a real explanation, was also partly a mere excuse. The truth was that the ignorant and negligent authorities in London had at last been awakened to the serious, if not terrible, results which might follow the total abandonment of all their rights and obligations in the American west. The Canadian fur traders argued that the new boundary would rob them of one-half to two-thirds of their trade. The angry Indians protested that they would not accept the sacrifice of hunting-grounds which the British had guaranteed by treaty. The fear of an Indian rising and the desire to keep the fur trade were the main reasons against the surrender of the posts. They were not separate and distinct arguments, but, in effect, two ways of putting the same argument. Fur traders and Indians were inseparable partners who cherished the same hope of stopping the advance of American settlement and the same ambition of preserving the fur-trading commercial empire of the west.

As the Canadian officials had predicted, the Indians did rise; but they rose, not against the British who had betrayed them, but against the Americans who now held their hunting-grounds in jeopardy. Naturally the United States believed that British officials had egged on the Indians to resist their new sovereign; but what really drove the tribes to make a last stand for their territories was the extreme demands of Congress for Indian land and the unauthorized advance of American frontiersmen. The Indians defeated the first two American armies that were sent against them; and these successes helped to persuade the British that they could still repair their broken faith with the tribes. They offered to mediate between the Americans and the Indians. They suggested the creation of a neutral Indian barrier state, which, conveniently for themselves, would be entirely on the American side of the new boundary. But this obvious effort to undo the Treaty of Paris collapsed during the course of 1794. 'Mad Anthony' Wayne defeated the Indians at the Battle of Fallen Timbers; and by Jay's Treaty, the British agreed to evacuate the western posts. During the summer of 1796, the last red-coats marched out of the territory of the United States; and it seemed as if the old empire of the St. Lawrence was ended for ever.

Yet, despite the cession of the posts, the fur-trading dominion south of the Great Lakes lingered for a few years longer. By Jay's Treaty, Great Britain and the United States granted to each other the right to pass freely over the new international boundary and to make free use of the lakes, rivers, and carrying-places on both sides for commercial purposes. Legally this privilege was reciprocal, but practically it was one-sided, for the Canadian fur traders were much stronger; and the officials of the United States, annoyed by this continuance of Canadian competition south of the line, sought to limit as narrowly as possibly the rights which had been granted by treaty. They were prevented, by the terms of the agreement, from levying duties on inland trade which were higher than those imposed on ocean commerce; but they could — and did — resort to the rather sharp practice of placing an arbitrary valuation, one-third higher than the prime cost in Europe, on goods which the Canadians carried in across their northern boundary. In 1805 they excluded all but American citizens from the trade of the newly purchased Louisiana; and when the British protested that Jay's Treaty had guaranteed the reciprocal right to pass freely, for commercial purposes, through 'the respective territories and countries of the two parties, on the continent of North America,' they were informed that Louisiana was an 'additional territory' and not included in the bargain. 'Your Memorialists,' wrote the despairing Canadian merchants, 'have for some time seen progressing, with extreme concern, a systematic plan to drive the British Indian Traders from the American Territory, by every species of vexation; and they must soon succeed if His Majesty's Government does not take up their cause with decision. . . .' Two years before the War of 1812 broke out, the Canadians had been driven by necessity to come to terms with John Jacob Astor, their principal rival in the south-west trade.

While the fur trade dwindled in the south and approached the limits of expansion in the north, the new British North America, with its new economic interests and political problems, was slowly and painfully developing in the rear. In the Maritime Provinces, the great northward movement of peoples from New England had spent itself at last with the coming of the Loyalists. Immigration did not cease entirely, for there were some colonists from the British Isles, including a number of Highland Scots, who settled in Cape Breton and the north-eastern part of Nova Scotia. But, on balance, the Maritime Provinces probably lost more people by emigration than they gained by immigration in the first two decades after the Peace of 1783. Some of the Loyalists, who were baffled by the problems of adjustment which faced them, left for the already more popular Upper Canada, and some for the once-hated United States. 'A few giddy, eccentric, and discontented characters have appeared,' wrote Edward Winslow in 1802, 'who, forgetting all the favours which they have received from our government, have made a voluntary sacrifice of their former honourable principles and professions, have sold the lands that were granted them, and meanly skulked into the United States.'

In the Canadas, on the contrary, the settlements which had been founded by the refugees of the War of Independence were growing steadily. On the heels of the Loyalists came a stream of American colonists who simply followed the natural path of westward migration around the lower lakes. Some of these people settled east of the Richelieu River in what came to be called the 'Eastern Townships' of Lower Canada; but the majority ventured further west, to fill up the gaps in the Loyalist settlements around Lake Ontario, and to penetrate the peninsula between Lake Erie and Lake Huron. The original Loyalists had numbered less than six thousand; but, on the eve of the War of 1812, there were perhaps eighty thousand inhabitants in Upper Canada. With only a sprinkling of British immi-

grants in this mass of frontiersmen from New York, Pennsylvania, and Vermont, Upper Canada was the most 'Americanized' of all the British provinces. Even Lower Canada,
which at the time of its creation in 1791 had contained only
a few British merchants in an overwhelming majority of
French Canadians, had now been invaded by thousands of
typical New England pioneers.

Though in both the Maritime Provinces and the Canadas
these new settlements remained primitive and largely self-
sufficient, they quickly began to develop the economic interests which were to distinguish them in the future. By
degrees the basic differences between the two economies of
British North America became more evident. Upper Canada and the much less important Eastern Townships were
purely agricultural frontiers — the first of their kind in the
northern provinces. In the Maritime Provinces, where the
sea and the forest were dominant and where fertile land
was relatively scarce, it was inevitable that agriculture
should be subordinate to fishing, lumbering, and trade. Far
from being able to export foodstuffs, Nova Scotia and New
Brunswick began to import wheat and flour from the United
States almost as soon as the Revolutionary War was over.
On the other hand, the untouched timber resources of Nova
Scotia, and particularly of New Brunswick, seemed to assure
the future of lumbering; and the people of Nova Scotia
argued, reasonably enough, that 'if the New England traders
could find a profit in sending their vessels to this coast to
fish, those who inhabit its borders can carry on the business
to much greater advantage.' The growth of the fishery in
cod, mackerel, salmon, and herring, the increase of sawmills
in Nova Scotia, the building of sloops, schooners, and square-
rigged vessels in New Brunswick in the years following the
peace, were all very encouraging. Merchants along the coast
began to take shares in schooners and fit out the assorted
cargoes for the West Indies trade.

In all these ways the new British North America, which

had been born of the American Revolution, was beginning to take on the form and character of the future. The new settlements had gained, though with painful difficulty after the first great spurt of the coming of the Loyalists. But they were still primitive, pioneer communities, which had yet to find a place for themselves, which were still groping for some form of economic good fortune; and it seemed unlikely that they could ever undertake the ambitious commercial rôles for which they had been cast during the reorganization of the Empire. On both sides of the Atlantic, it had been confidently predicted that the St. Lawrence would become the trunk-line of a second great commercial empire in which the manufactures of Great Britain would be exchanged for the natural products of the new American West. Obviously, the settlements in the region of the Lower Lakes, including those in Upper Canada, were still too weak to have any large surplus for export; and, instead of risking their wheat down the rapids of the St. Lawrence, the Upper Canadian farmers preferred to grind it into flour and sell it to the garrisons on both sides of the international boundary. The real test of the St. Lawrence as a trade route to the west lay in the future; but it was perfectly clear already that there were several factors which narrowed its chances of success. As it stood the route was difficult and costly. There was no good preferential market in the Empire for wheat and flour to offset the enormous transport charges to and from the interior; and worst of all, there was a real chance of serious competition from the Hudson River route through New York State. 'Mercantile Competition,' wrote a London merchant who was interested in the Canadian trade, 'will now most probably place these two Communications with the Sea, more strongly in opposition to each other. The question will be by which Rout can the necessary supplies be brought up, or the superabundant Produce carried down, *on the best terms,* from these extensive Countries bounding the sides of the Great Lakes.' The old rivalry of the New York route, which had first appeared long ago in the days of the French fur trade, now threatened to revive in the new age of western settlement and agriculture.

While the St. Lawrence had yet to meet its test, the Maritime Provinces were already failing in theirs. The northern provinces could no more supply the British West Indies than they had been able to supply the French West Indies a hundred years before. In their struggle to capture the trade from the United States, they were handicapped by distance, by high freights and insurance, and by lack of experience in the West Indies market. To make up their cargoes, they had to import, not only flour and provisions, but even lumber, from the United States, for once the timber closest to the navigable rivers had been devoured, the Maritime sawmills could no longer meet American prices. Even in the early days, when American ships were excluded from the islands, Nova Scotia and New Brunswick could not take full advantage of their chance. In 1793, when the war between Great Britain and revolutionary France began, and when a large portion of British shipping was diverted to war purposes, the governors of the West Indies were permitted to open their ports to American vessels if necessary; and the special privileges of the northern provinces were largely wiped out. 'What will be the event, time will discover,' wrote one merchant of Liverpool, Nova Scotia, 'but at present the prospect is very gloomy as we have no other dependence but the fishery and trade, having no farms to resort to when trade fails, for these reasons the war opperates more particular against this town, but is felt more or less by every traiding town in the province.'

And then, quite suddenly, the whole future of British North America was altered. The French Revolutionary Wars had caused the northern provinces nothing but trouble; the Napoleonic conflict brought them almost unqualified prosperity. With his navy destroyed at Trafalgar, with his hopes of invading England annihilated, Napoleon turned to the Continental Policy, political and economic — to the plan of smashing England by destroying the commercial foundation on which he believed her greatness was based. In one form or another, economic pressure had been used often enough in the past in both diplomacy and war; but in the ten years from 1805 to 1815 it was employed by so many great powers and on such a scale as to dwarf all previous experience. In the end, governmental stoppage of trade extended over virtually the whole continent of Europe, including Russia, as well as over the principal American neutral country, the United States. In 1806 and 1807, by the Berlin and the Milan Decrees, Napoleon completed his self-imposed blockade of the European continent against British trade. In January and November, 1807, Great Britain retaliated with the Orders-in-Council which virtually closed the Continent to neutral commerce. The United States, in its effort to uphold the commercial rights of neutrals, simply copied the economic methods of the belligerents. In 1807, under President Jefferson, an embargo was laid on all foreign-bound vessels in American ports; and this policy was continued by the Nonintercourse Act of 1809, which was imposed at different times against both Great Britain and France.

British North America felt the bracing effects of both the European and the American economic reprisals. The consequences of Napoleon's blockade turned out to be more permanent; but, while they lasted, the results of the Embargo and the Nonintercourse Act seemed almost equally beneficial. It was possible to stop traffic from American Atlantic ports to overseas markets, but it was incredibly difficult to sever all commercial connection with British North America. The provinces not only touched the United States, but they also touched the very sections of the Republic which were most opposed to the economic policy of Jefferson and Madison and quite prepared to disobey it. Down in Passamaquoddy Bay, storm-tossed American coasters put into

New Brunswick ports to get repairs — and to sell their cargoes. By sledges in winter and by great rafts in summer, the flour and lumber of New York and Vermont were brought down the Richelieu River route to Montreal. The American foodstuffs which had been sent directly to the British West Indies were now smuggled into the northern colonies; and, for the first time in their existence, the Canadas and the Maritimes had become the real source of West Indies supply. 'If,' declared a Canadian newspaper later, 'the last two Presidents [of the United States] are entitled to the honour of monuments, anywhere upon the globe, it is surely at Montreal.'

In the meantime, the Napoleonic blockade had suddenly created another, and an even more important market in Great Britain. For generations, ever since her own supply of wood had run out, the mother country had looked to the Baltic countries — Denmark, Norway, Prussia, Dantzig, and Russia — for the timber which was the vitally essential material of her merchant fleet and Royal Navy. During the first years of the century, when economic warfare grew more fashionable, Great Britain became slightly uneasy about this European source of her supplies; but it was not until the last moment, when Alexander of Russia had joined the continental blockade and threatened to turn the Baltic into a closed sea, that the British finally awoke from their complacency to a realization of the terrible seriousness of their situation. They then turned to the British North American provinces, whose prospects in general had never stirred their interests very much, and whose wood in particular they had frankly despised. The colonial preference on timber had never been sufficient to balance the high freights across the Atlantic; but between 1809 and 1812, the British Parliament raised the duties steeply, until the colonial preference on a load of square timber amounted to a little over £2, 16s. Contracts were awarded lavishly to firms who embarked their capital in the new British North American industry.

With one great stroke of fortune, British North America had found its justification and acquired its economic rights in the Empire. In their own weakness, the northern colonies had relied on Great Britain; and now, in its own temporary embarrassment, Great Britain had been obliged to fall back on them. Unwanted in some imperial markets, unsatisfactory in others, the new staple products had never yet found a real place for themselves; but now one of them had been lifted into pre-eminence as the vital raw material of imperial defence. At almost the last possible moment wood had succeeded furs as the great northern staple; wood had become the second 'crop' of both the Precambrian Shield and the Appalachian Highlands. This was no specialized business, like making boards and shingles, hoops, staves, and headings for the tricky West Indian market. Here the great buoyant red and white pine logs were simply squared, lashed together in rafts, and floated down the Saint John and the Miramichi in New Brunswick, and down the Richelieu and the Ottawa towards Quebec. Timber, the inexhaustible material, became virtually the sole support of New Brunswick, the great resource of the Canadas, the origin of traffic, population, and plenty for all British North America. In the suddenly crowded ports of Saint John and Quebec, the shipping tonnage employed in the colonial timber trade increased from twenty-two thousand tons in 1802 to one hundred and eleven thousand in 1814; and, at the end of the Napoleonic War, it was said that British North American timber required five times as much shipping as all the British imports from Asia.

Where all else had failed, the Jeffersonian Embargo and the Napoleonic blockade had apparently succeeded. 'Since the Northern Ports of Europe have been shut,' said the Canadian merchants with confident assurance, 'and the Embargo in operation, the Supplies of various kinds derivable from the British North American Provinces, and the Canadas in particular, have become objects of great national concern, and cannot but point them out as most valuable appendages of the Empire, meriting such a preference in the British & West India Markets, by Bounties, protecting Duties and other expedients, as shall assure to the commodities they are capable of furnishing, decided advantages over those from the United States or from other foreign nations.' The economic design of British North America since 1783, which was to co-operate with the Empire, and to compete with the United States in the new staples, seemed almost to have passed into the reality of achievement. The transition from furs to fish, and wheat, and lumber had been pushed a long way to completion; and the struggle for survival in the swift chances of North American politics seemed now to have some prospect of success. Even the War of 1812, which might have interrupted this evolution in mid-career and completely diverted the course of British North American development, actually formed only a dramatic episode in a trend which was already well established. To the surprise of most North Americans, including the Canadians themselves, the war confirmed the independence of British North America and completed its economic revolution.

[*IV*]

The War of 1812 was obscure in its origins and surprising in its development. Did the United States wish merely to punish Great Britain for her offences on the Atlantic or did she wish to extend her own empire in the centre of the continent? Were the Canadas invaded because they were desirable in themselves or simply because they were the only part of the British Empire which lay open to American attack? Outwardly, at least, the whole course of Anglo-American relations seemed to prove that it was Great Britain, not British North America, which had provoked the anger of the United States. The disastrous effects of the British blockades on American trade and shipping, the incidents arising out of

the British claim to search neutral vessels for absconding sea-
men, had goaded the American government to resort to its
policy of economic pressure, and, at the time of the *Chesa-
peake* affair, had almost united the American people in a
cry for war.

On the other hand, the Battle of Fallen Timbers and the
British surrender of the western posts had certainly not
brought a real peace in the centre of the continent. Impelled by the remorseless onward march of the American
frontier, the Shawnee chief Tecumseh and his fanatical
brother the Prophet had tried to rouse the tribes for a last
effort at resistance; and, though the British officials actually
did everything in their power to quiet the Indians on this
occasion, the Americans naturally believed that they had
fomented the native uprising. Despite the new boundary,
despite the surrender of the posts, the connections between
the Indians on the American side of the line and Canadian
officials and fur traders were suspiciously intimate and
friendly. They had fought for each other in the past, and,
as time would prove, they were to fight for each other one
last time in the future. At Tippecanoe, General Harrison
crushed the Indian revolt; but behind the Indians the American West could see a sinister British influence which loomed
in gigantic distortion over the whole frontier. It was the urgings of western men and the pressure of frontier states which
helped largely to bring on the war. No doubt the westerners
were angry with the British blockade, for it had closed their
markets in Europe; but no doubt also they hoped to secure
the free and uninterrupted expansion of their frontier at
the expense of the Canadas.

From the Americans' point of view, their declaration of
war in June, 1812, could scarcely have been better timed.
Napoleon was just about to set his Grand Army in motion
against Russia, and from then on until the spring of 1814,
everything that England had was invoked in the final titanic
struggle against France. There were less than five thousand

British regulars in the provinces when the war broke out. In the circumstances there seemed little hope that they could be reinforced, and even less that British North America could defend itself while Great Britain was distracted in Europe. The population of the northern provinces, which totalled less than five hundred thousand, to seven and a half million Americans, was probably less certain in its loyalty than it had been twenty-five years before. The Loyalists and their descendants were ready enough for a fight and they dominated society in New Brunswick and, to a lesser extent, in Nova Scotia. But in Lower Canada, which was far more open to attack, there were only a few British to offset a mass of dubious French and an even more dubious fringe of American settlers. In Upper Canada, which was the most exposed of all the provinces, the original Loyalist population had been surrounded and submerged by an influx of typical American pioneers who came with no particular affection for British institutions and a very real desire for free land.

Yet if British reinforcements seemed unavailable and Canadian loyalty was uncertain, there were at least comparable weaknesses on the other side. The war divided the United States only less seriously than the Revolution had done thirty years before and than the Civil War was to do fifty years later. The New Englanders refused to serve in the army, bought British treasury notes instead of United States bonds, and traded with Nova Scotia and New Brunswick almost as if they were friendly neutrals. The American government, weakened by the defection of this wealthy and powerful part of the community, had somewhat surprisingly prepared for the war of its own choosing by reducing the Regular Army, and thus it had to rely largely on untrained and undisciplined militia. The generals who led the long succession of these slatternly American armies in and out of Canada were, for the most part, lamentable incompetents; and the chaotic assortment of conflicting intentions which served them as a plan of campaign was even feebler. If, as the Thirteen Colonies had done before, the United States had invaded Canada by the Richelieu River and captured Montreal, it could have completely severed Upper Canada from all hope of assistance. The Americans could then have demolished at their ease the province at whose half-settled boundaries their armies kept nibbling ineffectually for three years.

The war was fought in two distinct and widely separated theatres — on the Atlantic Ocean and in the region of the upper St. Lawrence and Lakes Ontario and Erie. In the east, it was a purely naval conflict. New England, which was violently opposed to the war, virtually protected the Maritime Provinces from attack by land; and even on the ocean there was relatively little fighting, for the tiny American fleet could not possibly face the British navy in a stand-up engagement, and both sides had to content themselves with injuring each other's commerce as much as possible. American frigates did extremely well in occasional single-ship combats with vessels of the Royal Navy; and together with the swarming American privateers they took very nearly fifteen hundred British merchantmen as prizes. In this war on commerce, the provincials of Nova Scotia and New Brunswick copied the tactics of their relations south of the line; and their swift privateer, the *Liverpool Packet,* together with the *Retaliation,* the *Wolverine,* the *Sir John Sherbrooke,* and two score others, brought in slightly over two hundred American prizes in the three years of the war. In the main, however, the British method was not privateering but blockade, systematically imposed by the Royal Navy. By degrees the American privateers were hunted down, as the notorious *Young Teazer* was in 1813, and the American frigates and merchantmen swept from the seas. And the blockade, becoming ever more rigorous in execution and disastrous in its effects, was extended at length even to New

England, which had been spared for so long out of pure policy.

While the United States could not escape from the defensive at sea, its overwhelming superiority on land enabled it to take and keep the offensive for the greater part of the war. In the summer of 1812, three American armies assembled for the easy conquest of the Canadas. The main force, under General Dearborn, which was supposed to attack by the Richelieu River route, barely reached the frontier of Lower Canada late in the campaign; and this complete failure to strike at the vitally important Montreal was an accurate forecast of the bad strategy which was to paralyze the American offensive until the end of the war. Even so the Americans might have conquered the whole western part of Upper Canada, if their two secondary attacks on Niagara and Detroit had been carefully synchronized and driven home; but obligingly they let themselves be defeated in detail and at long intervals. Isaac Brock, the Lieutenant-Governor of Upper Canada, had only a tiny force of regulars, Indians, and somewhat doubtful militia to defend the two widely separated gateways into his province; but he received the capitulation of Hull and his entire army at Detroit and was back again at Niagara weeks before Smyth launched his belated October attack. The fifteen hundred Americans who had taken up a good position on Queenston Heights were gradually encircled, and killed or captured, while the New York militiamen, protesting that they had not engaged to serve outside their own state, looked on as interested spectators from the other side of the river. Curiously enough, the only successful offensive of the first year of the war was the British conquest of Michilimackinac. It was a typical western Canadian army of regulars, fur traders, and Indians which took the place without firing a shot. The fur-trading colony had begun to recover its lost dominion in the southwest; and Brock, though he had been killed in the first skirmish at the Battle of Queenston Heights, had done enough to restore the morale of Upper Canada.

In 1813, when the Americans had their great chance to deliver a knock-out blow, they frittered away their superior strength in widely dispersed, unco-ordinated, and ineffectual attacks. Their greatest success came late in the season on Lake Erie, where Perry defeated Barclay at Put-in-Bay, gained command of the lake, and sent Procter retreating eastward from Detroit with Harrison at his heels. This decisive naval action and the subsequent battle of Moravian-town in which Procter was defeated constituted the first real American triumph in the war; but fortunately for the Canadians its significance was almost purely local. It did not even interrupt British communications with Michilimackinac and the west, for supplies and reinforcements were simply re-routed via Lake Simcoe and Georgian Bay, and it had no influence at all on the fighting further east. On Lake Ontario, the American Captain Chauncey could never quite win the breathless naval construction race and establish a clear supremacy over Sir James Yeo; and while the two fleets took to their bases one after the other to await the construction of new vessels, or chased and banged each other around the lake, the American commanders scarcely knew what to do with their land armies and had to abandon every operation in the Niagara peninsula that they tried to carry out. It was, once again, only very late in the season when they finally decided on a twofold attack upon Montreal, which was intended to be the major effort of the year, but which, through wrangling and incompetence, never got anywhere. Hampton, advancing north-west from Plattsburg, was checked at Châteaugay; and Wilkinson, moving down the St. Lawrence from Sackett's Harbour, lost a minor engagement at Crysler's Farm, where one of his divisions was badly mauled by a British force half its size. And then, suddenly, the whole plan was thrown up.

Up to this point, the far weaker forces of the British had

kept them strictly on the defensive, except in the region west of Lake Erie. The year 1814, which saw the downfall of Napoleon and released the veteran British armies in Spain, abruptly reversed the rôles of the two combatants in North America and entirely changed the character of the war. It was impossible, however, for these British reinforcements to reach the Canadas until late in the season, and the United States was presented with a last chance to score an important strategic success. Its troops were now much improved, and really capable officers like Jacob Brown and Winfield Scott had replaced such pathetic incompetents as Hull, Smyth, Dearborn, and Wilkinson. Something might have been done, though the issue was doubtful on both land and lake; but between the bad strategy of Washington and the bad co-operation of Chauncey's fleet at Sackett's Harbour, the last chance was thrown away. Montreal or Kingston, the British naval base near the foot of Lake Ontario, were the real objectives; but with consistent perversity it was decided to make the main effort on the remote and strategically unimportant Niagara frontier. The American offensive, which got under way at last in July, was planned to capture the forts at the mouth of the Niagara River and to roll westward along the peninsula toward the head of the lake. Brown found the going difficult enough on land, for though Chippewa was a hard-fought American victory, Lundy's Lane was tactically a drawn battle. But what ruined the campaign was Chauncey's stubborn refusal to leave his base. Without naval support, Brown could not capture the Niagara forts; and after the hard check at Lundy's Lane, he threw up the drive to the west and retreated back to Fort Erie. The last major American enterprise had been a strategic failure.

Late in the season, when their reinforcements at last arrived, the British began their one and only important offensive of the entire war. Of the four main attacks which they carried out, two were intended to be mere raids, and two were serious efforts to recover vital territory which could compel a revision of the boundary of 1783. The raid on Washington, which was made in excessive retaliation for the burning of York in 1813, was a complete success; but the late attack on New Orleans was a disastrous failure. In the north, where the two major invasions were attempted, the results were equally mixed. Under Sir John Sherbrooke, the Governor of Nova Scotia, a British force took Castine, Machias, and Bangor, occupied the whole of Maine east of the Penobscot, and received the formal submission of the inhabitants, who seemed undisturbed at the prospect of becoming British subjects. In the Great Lakes region it was very different. Here the British planned a smashing blow, for they hoped to break in the boundary which Oswald and Shelburne had accepted back in 1783. In the far west, they did not need to take action, for the Indians and the British garrisons at Michilimackinac and Prairie du Chien were already holding down the region of the Upper Lakes; and it was too early to risk a major engagement on Lake Ontario, for the great ship which gave Sir James Yeo command of the lake at the very end of the war was not yet ready to leave the stocks. In these circumstances, Sir George Prevost, the Governor of Lower Canada, made an attempt on Plattsburg, the American base on Lake Champlain, which was as complete and deplorable a failure as anything in the entire war. Inside Plattsburg Bay, the tiny British flotilla was gradually overcome; and Prevost, having marched seven thousand of the Iron Duke's veterans down to Lake Champlain, marched them back again to Canada without striking a blow.

In this fashion the campaign and the war came to an end. Though the British had occupied more territory in three months than the Americans had done in three years of war, they had not won an unqualified decision; and the peace settlement, which was spread out over more than four years of argument, reflected this indecisive outcome. When the negotiations opened at Ghent, the second-rate British diplomatists who were as usual detailed to settle American affairs began by insisting that the international boundary must be revised in favour of the British provinces, and that an Indian barrier state must be created on the American side of the line. Steadfastly refusing to accept these changes, the able American commissioners clung determinedly to the boundary as laid down in the Treaty of 1783; and in the end Great Britain, whose interests at the Congress of Vienna were as important as her concerns at the Conference of Ghent appeared negligible, accommodatingly adopted the American position. Apart from this, and the fact that it ended the war, the Treaty of Ghent did little; and it was left for the Convention of 1818 to settle the more outstanding issues between the United States and British North America. The Convention did not deal with the disputed boundary between New Brunswick and Maine and it simply postponed the problem of sovereignty west of the Rocky Mountains. But it decided that the line west of the Lake of the Woods was to follow the forty-ninth parallel to the mountains; and although it permitted American fishermen to enter the bays and harbours of British North America for wood, water, shelter, and repairs, they were definitely excluded from the inshore fisheries of British North America.

Thus, though the United States had yielded a little on the Atlantic coastline, it was able to confirm its great diplomatic victory in the centre of the continent. The boundary of 1783 stood immovably; British North America had definitely lost its inheritance in the west; and the old unity of the St. Lawrence and the Great Lakes was gone for ever. The retreat of the Canadian fur traders south of the line became a rout which ended quickly in withdrawal. The United States, adopting a vigorous policy of economic nationalism in the interior, promptly decreed that nobody but American citizens could carry on the fur trade in its territories; and there was nothing for the Canadians to do but to hand over the wreck of the great business which Radisson, and Dulhut, and La Salle had founded a hundred and fifty years before.

Now the north-west trade alone was left to Montreal; and even the North West Company, the first great transcontinental concern in Canadian history, was travelling rapidly through its last victories to final surrender. In 1813, it had compelled Astor's Pacific Fur Company to sell out at Fort Astoria; and in 1815 it began a vigorous private war against the colony which Lord Selkirk had established near Lake Winnipeg, in the heart of one of its provision districts. To the very end of its existence, the company seemed its old self — as ingenious, as violent, and as successful as ever. But the terrible cost of pursuing a difficult and dwindling trade across a continent broke the men whom nothing else had been able to conquer; and in 1821 the North West Company was absorbed in the Hudson's Bay Company. The river city had been vanquished in the end. The far west was lost to Montreal. And henceforth the territory for which it had fought so long was held in trust for the future Dominion of Canada by the Hudson's Bay Company.

The long period of confusion and uncertainty which had begun in 1763 had ended at last. Despite three attempts — two of them armed attempts by the United States — to impose a political unity on the continent, the northern provinces had managed to keep their independence. A terrible price in territory had been paid for their survival; the population and enterprises of British North America had altered under the shock of war and revolution; and the old world of the Indians and the fur traders had vanished before the onward march of settlement and the new staple trades. The fight for a separate existence had changed much; but it had left the character and basic purposes of British North America virtually unaltered. The American Revolution and the coming of the Loyalists had confirmed the old alliance with an imperial European power; the War of 1812 intensified the old fearful and jealous rivalry with the United States.

CHAPTER FIVE

FREE TRADE AND
RESPONSIBLE GOVERNMENT

[*I*]

IN THE YEARS following the American Revolution, the second British Empire had been organized on roughly the same basis as the first. Certain changes had been introduced. A few alleged improvements had been made. But in all essentials the organization was the same. Once again the mother country and the colonies were linked together in a political and economic system which imposed mutual obligations and granted mutual privileges. The Old Colonial System was to be given a second chance; but it had failed in its first trial, and it soon began to look ominously as if it would fail in its second. In the first half of the nineteenth century, the mature nationality of Great Britain and the simple communities of British North America were both undergoing drastic changes which were likely to influence their relations with each other and with the outside world. But if the old imperial association was to be altered, how serious would the change be and how was it to be brought about? Was the partnership to be ended or were its terms merely to be revised? And in either case, was all this to be done by force or by mutual consent?

In North America, the British provinces had already entered that dangerous period of adolescence which had been the prelude to armed revolt in the Thirteen Colonies. The

French-speaking community of Lower Canada had taken on its permanent form long before this; and now the other societies of British North America were rapidly forming a distinctive character. This social process, which had begun before the American Revolution and was to continue until the middle of the nineteenth century, ran a somewhat similar course throughout the northern provinces. It was true, of course, that the environment and the chief economic interests varied greatly from province to province. It was equally true that in no two provinces was the mixture of ethnic and cultural groups at all the same. But in all British North America, except Lower Canada, the basis of settlement had been laid by colonists from the Thirteen Colonies and their successors, the United States. To these were now added a great army of migrants from the United Kingdom.

Thus the new stock continued to be English-speaking. But — and this was to be an important factor in the formation of British North American character — it now came almost exclusively from the British Isles where before it had come almost exclusively from North America. The depressions which recurred periodically in Great Britain from 1815 to the middle of the century, the continued unemployment, and the mounting distress drove the emigrants in bewildered thousands to the ports; and the timber trade, which had meant a heavy outbound cargo and a light return to British North America, supplied the cheap shipping which carried these people to the new world. In 1812, there had been less than five hundred thousand people in the northern provinces; by 1850 their number had increased to approximately 2.4 million. Throughout the north, the new arrivals from the British Isles, and the older immigrants from the United States, were joined in the common task of winning a new social well-being through adjustments and sacrifices; and everywhere there was the same interplay of different cultural heritages, the same conflict of different social groups, the same rivalry of different religious persuasions. Out of this

long and painful process there emerged several characteristic British North American societies, with distinctive
values, needs, and objectives of their own.

The Maritime Provinces were almost as extreme an example of cultural diversity as they were of economic and
political division. In Nova Scotia, which was the senior
province in the eastern group, there were the Acadians, who
had returned after the great dispersion, the pre-Loyalist
Yankees, the Loyalists, the various small groups of settlers
from the British Isles, and isolated and curious pockets of
people like the German Protestants at Lunenburg. Up
until the end of the eighteenth century, relatively few Scots
had reached the province; but they began to arrive during
the interval of the Peace of Amiens and, for a decade or so
after Waterloo, they came in a great wave which peopled
Cape Breton, Prince Edward Island, and the north-eastern
part of the Nova Scotian peninsula. The newcomers were
Presbyterian and Roman Catholic Scots who had left homes
in the Highlands and the Western Isles; and they totalled
over half of the forty thousand immigrants who were known
to have reached Nova Scotia in the period 1815-1838. Together with the pre-Loyalist New Englanders and the Loyalist refugees, the Scots formed the third most important
group in Nova Scotia. They were also the last large group
of settlers to make their homes in the peninsula. And thereafter the great population movements of the nineteenth
century largely passed the province by.

As in the past, the geography and the economic pursuits
of Nova Scotia helped also to make for the variety of provincial life. Within its small limits, the province was a country of violent contrasts. The good farm lands, the lush
river valleys, were never far away from rock and forest, and
almost always close to the sea. Men had to piece a livelihood together out of resources which were strangely varied,
which had been scattered by a none too lavish hand. Along
by the tidal reaches and up the short river valleys, stretched

the orchards and farms where they grew hay and root crops and fattened their cattle. The harbours of the long string of seacoast towns were white with fish spread out for drying; the beaches were cumbered with the scaffolding of half-built schooners. And far beyond the last red boulders of the rocky headlands lay the fishing-banks; and beyond these again were the remote markets of the West Indies, and the Mediterranean, and the Orient. 'The Nova Scotian, . . .' wrote Thomas Chandler Haliburton, in one of his best pictures of provincial life, 'is often found superintending the cultivation of a farm and building a vessel at the same time; and he is not only able to catch and cure a cargo of fish but to find his way with it to the West Indies or the Mediterranean; he is a man of all work but expert in none.'

When the Scots had closed the last frontier in Nova Scotia, the tumult of settlement gradually subsided in the province. It was as difficult, however, to knit together an integrated community out of these diverse peoples as it was to make Nova Scotia a political unit or an economic whole. Ever since the American Revolution, Halifax had been trying seriously to become the metropolitan centre of Maritime life — to take the place which Boston and the other New England towns had once held. Halifax was the seat of government and bureaucracy, the British naval and military base, the focus of trade with Great Britain, the stronghold of Loyalist political views and conservative social prejudices. With its wealth, its dignity and gaiety, its aristocratic codes and standards set by government house and garrison, Halifax assumed the right of social leadership in the colony. The Tory Haligonians — the young officers, dignified civil servants, comfortable merchants, and cultivated Church of England clergymen — tried to impose their cultural and religious standards upon the primitive community around them; and over on the Fundy side of the peninsula, the professors, judges, and professional men of the little college town of Windsor supported the capital in its defence of the British connection, the Church of England, and English cultural values. As early as 1787, shortly after the arrival of the Loyalists, Nova Scotia was made a bishopric — the first in North America — with a resident bishop who was expected to give vigorous leadership for the church in the second British Empire. In 1789, King's College, the Anglican academy at Windsor, was incorporated. In 1802, when it was chartered as 'King's College of Nova Scotia' and opened exclusively to members of the Church of England, King's became the first university in the second British Empire. One of its graduates, Thomas Chandler Haliburton, the author of various historical and political works and the creator of the *Sam Slick* series of humorous satires, was perhaps the most distinguished literary exponent of the Loyalist tradition in British North America.

Though the Loyalist contribution was an important one, it was not everywhere accepted. Halifax leadership was vigorous, but it did not go unopposed. Just as the outports fought to prevent the capital from restricting their direct trade with the United States and from centralizing all external commerce at her own docks, so they criticized Halifax's cultural standards, refused to recognize its privileged classes, and rejected its organized religion. The evangelical churches, the Methodists and particularly the Baptists, made rapid progress among the older settlements of English and New Englanders. The newly arrived Presbyterian Scots were reinforced by large numbers of people from the now rapidly declining orthodox Congregational churches in the community. The Roman Catholic Church, which had the allegiance of the Highland Scots of Antigonish as well as the returned Acadians, became a fourth competing religious group in the province. The retreat of the Church of England before these rival communions was symbolic of the decline of English class distinctions and cultural standards amid the incurable diversity of Nova Scotian life. In education, the dissenters attacked the exclusive claims of the church from two different points of view and with two different kinds of proposals. The Presbyterian Pictou Academy and the Baptist Acadia College were sectarian institutions; but Dalhousie College, whose cornerstone was laid by the Governor, Lord Dalhousie, in 1820, was the first beginning of a non-sectarian provincial university.

While Nova Scotia had largely passed through the first frontier stage by 1820, New Brunswick had barely begun to face the worst difficulties of settlement. In the years from 1815 to 1850, the 'province of the Loyalists,' 'the most gentlemanlike on earth,' was to suffer a great change in character and a considerable loss of gentility. Already, before the end of the War of 1812, a number of Acadians had reached the north shore of the province, on the Gulf of St. Lawrence, where they were to multiply prodigiously in the future; and after 1815, and particularly during the 1830's and 1840's, came the rush of British settlers, principally poverty-stricken and 'famine' Irish, which was the greatest mass migration that New Brunswick was ever to know. Even if the environment of the province had encouraged a diversified industry, even if a variety of jobs had been open to the immigrants, the necessary adjustments of colonization would have been many and painful. But the timber trade and the shipbuilding industry had become almost the sole economic support of the province ever since the days of the Napoleonic blockade; and the timber trade depressed the status of every other occupation and disturbed the whole business of settlement. 'It was an acknowledged evil of the lumber trade,' wrote an acute contemporary observer, 'that, so long as it was the leading industry of the province of New Brunswick, it overshadowed and lowered the social condition of every other. . . . The young and adventurous among the province-born men were tempted into what was considered a higher and more manly, as well as a more remunerative line of life; many of the hardiest of the emigrants, as they arrived, followed their example: and thus not only was the progress of farming discouraged, but a belief began to prevail that the colony was unfitted for agricultural pursuits.'

Though all unsettled British North America was covered with trees, the forest was omnipresent in New Brunswick in a sense which was peculiar to that province alone. In Upper and Lower Canada, natural forest lands were separated from natural farm lands by that fairly clean division between the rocky Precambrian Shield to the north and the lowlands of the St. Lawrence to the south. But in New Brunswick the fertile soil of the Saint John and the Miramichi river valleys sloped up to high, rocky ridges bearing magnificent stands of pine; and thus, just as lumbering overshadowed agriculture throughout the province as a whole, so it crowded farming even on the lands of the individual settler. For all practical purposes the population was divided into one group of lumbermen and labourers, who worked in the camps and shipyards, and another group of farmer-lumbermen, who tried to combine two occupations to the advantage of neither. 'My father,' wrote one man who remembered the pioneer days of the early 1830's, 'gave his attention to the farm during the summer-time. In the winter and spring, he was away in the woods, lumbering or logging. This routine was followed by most of the men on the upper Saint John; and not a few of them, when the long day was over, came home to thresh grain and attend to the needs of their livestock.'

Just as the timber trade weakened the economic basis of New Brunswick, so it disorganized New Brunswick society. Each in its different way, the various groups connected with lumbering and shipbuilding helped to demoralize the staid community of farmers, traders, and professional men which the Loyalists had hoped to create back in 1784. The farmer-lumberman, who had often tied up everything they owned to get capital for logging, were swept away in ruin by the coming of a depression. In Saint John and other ports, the native-born and the immigrant Irish formed a virtual proletariat which made its uncertain living in the speculative business of shipbuilding. In the upper reaches of the Saint John and the Miramichi, the most energetic and ambitious young men sought the companionship of the lumber camps in the winter, drove the great rafts of squared timber down the river when spring came, and spent the greater part of the summer in a long career of riotous living. With their dislike of the drab, continuous work of the farm, their impatience at the puritanical restraints of society, their love of rum, of gaudy finery, of uproarious companionship, the lumbermen were the *coureurs-de-bois* of the nineteenth century; and they swaggered about the streets of Saint John with the same jaunty and insolent assurance that the returned fur traders had once showed in Montreal. 'After selling and delivering up their rafts, they pass some weeks in idle indulgence; drinking, smoaking, and *dashing off,* in a long coat, flashy waistcoat and trowsers, Wellington or hessian boots, a handkerchief of *many colours* round the neck, a watch with a long tinsel chain and numberless brass seals, and an *umbrella.*' Like the *coureurs-de-bois,* whom they so clearly resembled, the lumbermen came to represent freedom, and quick wealth, and rich and varied experience for the entire community. In the autumn they drew the restless young farmers' sons away to the camps; and in the spring they brought their easy-going, hard-drinking standards to the ports with them.

With ever increasing difficulty, the Loyalist leaders tried to impose their ideal of the good society upon the province. Their church, the Church of England, was a privileged communion which had been identified with government and learning and polite society. Anglican missionaries, sent out by the Society for the Propagation of the Gospel, taught in many of the new schools; and King's College of New Brunswick, which received its charter in 1829, was under Anglican supervision from the first. These treasured institutions, these unquestioned cultural standards, were threatened in the strange and rather precarious world that had come into being with the timber trade. The Church of England was confronted on the one hand with masses of Acadian and Irish Roman Catholics and on the other with equally large numbers of evangelical Baptists and Methodists. The Loyalist squires, bureaucrats, and professional men, who had stood for education and breeding and class distinctions, now found their old leadership increasingly usurped by a parvenu gang of Scots and Yankee capitalists who ran the trade of the province, as well as its shipyards and its lumber camps. Even in politics, where the Loyalists controlled the council and monopolized the key jobs, the city of Saint John was leading an increasingly active and irreverent opposition to this decaying old Loyalist oligarchy. Fredericton, the little capital a hundred miles up the Saint John River, with its sleepy government offices, its cathedral church, and its grey-stone university overlooking the tranquil river, had become one of the last strongholds of the group of men who had hoped to make New Brunswick the pattern Loyalist province of British North America.

Though the migration to New Brunswick was large, it was only a fraction of the great army of people that travelled up the St. Lawrence to the Canadas. In the main, Upper Canada was the goal of these colonists; and Lower Canada was comparatively immune from the good and bad effects of this mass population movement from Great Britain. In the summer, of course, the poverty-stricken immigrants filled the old towns of Quebec and Montreal to suffocation, crowding every inch of the taverns, immigrant shelters, and hospitals, filling the ill-paved, ill-lighted streets with their quarrels and drunken merriment, and thrusting the problems of their poverty and disease upon a community which was totally unprepared to cope with them. A few of these newcomers found farms in Lower Canada on the territories which the British American Land Company had secured; and others, chiefly Irish, remained in Montreal and worked in the construction of the St. Lawrence canals. But the main body of the migration pressed tumultuously through Lower Canada, leaving only few and scattered detachments behind it; and French-Canadian society was never disorganized to the same extent as were other colonial communities by this thunderous invasion from overseas.

Yet if Lower Canada was not affected in the same way as the other provinces, it was none the less the centre of acute social unrest. Neither the English Canadians nor the French Canadians were greatly disturbed as a separate group; but the clash between them was becoming steadily more serious. It was a quarrel of two ethnic groups, two social classes, two cultural heritages, two vastly different sets of values. The Scots, English, and American merchants of Quebec and Montreal, sometimes supported by the settlers in the Eastern Townships, wanted to dominate the province and mould its character just as much as did the Tory 'Family Compacts' in Halifax and Fredericton. These merchants of Lower Canada, with their belief in progress and improvement, their commercial values, their big capitalist schemes, grew more and more irritated by the semi-feudal conditions in which they lived. They were irrepressible individualists in a society which emphasized corporate unity and was willing to sacrifice much for corporate survival. They were dynamic enterprisers in a community which stood for the permanence of rural life and the immutabilities of home and altar. They were willing and eager to exercise the leadership which would have been theirs in almost any other North American setting; but here was a people who did not share their spirit, who questioned their methods, and criticized their goals.

French-Canadian society, in fact, had changed extraordinarily little since the conquest. The church kept its old position, the seigniorial system was not abolished until 1854. For these quiet rural communities along the lower St. Lawrence, all the great excitements seemed to lie just beyond the horizon of time and space. The fur trade was dead and done with. Lumbering was a big business, carried on far up the Ottawa, in which French Canadians took only a subordinate part; and, until the achievement of responsible government, the civil service was largely monopolized by Englishmen who had come out to make careers for themselves in the colonies. Shut out from some employments in the world of commerce and politics, unfitted or disinclined to enter others, the French Canadians poured their ability and their energy into the church, the legal profession, and the farm. It was a somnolent, sheltered community, where life rumbled unhurriedly along in the smooth ruts of established routine around the whitewashed stone cottages, the seigniories, and the gorgeously ornamented churches. Here there was 'contentment, *gaieté de cœur*, politeness springing from benevolence of heart, respect to their superiors, confidence in their friends, attachment to their religion — a character, in short, resembling what Madame de Larochejaquelein describes as existing among that part of the French population which had not been poisoned by the age of Louis the Fifteenth and the Revolution.' The comparison was a favourite one; and to more than one visitor in the first half of the nineteenth century, Lower Canada seemed like 'a province of old France, without its brilliancy or its vices.'

The merchants of Quebec and Montreal and the settlers of the Eastern Townships struggled to free themselves from this apathetic conservatism which seemed to have slowed down the life of the whole province. They criticized the illiteracy of the French Canadians, their lack of enterprise and initiative, their stubborn adherence to the old forms and conventions. 'The population of this province,' wrote one pamphleteer indignantly, 'forms a small compact body inert in its nature, without one principle of percussion; and exhibiting its infant face, surcharged with all the indications of old age and decay.' Under the pressure of this attack, and in fear of the subjugation of their culture, the French Canadians drew together in an uncritical and unquestioning defence of the old régime in the St. Lawrence valley. In the assembly of the province, they defended the old laws and the feudal system. They showed unmistakably their dislike of immigration, banks, and land companies. They refused to vote money for the canals and public improvements by which the settlements in Upper Canada could find an outlet to the sea, and the St. Lawrence could compete with its American rivals.

The conflict of these two philosophies appeared inevitably in the cultural life of the province and retarded its development. French-Canadian education, the standards of which had been so largely maintained by the teaching orders from France, suffered seriously from the conquest and the papal suppression of the Jesuits in 1773; and the two ethnic groups who now lived together in the valley of the lower St. Lawrence could never agree upon a common plan of reorganization. For the French Canadians, education was still a department of religion which must remain under the control of the church; for the new English Canadians, education was becoming more and more a secular matter which ought logically to be placed under the supervision of the state. Hampered by these divided aims and by this lack of cooperation, public instruction made slow progress in this wealthiest and most populous province of British North America. The foundation stone of Laval University, the French-speaking, Roman Catholic institution in the city of Quebec, was not laid until 1854. McGill University of Montreal, which received its first large bequest from the wealthy Scottish fur trader, James McGill, was granted a charter as early as 1821; but apart from the medical faculty, which began its famous career in 1829, the university led only a very shadowy existence until the middle of the century. The Roman Catholic seminaries, where boys and young men were prepared for the priesthood and the professions, apparently did good work; but primary instruction was inadequate for both British and French, and the great mass of the *habitants*, during the early decades of the nineteenth century, seem to have been largely illiterate.

It was not until after the first quarter of the century had passed that the lower province began to show some signs of the new intellectual ferment. French Canada had remained singularly unaffected by the ideas of the French Revolution; it was singularly slow to respond to nineteenth-century liberalism in either its European or its British form; but in the 1830's and 1840's a few cross-currents began to cut across the main stream of French-Canadian development. The *Institut Canadien*, which was founded in 1844, was the first important organization to show the influence of the liberal anti-clerical views of nineteenth-century France. The *Institut* was established late — too late perhaps for its own successful growth; and already, even before its founding, a strong Roman Catholic revival had begun a movement in the opposite direction. In 1841, Bishop Bourget of Montreal journeyed to Europe; and in the next year, partly as a result of his visit, the Jesuits returned to Lower Canada as a teaching order. Bishop Bourget was a vigorous and creative churchman, with a great interest in education; but in the near future he was to prove to be one of the chief links between French Canada and the illiberal, ultramontane Roman Catholicism of Pope Pius IX. The next two decades were to resound with the intellectual battles between this leader of the diocese of Montreal and the *Institut Canadien*.

The great migration to British North America had its heaviest impact on Upper Canada; and for at least a quarter-century after the War of 1812, the province was the scene of great disorganization and unrest. Its problems differed essentially from those of provinces further east, for there was no basic cultural cleavage as there was in the population of Lower Canada, and the timber trade, which was centred largely in the Ottawa valley, never exerted an unsettling influence over the whole province as was the case in New Brunswick. Upper Canada was an almost purely agricultural frontier, in which scores of thousands of British immigrants were engaged, along with the older American settlers, in the painful task of making a new community. The new colonists — English, Scots, Ulster and Southern Irish — were, for the most part, poor, new to North America, and completely alien to its pioneer tradition. Unprepared and badly equipped to meet the loneliness, the poverty, the incessant, brutalizing toil of the backwoods, they often escaped complete shipwreck only by sacrifices in health and education which impoverished their cultural life and degraded their standards of living. It was only gradually that this heterogeneous mass of settlers began to win some kind of order and stability out of the unrest which their coming had created.

The migration did not make as much change in the social organization of Upper Canada as might have been expected. The governing class, attacked by the Reformers as 'The Family Compact,' was a group of judges, civil servants, bankers, merchants, and Church of England clergymen, a number of them related, and more English than the English in their devotion to the old order. This little oligarchy was not greatly increased or strengthened by the new British settlers, even though some of them were persons of good birth and social prominence, and though they all came from a land of rigid class distinctions. Often the poorest and most servile immigrants were found to be 'indefatigable in acquiring a knowledge of the Rights of Man, the First Principles of Equality, and the True Nature of Independence.' Often they aped the accents and manners of the North American settlers around them, copied their airs of casual independence, and sometimes found their greatest and most malicious pleasure in the 'freedom to wreak upon their superiors the long locked-up hatred of their hearts.' The settlers of good family and breeding, thrown into an unfamiliar and hostile environment and surrounded by Americanized neighbours who robbed them and watched their misfortunes with malevolent satisfaction, discovered that good name, education, refinement, and even capital were often powerless to save them from degradation. 'For seven years,' wrote Mrs. Moodie, a

woman of gentle birth and real intellectual distinction —
the author of that classic of frontier life, *Roughing It in the
Bush* — 'I had lived out of the world entirely; my person
had been rendered coarse by hard work and exposure to the
weather. I looked double the age I really was, and my hair
was already thickly sprinkled with grey.' There was to be
no landed gentry on the frontier of Upper Canada, as the
gentlemen immigrants from the old country discovered to
their amazement and disgust.

In religion, as in social organization, the old order, beloved
by the anglophil Loyalists, did not survive intact. Though
the prestige and power of the Church of England continued
to be great, it did not become the dominating church of the
community. It had never been legally established in the
province; but it was endowed with lands by the Constitutional Act of 1791 and for some time it was subsidized by
grants from Great Britain. Anglican clergymen were invariably given precedence in all official affairs of the colony,
Anglican doctrines were professed by the Governor and his
advisers, Anglican services were attended by the soldiers and
the quality of the little garrison towns. The arrival of scores
of thousands of immigrants, a large number of whom had
been unquestioning members of the Anglican Communion,
offered the church a great opportunity and at the same time
faced it with a tremendous problem. It soon became obvious that many of the Anglican clergy preferred the comforts
of town and the companionship of polite and sophisticated
congregations to the hard work of the frontier. They were
tied to their churches and bound by their ritual; and they
showed a gentlemanly aversion for the emotional outbursts
and the unorthodox pilgrimages through the country to
which the dissenting sects took so readily.

While the Church of England failed to take full advantage of its opportunities, the dissenting churches were rapidly winning success. The coming of large numbers of Scots
greatly strengthened Presbyterianism; but the most outstand-

ing phenomenon of the migration period was the advance of the evangelical sects, and particularly of the Methodist Church. With its system of regional conferences and local and itinerant clergymen, Methodism had both the centralized strength and the flexible mobility required for success in the backwoods. Its clergy and lay preachers were one with the simple congregations which they harangued and exhorted. Their fervour offered an emotional release from the stultifying toil and empty silence of the bush; their camp meetings provided the occasion for a lengthy and exhilarating social gathering. In Egerton Ryerson, who became the first editor of their new church paper, *The Christian Guardian,* the Methodists had a leader of great force and very considerable ability; and in 1825, Ryerson vigorously took up the cause of the dissenting churches against the attacks of Archdeacon Strachan, the Anglican leader in Toronto. In its bitter factional fights and its divided loyalties, Methodism reflected accurately enough the unrest of the time and the pull of rival English and American influences. As early as 1828, the Canadian Conference, in the light of public prejudice against the Americans, decided to break completely with the Methodist Episcopal Church of the United States. But though it united with the Wesleyan Methodist Church of Great Britain, this second alliance was not much happier than the first. In their impatience with control either by Americans or by Englishmen, the Methodists represented the growing nationalism of the Canadian frontier, just as they represented its restless democracy in their resentment at the privileges and claims of the English church.

In Upper Canada, the attempt of the Loyalists and the Anglican clergy to impose their cultural standards on the community was resisted just as strenuously as it was elsewhere. Within the province the means of education were woefully inadequate and its intellectual impoverishment was very real; but the Tory solution to the problem was partial and completely unacceptable to many. On the whole, the

Tories tended to emphasize secondary and higher education for the privileged few and to insist on Anglican control. The district grammar schools, first established in 1807, served only a fairly small and well-to-do class. Upper Canada College at Toronto, which was founded in 1829 with the help of public money, was a secondary school in the English manner and under Anglican supervision. The first charter for a provincial university, which was secured while Strachan was chairman of the board of education, would have set up an institution called King's College in which, as in Nova Scotia and New Brunswick, the Church of England exercised control. Against this system the dissenters and democrats in the province raised a clamour which lasted for decades. They tried to escape from the Anglican monopoly of culture either through sectarian colleges of their own, or through a non-sectarian, state-supported educational system. The Methodists founded Victoria College; the Presbyterians established Queen's University at Kingston. But it was not until after the union of Upper and Lower Canada in 1841 that a provincial system of free public schools was built up, and not until nearly the middle of the century that the old King's College was secularized as the University of Toronto.

North-west of the Upper Canadian settlements, which occupied the peninsula between Lakes Ontario, Erie, and Huron, stretched the endless rocky plateau of the Precambrian Shield. Beyond that again, and at the edge of the prairies by the forks of the Red and Assiniboine Rivers, lay the Red River settlement, the one important colony in the British north-west. After 1821, when the North West Company was incorporated in the Hudson's Bay Company, the Ottawa route to the west was abandoned and the fur trade carried on through Hudson Bay. But though Canada had lost contact with its old fur-trading empire, it had left an abiding mark on the little settlement at the forks of the Red and the Assiniboine Rivers. The original nucleus of the colony had been formed by the Scots settlers sent in by

Lord Selkirk in 1812; but it was not until 1821, when the union of the two companies released a number of old employees, that the settlement really began to grow. From that time, the colony was largely peopled by the half-breeds. These were the offspring of the unions which the French-Canadian Nor'Westers and the Scots and English factors of the Hudson's Bay Company had made with Indian women. A common bond united the two groups; but there were important differences between them. While the Scots and English half-breeds were often better educated and normally more industrious farmers, the *Métis*, or French-Canadian half-breeds, were an agreeable, irresponsible, and adventurous lot who trapped, hunted the buffalo, and freighted goods for the Hudson's Bay Company. In 1840, the little Red River settlement numbered slightly less than four thousand five hundred people. It was a typical fur-trade colony, primitive in its economic pursuits, simple in its culture and social organization.

By virtue of its original charter of 1670 and of a licence for exclusive trade which was renewed in 1838, the Hudson's Bay Company still held complete control of the whole British-American north-west. For years after the amalgamation of 1821, the chief difficulty which the company faced was the ancient, the traditional fur-trade problem of enforcing its monopoly; and not until 1849 did it give up the attempt to prevent the Red River colonists from trading with the American fur companies south of the line. In the meantime while the old style of fur-trading competition continued, a new and far more sinister danger was slowly approaching from the east. The peninsula of Upper Canada was being rapidly occupied, the outposts of American settlement were creeping towards the plains; and out in Oregon, the sudden coming of the pioneers soon brought to an end the territorial compromise which had lasted for nearly a quarter-century. By the Convention of 1818, the territory of old Oregon between the Spanish and the Russian claims was left open to both British subjects and American citizens. But the first group of American settlers reached Oregon in 1842. In the next few years, they were followed by even larger numbers, who clamoured for the assertion of American sovereignty in the region. And the agitation which followed was swiftly ended when, in 1846, the Treaty of Washington divided the disputed territory by prolonging the forty-ninth parallel as the international boundary to the ocean and by giving Vancouver Island to Great Britain. As soon as it could do so, the Hudson's Bay Company left American soil. Once again the fur trade had yielded to settlement. It was true that this defeat had come in a debatable land, where sovereignty was still undecided. But north of the forty-ninth parallel, in British-American territory, would the ultimate fate of the fur trade be very different?

In 1850, the future of the Hudson's Bay Company's territories was still uncertain; but, in the meantime, the provincial societies of the Canadas and the Maritime Provinces had formed the permanent bases of their character. Essentially they were North American communities. But their Americanism differed from that of the United States' communities to the south; and these differences had been modified but not seriously changed during the period of the great migration. If British North America was subject to pervasive influences from the United States, it remained in close and vital contact with Great Britain. In the main, its leaders during the first half of the century had been the Loyalists and their descendants; its leaders during the second half of the century were to come from among the British immigrants who had settled the provinces and determined their character.

Yet if the Americanism of British North America was its own, it was none the less impatient of political imperialism. And if, as seemed likely, the Old Colonial System was to be changed or ended, what new status would the provinces seek? Would they follow the path of the United States, or would they strike out some new course of their own? Would they declare for independence, or would they merely establish some new political relationship with the motherland?

[*II*]

In the twenty years that followed Waterloo, the prospect of a peaceful settlement looked good, for both sides approached the problem in a spirit very different from that of 1776. Great Britain, in particular, had greatly changed in her attitude to her colonies. There could be no mistaking it — she was less vitally interested in the second Empire than she had been in the first; and if this decline in interest was partly to be accounted for by the intrinsically smaller value of the surviving colonies, it was also partly to be explained by the widening activities of the mother country itself. Great Britain was passing through an age of reform and reconstruction which affected every phase of her national life. The rise of British industrial specialization and world commerce had created a new economic national interest, a new philosophy of free trade by which it could be justified, and a new class of manufacturers who were ready to fight for it with all the moral earnestness of Hebrew prophets. In the old Mercantile System, where the objective had been the monopoly of empire trade and shipping, colonies had been a real advantage; but in the new age of industrial capitalism, where everything was sacrificed for large-scale manufacture and foreign markets, colonies might become a positive embarrassment. The horrible truth was that they raised costs. Tariff preferences had been given to colonial products; taxation had been imposed to meet the charges for colonial defence. These increased costs of production inevitably prevented that maximum efficiency in cheap manufacture by which world markets — including, of course, the despised colonial markets themselves — could be conquered with ease. 'Little Englandism' was inevitably one of the most popular expressions of the new industrial nationality of Great Britain. And for the Manchester school, there could be no justification for the uneconomic loyalties and sentimental attachments of the old Empire.

This new attitude could take the form either of a negative lack of interest in the colonies or of a positive dislike for them. As might have been expected, it was in learned circles, where the new religion of 'political economy' was being developed, that antipathy to the Empire was most extreme during this period. The Utilitarians, the philosophic radicals, the classical economists of the late eighteenth and early nineteenth century — men like Bentham, McCulloch, and James Mill — repeated and amplified the attack which Adam Smith had first begun on the Old Colonial System. The *Edinburgh Review*, and the other journals which acted as the chief organs of propaganda for the fashionable new views, denounced the colonies from the same frank and realistic attitude of self-interest. 'We defy any one,' declared the *Edinburgh Review* in 1825, 'to point out a single benefit, of any sort whatever, derived by us from the possession of Canada, and our other colonies in North America. . . . There is not a man of sense in the Empire who does not look forward to the dissolution, at no distant period, of the connexion between Canada and England.' It was true that in Parliament these extreme criticisms were still voiced only by rather dubious radicals, and that officially England still clung stoutly to her empire. But the time would come — and come soon after the passage of the Reform Bill of 1832 — when those two sonorous voices of early Victorian orthodoxy, Mr. Richard Cobden and Mr. John Bright, would lead a veritable chorus in complacent denunciation of the Empire.

It was much more difficult for British North America to adopt such an independent attitude to the mother country. As the colonies developed, as they slowly approached maturity as North American communities, there was a natural tendency for them to reach out after the power to manage their own affairs. But, at the same time, this instinct for freedom was checked by a long tradition of dependence and a shrewd realization of its benefits. Politically the colonies depended for their very existence upon British arms and British diplomacy. Economically they were still primitive, staple-producing communities which were tied closely to imperial markets. British North America had a real part to play in a world where people lived and worked and travelled within wooden walls, where sails and mills were still driven by wind- and water-power, where seas and lakes and rivers and canals were still the highways of the world's traffic. Pre-industrial themselves, the colonies could make a direct and important contribution to a mother country which was still in the first stages of industrial development.

Now that furs had become the monopoly of the Hudson's Bay Company, the dominant export staple products of the Maritime Provinces and Canada were timber, fish, and wheat. In Nova Scotia, where those Jacks-of-all-trades the Bluenose skippers used to set out to peddle their small mixed cargoes of salt fish, flour, provisions, and lumber in the West Indies, the Canaries, Madeira, and Spain, there was probably the greatest variety of production and the widest horizon of distant markets. Prince Edward Island, where the fine trees had been cut down and where men were gradually deserting the sea, had become a tiny agricultural community. New Brunswick was like an enormous lumber camp which shared with Nova Scotia in the wood trade with the West Indies and shipped the great bulk of its forest products in the form of squared white pine timbers and deals to the British market. In Lower Canada and up the Ottawa valley, the forest dominated the lives of men in much the same way as it did in New Brunswick; and although wheat was the main cash crop of the new mob of settlers who were now making homes for themselves in the peninsula of Upper Canada, the export value of Canadian farm products did not definitely surpass that of Canadian forest products until after the middle of the century. Over almost all of British North America, it was the forest — the great sticks of red and white pine timber, the deals, the lumber, the shingles and sugar-box shooks — which gave men their livelihood and kept the civilization together which they had carried painfully to the new world.

In much the same way, the secondary industries of the provinces — such as flour-milling and lumber-milling — were all closely related to the staple products, were, in fact, little more than the first stage in their processing. By far the most complete and dignified of all these industries, as well as the most important, was the business of building ships. It was not until the third quarter of the nineteenth century, when the wooden ship was already hard pressed to compete with iron plates and steam-driven propellers, that the British North American industry reached the height of its achievement; but by the middle of the century the northern provinces already held fourth place in the world, in total tonnage of registered shipping, even though so many of their ships were built to be sold immediately abroad. All along the ragged coastline of British North America, from Quebec to Yarmouth and St. Andrews, the river ports were crowded with yards where the shipwrights and their foremen superintended the building of an annual fleet of ships which, like most other things in British North America, combined English and American traits in a distinctive fashion of their own.

In this period Nova Scotia built small vessels — sloops and schooners, brigs and brigantines — mainly for service in her own merchant marine. By the 1830's, Quebec was building large square-rigged vessels, of a thousand tons and over, for the British market; and along the North Shore and the Bay of Fundy, New Brunswick yards turned out a great variety of vessels, including numbers of those 'hardscrabble packets,' the 'timber droghers,' which carried the great loads of red and white pine to England and brought back the miserable cargoes of immigrants in return. In contrast with the hardwood ships of Great Britain and the United States, British North American vessels were almost invariably of soft-wood construction. Built of tamarac (hackmatack), spruce and pine, and often — particularly in the early days — jammed together as quickly and cheaply as possible for the timber trade, they took some time to win a decent rating at Lloyd's. But, as the middle of the century drew near, as the industry approached maturity, provincial or Bluenose ships gained in speed and solid simplicity of construction, Bluenose crews won a reputation for hard work and smart seamanship, and Bluenose masters and mates acquired their rather fearful notoriety for harsh and exacting command.

The markets for all these British North American products lay chiefly in Great Britain and her West Indian possessions. In the main, British North America was a producer of raw materials for an industrial metropolis; and, in so far as the northern provinces began to use the new techniques of iron and steam, they employed them chiefly to shorten and cheapen the carriage of their staple products to the markets of Great Britain. In 1809, eight years after the first steamer had appeared in Scotland and two years after Fulton's *Clermont* had run between New York and Albany, the *Accommodation*, built and engineered in Lower Canada for John Molson, made the journey between Quebec and Montreal. Within a decade, the first steamers had been launched on Lake Ontario; and in the early 1820's the Molson Line and the Torrance Line, the two main steamship lines on the lower St. Lawrence, had provided a small fleet of towboats to drag the great sailing ships up the river past the swift St. Mary's current to the harbour of Montreal. In 1831, a group of Quebec and Halifax capitalists, which included Samuel Cunard, launched the *Royal William,* a superb steamship which was intended to ply between the St. Lawrence and the Maritime ports and which in 1833 crossed the Atlantic, being the first vessel to use steam-power for the entire journey. By the 1830's Samuel Cunard of Halifax and Hugh Allan of Montreal, the two great British-American pioneers in transatlantic steamship service, stood at the open-ing of their careers.

Inevitably this speeding-up and cheapening of traffic on the lower St. Lawrence and the Great Lakes increased the pressure for the building of canals. More than ever before, the Industrial Revolution had exposed the weakness of the St. Lawrence route as a great waterway from inland North America to industrial Great Britain. Potentially, the St. Lawrence-Great Lakes system seemed unequalled as an avenue to the riches of the new west. But, in sharp contrast with the old and senile Mississippi, the northern waterway was youthful, wilful, and turbulent. Its continuity was broken at Niagara. It stumbled and faltered through long reaches of white and angry rapids between Lake Ontario and Montreal; and the Erie Canal, which was completed in 1825, though it was merely a long four-foot ditch, at least supplied a through route which contrasted sharply with the broken magnificence of the St. Lawrence. The merchants of Mon-treal, the great bulk of public opinion in the upper province, were desperately anxious to meet this revival of competition from the Hudson River route. But for a while it almost seemed as if the Canadas were politically and economically too weak to find an answer to the challenge. The first Lachine Canal was finished in 1825 — the very year that saw the completion of the Erie: the first ship passed through the eight-foot Welland Canal from Lake Erie to Lake Ontario in 1829; and in 1832, the British government completed the Rideau Canal, as a military work, from the Ottawa River to Lake Ontario. But these were only beginnings, mere ap-proaches to the heart of the problem, which was, of course, the series of tremendous rapids on the upper St. Lawrence. The trouble was, that by the fatal division of the province in 1791, there was no single political authority which could stand and fight for the river system. The English-speaking merchants of Lower Canada tried in vain to persuade the French-Canadian assembly to take action in the matter; and in 1834 the Province of Upper Canada took up its share of the burden alone.

But, though the Canadians tried to improve their river route, though they attempted to reduce the cost of British manufactures in Canada and to increase the profits of Canadian sales in Great Britain by lowering the transport charges to the mother country, they did not depend on these methods alone to raise the value and prestige of the St. Lawrence waterway. Like all British North Americans, they relied on the privileges of the Old Colonial System as an aid in their search for prosperity and in their struggle to meet American competition. The lumberers of New Brunswick and the Ottawa valley blessed the Old Colonial System for the timber preference. The farmers and millers of Upper Canada looked to it hopefully for a preference on wheat and flour. The merchants and fishermen of Nova Scotia expected that imperial tariffs and shipping regulations would keep the Americans out of the West Indies market. Economically, the hopes of the colonies were still centred in the Old Colonial System. And if, therefore, British North America was beginning to yearn for the blessings of local autonomy, she had at the same time a very real appreciation of the advantages of dependence.

Thus, though the reform of the Old Colonial System was a reciprocal process in which both Great Britain and British North America participated, the mother country very often took the first steps. In financial reform, which was of central importance, the initiative was largely hers. In the years which followed the downfall of Napoleon, the burden of colonial defence and upkeep began to look very large to British statesmen. During this period Great Britain kept about five to six thousand soldiers in the northern provinces. She constructed fortifications at Halifax, Quebec, and Kingston, and built the Rideau Canal, from the Ottawa River to Lake Ontario, at a cost of approximately eight hundred thousand pounds. These military expenditures were bad enough; but the civil expenditures, though they were much smaller, were even more objectionable. In every one of the provinces, Great Britain paid, or helped to pay, the salaries of a number of officials, both civil and religious. It seemed reasonable enough to ask colonies which had been granted representative institutions to foot the costs of their own civil government; and soon after the peace of 1815, the Colonial Office tried to persuade the provinces to take over the chief charges of their administration, which were to be set down in a regular civil list and granted for the life of the king or a given number of years.

The provincial legislatures looked at this British offer; and the more they looked at it the less some of them liked it. It was hard enough to give up British subsidies, even when their surrender was the price paid for full financial control; but it was far harder when full financial control seemed withheld by the conditions which the British had attached to their offer. In each colony at this time, a few revenues, including some customs duties and the income from natural resources, were under the control of the crown, and could be spent by the governor without the assent of the assembly. In each colony also the chief officers were appointed, and their salaries fixed by the crown without the consent of the people or its representatives. The assemblies, in short, were asked to underwrite a financial system of which they controlled neither the revenues nor the expenditures. They knew very well that the colonial civil service, as the British had set it up, was an expensive system, full of sinecures, absentees, and old-fashioned methods. In it there were happy people like the collector of customs in New Brunswick, who in 1828 received nearly three thousand pounds in fees, a sum which was approximately double the salary of the lieutenant-governor of the province. There were deserving characters like Thomas Amyot, the Provincial Secretary of Lower Canada, who had never set foot in the province he was supposed to serve, or like Adam Gordon, a clerk in the Colonial Office in London, who supplemented his no doubt modest salary by a completely unearned gratuity as 'agent' for the province of Lower Canada.

With all this in mind, the assemblies tried to strike a good bargain with the Colonial Office. But, at the same time, both sides were fairly anxious to have a bargain struck. Great Britain hoped to escape financial obligation and British North America was bound to acquire financial control; and gradually, first in one province and then in another, a deal was made, an agreement concluded, which brought the financial transfer one stage nearer to a close. Slowly, the imperial authorities got rid of the worst absentees and sinecures on the colonial salary list. In Nova Scotia they abolished the stupidly expensive system of fees for customs-house officers and permitted the provincial legislature to appropriate their salaries. In Lower Canada, they surrendered the proceeds of the Quebec Revenue Act to the control of the provincial parliament; and in New Brunswick, in 1836, they even handed over the revenue, though not the administration, of the crown lands and natural resources. In return for these and other concessions, the provincial legislatures either granted a civil list or made provision for some of the important salaries; and by degrees Great Britain's expenses for civil government in the colonies dropped down to the vanishing point. In only one province, Lower Canada, did the British programme meet complete failure. From the moment in 1818 when the proposal was first put forward, the Lower Canadian assembly on the one hand, and the governor and council on the other, were locked together in a furious quarrel which lasted with few interruptions for nearly two decades.

Along with these changes in finance, there went another and complementary group of reforms in commercial policy. Here again the reforming movement was a reciprocal process; but there was no doubt that Great Britain took the lead and played the larger part throughout. Her statesmen looked suspiciously at the timber preference and even began to question the imperial shipping monopoly. But the colonists still believed that these devices were their best means of meeting the competition from the United States; and they were certain that, ever since the War of 1812, the pressure from the Republic was becoming steadily harder and harder. In the interior of the continent, the State of New York completed the Erie Canal. On the Atlantic Ocean, the United States began a vigorous campaign of retaliation against the British Navigation Laws, in the hope of forcing its way into the carrying trade of the West Indies. The Republic was a far stronger competitor now, with a growing merchant marine. At last it became obvious that the Old Colonial System could no longer be maintained in the West Indies. And its failure in the West Indies was simply the first stage in its final collapse.

In the period 1822-26, the reforming Tories — William Huskisson and his associates — carried through the first serious reforms in the British Navigation Laws. In this rearrangement they discovered the method which was to be used hereafter in dividing the interests of the two imperial partners. The colonies surrendered their special privileges in exchange for a general freedom of trade: the mother country relaxed its control of empire trade in return for its release from its commercial obligations. In 1830, American shipping was at length permitted entry into the British West Indies; but by the Wallace-Robinson code of 1822 and the Huskisson legislation of 1825, the colonies had already been allowed to carry on a direct import and export trade with foreign states and possessions in both Europe and the Americas, and in both British and foreign shipping. In effect, the northern provinces had exchanged their doubtful monopoly in the West Indies for a competitive chance in the markets of Europe and the newly freed republics of South America.

[*III*]

So far everything seemed to have gone forward fairly successfully. It was true that in Lower Canada, where the French Canadians controlled the assembly, the executive and the legislature were in a state of perpetual warfare. But elsewhere the piecemeal revision of the Old Colonial System seemed to be proceeding quietly enough. The first British Empire had collapsed in revolution; but the second was changing through peaceful reform. If this bloodless revolution could be completed successfully, it would be a great achievement. Much had already been done. The prospects looked most hopeful for the future. And yet the strange fact was that a note of exasperation, a hint of violence, had already begun to creep into the discussions of the time. In the Maritime Provinces the public temper remained unexcited; but in Upper and Lower Canada there was an ominously mounting wave of discontent. Was it possible, even yet, that the second British Empire might end like the first — that an attempt would be made to substitute the revolutionary method of the Thirteen Colonies for the bargaining procedure of British North America?

In the Canadas, a large group of people was clearly dissatisfied with the slow pace of reform and resentful of the abuses and inequalities which still remained. The men who made up this radical party in the upper province were mostly farmers and unskilled labourers, with a sprinkling of mechanics and an even smaller number of innkeepers, teachers, and professional men. Their crusade was the crusade of the common man against the powerful individual and the great corporation — the crusade which periodically convulsed England in the quarter-century after Waterloo, which was sweeping the western American states and had triumphed in the election of Andrew Jackson to the presidency. The Upper Canadian radicals hated the Church of England and its close **relations to** the state, its efforts to control education, and **its** exclusive claims to the Clergy Reserves. They were furious that humble township schools should be neglected, while the district grammar schools were well equipped and the Governor generously supported Upper Canada College. To them such corporations as the Bank of Upper Canada and the Welland Canal Company were 'abominable engines of state' which corrupted government and oppressed the people. They hated the whole land-granting policy of Upper Canada — the system of crown reserves, of Clergy Reserves, of large grants to privileged individuals, which stood like uninhabited islands in the midst of general cultivation and blocked the whole development of the province. In the Huron Tract, in the north-west part of the province, there was deep discontent with the policies of that big land corporation, the Canada Company; and Colonel Talbot, the founder of the Talbot Settlement north of Lake Erie and the owner of an enormous property, was denounced as a local despot 'whose power is infinitely more to be dreaded than that of the King of Great Britain.' In the opinion of the radicals, the whole system of privilege and abuse was held together in its own interest by a little oligarchy of appointed executive and legislative councillors at Toronto called the 'Family Compact,' and by the network of little local family compacts, composed of appointed justices of the peace who governed the countryside.

On the whole, there were only superficial points of resemblance between this protest movement and that of Lower Canada. It was true, of course, that since the constitutions of the two provinces were identical, the Lower Canadians had much the same problem of an irresponsible oligarchy, and also true that they planned to solve it by a similar democratic method. But this political liberalism was largely skin-deep; and beneath it was a large, solid, and phlegmatic body of social conservatism. Though the Lower Canadian patriots hit at banks, land companies, and a few other Upper Canadian targets, their chief objectives, both positive **and nega-**

tive, were strictly their own. They opposed immigration and 'public improvements like canals with a stubborn consistency which was certainly alien to North America; and they defended their old institutions, their old laws, and their feudal landholding system with an uncritical jealousy which was beginning to look more than a little odd in the second quarter of the nineteenth century. With a good deal of truth as well as some malicious exaggeration, the British-Canadian merchants of Quebec and Montreal insisted that the guiding principle of their opponents' 'liberalism' was in fact 'the genius of feudality.' Feudalism, they pointed out, 'has at this day its admirers on the banks of the St. Lawrence and is the cherished idol of the pretended friends of freedom. It still exhibits the same despotic features, paralyzing industry, retarding improvements, and interfering with those rights which in better regulated states are the proud boast of every citizen.'

At first the leadership of the reform movement in both provinces was varied and fairly representative of its component interests. In Lower Canada, John Neilson shared a directing influence with the French-Canadian leaders; and in Upper Canada, Marshall Spring Bidwell, who was frequently speaker of the assembly, and the Methodist leader, Egerton Ryerson, had a large following. But as the crisis deepened, as anger flared higher at the failure of each attempt at redress, the moderates were superseded by extremists like Louis Joseph Papineau and William Lyon Mackenzie. These men had little enough in common at the beginning, though in the end they came to profess much the same political creed and to unite in the chances of a badly planned rebellion. Far from being in any sense a man of the people, Papineau was the seigneur of Montebello and a lawyer who had received the traditional seminary training at Quebec. Though he showed throughout a real skill in English parliamentary technique and though at the crisis of his career he became genuinely interested in French anti-clerical and republican

views, he could scarcely be called a really revolutionary reformer at this stage. Mackenzie, the emotional, voluble,
violently quarrelsome editor of the *Colonial Advocate* and
The Constitution, was a man of more profound political
convictions. Better read than many of his contemporaries,
with a wide circle of radical friends in both England and
the United States, and intensely interested in first principles,
Mackenzie was probably the only serious theorist of the
political and social revolution in the Canadas.

Both these men began to turn more and more to the inspiration and example of the United States. Mackenzie borrowed ideas extensively from Great Britain, and Papineau
perhaps slightly from France; but both agreed that the best
way of reforming the irresponsible Canadian oligarchies was
by recourse to the American method of popular election.
There were members of the Reform Party in Upper Canada
such as Robert Baldwin who preferred the British system
of responsible or cabinet government; but as early as 1835
Mackenzie was almost certainly among the group of radicals
who argued that 'elective institutions are the only safeguards
to prevent the Canadas from forming disadvantageous com-
parisons between the condition of the colonists and the ad-
joining country.' In much the same fashion, under the
leadership of Papineau, the Lower Canadian assembly resolved that 'the constitution and form of government which
would best suit this colony are not to be sought solely in the
analogies offered by the institutions of Great Britain' and
that 'the unanimous consent with which all the American
States have adopted and extended the elective system, shows
that it is adapted to the wishes, manners, and social state of
the inhabitants of this continent.' Both Mackenzie and
Papineau advocated American institutions; but it was Mackenzie who systematically explored the political philosophy
upon which they were based. He believed, with an almost
puritanical fervour, that government was a sacred trust to
be administered on behalf of the people; and, like the Ameri-

can revolutionaries sixty years before, he went back to John Locke and his commentators to find the theoretical basis of this emotional conviction. In effect, the radicals in both provinces sought to persuade a people whose grandfathers had rejected the gospel of Thomas Jefferson to accept the revised version of Andrew Jackson. They tried to induce the Canadians to re-enact the American Revolution sixty years after their ancestors had failed to take part in the original performance.

Obviously they faced enormous difficulties. The provincial oligarchies, which had grown up under the protection of the Constitutional Act of 1791, simply formed the core of a far larger force of anti-republican Loyalists. In Lower Canada, it is true, the strength of the Tory or 'Constitutional' party was largely confined to the towns of Quebec and Montreal; but in Upper Canada, where it was supported by the descendants of the Loyalists and by many of the new immigrants, including the Protestant Ulster Irish, with their Orange Lodges, the 'party of loyalty' dominated the eastern section of the province and even competed vigorously in the discontented west. Though the Conservatives attacked French Canada and emphasized the British connection, they were, in their own way, just as 'Canadian' as their opponents. From Frontenac and La Salle, from the departed directors of the North West Company, the Tories inherited the urge for the material expansion of Canada, the belief in the St. Lawrence as a great imperial trade route which was to dominate the interior of the continent. In both provinces, the party had the support of the big commercial interests as well as the adherence of the professional classes, the civil servants, and the churchmen. Even the two churches which were closest to the mass of the people — the Methodist Church in Upper Canada and the Roman Catholic Church in Lower Canada — broke with the extreme radicals as they drifted closer towards physical force. In number and popularity — at least in Upper Canada — the Tories were not a bad match

for the Reformers. They were fully their equal in violence.
'If you had been in London, . . .' wrote a farmer of their
conduct in an Upper Canadian election, 'you would have
seen a set of government tools called Orangemen, running
up and down the street crying five pounds for a liberal; and
if a man said a word contrary to their opinion he was
knocked down.'

This violent and profitless quarrelling, which was beginning to take on all the aspect of a civil war, reached its
climax in the middle 1830's. In 1834, the Reformers won
the elections in both provinces; and there followed a Tory
reaction, which moved rapidly forward in the next two years,
gaining force and momentum, and sweeping first the Canadian governors and finally the Imperial Parliament along
with it. The Quebec and Montreal Constitutional Associations were founded in the autumn of 1834. About a year
later, in December, 1835, a group of the younger 'Constitu-
tionalists' in Montreal tried to form a semi-military organization which they first christened the 'British Rifle Corps.'
Governor Gosford promptly dissolved the Rifle Corps by
proclamation; but it was obviously becoming more and more
difficult for the officials to keep up a show of impartiality between the two parties. In Upper Canada, they soon ceased
even to try. Sir Francis Bond Head, the new lieutenant-
governor of the province, saw the confused struggle in Upper
Canada in the straightforward terms of melodrama. The
British connection, cast in the appealing rôle of heroine, was
menaced by the villain of American republicanism; and Sir
Francis, rushing like a cavalier to the aid of distressed virtue,
led the delighted and reinvigorated Tories to a complete
victory in the general election of 1836. A sudden electoral
reversal such as this was impossible in Lower Canada, for
Papineau kept the loyalty of the great masses of French
Canadians; but the assembly at Quebec was after all an inferior legislative body, subordinate to the Imperial Parliament, which was rapidly losing what little patience it had

left for the *Patriotes* of the lower St. Lawrence valley. In March, 1837, Lord John Russell introduced a series of ten resolutions in the British House of Commons which declared that an elective legislative council and a responsible executive could not be granted, and which authorized the government of Lower Canada to spend money without a legislative appropriation, since the assembly had persistently refused to vote supplies.

It was the misfortune of the Canadas that this political crisis was accompanied by a major financial collapse. The boom of the last few years, which had obviously become more hectic and abnormal on both sides of the Atlantic, ended with a crash in North America in the spring of 1837. In the Canadas, the business crisis began as a financial panic, continued as a commercial slump, and ended as a fairly general depression. Almost everybody was affected. The government of Upper Canada, which had lost money in the failure of a London banking house and could float no more loans, was nearly bankrupt. The merchants, particularly in Upper Canada, where the Governor tried to force the banks to maintain specie payments, could get no credit and practically suspended operations. The stoppage of work on the Upper Canadian canals threw the immigrant labourers out of their jobs; and the failure of the wheat crop in Lower Canada brought real distress to the *habitants* in the winter and spring of 1837.

In these months of 'brass money and wooden shoes,' of misery and discouragement, the bitter sense of frustration became almost unendurable. The invective of the journals grew shriller, political speeches took on a tone of deliberate menace, the great parades and vast, shouting public meetings were like military demonstrations. In both provinces the leaders answered the violence of their opponents with threats of reprisal, and prophesied the outbreak of civil warfare with confidence and relish. 'Is then the country under the control of a lawless band of sworn villains?' Mackenzie inquired dramatically when his meeting at the village of Churchville was broken up by Orangemen. 'If so, the citizens will have to form, not only political unions, but armed associations, for mutual self-defence. . . . Sir Francis may find that an opinion is gaining ground that deeds are doing among us, which will have to be answered by an appeal to cold steel.'

In both provinces the rebellions were unplanned and misdirected to the last degree; but in Lower Canada there did not even seem to be a generally accepted revolutionary goal. The *Patriotes* founded 'Fils de la Liberté' associations in obvious imitation of the 'Sons of Liberty' of the American Revolution; and though they could not, of course, get the support of the Tory merchants, they tried to imitate the old American non-importation agreements by wearing either smuggled clothes or garments made out of cumbrous, iron-grey *étoffe du pays*. Outwardly procedure was all very much in the correct American Revolutionary tradition; but inwardly there was a noticeable lack of purpose. It was true that Papineau continued to radiate a bold defiance. The tribune of Lower Canada looked almost as if he had been specially made up for the part of a revolutionary leader. But there was a curious weakness behind the splendid determination of his face. Perhaps he did not know where he wanted to go. Perhaps he knew very well that he did not want to go in the direction of armed revolt. The agitation he had called into being was drifting aimlessly but irrevocably towards rebellion; but he could not bring himself to take hold of it, lead it, and direct it towards revolutionary objectives.

In Upper Canada, the radicals debated until the last possible moment between an armed mass demonstration and open revolt; but at any rate they had a clear understanding of their own first principles and of the kind of provincial order which they hoped to create. In the Declaration of the Toronto Reformers, adopted at a meeting in Doel's Brewery on July 31, 1837, the militant radicals set out the basis and justification of their movement. 'Government,' their declaration asserted, 'is founded on the authority, and is instituted for the benefit, of a people: when, therefore, any Government long and systematically ceases to answer the great ends of its foundation, the people have a natural right given them by their Creator to seek after and establish such institutions as will yield the greatest quantity of happiness to the greatest number.' This effort to modernize the American Declaration of Independence by substituting the Benthamite gospel of the 'greatest happiness' for the Lockian doctrine of natural rights was later abandoned; and Mackenzie returned to the pure principles of 1776. In the draft constitution for the State of Upper Canada which was published on the eve of the rebellion, he laid down an elaborate frame of government which included elective institutions, a careful separation of powers, a system of checks and balances, all obviously modelled on American examples. Perhaps the most original features of this constitution were the results of Mackenzie's hatred of economic privilege and social inequality. In the idyllic republic of Upper Canada there were to be no incorporated trading or banking companies; and labour was solemnly declared to be the only means of creating wealth. 'My creed,' said Mackenzie later, 'has been — social democracy — or equality of each man before society — and political democracy, or equality of each man before the law.'

The rebellion in Lower Canada began, almost accidentally, on November 6, 1837, in a street brawl in Montreal. It was as much Tory provocation as Patriot determination that began the clash which everybody had expected; and the members of the Doric Club, the 'fraternal' association which had replaced the British Rifle Corps, fought their way through the streets against the *Patriotes* and drove them into the St. Lawrence suburb. When Papineau and the other *Patriote* leaders left the city a few days later, they were really retreating from an embarrassing and untenable position; but the government, worried by the outbreak of violence, jumped to the mistaken conclusion that they had left to raise the countryside in a general rebellion. On November 16, it issued warrants for the arrest of Papineau and his lieutenants; and it was this abrupt move that provoked the *Patriotes* to armed resistance. In the Richelieu valley, which had been the stronghold of the agitation from the beginning, the *habitants* gathered at the two villages of St. Denis and St. Charles in half-armed and untrained bands. On November 23, at St. Denis, they gave a hard check to the tiny British force which had been sent against them; but two days later, at St. Charles, the regulars scattered them easily. Papineau removed himself from the country with the greatest possible expedition, and the rebellion in the Richelieu valley was over.

There was only one important centre of revolt still left. This was the village of St. Eustache, about eighteen miles north-west of Montreal, in the county of the Two Mountains. Under the leadership of two men, the plausible, mysterious adventurer, Amaury Girod, and the local doctor, the sombre and tenacious J. O. Chénier, over five hundred rebels assembled in the village in the first days after the 'victory' of St. Denis. It was an odd, inert insurrectionary force which waited, apparently without objective or purpose, until the government, in its own good time, was ready to take the offensive. In the crisp December days, the *habitants,* in their homespun garments, leather mittens, and long toques, strolled aimlessly up and down St. Eustache, carrying their rusty, broken-down muskets and smoking stumpy black pipes. The arrival of Sir John Colborne with an overwhelming force was the appropriate end of this fatuous conduct. The equivocal Girod escaped; but Chénier and about two hundred and fifty *habitants* barricaded themselves inside the buildings of St. Eustache and fought it out, until their death or capture ended the one real show of courage and resolution in the entire rebellion.

A week before the final end of the Lower Canadian revolt, the rising in the upper province began. Mackenzie, Lount, Gibson, Anderson, and the rest realized at least that they must make themselves masters of the capital, Toronto, as quickly as possible; and since the few troops in the city had been sent down to Lower Canada, there seemed outwardly a real chance of success. But the rebel force, which never numbered more than a few hundred men, was simply not strong enough for easy victory; and the one real hope of its leaders lay perhaps in an initial surprise. They frittered away their small chances in ineffectual bungling. At the last moment, the date of concentration at Montgomery's Tavern, nearly four miles north of Toronto on Yonge Street, was changed from December 7 to December 4. Doctor Duncombe, the leader of the rebels in the disaffected London District, never even began his march eastward towards Hamilton and Toronto before the whole Patriot cause had been lost on Yonge Street; and even in the Home District, close to Toronto, the rebels kept drifting into Montgomery's for days after the appointed date. In the meantime, while the Patriot leaders wrangled over grand strategy, the militia was pouring into Toronto; and on December 7, the very day in which the rebels had planned first to start the revolt, the loyal army which was to end it was forming up on the esplanade in front of Archdeacon Strachan's house.

It numbered nearly a thousand men. The Lieutenant-Governor, Sir Francis Bond Head, was there, formidable with a double-barrelled gun and a brace of pistols. The judges and crown officers stood side by side in the ranks with the merchants, mechanics, and labourers. In the brilliant early afternoon sunshine, the little force moved off with bands playing through streets which were bright with flags and loud with cheering; and, under the Lieutenant-Governor and Colonel Fitzgibbon, a veteran of the War of 1812, the main body, with two supporting columns, marched up Yonge Street towards the rebels. In less than half an hour the fighting was all over, for the Patriots, many of them armed only with pikes, pitchforks, and cudgels, were outnumbered and demoralized. 'Soon,' wrote a Loyalist eyewitness, 'a movement was visible through the smoke, on the hill fronting the tavern, where some tall pines were then standing. I could see there two or three hundred men, now firing irregularly at the advancing Loyalists; now swaying to and fro without any apparent design. We had by this time arrived within cannon shot of the tavern itself. Two or three balls were seen to strike and pass through it. A crowd of men rushed from the doors, and scattered wildly in a northerly direction. Those on the hill wavered, receded under the shelter of the undulating land, and then fled like their fellows.'

Though the Canadian rebellions had really ended, the Patriot agitation had barely begun. Mackenzie and a number of other Canadians fled to the United States, where their arrival awakened immediate and active support for the cause of 'Canadian freedom.' All along the northern border of the United States, Patriot Societies and Hunters' Lodges were organized for the express purpose of invading Canada. Hundreds of American citizens, as well as numbers of Canadian refugees, were openly recruited, armed, and drilled on American soil; and boats were secured, supplies collected, and expeditions organized, with little or no attempt at concealment. The Canadians, on their part, committed a serious act of provocation in the early stages of the trouble, for they destroyed, in American waters, the steamer *Caroline*, which had been notoriously engaged in supplying one of the first of these Patriot armies, established in Navy Island, on the Canadian side of the Niagara River. Under a series of quarrelling 'generals' — some American and some Canadian — who, with a few exceptions, maintained a fairly consistent record of cowardice and incompetence, the Patriots and the Hunters actually succeeded in carrying out half a dozen raids on Canadian territory in the course of 1838. Though the government of the United States and its re-

sponsible citizens were genuinely anxious to avoid unfriendly acts, the American neutrality laws were defective,
the state militia was lax if not openly sympathetic to the
Patriots, and the American courts simply would not convict
even notorious offenders among them. The invasions were
all stopped on the Canadian side, without much difficulty;
and the movement degenerated into a number of predatory
raids, marked by murder, arson, and robbery, which pretty
well justified the title of 'banditry' applied to them by the
Canadian Tories. As a whole, the Patriot movement
had the worst possible effects on the Canadian attitude to
republicanism and to the great neighbouring Republic itself. Through the Hunters and the Patriots, the rebellions
of 1837 had been linked with the foreigner and with a kind
of disreputable violence. And the Canadians, just when
they were beginning to forget the War of 1812, were again
reminded of how difficult the Americans seemed to find it to
let them work out their own destiny in their own way.

[*IV*]

The attempt to end the second Empire in the same way
as the first had failed completely. The shift away from the revolutionary tradition of the Thirteen Colonies and back to the
revisionary method of British North America was prompt
and instinctive; but it was all the more decisive as a result
of the mission of the Earl of Durham to the Canadas. At a
time when American principles had been discredited by
raids and rebellions, Durham restored British ideas and practices to their old prestige. In the persuasive, rhetorical
prose of his famous *Report,* he proved to Canadians, who
had once again rejected the American solution, that the
answer to their problems could be found simply in British
political technique. When he landed, at Quebec, in the
spring of 1838, the Canadas were completely without a sense
of purpose and direction. The country was full of defeat,

and apathy, and discontent. The constitution of Lower Canada had been suspended, the public works were stopped, the gaols were full of political prisoners, the trade of the St. Lawrence was at a standstill, and beaten and angry farmers were leaving the provinces by the thousand for the United States. Within a year, in a *Report* which still stands as one of the greatest state papers in the history of the British Empire, Lord Durham had laid down a programme for the reorganization of the Canadas in particular and the revision of the Old Colonial System as a whole.

If Andrew Jackson was the presiding genius of the Canadian rebellions, the spirit of Lord Durham brooded over the achievement of responsible government. The two men were as different as the philosophies they represented. John George Lambton, first Earl of Durham, was an aristocratic reformer who combined a Byronic temperament with an air of lordly breeding. He had the entrée to the elegant Whig inner circle; and, at the same time, he enjoyed the more grimy, but more solid, economic backing of large collieries in the Newcastle district. Proud, moody, and imperious, he lived, a little consciously, in the grand style. On his first day at Quebec, he rode up to the old Castle of St. Louis mounted on a fine white horse and clad in a brilliant uniform. His luggage took two days to land. The buffet at his supper parties glittered with family plate and racing trophies. It was as a political, not as a social, reformer that he had won his title of 'Radical Jack.' But he was warm-hearted and vigorous in his sympathies. He had taken a leading part in the passage of the English Reform Bill of 1832. And he was now to become the leader — and, indeed, the deity — of a small group of 'Colonial Reformers' in England, who almost alone stood for a positive faith in the Empire in the midst of general disillusionment.

After his whirlwind career of five months in the Canadas had been cut short when the shaky Whig ministry in England recalled him for exceeding his authority, Lord Durham presented his *Report on the Affairs of British North America* to Parliament in the late winter of 1839. It is a famous document; but both in its analysis of Canadian conditions and in its remedies for Canadian abuses, there was really very little that was new. Lord Durham, far from being an original philosopher from the mother country, was actually a brilliant popularizer of colonial ideas. In the first place, there were a number of reforms which he advocated, such as the introduction of a system of local self-government and the improvement of education, which were common property of the radical groups in all English-speaking countries; but, more important, the recommendations which he made for the central political difficulties of the Canadas had already been developed by Canadians long before he had ever given a thought to the crisis in British North America. About the only proposal he brought with him when he arrived in Quebec was the idea of a federal union of the British provinces; and though he was still clinging to this notion when he returned to England, it was, at that stage, an impracticable plan. In its place, Lord Durham substituted two ideas, which were the basic recommendations of the *Report.* One, the idea of legislative union, he took mainly from the Canadian Tories; the other, the idea of local autonomy, he derived from the Canadian Reformers. In the *Report,* the two principal political philosophies of the Canadas are combined and reconciled.

The policy of the legislative union of Upper and Lower Canada was simply another variant of that idea of unity and expansion which had moved New France in the days of Frontenac and La Salle and was to inspire the Dominion of Canada in the time of Sir John Macdonald and the Canadian Pacific Railway. For decades — in fact, ever since the division of the old Province of Quebec in 1791 — the Tories of Lower Canada, and in particular the merchants of Montreal, had believed that the only solution for the problems of the St. Lawrence region lay in the reunion of the two provinces

of Upper and Lower Canada. In the first place, they were
convinced that the St. Lawrence could only succeed as a
great international trade route on the basis of political
union. In the second place, they were equally persuaded
that the French Canadians — that backward, feudal, and
'anti-commercial' people — were the main obstacle to the
improvement of the river system and that their opposition
could only be overcome through the political union of the
two provinces. To a large extent Lord Durham shared
these views of material improvement and prosperity. Without question he believed that the unprogressive French
Canadians must be anglicized and assimilated in a legislative
union. The vigorous sentences of his *Report* echo the arguments which had become almost wearisomely familiar in
Montreal for decades past.

But if Lord Durham shared one of his main ideas with the
Tories of Montreal, he took the other one direct from the
Reformers of Toronto. Doctor William Warren Baldwin,
and his more famous son Robert Baldwin, were cultivated,
substantial, and extremely respectable Reformers who had
little enough in common with the journalists, innkeepers,
and farmers whom Mackenzie led into the Rebellion of
1837. While Mackenzie took his ideas from the theories of
John Locke and Thomas Jefferson, and the practices of the
American governments, the Baldwins drew their inspiration from the technique of cabinet rule in England as it had
gradually developed ever since the Revolution of 1688. At
Durham's own request, the Baldwins wrote him at length
concerning their own remedies for the Canadian political
problem and Robert Baldwin enclosed a letter, composed
two years previously for the Colonial Office, which contained
a full and forceful explanation of how responsible or cabinet
government could be applied to the Canadian constitution.
In all probability this letter converted Lord Durham. He
took up the idea and covered it with his enormous prestige. 'It needs,' he declared in the key passage of his *Report*,

'no change in the principles of government, no invention of a new constitutional theory, to supply the remedy which would, in my opinion, completely remove the existing political disorders. It needs but to follow out consistently the principles of the British constitution. . . . We are not now to consider the policy of establishing representative government in the North American Colonies. That has been irrevocably done. . . . But the Crown must, on the other hand, submit to the necessary consequences of representative institutions; and if it has to carry on the Government in unison with a representative body, it must consent to carry it on by means of those in whom that representative body has confidence.' In these words, Lord Durham simply recommended that the British system of cabinet government, whereby executive power is entrusted to a ministry responsible to Parliament, as Parliament is already responsible to the electorate, should be transplanted from the mother country to the colonies. A basic British political technique had been first applied to British North America by a Canadian. A British peer had presented the Canadian's solution to his countrymen with all the persuasiveness of his eloquent prose.

Durham's recommendation of legislative union applied, of course, only to the Canadas, in which his time on American soil had been wholly spent; but his proposal of responsible government was intended for all the British possessions in North America. The doctrine had been first suggested by a Canadian; but it was a Nova Scotian, Joseph Howe, who gave it perhaps its most adroit and persuasive defence. Of all the rather sober generation of Reformers who succeeded to the revolutionaries of 1837, Howe was by all odds the most picturesque personality. His warm-hearted humanity, his boisterous exuberance, his unashamed joy in political battle, and his fanatical loyalty for his native province have made him a legendary figure. He seemed marked for easy success. He had his moments of great achievement. But there was a curious vein of coarse violence in his character. Poverty drove him into an unseemly hunt for jobs; and the lost causes he took up are more numerous than his triumphs. But in 1839 these frustrations were still in the future. In the autumn of that year, in his four open *Letters to Lord John Russell,* Howe gave the practical case in favour of responsible government as it was only possible for a colonial to give it.

Lord Durham had advocated both responsible government and legislative union. The second was perfectly compatible with the Old Colonial System, the first was completely antagonistic to it. And the Old Colonial System, though it was weakened and tottering, was still standing with its supporters around it. Two little, vigorous men — the Colonial Secretary, Lord John Russell, in England and the new Canadian governor, Charles Poulett Thomson, Lord Sydenham — attempted to carry out the second part of Lord Durham's programme while steadfastly refusing the first. Russell and Sydenham were far from being reactionaries. Already 'Johnny' Russell had proved himself a liberal administrator in Ireland. And he was the same 'little fellow not weighing above eight stone' who had stood up in his place in the evening of that great day in March, 1831, to move the first reading of the Reform Bill. But, moderate and liberal though he was, he could not see how cabinet government could be carried on in a colony — how a colonial governor could at one and the same time take orders from responsible ministers in Great Britain and act in accordance with advice of his executive council in the colony. 'It may happen, . . .' he wrote in rejecting the principles of responsible government, 'that the Governor receives at one and the same time instructions from the Queen, and advice from his executive council, totally at variance with each other. If he is to obey his instructions from England, the parallel of constitutional responsibility entirely fails; if on the other hand, he is to follow the advice of his council, he is no longer a subordinate officer, but an independent sovereign.'

Sydenham, the ex-president of the Board of Trade in Melbourne's cabinet, the masterful little man with the efficiency expert's demand for quick returns and the autocrat's impatience with democratic processes, agreed with Lord John Russell's irrefutable logic. He came out to British North America determined to be his own prime minister and to put through a great programme of reconstruction based upon the legislative union of Upper and Lower Canada. It was very easy to carry the union in Lower Canada, for there the constitution had been suspended and legislative power entrusted to a small council. It was not too hard to persuade the legislature of Upper Canada that union was the one really satisfactory solution for its financial and economic troubles. Once the consent of the Canadas had been gained, the Imperial Parliament, in 1840, passed the Act of Union, which established the united province of Canada. The new system, which came into operation in the following year, brought a real shake-up in colonial government in the St. Lawrence valley. With the obvious intention of neutralizing the French-Canadian majority in the new united province, the old Lower Canada, or Canada East, as it was now called officially, was given the same representation in the assembly as Canada West. This open violation of representation by population was to cause trouble in the future. But, for the moment, it was the executive rather than the legislative branch which invited controversy. The executive — the governor's council — had suddenly become a far more powerful and flexible body than it ever had been in the old days when appointments to it were practically for life. It was now composed of heads of departments who were intended to hold office only so long as the public business seemed to require it and who were to sponsor and defend government policy in the legislature. Finally, by the terms of the Act of Union,

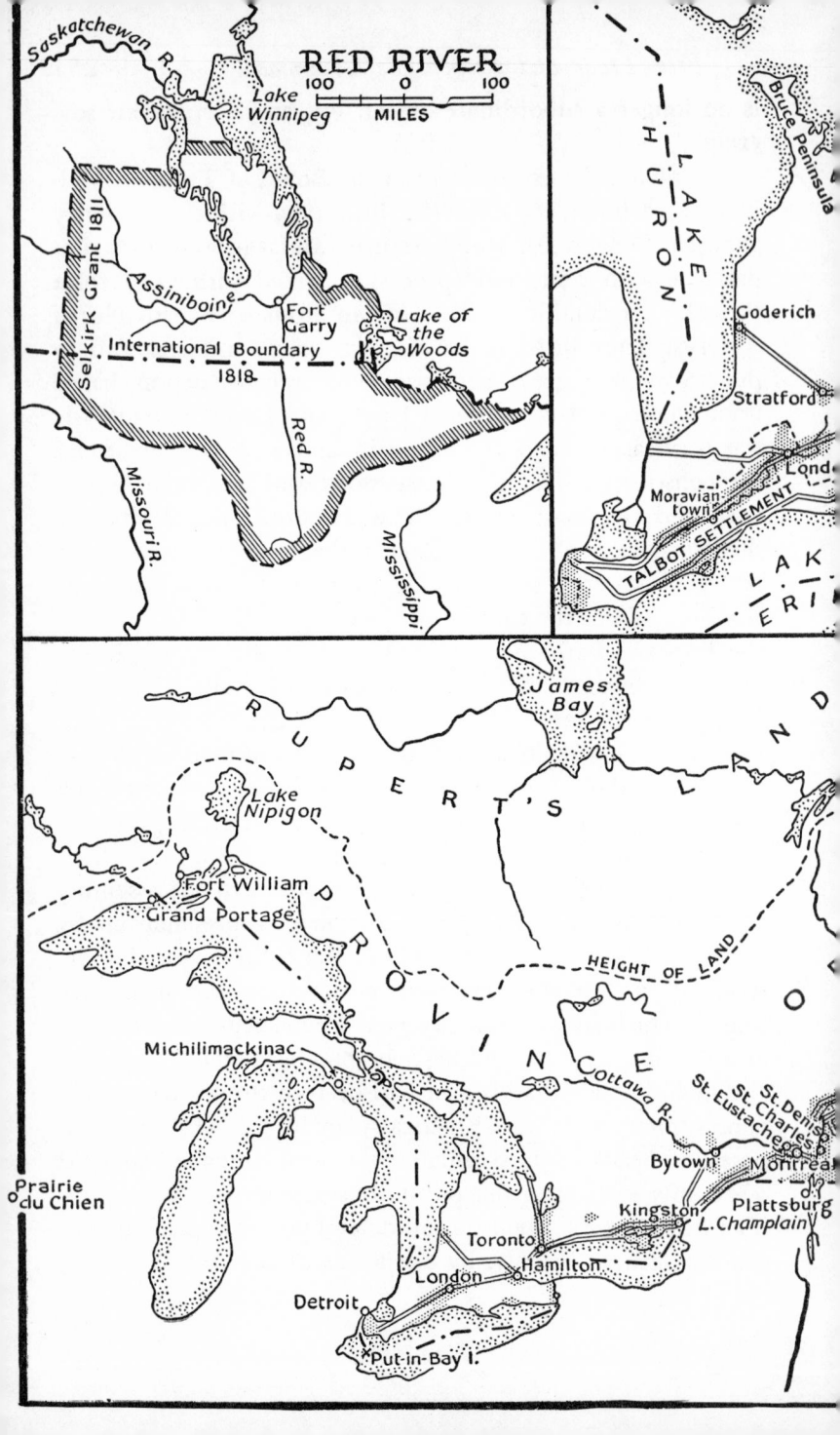

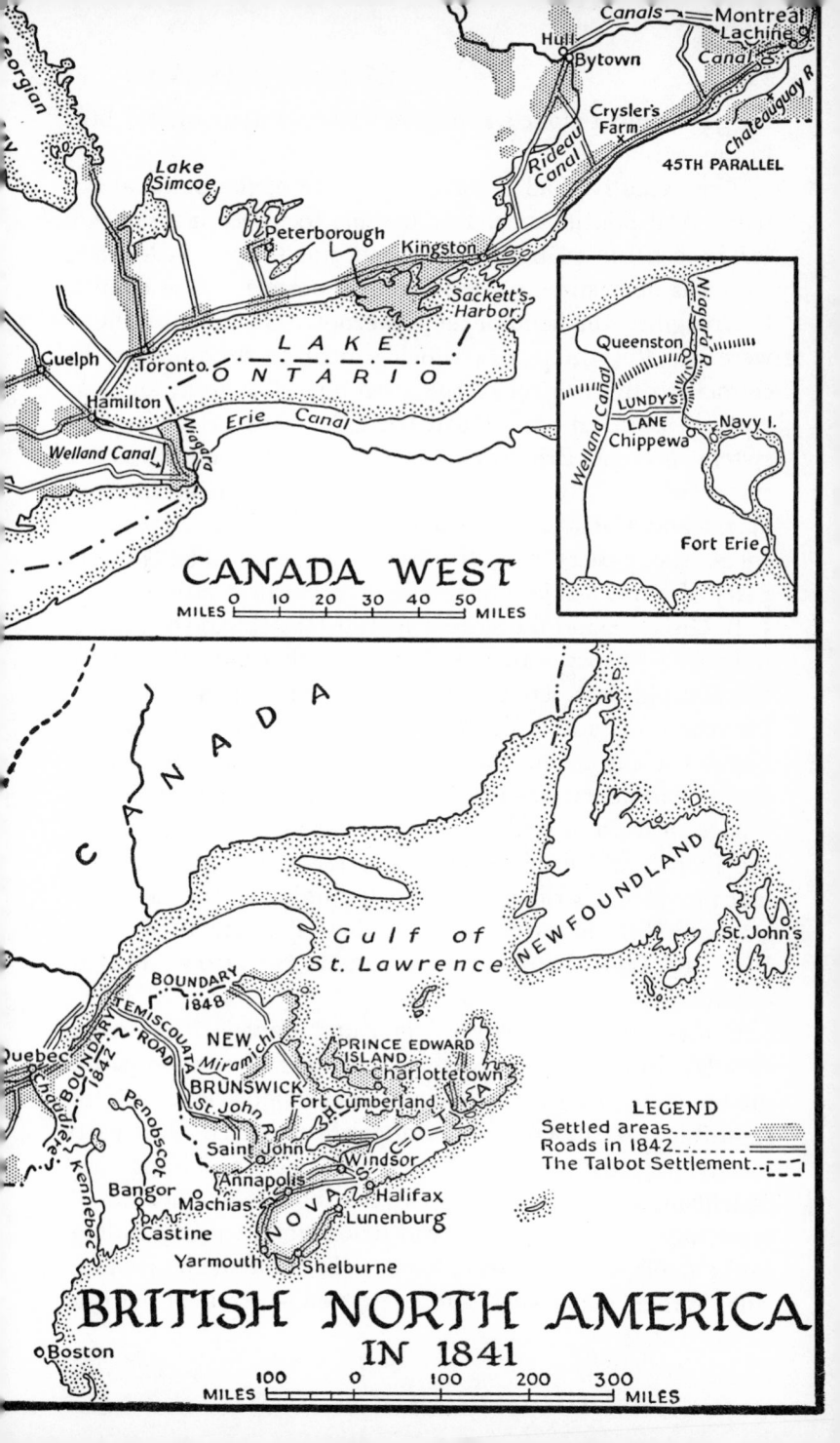

CANADA WEST

Georgian
Lake
Simcoe
Peterborough
Guelph
Toronto
Hamilton
LAKE ONTARIO
Kingston
Sackett's Harbor
Niagara
Erie Canal
Welland Canal

Hull
Bytown
Crysler's Farm
Rideau Canal
Canals
Montreal
Lachine
Lachine Canal
Chateauguay R
45TH PARALLEL

MILES 0 10 20 30 40 50 MILES

Queenston
Niagara R.
Welland Canal
LUNDY'S LANE
Chippewa
Navy I.
Fort Erie

BRITISH NORTH AMERICA IN 1841

C A N A D A

Gulf of St. Lawrence

NEWFOUNDLAND
St. John's

BOUNDARY 1848
TEMISCOUATA ROAD
BOUNDARY 1842
Quebec
Chaudière
Kennebec
Penobscot
NEW BRUNSWICK
Miramichi R.
St. John R.
Fort Cumberland
Saint John
Bangor
Machias
Castine
Annapolis
Windsor
N O V A   S C O T I A
Halifax
Lunenburg
Yarmouth
Shelburne
Boston
PRINCE EDWARD ISLAND
Charlottetown

LEGEND
Settled areas
Roads in 1842
The Talbot Settlement

MILES 100 0 100 200 300 MILES

the government alone was empowered to initiate money bills in the legislature.

The executive had become the centre of the political system. And politics inevitably became focussed in a struggle for its control. On the one hand stood Lord Sydenham, who was determined to use the new powers of the council to strengthen the hand of the Governor. On the other hand were the Reform parties which sought to subordinate the council to the control of the assembly. Coherent and disciplined political parties had been the basis of the cabinet system in Great Britain and they were indispensable to the success of the Reformers in British North America. In Nova Scotia and Canada, the two most politically mature provinces, the parties had developed furthest. The Reform party of Nova Scotia, under men like Herbert Huntingdon, J. B. Uniacke, and the stormy Joseph Howe, had the longest unbroken history. In the Canadas, the Reform tradition was also old; but here the Reformers had been weakened by the rebellions, and until the union the two provincial parties had never any reason for political co-operation. It was the supple and adroit Francis Hincks — a new and realistic personage in Reform ranks — who took up the task of bringing the French and English Reformers together; and when the first provincial parliament under the union opened in 1841, a united Reform party, led by Robert Baldwin for Canada West and Louis Lafontaine for Canada East, stood ready to confront the Governor.

If these parties in Nova Scotia and Canada had proved steadfast in their union, if they had not had to cope with a master strategist like Sydenham, they might have won responsible government a half-dozen years earlier. But party loyalty was still a new, and a rather uncertain thing; and Sydenham's appeal was almost irresistible for practical, moderate men. The Governor was determined to play Bolingbroke's rôle of the *Patriot King*. He wanted non-partisan rule, rather than party administration — practical reforms rather than 'useless discussions upon theoretical points of government.' There was something almost magical in his appeal. In 1840 — in his capacity as governor-in-chief of British North America — he journeyed down to Halifax and persuaded Howe and the other Reformers to enter a coalition government in Nova Scotia. In 1841, before the first session of the union legislature in Canada was over, he had converted the Reformers of Canada West; and even Francis Hincks — himself the author of the great Reform coalition — was to be found voting steadily for the measures of the Sydenham government.

In British North America, the first campaign for responsible government had failed. The Old Colonial System still stood in the colonies. It stood, almost equally stoutly, in Great Britain itself. In Great Britain, the Anti-Corn Law League had not yet converted the nation; and the Whigs, grown cautious under the aged and affable Melbourne, were still in office. The fiscal revolution in the mother country, the political revolution in the colonies — the two movements which threatened to destroy the second British Empire — stood for a last moment arrested in their course; and in this final phase of its existence, the Old Colonial System, as if it wished to be regretfully remembered, seemed to shower its benefits with a more lavish hand than ever before. It was true that, so far as Nova Scotia was concerned, the disappearance of preferences in the West Indies market was a serious blow; but, in compensation, Great Britain reduced the Nova Scotian tariff, increased the number of Nova Scotian free ports, and, at the same time, sent additional ships to aid the province in its increasingly vigorous struggle to keep the Americans out of the inshore fisheries. Partly persuaded by a memorandum drafted by Joseph Howe, the imperial government, in the autumn of 1838, decided to establish a regular steamship service to North America, *via* Halifax, for the carriage of mails; and it was the company headed by the Nova Scotian Samuel Cunard which won the contract, inaugurated the first regular transatlantic steam communication, and founded the fortunes of the great Cunard Line of the future. As for New Brunswick, her trade in ships and timber was still very largely with Great Britain; and the timber preference, which had not been seriously changed since 1821, was still a great advantage in the British market.

Perhaps the Province of Canada profited most from this last benevolent phase of the old imperialism. Sydenham was determined to pull the province together whether the Canadians liked it or not. He picked out all the most troublesome problems — education, local government, the Clergy Reserves — for legislative treatment; and — most important of all — he, and the British government back of him, were able to lift the financial burden which held the province back like a dead weight. Upper and Lower Canada went into union in 1841 with an uncompleted series of canals, a broken credit, and a combined debt of £1,325,000 currency. In his opening speech in the first session of the union legislature in 1841, Sydenham announced the news of the £1,500,000 imperial loan. It was his most splendid gesture. He seemed to sweep away both material obstacles and human opposition, as if with a magic hand. At first the British government wished the loan to be used to retire the provincial debt; but in the end it agreed that the money should be spent to complete the St. Lawrence canals — the project upon which all groups and parties in the province were now agreed. The St. Lawrence was no barge canal, like its famous rival the Erie, but a ship canal, nine feet deep. During the next few years, the sections at Lachine, Beauharnois, and Cornwall were pushed forward rapidly, while the Welland Canal between Lakes Erie and Ontario was deepened and improved. For the first time since the middle west appeared as a new market and a source of agricultural supplies, the St. Lawrence was at last approaching the point where it could throw in the full weight of its competitive strength.

It was a period of hope and achievement and prosperity. But it was soon over, for, in the meantime, the last lull in the history of the Old Colonial System had come to an end. In September, 1841, Lord Sydenham died and the Tories under Peel succeeded to political power in Great Britain. In the great British age of reform which lasted from Waterloo until the middle of the century, the Tories had played, on the whole, a rather embarrassing part. They had carried on the somewhat dangerous drudgery of economic change while their rivals, the Whigs, had walked off with the easy glory of political reform. This had been true of domestic matters; it was to be equally true in imperial affairs. When Peel became prime minister in the autumn of 1841, the forces which were making for a radical change in the British fiscal system were already approaching their goal. The tremendous growth of industrialism had already upset the economic balance of power within the United Kingdom. Though its great days were not yet over, the resources of British agriculture were already strained; and in the bad harvests of the late thirties and early forties, it could not provide a manufacturing nation with cheap bread. In these circumstances the middle-class opposition to protection for agriculture took on all the aspects of a great humanitarian crusade. In the centre of the Anti-Corn Law League, led by Richard Cobden and John Bright, was a hard core of British manufacturers who preferred, with a Christian humility which was a credit to them, to conceal their presence from the world. But the League's mixture of economics and moralizing, its ingenious appeal to humanity and self-interest, helped to win it the support of some of the agricultural labourers as well as of the mass of industrial workers. By the early 1840's it had become a most imposing political force.

In his first year of power, Peel — with the unsuspecting Tory party at his back — began the march which ended in free trade. He brought back the income tax in order to reduce the tariff; and in 1842 the reforming budgets began.

In that year both the timber duties and the Corn Laws were reduced. There was some compensation for Canadian farmers and grain merchants when the Canada Corn Act of the following year admitted Canadian wheat at all times to the British market under a fixed duty of a shilling a quarter; but the lumbermen of New Brunswick and the Ottawa valley could only find the new timber duties acceptable on the assumption that worse was coming. By the spring of 1845 Peel had really been won to the idea of free trade in wheat; but the public profession of his new faith was hastened by a most remarkable — a most awful — combination of circumstances. In the eyes of its believers, at any rate, free trade was not only economic orthodoxy; it was also Christian morality. There were even moments when it seemed to take on the awful grandeur of divine revelation. It was, therefore, entirely appropriate that Peel, who had been converted by the reasoning of Mr. Cobden, should have been stung to action by an unmistakable sign from God. That summer of 1845 the blight ruined the Irish potato crop and implacable rains beat down the half-ripened wheat crop in England. And in June, 1846, Peel's new Tory government repealed the Corn Laws.

The repeal of the Corn Laws was simply the most decisive and the most famous incident in the coming of British free trade. In 1842 the colonial timber preference had been reduced. It was reduced again in 1845 and for a third time in 1846; and after this last reduction, the preference which remained was hardly sufficient to offset the freight-rate differential in favour of Baltic timber. The blow which British North America had dreaded so long, which it had tried so hard to delay or to prevent, had fallen at last, crushingly. In effect Great Britain had broken away from her own empire; and with the repeal of the Navigation Laws in 1849, the Old Colonial System, which had sheltered and nurtured the northern colonies through the whole period of their uncertain youth, came at last to an end. For provinces which had been so closely associated with the mother country, so deeply dependent upon imperial benefits, this was a major catastrophe; and it was followed by a profound commercial depression, which magnified and distorted all the effects of these fiscal changes into monstrous shapes. In the eyes of British North Americans, the old Empire as they had known it was done and finished for ever.

But, in fact, it was not quite finished yet. Hitherto the reform of the Old Colonial System had been a bargaining process, in which each side had received advantages. But free trade was established in a spirit of pure self-interest and in complete disregard of the colonies. Great Britain was determined to win her own fiscal independence; but at the very same time she was doing her best to prevent the North American provinces from gaining a fresh instalment of local autonomy. The system of government which Lord Sydenham had introduced — the system by which the governor remained as his own prime minister at the active centre of a non-party administration — was continued, with the support of the Conservative Colonial Office in London, even though it soon began to run into difficulties. In Nova Scotia Howe and two other Reform leaders had been persuaded to enter a coalition government under the Governor, Lord Falkland, in 1840. In Canada — and this was, perhaps, the greatest triumph of the old system of colonial governance — the French Canadians, under their leaders Baldwin and Lafontaine, had joined the administration under Sir Charles Bagot in 1842. But the Reformers soon found that though their support was used their advice could very easily be disregarded. In the autumn of 1843 they withdrew from office in both provinces. And this resignation soon brought about the collapse of the Sydenham method. The Reformers closed their ranks in a resolute attempt to capture political power as united parties. The governors had to abandon the fiction of impartiality in a desperate effort to maintain their own personal control. Deserted by the Reformers, they were forced to identify themselves with the Conservatives. Hotly pressed by the opposition, they were obliged to take an active part in an increasingly vicious and unedifying political battle. And although Lord Falkland in Nova Scotia and Sir Charles Metcalfe, the new governor in Canada, managed to keep precarious legislative majorities until the end of their tenure, it was only by using — and abusing — the great prestige of their own office as well as the great affection of British North America for the imperial tie.

How long this could have gone on is doubtful. But in 1846 Peel broke his party to repeal the Corn Laws, and the Whigs, under Lord John Russell, came back into office. The new colonial secretary was the third Earl Grey, a brother-in-law of Lord Durham, and a firm believer in the Durham theories of colonial government. That Grey represented the best type of liberal constructive imperialism there can be no question; but there is also little doubt that the ease with which he persuaded himself and convinced his colleagues that a change was desirable in colonial government is partly to be explained by the prevailing anti-imperial sentiment of the day. Grey himself admitted to Lord Elgin in Canada that lack of interest in the Empire, and lack of belief in its continuance, had now infected many of the statesmen of central importance in the mother country. 'Unfortunately,' he wrote, 'there begins to prevail in the H. of Commons & I am sorry to say in the highest quarters, an opinion (wh. I believe to be utterly erroneous) that we have no interest in preserving our Colonies & ought therefore to Make no sacrifice for that purpose. Peel, Graham, & Gladstone if they do not avow this opinion as openly as Cobden & his friends, yet betray very clearly that they entertain it, nor do I find some Members of the Cabinet free from it, so that I am powerless to do anything wh. involves expense . . .' Great Britain had already withdrawn the economic benefits of empire; she was anxious — as Grey himself clearly revealed — to withdraw her military protection. And since she insisted so

strenuously upon her own freedom from imperial obligation, it was more than a little difficult for her to deny the
colonies their freedom from imperial control. The grant of
responsible government was not an isolated act of political
wisdom. It was simply a single incident in the long process
by which the Old Colonial System was tranformed.

Under Grey and the governors in the two most critical
colonies — Sir John Harvey in Nova Scotia and Lord Elgin
in Canada — responsible government was frankly and generously conceded. 'The object with which I recommend to
you this course,' wrote Grey to Harvey in the key dispatch of
November 3, 1846, 'is that of making it apparent that any
transfer which may take place of political power from the
hands of one party in the province to those of another is the
result not of an act of yours but of the wishes of the people
themselves. . . . In giving, therefore, all fair and proper support to your Council for the time being, you will carefully
avoid any acts which can possibly be supposed to imply the
slightest personal objection to their opponents, and also to
refuse to assent to any measures which may be proposed to
you by your Council, which may appear to you to involve an
improper exercise of the authority of the Crown for party
rather than for public objects. In exercising, however, this
power of refusing to sanction measures which may be submitted to you by your council, you must recollect that this
power . . . depends entirely for its efficacy upon its being
used sparingly, and with the greatest possible discretion. A
refusal to accept advice tendered to you by your council is a
legitimate ground for its members to tender to you their
resignation, a course they would doubtless adopt should they
feel that the subject on which a difference had arisen between you and themselves was one upon which public
opinion would be in their favour. Should it prove to be so,
concession to their views must, sooner or later, become inevitable, since it cannot be too distinctly acknowledged that
it is neither possible nor desirable to carry on the govern-

ment of any of the British provinces in North America in opposition to the opinion of the inhabitants.'

Thus, by the formal order of the Colonial Office itself, complete self-government in domestic affairs was to be granted to the British North American provinces. Lord Grey had left changes in administration to the 'wishes of the people'; and in the Nova Scotian and Canadian elections of 1847 the people unmistakably spoke their wish in favour of Reform. When the provincial legislatures met in the winter of 1848, the formal shift to the British system of cabinet government was made in accordance with the traditional British parliamentary technique. In each assembly a vote of want of confidence was proposed and carried, the existing government resigned, and a Reform ministry was instantly sworn in to take its place. Only a short interval separated the dénouement in the two provinces; but it was at least highly appropriate that the first responsible ministry in the British Empire was that formed on February 2, 1848, in the Province of Nova Scotia, the oldest British colony in the second Empire, the home of irrepressible local liberties, of firm but constitutional resistance to imperial claims.

In Nova Scotia the peaceful revolution was accomplished without trouble or disturbance. But in Canada the old order died very hard. The end of the Old Colonial System had driven the merchant Tories of Canada East into a state of desperation unequalled anywhere else in British North America. Montreal stood to lose more than other places from the establishment of British free trade. Montreal was far more frightened than her neighbours at the introduction of responsible government, for responsible government at once brought into office the 'unprogressive and anti-commercial' French. When, in 1849, the French seemed to flaunt their power in the new ministry, when the Reform administration introduced a measure called the Rebellion Losses Bill which distinguished somewhat imperfectly between the losses of Loyalists and those of rebels in the Lower

Canadian rebellion of 1837, the accumulated resentment of the Montreal Tories exploded in a burst of uncontrollable rage. In the late afternoon of April 25, when Lord Elgin drove away from the legislature where he had just accepted the Rebellion Losses Bill, he was pelted with volleys of refuse. A great crowd of furious English-speaking Montrealers assembled in the Champ de Mars that cool, windy spring evening to petition for the recall of the governor. As the night deepened, as the excitement grew, the legitimate assembly of citizens quickly became a passionate mob, which moved off abruptly towards the parliament buildings, with torches streaming redly in the darkness. While the frightened officials and members hurried from the legislature, the rioters stormed through the rooms and corridors, smashing furniture and breaking lights; and finally they fired the great piles of stationery which lay stored in a gallery at the west end. In a few minutes the fire was racing through the whole building; and the high wind drove the great ragged flames far into the sky.

In a day, the Conservatives of Montreal had gone almost as far as the rebels of 1837 in their appeal to force; and before the year was out they went even further in their departure from the British connection. That autumn of 1849 over a thousand merchants and politicians of Montreal signed a manifesto advocating the annexation of Canada to the United States. It was the first — and last — time that Montreal ever forgot its historic rôle as the city of the St. Lawrence River. It was the first — and last — time that it ever prepared to abandon its hereditary allies and join forces with its hereditary rivals. And the fact that it was provoked to this astounding, this unique, aberration is the best proof of the profound and hopeless despair of 1849.

Yet, apart from the original signatories, the annexation manifesto won practically no support in Canada. Though the United States was obviously interested in the movement, she discreetly refrained from taking any official notice of it;

and though British statesmen may have believed that the imperial connection was not likely to last a great deal longer, officially they set their faces against any break at that time. The fact was that a revolutionary change had taken place in the organization of the second British Empire; but, though this had caused great irritation in the colonies, and though it had occurred at a time when the United States was inspired by strong imperialist ambitions, it had not resulted in any change in the political allegiance of British North America.   The United States had obtained Oregon and Texas.   The Mexican War had left the Republic in possession of New Mexico and California.   But, so far as British North America was concerned, all the disputes of the 1840's had been ended peacefully, for the Ashburton Treaty of 1842 settled the international boundary in the east and the Treaty of Washington of 1846 determined it in the west. It looked as though British North America had survived a crisis without a change of character or purpose.   Yet the effects of responsible government in the colonies and free trade in Great Britain were not ended yet.   The colonies — and particularly Canada — were trading more with the United States, were more interested in the American market, than they had ever been before.   Obviously it had not yet been decided what their final position was to be in either the British Empire or the North American continent.

CHAPTER SIX

TRANSCONTINENTAL
DOMINION

[*1*]

THE THIRD QUARTER of the nineteenth century
was an age of expanding industrialism and triumphant nationality. The new inventions, the new techniques in steel and steam, the new methods of machine manufacture and railway transport, were visibly revolutionizing
the West European-American world; and on both sides of
the Atlantic the rise of the new industrialism was accompanied by a period of war and unsettlement out of which
there emerged a number of great national states. Perhaps
the most obvious and spectacular examples of this political
process were the unification of Italy and the creation of the
German Empire. But in both divisions of the English-
speaking world — the British Empire and the United States
— there were political reorganizations which were just as
drastic as anything that took place on the Continent. Under
the pressure from 'Little England' the loosely united second
British Empire began to break up into a number of quasi-
independent national states. Under the coercive power of
civil war the old divided federalism of the United States was
suddenly forced into a unity.

The coming of the new industrialism and the new nationality was bound to have the most serious consequences for
the British North American provinces. They had grown up

in the old world of business and politics. They were fairly well adjusted to an economic order characterized by wooden shipping, wind- and water-power, ocean and river transport. The economy of the Maritime Provinces was based upon the sea and the forest, and that of United Canada upon the St. Lawrence and the Precambrian Shield. Lumbering, agriculture, fishing, and shipbuilding were their staple industries; and they had a common interest in waterways, wooden shipping, and the carrying trade. By 1850 Canada had completed a most ambitious system of canals, and the tiny Maritime Provinces had risen to fourth place in registered tonnage of shipping in the entire world. For these provinces, the shift from wood to iron, from water-power to steam, from canals to railways, and from sailing vessels to steamships seemed at once ominous and encouraging. If it offered opportunities, it also posed problems. The only extensive deposits of coal then known to exist in British North America lay in Cape Breton Island, on the extreme east; and the only large body of iron ore so far discovered in the Precambrian Shield turned out, almost as if in mockery, to lie south of the international boundary. The new age of steam and steel was bound to involve many and unpredictable adjustments. It might mean the rise or the decline of the economics of British North America.

But the provinces did not only have to adjust themselves to the new industrialism; they also were forced to face the national policies and the great national states of the future. They had grown up in the old relatively tranquil world of small states, little provinces, decentralized federations, and great sprawling empires. It was their settled habit to think in terms of distant markets, of great commercial systems, both imperial and international, which extended far beyond their own boundaries. Their own interprovincial trade had not so far been great enough to suggest the idea of a British North American national economy. Their membership in the second British Empire had accustomed them to the idea of reciprocity, of exchange of fiscal privileges, of economic give and take. They were unprepared for the extreme and exclusive national commercial policies of the future. They were even frightened by the appearance of the great national states. Accustomed to a loose association with some great imperial power, the provinces had so far taken only a very academic interest in a national British North American political union.

From 1850 on, the northern provinces tried continually to adjust themselves to the new industry and the new economic nationalism. Appropriately enough, the impact of these two great new forces fell upon them first through the agency of Great Britain, the original industrial power. By financing the first railways in British North America, Great Britain helped to teach the new techniques of steel and steam to the provinces; and by adopting a national policy of free trade which sacrificed her colonial empire, she confronted the provinces with the first of those extreme national policies which were to govern international trade from then on. Railways proved to be the basis of industrial growth within the provinces; British free trade was the first of the shattering blows aimed by economic nationalism from without. From then on the constant operation of these two forces, one internal and one external, began to transform the character of the provinces, to change their connections with each other, to alter their relations with the external world. How would British North America stand the passage from wood, wind, and water to steel and steam? Could the provinces stick by their old international commercial systems and keep their old reciprocal trade agreements? Or would they be forced to frame national policies for British North America and create a British North American national state?

As soon as the English Corn Laws and timber duties had been repealed, British North America immediately began its instinctive search for new preferential markets. There was some, but not very much, interest in the prospects of interprovincial trade. In 1850, the Maritime Provinces and Canada permitted the mutual free exchange of their natural products; but for the majority of the provinces, and particularly for Canada, the American market was looked upon as the only thing that could compensate for the losses which had come through British free trade. Though Lord Grey at the Colonial Office was one of the new doctrinaire free traders who looked upon differential duties as an immoral commercial monstrosity, Lord Elgin, the Governor-General of Canada, sought to convince him that a preferential trade agreement with the United States was probably the only thing that would save the province from annexation to the Republic. British officials, spurred on by the urgings of the colonists, did their rather half-hearted best at Washington to secure a treaty with the United States. It was a hard job. The Americans were not particularly friendly to the British, they were completely indifferent to the colonials; and they had become so passionately absorbed in the struggle between North and South that other questions were often either neglected altogether or judged solely in the light of sectional fears and prejudices.

Fortunately for the provinces, the trade agreement was not the only issue outstanding between the United States on the one hand and Great Britain and British North America on the other. There was the matter of the North Atlantic fisheries. By the Convention of 1818, American fishermen had been excluded from most of the inshore waters of British North America except for the purpose of obtaining wood, water, shelter, or repairs. The disputes over the interpretation of this article, and the quarrels over the British attempts to enforce it, grew more frequent as the middle of the century drew nearer. At the very time when American fishermen, intent upon the inshore mackerel run, entered colonial waters more frequently to fish and smuggle, the Province of Nova Scotia, desperate with the disappearance of its last trade privileges in the West Indies, was more than ever determined to protect its one remaining asset from American encroachment. In 1852, after a new series of complaints and appeals from Nova Scotia, the British government announced that it would send out a small fleet to defend the inshore fisheries. This, though it was by no means the first show of force, produced a greater uproar than any of its predecessors. And it was to a large extent their common desire to avoid a serious clash over the fisheries, a clash which might conceivably lead to war, that persuaded the British government and the American administration to settle their outstanding problems in a trade and fisheries agreement.

Yet, in the spring of 1854, when the Earl of Elgin arrived in Washington, there was no certainty that a treaty could be negotiated with the American executive and accepted by the American Congress. Elgin had been a great colonial administrator. He now proved himself to be a suave and accomplished diplomatist. Reciprocity was borne along on the charming conviviality of a long series of dances, dinners, and supper parties. Elgin's guests used to depart 'pleased with the monarchical form of government in England; pleased with the republican form of government in the United States; pleased with each other, themselves, and the rest of mankind.' In 1853-54, under a Democratic Congress and administration, protectionist feeling in the Republic was at a temporary stand; and the various sectional interests likely to be affected by the treaty had in one way or another been conciliated. Even the basic political rivalry between North and South, which so long had blocked the treaty, now seemed actually to push it forward towards completion. In the minds of both Southerners and Northerners reciprocity with British North America was tied up with the annexation of British North America to the United States. But while the Northerners believed that reciprocity would promote annexation, the Southerners were now convinced that reciprocity would prevent or delay it. The passage of the Reci-

procity Treaty was, in fact, one of the last efforts of the South
to preserve the economic and political balance of power on
the continent. It was one of the South's last successes. For
the treaty was accepted in the same year that saw the passage
of the Kansas-Nebraska Bill, which in effect destroyed the
Missouri Compromise; and from that moment the struggle
between North and South for the control of the western
domain approached its final paroxysm.

By the Reciprocity Treaty of 1854, reciprocal free trade in
coal and fish, in farm and forest products, was established
between the northern provinces and the United States. This
free entry for unmanufactured produce was the great benefit which British North America obtained from the treaty;
and to get it she had to offer, not only an equivalent freedom
in her own market, but also additional and important concessions. American vessels were permitted to use the St. Lawrence River and the Canadian canals; and — much more significant — American fishermen were granted the liberty of
the inshore fisheries of British North America. It was true,
of course, that these privileges were supposedly balanced by
concessions on the part of the United States; but the navigation of Lake Michigan was scarcely an equivalent for the
navigation of the St. Lawrence and it could hardly be pretended that the American fisheries north of the thirty-sixth
parallel approached the value of the British North American.
The treaty was to remain in force at least ten years; it was
to continue beyond this period until twelve months after
one of the contracting parties had given notice of a desire
to terminate it.

In the meantime, while the northern provinces were making their first adjustments to the new national commercial
policies, they were also laying the bases of the new industrialism. There had been plenty of talk about railways in the
provinces during the 1840's; but it was not until the middle
of the century that serious construction began. And as soon
as railway projects of any size were considered, the vital

problem of railway strategy in British North America immediately appeared. Broadly speaking, the provinces had two alternatives from which to choose; they could either link British North America together in a national system, or they could build lines which would strengthen their old international trade routes in competition with the United States. On the one hand, there was the Intercolonial Railway, an all-British North American project with terminals in Halifax and Quebec, which would link the Maritime Provinces and Canada together; and on the other hand, there were separate Canadian and Maritime railway schemes, regional projects with American connections, which would seek an international traffic. The projected regional railway of the Maritime Provinces, which went by the resounding title of the European and North American Railway, was planned to run from Halifax through Saint John and southwestward to Portland, Maine. The Canadian regional scheme, which was finally embodied in the Grand Trunk Railway, called for a great trunk line which would extend the whole length of the St. Lawrence valley from the western boundary of Canada to the eastern ports of Montreal and Portland, Maine.

In 1850, when the crucial decisions were made, it was not clear for a time which of these two plans would be followed or whether they could not both be combined in a single great project. For a time the provinces held the most ambitious hopes. But it was soon discovered that while the obstacles to any colonial railways were great, the difficulties in the face of an Intercolonial Railway were likely to be insurmountable. In 1850, Joseph Howe thought he had secured the financial guarantee of the British government, as well as the financial co-operation of the different provinces, in a great scheme for building both the European and North American to the United States and the Intercolonial Railway to Canada. But Howe's assumption was the result of a most unfortunate misunderstanding. Earl Grey, at the

Colonial Office, insisted that his government had never dreamed of underwriting anything but a railway connecting the British colonies, which would follow a northerly route at a safe distance from the American border. The whole elaborate scheme fell to the ground with a crash; and although efforts were made in later years to unite the provinces again in support of the Intercolonial, no plan was ever adopted and acted upon. Whereupon the provinces turned back to their separate provincial projects. In Nova Scotia and New Brunswick, where private capital was extremely hard to come by, the two governments built short provincial railways which could be regarded as the first sections of the European and North American line. In Canada, three commercial companies, the Northern, the Great Western, and the Grand Trunk Railway, were founded largely with British capital and received extensive government support. Though the Northern and the Great Western were relatively small in comparison with the Grand Trunk, all three railways were planned to attract a part of the general east-west traffic of the continent. The Grand Trunk Railway, which stretched from Sarnia at the foot of Lake Huron to Montreal and Portland, reinforced the old commercial empire of the St. Lawrence and repeated in the new material of iron the ancient style of Canadian business life.

Though Canadian and American as well as British contracting firms took part in the construction of the British North American railways, all the lines were supposedly built in accordance with the English standard of solid construction with high original cost and low upkeep. How far this principle was honoured except in high original cost is doubtful; but here at any rate the resemblance between the English and Canadian railways ceased. Within a short time, all the engines and carriages on the northern lines followed the North American pattern set by the United States, whether they were built in the Republic or in British North America. Similarly train equipment and personnel did not differ markedly from American standards. English visitors, accustomed to 'civil and decent' guards and to compartmented carriages, were astonished by the condescending dignity of the Canadian conductors and the democratic promiscuity of the Canadian 'cars.' 'Those I am writing of,' observed an English visitor, 'are like large caravans, some 40 feet long, and not like the English ones, divided into three compartments. . . . I have counted forty-four people in one carriage. . . . The conductors generally are civil fellows, but fearfully off-hand. . . . Wood is used instead of coal, and the nuisance from the *"smuts"* is intolerable. You will get nothing to eat or drink on the way, but the vilest of compounds, and no time to stow them. A cup of tea, if you don't sit down to drink it, is 25 cents; and a bottle of beer — ugh! (Bass, Allsop, hear me!) 50 ditto.'

In its strategy of railways, as well as in its commercial policy, British North America had strengthened its old trade routes and reaffirmed its old dependence on external markets. It looked as if the United States had simply been substituted for Great Britain — as if British North America had merely turned from a European to an American empire. There was more than a little truth in this view; but it was by no means a completely satisfactory interpretation of what was happening. The interest of the colonies in interprovincial trade and their efforts to begin the Intercolonial Railway at least suggested a new belief in closer relations among themselves. And there was other evidence as well of a vague general belief in a new British North American nationality. For the first time both Maritimers and Canadians were becoming excitedly aware of the enormous inheritance of property which was still left to Great Britain on the new continent. Already there were a few Maritimers who began to look upon the whole of British North America as a potential hinterland for their Atlantic ports. The Canadians, whether or no they took much interest in the east, were becoming fascinated by the prospects of a British-American north-west. There was nothing new, of course, in western ambitions. Montreal had always been absorbed in the west, had staked everything upon the St. Lawrence as a trade route to the west. But the old empire of the St. Lawrence had been, at least in intention, a commercial, an international, dominion; and ever since 1821, when the fur trade had been transferred to Hudson Bay, it had sought its traffic in the staple products of the new middle-western states. The new Canadian interest lay not so much in the international west as in Rupert's Land and the North-West Territories, the domain which had been granted to the Hudson's Bay Company. And perhaps equally significantly, these lands were looked upon not merely as the path of a trade route, but as the new frontier of British-American settlement.

There were several reasons for this new interest. In the first place, the Canadians suddenly discovered that they themselves were concerned in the north-west; and in the second, they became apprehensive that the Americans were likely to forestall them. The fact was that the last frontier had virtually been closed in Canada West. The Bruce peninsula, between Lake Huron and Georgian Bay, was rapidly occupied in the late 1840's and early 1850's. South and west of the old, settled districts of Canada West there was nothing but the United States, into which scores of thousands of immigrants and native Canadians were already travelling. North and west was the Precambrian Shield or Laurentian plateau — that vague wild country of scarred rock, massed evergreens, lakes, rivers, and spillways, which they knew as the dominion of the lumbermen. The mistaken effort to invade this natural forest land, to open a way for a last influx of settlers by means of colonization roads, was tried in the 1850's and proved a costly and a complete failure. The good lands of Canada were occupied. But far to the north-west, beyond the great barrier of the Laurentian plateau, there lay a new domain of hundreds of thousands of square miles between Lake Winnipeg and the Rocky Mountains.

This new interest of the Canadians was not the only, nor perhaps the most important, external factor which now served to endanger the old order of things in the Hudson's Bay Company's lands. The company's domain was suddenly threatened from all sides, where before it had seemed so remote, so secure, so inaccessible. By the original charter of 1670, the company held proprietary rights to a vast, vaguely defined territory surrounding Hudson Bay; by letters-patent of 1849, it had been granted title to Vancouver Island; and over all the remainder of the British north-west as far as the Pacific coast, it held an exclusive licence to trade which in 1838 had been renewed for twenty-one years. The entire region was still a fur-trade empire. Though Vancouver Island had been granted to the company on the express condition that it should promote colonization and settlement, only a handful of Hudson's Bay Company servants were ever brought out. Though Lord Selkirk's settlement close to Lake Winnipeg, at the forks of the Red and Assiniboine Rivers, had been established far back in 1812, in 1849 it was composed only of two small groups of French half-breeds and Scottish settlers, who together numbered only a little over five thousand people, and who made their living by catering to the fur trade. Within the licensed and chartered territories of the Hudson's Bay Company, the old order seemed unchanged and unchangeable. But outside the west was full of the tramp of advancing settlement. And settlement was the hereditary enemy of the fur trade.

Curiously enough, the attack began on the Pacific coast. The American frontier leaped over the almost empty western half of the continent to settle Oregon; and when the Treaty of 1846 prolonged the forty-ninth parallel as the international boundary to the coast, the Hudson's Bay Company abandoned the Columbia River region, where its Pacific headquarters had once been established. Already the advance guard of American settlement had accomplished much; and behind it followed the enormous main body of migrants, which, with the help of the new railways, was now moving with ominous swiftness towards the plains. In 1852 the railway from the east reached Chicago. It touched the Mississippi in 1854, the Missouri in 1859. Minnesota, which had been a territory with six thousand frontiersmen in 1850, became a state in 1858 with a population which reached one hundred and seventy-two thousand two years later. The little settlement on the Red River stretched out towards this advancing army of people which threatened to surround and engulf it. In 1856, over five hundred Red River carts loaded with peltries made the overland journey to the American outposts; and the frontiersmen were astonished to see Scots settlers, in brightly coloured *capotes* and *mocassins*, emerge out of the even more remote north-west. Even the company soon began to bring in the mails as well as some of its own supplies from the south. The transport and communication system of the Hudson's Bay Company, which had been completely cut off from Canada in 1821, was now partly diverted away from Hudson Bay itself and towards the southern route through the United States.

In the meantime, the pressure became even more serious on the Pacific coast. In the centre of the continent, the wave of exploitation and settlement had still merely threatened the territories of the Hudson's Bay Company; but in the ultimate west the actual invasion was just about to begin. After the Treaty of 1846, there was barely a last decade of peace. Far in the south the California gold rush reached and passed its climax, leaving behind a disbanded army of skilled prospectors and miners who searched restlessly up and down the coast for the deposits which everybody believed must lie somewhere in the region. In 1855, gold was discovered in the Columbia River, just north of the international boundary. It was found in the Thompson and Fraser Rivers in 1856. In the spring and summer of 1858 the tent city of Victoria sprang into existence; and thousands of miners, crossing to the mainland, began to push up the Fraser, testing every bar of sand for gold.

In the dozen years from 1846 to 1858 it became obvious to everybody that the end of the Hudson's Bay Company rule was rapidly approaching and that the ultimate fate of the British American north-west would soon be decided for ever. Throughout British North America there were people everywhere who were vitally concerned in the outcome. 'The Maritime Provinces which I now address,' said Joseph Howe in 1851, in support of the Intercolonial project, 'are but the Atlantic frontage of this boundless and prolific region — the wharves upon which its business will be transacted and beside which its rich argosies are to lie. . . . See that you comprehend its destiny and resources — see that you discharge, with energy and elevation of soul, the duties which devolve upon you in virtue of your position.' Undoubtedly there were western expansionists in Nova Scotia and New Brunswick; but they were more numerous in Canada than in the Maritime Provinces, and more numerous in Canada West than Canada East. Ever since the collapse of the North West Company in 1821, Montreal had sought its commercial empire in the middle-western American states. It had supported the St. Lawrence canals and then the Grand Trunk Railway in an effort to compete with New York for this western traffic. Montreal, and Canada East, and the Liberal-Conservative party, which was strongest in Canada East, represented this old, international form of Canadian imperialism. But Toronto, and Canada West, and the Reformers or 'Clear Grits,' who drew their chief support from the western part of the province, had already begun to dream of a new national Canadian Empire in the British American north-west.

The Grits, who were the true heirs of the Mackenzie tradition, drew much of their strength from the agrarian frontier. It was they who first awoke to the fact that Canada West was an occupied country and that the only remaining frontier of British North America lay far away in the territories of the Hudson's Bay Company. As early as the late forties, George Brown, who became a leader of the Reform party and whose newspaper, the Toronto *Globe,* grew to be the Bible of the Clear Grits, had interested himself in the north-west; and in their convention in 1857, the Reformers made the incorporation of the north-west into Canada a plank in the party platform. The domain of the Hudson's Bay Company appealed to these men as a field for settlement — as an agricultural frontier. But it had not yet sold itself to the business, banking, and railway interests of the province as a practical project. And the Canadian government still hung back before the task of taking it over. In 1857, two years before the expiration of the company's twenty-year trade monopoly, when a select committee of the imperial House of Commons sat down to consider the whole problem of the future of Rupert's Land and the North-West Territories, the policy of the Canadian government with respect to westward expansion was still cautious to a degree. Ch:ef Justice Draper, who attended at the committee's request to give evidence on behalf of Canada, voiced the general hope that his province would eventually inherit the greater part of the Hudson's Bay Company's territories and that a railway would one day link them with the St. Lawrence. But he admitted that Canada was not yet ready to take up the burden of the whole north-west and suggested that a gradual, piecemeal expansion was alone possible. In somewhat guarded language, the committee's *Report* recommended that the Red and Saskatchewan River district should be ceded to Canada and that the company's trade and proprietary rights should be extinguished on the Pacific coast.

This awakening interest in Rupert's Land and the North-West Territories was not the only manifestation of a new urge towards a British North American nationality. Just as the idea of a British-American north-west was beginning gradually to compete with the far older concept of an international western commercial empire, so the policy of economic self-sufficiency was rising to challenge the historic policy of economic dependence. In the past, British North America had always been a staple-producing country, which had hoped to sell its products in preferential markets, and in return was quite prepared to import the vast bulk of its manufactures from outside. The provinces had no tradition of native industry. They had always stood for low tariffs and reciprocal preferences; and though the Reciprocity Treaty of 1854 had only concerned natural products, there is no doubt that American manufacturers were induced to accept it in the hope that with the general opening of trade they would have a better chance of taking the place of the English in supplying the provinces with manufactured goods. But the beginning of reciprocity coincided with the coming of the railway; and the railway — the first phase of industrialism in the northern provinces — was destined to do strange things with the economies of British North America, and even stranger things with the commercial policies of several of its governments.

In the first place, the railways had been extremely expensive and the cost had largely been borne by the state. From the first the governments of the northern provinces had accepted the view that they must open avenues for settlement and exploitation, that they must clear and prepare the way for the colonist and the capitalist. This assistance was just as necessary in the railway age as it had been in the canal period. State aid for the railways was financially essential, for otherwise private capital might not be forthcoming; and to many it seemed politically desirable as well, for, as Joseph Howe said, 'the policy on which we are acting in Nova Scotia, is *to keep the great Highway which must pass through our Country into the United States, under the Control of the Government.'* In the Maritime Provinces, where private funds were even more difficult to get than in Canada, the provincial governments frankly undertook the construction and management of their own railways. In Canada, where the Northern, the Great Western, the Grand Trunk, were supposedly independent commercial companies, the province helped to support them with loans and subsidies. In 1850, there had been only a few miles of railway track in the whole of British North America; in 1860, there were from two to three hundred miles in the Maritime Provinces and slightly over two thousand in the Province of Canada. The whole British North American system cost approximately one hundred and sixty million dollars, of which Canada, with an expenditure of one hundred and forty-five million, contributed by far the bigger share. A large part of this capital had been supplied by private investors, chiefly in Great Britain; but a large part had also been contributed by the state. Nova Scotia and New Brunswick had put nearly eleven million into their provincial railways; and the Province of Canada had granted or loaned nearly twice as much to the Grand Trunk, the Northern, and the Great Western Railways. Thus provinces which were principally dependent upon a low tariff for revenue had loaded themselves with a large and dead-weight debt.

In the meantime, while the railways were bringing these changes in public finance, they had already begun to effect an even more important revolution in the economic life of British North America. The railways supplied the first basis of industrialism. They enlarged the economic horizon of the provinces and quickened the progress of their exploitation. British North America remained a region in which staple products were produced for export by lumbermen, fishermen, and farmers; but, in the age of steam and iron and steel, these old staple industries were changing and were being supplemented by others. Industrialism quickened the growth of the Nova Scotian coal industry, hastened the shift from the old square-timber trade to the production of sawn lumber for the American market, and foreshadowed the rise of mixed farming in the wheat-growing areas of Canada West. Steam-power began to replace water-power in flour-mills and lumber-mills; new tools, saws, implements, and machines were remaking the whole pattern of labour in the forest and the farm. Industrialism had affected the conduct of the old staple industries. But it did more: it brought manufacturing to British North America for the first time.

Up until the middle of the nineteenth century, the northern provinces had practised almost literally the ancient mercantilist maxim that colonies should export raw materials and import manufactured goods. Their one great secondary industry had been the wooden shipbuilding business of the Maritime Provinces and Quebec city. The coming of the iron ship meant the inevitable downfall of wooden ship-building; but, on the other hand, the railways brought in the new industrial materials, the new industrial tools, techniques, and machines, the new skilled industrial workers. It was true, of course, that progress towards industrialization was largely confined to the Province of Canada and limited to a small number of lines. Apart from the mere processing of primary materials, such as flour-milling and lumber-milling, which accounted for over forty per cent of total Canadian industry as late as 1871, British North American manufactures usually relied for success on cheap local supplies of raw materials or on the natural protection of heavy transport charges from abroad. The provinces, and particularly Canada, began to make clothing, boots and shoes, furniture, agricultural implements, tools, boilers, engines, and castings. But though efforts were made to work the small available local supplies of iron, British North America developed no primary iron and steel industry during this period; and in the making of paper, cotton and woollen textiles, machinery and fine-edge tools, her manufactures still had to face very serious competition from imports.

So long as the boom lasted the local manufacturers found it easy to extend their business, and the provincial governments found it possible to support their debts. The Crimean War and the consequent high prices for wheat, which coincided with the building of railways and the heavy imports of capital equipment, brought a great wave of prosperity. But in 1857 the good times came suddenly to an end, with disastrous results for Canada, the province which had plunged most adventurously in railways and had advanced furthest along the path to industrialization. The provincial government had to support heavy fixed interest charges on the proceeds of a low tariff. The manufacturers had to fight for their share of the local market in the face of declining prices and dwindling demand. The new forms of transport, which had done so much to promote Canadian industry, now confronted it with its most serious competition; the new ships and railways could now bring goods from mature manufacturing countries like Great Britain at prices which the Canadians could not hope to meet. In April, 1858, the newly formed Association for the Promotion of Canadian Industry met in general session at Toronto and petitioned the government for a substantial increase in the tariff.

The manufacturers did not suffer alone. Fortunately for themselves, their distress coincided with the very real financial embarrassment of the Canadian government. If the manufacturers thought they needed protection, the government knew that it must have increased revenue; and during 1858-59, under the leadership of its finance ministers, William Cayley and Alexander Tilloch Galt, the Conservative government sharply raised the tariff. Galt, who succeeded Cayley in 1858 and became the real sponsor of the tariff, was a new and vital force in Canadian politics. He had been a commissioner of the British American Land Company — a promoter of the St. Lawrence and Atlantic Railway, which had eventually been absorbed by the Grand Trunk; and in the Conservative cabinet he stood for the drive and energy of the big business of Canada East. He insisted, of course, that the new duties had been established for revenue purposes only and that any protection they afforded to Canadian industry was incidental to the main object of getting money to pay the canal and railway debt. The province, he argued, had cheapened the cost of British manufactures in Canada, and raised the value of Canadian products in England, by its expenditures on canals and railways. The traffic which poured over the new Canadian transport system could very well afford a small toll; and the government, which had helped to supply the system, badly needed the money. The argument was sound enough; but while Galt could justify the change, he could not minimize its importance. Traditionally Canada had been committed to low duties and reciprocal preferences. But now, in the national interest, she had suddenly raised the tariff. Within ten years of the coming of the railway and the beginning of industrialization, an important change had already been made in the traditional commercial policy of British North America.

These new economic tendencies were important; but equally important was the new direction in political thinking which accompanied them. Along with these shifts in tariff policy, and this anxious concern for the British-American north-west, there went an awakening interest in the problem of British-American union. During the 1850's most people who were concerned with policy — the Colonial Office administrators in London, the governors in the colonies, and the members of their executive councils — found themselves speculating on the subject of British North American union. Their approaches to the problem were extremely tentative. Their solutions — so far as they reached solutions — were varied and vague. But, broadly speaking, those who busied themselves with the problem could be divided into two schools of thought. There were those who thought in terms of regional unions — the union of the Maritime Provinces — of Canada and the north-west — of British Columbia and Vancouver Island. There were also those who hoped for a general union, either legislative or federal, of British North

America as a whole. Thus the two contrasted economic policies — the policy based on regional interests and external trade on the one hand, and the policy of economic union and the home market on the other — had their counterparts in the political world. The two solutions certainly differed; but people did not look upon them as inevitably exclusive and contradictory, and very often regional unions were regarded merely as first steps towards the desirable national union of the future. 'Now, sir,' said George Brown in a speech of 1859, in which he supported the federal union of Canada East and Canada West alone, 'I do place the question on the ground of nationality. I do hope there is not one Canadian in this assembly who does not look forward with high hope to the day when these northern countries shall stand out among the nations of the world as one great confederation. What true Canadian can witness the tide of immigration now commencing to flow into the vast territories of the North-West without longing to have a share in the first settlement of that great and fertile country? . . . But . . . is it not true wisdom to commence the federative system with our own country, and leave it open to extension hereafter, if time and experience shall prove it to be desirable?'

There were many approaches to union; there were many people who started to move towards it; but there was one group, above all, that began to force the pace. Colonial Office clerks scribbled minutes on union; colonial governors wrote lengthy dispatches on union; Maritime politicians made speeches, and moved resolutions on union. But it was the Canadians who had been driven, by the mere pressure of the difficulties in their own province, to believe that some kind of political reorganization was absolutely essential. Ever since their union in 1841, Canada East and Canada West had been coming gradually to realize that, though it was impossible for them to live economically apart, it was almost equally difficult for them to live politically together. Their union had never been organic. They remained two different cultures — one emphatically British and one ineradicably French. They continued as two virtually distinct political entities. By a fatal flaw in the Union Act of 1840, the two divisions of the province had been given equal representation in the provincial assembly, irrespective of population; and this legislative equality had tended to preserve their separateness and to prevent unity and stability in their government. Politically the province was a dualism in an uneasy state of balance.

Nobody knew this truth better than the Canadian parties. Both were loose associations of French- and English-speaking Canadians, not unequal in numbers, and continually uncertain as to their following. The Tory party, christened 'Liberal-Conservative' in a burst of inspiration, had been formed in 1854 by the union of the French-Canadian Roman Catholics under Georges E. Cartier and the English-speaking Tory and moderate groups under John A. Macdonald. A generation before, when Papineau had thundered against the shopkeeper aristocracy of Montreal and when the Tory merchants had demanded the anglicization of French Canada, such a union would have appeared unnatural and almost indecent. But in the meantime a number of things had served to legitimize it. In the first place, the English-speaking Tories had come to realize, as a result of the bitter experiences of the 1840's, that co-operation with the French was essential to political success in the united Province of Canada, and that co-operation could only be bought by a frank recognition of the cultural dualism of Canadian life. In the second place, the French Canadians had come to realize the religious perils and the pecuniary disadvantages of eternal opposition to wealth and authority. In the 1840's they had come to terms with commercial capitalism; and the fact that Georges E. Cartier, an ex-follower of Papineau, was solicitor for the Grand Trunk Railway showed how thoroughly the French Canadians could accommodate themselves to big business once they got started. In the meantime, while they had been

losing their old dislike of public works and capitalist enterprises, the Roman Catholic Church had been planting in
them a new horror of liberalism. The break of the Canadian
church with the *Patriotes* in 1837 was followed by the far
more important rupture between the Papacy and the revolutionaries of 1848 in Europe. Pius IX, once reputed a liberal,
became a strong reactionary. Certain members of the
hierarchy in Canada fervently followed his example. They
went so far as to attack political liberalism and to support
Macdonald and Cartier. And the strange result of all this
was that the Conservative party relied on the contrasted
support of French peasants and English business men, of
Roman Catholic priests and Tory Orange leaders.

The Reform or Liberal party was an even more uncertain
union. Like its rival it was composed of two sections, the
Parti Rouge of Canada East, led by A. A. Dorion, and the
Reform party of Canada West, dominated by George Brown.
The two groups were largely influenced by North American
values, and the western Reformers in particular tended to
represent the interests of the agrarian frontier. But like all
British North American parties, including their rivals the
Conservatives, they inherited a large part of their political
philosophy from England and the Continent. With respectful admiration, the Reformers of Canada West took many of
their notions from the Manchester school and the Gladstonian
Liberals. The *Rouges,* with an independence which was
new in French Canada, derived much of their democracy
and their moderate anti-clericalism from the European revolutionaries of 1848. The two groups had a number of things
in common; but their concern for local interests and local
autonomy tended to drive them apart. Intrinsically, moreover, the *Rouges* were weak and growing weaker. They had
tried to awaken French Canada with a democratic spirit derived from revolutionary France; but they — and their newspapers and their society, the *Institut Canadien* — were systematically hunted and harassed by the clergy.

In the years 1857-59, during which the pattern of the future Canadian nationality began to appear in its first pale outline, the two Canadian parties were formally taking their stand on the pressing problem of constitutional change. The differences between the two solutions should not be exaggerated, for some of the leaders on both sides were already dreaming, in a romantic fashion, of a transcontinental British North American union. But, so far as the immediate Canadian problem was concerned, their proposals were widely at variance. At first the Reformers, who thought less in terms of big unions and more in terms of local autonomy, could scarcely agree on a solution. George Brown and the Grits of Canada West were suspicious of Roman Catholic Canada East and resentful of the fact that she continued in possession of half the seats in the provincial legislature despite the smaller numbers of her people. They proposed representation by population, which would have settled the problem simply by giving Canada West a majority in the united parliament; and there were a number of English-speaking Reformers and a much larger number of French-speaking *Rouges* who preferred a complete dissolution of the union of 1841 to this drastic remedy. The Conservatives had a much stronger tradition of political centralization and western empire. A generation before, their predecessors had been struggling vigorously for the union of Upper and Lower Canada. But now they hesitated to commit themselves to a much vaster political enterprise; and for a while they did little more than expose the weaknesses of their opponents' plans. In 1858, however, the first really serious breakdown in government led them to go a long step further. The Conservatives began to take up the cause of British North American nationality.

In 1858, during the ministerial crisis of that year, A. T. Galt entered the reorganized Conservative government, as minister of finance. He entered on condition that the party adopt the general federation of the British North American provinces as a plank in its platform. This was the first real sign that the railway and business interests of Canada East were likely to throw their weight in favour of federal union; but it remained a portent merely, for when Canada sought to start negotiations, its project was received with chilly indifference or almost open hostility by the other provinces and the Colonial Office. In the following year, 1859, the Reformers, meeting in convention at Toronto, abandoned their two radical solutions of the past, which would have antagonized either one or the other section of the province, and adopted the plan of a loose federal union of Upper and Lower Canada alone. The two alternatives — general federation or local federal union — had thus been laid down; and throughout British North America it looked as if the forces back of the regional plan were likely to be stronger.

[*II*]

In April, 1861, when the Confederate guns opened upon the Union fort in Charleston harbour, a conflict began which was to have an indirect but decisive influence upon the fortunes of British North America. In fact, the American Civil War brought about the second great political and economic reorganization in the English-speaking world. It opened the way for a new unified and industrialized nationality through the overwhelming defeat of the South. Up to 1861, though with increasing difficulty, the South had managed to keep a precarious balance of economic and political power within the United States, and hence upon the North American continent as a whole. The South had defended those political institutions and economic interests with which the northern provinces had been identified since the beginning of their history. It had taught the continent its ideas of equalitarian democracy, had preached the doctrine of local autonomy for the benefit of little states and provinces, and had stood for the interests of agriculture, commerce, and international trade. In the end, as the passage of the Reciprocity Treaty showed clearly, the South had been driven openly to include British North America in its defence against the imperialism of the northern states. A war which threatened the integrity of the South threatened the whole balance of power in North America.

Within a year of the opening of the war this truth had been brought home to British North Americans with dramatic abruptness. As soon as the news of the fall of Fort Sumter reached England, it was decided to reinforce the North American garrisons, which had been rather dangerously reduced. This was simply a precautionary measure, the result of no crisis; but before the year was out a real threat of war between the United States and Great Britain suddenly appeared. On November 8, 1861, the captain of the U.S.S. *San Jacinto* stopped the British mail packet *Trent* en route to England and took from her by force two Confederate agents, Mason and Slidell. Over in London, in the wild haste of what looked to be certain war, they put together an expeditionary force of nearly fifteen thousand men for British North America; and that winter the reinforcements were carried in sleighs through the piled drifts of the Temiscouata Road overland from New Brunswick to Canada. Then the United States restored the arrested southern diplomats and the worst peril abruptly ended. But it had cost Great Britain nearly a million pounds to get the reinforcements to Canada, and nearly a million more to maintain her total forces in British North America during the financial year 1862-63. Thus the *Trent* crisis suddenly revealed the danger in which the American Civil War might involve British North America. It brought up, in a particularly acute and embarrassing form, the whole problem of imperial defence in the new world.

As the war continued, it became obvious that even though the threat of actual invasion might be postponed, the end of friendly economic relationship was almost certain. In Washington, the war brought about the triumph of the men who stood for large-scale manufacture, transcontinental railways, and western exploitation; and they proceeded to work out the North American variant of the new economic national-ism. Even before the war, opposition to the Reciprocity Treaty had been growing among American manufacturers, and the new Republican Party had declared for a protective tariff. The war silenced the old southern defence of inter-national trade and low tariffs; and it gave the new national policy of protection a double justification. It thrust forward the growth of American industry while at the same time it enormously increased the need for public revenue. With the excuse of the national financial emergency, the Morrill tariff was steadily increased; and the whole policy represented by the Reciprocity Treaty grew more and more out of date and discredited.

In addition, the North stood for a vigorous national ex-pansion. The withdrawal of the southern states removed the last checks and inhibitions from the northern strategy of western advance. In 1862, the Free Homestead Law was passed. The Union Pacific was chartered in 1862, the Northern Pacific in 1864. The use of these new techniques in western settlement seemed to threaten the encirclement and the penetration of the few British outposts in the plains and on the Pacific. There were steamships on the Red River now. The mails and even some of the Hudson's Bay Com-pany supplies were coming in from St. Paul; and the citizens of the new state of Minnesota began to show a great curiosity in the fate of the Red and Saskatchewan River districts. On the Pacific slope, where the gold rush in the Fraser valley had brought in some twenty thousand people in the two years from 1858 to 1860, it seemed as if the region would become American through the ease and completeness of its peaceful penetration. Sir James Douglas, the Governor of Vancouver Island, who in 1858 became governor of the newly created mainland province of British Columbia, fought to preserve

British rule against the picturesque California tradition of duels, lynchings, vigilante justice, and miners' self-government. But Vancouver Island and British Columbia were simply part of a long seaboard which was connected by American steamships, American express stages, and American commercial houses with the metropolitan centre of San Francisco. And in the depression which followed about 1865, when the brief mining boom collapsed and the population sank to roughly ten thousand people, it looked as if the region might find little reason and less zeal to defend its independence from the neighbouring states.

The ominous change which seemed to come over the United States during the Civil War strengthened every force in British North America which was making for national union. Up to this time, the northern provinces had done little more than exchange one kind of dependence for another. After 1846, they had sought trade privileges in the United States which would compensate for their vanished preferential markets in Great Britain. They had exchanged the warm shelter of the Old Colonial System for that of the Reciprocity Treaty. But here was a new United States, military in character, expansionist in spirit, and increasingly exclusive in its commercial policy. It looked as if the privileged connection with the Republic was doomed. It looked as if the provinces would soon be forced to take a new stand, to adopt a new policy, from a rapidly dwindling number of possibilities. And if they wished to survive in the new world, it was certain that they would have to rely far more upon themselves than ever before. Great Britain showed no intention of admitting them to the old privileges and covering them with the old protection. The American Civil War, far from rejoining the partly severed bonds between Great Britain and the colonies, helped to bring about the final break in the old imperial tie.

As early as July, 1861, before the Civil War had had time to exert any influence, a British parliamentary select committee had reported that it was 'desirable to concentrate the troops required for the defence of the United Kingdom as much as possible, and to trust mainly to naval supremacy for securing against foreign aggression the distant dependencies of the Empire.' In the *Trent* crisis Great Britain made a military re-entry of North America; and in the rush of imperialist sentiment which followed, the new principle of empire defence was forgotten for a moment. But in March, 1862, when the bills for the Canadian reinforcements came up, the House of Commons for the first time passed a resolution calling upon the colonies to take part in their own defence. If the colonies — and particularly the most exposed colony, Canada — had made at least a gesture in reply, Great Britain would probably have been satisfied. But in the summer of 1862, the Canadian legislature threw out the new militia bill, sponsored by the Macdonald-Cartier government, which would have devoted an annual expenditure of about a million dollars for defence.

There were two main reasons for this unexpected behaviour. In the first place, to the amazement and disgust of the British, the Canadians had not as yet become very excited over the alleged danger of the great new military machine which the North was building up. In the second place, they were convinced that if war did come, it would come as a result of a diplomatic duel between two rival imperialist powers, Great Britain and the United States, in which the Province of Canada would have little if any voice. In effect Canada seemed to imply that if Great Britain wanted large forces in North America in preparation for a war of her own choosing, she could very well afford to pay the biggest part of the bill herself. This attitude goaded many Britishers to fury; and in the summer of 1862, after the defeat of the militia bill, a certain number of English journalists and parliamentarians leaped upon the St. Lawrence colony for its spineless failure to accept its new responsibilities. 'My opinion is,' said Roebuck, member for Sheffield in the House of Commons, 'that the people of Canada have been led to believe that we consider them of such wonderful importance that we shall undertake any expense to maintain dominion over them. What I want them to understand, and what I want our Government to make them understand, is that we do not care one farthing about the adherence of Canada to England. . . . The only chance of benefit we ever expected from our colonies was perfect freedom of trade. What has Canada done in that matter? The Canadians have laid twenty per cent upon the introduction of all English manufactures into their country. . . . ' The American Civil War convinced these English manufacturers and free traders that the colonies were not merely a useless but also a perilous possession. From that moment the pressure in favour of Great Britain's final withdrawal from her military responsibilities in inland North America became stronger than ever.

If British North America was still a little unconcerned over the danger of American invasion, it was becoming more and more worried over the meaning of American expansion westward. As the frontier of American settlement and exploitation, speeded onward by the railways, moved inexorably across the continent, the concern for the future of the British north-west became at once more general and more urgent. 'The non-occupation of the North-West Territory,' declared George Brown's *Globe,* 'is a blot upon our character for enterprise. We are content to play drone while others are working. We settle down quietly within the petty limits of an insignificant province while a great empire is offered to our ambition. . . . If Canada acquires this territory it will rise in a few years from a position of a small and weak province to be the greatest colony any country has ever possessed, able to take its place among the empires of the earth. The wealth of four hundred thousand square miles of territory will flow through our waters and be gathered by our merchants, manufacturers, and agriculturists. Our sons will occupy the chief places of this vast territory, we will **form** its institutions, supply its rules, teach its schools, fill its stores, run its mills, navigate its streams. . . . We can beat the United States if we start at once. It is an empire we have in view and its whole export and import trade will be concentrated in the hands of Canadian merchants and manufacturers if we strike for it now.'

As the urge for a new land frontier began to develop into this robust imperialism, the supporters of western expansion became more numerous and more varied in character. The policy of a British North American west, which a few years ago had been urged chiefly by the journalists of Toronto and the Grit party of Canada West, now began to be taken up by the railway and commercial interests of Montreal. Up until after the middle of the century Montreal regarded the St. Lawrence as an international trade route whose sources of supply lay in the American middle west. Like the St. Lawrence canals, the Grand Trunk Railway was designed to compete with New York and the other American Atlantic ports for the trade in wheat and flour with the agricultural west; and like the St. Lawrence canals also, it failed to attract more than a modest share of the traffic. By 1860, it was obvious that the old design of the commercial empire of the St. Lawrence had failed as badly in the new age of steel and steam as it had in the old era of wood, wind, and water. The very completeness of the failure was registered in the chronic weakness of the Grand Trunk, which would have been bankrupt if it had not been for the mercy of its creditors. The old strategy had failed. But was there not a possible change of plan? Jn 1861, Edward Watkin, the new president of the Grand Trunk Railway Company, came out to Canada in a last effort to pull the property together. He reached, almost immediately, a revolutionary decision. He discovered that it was not retrenchment, but an enormous expansion, which could alone save the Grand Trunk. He came to believe in a transcontinental British North American railway which would be extended eastward to the Maritime ports of Halifax and Saint John and westward across the prairies to the Pacific.

In the meantime, while the railwaymen were developing a new interest in British North American transport, the manufacturers were winning a new and larger share of the British North American market. The Civil War gave an impetus to the trade carried on under the Reciprocity Treaty, though the impetus was smaller and came later than the northern provinces had at first expected. In the closing years of the war, agricultural produce from the Province of Canada moved in very large quantities across the boundary, and in 1864 the wooden shipbuilding industry of the Maritime Provinces reached its all-time peak of production. But, in addition to its influence on the old staple industries of the northern provinces, the American Civil War also affected their new industries based on steam and iron. 'I trust,' said James Watson, president of the Manufacturers' Association of Ontario, at a later period, 'I trust it will be borne in mind that the rapid development of manufacturing in this country during the past few years is almost entirely due to the peculiar position of the United States from the commencement of the late civil war.' Inevitably the war and the economic dislocation resulting from it focussed the manufacturing industry of the United States upon the home market. The import of dutiable articles into British North America declined rapidly as the war went on; and there were probably a good many Canadian manufacturers like Edward Gurney of the Gurney Stove Company, who declared in 1876 that his business had quadrupled since 1861 and that, in effect, it was the wartime rise in values in the United States which had given him the home market.

It seemed, in the early 1860's, that there was both greater need for union and more powerful support in its favour. Yet Galt's scheme for a general federation was not revived. Even the plans for complete interprovincial free trade and for intercolonial railways — which might have provided an

economic basis for future political union — always seemed
to end in failure. In 1862, the representatives of Nova
Scotia, fearful of competition from the more advanced Canadian manufactures, turned down the plan for a customs
union among the provinces; and in the following year,
Canada, on what seemed to the Maritime Provinces to be a
specious technicality, rejected an agreement to build the
Intercolonial Railway. So far as the west was concerned,
Canada was anxious eventually to secure possession of Rupert's Land and the North-West Territories, while Watkin
and the Grand Trunk Railway were now eager to obtain a
monopoly of western transport and communications. But
the negotiations between the province and the railway on
the one hand and the Hudson's Bay Company on the other —
with the imperial government as an intermediary benevo-
lently disposed to the Canadian interests — pursued an involved and mysterious course which never seemed to end in
anything definite and constructive.

In these depressing circumstances, which seemed to block
the hope of any general union, political or otherwise, the
alternative plan of regional unions was again revived. The
most ambitious of these projects was the scheme to unite the
three colonies of Nova Scotia, New Brunswick, and Prince
Edward Island into one province with a single legislature
and government. On the whole, the politicians, press, and
public of Nova Scotia and New Brunswick had shown merely
a languid interest in the scheme. Prince Edward Island in
particular was solidly opposed to it, since union would certainly mean the transference of the capital to the mainland
and the downfall of Charlottetown. The governors of the
Maritime Provinces, and particularly those of New Brunswick,
who looked upon Canada with a slightly jealous eye, supported Maritime Union, chiefly as an antidote to a general
federation of British North America. The Colonial Office
in London, though the time had long gone by when it would
take the initiative in such a matter, gave the project its pri-

vate benediction. Maritime Union was largely a product of British officialdom; and it is not very surprising that it made very slow progress in public favour. Not until the winter of 1864 did the three provinces agree to hold a joint conference to discuss the proposal. By midsummer of 1864 they had made only a few desultory preparations for it. The very place of meeting had not even been chosen, when the three governments were shocked to receive a most surprising communication from Canada. The Canadians requested not only the privilege of attending the conference but also the liberty of laying an alternative proposal before its delegates.

The fact was that the long-awaited crisis had at last arrived in the affairs of the distracted Province of Canada. On March 21, after less than a year of office, the new Reform administration resigned; and on June 14 the Conservative government which followed it was defeated in the House by two votes. It was obvious that what the province needed was not so much a new ministry which would repeat the short, uneasy career of its predecessors, as a new constitution which would give at least the hope of some governmental stability for the future. For ten days the representatives of the different parliamentary groups negotiated. On June 22, George Brown, with two other members representing the Reformers of Canada West, agreed to join with the Conservatives in a coalition government pledged to end the impasse in Canada through fundamental constitutional change. But what kind of constitutional change? Back in 1858 Galt had won the Conservatives over to the idea of a general federation of British North America. In 1859 Brown had persuaded the Reform Convention to adopt the plan of a federal union for Canada East and Canada West. Both these schemes found a place in the published platform of the new coalition government; but Brown's solution was put second and dependent upon the failure of the first. The design of a federation of all the provinces had triumphed.

In the end, it was a political crisis — a product of the basic sectionalism of the province — which had driven Canada to face the need of constitutional change. But once this fundamental decision had been reached, the province instinctively selected the plan of reorganization which seemed most in accordance with its own ambitious past and towards which all the circumstances of the present seemed to be driving it. The Maritime Provinces had begun a half-hearted investigation of regional union; Canada had gone off on a crusade for a general federation of all the provinces. Which of the two solutions would win?

On September 1, when the Provincial Secretary of Prince Edward Island, W. H. Pope, rowed out in a small boat across Charlottetown harbour 'with all the dignity he could' to meet the Canadian delegation which had come down in the government steamer *Queen Victoria,* the two union movements came into open competition. The Charlottetown conference had convened for the first time that morning. Samuel L. Tilley, member of an old Loyalist family, Prime Minister of New Brunswick and perhaps the best financial expert in the Maritimes, headed the delegation from his province. Charles Tupper, vigorous, downright, and aggressive, led a non-partisan Nova Scotian group, which significantly — and ominously — failed to include the veteran Joseph Howe. The Prince Edward Island government, with Colonel J. H. Gray as prime minister, had been placed in a somewhat awkward position as host to a conference of whose ostensible purpose it highly disapproved; and the Islanders' efforts at hospitality were still more seriously embarrassed by the fact that the Charlottetown hotels were jammed with people, who — with true British North American calm in the face of great events — had poured into the capital, not to watch the conference, but to go to a circus which had also just arrived.

The conference had barely assembled on the morning of September 1 when a telegram was handed in announcing the imminent arrival of the Canadians. The meeting at

Charlottetown had been called for the express purpose of considering a legislative union of the Maritime Provinces; but, on receipt of the telegram and with a rather significant readiness, the Maritime delegates decided to postpone consideration of their own project until after the Canadians had been heard. Maritime Union had never been a party issue or a political cause; and each Maritime delegation was a non-partisan group of rather puzzled Reformers and Conservatives. With all this the position of Canada was in almost complete contrast. The Canadian delegation to Charlottetown was composed of the chief members of the new Canadian cabinet, preaching a doctrine in which they believed their political salvation to lie, with all the fanaticism of converts. The Maritime Provinces held a few inconclusive meetings on their own regional union. But it was the Canadians who monopolized most of the secret sessions of the conference; and at the balls, dinners, and public meetings which were held as the delegates moved on from Charlottetown to visit Halifax, Saint John, and Fredericton, the talk was always of some grand general union of British North America. By September 16, the wandering delegates began to disperse; and oddly enough the main result of a conference which had been called to discuss Maritime Union was the decision to hold another formal conference at Quebec on October 10 for the purpose of considering a general federation of British North America.

Quebec was overclouded and dank with rain as the delegates began to arrive. In the main the company was the same as had assembled at Charlottetown a little over five weeks before; but for the first time there was a small deputation of two delegates from Newfoundland. All the sessions of the conference were held in a fairly new brick building, perched on the edge of the cliff overlooking the river, which had been built as a post office and which at that time housed the Canadian legislature pending its removal to the nearly completed buildings at Ottawa. North-eastward lay the

island of Orleans, where Cartier's men had gathered the ripe
fruits of autumn far back in 1535. South-westward was the
site of the old castle of Saint Louis, where the French governors had planned the seizure of the west, and beyond, the
Plains of Abraham, where their empire had been overthrown.
Through the tall windows of the second-storey room in which
the delegates sat, they could see the St. Lawrence — the River
of Canada — moving slowly through its broadening estuary
towards the sea. The rain drummed persistently on the windows; but nothing could destroy the overpowering effect of
that panorama. The rock was the beginning and end of
everything in Canada — the first outpost of expansion, the
last citadel of defence. Quebec had been the origin of the
empire of the St. Lawrence; it was to be the genesis of the
Dominion of Canada.

When sixteen days later the delegates left Quebec for a
tour of the upper part of the province, they had practically
finished the seventy-two resolutions, known ever since as the
Quebec Resolutions, which were intended to be the basis
of a federal union of the provinces. There was still a long
distance to go before an imperial statute based upon these
resolutions would unite the provinces together; but in that
tense and excited autumn and winter of 1864-65 it looked as
if every external force to which British North America was
subject was driving the provinces into union. As the American Civil War moved swiftly towards its conclusion, as Sher-
man cut his swath of desolation through Georgia from At-
lanta to the ocean, the United States found time and cause
to look abroad with irritation at neighbours whose opinions
and conduct had been annoying during the years of struggle.
The destruction wrought by the *Florida* and the *Alabama*
had already angered the Americans with Great Britain. Now
their attention was suddenly turned to British North
America, where a few ineffective efforts by Confederate
agents operating from the Canadian side had their climax in
a raid on St. Albans in Vermont. Suddenly the Congress and

the administration adopted a stiffer tone. Passports were required from British North Americans visiting the United States. A threat was made to repeal the laws permitting Canadians to import and export through the United States in bond; and notice was served that the United States would no longer consider itself bound by the Rush-Bagot agreement of 1817 limiting naval armaments on the Great Lakes. Finally, and, as it turned out, most serious of all, Congress decided, early in 1865, that the Reciprocity Treaty must come to an end.

The possibility of a war with the United States in which Canada might be invaded turned Great Britain back to the anxious consideration of her commitments in America. The United States was now a formidable military power, with an army which would soon be freed for new adventures; and Canada, so Lieutenant-Colonel Jervois had insisted in his report of 1864 to the War Office, could be defended only in part and with great difficulty. The 'Little Englanders' argued that the province was indefensible and that in any case Great Britain had no interest in it to safeguard except perhaps the military reputation of the British soldiers who had mistakenly been placed there. 'I cannot see,' wrote Richard Cobden realistically, 'what substantial interest the British people have in the connexion to compensate them for guaranteeing three or four millions of North Americans living in Canada, &c, against another community of Americans living in their neighbourhood.' The Manchester horror of giving something for nothing had not infected everybody; the great Manchester plan of letting the Empire go because Great Britain derived no military help nor obvious pecuniary advantage from it, had by no means led the Imperial Parliament into a declared policy of abandonment. In fact, in 1864 the Imperial Parliament reaffirmed its determination to defend any portion of the Empire which was attacked with all the resources at its command; and, on its part, the Canadian Parliament now began to honour its obligation of self-defence far more effectively than before. The situation had definitely improved since 1862; but behind the scenes the two governments continued to debate and argue over their joint military responsibilities in North America. Great Britain was, if possible, more determined than ever to escape from the burdens of administration and local defence in the northern colonies. The new colonial secretary, Edward Cardwell, was intensely interested in the problem of imperial defence. Seven years later, as secretary of war, he was to make his reputation as the man who reformed the British army, and 'called back the legions' from the colonies. Like so many Englishmen of his generation, he wished to see the British North American provinces stand on their own feet, and assume responsibility for all the British territories in the new continent. And now, as he read the dispatches announcing the results of the Quebec Conference, he saw how this could be achieved. The earlier plan of British North American union had been proposed merely by the Conservative party of the Province of Canada; but here was a federal scheme sponsored by a coalition Canadian government, and apparently accepted by all the other provinces in solemn conference. In the Quebec Resolutions, Cardwell could see the project of a state which might prove strong enough to relieve Great Britain of her responsibilities, and resistant enough to preserve the whole of British North America from annexation by the United States. He closed at once with this scheme of federal union. And from that time forward all the influence of the British government was used to push the plan to its conclusion, and all its diplomatic power was employed to protect the reorganization until it was complete.

Even so, even with all these powerful influences in its favour, the scheme was very nearly wrecked in the next few years. For a time it looked as if English-speaking Canada, and Canada West in particular, was practically alone in its support of Confederation. French-speaking Canada East was uncertain and divided, for undoubtedly it would have only

a minority, though a powerful minority, in the united legislature. But the strongest opposition of all came from the
Maritime Provinces, where geography and history had nour-
ished a spiritual separateness and an instinct for local autonomy. If Canada had a tradition of western empire which
fitted in well with the new age of great continental nationalities, the Maritime Provinces belonged to the old world
of wind-borne commerce, low tariffs, foreign trade, and local
freedoms. Though there were people in Nova Scotia and
New Brunswick who hoped that the Intercolonial Railway
might bring the traffic of a half-continent to the ports of
Halifax and Saint John, there were others, probably more
numerous, who continued to rely on the old trades of the
Atlantic Ocean, or looked forward to the prosperity which
they expected to follow from the extension of the Maritime
railways down to the United States. 'Look at the geographical position of this continent,' said one of the anti-confederates in Nova Scotia, 'and consider what seems to be the
most natural arrangement. We have thirty millions of people directly before us, in every way more convenient to us
than Canada; they are of the same stock, same feelings, as
ourselves. . . . I do not think that the people of Nova
Scotia want annexation to the United States, but why should
you drive them against their interests and inclinations into a
union with Canada — with which they have no natural
means of communication, and no sympathy?'

Confederation, to these Maritime anti-confederates, was an
unnatural union which would result in increased financial
burdens and a loss of local political power. Without exception, the anti-confederate orators expatiated on the size
of the Canadian debt and the height of the Canadian tariff.
Actually the difference between the two regions in respect of
public finance lessened rapidly as the Maritime governments got more deeply involved with railways; and, on the
eve of Confederation, the tariff of New Brunswick was probably the highest, by a small margin, in British North America.

In 1864-65, it was still possible to take up a very superior attitude to the Canadian tariff and to prophesy gloomily that the scale of Canadian taxation would likely provide the model for the new federation.   It was even easier to attack the Quebec scheme on the ground that it would reduce the local legislatures to complete insignificance and that Maritime representation in the Federal Parliament would be pitiably small.   'Our nationality,' said one journalist sadly, 'would be merged into that of Canada; we would be made use of by the Canadians, as were the Israelites of old by the Egyptians, to dig their canals.'

In the Canadian legislature, where the coalition government was in secure control, the Quebec Resolutions were accepted without change and by comfortable majorities. But the reaction in the Maritime Provinces threatened to sweep the whole scheme into the discard.   Prince Edward Island and Newfoundland rejected the Quebec Resolutions outright.   In Nova Scotia, where Joseph Howe was leading a crusade against acceptance with all the energy of his vigorous and slightly embittered nature, the Prime Minister, Tupper, did not even dare to put the resolutions to a vote in the lower house; and in New Brunswick, where Premier S. L. Tilley decided to risk an election in March of 1865, the anti-confederates, led by A. J. Smith, won a smashing victory at the polls.   Without New Brunswick — the watershed between the seaboard and the interior — the union was hopeless.   But might not this electoral decision be reversed?   The Canadians and the British — the two vitally interested parties — were still able to hope.   The Colonial Office began to use all the pressure at its disposal to induce the old Loyalist province to follow the wishes of the motherland.   The Canadian government was ready to spend its money lavishly in the lucky chance of a new election.

Fortune favoured them.   For the Smith government the obvious alternative to Confederation was the old regional scheme of closer railway and trade connections with the

United States; but in 1865-66 everything seemed to unite to make this impossible of realization. The Smith government was not able to push through the 'western extension' of the European and North American Railway to the American border; and in March, 1866, the Reciprocity Treaty came to an end. When Prime Minister Smith, along with other British North American leaders, journeyed down to Washington in the early winter of 1866 to see if the treaty could not be renewed, J. S. Morrill and the other protectionists of the Ways and Means Committee had only a very singular proposal to make to them. The Americans proposed that, in return for the inshore fisheries of British North America, the United States might agree to reciprocal free trade in five articles of national importance. These were rags, firewood, unwrought burr-millstones, unfinished grindstones, and unground gypsum or plaster. After this revelation of the new national exclusiveness, there was not much that the British-American delegates could do but go home. Evidently there was no hope of favourable trade relations with the post-bellum United States. Even the future of political relations looked uncertain. The Republic, it was true, had not followed up the threat it had made after the St. Albans raid; but the Fenians, who hoped to liberate Ireland by the somewhat circuitous route of conquering British North America, plotted invasions from the American side of the line and threatened to break the peace between the northern provinces and the United States.

The bottom had really been knocked out of the anti-confederate policy in New Brunswick. The Smith government grew weakened and divided. Finally the Prime Minister was manoeuvred into handing in his resignation. In the election which followed in the spring of 1866, Tilley was supported by Canadian funds and British moral pressure and the Confederationists routed their opponents badly. The union cause was suddenly set in motion again. The legislatures of Nova Scotia and New Brunswick never accepted the Quebec

Resolutions; but they appointed delegates to discuss a plan of union in co-operation with Great Britain and Canada. Late that autumn the representatives of the three provinces met in the Westminster Palace Hotel in London; and in the following March, the British North America Act, uniting Canada, Nova Scotia, and New Brunswick, passed the Imperial Parliament. By royal proclamation the Act was to come into force on July 1, 1867.

[*III*]

In large measure, the federation of British North America was a response to the revision of the Old Colonial System and the outbreak of the American Civil War; and like these two movements for national reorganization, it was essentially an experiment in the new nationality. Consciously, with a glad sense of release from the past, and an excited confidence in the future, the 'Fathers of Confederation' turned their backs on the pettiness and inferiority of provincialism and dependence. Every new constitution has to be launched with the champagne of rhetoric; but there was a sincerity in their grandiose prophecies which was the real mark of British North America's coming-of-age. The new nation was to have a half-continent as its homeland, a strong national government as its sovereign, and a new name and station in the world at large. Macdonald confidently expected that a 'healthy and cordial alliance' between Great Britain and Canada, as virtual equals, would soon take the place of the old imperial relationship. He spoke of 'founding a great British monarchy in connection with the British Empire'; and at London he and his colleagues fought hard for the title of the 'Kingdom of Canada.' This last ambition was thwarted, for the British were fearful that the title would annoy republican America. It was not the first nor the last time that Canada sacrificed her hopes on the altar of good relations between Great Britain and the United States. But this failure to secure the appropriate title should not obscure the scope of the original design. In its emphasis upon expansion, national unification, and independence, Canadian Confederation was a typical experiment in nineteenth-century nation-building.

The constitutional basis of the new experiment was the British North America Act of 1867. This statute was a characteristic product of the political experience of English-speaking peoples; but despite the popular impression to the contrary, it owed far more to the Constitution of Great Britain, and of the second British Empire, than it did to the Constitution of the United States. Naturally enough, the Fathers of Confederation were thoroughly familiar with the American federal system. They were prepared to defend it, up to a point, as another example of the federal principle; and John A. Macdonald went so far as to declare that the American Constitution was 'one of the most skilful works which human intelligence ever created.' But the prevailing note was one of criticism. In general British North Americans had little liking for the American presidency, which, as a solution of the problem of the executive, they regarded as distinctly inferior to their own system of responsible, or cabinet government. And they were deeply suspicious of the doctrine of 'States' Rights.' States' Rights, as one British American journalist put it, was 'the Guy Fawkes lurking under the federal building' that had caused the immense upheaval of the American Civil War.

These criticisms were simply expressions of the two fundamental constitutional preferences of British North America. One of these preferences, and indeed the most fundamental, had been determined a full generation before, in the long struggle which had ended with the defeat of the Canadian rebellions and in the adoption of responsible government. The American theory of a government limited by the prior existence of natural and inalienable rights, separated into executive, legislative, and judicial compartments, and organized in an elaborate system of checks and balances, had gone down in disgrace with Mackenzie and Papineau. The historic British conception of a sovereign parliament, as the basis and guarantee of a great unwritten constitutional heritage of administrative practice and individual liberties, had triumphed in the victories of Baldwin, Lafontaine, and Howe. The continuance of this system was the first desire of the Fathers of Confederation. The opening sentence of the British North America Act asserts that the northern provinces have expressed the desire to be federally united, 'with a constitution similar in principle to that of the United Kingdom.' This fundamental principle of parliamentary sovereignty and responsible government ensured that, at bottom, Canadian federalism must differ radically from American federalism, with its basis in a written constitution and its reliance on the interpretation of the courts.

The second major constitutional preference of British North America was against States' Rights and in favour of a strong central government. This choice, which was made deliberately and emphatically at the time of the Charlottetown and Quebec Conferences, showed the same reliance on British constitutional forms and practice. Outwardly it might have seemed that British North America, by adopting the federal principle and embodying it in a statute, the British North America Act, had in fact adopted a system similar in principle to that of the United States. But American federalism, despite its renown, was only one of a number of federalisms, ancient and modern; and, as a matter of fact, British North Americans did not have to look very far in either time or space before they discovered another rather informal federal system, with which they were all perfectly familiar and which they infinitely preferred to the American. This was, of course, the Old Colonial System of the second British Empire, with its sovereign Imperial Parliament and its dependent colonial legislatures. And from the Old Colonial System the political theory and the political ma-

chinery of the British North America Act were very largely
derived.

It was through the Old Colonial System that the new
Canadian federal system inherited a theoretical basis which
made a full-fledged theory of States' Rights completely impossible. The British North American provinces were not
independent states, but integral parts of the Empire. They
could not, as the London *Times* observed, 'delegate their
sovereign authority to a central government because they do
not possess the sovereign authority to delegate.' The new
Canada was not the result of a compact or treaty between
free and autonomous provinces; it was the creation of the Imperial Parliament, which, in accordance with the procedure
laid down already on previous occasions, was advised by the
proper authorities in the provinces, who had previously consulted among themselves. The long process of debate and
discussion which preceded the passing of the British North
America Act differed in both fact and theory from the
method used in the adoption of the American Constitution;
and of this truth the Fathers of Confederation themselves
were very well aware. 'At the time of the framing of their
constitution,' wrote J. H. Gray, a New Brunswick delegate
to the Quebec Conference, 'the United States were a con-
geries of independent States, which had been united for a
temporary purpose, but which recognized no paramount or
sovereign authority. The fountain of concession therefore
flowed upward from the several states to the united government. The Provinces, on the contrary, were not independent States; they still recognized a paramount and sovereign
authority, without whose consent and legislative sanction the
Union could not be framed. True without their assent their
rights would not be taken from them; but as they could not
part with them to other Provinces without the Sovereign
assent, the source from which those rights would pass to the
other Provinces when surrendered to the Imperial Government for the purposes of confederation, would be through

the supreme authority. Thus the fountain of concession would flow downward, and the rights not conceded to the separate Provinces would vest in the Federal Government, to which they were to be transferred by the paramount or sovereign authority.'

The federal system which had been born of the British Empire showed everywhere the plain marks of its origin. The Dominion was not only the creation, but also, in a large measure, the heir of the Imperial Parliament; and the provinces were expected to stand in much the same relation to the new federal authority as they had to the old imperial sovereign. 'The General Government,' said Macdonald, 'assumes towards the local governments precisely the same position as the Imperial Government holds with respect to each of the colonies now.' Everything was done to prepare the Dominion for its new and exalted station. The federal powers of taxation were unlimited. The federal legislature was given the name of 'parliament,' a proud title which no British colonial assembly had yet officially borne; and, perhaps even more important, the federal government was granted all the controls which the imperial government had exercised in the past over the colonies. The Dominion was to appoint the lieutenant-governors of the provinces. The lieutenant-governors, described officially as 'officers of the Dominion,' were empowered to reserve provincial legislation for Dominion approval on Dominion instructions. And even if a provincial bill had received the lieutenant-governor's assent and had become law, it was still possible for the federal government to disallow it. In no respect whatever was provincial jurisdiction to be absolute.

In its organization, as well as in its general position, the new federal government was the legitimate descendant of the Old Colonial System. Executive power was vested in the governor-general, who could act only on the advice of his constitutional advisers, the members of the cabinet, in accordance with the well known principles of responsible government. Legislative power was entrusted to a legislature of two houses, the Senate and the House of Commons; but there was no particular significance in this somewhat curious mingling of British and American terms. The House of Commons was based on the idea of representation by population, with Quebec (Canada East) being given a total permanent representation of sixty-five members and the other provinces in proportion according to population. As for the Canadian Senate, its only American feature was its name, which was Roman anyway. Its real direct ancestor was the British American legislative council, which had been established as far back as 1791. At the Quebec Conference, no delegation, and not even a single member, proposed that each province, irrespective of size and population, was to have the same number of representatives in the federal upper house. In the end, after much debate, a regional scheme was adopted by which twenty-four senators were allotted to the Maritime Provinces collectively, twenty-four to Quebec, and twenty-four to Ontario (Canada West). Moreover, these senators were not to be elected for a term of years either by the legislatures or the peoples of the different provinces. They were to be appointed by the federal government, and for life.

Everybody, both supporters and opponents of Confederation, expected that under the new system the provincial governments would have only a minor and subordinate rôle to play. In one of the drafts of the British North America Act the future lieutenant-governor was given the title of 'superintendent'; and throughout the discussion of the Quebec Resolutions, speakers persistently referred to the future provinces in municipal terms. In Macdonald's mind, one of the chief reasons for simplicity in the organization of the provincial legislature was that it would 'under the circumstances of the General Legislature, be more of the nature of a municipal than a legislative body.' Actually there was not much fundamental change in the structure of the provincial governments, for though Ontario was to have only a single-chamber legislature, Quebec, Nova Scotia, and New Brunswick each kept a legislative council as well as a house of assembly. The provinces, as Macdonald explained in the debate on the constitutions of Quebec and Ontario, were to be 'miniature responsible governments.' In exactly the same way as the federal cabinet, the executive councils of the lieutenant-governors were to be responsible to the provincial assemblies, 'according to the well-understood principle of the British Constitution.' Financially, the provinces were restricted to direct taxation, which in British North America at that time meant taxes on real estate; and such was the general reluctance to impose direct taxation that a scheme of unconditional subsidies, paid by the Dominion to the provinces, had to be written into the British North America Act.

In the distribution of legislative powers between the provinces and the future Dominion, the Fathers of Confederation showed equally clearly their deliberate rejection of American principles and their deliberate preference for a strong central authority comparable to the sovereign Imperial Parliament. There could be no theory of provincial sovereignty in the Old Colonial System; there was to be no legislative basis for the doctrine of States' Rights in the new confederation. At Quebec the delegates unanimously resolved that general or residuary powers were to lie, not with the local, but with the general legislature. The provinces were given the power to deal with a specified number of local matters; and the Dominion was authorized to legislate on the vast residue of questions of common interest to the whole nation. For greater certainty, but not so as to restrict the generality of this grant, the residuary authority — these 'high functions and almost sovereign powers,' as Lord Carnarvon called them in the House of Lords — were illustrated by a long list of specific examples. 'We have strengthened the General Government,' said Macdonald. 'We have given the General Legislature all the great subjects of legislation. We have conferred on them, not only specifically and in detail, all the powers which are incident to sovereignty, but we have expressly declared that all subjects of general interest not distinctly and exclusively conferred upon the local governments and local legislatures, shall be conferred upon the General Government and Legislature. . . . This is precisely the provision which is wanting in the Constitution of the United States. It is here that we find the weakness of the American system — the point where the American Constitution breaks down. It is in itself a wise and necessary provision. We thereby strengthen the Central Parliament and make the Confederation one people and one government, instead of five peoples and five governments, with merely a point of authority connecting us to a limited and insufficient extent.'

Yet, though the new nation was intended to be strongly unified, it was none the less based upon a cultural diversity. There were two main ethnic groups in the Dominion — French and English; there was a great variety of religions; and any attempt ever made to assimilate these minorities had been given up long before 1867. The Fathers of Confederation accepted the principle that a limited number of safeguarding clauses should be put into the British North America Act to protect minority rights without sacrificing national unity. The Protestant and Roman Catholic religions were given certain guarantees in respect of separate or sectarian schools. The English and French languages were both to be used in the acts and official records of the Parliament of Canada and the legislature of Quebec; and either language might be employed in the debates of these bodies or in pleading before the courts of Quebec or the Dominion. Finally, the civil code of Quebec was protected from alteration except at the hands of the provincial legislature. The scope of these guarantees should not be exaggerated; but, at the same time, they were important principles of national unity. The new nation was to be based on a broad spirit of cultural tolerance and goodwill. 'We were of different races,' said Cartier, 'not for the purpose of warring against each other, but in order to compete and emulate for the general welfare.'

[*IV*]

On the first Dominion Day, July 1, 1867, the new North American federal union began its official existence. Its authors had already accomplished much; but, in a very real sense, the largest part of their programme still awaited completion. Only a portion of British North American territory had as yet been included in the new union. In the east Newfoundland and Prince Edward Island still held aloof; and, even more important, the whole future of Rupert's Land, the North-West Territories, and British Columbia was still uncertain. The absence of Prince Edward Island would have been a serious disadvantage in framing a policy for the fisheries; but the failure to include the west would have completely frustrated the expansionist urge which was one of the main propelling motives back of Confederation. Could the Dominion realize these ultimate objectives? Would it be permitted to do so? In 1867 it still seemed that the new nationality was still in jeopardy — that its expansion was problematical, even if its very existence was not endangered.

It was a time when liberals and democrats everywhere were in raptures over the new small nationalities of Europe. But Canada started off on its career without arousing the slightest enthusiasm or winning more than perfunctory goodwill. The attitude of even Great Britain and the United States, the two English-speaking countries with which the provinces had always been most closely associated, was an attitude of complete indifference, qualified on the one side by a bored sense of obligation and on the other by an unmistakable feeling of hostility. When the debate on the British North America Act was on, the English Parliament could scarcely conceal its excruciating boredom; and when the ordeal was over, it turned with great relief to a really national problem — the English dog tax. In one of his occasional sardonic comments, Macdonald declared that English officials treated the Canadian union 'as if the B. N. A. Act were a private Bill uniting two or three English parishes.' As for American legislatures and American politicians, their most frequently expressed opinions were those of suspicious hostility. What might be called the official greeting of the Congress of the United States to its new northern neighbour was expressed in a resolution passed after brief debate in the special session of 1867. The resolution asserted that the people of the United States regarded with great anxiety the proposal to form a British-American confederation on a monarchical basis, since the new union would be in contradiction to the frequently expressed principles of the United States, antagonistic to its interests, and calculated to perpetuate and increase existing embarrassments.

The conclusion of the Civil War, which released all the pent-up expansive forces in the United States, had inevitably intensified its imperialism. The subjugation of the defeated South was accompanied by a vigorous campaign for the annexation of the still independent North. The heart and centre of this movement was a small group of vociferous Radical Republicans — Zachariah Chandler, N. P. Banks, Charles Sumner, Benjamin F. Butler, and others; but the urge for the acquisition of British North America had its supporters in the administration itself as well as in Congress. In the summer of 1867, W. H. Seward publicly affirmed his belief that Nature had intended that the whole continent should come 'within the magic circle of the American Union'; and even President Johnson, in his last annual message, alluded vaguely to the prospect of the acquisition of 'adjacent communities.' The new President, Ulysses S. Grant, was more determined and outspoken in his desire to acquire Canada; and his secretary of state, Hamilton Fish, brought the matter up on several occasions in discussion with the British minister at Washington. The purchase of Alaska had aroused an acquisitive interest in the north Pacific coast; the economic dependence of Red River on St. Paul had awakened a strong annexation sentiment in Minnesota. The threat to the Canadian west was most serious; but over the whole of British North America hung the enormous danger of the *Alabama* claims, which, in the minds of many influential Americans, including that of the new President, might be liquidated best by the cession of the new Dominion.

The race for the Pacific, the rush to include the domains of the Hudson's Bay Company within the new nation, was the most urgent task which faced the government of Canada. It was attacked immediately. In 1869 an agreement was concluded whereby the Hudson's Bay Company consented to cede to the crown its territorial rights in return for a compensation of three hundred thousand pounds, to be provided by Canada; and this chartered territory, known as Rupert's Land, together with the North-West Territories over which the company had held the monopoly of trade, were to be transferred by Great Britain to the Dominion. Canada decided that the whole region was to be administered by a lieutenant-governor with an appointed council; and early in the autumn of 1869, William McDougall, one of the Grits who, with George Brown, had taken an active part in the campaign for the acquisition of the west, departed for his new government by way of the United States. He never reached his destination. He was stopped at the border by the agents of a 'provisional government' which had just been set up in the Red River settlement. The first attempt of Canada to forestall the United States and to grasp the British-American west had opened with a rebellion.

The resistance at Red River was one of the last episodes in the retreat of the fur trade before the advance of agricultural settlement. The Red River colony was a typical fur-trade colony; and, though it had developed and progressed, it still bore the plain marks of its origin. In 1869, its population was composed of Hudson's Bay Company officers, English, Canadian, and American traders, Scots and English settlers, and English and French half-breeds. The French half-breeds, the Métis, who hunted the buffalo, fought the Sioux Indians, and freighted goods for the Hudson's Bay Company, were the most politically conscious and effectively organized part of the community. They had a defiant sense of their own identity as a 'peculiar people' — a 'new nation'; and they and their clergy, the French missionary priests, were convinced that the distinctive Métis way of life would be threatened by the coming of a great mass of Protestant, English-speaking immigrants. The advance guard of the Canadians — merchants and civil servants — did not quiet these fears; and neither the British government nor the Hudson's Bay Company made any effort to explain Canada's good intentions and prepare the way for the transfer. A large part of the Red River community was either indifferent or unsympathetic to union with Canada. But it was the Métis who began the resistance and provided its leader, Louis Riel.

Riel was a clever but unstable and dictatorial man, who had a real skill in organizing resistance and a sure sense of vital political objectives. The Métis seized control of the colony; a provisional government was founded; and a convention of French and English settlers decided upon terms of union with Canada and elected delegates to represent their views at Ottawa. The Canadian government was anxious to meet the wishes of the Red River community as a whole; but Riel, the president of the provisional government, and his clerical advisers, were determined, above all, to secure corporate privileges for the Métis. The list of 'rights', which the convention had accepted, was deliberately altered in the special interests of the French, before it was presented at Ottawa. Riel could be arbitrary. He was also quite prepared to use violence. He permitted the execution of Thomas Scott, a young Irish Canadian, who had dared to question the authority of the provisional government.

In the meantime the federal government was troubled by both embarrassment and fear. It had to please Quebec, which sympathized with the French-speaking Métis. It had to satisfy Ontario, which clamoured for the blood of the murderers of Scott. Above all, it had, with all possible speed, to stop the trouble and complete the transfer of the territory to Canadian jurisdiction. The policy which it wisely adopted combined the reality of conciliation with a show of force. The British government had announced that the imperial troops would be withdrawn from inland Canada in 1870. But it was persuaded to make one last gesture for imperial solidarity; and in the summer of 1870 Colonel Garnet Wolseley led a mixed force of British Regulars and Canadian militia out to Red River. Its purpose, of course, was not to attack the settlement, but to take control of the situation, and to prove to the world in general, and the United States in particular, that the whole British Empire was back of the Canadian acquisition of the British American north-west. In the meantime the federal cabinet had received the representatives from the Red River settlement; and in 1870, while it was still essentially a fur-trade colony, the district was made into the Province of Manitoba. In the new province, the French and English languages were to be officially equal; and Protestants and Roman Catholics were to have separate schools. All this seemed to imply that the Métis were to continue as a major part of the population. But, by another clause of the Manitoba Act, the natural resources of the province were transferred to the Dominion. And the Dominion planned to use the land of the prairies to support the railway and to attract the immigration which would bring the old primitive culture of Red River to an end.

After Rupert's Land and the North-West Territories had been united with Canada, the one vulnerable region still remaining outside Confederation was the Pacific slope. Since the collapse of the gold rush, the whole district had been in economic and financial difficulties. It was politically immature as well, for it had not yet won responsible government and its legislature was only partly elective. In 1866, with the idea of reducing costs and effecting economies, the mainland and Vancouver Island had been united in the Province of British Columbia. But the financial weakness and the isolation of the colony continued; and apart from Confederation there did not seem to be any really promising avenue of escape. A petition prepared towards the close of 1869, which requested the annexation of the province to the United States, was signed by only one hundred and four people, among whom were a curiously large number of Germans and Jews; and for the great mass of the roughly ten thousand inhabitants of the province, even including its most stubborn anti-confederationists, union with the American republic never seemed in the least a desirable solution. The Governor, the official clique, the Hudson's Bay Company officials and their friends, undoubtedly would have preferred to keep the province as a separate dependency of the crown; and for a while the Colonial Office in Great Britain appeared to think that the time was not yet ripe for a change in its status. But the strongest popular movement in the province was in favour of union with Canada; and when Governor Seymour died in the summer of 1869 and when, above all, the approaching transfer of the Hudson's Bay Company's territories to Canada ensured that the whole north-west was to belong to the new Dominion, the British government hesitated no longer and threw the whole weight of its influence in favour of British Columbia's immediate entrance into Confederation. In 1870 delegates from the province journeyed to Ottawa to discuss the terms of union with the federal government; and the Dominion made its famous promise to begin a railway to the Pacific in two years and to complete it in ten. In July, 1871, British Columbia — granted at

length a fully elective assembly and responsible government
— entered Canadian Confederation.

From its inception the federal movement in British North
America had been influenced and hurried forward by the
pressure from Great Britain and the United States. On the
one hand was the American urge towards annexation; on the
other was the British desire for withdrawal from North
American commitments. The danger had always been that
these two factors, which had helped to persuade British
North America to unite, would destroy British North American union before it was completed. By the end of 1870 that
danger was really over. American jingoism reached its climax in 1870; but no formal move was made to annex the
north. British troops left central Canada in 1871; but not
before the survival of the Dominion as a continental power
had been pretty thoroughly assured. At every stage in the
movement towards Confederation, at every stage in the expansion of Canada, Great Britain had given her help, political and military; and all the while she had repelled every
American suggestion that British North America should be
abandoned either to smooth the way towards an Anglo-
American agreement or even to liquidate the *Alabama* claims
themselves. When Secretary of State Fish suggested that
Great Britain should 'withdraw entirely from Canada,' Sir
Edward Thornton, the British minister to Washington,
shook his head. 'Oh,' he replied, 'you know that we cannot
withdraw. The Canadians find great fault with me for say-
ing as openly as I do that we are ready to let them go whenever they wish, and declare they do not desire it.' To the
Radical Republicans, and even to President Grant and his
cabinet, Canada apparently seemed like so much territory
which could be handed over in compensation for alleged
wrongs with complete disregard for the wishes of its population. But though many influential Englishmen believed
that the imperial tie would likely snap in the near future,
they were very well aware that the overwhelming bulk of

Canadians still wished to see it maintained. In the meantime, while Great Britain refused to be drawn by American offers, Canada was being extended to the Pacific with resolute speed. And finally, in the autumn of 1870, Secretary Fish himself reached the unwelcome conclusion that Great Britain would not abandon Canada and that there was little prospect of getting half a continent for the *Alabama* claims.

A sudden relaxation of the diplomatic tension immediately followed. The powers established the Anglo-American Joint High Commission, and the resulting Treaty of Washington of 1871 settled the outstanding disagreements which had arisen since the opening of the Civil War between the United States, Great Britain, and British North America. In recognition of Canada's new status in the British Empire, her prime minister, Sir John Macdonald — he had been knighted at Confederation — was made a member of the British commission to Washington. His part was a thankless one. Canada had to weigh the vital benefit of peace between Great Britain and the United States against the sacrifices she might be called upon to make for it. She was a small power faced by two very great powers who were determined to make a settlement in part at her expense; and like other small powers in a similar situation she soon became the nuisance of the conference in her frantic efforts to escape becoming a burnt offering on the altar of Anglo-American friendship. Sir John went down to the conference with the hope of winning a trade agreement which would resemble the Reciprocity Treaty of 1854. His two main bargaining assets were the navigation of the St. Lawrence River and the Atlantic inshore fisheries. But the British commissioners had no particular pride of ownership in those properties and the Americans had the bargainer's instinct for depreciating their value. In the end the free navigation of the St. Lawrence was conceded for ever in return for similar privileges on three remote Alaskan streams. The inshore fisheries were handed over for a period of years in exchange for the American fisheries north of the thirty-ninth parallel, the free entrance of Canadian fish and fish-oil into the American market, and the hope of obtaining a money payment in addition, if a commission of arbitration decided that the value of Canadian fisheries was greater than that of the American. The *Alabama* claims, resulting from British breaches of neutrality during the American Civil War, were to be submitted to arbitration; but as for American breaches of neutrality at the time of the Fenian raids on Canada, the United States bluntly refused to discuss compensation on the technical ground that the matter had not been mentioned in the original agenda of the Joint Commission.

While in the United States the Treaty of Washington was regarded with general complacency, in Canada it was the object of bitter attack. Yet, in its own rather grudging fashion, the treaty was in effect a recognition of Canada as a North American nation of transcontinental extent. The new nationality had been born in the shadow of British indifference and American hostility — in the danger of Anglo-American misunderstanding. At a time when Great Britain was anxious to reduce her American commitments and when the United States was just emerging from a great civil war, the Fathers of Confederation had risked a complete reorganization of British North America. In 1871 their new Dominion extended to the Pacific. In 1873, with the entrance of Prince Edward Island, it included all the Atlantic provinces except Newfoundland. Great Britain had supported, and the United States accepted, these changes. And the Treaty of Washington ended all important differences between the English-speaking peoples without seriously affecting the new nation which had been founded among them.

CHAPTER SEVEN

THE STRUGGLE FOR
NATIONAL UNITY

[*I*]

IN 1873, when Prince Edward Island entered Confederation, the physical structure of the Dominion was complete. *A mari usque ad mare* — the heraldic device of the new federal union had been justified within six years of its foundation. It was a not unimpressive beginning; but, at the same time, most people were conscious of the enormous task which lay ahead. The half-continent which had fallen to the new nation was occupied by a population of four million people, separated into larger or smaller groups by vast distances of unsettled territory, and divided in religion, cultural heritage, and economic interests. The elements of nationhood were there, the urge towards nationality existed, the demand for a new position in the world could not be denied; but in 1873, the national objectives were still a little vague and the national policies were as yet undetermined. 'We are engaged in a very difficult task,' said Edward Blake, the rising hope of the Reform party, in his speech at Aurora, Ontario, in 1874 — 'the task of welding together seven Provinces which have been accustomed to regard themselves as isolated from each other, which are full of petty jealousies, their Provincial questions, their local interests. How are we to accomplish our work? How are we to effect a real union between these Provinces?'

This search for the national policies which would produce the true Canadian nationality was to occupy the last quarter of the nineteenth century. In one form or another, the search lasted a long time; but it was never keener or more daring than in the early 1870's. Spurred on by the fact of Confederation itself, by the withdrawal of the imperial troops, and by the apparent sacrifice of British American interests at the Treaty of Washington, the Canadians set out to explore all the numerous problems which related to their national organization and their international status. It was an intellectual quest in which many people participated, which took many forms; but perhaps the movement known as 'Canada First' was its purest and most disinterested, as well as its most naïve, expression. Canada First was formed in the early 1870's by a group of young Toronto business and professional men. Its object was to unite Canadians on a lofty plane of non-partisan loyalty for their country; and it went in for a cultivated literary propaganda which was characterized by an irrepressible youthful urge towards poetry and prophecy. The first leader of the movement, W. A. Foster, was an able lawyer with literary ambitions and a taste for some of the more blowzy flowers of nineteenth-century rhetoric; and Charles Mair, the poet, was also a member of the group. Mair's verses were highly uneven, full of his own lapses of taste and the echoes of other people's successes; but he was one of the first to interpret the Canadian scene and, at its best, his poetry shows an acute and sensitive awareness of its beauty. Foster made an even more direct contribution to the movement by writing what in effect became the party's manifesto. In 1871 he published a pamphlet called 'Canada First; or Our New Nationality.' 'As between the various Provinces comprising the Dominion,' wrote Foster, 'we need some cement more binding than geographical contact; some bond more uniting than a shiftless expediency; some lodestar more potent than a mere community of profit. . . .' He and the young men who followed him believed fervently in 'the cultivation of a Canadian national sentiment.' They exalted the unifying force of Canadian nationality; and it was, perhaps, too much to ask them to describe its characteristics and to indicate how it could be cultivated. At this stage, they simply represented the naïve, confused, and urgent aspiration towards national unity.

At first sight, it might have seemed difficult to discover anybody more remote from these youthful ideals, more incapable of realizing them, than the Prime Minister and leader of the Conservative party, Sir John Alexander Macdonald. Macdonald had no particular objection to 'community of profit'; he had been known to practise 'shiftless expediency.' There was no doubt that Canada First highly disapproved of him. And yet, though he seemed such an unlikely champion for a crusade, the story of Canadian nationality seemed to write itself around him from the start. In 1873 he was still two years short of sixty; but already he was enveloped in the mysterious prestige of the elder statesman. The enormous nose, the hair curling thickly over the ears, the faintly Disraelian cast of countenance, were the picturesque features of innumerable cartoons. There was about him an air of jaunty distinction, an air of assured, casual, and friendly expertness. In the alien atmosphere of the nineteenth century he seemed to evoke a ghost of the old eighteenth-century idea that government was a craft which could be practised best by gentlemen amateurs. Unphilosophical, intensely practical in his shrewd, rather indolent fashion, he brought a broad humanity to his basic assumption that politics was simply the art of the possible in the management of living men. He knew the Canadians as nobody has ever known them since. He met them in crowded hotels and committee rooms, in the long, lamplit winter sessions of the House of Commons, on the interminable train rides from Rivière du Loup to Sarnia, and out in country fairgrounds and shaded picnic places where the farm people used to congregate on long summer afternoons to hear him speak. He knew all the faces. He threaded his way through the intricacies of Canadian politics like a man crossing a room which is crowded with his friends. Sceptical, tolerant, easy-going, the suave contriver of compromises and reconciliations, the 'Old Tomorrow' of innumerable and notorious postponements, he seemed almost to practise opportunism as an art for its own sake. Yet in him there existed certain ultimate objectives, certain subterranean loyalties, which in the end gave to his career a marked character of unity and design. He was not a political philosopher but a nation-builder. His work was essentially a great effort in economic and political nationalism.

In a sense the first task was to build a party. Macdonald had his programme ready; but to carry it out he needed political power, and to keep political power he needed a national party organization. The nucleus of this national party organization was, of course, ready. It was simply the Liberal-Conservative party of the old Province of Canada, which had already proved its marvellous capacity to assimilate the repugnant and to reconcile the irreconcilable. With apparent ease the party which Macdonald had founded back in 1854 had united the *habitants* of rural French Canada with the great railway and business interests of the cities. It had linked — and this had been its most tremendous achievement in reconciliation — the Orange Order of Canada West with the Roman Catholic hierarchy of Canada East. In the politics of Confederation, these two central Canadian forces, the railway and business interests on the one hand, and the Roman Catholic Church on the other, were to prove two of the strongest factors in the maintenance of Macdonald's power.

The Roman Catholic Church of French Canada had an old tradition of illiberality and Ultramontanism. And when Pius IX, estranged by the Revolution of 1848, began the attack on European liberalism, there were prelates in Canada

— such as Bishop Bourget of Montreal and Bishop Laflèche of Three Rivers — who resumed with pleasure the old and congenial crusade. Confirmed in their most obscurantist prejudices by the publication of Pius IX's *Syllabus of Errors* in 1864 and immensely uplifted by the declaration of papal infallibility in 1870, they moved deliberately forward to complete the wreck of the *Rouge* party and the *Institut Canadien,* which provided the only opposition in Quebec to Macdonald's Conservative machine. The *Rouges* had incurred clerical displeasure by criticizing religious orders and by supporting non-sectarian state education. The *Institut* had erred even more deplorably. It had admitted Protestants and English Canadians to its ranks. It had included a few Protestant and sceptical volumes in its library. With great temerity it had debated such dangerous questions as 'Can the establishment of a large number of monastic houses contribute to the progress of a country?' Could conduct such as this, so tainted with the vicious principles of reason and tolerance, so unhappily reminiscent of the worst excesses of the French Revolution, be tolerated in a Christian community?

Evidently there could be only one answer to this question. Bishop Bourget, having exhausted his own powers of intimidation, turned to the arsenal in Rome. In 1869 most satisfactory papal thunderbolts were launched against the *Institut*: and the bishop was able to announce that the Sacraments would be forbidden to its members. In the same year, Joseph Guibord, a devout Roman Catholic and one of the surviving members of the *Institut,* died suddenly of a paralytic stroke, without the last rites of the church; and the clergy duly refused to permit him to be buried in the consecrated ground of a Roman Catholic cemetery. The *Institut,* which was close to death itself, determined to exhaust its last ounce of strength in the defence of Guibord's civil right to Christian burial in his own church; and while the remains were given a temporary resting-place in a Protestant vault, the society fought the case from court to court until, in the Judicial Committee of the Privy Council, it secured a last favourable decision. This pronouncement by the highest civil authority in the land might seem to have settled the matter; but a part at least of the Roman Catholic population of Montreal refused to take this lax view of the situation. The hearse was stoned away from the cemetery on the first attempt to bury Guibord; and when, on a rainy November day of 1875, his body was at last lowered into the earth of the Côte des Neiges cemetery, a mixture of cement and scrap-metal was carefully poured over the coffin. This was intended to protect the remains from the physical violence of the Roman Catholic laity; but naturally it was no defence against the ghostly powers of the priests. By a special and somewhat unusual clerical operation, Bishop Bourget deconsecrated the patch of ground in which Guibord lay. And the church thus snatched victory out of the very jaws of defeat.

'The *rouge* party and the *Institut*,' declared the newspaper *La Minerve* triumphantly, 'have dug their own grave in digging that of Guibord.' It was only too true. The *Institut* did not long survive its final victory; and the old *Parti Rouge* soon followed it into oblivion. Brandishing their spiritual weapons, the clergy openly pursued the fleeing *Rouges* into the mundane world of politics. To vote for a Liberal or Reform candidate, many priests assured their parishioners, was undoubtedly a sin. The only question was as to the extent of its gravity. Some priests conceded that a Liberal vote was merely a serious fault; others insisted that it was a mortal sin. 'Si tu veux aller en enfer,' one curé is alleged to have said to a parishioner, 'tu as une belle chance. Vas voter du côté des libéraux.' In the Quebec bye-elections of 1876, these persuasive methods helped to secure handsome majorities for the Conservative or *Bleu* candidates. The few surviving *Rouges* were so terrorized that for some time they hesitated to seek the redress which the law now provided;

and even when they took the matter to the courts and the courts disallowed several elections on the simple grounds of undue clerical influence, they were still not satisfied. The fires of Gallicanism had been pretty effectively smothered in them. The decision of the civil power was not now sufficient. What they wanted was the favourable verdict of Rome. In the end Rome tolerantly explained that the prohibition of Catholic liberalism did not necessarily extend to Liberal political parties. Possibly clerical influence declined after the general election of 1878. Possibly it merely became a little less open and flagrant. But, at all events, the hold of the *Bleus* and of Sir John Macdonald on Quebec remained unbroken.

A party which could retain the energetic assistance of the Roman Catholic clergy at Quebec without losing the warm support of the Orange Order of Ontario was surely an organization endowed with almost magical powers of reconciliation. In the first few years after Confederation, Macdonald applied this method of balancing interests, of reconciling loyalties, which had succeeded so well in central Canada, to the task of building up a continental Liberal-Conservative party. 'How are we to effect a real union between these Provinces?' asked Edward Blake virtuously. 'Can we do it by giving a sop now to one, now to another? . . . ' Sir John might have replied that the method was certainly not a cure-all; but that, within limits, he found it to be extremely effective. He gave Nova Scotia a larger subsidy in 1869, in open violation of the 'final and unalterable' financial terms of the union. He granted the new western provinces more parliamentary members than they were entitled to, in complete disregard for the principle of representation by population. Manitoba was given special guarantees for its French and Roman Catholic minority. British Columbia was promised a railway in ten years. This ingrained bargaining habit, this deplorable disposition 'to buy love and purchase peace,' as Edward Blake called it, resulted in the Dominion of Can-

ada and in its first principal by-product, the national Conservative party.

Macdonald had to create a party. It was his first task —
there were, no doubt, many times when he was driven to regard it as his most important task. But it was far from
being all he wanted to do. Once he had accepted the scheme
of Confederation, he had tried to make it the vehicle of all
his political ideas, and the instrument of all his political
ambitions. In the Quebec and London Conferences, he had
laid the basis for a strong, centralized, and expansive Canada;
and now, in the years which followed Confederation, he committed his party and his country to all the basic national
policies, political and economic. For him, the one fact of
overwhelming importance in Confederation was Canada, the
new nation, with its new federal government. He saw it, in
external affairs, as a virtually autonomous power in friendly
relation to Great Britain. He conceived of it, in domestic
matters, as a paramount authority surrounded by subordinate and semi-municipal provinces. According to his official
opinion, the lieutenant-governor of a province, far from
being a separate representative of the crown, was an 'officer
of the Dominion' charged with the protection of federal interests. On federal instructions, the lieutenant-governor
could reserve provincial bills for the signification of the
pleasure of the federal government; and if, despite his vig-
ilance, unacceptable measures were made into provincial
statutes, these could be disallowed by the federal government on the recommendation of its minister of justice. In
Macdonald's considered opinion, disallowance was proper
and desirable, not only if the acts in question were *ultra vires*
of the provinces, but also if they conflicted with federal interests, or if they violated those principles of equity and
natural justice which were embodied in the unwritten constitution of Great Britain and her colonies. Macdonald was
determined to maintain federal supervision over the activities of the provinces; but he was equally determined to pre-

vent provincial interference in the affairs of Canada. In all the early amendments to the British North America Act, the Parliament of Canada, through a joint resolution of the Senate and the House of Commons, requested legislation by the Imperial Parliament; and the few feeble efforts of the Reformers to insist that amendments required the unanimous or practically unanimous consent of the provinces were unceremoniously disregarded.

Only less important than those constitutional usages were the economic policies designed to enlarge and integrate the Dominion; and here again, in the first few years after Confederation, the Conservatives under Macdonald began to work out an aggressive policy of economic nationalism which attracted some of the strongest interests in the country. The Quebec Resolutions foreshadowed western expansion and transcontinental railways; the abrogation of the Reciprocity Treaty necessitated a new commercial policy. But the plans for western settlement and railways were still vague and the hope for a positive trade policy still more indefinite. In 1866, the year before Confederation, the Province of Canada had carried out a final reduction of its tariff as a gesture of goodwill and assurance to the tax-frightened Maritime Provinces; and for the first few years after 1867, the new Dominion customs duties were a moderate compromise between the old Galt tariff and that of Nova Scotia. Evidently people placed their hopes not so much upon the development of industry as upon the growth of general commerce within the free-trade area of four million people which Confederation would create. But railways, as Galt had shown, were inextricably linked with fiscal policy, which in turn was linked with industrialism. And large-scale industry, helped on by the stimulus of the American Civil War, made rapid progress in the years from 1860 to 1872.

In Canada the Liberal-Conservative party was the first to become aware of this portentous change. Sir John found the Canadian manufacturer where Galt and Cayley had left him; and he discovered the **Canadian** workingman for the first time. At first the Conservatives did little more than appropriate the magical name of 'National Policy.' 'The time may soon come,' said Finance Minister Rose in 1869, 'when we may require to have a national policy of our own, no matter whether that national policy may sin against this or that theory of political economy.' This looked impressive and vaguely threatening, but sounded a little hollow. The very next year the Conservatives proceeded to put a little content into their empty but resounding phrase by linking the 'National Policy' with a slight but definite increase in the tariff. It was not a particularly successful venture, for next year, when the Prime Minister was away in Washington, the new duties were repealed. But early in 1872 Sir John made one of his periodic visits of personal reconnaissance to the 'west' — by which he meant Ontario from Toronto to Sarnia. His nose, that large, sensitive, and unerring organ, detected the unmistakable sniff of a fresh growth of protectionist sentiment; and to his astonished and sceptical intimates he explained that it was time to bring out the National Policy once more. 'It is really astonishing,' he wrote to George Stephen, the future president of the Canadian Pacific Railway, early in 1872, 'the feeling that has grown up in the west in favour of the encouragement of home manufactures. I am sure to be able to make considerable capital out of this next summer.'

Before that time came Sir John had made his second great discovery — the workingman of the new industrial cities of Toronto and Hamilton. Organized labour, as well as organized associations of manufacturers, was a portent of the rise of the new industrialism. A number of the new national unions of the United States had crossed the border into Canada; the agitation for the nine-hour day had been carried over the ocean from England; and in March, 1872, the Toronto local of the Typographical Union went on strike for the nine-hour day without reduction of pay. The strike was suggestive enough in itself; but its political importance was magnified out of all proportion by the fact that George Brown, the old leader and the unfailing mentor of the Reformers of Canada West, was the editor and proprietor of the *Globe*, the principal Liberal paper in Toronto. With all the doctrinaire conviction of a Manchester Liberal and all the virtuous anger of an injured capitalist, he put himself at the head of the employers' committee which fought the strike. He assured his readers that in Canada there was 'no such class as those styled capitalists in other countries,' that 'the whole people are the capitalists of Canada,' and that the printers were 'foreign agitators' who had simply imported an unnatural strife into the peaceful Dominion. On April 16, 1872, he and the other master printers had thirteen strikers arrested on a charge of criminal conspiracy in restraint of trade. At this point, when Brown had thoroughly committed himself and compromised his party, Sir John Macdonald rushed to the deliverance of the working class. In June, 1872, he pushed through Parliament the Trades Union Act, which freed Canadian unions from the old common-law restrictions as combinations in restraint of trade. Even from the point of view of the Reformers, this was a most exasperatingly respectable measure, since it was based upon Gladstone's British statute of the previous year. On June 19, John Hewitt, corresponding secretary of the Toronto Trades Assembly, wrote to Sir John informing him that the Canadian unions desired to make a presentation to Lady Macdonald in appreciation of her husband's 'timely efforts in the interests of the operatives of this Dominion.' The basis of Canadian Tory democracy had been laid.

That summer, in the general election of August, 1872, the Conservatives made their first direct appeal to the industrial classes of Canada by advocating a tariff with incidental protection to home industry. Sir John announced the programme in Hamilton, which he had shrewdly realized was the most specialized manufacturing city in the Dominion;

and in Montreal, Toronto, Hamilton, Brantford, and a few other western towns, a deliberate effort was made to link manufacturers and workingmen in support of the new protectionist planks. In Hamilton the Conservatives had perhaps their greatest triumph, for they ran a labouring man in one of the ridings of the city and elected him; and on August 16, he came over to Toronto for a great labour rally in the market place and a torchlight procession through the city. Sir John was there in his new and enchanting guise of the 'workingman's friend.' Nothing, said the *Globe* sourly three days later, could be so disgraceful 'as a sight of the hard-featured, drunken crowd round the hack of the Prime Minister, with Sir John bending over to catch a dozen hands at once, joking with this, pretending to know that, calling on the "boys" to be sure to be at the polls by eight o'clock, and playing fugleman to the cheers which two or three drunken loafers were continuously calling forth. . . . We shall not say that they had only "a shirt and a half among them," or that they had plundered the scare crows of half a county. It was not their clothes, but their bearing, their looks, their unredeemed hard-facedness, and their fantastic efforts at getting up a show by poking some smoky lamps in the face of the glorious full moon as she shone in a clear Canadian sky, that gave the whole such an air of ludicrous absurdity and broken-down blackguardism which the central figure in the not very magnificent cab fitly crowned and completed.' Brown never showed a greater talent for the inappropriate than in this passage. His sneers at the ragged clothes of the 'workingman' were taken up and repeated gleefully by Conservative papers throughout the country.

The election of 1872, however, is notorious in Canadian history not so much because of the part played by labour or manufacturing capital, as because of the enormous influence of the railways. The Conservatives had taken up the cause of transcontinental transport with greater vigour and fewer qualifications than they had the policy of protection. The Quebec and London Resolutions had required the immediate construction of the Intercolonial Railway between Halifax and Quebec; but, so far as western transport was concerned, they merely asserted that communications were important and would be undertaken as soon as the state of the finances would permit. The Conservatives proceeded to honour the conditional, as well as the unconditional, promise, and carried out their programme in a spirit of uncompromising economic nationalism. The construction of the Intercolonial was pushed forward rapidly along a northern route which was selected in part to avoid proximity to the United States; and in 1871 the government contracted to begin a Pacific railway within two years, and to complete it within ten of the entrance of British Columbia into the union. The Grand Trunk Railway was soon eliminated from the race for the Pacific charter, for though it had dreamed of westward extension ever since the coming of Watkin, it refused to change its view that the best route west was *via* Chicago, south of the Lakes. The government was determined upon an all-Canadian railway, north of Lakes Huron and Superior. In aid of this enormous undertaking it was prepared to offer thirty million dollars and a land grant of fifty million acres to the company which would build the line.

Two syndicates, or 'rings,' as they came to be called, began to compete for the prize. One, called the Interoceanic Railway Company, composed largely of Toronto capitalists, was headed by D. L. Macpherson, who had risen to prominence as a partner in one of the largest contracting firms in the country. The other, the Canada Pacific Railway Company, made up chiefly of Montrealers and a number of Americans who were connected with the Northern Pacific, was led by Sir Hugh Allan, the president of the Allan Line of ocean steamships. Outwardly, Allan seemed to be the more obvious choice. Like so many Canadians of his generation, he had come out from Scotland as a young man; and beginning with nothing, he had built up a fast ocean steamship service using the St. Lawrence route. As was fitting, he had been knighted for his services to Canadian commerce; and he was by this time a figure of great solidity and respectability in Canadian commercial life. His company, however, was seriously weakened for lack of Ontario support, and heavily compromised by the presence of so much American capital. Politically, it would not do; and when, early in 1873, the charter was finally drawn up, it was awarded to a new company, the Canadian Pacific Railway Company, which commanded a much broader Canadian backing and from which the Americans were carefully excluded. But Allan was still president of the company. He had sacrificed too many interests and made too many enemies; and chance gave them the opportunity of bringing about his ruin. When Parliament opened in 1873, L. S. Huntingdon charged that Allan and his friends had given the government substantial financial aid in the election of 1872 in return for the promise of the Pacific charter. In July, the Montreal *Herald* published a number of letters and telegrams which proved without question that during the election the ministers had repeatedly called on Allan for funds.

The affair — the 'Pacific Scandal' as it was called — broke the first Canadian Pacific Railway Company. It broke the Conservative government; and for a time it seemed as if it would break Sir John Macdonald as well. It was, of course, not a case of personal bribery, but of party funds. There was no doubt at all that the ministers had asked and accepted very large amounts of money (totalling three hundred and fifty thousand dollars in all). But they insisted, realistically enough, that political parties habitually got their funds from the contributions of friends; and that Allan's gifts in particular had brought him no special advantage since the company to which the charter was eventually granted was essentially different from his original syndicate. The defence was not entirely unreasonable, but it was not surprising that the country found it completely unsatisfactory. In November, 1873, Macdonald resigned. Alexander Mackenzie formed a government and when he appealed to the people early in 1874, he was triumphantly returned. The national policies rested in suspense. What would the Liberals do about them? Would they carry on from the point at which the Conservatives had left off, or would they form new and radically different policies of their own?

[*II*]

The Reform or Liberal party which took office in the autumn of 1873 was a very different organization from the Conservative party led by Macdonald. The history of the previous six years had brought the Reformers neither unity nor prestige. The Canada West section of the party had joined the Great Coalition of 1864 to support Confederation; but George Brown had retired from the union ministry late in the following year and in 1867 the Reform convention of Ontario had expressly repudiated the principle of coalition. For six years, therefore, the party had remained in opposition; and its triumphant electoral victory early in 1874 was perhaps less a reflection of its own strength than a sign of the overwhelming disrepute of the Conservatives. In Quebec, the few remaining *Rouges* were being hunted down with a tireless and remorseless efficiency by the Church. In the new western provinces the party scarcely had a foothold; and the relations between the Reformers of the Maritime Provinces and those of central Canada were none too close or friendly in these early days. The great centre of the party's strength was the Province of Ontario; but even in Ontario there were differences and divisions which were reflected accurately in Reform leadership. George Brown, the old leader of the Reformers in Canada West, had retired from active political life; but from the editorial office of the Toronto *Globe* he still brooded over the fortunes of the party like a brilliant,

imperious, and scolding matriarch over the affairs of an ill-
assorted and distracted family. There were two principal
choices for the place he had left vacant. On the one hand,
there was the ex-stone-mason, Alexander Mackenzie, with
his peculiarly bleak Scots visage, his rude skill in debate,
and his angular Puritan rectitude in administration. On
the other hand, there was Edward Blake, the University
man, the brilliant lawyer, with his cold intelligence, his instinct for refined and elaborate argument, and his curious
temperamental variability. It was a strange contrast. Mackenzie was chosen leader, at Blake's own request; but Blake
was young, distinguished, and imperious; and it was clear
that he had only just begun his enigmatic part in the history
of the Reform party.

The Liberals took office at a highly curious conjunction
of circumstances. The Great Depression, which began in
1873, wrecked the Reform administration in the end; but
in the beginning, the political, if not the economic, circumstances looked unusually favourable. The national spirit,
which had been awakened by Confederation, by the recall of
the British troops and the negotiation of the Washington
Treaty, stood at its zenith. There was a new sense of political maturity in the country, a new zestful confidence in the
future, a new desire for independent experimentation. What
lay ahead was still invitingly uncertain. The relations of
the new country with the United States and Great Britain
had not yet been determined; the national policies designed
to unite the Dominion were still to be decided upon. All
that the Conservatives had tried to do had been involved in
their discredit and apparent ruin. The Reformers, strengthened by the moral reaction in their favour, spurred on by
the growing confidence in Canada's future, had apparently
been given the chance to identify their party with the hopes
and aspirations of the country in its first youth.

Almost immediately the Reformers were presented with
their first challenge. It came from those people who be-

lieved that the new nationality created by Confederation inevitably involved a drastically changed relationship with the United Kingdom. Ever since 1867, a number of prominent people, both Reformers and Conservatives, had shown themselves restive at the imperial tie, had even expressed a wish for independence; but in its purest and most positive form the urge for a new status for the new Canadian nationality was represented by the youthful group known as Canada First. In 1873-74, at a moment when the Pacific Scandal had brought about a violent upset in public affairs, the group which claimed W. A. Foster as its minor prophet moved out into the open. The young members of the society had founded a new club, the National Club, in Toronto; they had begun a good critical journal, *The Nation*. But these efforts left them unsatisfied; and they were drawn rapidly, and by an irresistible fascination, into the realm of politics. They persuaded themselves that the old names of Liberal and Conservative meant nothing except perhaps a tendency to corruption; that a new national party was needed to express the hopes and ideals of the brave new world of Confederation. And in 1874 they founded the Canadian National Association. Its platform was a rather odd collection of proposals, whose chief connecting link was the vague forward-looking air which they had in common. Obviously the most interesting and the most controversial suggestions of all had to do with the imperial relationship. Here the party's published platform simply advocated 'British Connection, Consolidation of the Empire — and in the meantime a voice in treaties affecting Canada.' This appeared to imply imperial federation; and there were imperial federationists in Canada First. But there were also Canadian nationalists who had already begun to think in terms of independence.

What attitude would the Liberals take to the ideas of Canada First? How far would they sponsor the apparently rising demand for a change in the imperial relationship which the Canadian National Association embodied? These were highly embarrassing questions; and it soon became clear that, so far as the British connection was concerned, there were evidently two schools of thought in the Reform party. With some difficulty, the unpredictable Edward Blake had been persuaded to become a member of the Reform government in the autumn of 1873. But he withdrew early in the new year, in one of his periodic fits of ostentatious independence; and in the autumn of that year, in a speech delivered at Aurora, Ontario, he endorsed all the main parts of the programme of Canada First, including its proposed imperial federation. 'It is impossible,' he told the electors of North York dramatically, 'to foster a national spirit unless you have national interests to attend to. . . . The time will come when that national spirit which has been spoken of will be truly felt among us, when we shall realize that we are four millions of Britons who are not free. . . . Tomorrow, by the policy of England, in which you have no voice or control, this country might be plunged into the horrors of a war. . . . We must find some common ground on which to unite, some common aspiration to be shared, and I think this can be found alone in the cultivation of that national spirit to which I have referred.'

In the midst of the general astonishment and execration which followed this speech, the members of the Canadian National Association alone were full of rapture. They were convinced that they had found their man. They believed that Blake was simply the forerunner of an army of Reformers who would make a great new Liberal Party out of Canada First. But they made two bad miscalculations. They underestimated the old-fashioned loyalty of the Reformers and they overemphasized the stability of Edward Blake. The Reform party drew much of its inspiration from English Liberalism; but it had never accepted the anti-imperial views of the Manchester men; and the Reform party leaders, though they felt it prudent not to do more with Blake than to dismiss his views as harmless speculation, relieved their outraged feelings by a violent loyalist attack on the nationalism of Canada First. As for Blake himself, he grew tired of his new friends and his new views in short order. In 1875, having had his rather dramatic fling of independence, he relapsed again into respectable conformity as a member of the Reform administration at Ottawa. This was the end of Canada First. The *Nation* ceased publication; the National became an ordinary club. There was evidently small hope of a radical nationalist party in the Dominion.

At the same time there seemed equally little prospect that the old Reform party would support any serious change in the imperial relationship. It was true that in 1875 the Reformers pushed through a Supreme Court Act which purported to abolish appeals to the Judicial Committee of the Privy Council in England, and that in 1876 Edward Blake, the new minister of justice, obtained alterations in the commissions and instructions of the governor-general which discouraged that officer from regarding himself as a protector of imperial interests, with power to act independently of his constitutional advisers in Canada. But the clause in the Supreme Court Act abolishing appeals to Great Britain turned out to be inoperative; and probably the imperial authorities failed to disallow the statute precisely because they knew it to be inoperative. The Reformers did not re-draft and re-enact the defective clause. Apparently they lacked the courage to do so in the face of British disapproval. And thus the appeals continued — with disastrous consequences for the future. In all essentials, the official Reform view of the British connection did not seem to differ markedly from that of the Conservatives; and the Reformers showed no more hardihood than their opponents in pressing Canadian claims against the resistance of British officials.

If the Reformers failed to anticipate the growing Canadian urge for a new status in the world at large, they failed even more completely to satisfy the Canadian demand for policies which would link the country together. Their most notorious failure, of course, was in the project for a Pacific railway. George Brown had been the pioneer propagandist for the acquisition of the west, the earnest advocate of forestalling the Americans by British communication with the prairies. But when it came down to the concrete problem of means, the Reformers in Parliament denounced what they regarded as Sir John's insane agreement to complete the railway within ten years of British Columbia's entrance into Confederation. The unimaginative, upright Mackenzie and the brooding, hypercritical Blake were suspicious and disdainful of Macdonald's jaunty confidence in the future, and his easy, casual familiarity with great corporations and big business men. When the Liberals came into office in 1873 and took over the wreckage of the Pacific scheme, they found that there were many good reasons for continued caution. The uncompromising Blake was ready to postpone the whole affair indefinitely and take whatever consequences followed. 'If under all the circumstances,' he told his audience at Aurora in 1874, 'the Columbians were to say "You must go on and finish this railway according to the terms, or take the alternative of releasing us from Confederation," I would — take the alternative.' There were few Reformers who shared Blake's temperamental pessimism; but they all agreed with his caution. For by this time the depression had come in earnest; and it was drying up the capital markets and causing a steady decline in Dominion revenues. The Reform government was prepared to build portage railways between the lakes which would link Manitoba with central Canada. It undertook surveys for the whole route to the coast. It even began construction in British Columbia. But it would not start to build westward from Winnipeg until the whole route had been determined; and, as a result, it soon found itself in a prolonged and acrimonious row with British Columbia. The cloudy impression that perhaps the Reformers were not as zealous as they might be for the great Canadian transcontinental railway took the shape of a positive conviction in the minds of many people as the years went by.

The second example of the inability of the Reform party to meet the demand for a national economic programme lay in its failure to devise a new and striking commercial policy. Up to this time both parties had agreed in supporting a system of 'modified free trade.' But in 1872 Sir John Macdonald had coquetted with protection and deliberately sought the support of manufacturers and working class; and, as a natural result, the Reformers had tended to stress the interests of the primary producers and to defend the old Canadian tradition of low tariffs and foreign trade. If the Reform party could have secured a reasonable reciprocity treaty with the United States, its credit would have been immensely increased. In 1874 it made an eager attempt to regain the lost American market. George Brown, a straightforward, moderate, and incredibly optimistic diplomatist, was appointed plenipotentiary along with Sir Edward Thornton, the Minister to Washington, to present the Canadian proposals for a new treaty which would have given the United States the liberty of the inshore fisheries without money compensation, and which would have established mutual free trade in manufactures of wood, iron, and steel as well as in natural products. Though the proposal was designed to conciliate the United States by opening the Canadian market to important groups of American manufactures, Hamilton Fish, the American Secretary of State, remained uninterested in Brown's concessions. The draft treaty which eventually resulted from their discussions was sent to the Senate with a frigid presidential message which practically invited rejection. And in due course the Senate accepted the report of its Foreign Relations Committee that the draft should not even be discussed.

Once again the United States had blocked a return to the old Canadian policy. The most promising proposal of the Reformers had been rejected. But the demand for some kind of government action continued to grow with the depression; and the nature of the depression itself seemed to suggest another form which that action might take. Even more obviously than the slump of 1857-59, the Great Depression revealed how far the new industrial system and the new transport system of the English-speaking world had combined to reduce the prices of manufactured goods. In the period 1873-79 the price level of Canadian imports, which were mainly manufactures, dropped 26 per cent while the price level of Canadian exports, which were mostly natural products, declined by only 8 per cent. For the whole country the terms of trade were not unfavourable; but for the merchant and manufacturing groups, the depression brought disastrous effects. In the fourteen months from January 1, 1875, to February 23, 1876, the total liabilities of firms failing in Canada amounted to nearly twenty-seven million dollars. And of this total the bankrupt manufacturers accounted for about a fifth. In view of the general position of manufacturing in the Dominion at that time, this was not a small share. And it quickly drove the manufacturers to organize and protest. They had a tradition of lobbying, they had the example of the United States to spur them on, they had a simple comprehensible solution for their difficulties which the merchants certainly lacked.

Beginning in the summer of 1874, when the publication of the terms of the Brown-Fish draft treaty jarred almost the whole Canadian business world into protest, the demand for a national policy of protection strengthened with the seriousness of the depression. In the autumn of 1875, that new and vigorous group, the Manufacturers' Association of Ontario, held a well-attended meeting in Toronto which pressed for an upward revision of duties; and in January, 1876, the Dominion Board of Trade, the national business organization which had been founded a few years before and which had so far refused to abandon the principle of 'modified free trade,' went over to protection by a small majority.

Apart from the coal interest of Nova Scotia, there were few groups in the Maritime Provinces which favoured protection. It encountered strong opposition from the merchants in old-established commercial towns like Montreal; and even among the manufacturers themselves there were many individuals who would have preferred a large measure of free trade with the United States on the assumption that they could compete successfully for a share in the American market. When one manufacturer of agricultural implements appeared before the parliamentary committee on the depression in 1876 and was asked what he thought of reciprocity with the United States, he replied, 'We would hold up both hands for that.' But there were many manufacturers — more perhaps than has been realized — who were already frankly dubious of this alternative; and in any case Brown's failure in 1874 had made it seem impossible of realization. In the circumstances, everybody could agree on the principle that, if Canadian industry was to be shut out of a wider market by the towering American tariff, it could not afford to share the small market which remained. 'Reciprocity of trade, or reciprocity of tariffs' was the slogan to which all manufacturers could afford to subscribe.

The demand for protection, which was, of course, strengthened by the general cry for some remedy for the depression, was the most serious political portent of these early depression years. The two parties, though even they were not fully aware of its vital importance for the future, began to look upon the problem of the tariff with eyes of wary respect. Up to this time the general conviction that a low tariff was best for Canada had been modified of necessity by the assumption that direct taxes were impossible in the Dominion, and that, as a result, the bulk of the national revenue must be derived from customs duties. It would therefore have been quite legitimate for the Reformers, particularly in times of depression, to raise the tariff in the sheer need of national revenue, and to take gratefully, though unostentatiously, whatever support they got from the manufacturers as a result.

This had been essentially the Cayley-Galt manoeuvre of 1858-59. For a while it looked as if the Reform party might repeat it. In 1874, the government carried through Parliament a slight increase from 15 per cent to 17½ per cent in the general rate on manufactured goods. Even the unbending Mackenzie was not above reminding the electors that it was his administration that had raised the tariff; and in both Hamilton and Montreal Reform candidates in bye-elections appealed for the support of manufacturers and workingmen on the ground that their party was more likely than its rival to establish protective duties. As the time approached for the budget speech of 1876, the demand for protection in the ranks of the Reform party itself grew steadily heavier. Perhaps the Finance Minister, Richard Cartwright, was in favour of the raise. A number of Ontario members certainly counselled it. The press as a whole simply assumed that it would take place. And then something happened. At apparently the last moment, the free-trade Reformers of Nova Scotia threw their whole weight against the change; and their protests must have reawakened the dormant Scots conscience of Alexander Mackenzie. In the summer of 1875, when on a visit to Dundee, Scotland, which was his birthplace, he had announced that 'the principles of Richard Cobden were the principles of civilization.' And now the imperative appeal of Cobden and of civilization recalled him to his duty. Cartwright had not been long on his legs on February 25, 1876, when it was revealed to his astonished listeners that the tariff was not going to go up.

Tactically, this was a slight surprise to the Conservatives; but strategically it was an enormous advantage. Macdonald hastened to grasp the opportunity which had been offered him. He believed that protection would be popular as a national war-cry, that it would be supported by powerful business groups; but he was aware also of the class and sectional interests which were likely to oppose it. To meet this opposition, he relied upon the very argument which the Reformers had rejected. What the Conservatives wanted, he explained, was merely 'incidental protection.' Everybody knew that financial need really determined the rate of taxation in Canada, and that the depression had brought a decline in revenue which must be made up in some way. The tariff — the principal source of Canadian revenue —would obviously have to be increased. But the new burden could be distributed in various ways; and all the Conservatives asked was a 'readjustment' or 'rearrangement' of the duties which would give the greatest protection to home manufactures. 'The Government [Reform] press here,' wired John Boyd of the Saint John *Telegraph* to Macdonald, 'state that you propose to raise the tariff generally to 35 per cent. Can I contradict this?' Macdonald's reply was prompt and very emphatic. 'It is an absurd falsehood,' he wired back; 'neither at London or elsewhere have I gone beyond my motion in Parliament, and have never proposed an increase but only a readjustment of tariff.'

Thus, by a strategy which the Reformers could almost as legitimately have employed, Macdonald gained the backing of important groups and the support of a frustrated and desperate national sentiment. By this time it was obvious that the Reform administration was drifting in a desultory fashion towards the rocks. In the midst of a depression, which gave a terrible emphasis to every lack of success, it had failed to make any progress with the old policies, and had hung back in prudence and honest distrust from the new. It had alienated almost every interest, material or spiritual, which saw in Confederation the beginning of a fuller, richer national existence. In September, 1878, when Mackenzie appealed to the country in a general election, he was defeated in every province of the Dominion except New Brunswick. Macdonald returned to power; and from that moment the uncertainty, the hesitation, and the failure which had marked the ten years from Confederation seemed miraculously to end. Macdonald had his mandate; he had settled upon his policies; and he was favoured, far more than perhaps even he was aware, by a brief return of good times. The Conservatives had found their answers to the riddle of national unity; and for the next half-dozen years they plunged into a wild career of economic and political nationalism.

Of the three interrelated national policies of western settlement, transcontinental railways, and protective tariffs, it was the third upon which the Conservatives began. Though this precedence was largely accidental, there was a certain definite appropriateness about it. The tariff was an instrument of vast emotional significance as well as of great practical value; and of the three methods adopted for the attainment of national expansion and unity, the tariff significantly was the only one which ever came to be dignified by the title of the 'National Policy' in capitals. In international affairs, the tariff asserted the principle of independence as against Great Britain and the United States. In domestic matters, it expressed the hope for a more varied and self-sufficient national life. It was intimately and vitally related to the other national policies. By means of the tariff, the settlement of the west would provide a national market; and this national market would supply east-west traffic for Canadian transcontinental railways and areas of exploitation for eastern Canadian industry.

Samuel Leonard Tilley, the veteran pre-Confederation leader in New Brunswick who had spent the past few years vegetating as lieutenant-governor of his native province, moved up to Ottawa to act as the minister of finance in the new Conservative government. As late as August, 1878, Tilley had been reassuring an attentive audience in Saint John that the Conservatives had no desire for 'increased taxation' but simply wished for a 'readjustment' of the existing rates. 'Readjustment' was a soothing word breathing restrained and modest purpose; but the proposals which Tilley made in his first budget speech of 1879 suggested that his ideal was not a rearrangement but a re-creation. The tariff of 1874 had been a simple affair, on a straightforward *ad valorem* basis. Primary products entered free; partly processed goods paid 5 to 10 per cent and most finished manufactures 17½ per cent. In place of this uncomplicated revenue tariff the Conservatives proposed and carried an elaborate schedule, with substantially increased rates which included a number of specific duties designed to stiffen the resistance of the tariff in times of depression. The most important types of cotton, woollen, and silk textiles now bore a variety of rates, which, on the basis of the import valuations of 1789-80, had *ad valorem* equivalents which hovered in the neighbourhood of 30 per cent. The duties on castings, boilers, tanks, engines, and agricultural machinery were increased to 25 per cent. Boots and shoes, harness, and saddlery now paid 25 per cent, hardware 30 per cent, furniture and ready-made clothing 35 per cent. Protection was given to Nova Scotia coal, to the petroleum industry of western Ontario, and to agricultural products, though here the duties could have little or no effect, since the country was on an export basis in respect of most farm commodities. For the whole of Canada, and particularly for the Maritime Provinces, this was the greatest fiscal revolution which had yet occurred in their history.

Yet there was only a short interval before the government sponsored its second great national undertaking, the Canadian Pacific Railway. This time there was no very serious competition between rival syndicates; and on October 21, 1880, Sir Charles Tupper, Minister of Railways and Canals — the second Maritimer to preside over the launching of one of the new national policies — concluded an agreement with a group of resolute and experienced men for the construction of a railway from central Canada to the Pacific Ocean. It was very largely a North American association. Kohn, Reinach and Company of Paris, and Morton, Rose and Company of London both had an interest in the venture; but on the whole, despite the fact that the Canadian government had appealed for the support of English capital, London had only a small share in the financing, direction, and construction of the Canadian Pacific Railway. In fact the dominating interest in the syndicate was a group of Canadians — George Stephen, Duncan McIntyre, Richard B. Angus, and Donald Smith — whose activities centred chiefly in Montreal and who had had a varied experience in manufacturing, railways, and finance. Several members of this group, including Stephen and Angus, had just scored a spectacular success out of the St. Paul, Minneapolis, and Manitoba Railway in the State of Minnesota; and their choice for the position of general manager in the Canadian Pacific was the American-born William C. Van Horne, who had an unbroken record of triumph in the management of small middle-western American railways. This American experience and these American contacts were valuable; but they were a very different thing from Allan's heavy dependence on American capital in the original syndicate of 1872. Appropriately enough, this new reassertion of Montreal's ancient dominion over the north-west came primarily from a group of the river city's own citizens with characteristic Scotch-Canadian names.

The Canadian Pacific Railway was a commercial organization which won its astounding success partly through brilliant individual enterprise and partly through heavy government support. The group which George Stephen headed did not look upon itself as an association of financiers engaged in a giant and highly lucrative job of company flotation. They were practical railwaymen who wanted to build, and run, and hold on to a railway. 'There are two ways,' wrote Stephen to Macdonald, 'by which you can get the road built and operated: one by getting up a financial organization such as Allan contemplated and such as Jay Cooke & Co. got up for the construction of the Northern Pacific Railway. . . . A scheme of this nature involves the issue of a large number of Bonds. . . . The outcome . . . is that the real responsibility is transferred from the Company to the people who may be induced to buy the Bonds, while the Company or the projectors pocket a big profit at the start out of the proceeds. . . . The other plan, and the one I should have followed . . . would have been to limit the borrowing of money from the public to the smallest possible point . . . to have looked for a return of our own capital and a legitimate profit entirely to the growth of the country and the development of the property. . . . '

Yet if the company was dependent on the financial genius of Stephen and the driving, constructive energy of Van Horne, it was equally dependent upon the assistance of a government which was determined upon a transcontinental railway as an instrument of national unity and expansion. By the terms of the original contract, the government agreed to give the company a money subsidy of twenty-five million dollars, to hand over those sections of the transcontinental line completed under the Mackenzie administration at a cost of nearly thirty-eight million dollars, and to make a grant of twenty-five million acres of land, distributed in alternate sections of six hundred and forty acres, within a belt twenty-four miles deep on either side of the railway running all the way from Winnipeg to the mountains. In addition, the company's capital, as well as its grounds, buildings, and rolling stock, was to be forever free from taxation; and for twenty years, by the careful exclusion of all competing lines to the American border, it was to enjoy a monopoly of the traffic of western Canada. These were formidable privileges. The Liberal opposition condemned them as wantonly lavish; but it turned out in the end that they were far from enough. Influenced in part by the Grand Trunk Railway and by competing American roads, the money markets of London and New York were cold or hostile to the project. 'Jumbo, the big elephant bought by Barnum, is a matter of ten times more interest to London than twenty Colonies,'

Stephen wrote bitterly to Macdonald from the old country; and late in 1883 he was complaining that 'things have gone to the devil in New York.' Again and again, the government had to come to the rescue of a company which was living literally from hand to mouth. Macdonald grew wary and suspicious of Stephen's importunities; and Stephen, who had sold or pledged everything he owned, was bitterly reproachful of Macdonald's delays. Right down to the summer of 1885, when the government came to the company's assistance for the last time, it was still touch and go with the whole enterprise.

In the meantime, the line was being driven headlong westward under the direction of the imperious William Cornelius Van Horne. It was to be an all-Canadian railway in conformity with the firm decision to build north of Lake Superior, and yet a competing North American road, in the tradition of Montreal's historic struggle with its American rivals. In part it followed, and in part it deviated from, the route which Sandford Fleming had chosen as government engineer-in-chief during the Mackenzie régime. In the eastern section from Lake Nipissing to Winnipeg, the line followed Lake Superior rather than the height of land to the north, in accordance with Fleming's recommendation. For miles and miles the track hugged the gaunt shoreline, tracing the sweeping curves of the lake, past scarred ungainly masses of Precambrian rock and bent and tattered jack pines. Westward from Lake Winnipeg, Fleming and the government had projected a route which would traverse the northern fertile 'park belt' of the prairies and reach the Pacific via the Yellowhead Pass; but the Canadian Pacific directorate abandoned this in favour of a much more southerly line which was intended to strengthen the company's monopoly of the Canadian prairies and to enable it to compete for traffic originating in the United States. By the terms of the new agreement which resulted from this change of plan, the pass through the mountains had to be at least one hundred miles north of the international boundary. The Kicking Horse Pass offered a way through the Rockies; but beyond these again lay the towering slopes of the Selkirks. In 1881 the prospectors searched in vain for an outlet. It was not until the summer of 1882, when the railway was rapidly approaching the mountains, that Major Rogers, the American engineer, at last discovered the pass through the Selkirks which bears his name.

In more than one way, George Stephen (Lord Mount Stephen) resembled that long-dead Scots Canadian, Simon McTavish, who had founded the North West Company, the first great Canadian concern to cross the continent. The two men shared an imperial outlook, a consummate financial ability; and in Stephen there was something of that primitive clan and family spirit which had been such a strong compulsion in the life of the old eighteenth-century grandee. Far back in Scotland, in the valley of the Spey, close to Dufftown, where George Stephen was born, there was a rock called 'Craigellachie,' known to both Stephen and his cousin Donald Smith as the meeting place of the clan Grant, when the fiery cross sped through Speyside calling the clansmen to battle. Once, in the dark autumn of 1884, when the railway seemed threatened with disaster, Stephen had pledged and fought his way to a small advance in London; and, in a moment of passionate exultance, he cabled Smith back in Montreal with nothing but the battle slogan of the Grants. 'Stand fast, Craigellachie,' ran the message. And when, on November 7, 1885, the last spike of the railway was driven in at Eagle Pass, in the heart of the mountains, the spot was named Craigellachie in memory of that ancient rock. There were no brass bands or troops of officials in attendance at Craigellachie that November day; and the spike, unlike that which had been used for the Northern Pacific two years before, was plain iron and not gold. Van Horne looked on, conspicuous with his great bulk, his broad impassive face, his scrutinizing eyes, while Donald Smith drove the spike home;

and when someone called upon the general manager to make
a speech, Van Horne replied laconically, 'All I can say is that
the work has been well done in every way.' It was all over.
By contract they had been given ten years to finish the railway. They had completed it in five.

With the completion of the Canadian Pacific Railway,
the Conservative programme of economic unity and expansion had been fully rounded out. Emboldened by the success of its own mission, strengthened by the tide of national
feeling which it had itself evoked, the Macdonald government continued to assert its supervisory control over the
provinces and began to insist upon a new and more dignified
national status in the world at large. For reasons of concrete national interest, as well as on grounds of loyalty and
emotional attachment, Macdonald believed in the British
connection; but he believed also that, under the new colonial
system, the connection between Great Britain and Canada
must more and more approximate the relationship of friendly equals. It had already been established, by the appointment of Macdonald in 1871 and Brown in 1874, that Canadians must play a large part, as fully accredited plenipoten-
tiaries, in the negotiation of all commercial treaties with the
United States. But what about commercial treaties with
other foreign powers? And what about Canadian external
interests during the long intervals between such negotiations? Should Canada establish her own agents in foreign
countries or should she continue to rely on the British diplomatic service?

Macdonald looked at these questions with an assertiveness
tempered by caution. Blake pressed him to establish a resident agent in Washington; but he remained content with
the British ministry to the United States for the ordinary
routine of Canadian-American relations. On the other
hand, he was far less satisfied with the channels of communication between Canada and Great Britain itself; and he and
Tilley and Tupper prepared a memorandum in which they

set forth the need for a permanent representative of Canada in London, who was to have the title of Resident Minister, or some name of equal import, who should enjoy virtual diplomatic honours in official circles, and who could be accredited as Canadian plenipotentiary to European courts. The implications of this somewhat daring proposal were immediately appreciated in London; and the methods of polite frustration were duly applied by Sir Michael Hicks Beach. Though the status of the Canadian representative would be worthy of his important functions, it obviously could not be diplomatic in character, he suavely reminded the Canadians. Eventually the title 'High Commissioner of Canada in London' was decided upon. Sir A. T. Galt, the first high commissioner, returned home in a rage after a few years; and it was not until the appointment of Sir Charles Tupper, who though equally aggressive was somewhat more adroit than Galt, that the office began to pay any dividends to Canada.

In the early 1880's the drive and purpose of Macdonald's nationalism were clearly apparent. With a new government, a new series of national enterprises, and a new wave of prosperity, the Dominion stood at the zenith. It was superb with promise and with achievement. It looked confidently into the future. But it could not foresee the long train of disappointments, divisions, and frustrations which in the end were to ruin the Conservative party and very nearly to break the Dominion of Canada itself.

[*III*]

The furious controversies which in the 1880's threatened to divide Canada into its component parts, had their origin in a variety of causes, cultural and political as well as economic; but almost all of them were aggravated by the Great Depression and a number were directly inspired by it. For over twenty years, the depression continued virtually un-

relieved. The brief trade revival which had accompanied
the introduction of the National Policy and the commencement of the Canadian Pacific Railway faded away in the
gloom of renewed failures and disappointments. The slump
deepened. It broke the naïve hopes which had been held
for Canada at Confederation. It revived the old regional
divisions within the country by frustrating the national policies which were intended to unite them.

The country grew with most discouraging slowness. In
1871, the population had been 3,689,257. Twenty years
later, in 1891, it had only reached 4,833,239. The greater
part of this increase was attained during the first decade;
and, during the second, from 1881 to 1891, the percentage
increase dropped to twelve per cent. In the meantime, while
the provinces of eastern Canada barely held their own, or
suffered an absolute decrease in population — while immigration, after its brief spurt upward from 1881 to 1884,
began to decline once more — the movement of people to the
United States began to reach the most alarming proportions.
It was bad enough to lose the new immigrants, a number
of whom left sooner or later for the United States; but it
was far more calamitous to be deprived of a great number
of the native stock itself. Back in 1850, there had only
been about one hundred and fifty thousand Canadian-born
in the United States; but by 1890 there were very nearly a
million. 'There is scarcely a farm house in the older provinces,' said the Toronto *Mail* gloomily, in 1887, 'where there
is not an empty chair for the boy in the States.'

The weight of the depression lay on the whole country,
but in a varied and unequal fashion; and perhaps the Maritime Provinces suffered most. In Nova Scotia, New Brunswick, and Prince Edward Island, the depression coincided
with even more drastic, long-run changes in economic circumstance. The fortunes of the Maritime Provinces had
been bound up with the old, pre-industrial techniques and
trades and markets; and in the period after 1875 they were

obliged to adjust themselves more and more drastically to industrialism in general and to something which might be regarded as one of its expressions — the new Dominion of Canada. The American Civil War and the period of reconstruction which immediately followed formed the last great period in the history of wooden sailing ships and wooden shipbuilding. From then on the iron steamship gradually silenced the scores of little shipyards along the long coastline of Nova Scotia and New Brunswick, drove the sailing ships of the Maritimes into more and more unproductive routes and cargoes, and forced the shipwrights and sailormen into the fishery or agriculture and often into exile. Though the fishery expanded, partly as a result of the decline of shipbuilding, it also was an industry which was forced to adjust itself to accumulating change. The old dried-fish markets of the eighteenth century, for which the whole Atlantic seaboard had fought so tenaciously in the days of the wooden sailing ships, now seemed to shrivel into relative insignificance. As the production of beet sugar rose, the West India islands entered into a long period of absolute decline. The United States, which had been required by the Halifax Award of 1877 to pay four and a half million dollars in compensation for the excess value of the Canadian inshore fisheries over its own, gave notice of the abrogation of the fisheries articles of the Treaty of Washington in 1883. In 1885 Canadian fish were once more subjected to the heavy duties of the American tariff.

If, however, the Maritimes were losing in the old trades and markets of the Atlantic seaboard, they were making few compensating gains in the vast continental area which was opened to them with Confederation. Before 1867 they had fondly hoped that the Intercolonial Railway would pour an accumulating traffic into the national ports of Saint John and Halifax; and that Maritime coal and iron would form the basis of a manufacturing industry which would supply the whole Dominion. As the dull years of the depression dragged on, it began to seem more and more unlikely that these hopes would be realized. With the coming of the railway and the steamship, Saint John and Halifax gained at the expense of the little Maritime outports; but they competed very unequally with great metropolitan centres like Montreal and New York. From the very first, it seemed natural and inevitable that Maritime coal should move up to the more mature industries of the St. Lawrence valley rather than that industries should come down to Maritime coal. In the 1870's the manufacturers of Quebec and Ontario began to invade Nova Scotia, New Brunswick, and Prince Edward Island in force; and by the time of the general election of 1878 the Halifax *Chronicle* was raging that the only 'slaughtering' [dumping of goods] that the Maritimes knew anything about came, not from foreign countries, but from Ontario and Quebec.

Far from alleviating the difficulties of the economic transition which the Maritime Provinces had to face, the National Policy of the tariff probably intensified them. The main special advantage for the Maritimes which was contained in the budget of 1879 was the duty of fifty cents a ton on coal which was raised to sixty cents in 1880. So far as the great bulk of consumers' goods was concerned, the manufacturers of Ontario and Quebec obviously got the lion's share of the new protected national market. 'The people of Nova Scotia know the Ontario or Quebec man,' declared the Halifax *Morning Chronicle* bitterly in 1886, 'but we know him principally in the shape of the commercial traveller. He comes here to sell, but he buys nothing but his hotel fare and in this respect he makes a rather ostentatious display. He is usually a genial enough sort of person, has a diamond ring, smokes fair cigars, "sets them up with the boys" in an offhand way, and generally conveys the impression that in his own estimation he is a very superior being, whose condescending patronage it is a great privilege to enjoy. He spreads himself periodically throughout this province, in number he equals the locust and his visit has about the same effect. He saps our resources, sucks our money and leaves a lot of shoddy behind him. He has been able — at least the people whose agent he is — to have laws passed that compel us to buy his wares or submit to a tremendous fine if we purchase from John Bull or brother Jonathan.'

Costs for the fishermen and farmers of the Maritimes did not increase as much as might have been expected under the tariff, for during the depression the decline in the price of manufactured goods was relatively much greater than that of primary products; but the new duties robbed the seaboard, as well as the rest of Canada, of much of that advantage in the terms of trade which might otherwise have mitigated some of the bad effects of the slump. Confederation and its national policies had not created the basic problem of the Maritime Provinces; but, on the other hand, they had not greatly alleviated its bad effects. It was difficult and politically unrewarding to tilt at world forces like the Industrial Revolution and the business cycle; but it was well worth while to run down the Dominion. In 1886, W. S. Fielding, the new Liberal prime minister of Nova Scotia, moved a series of resolutions in the legislature which ascribed the 'unsatisfactory and depressed condition of the province' to Confederation and declared that secession from the union was the only real solution of its woes. Fielding had become the political expression of the economic crisis of the Maritime Provinces; and in the Nova Scotian provincial election of 1886 he was triumphantly returned to power.

In the meantime the perplexities of the Dominion were growing in the west. The prairies, as well as the seaboard, had entered a real period of transition; but while in the east they faced a slow shrinkage of opportunity, in the west they stood on the edge of an enormous expansion. In both regions the inevitable and painful process of change was complicated by the depression. It had intensified the troubles of the Maritime Provinces and for years it frustrated the high hopes for the west. There were other reasons, of course, for the slow development of the Canadian prairies in the first two decades after Confederation: the lack of accessibility until the railway was built, the supposedly superior attraction of the United States for immigrants, the first long train of prairie disasters — grasshoppers and torrential rains in the 1870's which were followed by drought and untimely frosts in the early years of the following decade — all these played their part in discouraging settlement. But a real burst of prosperity, such as that of the first decade of the nineteenth century, would have quickened the region into life; and this prosperity simply did not appear. In 1881, the population of the new Province of Manitoba was just a little over sixty-two thousand and that of the North-West Territories had not quite reached seven thousand. When the railway first went through, the trade revival of 1879-1883 had its western counterpart in the Manitoba boom, which threw the province into a momentary speculative frenzy, only to die away again in disappointment and apathy.

All this increased the burdens of the young community and aggravated its emerging resentment with eastern and central Canada. In the 1870's, when the Pacific railway project had been so long postponed, British Columbia had been the most obstreperous of the new provinces; but in the 1880's Manitoba and the North-West Territories replaced the Pacific slope as the chief centre of protest and disaffection. Without much difficulty and within a relatively short time, Manitoba acquired a long list of grievances. A prematurely created province, far more immature than any of the others, including British Columbia, it had been forced to accept the standard financial arrangement with the Dominion; and, partly as a result of this, it was hard up from the start. Unquestionably all its hopes for the future were bound up with rail transport to the east and with large-scale immigration; but although it supported the national policies for western development, it soon came to believe that far too much of the burden of them was laid on its own shoulders. The Dominion government's retention of the natural resources of the prairies was sensible enough, since only the Dominion could plan an effective national land and immigration policy; but, on the other hand, the province was left without its lands and without a subsidy in lieu of them. Again, it had begged and prayed for the railway — there could be no doubt of that; but it soon discovered that a twenty-year monopoly clause which kept competition out and rates up was a good price to pay for the Canadian Pacific Railway. When the provincial legislature tried to charter railways running south and south-east to connect with the American roads at the border, the Dominion promptly disallowed the statutes. In the middle 1880's the accumulation of these grievances had stirred up a general agitation; and John Norquay, the half-breed prime minister of the province, put himself at the head of it.

This agrarian protest against exploitation, which was common to the prairies as a whole, was accompanied in the North-West Territories by far more primitive kind of resistance. The great majority of the settlers who arrived in the Territories in the 1880's naturally made their homes in the southern part of the region, in fairly close proximity to the Canadian Pacific Railway; but further north, in the valley of the Saskatchewan River, there were older settlements, founded by migrants who had trekked westward along the waterways in previous decades and who represented a profoundly different type of culture. The Métis, or French half-breeds, embittered by the collapse of their rebellion at Red River and completely estranged from the alien civilization which was visibly remaking their old homeland, moved west to found the settlements of St. Laurent, St. Louis, and Batoche, in the wild free land of the Saskatchewan valley. Their old, half-nomadic way of life had been based upon the fur trade and therefore closely related to Indian culture. They were in part Indian in origin; and in their last struggle for survival on the banks of the Saskatchewan they were joined by the Indians, whose existence had also been brought to a final crisis by the coming of settlement on a large scale.

In contrast with the western United States, where constituted authority often toiled ineffectively in the rear of the adventurous plainsmen, the Canadian prairies were governed and policed before they were occupied by settlers on any large scale. It was true that a separate government for the Territories was not established until 1877 at Battleford; but as early as 1873, only four years after the transfer of the Hudson's Bay Company's territories, Sir John Macdonald introduced the bill which founded the North-West Mounted Police, the present Royal Canadian Mounted Police. In July 1874, a small force of nearly three hundred men, in the scarlet tunics, grey breeches, and round, flat-topped forage caps of their first service uniform, set out for the north-west. Sir John had determined that there would be 'as little fuss and feathers' as possible and the police were strictly a civil organization. But from the first they had the high standard and the strict discipline of a crack regiment, and the colour of the tunic was deliberately adopted to assure the Indians that the ideal of the force was the honour and fair dealing which they had associated with the British red-coats. In short order the police chased out the unscrupulous whiskey traders who had crept in from south of the border and were demoralizing the Indians; and it was not long before the chiefs were properly grateful for their new peace and security. 'If the police had not come to the country, where would we all be now?' asked Crowfoot, head chief of the Blackfoot nation. 'Bad men and whiskey were killing us so fast that very few, indeed, of us would have been left today. The police have protected us as the feathers of the bird protect it from the frosts of the winter.'

Yet the police were simply the forerunners of an army of government officials and agents whose fundamental purpose was to make ready the land of the west for the coming of the settlers. The old order was gone for ever. And the new régime had not yet brought the hoped-for good fortune. Each of the principal groups in the north-west — the white settlers, the Indians, and the Métis — revealed ominous signs of discontent and unrest. The brief burst of prosperity had ended in 1883; and the white settlers, who for a few short years had enjoyed the good crops and high prices of the boom, were suddenly confronted with the frosts, ruined harvests, and deflated land values of renewed depression. The Indians had been obliged to adjust themselves to the vastly changed circumstances of life on the reserves during a period of exceptional difficulty; and the Métis, who could no longer earn their accustomed livelihood as hunters of the buffalo and carriers for the Hudson's Bay Company, had become reluctant squatter farmers. Despite the inevitable delays which accompanied the settlement process, they had been treated, on the whole, with real consideration; and, in particular, the rectangular survey of the north-west had been carefully modified so as to preserve their long, narrow river lots. But the Métis claimed in addition that they shared with the Indians in the original title to the land of North America and could prefer an equally valid claim for compensation. The Canadian government, under the terms of the Manitoba Act, had already granted 1,400,000 acres in land and negotiable scrip to the half-breeds; and, in the opinion of western experts, such easily squandered compensation brought no permanent benefit to a restless and improvident people. The Métis demand remained ungranted; the Métis discontent deepened the unrest of the region. And it was in these circumstances that the people of the North Saskatchewan valley invited Louis Riel to return and to lead them in a constitutional agitation for the redress of grievances.

By the summer of 1884, Riel was back again in Canada. His power of leadership was as great as ever, his sense of vital revolutionary objectives was as sure as before. But he exhibited a curious mixture of motives and he completely misjudged the political conditions of the north-west of 1885. In public, he seemed devoted to the Métis cause; in private, he showed

CANADA, 1885

100 0   100 200 300 400 500
MILES

an unexpected readiness to abandon his followers for money. And although the Canadian government decided, at the last moment, to recognize the aboriginal title of the Métis and to grant them compensation in land and scrip, the public announcement of the establishment of a commission to carry out these purposes mysteriously failed to prevent the explosion. Riel imagined that he could achieve the bargaining power he had possessed in 1870. In reality his position was desperate. By this time the priests of the Roman Catholic church were implacable in their opposition to the agitation. The white settlers and the English-speaking half-breeds abruptly withdrew. And Riel was left with the Métis — the French half-breeds of Batoche and St. Laurent — and a few small bands of Indians. Late in March, 1885, the Métis drove back a small detachment of Mounted Police at Duck Lake; and the Indians, under Big Bear and Poundmaker, terrorized the valley of the North Saskatchewan. But nearly eight thousand troops — Canadians this time in place of the British who had been sent out to Red River in 1870 — were rushed west with determined speed by the new railway. The main body of the half-breed insurgents was driven in at Batoche, and the Indian resistance collapsed quickly thereafter. Riel was taken prisoner on May 15. At his trial in Regina, his lawyers sought to defend him on grounds of insanity; but Riel himself vigorously repudiated the plea. The court found him guilty and he was sentenced to be hanged.

In the meantime, while the seaboard and the prairies were producing protest movements, rebellions, and threats of secession, the central provinces of Ontario and Quebec were marked also with a good deal of unrest. Central Canada, under the operation of the National Policy of protection, was becoming ever more clearly distinguished from the rest of the country. The industrialization of the region continued steadily, despite the depression. The drift to the cities was unmistakable. Labour agitation in Ontario rose to a climax in 1887; and at the same time the still important farming interest in the province grew more and more dissatisfied with the protective tariff. The material for an attack on the Dominion and its national policies was accumulating; but up until the outbreak of the North-West Rebellion, Ontario alone had taken up the fight with the central government. While Quebec remained placid under the rule of Conservative prime ministers who were friendly to Sir John, Ontario bristled truculently under the leadership of the Liberal, Sir Oliver Mowat. Sir Oliver, who had become a provincial establishment in somewhat the same way as Sir John had become a national institution, had fought a long series of engagements with Ottawa over the federal power of disallowance. There was no more ardent supporter of provincial rights than he.

At this point Quebec, which had hitherto been the most tractable of all the provinces, was suddenly roused to an outburst of nationalist fury by the execution of Louis Riel. Outwardly Riel might have appeared a very unpromising candidate for the rôle of French-Canadian martyr. He was of mixed blood, his religious orthodoxy was highly dubious, he had been twice guilty of rebellion. But these faults were forgotten in a rush of sympathy for the man's cause and a wave of pity for his sufferings. In Riel the citizens of Quebec saw another patriotic Papineau who in the far west had defended a little colony of French blood and French culture against the oppression of the English. While in Ontario the people raged for the punishment of the dastardly rebels, in Quebec they begged for clemency for the misguided patriots. It was due to the influence of French Canada and the pressure of French-Canadian members in Sir John's cabinet that Riel was several times reprieved for brief periods and that a special commission was appointed to investigate his insanity. But the commission found, as the courts had found already, that the prisoner was a responsible being, and accountable for his actions. The Cabinet decided that the execution of the sentence should be postponed no longer; and Riel was hanged at Regina on November 16, 1885.

The execution of Louis Riel revived the old importance of ethnic and cultural differences in Canadian life. The agitation over the fate of the Métis leader, which brought out again all the chief contrasts which separated the country's two main ethnic groups, began a political revolution which fundamentally altered the whole balance of Canadian public life. Ever since Confederation, the Roman Catholic Church of French Canada, ultramontane in belief and illiberal in spirit, had helped materially to keep Quebec faithful to political conservatism. The movement represented by the *Institut Canadien* and the *Parti Rouge,* which drew much of its inspiration from the continent of Europe, had made a genuinely liberal attempt to break this domination; but the *Institut* and the *Parti Rouge* had been broken themselves under the unrelenting attack of the clergy. It was not the liberal philosophy of Europe, but the nationalist passion of French Canada, which, in the end, undermined the hold of the Conservative machine and the Roman Catholic clergy in the Province of Quebec. From the day of Riel's execution, a shift in political allegiance was probable, if not inevitable, in French Canada. It came more swiftly in the provincial than in the federal field. After a year of confused struggle, the province was swept from its traditional Conservative allegiance, and Honoré Mercier climbed into power early in 1887 as the champion of the outraged national feelings of his French-Canadian countrymen. In the federal field, Langevin and Chapleau, the two principal French Canadians in Sir John's cabinet, accepted the majority decision on Riel's fate; and their stand helped to stop any sudden and general defection from the Macdonald government. But in the federal general election of 1887 Sir John began to lose seats in Quebec, and this loss was simply the ominous prelude to the great Conservative downfall of 1896.

In 1887 the long train of regional discontents and national discouragements at last reached its climax. Foster's pamphlet on 'Canada First' was barely fifteen years old; but already it seemed like an oddity of the remote past, buried and forgotten under an avalanche of catastrophes. The national policies had not brought the unity and expansion of the country. The provinces, divided by cultural antagonisms and economic jealousies, were quarrelling among themselves and with the federal government. The air was heavy and sullen with disillusionment — with disgust for the present and disbelief in the future; and a movement, which was essentially an attack upon the basis of Confederation, began to gather strength. Sir John Macdonald had fought to establish a centralized, self-sufficient Canadian nationality; but now the political relationships within the Dominion were suddenly questioned and its position in the English-speaking world as a whole was again made the subject of dispute. Ever since the defeat of 1878 the Liberal party had tended to minimize the differences between it and the government; but now it moved boldly to take the lead of what looked like a great national protest movement.

The attack upon the Macdonald conception of the preeminence of the Dominion and the subordination of the provinces was launched by Honoré Mercier in the summer of 1887. That autumn five provincial delegations, headed by five provincial prime ministers — Fielding of Nova Scotia, Blair of New Brunswick, Mercier of Quebec, Mowat of Ontario, and Norquay of Manitoba — assembled in conference at Quebec, where the Fathers of Confederation had met twenty-three years before. By Macdonald's decision, the Dominion was not represented at the Conference; the provinces of British Columbia and Prince Edward Island remained aloof; and, with the exception of Norquay, all the provincial prime ministers were Liberal in politics. This enabled the Conservatives to insist that the Conference was really a partisan assembly, whose objective was not constitutional improvements, but bigger subsidies from the Dominion to the provinces. But, at the same time, the meeting at Quebec was a disturbing portent, which could not entirely be explained away. There was no provision for interprovincial conferences in the British North America Act; and in the absence of any specific procedure for the amendment of the constitution, the provinces simply assumed that they could change the statute in the same way as they had laid the basis for it at Quebec in 1864. In the resolutions of the Conference of 1887 there was certainly included a scheme for larger federal subsidies for the provinces; but in addition there were a number of suggestions for constitutional reform, which included the abolition of the Dominion power of disallowance and the provision that one half of the federal senators should be nominated by the provinces for life.

In the meantime, while this attack on political centralization was under way, the movement against economic nationalism was also gaining strength. The National Policy of protection was by now a vital element in the tripartite Conservative programme of western settlement, transcontinental railways, and protected industry; but the tariff was the last of the trio, the most unequal in its effects, and the most vulnerable politically. In 1886-87, a widespread demand arose that the commercial policy of Canada should be drastically changed so as to encourage a far greater measure of trade with the country's two traditional markets, Great Britain and the United States. People talked, rather vaguely, of some form of imperial federation which might give Canada trade preferences in the United Kingdom; but they talked more frequently, and with far more conviction, of commercial union, or its less frightening alternative, unrestricted reciprocity with the United States. In reality the two schemes were almost equally naïve. The assumption that Canada could persuade free-trade England to adopt a tariff was scarcely less absurd than the idea that she could induce protectionist America to take up free trade. But the Liberal party, which had been nearly ten years in opposition, was not in the mood to be too critical. As late as the general elections of the winter of 1887, Edward Blake, the Liberal leader who had succeeded Mackenzie, justified the tariff on the old ground of the need for revenue. But the defeat which resulted from this election was too much for him; and once again — and for what, perhaps to his own surprise and regret, turned out to be the last time — he handed in his resignation. Wilfrid Laurier, the French Canadian, the ex-member of the old *Parti Rouge,* succeeded to the Liberal leadership; and in 1887 he and his principal lieutenants committed the party to the policy of unrestricted reciprocity with the United States.

In 1887, the campaign against the Macdonald national policies, against the Macdonald conception of Confederation, at last reached its height. 'It is not improbable,' said the Montreal *Gazette* gloomily, in an editorial on the interprovincial conference, 'that the people will, sooner than many now imagine, be called on to determine whether the work accomplished in 1867 is to be undone, whether the Confederation is to be preserved or allowed to lapse into its original fragments preparatory to absorption into the United States. The signs of the times point to the imminence of so momentous an issue. The pro-provincial attitude of the Liberal party, its advocacy of commercial union, the anti-British tone of its press, and the present conference in which the representatives of every element hostile to Canada are found, all indicate that the Liberal party is arraying its force for an effort to smash the Confederation.'

[*IV*]

In 1887 Macdonald was seventy-two years old. He had been born — how far away it must have seemed — in the year of Waterloo. His career had spanned the winning of responsible government, the achievement of Confederation, the transcontinental extension of the Dominion. In 1884, he had been given banquets in Toronto and Montreal for the fortieth anniversary of his entrance into public life. In large measure his programme had been finished with the completion of the Canadian Pacific Railway; and in all sincerity he wanted to retire. But, with one of those amazing changes which make the drama of war and politics, he was driven from his position of triumph and security and put into a state of desperate defence. In his mind, his own personal ascendancy, the Conservative party, the national policies, and the Dominion of Canada itself were all linked in mysterious but essential association. And they were all threatened. He was an old man now, but his back was to the wall. He summoned up his vast reserves of power, of experience, of ingenuity, for what was perhaps the greatest fight of his entire career.

The opposition to Macdonald was formidable; but he did not stand alone. He had to meet and defeat the impulses and demands which had grown out of provincialism and depression; but, at the same time, he was sometimes supported, perhaps unconsciously, by new loyalties of a non-material order, as well as by old economic and political ambitions which had arisen long before the slump. Back of him was the ancient urge, which had persisted in the St. Lawrence region ever since the French régime, towards a strong and centralized political union — a union which would be allied with Great Britain and independent of the United States. Back of him also, at least in part, were those institutions, ideas, and emotions, cultural and religious in nature, which had begun to cluster around Confederation, as the final embodiment of this old British North American urge to unity. Confederation had been achieved first on the political and economic plane. But Foster and the young men of Canada First had believed that a cultural unity would follow these material achievements — would, in fact, be the best sign and guarantee of their success. Surely the depression had left Foster and his band in ignominious discredit? But had it — entirely? A memorial volume of essays, by the departed leader of Canada First, was published in 1890. And by that time, despite the depression, despite the shaky insecurity of the material basis of Confederation, were there not some faint, hesitating, premonitory signs of that Canadian culture, of that spiritual unity, which Foster had foretold?

Certainly the period saw the founding of important Protestant national churches, the growth and reorganization of the national system of education, and the first beginnings of the new national letters. It was a time when some of the old, petty internal rivalries disappeared, when the old feeling of colonialism was weakened. The divisions which had existed so long in the Protestant churches did not long survive Confederation. In 1875, the various Presbyterian bodies came together to form a single Canadian communion; and by two unions, of 1874 and 1884, the different Methodist groups agreed to join in a single national Methodist Church. The Royal Society of Canada was founded in 1881. The establishment of a branch of Laval University in Montreal in 1878 — a branch which subsequently developed into the University of Montreal — suggested the increasing interest in higher education in the Province of Quebec; and in 1887, when Victoria College and the University of Toronto agreed to unite, there began the process which was to bring together four colleges and universities, whose conflicts had often troubled the early history of Canadian education, in the enlarged federal union of the University of Toronto. The last two decades of the century saw the steady advance — particularly in the English-speaking universities — of higher education in the natural sciences and its beginning in the social sciences and history. The formal basis of a culture had been laid. And perhaps more surprising, in view of the omnipresent sense of economic failure and political frustration, there appeared the first groups of recognizably Canadian authors.

In 1880, Charles G. D. Roberts (Sir Charles Roberts) published his *Orion and Other Poems;* and Archibald Lampman, a young undergraduate at Trinity College, Toronto, discovered in the book that new sense of freedom from cultural colonialism which was beginning to excite a few of the young men of his generation. 'Like most of the young fellows about me,' wrote Lampman, 'I had been under the depressing conviction that we were situated hopelessly on the outskirts of civilization, where no art and no literature could be, and that it was useless to expect that anything great could be done by any of our companions, still more useless to expect that we could do it ourselves. I sat up most of the night reading and re-reading *Orion* in a state of the wildest excitement. . . . It seemed to me a wonderful thing that such work could be done by a Canadian, by a young man, one of ourselves.' This sudden realization of creative capacity, this awakening belief in the possibility of a Canadian culture, was more widely diffused, and more nearly justified, than it had ever been before.

The French school founded by Octave Crémazie was the first of the new literary groups; and Louis Fréchette, who was perhaps its most distinguished member, published his first book of verse as early as 1865. The principal English group was made up of four friends, Charles G. D. Roberts, Archibald Lampman, Duncan Campbell Scott, and Bliss Carman, who were all born between 1860 and 1862. Fréchette and his friends drew some of their easy eloquence and swelling rhetoric from the example of Victor Hugo; Lampman was inspired to a number of his rich effects by Keats; and there were influences of Swinburne, Tennyson, and Arnold in the poetry of Roberts and his friends. Without question, the Canadians employed their considerable degree of technical skill within the main tradition of French and English nineteenth-century romantic poetry; but they were Canadian also in their concern for the native environment, and their efforts to describe and interpret its distinctive features. Fréchette and his associates found the dominant themes of their inspiration in the countryside of Quebec, in the history and the faith of the French-Canadian people. The members of the English-speaking group of 1861 were linked with their native country chiefly through their absorption in the Canadian landscape and their sensitive and accurate rendering of its moods. Lampman, Carman, and Roberts were somewhat commonplace philosophers who specialized in a rather vague and diffuse type of personal emotion; but they were also accomplished and serious artists who made Canadians aware of Canadian nature through the tradition of nineteenth-century romanticism.

In one way all this was remote from the political struggle of the period; but in another and perhaps more fundamental way it was not. If the material influences of the period were making for weakness and division, the cultural and spiritual forces of the time were exerting some influence on the side of unity and strength. The scholars who founded the Royal Society, the clergymen who established the national churches, the poets who painted the national scene and evoked the national history, were all strengthening and enriching the loose, coarse fabric of Canadian life; and when depression and political division seemed to threaten the continuance of the new collective existence, these emotional and cultural forces became involved in the struggles. It was true that there were two literary schools, French and English; but while at times they helped to feed the ethnic quarrels of the period, they also served to promote the ideal of national unity. There were advantages as well as disadvantages in the position occupied by Macdonald. Through his long career, his long tenure of office, he had come to seem almost the embodiment of Canadian nationality. If, on the one hand, he was the almost guiltless victim of the world depression, on the other, he was the somewhat undeserving beneficiary of the national ideal. There was a curious balance of forces within the country. And the outcome was uncertain when Sir John began the last fight of his career.

The Liberal party had taken up the cause of provincial rights in domestic affairs and of 'continentalism' in external relations. Within Canada the design of a strong centralized government was threatened; and Sir John struggled to save the concept of the Fathers of Confederation from defeat. He succeeded at least in frustrating the extreme demands of the Interprovincial Conference of 1887. The work of that body was studiously ignored or openly ridiculed. And the provincial prime ministers, having triumphantly finished their resolutions, were in the uncomfortable position of not knowing quite what to do with them next. They got less help than they might have expected from the federal Liberals. The federal Liberals, it was true, had shown a tender concern for provincial rights. But they had also displayed a marked moral disapproval of larger subsidies as mere bribes to discontented provinces. And since constitutional proposals and bigger subsidies were inextricably mixed up in the programme of the Conference of 1887, it was a little difficult for the federal Liberals to say anything very flattering about it. The work of the Conference, having been duly declared imperishable by its authors, was forgotten in short order. The direct attack on the constitution had failed. But if the provincial and federal Liberals could not see eye to eye on all the proposals of 1887, they could at least unite heartily to denounce disallowance. And here Macdonald felt obliged to retreat. The effort to prevent Manitoba from chartering railways to the international boundary in competition with the Canadian Pacific Railway was abandoned, just as the attempt to fight Ontario legislation had been given up a little while before. Soon there would be other provincial statutes — the Jesuits' Estates Bill of Quebec, the Schools Act of Manitoba — which important groups among Conservatives would clamour to have disallowed. And warily Macdonald and his successors would refuse them.

The most serious offensive, however, was directed not against the constitution, but against the national economic policies. The most revolutionary proposal was that Canada should enter into a completely new economic relationship with the United States. In his gradual strategic retreat, Sir

John consented to make a few changes in the Conservative economic programme; but as often as not these changes strengthened the national policies rather than moderated them. In 1888, as a concession to the indignant west, the 'monopoly clause' of the Canadian Pacific Railway charter was repealed; but a year before, the government had tried to soothe the grievances of Nova Scotia by granting bonuses and increased duties on coal and primary iron and steel, with the idea of building up a large national iron industry in Cape Breton and mainland Nova Scotia. Rounded out in this fashion, the National Policy of protection was simply continued, without any serious modification at all. Macdonald remained true to the ideal of a diversified, partly industrialized national economy, which would not be entirely dependent on the markets of Great Britain and the United States. He wanted to escape commercial union or unrestricted reciprocity with the United States. But he was equally determined to avoid imperial federation and an imperial customs union with Great Britain.

In theory, of course, the Conservatives were in favour of imperial unity. The change which came over the British attitude to the Empire after 1875 ought to have delighted them. The early Victorians in England had comforted themselves with the thought that the Empire could not last for ever; the late Victorians discovered with delight that it was still in existence. The colonies, which had been previously regarded as 'retainers who will neither give nor accept notice to quit,' were now looked upon as promising children whose affection it would be highly desirable to cultivate. For generations the overseas possessions had languished in the shadow of imperial neglect. They were now haled, blinking, into the sunshine of Britannic favour. J. A. Froude and J. R. Seeley founded the new school of imperial propaganda; and in 1884 the Imperial Federation League was established in London. These blandishments were very respectfully received by a number of Conservatives in Canada; and Sir

John even became a member of the Imperial Federation League. But in reality the imperial federationists had no more effect on his conception of the Empire and of Canada's place in it than the Manchester men had had a generation before. All along he had believed firmly in the British connection; but he would never permit it to become a fetter on Canadian autonomy. He told a British editor in 1888 that a common legislature for the Empire was 'altogether impracticable.' He had no desire to sink Canadian fiscal independence in an imperial customs union. And he saw no reason why the Canada which Great Britain had defended so reluctantly should now rush to the assistance of the mother country in every small imperialist war. 'The Suez canal is nothing to us, . . .' he wrote in 1885 when a Canadian contingent was suggested for the Sudan. 'Why should we waste money and men in this wretched business? England is not at war, but merely helping the Khedive to put down an insurrection, and now that Gordon is gone, the motive of aiding in the rescue of our countrymen is gone with him. Our men and money would therefore be sacrificed to get Gladstone and Co out of the hole they have plunged themselves into by their own imbecility.'

For the Conservatives, therefore, imperial federation was almost as objectionable as commercial union with the United States. They stuck by their old programme of economic and political nationalism, of which the protective tariff was one of the chief expressions; and it was on the basis of the National Policy of protection that Sir John went into his last election, the winter election of 1891. The Conservatives argued that the Liberal policy of unrestricted reciprocity with the United States would necessitate direct taxation and would involve discrimination against British products. But, in the desperate circumstances of the moment, it was very hard to oppose the natural desire for change. The slump was at its nadir. The country was full of profound despair. The only really solid foundation of the Conservative party was the enormous prestige of an old man of over seventy-five years, who, in a curious half-questionable, half-legitimate way, had come to represent the unrealized ideal of a Canadian nationality. He toiled up and down the country in bitter winter weather. He put into his election manifesto the last cunning and the final wisdom of his career. The manifesto was politics. It was party propaganda. And yet for him it was perhaps none the less the truth. 'The question,' he told the electors, 'which you will shortly be called upon to determine resolves itself into this: Shall we endanger our possession of the great heritage bequeathed to us by our fathers, and submit ourselves to direct taxation for the privilege of having our tariff fixed at Washington, with the prospect of ultimately becoming a portion of the American Union? . . . As for myself, my course is clear. A British subject I was born — a British subject I will die. With my utmost effort, with my latest breath, will I oppose the "veiled treason" which attempts by sordid means and mercenary proffers to lure our people from their allegiance.'

Was this the real issue? Did unrestricted reciprocity in effect mean the abandonment of the whole idea of a separate and independent Canadian nationality? Sir John had said so in his manifesto. The Conservatives fervently agreed with him. And — what was more surprising and almost equally important — so did Edward Blake. From the start, Blake had disapproved of the new Liberal plank of unrestricted reciprocity. He had retired from the leadership, but not from the party nor from his seat in the House of Commons. And when the election of 1891 was suddenly sprung upon the country, it placed him and the other Liberal leaders in an impossible situation. Blake decided that he would not run, that he would give up his political career. He made this extreme sacrifice in order to avoid disrupting the party; but his withdrawal without explanation in the crisis of an election inevitably aroused suspicions of a Liberal split. The Conservatives made the most of Blake's mysterious re-

tirement. Blake, they confidently announced, was dumb because he agreed with Macdonald and not with Laurier. And
when, on March 6, 1891, the day after the election, Blake at
length broke silence by publishing his letter of resignation
to the West Durham Liberals, it was revealed that the Conservatives had been right. The ex-leader did believe that
unrestricted reciprocity would lead inevitably toward political union with the United States. And his letter completed the division and the rout of the Liberal party.

Sir John had won this last election. One night late in the
campaign, after a long day's speaking in harsh weather, he
was found lying across the bed of his private railway car, his
face ashen and exhausted. He never really recovered from
the effects of this chill; and one day early in May there was
suddenly something wrong with his speech. He told his secretary, Joseph Pope, that he was afraid of paralysis and that
he seemed to feel it creeping over him; and late on the afternoon of May 29, there came a last serious stroke, which could
only mean the end. Across the front page of one newspaper
were printed the three words 'He is dying'; and for eight days
he lay silent, while the messages poured in from all over the
Empire, and the whole of Canada waited for the bulletins
from the sickroom. They had told him in England that his
country could not be called a kingdom; but perhaps he had
beaten them in the end by making himself a king. His memory was a long list of Canadian names, an endless procession
of Canadian faces, a vast panorama of the Canada he had
helped to create. He had embraced a cause which had been
weakened by the rivalries of cultures, and discredited by the
tragedy of the depression. And he had clung to it to the end.

With the death of Macdonald, the battle for the original
national policies, for the original concept of a strong national
unity, entered upon its last agonizing stage. The election of
1891 had defeated unrestricted reciprocity and ended the so-
called 'continentalism' of the Liberals; but it had not
smothered the excitement which had been awakened by the

execution of Riel. For ten years after 1885, the conflict of cultures broke out throughout the country in fierce and widely separated fires. In Quebec Honoré Mercier soon showed how much the new nationalist Liberals differed from the anti-clerical *Rouges*. The *Rouges* had been inclined to criticize religious orders; but Mercier, looking about for some bold and striking measure with which to signalize the coming of the Liberals to office, found in the Jesuits' estates the very opening he wanted. The Jesuits had come back as a teaching order to Canada and had taken an aggressive part in Bishop Bourget's anti-Liberal campaign. Mercier had been educated at their college. And in 1888 he pushed a bill through the provincial legislature which gave the church authorities in Quebec a large money compensation for the Jesuits' estates which had been confiscated far back at the time of the British conquest. This raised a furore in Protestant Ontario. It helped indirectly to start an agitation in Manitoba against denominational schools. And in 1890 the legislature of that province passed a statute which established a completely non-sectarian educational system.

It was the Manitoba schools question which revived the question of provincial rights and broke the Conservative government. The Roman Catholic minority believed that its rights and privileges had been violated. It sought to have the new school law declared *ultra vires*; but the courts sustained the province. It petitioned the Dominion to disallow the act; but the Conservative government refused to intervene. There was one chance left. By the terms of the Manitoba Act, a religious minority might appeal to the Dominion against a provincial statute which affected its educational rights and privileges, and if necessary the Dominion might even itself pass remedial legislation to protect those rights. The Judicial Committee of the Privy Council decided that in this particular case an appeal did lie from the minority to the Dominion. The government heard the appeal, ordered Manitoba to supplement its school legislation in the interests of the Roman Catholics, and Manitoba refused. What was the Dominion to do? The French-Canadian members of the cabinet and the Roman Catholic hierarchy pressed for remedial legislation; the Protestant Conservatives were resolutely opposed to any federal interference with Manitoba's nonsectarian schools. Divided within itself and led in rapid succession by four different prime ministers, the government decided for interference, and plunged blindly towards its doom.

Before the remedial bill could be jammed through the House, the legal end of the Parliament approached and the government appealed to the country. Inevitably the general election of 1896 was fought upon the issue; and the Liberals took up their position for the battle of provincial rights on ground which could not have been more favourable if they had themselves selected it. The government, virtually at the request of the Roman Catholic hierarchy, was about to coerce Manitoba. Naturally, English Canada voted against the Roman Catholic hierarchy. And French Canada, which ought to have voted for the Roman Catholic hierarchy, voted instead for its favourite son. The two votes put Wilfrid Laurier into power. The Bishops had been defeated in Quebec. It looked like a miracle. But was it, after all, a real deviation from French-Canadian nature? Had the bishops been beaten by the principle of anti-clericalism or the sentiment of nationality? Provincial rights had triumphed over the Dominion's attempt to uphold the guarantees for minorities. But had not this result been achieved in large measure by those cultural loyalties and religious passions which had reawakened with the execution of Riel?

In the meantime, while the doctrine of provincial rights was triumphing politically in the election of 1896, the Dominion was losing case after case in the courts. The defeat of the federal government's superintending powers over education would not in itself have been very serious; but the decisions of the Judicial Committee of the Privy Council which occurred at about the same time brought changes of a very different order in the Canadian constitution. The Judicial Committee of the Privy Council, which had remained the supreme court of appeal for the Empire, faced what was certainly a novel and difficult task in the interpretation of the British North America Act of 1867. The Committee was composed of Britishers, who knew little about Canada and who were as inexperienced in the workings of a federal system as it is only possible for citizens of a unitary state to be. For a number of years, however, the members of the Committee seemed almost as concerned as had been the Fathers of Confederation themselves to emphasize the scope of the Dominion's residuary power to legislate for the 'peace, order and good government of Canada' in all matters not exclusively assigned to the provinces. By the judgment in *Russell* v. *The Queen* (1882), the Committee decided that the Federal Parliament could legislate under the residuary clause for genuine national objects even though such legislation might incidentally affect 'property and civil rights in the Province'; and it was thus laid down temporarily that the Dominion was not to be prevented from making laws upon the general or national aspects of a matter simply because the local and particular aspects of the same matter might have been entrusted to the provincial legislatures. This so-called 'aspect doctrine' might have been the starting-point of an important trend of interpretation; but it had not been established for long when it was abruptly and even violently reversed. This reversal coincided with Lord Watson's tenure of office in the Committee.

According to his pupil and admirer, Lord Haldane, Lord Watson dominated the Judicial Committee during the crucial decisions of the 1890's. From some quarter Watson seems to have acquired certain theoretical views on the nature of federalism; and it was possibly in the light of these prepossessions that he set out to interpret the terms of the British North America Act. He became convinced that the residuary clause, as expounded in *Russell* v. *The Queen*, might possibly imperil the federal nature of the constitution by its undue enlargement of Dominion powers; and in the so-called 'Local Prohibition Case' of 1896, he tried to reach what seemed to him a more acceptable compromise as between the local and central authorities. Admittedly there were certain peculiarities in the technique of his interpretation. At times his paraphrases of the British North America Act were decidedly free. He even — on occasion — misquoted it. By the plain terms of Section 91 of the Act, the enumerated powers of the Federal Parliament were simply declared examples or illustrations of its residuary authority; but Lord Watson virtually separated the residuary power from the enumerated powers and declared that the former was supplementary and inferior to the latter. On the basis of this analysis he decided that the Dominion, while legislating under the enumerated powers, might incidentally affect matters which had been entrusted to the provincial parliaments; but that, when making laws under the 'peace, order and good government' clause, it could not 'trench upon' provincial powers except in the special circumstances of a crisis. In effect, the decision in *Russell* v. *The Queen* had been overruled.

This was a judgment of crucial importance in the history of the Canadian constitution. At one stroke, the jurisdiction of the Federal Parliament was restricted, for most purposes, to the specific enumerated powers of Section 91. The residuary authority, which the Fathers of Confederation had regarded as the central buttress of their work, was reduced to insignificance as an emergency power in cases of crisis which had yet to be defined; and thus the examples had swallowed up the principle which, by the plain terms of the Act itself, they were intended to illustrate but not to restrict. Inevitably from that moment the legislative competition between the Dominion and the provinces settled down to a conflict between the enumerated powers of each; and, in this rivalry between the specific heads of Sections 91 and 92, there were certain very real advantages on the side of the provinces. 'The regulation of Trade and Commerce,' which had been granted to the Dominion, was a specific power of wide and general meaning; but the provincial right to legislate in relation to 'property and civil rights in the Province' perhaps possessed an even wider and more inclusive significance. It was, in fact, this particular provincial power — clause 13 of Section 92 — which was, in the future, to become virtually the real residuary clause of the Canadian constitution.

And so the first quarter century of Confederation came to an end. The whole conception of a separate Canadian nationality had been subject for two decades to pitiless attack. Yet the Dominion still stood. So long as Sir John Macdonald remained to defend it, it had stood almost intact, and the losses it had suffered and the discredit it had incurred thereafter came as a result of changes which he could not have foreseen or could not have prevented. He had tried to found a real national unity; but the long drawn out consequences of the execution of Riel had undermined his work. He had tried to establish a strongly centralized federation; but the courts had fundamentally altered the constitution which was the principal monument to his fame.

CHAPTER EIGHT

NATIONAL SUCCESS AND IMPERIAL REORGANIZATION

[*I*]

ON AN AFTERNOON in late August, 1896, the members of the House of Commons assembled in their chamber for the first session of the eighth, the newly elected Parliament of Canada. A short while before they had been sworn in. That venerable parliamentary official, the Gentleman Usher of the Black Rod, had then invited them to the Senate; and there the Speaker of the Senate had informed them, in the time-honoured phraseology, that 'His Excellency the Governor General does not see fit to declare the causes of his summoning the present Parliament of Canada until the Speaker of the House of Commons shall have been chosen according to law; but tomorrow, at the hour of three o'clock in the afternoon, His Excellency will declare the causes of his calling this Parliament.' The members had returned to the Commons chamber, where the mace still lay under the table, awaiting the election of a speaker. The room was rapidly filling up. Most of the ministers were in their places. And then everybody's gaze was suddenly fixed upon the tall, slight figure of a man who had just entered. He was well — even elegantly — dressed; people had noticed his gloves, stick, and silk hat at the swearing-in ceremony a little while before; and he had about him an air of unassuming but graceful distinction. There was a burst of cheering. And then Wilfrid Laurier, the new Liberal prime minister of Canada, took his seat to the right of the Speaker's chair, in the place which Sir John Macdonald and his successors had occupied for nearly twenty years.

It is seldom that the fortunes of a country change so dramatically as they did for Canada when the Liberals arrived in power in 1896; and it almost seemed as if Wilfrid Laurier suggested the coming of the new era in his own person. He was a very different man from the long line of Loyalists and Scots Canadians who had made, and governed, and exploited the country for so many years. He was a Roman Catholic, a French Canadian, a descendant of that far-off François Cottineau *dit* Champlaurier who had reached Quebec with the Carignan-Salières regiment in 1665. There was about him that charming air of old-fashioned courtesy which has so often been the special gift of his people to Canadian affairs. His gracious manner was instinctive, his sunny friendliness was genuine; and yet there was a subtle difference between these qualities and the jaunty good-fellowship of Macdonald. A touch of dignified reserve, a suggestion of fastidious aloofness, always remained with Laurier. And people became only gradually aware that in him there were hidden reserves of power, of stubborn will, of calculating shrewdness. He was at once more studied and elegant, and more remote and subtle than Sir John.

All this was true. The new prime minister's personality was distinctive and unmistakable. And yet — it was very odd — the longer he and his party remained in power, the more striking became a certain fundamental resemblance between him and his departed rival. They were both tolerant, easy-going political amateurs, interested in broad general questions rather than in detailed specialties. They shared a common belief in moderation, a common dislike of haste, a common preference for compromises and reconciliations. They grew equally fond of old faces and old loyalties, and there was a curious unacknowledged affinity be-

tween their ultimate aims and even their basic policies. As
time went on, as the first months of Liberal power gradually
lengthened into years, it became more and more obvious
that what had happened in the exciting new Canada of the
late nineteenth and early twentieth century was not so much
a change of government and leader, or even a change of
national strategy, as a complete and violent change of circumstances. Macdonald and Laurier were both passionate
Canadian nationalists; but the problems of nationality which
confronted them were sharply contrasted. Laurier was able
to solve with ease some of the difficulties which had baffled
Macdonald; but behind these, growing out of these, were
other problems which Macdonald had scarcely dreamed could
exist. Sir John, after all, had been concerned mainly with
the expansion of continental Canada; but, for what was
really the first time, Laurier faced the question of Canada
in world affairs.

The world through which the new Liberal government
set out to conduct Canada in the last years of the nineteenth
century was a world of strange contradictions, in which
present good fortune was overhung by the shadow of approaching trouble. But, in the first prosperous years of the
new régime, Canadians were scarcely even aware of the
political menace which had already crossed the horizon.
They were obsessed by the overwhelming fact that at last
the depression had lifted and that the expansion which
Canada had failed so long to achieve was at length at hand.
The new prosperity was real and general; and, in addition,
it had several important features which were especially
favourable to raw material-producing countries like Canada.
In a very real sense, the new manufacturing machine seemed
to have outrun its supply of foodstuffs. The huge industrial
cities, with their mobs of workers, created a persistent and
increasing demand for the cereals of the western North
American plains. Prices were rising; but they rose relatively
higher for natural products than they did for manufactured

goods; and once again, as even during the depression, the terms of trade for Canada were distinctly good. In the past, the manufactories of western Europe had come to look chiefly to the western United States for their supplies of wheat and flour. But in the 1890's, the frontier reached its appointed limit in the United States. The good lands had been taken up. But up north, in the Canadian prairies, a new land, untouched, unwasted, lay awaiting exploitation. The long, serpentine column of migrants, which for generations, for centuries, had been crossing and recrossing the international boundary between Canada and the United States, turned north again, for the last time. From 1760 to 1815 it had moved up from New England and New York into British North America. From 1850 to 1900 it had turned south-west again from Canada into the middle-western American states. Now it began the final march northwestward towards the last region of free and untouched land which remained on the North American continent.

The whole world seemed ready to hasten the exploitation of the Canadian west. Experienced and inexperienced, the settlers came in scores of thousands from central Canada, Great Britain, the United States, and Europe. The capital and capital goods were available in greater volume than ever before and at rates so low as to be totally unprecedented in the history of the West-European and American world. The new shipping, which had come into being since the decline of the old sailing vessels, could transport the great piles of grain and flour to the markets of Europe at freights which kept falling and falling until 1908. Even the technical problems of farming and home building in a rolling, grassland region with relatively few trees and a rigorous, semi-arid climate had been solved slowly and painfully by settlers and governments on both sides of the international boundary. The special requirement of the Canadian prairies, the need for a spring wheat which would mature early enough for the short growing season of the north-west, was almost dramatically satisfied at the very moment when the settlers were pouring into the region like an army. Red Fife, the hardy, prolific wheat with the fine milling qualities which had been brought from Scotland to Upper Canada by Duncan Fife far back in the nineteenth century, had become universally popular in its first North American homeland, had travelled with Canadian emigrants into the American middle west, and now returned to Canada again in the company of the last north-west migration. In the agricultural experimental stations which Canada set up in the prairies, William Saunders began to cross Red Fife with a number of other hardy varieties from Russia and northern India. His son, Charles E. Saunders, who was appointed Dominion Cerealist and later knighted for his achievements, continued and completed these experiments. By 1908 he had produced a wheat which excelled the old Red Fife in every department and matured approximately a week earlier. This was Marquis wheat. The Canadian west had been given its appropriate cereal at the very moment when it was at last ready to go into full production.

The swiftness with which the Canadian west was occupied and exploited was an astonishing example of the way in which the instruments and techniques of modern industrial capitalism could put an empty and untouched region to work. With every advantage in its favour, with the forces of the world converging momentarily to people the Canadian west, the government of Canada had little more to do than to direct the abundant energies at its disposal. This task was carried out with considerable ability. The twin pillars of Canadian land policy in the west were the free homestead system and the railway land-grant system as embodied in the enormous concession made to the Canadian Pacific Railway. Under Clifford Sifton, the new Minister of the Interior, who as Attorney-General of Manitoba had led the fight for non-sectarian schools in his province, the federal government plunged into a systematic campaign of publicity, with advertisements in thousands of papers, immigration agents everywhere on two continents, and great excursion trainloads of pressmen and farmers to behold the wonders of the 'last, best west.' Immigration, which had dwindled down almost to a single file of settlers, began to crowd out again towards the proportions of an army. In 1896, only 16,835 migrants had come to Canada — the lowest number since Confederation. There were 55,747 in 1901 and 211,653 in 1906. Already, even in these early days of settlement, production on the prairies began to mount rapidly. The days of the great five-hundred- and six-hundred-million bushel crops were still in the future; but already western agriculture was taxing the transport system east. In 1902, barns, elevators, terminals, and freight cars were packed and bursting with the wheat which sought to get through the bottleneck of the main line of the Canadian Pacific from Winnipeg to the head of the lakes.

What advantage would the Liberals try to take from this burst of good fortune? How would they attempt to direct and control it and by what national policies? Ten years before, when the campaign for unrestricted reciprocity was getting under way, the Liberals had presented themselves as 'continentalists' who denounced the economic nationalism of the Conservatives — as free traders who defended the natural trade routes of Canada against uneconomic railways and protected manufacturing interests. This Canadian variant of Manchester economic morality had reached a shrill crescendo in the general election of 1891; but it died softly away during the next few years, as the American market began to seem more unattainable and — somewhat surprisingly — less vitally necessary. On the one hand, the uncompromising McKinley tariff of 1891, followed by the even more uncompromising Dingley tariff of 1897, seemed to prove that there was no hope of the United States' reducing its tariff barriers to Canadian produce. On the other hand, the phenomenal growth of exports to the British market began to convince everybody that the economic future of Canada lay in its trade with the United Kingdom. Ever since Confederation, Great Britain and the United States had purchased between them, and in not unequal shares, the vast bulk of Canadian export staples; but from 1891 on the percentage of the total sent to the United States had been steadily declining and the percentage of the total sent to Great Britain had been just as steadily increasing. In 1896, the year the Liberals came into power, fifty-seven per cent of Canadian exports were shipped to the mother country. And it was at this highly appropriate moment that Joseph Chamberlain, the new Colonial Secretary of Great Britain, began his enthusiastic campaign for Empire trade and an imperial customs union.

The fiscal re-education of the Liberals was now complete. With the most accomplished dexterity, they abandoned their old policy and paid that of their rivals the supreme compliment of adoption. Most people naturally expected that Laurier would make Sir Richard Cartwright his new Minister of Finance. But Sir Richard was one of the old Reformers, an unrepentant low-tariff man, a warm friend of closer trade relations with the United States. His reward for his long services to the Liberal party in the days of its adversity was the relatively unimportant portfolio of Minister of Trade and Commerce; and it was W. S. Fielding, the veteran Liberal Prime Minister of Nova Scotia, whom the shrewd and realistic Laurier appointed as his Minister of Finance. The tariff which Fielding proposed in his first budget speech of 1897 may have slightly decreased the general level of Canadian protection; but it made no vital change in the Canadian fiscal system and its two major innovations actually increased the anti-American character of the tariff. The offer of reciprocity with the United States, which for years had been inserted in all Canadian tariffs, was now pointedly omitted, while at the same time there was included a clause which offered a reduction of duties of one-eighth to countries prepared to reciprocate. This reduction, without any *quid pro quo*, was immediately granted to Great Britain. In the next year, 1898, a special British preference, one-quarter lower than the general tariff, was created. Thus, in less than a decade, the Liberals had shifted from unrestricted reciprocity with the United States to imperial preference for Great Britain. Fewer than ten years before they had been dubiously regarded as probable annexationists; now they were made the blushing recipients of a poetical tribute from the Empire's unofficial poet laureate, Rudyard Kipling.

Surprisingly, in view of their past professions, the Liberals had strengthened the east-west trade route with Great Britain. Even more surprisingly, they did this at about the time when conceivably they might have obtained the very kind of reciprocity treaty with the United States which they had always been supposed to want. In 1898, a Joint High Commission was established to settle some of the outstanding issues between the United States and Canada, including the Pacific and Atlantic fisheries and the Alaskan boundary dispute. The Commission was interesting enough in itself, for, in sharp contrast with the Joint High Commission of 1871, in which Sir John Macdonald had been the only British North American representative, the British delegation in 1898 included one Englishman, four Canadians, and one Newfoundlander. The composition of the Commission was thus very novel; but equally novel was the attitude of self-confident indifference with which it was regarded by the Canadian press, including those very Liberal papers which a few years before had been so ardent for unrestricted reciprocity with the United States. 'The people of this country,' declared the Toronto *Globe*, the old friend of North American commercial union, 'would be glad to extend their trade with the United States upon fair terms, but the time when the markets of the United States were essential to their prosperity, if it ever existed, has gone by, and if our neighbours do not believe that Reciprocity would be profitable to themselves, they are welcome to go their own way in peace, while Canada will return with renewed energy to the development of her own resources and industries on independent lines. . . . We can say with absolute certainty that Canada is reasonably satisfied with things as they are and that there will be no great disappointment in this country if the Commissioners part without accomplishing anything but an exchange of some good wishes.'

Apparently the Canadian government shared this mood of self-confidence and complacency. After two lengthy sessions, one in Ottawa and one in Washington, the Joint High Commission broke up, having accomplished precisely nothing. It had failed completely to come to an agreement in the matter of the Alaskan boundary, and this was the real reason for its end; but it was curious that, despite this failure, the British delegates made no effort to finish the other business on the agenda, though invited by the Americans to do so. 'Now, Sir,' said Sir Wilfrid later in the House of Commons, 'the hon. gentleman [the leader of the Conservative party, Tupper] assumes that in all these negotiations we have been begging for reciprocity. . . . Let me tell the hon. gentleman that in this matter, as in all others, and especially in this one he is mistaken. I have no right to speak of what took place in the commission, but I have a right to refer to what is now in the minds of the Canadian people; and if we knew the hearts and minds of our people at present, I think I am not making too wide a statement when I say that the general feeling in Canada to-day is not in favour of reciprocity. There was a time when Canadians, beginning with the honourable gentleman himself, would have given many things to obtain the American market; there was a time not long ago when the market of the great cities of the union was the only market we had for any of our products. But, thank Heaven! These days are past and over now.'

Evidently a day of new enlightenment had dawned for the Liberals. They had changed their views on the protective tariff. They were also revising their old opinions on the problem of all-Canadian transport. From the moment of triumph in 1896, the new government, with the full support of such influential Liberal papers as the Toronto *Globe*, had shown a real determination to strengthen the east-west Canadian route at every point in competition with the United States. It proceeded to subsidize all-Canadian trans-continental lines and to bargain for lower freight rates within Canada. In 1897, by the Crowsnest Pass agreement with the Canadian Pacific Railway, it agreed to give financial support to the new Crowsnest line in return for substantial reductions in the rates between central Canada and the prairies. Six years later, in 1903, when Prime Minister Laurier announced the government policy which was to provide new transcontinental lines, he made as fervent an appeal to economic nationalism as any that the Conservatives had ever uttered. 'We consider,' he declared, 'that it is the duty of all those who sit within these walls by the will of the people, to provide immediate means whereby the products of those new settlers may find an exit to the ocean at the least possible cost, and whereby, likewise, a market may be found in this new region for those who toil in the forests, in the fields, in the mines, in the shops of the older provinces. Such is our duty; it is immediate and imperative. . . . Heaven grant that it be not already too late; heaven grant that whilst we tarry and dispute, the trade of Canada is not deviated to other channels, and that an ever vigilant competitor does not take to himself the trade that properly belongs to those who acknowledge Canada as their native or their adopted land.'

With an odd echo of the old days of 1872, when the two 'rings' had struggled for the original Pacific railway charter, there was a new rivalry between two companies for government favour and support. But — and this was a difference which made it very difficult for the government to impose an ideal solution — the competition was not now between two mere syndicates, but between two already existing railways, with extensive properties and great ambitions. One of these was, of course, the old Grand Trunk Railway, which, having staggered through the depression, now entered upon one of its brief, recurrent periods of recuperation. The other was the Canadian Northern Railway, which had just recently sprung into existence under the enterprising, the ingenious, the almost magical manipulations of William Mackenzie and Donald Mann. In 1895-96, the years which saw so many significant changes in the fortunes of Canada, these two companies began to loom up as possible competitors of the Canadian Pacific's monopoly in the Canadian west. In 1895, the Grand Trunk got a new general manager, Charles M. Hays, an American who had pulled the Wabash Railway out of difficulties in his early thirties. In 1896 Mackenzie and Mann obtained their first charter for a railway in Manitoba. The Canadian Northern, which developed rapidly in the next few years, was at first a western network solely, with a line to Port Arthur at the head of the Lakes. The Grand Trunk was, of course, a central Canadian railway, roughly paralleling the St. Lawrence navigation system, with a splendid main line which by this time stretched from Montreal to Chicago. At the opening of the nineteenth century, both railways were still regional systems; but the success of the east-west route, the apparent triumph of the design of all-Canadian transport, had roused in both of them a desire to rival the Canadian Pacific Railway.

In retrospect, it seems obvious that the government should have used its very great influence to persuade these two roughly complementary railways to co-operate with each other in a unified scheme. In theory this was the best solution; but in practice almost nobody wanted it. The government could no more resist the various provincial and regional pressures upon it than it could escape from the prevailing optimism of the time; and in the end it gave lavish assistance to both the Canadian Northern and the Grand Trunk in their transcontinental schemes. The first of these big enterprises to get under way was a curious hybrid of private capital and government ownership known as the National Transcontinental-Grand Trunk Pacific. The Canadian government undertook to build a line, called the National Transcontinental, from Moncton, New Brunswick, to Winnipeg and to lease it to a subsidiary of the Grand Trunk, the Grand Trunk Pacific Railway, which in turn was to construct a line of its own from Winnipeg to Prince Rupert, on the Pacific coast, *via* the Yellowhead Pass. In the meantime, the Canadian Northern had already been buying up short lines in central Canada; and from 1908 to 1915 it proceeded to complete the last expensive links in a third transcontinental which stretched from Quebec to Vancouver. As a result of these spectacular achievements, the mileage of the Canadian railways rose from 18,140 in 1901 to 30,795 in 1914. There were more miles of railway in Canada for each one thousand inhabitants than there were in any other country in the world. The cost had been enormous; and it was largely borne by the Canadian government, either by direct contributions or by guarantees for railway bonds. The Dominion spent 155 million dollars on the National Transcontinental and the ill-fated Quebec bridge. It guaranteed 35 million dollars of Grand Trunk Pacific Railway bonds and nearly 60 million dollars of Canadian Northern bonds. In 1867, at the time of Confederation, the public debt of British North America had been approximately 96 million dollars; in 1913 — and very largely as a result of the heavy expenditures on railways, canals and harbours — it had risen to roughly 521 million dollars.

For the first time in history, the whole of transcontinental British North America was marching in unison through a period of unexampled prosperity. By every material test the

rate of achievement was high. Production of wheat increased from 55 million bushels in 1901 to 132 million in
1911. Net value of manufactures rose from 215 million
dollars in 1901 to 565 million in 1911. It was a national success, in which all regions participated, which linked all
regions for the first time in a common material interest based
on the vast expansion of the wheat-producing west. To be
sure, there were other enterprises, more regional in character, which got under way at about the same time. The
pulp-and-paper industries and the great hydro-electric power
developments of Ontario and Quebec date from this period.
The gold of the Yukon, the lead, zinc, and copper of British
Columbia, the silver and nickel of northern Ontario, were
all important novelties in Canadian economic life. But, for
a while at least, the expansion of the prairies overshadowed
everything else. The settlement of the west, the building of
its houses and barns, the provision of its community equipment, the inward transport of its needed manufactures, and
the carriage of its produce outwards to the markets of the
world was a great, exciting communal adventure in which
all the provinces took a larger or smaller part. British
Columbia provided lumber for building construction. The
Maritime Provinces built rails and rolling stock for the new
transcontinentals. Central Canada manufactured tools, and
clothes, and furniture for the hundreds of thousands of new
consumers who had suddenly appeared in the west. It was,
in view of the widely separated and extremely varied regions
of the Canadian economy, a closely connected, interde-
pendent system. It was national in extent; and its industrial, financial, and transport centre lay in the provinces of
Ontario and Quebec. From the days of the fur trade onward, the economic life of British North America had shown
an irresistible tendency to concentrate in the region of the
lower St. Lawrence valley. And the new centralization,
based ultimately on western wheat, was as great as any of its
predecessors.

[*II*]

This amazing economic success of Canada was the central fact of the period. The country filled out, took form and life and vigour. Regional inequalities and provincial discontents seemed to dwindle away in the achievement of a general well-being. The consciousness that the old national objectives had at length been triumphantly attained, created, for what was almost the first time, that common sense of achievement in the past, that common confidence in the promise of the future, which are the marks of an emerging nationality. Canada had solved — or seemed to have solved — its own internal problems. It could look abroad. It was ready and eager to express its new feeling of national consciousness, to claim the status in world affairs to which it now felt entitled. But the time was past when it could do this without danger. And the fortune or misfortune of its destiny was that the world in which it was burning to assert itself was a world which threatened to involve it in trouble. When for the first time in its history Canada began to look anxiously beyond its borders, the horizon of world affairs was perceptibly darkened with approaching trouble. International society was overshadowed with imperialist rivalries and threatened with imperialist wars; and these new impulses, far from being remote from the Dominion, showed themselves as vigorously as anywhere in Great Britain and the United States. By a curious coincidence the mother country and the Republic emerged from their splendid isolation at about the same moment of time. Impelled both by a sense of widening opportunities and by a sudden realization of increasing danger in a world which was now crowded with great aggressive national states, the two English-speaking powers plunged together into a course of direct action in world affairs. The change came somewhere about the middle 1890's. The United States began to show an imperialist interest in the Americas, and Great Britain an immediate concern for the balance of power in Europe. The United States fought the Spanish-American War and Great Britain the war in South Africa.

It was through Great Britain that Canada was first brought into touch with this exciting new world. During the greater part of the nineteenth century, the mother country had been opposed to entangling alliances in Europe and unenthusiastic about the relationship with the self-governing colonies. But it was hard to remain quite so complacent in the dangerous days with which the century ended; and Great Britain began to show a marked interest in both the imperial connection and a European entente. This urge to make new friends and to cultivate old relationships was perfectly embodied in Joseph Chamberlain, who became Secretary of State for the Colonies in the new Salisbury administration in 1895. Chamberlain was the son of a dissenting shopkeeper, a successful manufacturer of screws in Birmingham; and his appointment to the Colonial Office was not without its symbolic significance. Manchester — in the person of Richard Cobden — had done its utmost to destroy the British Empire; Birmingham — in the person of Joseph Chamberlain — would earnestly endeavour to unite it again. People were astonished that Chamberlain, who had his pick of any office in the cabinet, should have decided upon the hitherto lowly Colonial Office. But Chamberlain knew better than most what the world of the future was going to be like; and he proceeded to make the Colonial Office the seat of his own personal ascendancy in the cabinet and the centre of a completely new policy in external affairs. It was Chamberlain who inspired and led the negotiations for a German alliance. It was Chamberlain who set about enthusiastically to reorganize and centralize the British Empire.

His first great opportunity came with the celebration of Queen Victoria's Jubilee in 1897. This second Jubilee, the Diamond Jubilee, was an even more imperial pageant than its predecessor had been ten years before. The princes, prime ministers, and potentates of an enormous empire were present. The troops of every colour and creed, from every dependency and self-governing colony, marched through the packed London streets: and a picked Canadian contingent of Grenadiers, Highlanders, troopers of the Governor-General's Body Guard, and expert, scarlet-coated horsemen of the Royal Canadian Mounted Police followed Sir Wilfrid — plain Mr. Laurier no longer — through cheering crowds in the long Jubilee procession. Through the colour and splendour of those early summer days, through a long series of dinners, receptions, addresses, and reviews, Mr. Chamberlain shepherded his guests, the colonial prime ministers, with every mark of attention and honour. And the new order of close and friendly co-operation between the mother country and the colonies was admirably suggested in a photograph taken at the Colonial Office which showed Chamberlain, with monocle, white waistcoat, and immaculately pressed trousers, seated impressively in a throne-like chair, while his colonial premiers stood in respectful rows behind him.

The Colonial Conference was, in fact, perhaps the most important political incident of the Jubilee of 1897. Actually, it was not the first of its kind, for previous meetings of a somewhat similar character had been held in 1887 and again in 1894. But it was the first conference which was attended by the prime ministers of the self-governing colonies in a body and the first conference also which was taken seriously by British officialdom. Obviously there were three chief aspects of imperial relations — commercial, political, military. There were three obvious means by which the Empire might be more closely related — a customs union, or *Zollverein*, an imperial council or parliament, and a unified, centralized system of imperial defence. The old Imperial Federation League had struggled in vain to find a way of achieving these unities; but it was the 'great dream' of Chamberlain's life to succeed where others had failed. He made a strenuous effort at the Conference. He was at his best — business-like, straightforward, enthusiastic, and persuasive.

Yet, in the main, the colonial prime ministers either opposed or passively resisted this pressure. It was true that in public Laurier made a few grandiloquent references to a grand imperial council or an imperial legislative body; but in the sessions of the Colonial Conference, where alone serious decisions were made, he supported, and often led, the other colonial prime ministers in their defence of colonial autonomy against imperial centralization. The fact was that Laurier held very much the same view of the imperial relationship as Macdonald had voiced far back at the time of Confederation; but he had to meet and defeat a very different British effort at revision. Macdonald and the colonial statesmen of his generation had struggled to preserve the imperial connection from the attempts of Cobden and the Manchester men to sever it completely. Laurier and the premiers gathered together in the Colonial Office in 1897 sought to prevent Chamberlain and his associates from tightening the imperial tie into a confining band. Ever since the struggle for responsible government — instinctively at first, but with gradually increasing sense of purpose and direction — Canada had sought to transform the Empire into a commonwealth of free and autonomous nations, united by complementary interests, similar institutions, and common ideals. Even yet, Laurier could not see this novel political objective clearly in all its details; but he knew that the Canadian conception must be saved from Chamberlain just as it had been saved from Cobden — that the effort to regiment the Empire into a closed and centralized system must be stopped. This struggle against the second of the two extreme British plans for the Empire lasted for years. The Colonial Conference of 1897 was simply the first round of the fight; but obviously it was not Chamberlain's. 'The Prime Ministers here assembled,' ran the principal political resolution of the Conference, 'are of the opinion that the present political relations between the United Kingdom and the self-governing Colonies are generally satisfactory under the existing condition of things.'

The South African War — that ominous explosion of trouble with which the century closed — brought out, in another way, these conflicting tendencies within the changing Empire. Chamberlain, of course, hoped that the war would bring into reality his scheme of unified imperial defence. He wanted the self-governing colonies to send official contingents to South Africa; and there is no doubt that the two imperial representatives in Canada, the new Governor-General, Lord Minto, and the General Officer Commanding the Canadian militia, Major-General Hutton, were anxious to have Canada take an active part in the war. Lord Minto was a soldier-sportsman who had had no political experience before coming to Canada, but who had acquired a good deal of practical knowledge of the Empire during his military career. He was, as Laurier remarked later, 'absolutely untrained in constitutional practice'; but, though he could be 'stiff' in defence of his views on military matters, he became a good constitutional governor, with a tactful manner, and a shrewd sense of the powers and limitations of his office. When the issue of a Canadian contingent to South Africa became uppermost, Minto did not hesitate to put 'the imperial view of the question strongly before Sir Wilfrid'. But, at the same time, he had come to understand Canadian opinion and to appreciate Laurier's difficulties; and he took care not to urge a step whose wisdom in private he considered doubtful. Major-General Hutton was a good deal less tactful and discreet. His main purpose was to reform the Canadian militia and to make the Canadians military minded; and he suffered from an inveterate inability to realize that he was the servant of the government of Canada and not an independent military autocrat. Hutton may have wished — and worked — to commit the Canadian government to military participation in the South African War; but his authority and influence were, of course, extremely limited, and he was powerless to affect the final decision.

Imperial pressure did not take Canada into the war. Her entrance was the result of a deliberate national decision; and this decision was even more an expression of awakening national consciousness than it was of grateful imperial loyalty. In the end what decided the government to send an official contingent was a great mounting wave of public opinion which reached its climax in the disasters of 'Black Week' when Buller, Gatacre, and Methuen all met their tragic reverses in South Africa. French Canada, in general, looked without much concern or interest upon the struggle; but English Canada identified itself emotionally with the security and prestige of the Empire, and morally and intellectually with the cause of the disfranchised Outlanders in the Transvaal. Thus, at the moment when a turbulent world began for the first time to press in upon her old isolated security, there appeared, in its first simple form, the prime difference which separated French from English Canadians in their attitude to the external world. It was a new, but terribly complex phase of the old endless problem which from the first had conditioned Canada's growth and moulded her character. It was a crucial aspect of national unity which haunted Sir Wilfrid for the last twenty years of his life. 'If there is one thing,' he declared in the debates of 1900, 'to which I have given my political life it is to try to promote unity and harmony and amity between the diverse elements of this country. My friends may desert me, they can withdraw the trust which they have placed in my hands, but never shall I deviate from that line of policy. Whatever may be the consequences, whether loss of prestige, loss of popularity, or loss of power.' Confronted by the rising clamour of English Canada for intervention in South Africa, Sir Wilfrid, a French Canadian himself, decided that an apathetic French Canada must accept the decision of the majority.

Nearly thirty years before, in December, 1871, the last of the old British garrison regiments had marched, homeward-bound, down to the quays of Quebec singing 'Auld Lang Syne.' And it was from Quebec that the Second Royal Canadian Regiment sailed on the afternoon of October 30, 1899, for South Africa. There had been a great review in the esplanade — with speeches by Minto, Laurier, and Hutton; and then the troops swung through the steep and twisting streets of the old city down to the river. The crowd filled every dock on the waterfront, clustered over the palisades, and lined the great walls of the citadel. The deck of the Allan liner *Sardinian* was thick with dark tunics and white helmets; the men had climbed high into the rigging, and one soldier swung his cap from the top of the first mast. Then the big steamer cast off, the first gun of the citadel roared out, and the crowd crashed into the strains of 'God Save the Queen.' In the clear late-afternoon sunlight of autumn, the *Sardinian* stood out down the St. Lawrence, escorted by a little fleet of gaily decorated tugs and pleasure boats, heralded by the booming guns of the citadel and the screaming whistles of the river craft. Then in a little while the sun went down over Quebec; and from the decks of the *Sardinian* they could watch the spires and ramparts against a gaudy sky — they could see the long dark blue line of the Laurentians topped by a clear yellow light that dwindled into green. As it grew darker, the ship settled into the long journey down the river towards the open sea. She passed Grosse Isle at seven o'clock and l'Islet at eight-twenty. It was a fine night, with a clear, starry sky.

In all, about seventy-three hundred Canadians crossed the ocean to fight in South Africa. It was a relatively small number, but these were still the days of small British armies; and it began a completely new chapter in the military history of the Empire. The armed partnership in South Africa was an important step in the advance of the new colonial nationalities — an important stage in the long ascent from Empire to Commonwealth. It did not mean, as Chamberlain discovered in the new Colonial Conference of 1902, that Canada was any more prepared to accept a centralized imperial system, either political or military; but it did mean that Canada recognized that there were imperial wars in which her interests, either material or moral, might require her to engage as an independent power. 'What we have done,' said Laurier proudly in the debates of 1900, 'we have done . . . in the plenitude, in the majesty of our colonial legislative independence. . . . I am free to say that whilst I cannot admit that Canada should take part in all the wars of Great Britain, neither am I prepared to say that she should not take part in any war at all. I am prepared to look upon each case upon its merits as it arises. . . . I claim for Canada this, that, in future, Canada shall be at liberty to act or not to act, to interfere or not interfere, to do just as she pleases, and that she shall reserve to herself the right to judge whether or not there is cause for her to act.'

In the meantime, while this struggle over the reorganization of the Empire was still going on, it became involved in the problem of Anglo-American relations. Just as Great Britain sought new agreements in Europe and Asia, so she hoped for a more cordial understanding with the United States of America; and Canada, as a power which was politically within the British Empire, and geographically within the North American continent, was vitally concerned in the growth of this new Anglo-American friendship. The interests of Great Britain and the United States ranged widely over oceans and continents; but some problems of their relationship directly affected Canada, and of these the most immediately important was the controversy over the Alaskan boundary. Ever since 1898, when the Yukon gold rush had suddenly magnified the importance of the north-west coast, the boundary of the Alaskan panhandle had remained in dispute between Canada and the United States. And now, while the almost friendless Empire faced the tragic embarrassments of South Africa, the whole question of an Anglo-American understanding — which would necessarily include the Alaskan boundary — was suddenly raised again.

The definition of the Alaskan boundary almost invited trouble. The ultimate authority in the matter was the Anglo-Russian Treaty of 1825; but, so far at least as the southern part of the boundary was concerned, the treaty spoke in somewhat ambiguous phrases. According to its terms the boundary, from the Portland Channel north, was to 'follow the summit of the mountains situated parallel to the coast' so long as this crest was to be found within ten marine leagues of the sea; and in case at any point it extended beyond this limit, the boundary was to be 'formed by a line parallel to the windings of the coast and which shall never exceed the distance of ten marine leagues therefrom.' Thus the treaty itself apparently included two alternative boundaries. Far more than most such documents, it invited a legitimate division of opinion as to its meaning. The United States insisted that there was no mountain range situated parallel to the coast which conformed to the terms of the treaty and that therefore the boundary must everywhere be drawn ten marine leagues from the shore and so as to conform to its every sinuosity. Canada, on the other hand, affirmed that there were mountains fairly close to the ocean and that the boundary could be drawn along them parallel to the general trend of the coast. By the first interpretation Canada would be entirely excluded from the ocean; by the second she would be given access to the sea.

Unfortunately there was at least one serious flaw in the Canadian case. All the maps, including the British maps, gave the unbroken strip or *lisière* for which the United States contended; and until the Yukon gold rush brought a sudden commercial value to the coastline, Canada had never challenged this apparently accepted interpretation. There was thus some reason for the United States' conviction that the Canadian case had been trumped up. But, on the other hand, Canada did not feel in the least estopped from presenting it. The Canadians considered that, by the actual terms of the Treaty of 1825, their legal argument was good. Moreover they were convinced that their political position was excellent. The cause of English-speaking friendship was advancing and a general settlement of several outstanding Anglo-American difficulties was about due. Great Britain owed Canada something for her help in South Africa. And — even more important — the United States was soon to be under even greater obligation to Great Britain for a major concession in Central America. In other words, Canada might gain access to the sea through the Alaskan panhandle either as a legal right or as a political *quid pro quo.*

For the fact was that the United States was about to demand — and to secure — the unconditional surrender of British treaty rights in the project of a canal through the isthmus between North and South America. This was the scheme which eventually resulted in the forcible creation of the Republic of Panama and the building of the Panama Canal by the United States; but, in the middle of the nineteenth century, when the arrangements for the canal were first made, no such outcome had even been contemplated. By the Clayton-Bulwer Treaty of 1850, the two contracting parties, Great Britain and the United States, had agreed to construct and maintain a canal through the isthmus on terms of perfect equality. In 1850 the Republic had formally accepted the idea of a partnership; but now in 1900 she was determined upon complete and exclusive control. In her search for a cordial Anglo-American friendship, Great Britain was even prepared to consider this enormous concession; but she and Canada naturally assumed that it could only be granted as part of a general settlement which would be marked by equal generosity on both sides. In their opinion, even the full satisfaction of Canada's claims on the northwest coast could hardly be more than an adequate return for the surrender of British treaty rights in an enterprise of such vast commercial and political significance as the isthmian canal. But the United States refused to make any territorial concessions whatever in Alaska; she even refused a much more modest British and Canadian proposal to submit the Alaskan boundary to arbitration — though arbitration was the method traditionally used to settle such Anglo-American disputes and though the United States had just forced Great Britain to accept it in the matter of the Venezuela boundary. In short, what the United States intended to get was the complete surrender of British treaty rights in the canal project without any compensation whatever.

For a moment, the British hesitated. Could they ask Canada, whose troops were even then fighting for the Empire in South Africa, to surrender the one bargaining asset she possessed in the Alaskan boundary dispute? It turned out, in the end, that they could and did; and Canada, for whom surrender to pressure from the United States was becoming a somewhat familiar exercise, gave way at Great Britain's request. In February, 1900, at a time when the Empire faced the worst crisis of the South African War, Sir Julian Pauncefote for Great Britain and John Hay for the United States signed a new isthmian canal agreement which modified the old Clayton-Bulwer Treaty. This new arrangement empowered the United States to build and manage the canal; but it also provided, in terms modelled on those of the Suez Canal Convention, that the canal would be free and open in peace and war to the ships of all nations, and it invited other powers to join with Great Britain and the United States in maintaining this fundamental neutrality by collective guarantee. These provisions were by no means acceptable to the American Senate. The rules of free navigation which Great Britain found quite satisfactory in the Near East were too binding for the United States in Central America. And so, in November, 1901, Great Britain gave way a second time and a new Hay-Pauncefote Treaty completed the exclusive control of the United States over the canal. Thus, at a time when the rest of the world was largely hostile, the new Anglo-American friendship had been maintained; and Canada — as well as Great Britain — had contributed to the heavy price paid for it.

Once the isthmian business was settled to its entire satisfaction, the United States turned back to the Alaskan dispute. Like the problem of the canal, the problem of the boundary ultimately depended upon a treaty; but the United States did not look upon these two solemn engagements in exactly the same fashion. In the eyes of the American administration, the Clayton-Bulwer Treaty of 1850 was a preposterous document which must be entirely abrogated; but the Anglo-Russian Treaty of 1825 was a sacred text which must be rigidly enforced. The new President of the Republic, Theodore Roosevelt, who had succeeded on the assassination of McKinley, was convinced that the Canadian case in Alaska, when tested by the actual terms of the Treaty of 1825, was completely worthless. He compared it to the right of some Scandinavian country to the ownership of the Orkney Islands. 'The claim of the Canadians,' he declared in a further illustration of the same argument, 'for access to deep water along any part of the Alaskan coast is just exactly as indefensible as if they should now suddenly claim the island of Nantucket.' Since Alaska was not an island under the exclusive sovereignty of the United States, but a segment of a continent whose boundary marched throughout with that of Canada, the relevance of this emotional appeal to Nantucket was not very clearly apparent. But it was, at all events, fairly certain that the President would not give way an inch. His frequently repeated motto in the conduct of foreign relations was: 'Speak softly and carry a big stick, you will go far.' And in March, 1902, he proceeded to obey the second, if not the first, part of this pious injunction by sending troops to southern Alaska.

The President was quite prepared, if necessary, to use force — 'to run the line as we claim it, by our own people'; but in the meantime he was still willing to get his way by peaceful methods of his own choosing. Canada suggested reference of the matter to the Hague Court, or arbitration with some neutral outsider as umpire; but these proposals were summarily rejected. The Americans, convinced of the legal strength of their own case, would consent to nothing but a strictly judicial settlement: and the Canadians, intimidated by the prospect of trouble which as Roosevelt complacently remarked 'would be death for them,' had no course but to accept the American ultimatum. By the agreement of January, 1903, the Alaskan boundary was to be determined by a tribunal which was to consist of 'six impartial jurists of repute who shall consider judicially the questions submitted to them, each of whom shall first subscribe an oath that he will impartially consider the arguments and evidence presented to the tribunal and will decide thereupon according to his true judgement.' Three jurists were to be nominated by each party to the dispute.

The terms of this agreement had been virtually dictated by the American administration; but curiously enough, they were not instantly accepted by the American Senate. The Senate, in fact, was worried about a point of capital importance. If the projected tribunal were to reach a majority decision in the Alaskan dispute, obviously one of the impartial jurists would have to vote against his country's case. What if he should be an American? Admittedly the chances of this dreadful possibility's occurring did not seem to be very great. But the words 'impartial' and 'impartially' in the treaty had a very ominous look to them; and, after all, it was better to be safe than sorry. With all this in mind, the senators — according to Henry Cabot Lodge's delightfully candid memoir — 'could not agree to having anybody on the tribunal who would yield on the Canadian claim.' The government hastened to remove these senatorial apprehensions by revealing the names of the American nominees. These were Elihu Root, the Secretary of War, who had dispatched the troops to Alaska, George Turner, senator for the State of Washington, which was violently opposed to any concession to Canada, and Henry Cabot Lodge himself, who had publicly condemned the Canadian case. 'When these selections were made known in confidence to the Senators,' wrote Lodge, 'there was no further objection to the treaty. . . .' On the whole, the contented acquiescence of the senators was not very surprising. Neither was the furore which arose in Canada when the President's appointments were announced.

The three impartial jurists nominated by Great Britain and Canada were Lord Alverstone, Lord Chief Justice of England, Sir Louis Jetté, Lieutenant-Governor of Quebec and a former justice of the Superior Court of that province, and Allen B. Aylesworth, a leading member of the Ontario bar who subsequently became Minister of Justice for Canada. Obviously the British delegation was not a unit, for it was composed of representatives from two countries; and to win the decision — since the solidarity of the American delegation had been so thoroughly assured — the United States had merely to detach Lord Alverstone from his colleagues. Supposedly this was to be done by legal arguments before the tribunal. But was that any reason to neglect diplomatic pressure upon the British cabinet? Apparently it was not. For, in a series of letters, messages, and intimate conversations, which began long before the tribunal opened, the United States sought to impress the British government with the dire consequences which might follow if the commissioners failed to reach a satisfactory solution. And, as the legal proceedings drew towards their crisis in the early days of October, 1903, this diplomatic pressure was renewed and intensified behind the scenes. Having uncompromisingly rejected diplomacy for law, the Americans now proceeded to strengthen law with diplomacy. The results of these additional precautions were certainly all that could be desired. As Theodore Roosevelt put it later in his straightforward way, the British government 'tipped the wink to the Chief

Justice.' In fact, the British government appeared to do even better. It tipped a fresh wink whenever the Americans thought that Lord Alverstone seemed to stand in need of one.

By the award of the tribunal, the United States was given an unbroken *lisière* nearly as wide as she had claimed, together with two of the four small islands at the mouth of the Portland Channel. As a whole, the award looked more like a diplomatic compromise than an inflexible judicial decision; and the settlement of the islands seemed particularly dubious, for both sides had claimed them as a group, and no arguments nor evidence whatever had been presented to the tribunal for their partition. Unquestionably the United States had a strong legal case in her favour; but the long train of circumstances which had led up to the award, and the background of brutal imperialism on both sides of the Atlantic against which it was set, produced a nationalist reaction in Canada more violent and sustained than anything in the history of the country. The Canadians believed that they were simply the duped victims of American and British imperialist power politics; and in the first days of furious indignation which followed the rendering of the award, even Sir Wilfrid Laurier gave expression to this double resentment which was so characteristic of Canadian nationalism. 'I have often regretted, Mr. Speaker,' he said, speaking in Parliament with an ungrammatical emotion which was strange to him, 'and never more than on the present occasion, that we are living beside a great neighbour who I believe I can say without being deemed unfriendly to them, are very grasping in their national actions, and who are determined on every occasion to get the best in any agreement which they make. I have often regretted also that while they are a great and powerful nation, we are only a small colony, a growing colony, but still a colony. I have often regretted also that we have not in our own hands the treaty-making power which would enable us to dispose of our own affairs. . . .

It is important that we should ask the British Parliament for more extensive powers so that if we ever have to deal with matters of a similar nature again, we shall deal with them in our own way, in our own fashion, according to the best light that we have.'

The reassertion of independence against both the United States and Great Britain was not, however, the only consequence of the Alaskan dispute. The award not only hastened the growth of the new relationship within the British Empire; but it also helped to promote a more general realignment among the English-speaking peoples. In 1904, the settlement of the outstanding disputes between France and England was to lay the basis of the Anglo-French *Entente;* but already, in 1903, the award of the Alaskan tribunal had removed the last serious barrier to a less formal, but no less real, Anglo-American understanding. In its own way, the settlement of the Alaskan boundary helped to prepare the English-speaking peoples for the trials of the future. It was a factor of some importance in the rise of Canadian nationality, in the emergence of the British Commonwealth, and in the growth of Anglo-American friendship.

[*III*]

The Canada which responded to these political shocks and to the economic stimulus of western expansion was growing rapidly, and rapidly assuming its modern composition and character. The period from 1896 until the beginning of the War of 1914-18 saw the third and greatest migration of peoples which had ever come to British North America. The pre-Loyalist Yankees and the Loyalists of the eighteenth century had assured the English-speaking character of the northern provinces. The English, Scots, and Irish immigrants of the first half of the nineteenth century had filled out the old provinces and solidly occupied the more accessible parts of the half-continent. And now, for what was really the first time, a great new twentieth-century influx of British, Americans, and Europeans realized at last the continental nationality which it had been the objective of Confederation to achieve. The population of the Dominion, which was 5,371,315 in 1901, rose to 7,206,643 in 1911. It was an increase of nearly 35 per cent, which was more than three times the percentage increase for the two previous decades.

The most spectacular feature of this last great migration was, of course, the peopling of the western prairies. The Loyalists of the eighteenth century and the British immigrants of the ninteenth had each created new provinces; the settlers of the twentieth century brought Saskatchewan and Alberta into being. Nowhere else throughout the country was there anything to compare with the startling growth of these two provinces. Prince Edward Island suffered an absolute loss of population during this period. Nova Scotia and New Brunswick made only slight relative gains. Quebec and Ontario did considerably better with increases of nearly 22 per cent and 16 per cent respectively within the decade 1901-1911. The central provinces, with over 4.5 million inhabitants in 1911, still made up the great bulk of the Canadian people; but it was at least significant that whereas Quebec and Ontario held 75 per cent of the total Canadian population in 1881, and 70 per cent as late as 1901, their share had now fallen to about 63 per cent. The fact was that the centre of gravity of the Canadian population was moving rapidly westward. Of the gain of nearly two million people which was recorded for the whole of Canada in the ten years 1901-1911, well over a million were distributed through the three Prairie Provinces and British Columbia. In a single decade the percentage increase of population for Alberta was over 400 per cent, for Saskatchewan nearly 440 per cent.

The overwhelming majority of the million new people who came to the three Prairie Provinces in the decade 1901-1911 were English-speaking in origin. It is possible from the

homestead entries of the period to get some general idea of
the respective nationalities of these English-speaking stocks.
Canadians, including those returned from the United States,
entered 82,383 homesteads in the decade 1900-1910. American entries for the same period totalled 82,995, British
50,319, and all other nationalities approximately the same
number as the British. Thus the United States made a contribution to the settlement of the Canadian prairies which
was large in point of numbers and even greater in terms of
knowledge and resources. The American settlers, who were
very often dry farmers of experience with considerable
capital, adapted themselves to the rigorous, semi-arid conditions of the short-grass Canadian prairie with an ease and
success which the Britishers, and even the Canadians from
the wooded regions of the east, found it difficult to match.
In addition, a considerable number of the foreign-born, including many Germans and Scandinavians, came to Canada
from the United States, where they had already become more
or less adapted to the North American environment.

Yet, despite the predominance of the English-speaking
stocks in the great migration of the early twentieth century,
a new and strange element had entered the composition of
the Canadian people. It was true, of course, that ever since
the conquest of 1763, British North America had never been
a racially homogeneous country. In large measure, its character and history had been formed by the presence of the
two nationalities, French and English; but though for a hundred and fifty years it had been a cultural dualism, it had
never yet become a melting-pot of races. In 1871, in the first
census after Confederation, British and French had together
totalled 92 per cent of the population; and the only important group of a different European origin had been the
Germans, with a little less than 6 per cent of the population.
In 1911, and chiefly as a result of the great immigration of
the previous decade, this situation had unmistakably changed.
It was true that the British and French still stood in much

the same relationship to each other. There had been nearly twice as many British as French in 1871; and the ratio was about the same in 1911. But in 1911 — and this was the great change — British and French together only totalled 83 per cent of the population. Thus the European stocks other than French had now approximately doubled their percentage of the whole. The largest increases, in the decade 1901-1911, were among the Germans, Scandinavians, and Ukrainians; but, in addition, there were now small minorities of Russians, Austrians, Italians, and Poles.

A large proportion of these people found their way to the Canadian prairies. Very frequently they tended to cluster together to preserve the language, the religion, the social habits and cultural values which made up their way of life. For example, there came to be large and fairly compact settlements of Ukrainians and German Roman Catholics in both Saskatchewan and Alberta. To a greater or lesser extent these cultural islands sought to resist the levelling tide of North American civilization; and, in the case of bloc settlements which were organized as community enterprises by single groups, this resistance was often continued for some time. Perhaps the most prolonged and uncompromising opposition was offered by the Mennonites and Doukhobors, who had come to Canada directly from overseas and who were distinguished not merely by nationality and language but also by a stark and unyielding sectarian spirit. The Mennonites, who made their first settlement in southern Manitoba as early as 1873, were the descendants of a far-wandering group of Dutch and Germans who had migrated first to East Prussia and then to Russia long before they crossed the ocean to the North American continent. Far more than the older Mennonite settlements in Ontario, which had learnt long ago to adjust themselves to the surrounding society, the new colonies on the prairies were marked by a hard theocratic community organization and by an extreme puritanical simplicity of life. Finally, the Doukhobors, who made their first settlements in what was to become Saskatchewan in 1899, were an illiterate peasant sect from Russia, which had been hardened by an even more terrible history of persecution. They were like the Mennonites in their pacifism and their religious simplicity; but their communistic system of land-holding was an even more peculiar distinguishing feature.

Beyond the Lake of the Woods, the rock-edge of the Pre-cambrian Shield, which had followed the north shore of the lakes all the way from Georgian Bay, struck sharply north-ward towards the Mackenzie River basin. As the trains drove westward from Ontario into Manitoba, the trees thinned out, the scarred rock dwindled, the land spread away in dead levels that reached towards incredibly remote horizons. The whole enormous region, with its gently rolling plains, its short, waving grasses, its small clumps of willow and poplar, and its deep-cut, sluggish, muddy inland rivers, prolonged itself in endless repetitions towards the mountains. It was stamped, as only such a region could be, with the solemn marks of monotonous uniformity. It seemed constant and unfailing in the very austere regularity of its features. And yet, within this interminable outward sameness, there lurked a strange variety of elements, a capricious uncertainty of con-ditions, an almost savage whimsicality of mood. The varia-tions, both of time and place, seemed infinite. There were contrasted zones of soil and changing cycles of weather. There were hazards of frost and hail, calamities of blight and insects, chances of drought and rainfall.

Northward from the international boundary, the land flattened out in a series of roughly concentric soil zones, bounded on the east by the Precambrian Shield and on the west by the Rocky Mountains. First came a great lop-sided triangle of short grass country, the light brown, semi-arid soil zone, which had the international boundary for its base and which occupied south-eastern Alberta and south-western Saskatchewan. Beyond this triangle, and all along its cir-cumference, stretched a broad, irregular strip of prairie country which was distinguished from the central plains only by its darker brown soil, its longer grasses, its slightly heavier rainfall. North of this, again, was the black soil zone, the so-called 'park belt,' which encircled the brown-soil zones in a great arc stretching slowly north-west from the Red River valley to the Edmonton district and dipping sharply south again to the forty-ninth parallel. The park belt, with its richer soil, its more certain rainfall, its recurring patches of wood, was the last and best of the usable prairie regions. North, north-east, and west of the black-soil belt, the woodland thickened promisingly for a while; but the good earth petered out in grey, inferior, stony soils, varied by stretches of marsh and muskeg, which sloped slowly away northward towards the treeless barrens of the Mackenzie River basin.

The settlers proceeded to occupy and use almost the whole of this country with little guidance, with little discrimination, and at headlong speed. At first, in the early years of the great migration, settlement was largely confined to the park belt and the tall grass prairie; and the new frontiersmen avoided the high plains of the south-west. Back in the nineteenth century, when he had made his exploratory survey of the Canadian prairies for the British government, Captain Palliser had described this southern brown-soil region as a semi-arid desert, unfit for cultivation; and ever since the Canadian Pacific Railway had first gone through, 'Palliser's Triangle,' the high, flat country south of the South Branch of the Saskatchewan River, had been given over almost entirely to ranching. But now the migrants swarmed into the southern plains, deceived by several unusual seasons of heavy rainfall. The ranching leases were terminated; the new barbed-wire fences menaced the life of the cattle; and gradually the great herds were broken up. Everywhere, north and south, the whole country began to give itself over more and more to the great export specialty of wheat. Even in Palliser's Triangle, the familiar western farming routine of fall plowing, spring seeding, and summer fallowing established itself. The government had conceived the quarter section of one hundred and sixty acres as the probable unit of production; but it was soon realized that wheat-growing within such a small area would with difficulty bring a livelihood. The average farm grew bigger in the north and bigger still in the relatively infertile south. In contrast with the older farming regions of central and eastern Canada, even the park belt of the prairies was to remain sparsely settled and the flat endless plains of Palliser's Triangle emptier still.

In such a region, the building of schools and churches, the advance of cultural and spiritual life, would obviously meet with many difficulties. But, on their part, the new national churches of Canada were far better equipped than they had ever been to cope with the settlement of this last frontier. They had inevitably to deal with settlers who were absorbed in the business of getting a living — who were obsessed with the tasks of mastering a harsh, exacting, and uncompromising environment. They had to grapple with the enormous distances, the great lonely farms, the thin scattering of huts and shacks and houses. They had to meet and overcome the jealousies and rancorous clashes of different languages and religions, and the dull, sullen hostility of peculiar group communities. But they were now churches which had grown in unity and prosperity with the development of the country — which had gained in experience and wisdom through the old struggles in central Canada and the long years of depression in the west. If there was less spiritual fire than there had been in the old days, there was as much dogged courage and far more friendly co-operation. In particular, the Methodists and Presbyterians went a long way in making arrangements to cover the new western field. In religion, as in many other things, the west made its contribution to national unity; and the United Church of Canada, which in 1925 brought the Methodists, Presbyterians, and Congregationalists together, was in large measure the result of that friendly co-operation in the mission fields of western Canada in the first decade of the twentieth century.

In education as well, the Prairie Provinces escaped many of these agonizing difficulties which had frustrated the early cultural growth of central and eastern Canada. The west was never a subsistence-farming region in the old pioneer fashion. From the start it went in for commercial agriculture. Wheat was a cash crop which enabled the new provinces to pay for a school system fairly rapidly; and the normal schools and universities of the east readily provided the teachers who were needed. Even in the old vexed problem of religion and education, the west had learned from the experience of Ontario, and the North-West Territories — which subsequently became the provinces of Alberta and Saskatchewan — had profited still more from the success of Manitoba in its struggle against sectarian schools. The federal statute of 1875 had set up a dual system of schools, Protestant and Roman Catholic, in the Territories; but the territorial assembly, heartened in its desire to reform this system by the action of Manitoba, reduced the privileges of the Roman Catholic minority to a minimum and gained most of the advantages of unified state control. In 1905, when the autonomy bills creating the provinces of Saskatchewan and Alberta were being drafted, there was at first included in them a provision re-establishing the old territorial school system as it had been back in 1875. This decision, one of the most curious in Laurier's entire political career, was made when Clifford Sifton and W. S. Fielding were absent from Ottawa. The manoeuvre was presumptuously obvious, in sharp contrast with Sir Wilfrid's usual accomplished strategy. It was also a colossal failure. The resignation of Sifton, the revolt of the cabinet, the restlessness of the party, all combined to force Laurier to accept a revision of the clauses; and the episode passed over, leaving nothing but a thin, trailing cloud of suspicion behind it. The territorial school system, unaltered by federal action, expanded rapidly after 1905, with relatively little friction in Saskatchewan and even less in Alberta. In 1911, of the total population ten to fourteen years of age, 65 per cent was attending school in Saskatchewan and nearly 66 per cent in Alberta. In the same year, the percentage for the old-established Province of Ontario was about 84 per cent and the average for the whole of Canada nearly 78 per cent.

In the sphere of higher learning, the new western provinces carried out the plan of a non-sectarian, provincial system of education even more thoroughly than Manitoba had been able to do. Manitoba, it was true, had founded a provincial university as far back as 1877; but while the Great Depression continued and provincial poverty remained, she was obliged to starve the institution. For thirty years Manitoba relied for higher education upon its small denominational colleges; and thus, when the University of Manitoba at length began its effective career, it was inevitably based upon a federal union somewhat resembling that of the University of Toronto. There was no repetition of this complex history in Saskatchewan and Alberta. In both provinces the idea of a non-sectarian, publicly supported provincial university triumphed easily. The University of Alberta was opened in 1908, and the University of Saskatchewan in the following year.

In the meantime, while the great mass disturbance of settlement was reaching its peak in the west, another revolution among the people, different in character but almost equal in magnitude, was taking place in eastern and central Canada. The old, largely rural central provinces, which had endured the Great Depression with so little change, were now subjected to a greater shift in population than they had known from their first settlement. In the decade 1901-1911, great numbers of people began to move out from the farmhouses and villages of a large proportion of the rural counties of Ontario, Quebec, and Nova Scotia. Many set out to make new homes in the west. A few pushed up to the new pulp-

and-paper districts in the north and to new mining areas like Cobalt. Others — and there were a large number of these — moved into the commercial and industrial cities which were springing up to serve the suddenly prosperous national market of Canada. Vancouver, Winnipeg, and Hamilton all made rapid advances in this period. But they were regional, not national cities. The really national centres, the cities which belonged to the whole country and which held the whole country in tribute, were the metropolitan centres of Toronto and Montreal.

In 1911, the population of Montreal proper was approximately four hundred and ninety-one thousand, and that of Toronto about three hundred and eighty-two thousand. They were not mushroom cities by any means, for Montreal was one of the oldest important ports on the continent, and Toronto had been growing steadily for over a hundred years. In experience and character, as well as in power and status, they could stand for the new Canada of the twentieth century. They were both focal points in a radiating network of economic power — active centres in a great centralized national system of railways, banks, financial houses, and manufactories. But Montreal, the river city which had been the capital of the fur-trading empire of the St. Lawrence, was far more completely fitted to become the focus of the new national unity based on wheat. It stood where the traffic from the prairies was exchanged for the cargoes from the ocean, where the long trains and loaded lake-boats from the west met the freighters and liners from Great Britain. It symbolized the triumph of the east-west route — the success of a system which was at once transoceanic and transcontinental.

Moreover, it expressed the varied culture of Canada in ways which it was impossible for Toronto to rival. Toronto was solidly British. There were dozens of miniature Torontos all over English-speaking Canada. But Montreal, the one great city in which French and British stood on a footing

of relative equality, was fundamentally exceptional. Toronto was a cleanly, home-loving, self-centred, somewhat
puritanical town, with a serious concern for education, and
a growing interest in the arts. Winnipeg and Vancouver re-
acted against Toronto with all the spirit of a young girl
revolting against a mother whose chief features she is already
beginning to duplicate with painful fidelity; but Montreal,
somehow or other, was lifted above criticism as an acknowledged metropolis, imposing, complicated, and mysterious.
In its domes and spires and towers, there was a Scotch so-
briety mingled with a piety which was strongly French and
Roman Catholic. Its hotels and clubs, its squares and statues,
its wide avenues and long sombre business streets, suggested
both a solid British opulence and a Gallic interest in design.
And in the dingy regions which lay outside these bright show
places and prosperous suburbs, the squalor of a British manufacturing town seemed to combine with the ambiguous dis-
reputableness of a European port.

The rise of the Canadian cities — Montreal, Toronto, Vancouver, Winnipeg, Hamilton, and others — brought up the
usual problems and disturbances of industrial civilization.
In some important ways, the English-speaking towns did not
do badly for their new armies of citizens. With the help of
Andrew Carnegie, they began to build new public libraries.
They showed an awakening interest in technical education.
The Canadian police had always been quick to catch crimi-
nals and the Canadian courts equally quick to convict and
punish them. The rural background and the British heritage of the great majority of the new city dwellers put a hard
check on civic corruption and organized crime; and there
were to be few armed gangs in the downtown districts of the
east, just as there had been few picturesque desperadoes on
the western prairies. In other and more novel matters, in
questions of social welfare and public health, the Canadian
cities were more traditional and ineffective. Their governments and social leaders tended to minimize the effects of

unemployment; they kept on dealing with prostitution and venereal disease by police raids and taboos; and they concentrated, with puritanical fanaticism, upon a few questions of personal conduct, such as cigarette-smoking and temperance in liquors. The churches, which had done so well in the west, were never quite so successful in winning the support of the urban working class; and it was probably the Salvation Army, which sought the fringe of society in somewhat the same way as the Methodists had been doing a century before, that came closest to the urban proletariat at this time.

Inevitably, the rise of the city brought changes in the class structure of central Canada. The status of all groups which were linked with industrialism was improved. The manufacturers, who had been steadily rising in importance in the previous half-century, now took an even more prominent place among the bankers, professional men, railwaymen, merchants, and lumber magnates who made up the Canadian leading class; and the Canadian Manufacturers' Association, which was reorganized in 1900, was a significant indication of their new power in the community. As for labour, it met greater difficulty in its effort to win an accepted status. The decline of the labour movement which accompanied the Great Depression of the late nineteenth century had gone further in Canada than in the United States, for the Dominion was much weaker industrially than its neighbour; and when trade-union activity began to revive after 1896, it was hampered by conditions which were peculiar to the northern country. The Trades and Labour Congress of Canada, the counterpart of the American Federation of Labor, was the strongest labour organization in the Dominion; but after its reorganization in 1902, it contained only the international trade unions whose headquarters were in the United States; and it naturally invited attack from the Roman Catholic Church in Quebec and from the new nationalist forces within the country as a whole. The employers were, of course, most vociferous in their denunciation of foreign labour agitators from the Republic; but they were joined by the leaders of the new Canadian Federation of Labour which was formed by a number of Canadian unions in 1902, and which tended to appeal to nationalist sentiment. The industrial workers, who faced the hard task of establishing themselves in provinces which were still partly rural in character and largely individualist in philosophy, were themselves weakened by inward divisions and conflicting loyalties.

It was perhaps in the Province of Quebec that the coming of industrialism and the rise of the cities threatened the most serious troubles for the future. Yet the cultural life of the province remained almost unaltered. Once again its conservatism was emphasized by contrast with the radicalism of France, where, in these very years, the Dreyfus case began a revolution which ended in the limitation of the religious orders, the suppression of clerical teaching, and the separation of church and state. In the main, the French Canadians were anti-Dreyfusards who denounced the triumph of the 'godless schools' and deplored the abrogation of the Napoleonic Concordat with the Papacy. In Canada, during this period, the hierarchy lost the battle for sectarian schools, so far as the new western provinces were concerned; but in Quebec education remained under virtually complete clerical control. While instruction in the natural and social sciences made progress in the Maritime Provinces and Ontario, and while the whole of English-speaking Canada began to grow interested in technical education, Quebec clung to an educational system directed by priests and lawyers which continued to turn out more lawyers and priests. In the new, growing industrial centres of the province, English-speaking managers, technical experts, and foremen began to dominate, just as English capital dominated in the financing of the new manufactories. The control of the new industrial system of the province was slipping into culturally alien hands; and though a French-Canadian labour force was rapidly developing, a vigorous and an increasingly successful attempt was made to separate it from the rest of working-class North America by denouncing the international unions of the period. 'With the greatest anxiety,' declared Archbishop Bruchési in an important pastoral of 1903 on the labour question, 'do we see the labour organizations of our city seeking for affiliation with foreign associations. The majority of the leaders and members of those international unions have nothing in common with our temperament, our customs, or our faith.'

These various urban troubles, in Quebec and elsewhere, were simply symptoms of a much more general excitement. The sudden, vast expansion of the country had brought many disturbances and problems. And yet, despite the class conflicts and ethnic divisions of the new Dominion, despite the enormous confusion and unsettlement of the migration period, there was a new transcendent sense of nationhood which seemed, in some degree at least, to reconcile and integrate the whole. The churches, the business groups, the workers, had all given their associations a nationalist form and had crossed the continent like governments and railways before them. The first large-scale co-operative works in Canadian history — the *Makers of Canada* series and the series *Canada and its Provinces* — were both launched during this period; and the Canadian Club movement, which expanded vigorously towards the end of the first decade of the twentieth century, provided a social and fraternal channel for the spread of the new Canadian national feeling. The popular symbol of this naïve, youthful, self-confident Canadianism came to be the cartoon figure of Jack Canuck. Jack was a young, clear-eyed, and highly muscular personage, whose rolled-up shirt sleeves, stiff-brimmed hat, breeches, and leggings appeared to suggest a kind of cross between the working clothes of a farmer and the uniform of a trooper in the Royal Canadian Mounted Police, and whose ingenuous and open countenance radiated with honesty, uncorrupted virility, and shining moral purpose. Supposedly, Jack looked forward to the future with radiant assurance. But in actual fact, there was — or there ought to have been — a puzzled frown upon his face. For he had yet to complete the restatement of Canada's foreign policy — of the policy which British North America had followed, with a groping, instinctive consistency, ever since its foundation in the eighteenth century. And it was not long before this effort at redefinition became a controversial process which awakened old minority protests and created new ones.

[*IV*]

The first of these controversies was precipitated by the naval scare of 1909. The alarming discovery of Germany's progress in naval construction supplied the main reason for the Imperial Defence Conference of that year; and the Imperial Defence Conference, if it did not entirely demolish Chamberlainism, left remarkably little of it surviving. In the Colonial Conferences of 1902 and 1907, all previous efforts to convert the Empire into a centralized, exclusive, and intimidating organization had been frustrated — largely at the instance of Canada; and the long process which was to end in the creation of a commonwealth of free and autonomous British nations moved slowly towards its conclusion. The projects of an imperial parliament and an imperial customs union had both been rejected. And now, in 1909, the Conference finally gave up the plan of a centralized system of imperial defence.

Bit by bit, Canada had been assuming the burdens of its own protection. As far back as 1871, the British soldiers had left the central provinces. Even the small garrison at the naval base of Halifax had departed during the South African War; and the naval bases themselves at Halifax and Esquimalt had been taken over by Canada in 1905, as a result of Lord Fisher's concentration of the imperial fleet in home waters. Now, finally, in the Defence Conference of 1909, the Admiralty abandoned its stubbornly held principle that the imperial fleet was one, and its long-cherished hope that the colonies would contribute to it. The Conference accepted the scheme of separate colonial naval units. And this policy Laurier readily agreed to implement by legislation. Up to that time, he had specialized in the somewhat fatiguing task of inventing courteous Canadian refusals to hearty British invitations. But he could be positive as well as negative. And he proceeded to show it.

In January, 1910, the Prime Minister introduced his Naval Service Bill in Parliament. The bill called for a small Canadian navy of cruisers and destroyers, which would be under the independent control of the Canadian government, but which might, with the concurrence of the Canadian Parliament, be put at the disposal of the Admiralty in time of an imperial emergency. In Sir Wilfrid's view, this acceptance of the last burdens of self-defence was simply an important step in the slow evolution of the Empire, a logical corollary of that Canadian political autonomy for which he had fought so long. 'I do not pretend to be an Imperialist,' he declared, 'neither do I pretend to be an anti-Imperialist. I am a Canadian, first, last, and all the time. I am a British subject, by birth, by tradition, by conviction — by the conviction that under British institutions my native land has found a measure of security and freedom which it could not have found under any other régime.' These loyalties had found their satisfaction in the new imperial relationship; and the Canadian navy was simply the physical expression of the freedom which Canada had won within this 'galaxy' of British powers. A mere contribution to the British navy would have smacked of tribute to Caesar and left unsolved the problem of self-defence. 'That is not the conception, the true conception, of the British Empire, the conception of new, growing, strong and wealthy nations, each one developing itself on the line of its own needs and conditions, but all joining in the case of a common danger, and from all points of the earth rushing upon a common enemy.'

Thus the new Canadian navy could act simply for the local defence of Canada, or it could participate in the general wars of the British Empire. Laurier hoped that Canada could escape from what he called 'the vortex of European militarism'; and he determined that the country would remain as aloof as it was legally possible for it to do. He believed, of course, that Canada was formally bound in international law by the actions of Great Britain. 'When Britain is at war, Canada is at war,' he declared simply; 'there is no distinction.' But though he admitted that Canada, even in her new-found autonomy within the Empire, would be legally involved in every British war, he insisted — in the same way as he had done at the time of the South African War — that the extent of her participation would be determined by the nature of the conflict in each case. 'If England is at war,' he declared, 'we are at war and liable to attack. I do not say that we shall always be attacked, neither do I say that we would take part in all the wars of England. That is a matter that must be determined by circumstances, upon which the Canadian Parliament will have to pronounce and will have to decide in its own best judgment.' To preserve this independence of judgment, to maintain this freedom of choice in external affairs, had been one of Laurier's principal motives in his campaign for Dominion autonomy. It was, in part, for this reason that he had rejected the plan of an imperial parliament and an imperial council. It was for this reason that he disliked even the idea of regular consultation between Great Britain and the Dominions. He had little desire for a voice in the framing of a common imperial foreign policy. In his view, the giving of advice involved the acceptance of responsibility which he was anxious Canada should avoid.

The Laurier Naval Bill was opposed from two violently contrasted points of view, which, nevertheless, had their roots in a common colonialism. It was opposed both by the English-speaking imperialists who desired a contribution to the British fleet rather than the creation of a Canadian navy, and by the French-speaking 'Nationalists' who wanted neither the one nor the other. For Sir Wilfrid, the 'Nationalist' opposition was by far the more politically important of the two. For fifteen years, ever since the election of 1896, he had enjoyed the almost unanimous support of Quebec. He had become the acknowledged spokesman of his people, the official interpreter of French Canada to the Dominion and the external world. And now, when he stood apparently at the height of his power, the 'Nationalist' movement threatened both to supplant him in his native province and to divide the Canadian people which it had been his principal object to unite.

The leader of this new French-Canadian 'Nationalist' movement was Henri Bourassa. A descendant on his mother's side of Louis Joseph Papineau, Bourassa was a man of real intellectual power, as well as an orator of fire and genuine eloquence. At the time of the South African War, when he had first come into prominence by his opposition to Canadian participation, he had declared himself to be a 'Liberal of the British school,' an ardent disciple of Burke and Bright and Gladstone. But, in actual fact, he was to make his fame as perhaps the most brilliant representative of extreme French-Canadian nationalism, with its typical conservative instincts and clerical affiliations. According to his own story, subsequently related in parliament, he took an active part in the formation of the original educational clauses in the Autonomy Bills which set up the provinces of Saskatchewan and Alberta in 1905. When this not very adroit manoeuvre to revive the lost privileges of the Roman Catholic minority in the west had collapsed under the attack of Clifford Sifton, W. S. Fielding, and others, Laurier sensibly gave in and consented to have the offending clauses redrafted. But Bourassa apparently still believed that the bills could be pushed through. And Laurier's capitulation enabled him to ingratiate himself with the younger clergy of his province, and to put himself forward as the champion of those French Catholic interests which the Prime Minister had betrayed.

The Naval Bill of 1910 gave Bourassa a chance to broaden his attack against Laurier. Here again, in the matter of national defence, he presented himself confidently as a nineteenth-century British Liberal. According to his own statement, he held the Cobdenite belief that friendly separation was the eventual destiny of mother country and colonies. But there had always been, and there continued to be, a large element of colonialism in French-Canadian 'nationalism.' In the eyes of French Canada, the security of dependence looked perhaps even more satisfying than the freedom of independence; and, in his attitude to Canada's supposed eventual separation from the British Empire, Bourassa reflected these instinctive French-Canadian views. As he himself frankly explained on one occasion, he preferred to remain in a state of dependence for some time to come, because, as a Canadian, he wanted protection against the United States, and because, as a French Canadian, he wanted protection against English Canada. Such a conveniently adaptable theory of nationalism would not likely inspire any very vigorous efforts for self-defence at any time; and in that age of imperialist power politics, the Quebec 'Nationalists' remained suspicious of almost any Canadian armaments at all. They attacked the Laurier Naval Bill with the utmost heartiness. They insisted that, in reality, the projected Canadian navy was simply an outright contribution to British imperialist wars.

The opposition of Robert Laird Borden, the new Conservative leader, to the Laurier Naval Bill was of a very different character. If Borden's case against the projected Canadian navy was in part mere political sleight-of-hand, it was also in part political statesmanship of a high order. As a party leader, he obviously had to make an effort to unite in his own favour the two different and extremely contradictory protests which had been voiced against the Laurier policy. He accepted the idea of an emergency contribution of dreadnoughts to the British navy — that was for the Ontario imperialists: he took up the argument that nothing permanent should be done until the electorate had pronounced — that was for the Quebec 'Nationalists.' But he also combined and reconciled these discordant views in a more general and fundamental theory, which, in the end, became his principal contribution to the politics of the British Commonwealth. Borden contended that before Canada embarked upon a permanent scheme of defences, for both local and imperial purposes, she must come to an arrangement with Great Britain which would give her a voice in the control of imperial foreign policy. Unlike Laurier, who feared commitments, Borden was willing to accept military responsibility in return for a share in political power. The two men were equally strong Canadian nationalists; their two doctrines rested with equal solidity upon the principle of Canadian autonomy. But while Laurier stood for an attitude of disinterested aloofness within the Empire, Borden believed in the policy of regular consultation among its constituent members.

The Naval Bill was passed in 1910; but the issue obviously was not settled. And, in the meantime, while the problem of the imperial connection had created these divisions within the country, the old and controversial issue of Canadian relations with the United States was also emerging once more. Already the new policy of national defence had stirred up opposition in Quebec; and, as Sir Wilfrid discovered in his western tour during the summer of 1910, the old National Policy of the tariff was now arousing unrest and resentment in the Prairie Provinces. Curiously enough this western tour was the Prime Minister's first visit to the country which had almost literally come into existence dur-

ing the rule of his administration. Perhaps the trip was
fondly conceived as a triumphal progress. Its first few days
were uneventful and reassuring; but at Brandon, Manitoba,
on July 18, there descended upon Sir Wilfrid a great deputation of argumentative farmers, with long lists of grievances,
and from that day forward the Grain Growers' Association
of Manitoba, the Grain Growers' Association of Saskatchewan, and the United Farmers of Alberta almost monopolized
the tour. These organizations, which dated back to 1902 and
which had become the vigorous expression of western agrarian interests, urged upon Sir Wilfrid the establishment of
government-owned terminal elevators and the construction
of a railway to Hudson Bay. On the whole, these were politically innocuous requests; but along with them went another
which was emphatically dangerous — a persistent and irrepressible demand for a reduction of the tariff. In the
autumn of that year, the new national farmers' organization,
the Canadian Council of Agriculture, took up and general-
ized the agitation which the western settlers had begun. On
December 15, the biggest delegation which had ever descended upon Ottawa met in the city's opera house to draw
up the final agrarian programme; and next day the House
of Commons Chamber was packed with nearly a thousand
farmers from all parts of the country who had come to re-
state their demands of the summer and to insist that an
increase in the British preference and a large measure of
reciprocal free trade with the United States were vital necessities for Canada.

For a number of reasons the government was disposed to
listen seriously to this proposal of a trade treaty with the
United States. In the first place, ever since the award of the
Alaskan tribunal in 1903, the relations of the two countries
had steadily improved. In 1909 the International Joint Commission had been established to settle questions relating to
the boundary waters of Canada and the United States, and
to deal with other matters which might be referred to it by

the two powers. In 1910, the everlasting problem of the North Atlantic fisheries was referred, not to a special tribunal of impartial jurists, but to the Hague Court, which the United States had rejected for the settlement of the Alaskan dispute in 1903; and Canada and Newfoundland had the satisfaction of seeing their principal contentions respecting the Convention of 1818 — contentions which the United States had refused to acknowledge for nearly a hundred years — accepted and confirmed by the Hague Tribunal. Even in the old and provocative matter of the tariff the two countries were obviously ready to be more accommodating. In 1907 the Canadian Parliament had set up an intermediate tariff, approximately midway between the British preference and the general rates, which was to be granted to other countries by commercial treaty. In 1909, the United States, by the Payne-Aldrich Act, had established a set of maximum rates, approximately twenty-five per cent above the general tariff level, which were to be applied to countries allegedly discriminating against the Republic. Since the United States regarded the intermediate tariff which Canada had granted France by commercial treaty as an unfair discrimination against itself, there was a real chance of a tariff war in 1910. But both sides were anxious to avoid such a struggle. They came together to settle the matter amicably in the winter of 1910. And it was at these conferences that the magic word 'reciprocity' was uttered once again.

The fact was that both governments were inclined to favour a broad trade agreement. In large measure — and it is important to note this — their arguments were political. Both President Taft and Prime Minister Laurier were beset by embarrassments and anxieties. In the United States there was an unexpectedly strong reaction against the tariffs of 1909 and the whole American press was vociferously demanding a reduction in the price of newsprint from Canada. In the Dominion, Quebec was in full revolt against the Naval Bill, and the united farmers, joyously conscious of their new-found strength, had launched a concerted attack upon the tariff. For both harassed governments reciprocity appeared as a pacifying arrangement which might forestall criticism and quiet unrest; and such was their sudden eagerness for a trade treaty that they were even willing to reconcile their previous serious differences of opinion about its character. Ever since the old Reciprocity Treaty had been abrogated in 1866, the United States had made it perfectly clear that, if she ever consented to negotiate a new trade agreement with Canada, it would have to include a comprehensive list of manufactures. Ever since the Canadian Liberals had abandoned their old plank of unrestricted reciprocity, Canada had made it almost equally clear that she preferred a reciprocal trade agreement in natural products only. The two positions seemed irreconcilable; but the political necessities of the moment proved that they were not. In the brief negotiations of the late autumn and winter of 1910-11, each side relented a little. Canada consented to include manufactured, as well as natural, products; and the United States agreed to accept a specific, instead of a comprehensive, list of manufactures. The final agreement, which was reached by an official exchange of letters on January 26, 1911, provided for reciprocal free trade in grain, fish, fruits, vegetables, farm animals, and for lowered duties on food products such as meats, canned goods, flour, biscuits, pickles, as well as on agricultural implements, engines, and a variety of other articles. The agreement, at the request of the Canadians, was not to be embodied in a treaty; it was to be carried out by concurrent legislation in the two countries.

The Canadian government had negotiated the agreement with the most surprising promptitude; but it showed the most unaccountable delay in doing anything about it. Laurier, of course, was anxious that American legislation should come first. An old-fashioned parliamentarian, he was reluctant to apply the closure in debate. And during the summer of 1911 he was obliged to go to England to attend the coronation of King George V. The government failed either to get the agreement accepted in the existing Parliament or to go to the country on the issue while it still had the advantage of the initiative; and as the winter of 1911 drifted into spring and summer, the opposition had time and opportunity to organize itself, to marshal its arguments, and to devise its emotional appeals. As the months went by, the public protest took on the most formidable proportions. It was voiced, not merely by the Conservatives under R. L. Borden, but also by a number of prominent Liberals, led by the aggressive Clifford Sifton, who now abandoned his party. It was backed by manufacturers, bankers, railwaymen, millers, meat-packers, fruit-growers, with all the power and influence which they possessed.

What is the explanation of this suddenly mounting wave of opposition against an agreement which was, in so many ways, so obviously favourable to Canada? It has sometimes been suggested that the movement against reciprocity was, in effect, the successful result of a conspiracy of the Canadian Manufacturers' Association. There can be no question that the organized industrialists of Canada did their effective utmost to rouse a protest against the agreement; but to see in their efforts alone the sufficient explanation of the defeat of reciprocity is to neglect or minimize several other important factors in the situation. In the first place, the policy of a broad reciprocal trade treaty with the United States, far from being a recognized national objective of the period, had been virtually forgotten for nearly twenty years by press, parliament, and people. The Liberal party, once its old leader Edward Blake had finally betaken himself to Great Britain, unostentatiously dropped its plank of unrestricted reciprocity. The Toronto *Globe,* the greatest Liberal newspaper of Ontario and the old champion of the commercial union with the Republic, ceased significantly to enlarge upon the wonders of the American market. Trade policy was by no means a central issue in any of the elections of

1896, 1900, 1904, and 1908. The fact was that, in all essentials, the Liberals had simply continued the economic nationalism of their predecessors. The east-west transport system, protected by tariffs against the United States, and concentrated on the export of staples to Great Britain, had proved an independent success; and during his long term of office Laurier had repeatedly expressed the satisfaction of Canadians in this achievement and their resulting complacent indifference to the long sought after markets in the United States. Canada was not impelled to reject reciprocity with the United States because she preferred an imperial customs union with Great Britain. On the contrary, she was moved to turn down the offer of William Howard Taft for exactly the same reasons as she had previously rejected the offer of Joseph Chamberlain. She preferred, as far as possible, to stand on her own. She was proud of her independent success. She was anxious to avoid too intimate economic connections with either Great Britain or the United States.

In addition, the political factor played a large — and probably a decisive — part. William Howard Taft was the heir of 'My policies' in more senses than one. While, on the one hand, he took over the legacy of trouble which Roosevelt's crusades had left at home, on the other hand he inherited the accumulation of resentment and suspicion which Roosevelt's foreign policy had awakened abroad. The great majority of the Canadians who voted in the election of 1911 had watched the American intervention in the Venezuela boundary dispute, the founding of the American Empire in the Caribbean and the Pacific, the American participation in the politics of the Colombian Republic, and, above all, the American diplomatic victory in the Alaskan boundary dispute. From this record of the past, the Canadians drew the conclusion that an active policy of American imperialism was at work; and from American pronouncements regarding the reciprocity agreement, they came to nurse the resentful suspicion that this policy might soon be directed against themselves. There were a number of statements respecting the trade agreement, notably those by President Taft himself, which were torn from their context and misused by frantic Canadian nationalists. But there were other statements so naïvely and complacently frank in their imperialism that it would have been impossible for even the Conservative campaign strategists to have improved upon them. 'I am for it,' said J. Beauchamp ('Champ') Clark, Democratic Speaker-Designate of the House of Representatives, of the reciprocity agreement, 'because I hope to see the day when the American flag will float over every square foot of the British North American possessions clear to the North Pole. . . . I have no doubt whatever that the day is not far distant when Great Britain will joyfully see all her North American possessions become part of this Republic. That is the way things are tending now.' There was, of course, a swift official disclaimer of all such improper aspirations. The American government hastened to assure an uneasy and sceptical Canada that there were no ulterior motives back of the reciprocity agreement and that it carried no political implications whatever. These disavowals were repeated widely through the United States, by the press and by prominent people. But a number of irrepressible American congressmen continued to interrupt this reassuring chorus by intoning the discordant strains of 'Manifest Destiny.' This disclosure aroused that unsleeping hatred of North American continentalism which is one of the strongest elements in Canadian nationality. 'We must decide whether a spirit of Canadianism or of Continentalism is to prevail on the northern half of this continent,' declared R. L. Borden in his final message to the Canadian people on the eve of the election. Canada had rejected an exclusive British Empire centralized in Great Britain; but she was equally determined to oppose a continental system dominated by the United States.

The general election, which was held on September 21, 1911, ended in the resounding defeat of the Laurier government. The 'Nationalists' of Quebec, who resented commitments to Great Britain, and the nationalists of the rest of Canada, who feared and hated the domination of the United States, joined in a questionable alliance to overthrow the Liberals. On September 25, Robert Laird Borden entered Ottawa in triumph, like a conqueror. A hundred men drew his carriage for miles through streets which were packed with crowds and brave with fluttering flags. For fifteen years, Canada had been ruled by a French Canadian, a Roman Catholic, a suave, distinguished man who concealed a real will and tenacity of purpose beneath his gracious outward manner. The new Prime Minister of the country was a Nova Scotian, a descendant of Scots and Loyalist stock, a man whose deep voice, rugged head, and rather solemn countenance seemed also, in their different way, to suggest a spirit of stubborn resolution. In many obvious ways, the two leaders stood in marked contrast to each other. But they were both nationalists who faced similar circumstances — similar problems; and though they differed on the wisdom of imperial collaboration, they agreed on the necessity of autonomy. Borden had gained political power through a nationalist crisis. He was to lead the country through the greatest nationalist crisis that Canada had ever known.

[V]

On August 4, 1914, when Great Britain declared war on the German Empire, every Canadian assumed that his country was automatically involved. It was true, of course, that Borden had not yet gained the voice which he sought in imperial foreign policy, and that Canada had taken virtually no part in the conduct of the diplomacy leading up to the war. Borden had hoped to make Canada an active partner in a collective empire, with a voice in its collective foreign policy, as well as a share in its important collective wars. But his bill for an emergency contribution of dreadnoughts to the

British navy — which was simply the first step in his defence policy — was defeated in the Liberal-controlled Senate; and before he could reframe his policy and make a definite arrangement with the British government the war supervened. In 1914, therefore, Canada still remained in the political aloofness in which Laurier had left her, and still supposedly held the freedom of choice for which he had fought. Her choice — which was automatic and took no thought of possible alternatives — was in favour of instant and active participation. In this choice, Laurier himself heartily concurred. He had always insisted that the Empire might be confronted with a life-and-death struggle which Canada's every material and moral interest would require her to join; and perhaps he had merely failed to realize that, in the political circumstances of the moment, almost any small dispute would likely be distorted into a stupendous conflict. But if this was a defect of his policy, it was a defect which was exposed only by the collapse of a world order which many people besides himself had continued to believe was immutable.

In view of the sharp conflicts over external relations which had marked the last few years of its history, Canada entered the war with an almost unbelievable unanimity. To be sure, there was, from the very beginning, a slight but significant difference of opinion as to whether the country was involved in the war as a principal and committed to the totality of its powers. This difference was ominous for the future; but at the moment it was very inconspicuous; and the whole of Canada seemed united in its conviction of the justice of the cause and in its acceptance of Canadian participation. In those early days of August, 1914, parades, decorations, cheering crowds, and patriotic speeches were everywhere the outward manifestations of a spirit which pervaded the entire country. The special session of Parliament, which was called in the latter part of August, unanimously endorsed Canada's entrance into the war. Political leaders, both federal and provincial, Liberal and Conservative, French and English, accepted the conflict without question; and even Bourassa, the leader of the Quebec 'Nationalists,' declared that it was 'Canada's national duty to contribute, within the bounds of her strength, and by means which are proper to herself, to the triumph, and especially to the endurance, of the combined efforts of France and England.' In those first months of war, it looked as if the wrangles over external relations were to end in the *union sacrée* of war — as if the national solidarity which had been gained through the labour of western settlement would be completed by the brotherhood of arms.

The war, which thus forwarded the cause of national unity, inevitably raised the consequence of the national government. The leadership which the federal administration had assumed during the settlement boom in the west was confirmed and strengthened by participation in the crisis overseas. The war effort demanded federal control; the war patriotism bolstered federal prestige; and the national government advanced both within the sphere of the British Empire and within the sphere of the Canadian federal system. This wartime rise in the importance of Canada with respect to the provinces of which it was composed, and the empire of which it was a part, naturally began at home in the first days of the war. The constitution, as it had developed under the decisions of Lord Watson, in the last decade of the nineteenth century, might very well have prevented that type of centralized, national control which this twentieth-century war seemed from the first to require. But even though Lord Watson had insisted that the federal government, by virtue of its residuary authority to legislate for the peace, order, and good government of Canada, had no right 'to encroach upon' the exclusive powers of the provincial governments, he had at the same time admitted that 'some matters, in their origin local and provincial, might attain such dimensions as to affect the body politic of the Dominion and to justify the Canadian Parliament in passing laws for their regulation or abolition in the interest of the Dominion.' Under the abnormal circumstances of the war, these conditions at last seemed to have been realized. Now, for perhaps the first time, the crisis justified emergency legislation under the 'peace, order, and good government' clause. By virtue of the War Measures Act, which was passed during the special session of August, 1914, the federal government began slowly but inexorably to do a number of things which it would never have dreamed of doing in time of peace. The curious dual constitution was already in process of formation. And, in the end, Canada was to be the slightly mystified and highly embarrassed possessor of two federal systems: one for times of peace and one for periods of war.

Equipped with these exceptional powers, the federal government began to order the war effort on a big scale. It had much to do. Though in the past the fate of empires had been decided in Canada, and though in recent times a Canadian contingent had crossed the ocean to fight abroad, the Canadians were, in general, a profoundly unmilitary people with only a most amateurish fighting machine. When he arrived in power in 1911, Borden had curtailed the construction of Laurier's Canadian navy in order to substitute his own plan of defence; but when his first naval bill had been rejected in the Senate, he had temporarily dropped the subject, and in 1914 the whole problem of naval services still rested in suspense. The army, to be sure, was in a better position than the new 'tin-pot' navy. Under the Liberal minister of militia, Sir Frederick Borden, and under the Conservative Sam Hughes, who succeeded him in 1911, the army had certainly been rescued from the almost laughable state of incompetence in which it had languished during the long years of nineteenth-century peace. In 1914, there was a very small permanent force of about three thousand men, and a body of non-permanent active militia with a strength of about seventy-five thousand. This was the small and dubious foundation upon which the Canadian Department of Militia had to build.

It worked swiftly. In the late summer and early autumn the first division was assembled at Valcartier Camp, close to Quebec. On October 1, the contingent sailed for England — the largest armed force which up to that time had ever crossed the Atlantic; and less than four months after its arrival on Salisbury Plain, on a rainy day in early February, 1915, the first transports bearing the Canadian Expeditionary Force to the continent docked at the little port of St. Nazaire, at the mouth of the Loire River, in France. The first few novel weeks were uneventful; but early in April the division was transferred north to the low-lying Ypres salient, at the extreme left of Smith-Dorrien's Second Army; and here, at five o'clock on the afternoon of April 22, before a gentle north-east wind, the Germans opened the first poison-gas cylinders of the war. The low-lying, sluggish cloud of yellow-green chlorine drifted inexorably over the French trenches to the immediate left of the Canadians. The French line broke in panic; the African Zouaves fled in incoherent terror. The entire salient — with this great ragged hole torn out of it — was in peril. But the Canadians threw back and prolonged their line so as to form new contact with the French. These thin defences repulsed the fresh German attacks; and what seemed at first to be the imminent, the inevitable, break-through was averted.

In those few terrible days, the Canadian contingent established its quality. Soon it began to grow in size, as well as in experience and repute. That September, when the second division arrived in France, the force was transformed into a separate Canadian Corps; and the command which Sir Julian Byng took over in the spring of 1916 reached its definitive total of four divisions before the year was out. At St. Eloi in April, 1916, and the battles of Mount Sorrel in the following June, the 'Byng Boys' fought some of the most heroic defensive actions of their long career in the ill-fated

Ypres salient. Then, in September, 1916, the Corps left the churned, muddy flats of Flanders for the rolling, upland country of the Somme, where the principal allied offensive of that year was already raging through a series of furious and costly battles. It was on the Somme front, in the great attack of September 15, when the tanks were first used and when the Canadians took Courcelette, that the Corps won its reputation for terrible striking power. 'The Canadians,' wrote Lloyd George in his War Memoirs, 'played a part of such distinction [on the Somme in 1916] that thenceforward they were marked out as storm troops; for the remainder of the war they were brought along to head the assault in one great battle after another. Whenever the Germans found the Canadian Corps coming into the line they prepared for the worst.'

In the meantime, while the Canadian Corps was winning prestige abroad, the Canadian economy was responding in vigorous and unexpected ways to the war at home. Certain obvious contributions to the war effort Canada was prepared to make at once and in great volume. The construction of the great transcontinental railways and the settlement of the Prairie Provinces had brought into existence a great wheat-producing area which was immediately ready to go into full production for the provisioning of war-ravaged Europe; and the wonderful crop of 1915 resulted in the greatest export surplus of wheat on record up to that time. The war gave the Canadian newsprint industry a new opportunity; it brought a great stimulus to the mining of copper, lead, and nickel in the complex ore-bodies of the Canadian Shield; and, as might have been expected in view of high ocean freights and British industrial preoccupations, it strengthened and increased the hold of the Canadian manufacturers on the national market. On the whole, these enterprises were all in the main stream of Canadian economic development; but, though in 1914 the country could produce its own militia rifles, as well as small quantities of ammunition for small-arms and field-guns, it had no munitions industry of any importance whatever; and here perhaps the most dramatic effort of the war was made. Under the stimulus of the orders of the Canadian government and of the Imperial Munitions Board, the Canadians turned to the manufacture of shells, high explosives, ships, and aeroplanes. By 1917 between a quarter and a third of the shells fired by the British armies on the western front were made in Canada; and it had been shown that the new industrial strength of the Dominion was a vital factor in the military triumph of the Empire.

In various and compelling ways, these achievements, both foreign and domestic, pushed forward the recent great advance of Canadian nationalism which had first begun when Laurier became prime minister in 1896. In these months of tremendous accomplishment, the rise towards the maturity of nationhood was swift and confident, both at home and abroad; but it was abroad, rather than at home, that the problems incidental to this new position were solved with greatest ease and most conspicuous success. After all, the assumption of complete control over the Canadian armed forces overseas and the demand for a voice in the framing of imperial policy in Europe were legitimate corollaries of that status towards which the country had been striving instinctively for so long; and Sir Robert Borden, who, unlike Laurier, had been ready even before the war to exert influence and to accept responsibility within the Empire, was now in a position to demand the voice in affairs to which Canada's magnificent contribution entitled him. 'It can hardly be expected,' he wrote bitingly to the Canadian High Commissioner in London, in January, 1916, 'that we shall put 400,000 or 500,000 men in the field and willingly accept the position of having no more voice and receiving no more consideration than if we were toy automata. Any person cherishing such an expectation harbours an unfortunate and even dangerous delusion. Is this war being waged by the

United Kingdom alone, or is it a war waged by the whole Empire?'

In the autumn of 1916 the overdue reorganization of the Canadian war effort overseas began. A Ministry of the Overseas Military Forces of Canada, headed by a member of the Canadian cabinet, was established in October. In December, a Canadian General Staff, with head-quarters at London, assumed control of the training of all the forces from the Dominion in England. In the same month, the leisurely political combination of Asquith and Bonar Law collapsed under the attacks of the dynamic Lloyd George; and the new British leader immediately invited the prime ministers of the self-governing colonies to London and subsequently set up the Imperial War Cabinet. Sir Robert Borden, who had battered against the closed doors of London for months, spent the time from February to May of 1917 in deliberating with the Imperial War Cabinet and the Imperial War Conference in England. Under Lloyd George, the unconventional political genius of the war, the Borden conception of the Commonwealth was realized; and the foreign policy of the Empire became a collective policy, worked out in common by Great Britain and the Dominions through continuous consultation. In June, 1917, when the Canadian Arthur Currie succeeded Sir Julian Byng in command of the Corps in France, the nationalization of the Canadian effort overseas may be said to have reached its logical end.

For the Canadians in France, the year 1917 — the third year of the war of attrition — was crowded with a long line of brilliant and bloody victories. The Corps stood at the height of its power. In its superb physical fitness, its ruthless self-confidence, its immense powers of individual initiative and adaptability, and its proud and jealous consciousness of corporate unity and accomplishment, the force was second to none among the units of the British army in the west. Through the great battles of that year, through Vimy Ridge, Hill 70, and the macabre horror of Passchendaele —

from the mining and industrial region about Lens back again to the churned, oozing flats of the Ypres salient, the Canadians won position after position of vital strategic importance in that conflict of limited objectives, small gains, and terrible casualties. But the victory at the ridge of Vimy was perhaps the most perfect of them all; and it is at Vimy, appropriately enough, that the twin gigantic columns of the Canadian war memorial soar into the sky.

The ridge commanded the entire Lens-Arras landscape. Strategically, it was the key of the region; but it masked its immense significance with unassuming and modest disclaimers. It stood, on the average, not more than four hundred feet above sea-level. On the west side, as they saw it from the British lines, it rose gently, in easy, open, inviting gradations, towards an almost imperceptible crest-line. But, on the eastern side of the long, curving heights, the land fell away abruptly in steep, heavily wooded slopes. The whole ridge was covered with a maze of trenches, mined with an elaborate network of dug-outs and tunnels, protected by a massed concentration of guns which stood in concealment on the reverse side of the slope. It was this formidable stronghold which Foch's men had failed disastrously to take in the September offensive of 1915; and it was here, on April 9, the first day of the 1917 battle of Arras, that the Canadian Corps began its long and minutely prepared attack. Under a sombre sky, in the thick of a storm of sleet and snow which was the last stroke of the severest winter in twenty years, the Canadians pressed forward over the slippery, shell-torn slopes towards the ridge. By the evening of April 9, they had won the greater part of the heights; by the next day they had completed and consolidated their hold. In a battle which was more generally successful than any which the British armies had yet fought in the west, the capture of the Vimy Ridge was at once the most dramatic and the most important episode; and, in the history of the Canadian Corps, it became the perfect example of that mixture of preparation, timing, cohesion, and impetuous dash which made the secret of its success.

At home, in the meantime, the politicians were fumbling with the financial and economic difficulties of the war effort, as well as with its even more subtle problems of human relationships. The country which, almost overnight, had grown the last inches into maturity was now suddenly confronted with the burdens and distractions of its new state. Financially, Canada had always been a debtor country, reposing complacently on the comforting assumption that the fount of British credit would never run dry. No large-scale effort had ever been made to persuade the Canadians to invest in their own government loans; and in 1914, less than seven hundred thousand dollars of the five hundred-million-dollar Canadian debt was owned in Canada. In these circumstances it was a profound shock when the administration discovered that the familiar sources of capital had been exhausted and that the Dominion might have to finance a large part of the British purchases in Canada as well as pay for the entire national war effort at home. How was all this to be done? It seemed impracticable to get the major part of the required funds by taxation, for the country's tax system was extremely immature and, in the past, the federal government had derived most of its revenue from customs and excise duties. Canada did impose a business profits tax in 1916, and a personal income tax in the following year; but unquestionably the greatest financial resource of the government was the Victory Loans which were floated frequently, and in ever increasing size in the latter years of the war. To a considerable extent the success of these loans may be attributed to the greatly increased bank credits which were made to the Canadian government, the Imperial Munitions Board, and to private industry. These inflationary methods helped to bring about a wartime boom which was accompanied by rising money incomes and larger profits. But it was accompanied also by a swift increase in prices, a drastic rise in the cost of living, and a marked augmentation of general social unrest. In this tense and uncertain atmosphere of prosperity and discontent, the trade unions and the farmers' organizations began to grow rapidly in power and assertiveness.

The demands of the armed services, the increase in production, and the financial policies of the country inevitably forced the government to extend its activities still further. The war effort had overnight become a monopolizing and dangerous leviathan which apprehensive people wanted the authorities of Canada to control. Up to that time, nobody had seriously questioned the system of free enterprise; the government had no machinery to regulate its operations; and yet the state was reluctantly and almost protestingly driven by the sheer, insistent pressure of public opinion to undertake a system of controls. This increase of governmental responsibilities began in a very tentative fashion in the autumn of 1916. In the spring and summer of 1917, after the United States had entered the war, the system of controls was extended; and during 1918 and the first hectic months of 1919, the planned economy of wartime began to take on a more nearly complete shape. It was relatively easy for the Board of Grain Supervisors to dispose of the wheat crop, and for other boards to deal with the distribution and sale of such important single commodities as coal and newsprint. But the attempt to apply over-all controls to the entire economy was a much more ambitious and difficult business. The Food Controller, whose office was set up in 1917, concentrated on the conservation and the fair distribution of foods, and on the prevention of hoarding. The War Trade Board, established in the winter of 1918, regulated the import, export, and allocation of important and scarce materials. It was the Cost of Living Commissioner, whose appointment dated back to the autumn of 1916, who found himself in the most anxious and perplexing situation of all. Regarded with approval by the public, and with embarrassment by the government, he was expected, with the aid of inadequate information and insufficient powers, to control a situation which the government itself, by its inflationary policies, had made largely uncontrollable. On the whole, these wartime boards were only partly successful, since their activities were never really integrated with the financial aspects of the government's policy. They aroused — but did not satisfy — that confused general demand for an equitable control of the whole enterprise of the war. They left unappeased that growing conviction of injustice which threatened to disrupt the moral unity of the Dominion.

It was, however, a political, not an economic, question which finally broke the solidarity which had been growing so steadily ever since 1896 and which seemed to have reached a triumphant completion with the war. In the first months of the conflict, everybody had taken voluntary enlistment for granted, just as everybody had assumed that free enterprise was part of the order of nature; but now the first, as well as the second, assumption began to be seriously questioned. Canada had committed herself, in the face of the terrible casualties which were characteristic of the western front, to the maintenance of four divisions in the field. By the end of 1916, about three hundred and eighty-five thousand Canadians had voluntarily enlisted. It was an impressive enough total, for, since the population of the United States was more than twelve times that of Canada during the war, it was equivalent to nearly five million Americans. But at the beginning of 1916, Sir Robert had set the objective of five hundred thousand men; and during his long stay in England with the Imperial War Cabinet in 1917, the terrible need for men was brought home to him. He came back to Canada in the spring of 1917 determined to introduce a conscription law. And it was this conscription law which was at once the principal expression of the new wartime national unity and the chief cause of its disintegration.

From the beginning there had been some significant variations in the attitude of Canadians to the war. The legitimacy of the conflict was never called in question, nor the necessity of Canadian participation; but there were latent differences of opinion regarding the character and the extent of the contribution which Canada ought to make. These differences inevitably affected the response to the call for enlistment. The towns were readier than the countryside, the prairies more eager than the Atlantic seaboard; and, above all, it was observed that the proportion of enlistments achieved by any social group appeared to vary almost inversely to the length of its connection with Canada. On the one hand, the British-born — the new arrivals with a large proportion of unattached males of military age — gave the highest percentage of their numbers to the armed services, and, on the other hand, the French Canadians unquestionably gave the lowest percentage of theirs.

The French Canadians were the oldest, the original Canadians. With only a reasoned respect for Great Britain and with little more than a critical and uneasy attachment to the anti-clerical and republican France of the twentieth century, they were single-minded in their affection for their own homeland. But their Canadian nationality was, to some extent, localized to the Province of Quebec, and, as Bourassa had shown, qualified by a large vestige of colonialism. They were far more concerned to defend the values of their provincial culture in Canada than they were to protect the interests of Canada in the world at large; and naturally, when Ontario established a new regulation limiting the use of French as a language of instruction and as a subject of study in the province, their feelings were aroused as they had never been by the conflict in Europe. The French Canadians were not alone in their instinctive antagonism to conscription. The measure was opposed by organized labour, and it was accepted by the farmers only on the condition that liberal exemptions would be granted to their sons. But French Canada undoubtedly was the largest single bloc of resentful opposition to the bill. The country, which seemed to have been united by western settlement and war, was breaking apart once more on the old familiar cultural lines.

This fatal division was completed and emphasized by the formation of the Union Government in October, 1917. The purpose of this political reorganization was, of course, not division but unity. Like the *union sacrée* in France and the Lloyd George War Cabinet in Great Britain, the Union Government was regarded by its authors as a national, non-partisan administration which could best administer the final effort of conscription at this extreme crisis of the war. The design was a generous and patriotic expression of the new national feeling; but, in the circumstances, it could simply not be realized in its entirety. Sir Wilfrid Laurier, who had welcomed the party truce at the beginning of the war and who had co-operated actively in the war effort throughout, would not accept the principle of conscription and would not consent to join a union government pledged to carry out the newly passed conscription law. The old leader's conviction was unshakable: but he was confronted now by a mass determination which was as strong as his own. Led by the westerners, the conscriptionist Liberals entered Sir Robert's Union Government; and the remnant of the divided and weakened party which followed Laurier soon found that its one really solid base was the Province of Quebec. In the general election of December, 1917, the Conservatives and the conscriptionist Liberals swept the rest of the country. It was true, as the popular vote showed clearly enough, that, including the huge total in Quebec, there was a very large minority vote against the Union Government; but in terms of actual parliamentary seats, a united Quebec faced a virtually united English-speaking Canada. After twenty years of growing national unity, French Canada seemed again to stand in isolation; and the man who had given his life to the reconciliation of the two cultures in Canada was left at the end of his career with the leadership of his own people.

This flawed achievement at home was in marked contrast with the unbroken success abroad. In this last year of the war, in a great variety of services, the Canadian war effort was increased in size and maintained in effectiveness. The Canadian Army Medical Corps, the Canadian Forestry Corps, the Canadian Railway Construction Corps, were at work, in increasing numbers, in various parts of Great Britain and Europe. Inspired by the German submarine campaign, the Royal Canadian Navy had grown into a stout little fleet of small but active vessels which were engaged chiefly in coastal patrol. When the war ended, a separate Royal Canadian Air Force was just in process of formation; but from the beginning the Canadians had taken a very active part in the various imperial flying services. Canada contributed about twenty-four thousand men to the war in the air. In November, 1918, the Canadians, above eight thousand in number, numbered well over a quarter of the total officer strength of the Royal Air Force; and Colonel W. A. Bishop, with his incredible bag of seventy-two enemy planes, was simply the most spectacular of a number of Canadian 'aces' in the air. All these services stood outside the central effort which was, of course, the Canadian Corps in France. In all, six hundred and twenty-eight thousand Canadians served in the armed forces; and four hundred and twenty-five thousand went overseas.

Even in 1918, even in that year of madly changing military fortunes, the Canadian Corps had both the strength and the luck to maintain its career of unbroken victory. When the German high command made its supreme effort in March and when Gough's Fifth Army broke in dissolving confusion, the First Canadian Motor Machine Gun Brigade was swiftly moved to this field of disaster, where it fought for almost three continuous weeks of heroism. As the crisis deepened, the Canadian Corps was broken up to help stop gaps here and there; but it took no very important part in the great defensive battles of the spring of 1918, and there was therefore all the more reason for the British to use it when they began their heavy share of Foch's massive offensive of that summer. Secrecy was vital. To the Germans, the Canadian Corps was a bright spear of battle which had not been blunted in the reverses of the spring. The Corps had come to stand for sudden, and calculated, and murderous attack; and now its presence on the front line was more than ever certain to cause alarm. The mystification was elaborate. From the Arras front, where the Corps stood concentrated, two battalions were actually sent north to Kemmel, in the Second Army area; and with them went the wireless equipment of all four Canadian divisions, which began ostentatiously to buzz messages for the Germans to pick up. In the meantime, the entire Corps was transferred south, in secrecy and with incredible speed, to the region east of Amiens, where the surprise attack of the Fourth British Army was to be launched. At dawn on August 8, after a last night of feverish preparation, the Canadians and the Australians attacked and broke through for gains of seven to nine miles which at that time were unprecedented on the western front. August 8, in the often quoted words of Ludendorff, 'was the black day of the German army.'

The second phase of 'Canada's Hundred Days' — the name which has been given to the period from August 4 to November 11, 1918, in the history of the Canadian Corps — began on August 26, after only a brief interval. The Corps was sent back once more to the Arras sector and to the First British Army. Once again the Canadians were to form the spear-head of an attack; but this time their objective was that terrible, that supposedly impregnable line of defences which the enemy had constructed for his final retreat. On September 2, the Canadians cut clean through the so-called Drocourt-Quéant 'switch-line,' an elaborate and sinister maze of trenches which linked up with the Hindenburg Line; and on September 27, as part of the left flank of the massed British attack on the Hindenburg defence system, they crossed the Canal du Nord and began the sanguinary drive which ended early in October with the capture of Cambrai. Then, while the negotiations for peace had already begun, the whole German resistance began gradually to go to pieces. The Canadians joined in the furious general pursuit; and on November 11, 1918, soon after dawn, the pipe band of the 42nd Royal Highlanders of Canada was playing through the streets of Mons. It was the town where, far back in the days of August, 1914, the British had fought their first battle of the war; and now, in the closing moments of the struggle, the chimes played 'Tipperary' to welcome the Canadians. The war was over.

For Canada, the Peace Conference at Paris brought to an appropriate conclusion the long struggle for the establishment of Canadian nationality in the world at large. Sir Robert Borden, who was active and well-liked at the conference, had some contributions of value to make concerning policy; but unquestionably his most important object was to secure public recognition of the Dominion status for which he and Sir Wilfrid Laurier had fought so long. At Paris, the British Empire panel, which was virtually a continuation of the Imperial War Cabinet, included representatives of the Dominions; but Sir Robert, backed by the other Dominion prime ministers, successfully insisted that, in addition, these self-governing British nations should have separate representation in the general sessions of the conference, on exactly the same footing as the other smaller independent powers. When the long negotiations were at length concluded, the peace treaties were signed separately on behalf of the King, for Canada and for each of the other Dominions; and, in addition, the Dominions were all recognized as original members of the League of Nations with separate representation in the League Assembly and in the International Labour Organization.

In February, 1919, while Sir Robert Borden was winning these triumphs in Paris, Sir Wilfrid Laurier was dying in his house in Ottawa. It was a sudden stroke of paralysis which closed the long career; there was only a brief interval before the end; and the whispered words 'C'est fini' alone broke the silence of these last few hours of unconsciousness. The words suggested the stoicism which was so characteristic of Laurier's race, and the fortitude which was so marked a feature of his own personality. The phrase might even have served as the appropriate epigraph for the major effort of his career. But Laurier stood for the inward harmony, as well as the outward recognition, of Canada; and the bitterness and division of the last few years seemed to have postponed the realization of this aim into the indefinite future.

CHAPTER NINE

THE SEARCH FOR PEACE
AND SECURITY

[*I*]

O N MARCH 19, 1919, the 'Princess Pats' — Princess Patricia's Canadian Light Infantry — marched through the streets of Ottawa to receive a national welcome from the Governor-General of Canada. Famous for battle honours which stretched unbroken from St. Eloi to Mons, they had been cheered at every station along the railway line from Halifax to Ottawa; and at the capital they marched in full fighting dress with rifles and fixed bayonets through miles of frantic crowds to the Governor-General's dais on Parliament Hill. The wild enthusiasm of their reception was repeated for every unit of the Canadian Corps through those months of spring and early summer; and the cities, towns, and villages of the country welcomed back their regiments and battalions with flags, fireworks, and searchlights, and packed, gesticulating crowds. In July, Parliament recorded its gratitude to the armed services in solemn resolutions. The Ministry of Soldiers' Civil Re-Establishment and the other boards and commissions concerned with reconstruction were working feverishly to cope with the thousands of soldiers who returned daily in those exciting months of 1919. The boys had come home. It was now time for the world they had been promised — the world which was fit for heroes to live in — to materialize.

Unfortunately this never happened in quite the way that had been anticipated. Some people refused to believe the brave new world had arrived. Other people were certain that if this was the new world, they much preferred to remain in the old. In the profound unsettlement of the first post-war years, the form of the future was still largely hidden behind cloudy and angry ambiguities; and all that seemed certain was that the old order had been wrecked, the old conditions undermined, the old assumptions contradicted. Ever since Confederation, Canada had rested and relied upon two systems, one international and one national, which she had found generally satisfactory and which she had fondly believed were immutable. On the one hand, she had comfortably enjoyed the benefits of that world order of peace which had been maintained by Great Britain in the nineteenth century through the power of her navy; and, on the other hand, she had realized some of the advantages of nationality through the operation of certain generally accepted national policies. These two bases of her existence were now either altered or threatened. A new and untried political system, embodied in the League of Nations, had apparently taken the place of the old world order of the nineteenth century. A new and vague philosophy of economic controls and social security, expressed in class and regional protests throughout the country, seemed to threaten the old unity of Macdonald and Laurier.

From the very start, the new international system appeared disquieting. From a variety of motives, which she would have found it difficult to analyze, but which had always forced her to be concerned with external markets and transatlantic politics, Canada had not hesitated seriously to join the League of Nations; but the fact that she could not be content with North American aloofness did not mean that she was immune from those apprehensions of European affairs which so troubled the United States. Article X of the League Covenant, which committed League members 'to respect and preserve as against all external aggression the territorial integrity and existing political independence of all Members of the League,' had troubled Sir Robert Borden since the moment of its framing in Paris; and before the article was attacked in the United States, he protested against it in a secret memorandum which has been regarded as one of the best critiques of this system of mutual guarantees. His criticisms were repeated with equal fervour, if with inferior ability, when the whole subject was laid before the Canadian Parliament. In the end Parliament ratified the peace treaties, without a division; but several people voiced the uneasy suspicion that Canadian autonomy, which had just been disentangled from the British Empire, was now compromised by the collective system. 'In military matters,' said Rodolphe Lemieux, 'we are governed also by and from Ottawa, and not by and from London; and we do not want to be governed by and from Geneva.'

But if the new order looked potentially dangerous abroad, there was real and immediate trouble in the state of affairs at home. The first outbreaks in Canada were obviously the result of the policy of military conscription; but, as the war ended in armistice and armistice in peace — as the inflationary boom of 1918-19 collapsed in the depression of 1920 – this political grievance became only part of a confused, angry accumulation of social hatreds and political animosities. The Easter riots of 1918 in Quebec against conscription, the massed demonstrations of the United Farmers of Ontario in the following May, the angry resolutions proposed in the annual convention of the Trades and Labour Congress which met in Quebec in September of the same year, were supported by something more than dislike of the manpower policies of the federal government. They were fed by a bewildered sense of social injustice which war riches and profiteering had created at home, and by the uncertain hope of economic security and social welfare which the Russian Revolution had aroused abroad. And these grievances took visible form in farmer and labour parties which attacked the old national policies and the old national parties which had sponsored them.

In 1918 and 1919, the agitation grew rapidly in Ontario and the western provinces. It was partly agrarian and partly industrial in character; but, on the whole, the farmers were by far the most important factor in the new movement, and it was they who took over its direction and control. So far as labour was concerned, the most important event was the withdrawal of the western members from the Canadian Trades and Labour Congress and their formation of the One Big Union in 1919. The O. B. U. was based upon the novel and striking idea of uniting all workers in a 'modern and scientific organization by industry instead of by craft.' But its career was prejudiced by the failure of the great Winnipeg strike in the spring of 1919; it never won the support of the much stronger trades-union movement of eastern and central Canada; and perhaps the main result of this sudden outburst of western industrial radicalism was an increase in general working-class unrest in the country and a strengthening in the general protest against the labour policies of the federal government. On their part, the farmers were already mobilizing these various bitter discontents in support of agrarian political action. Their associations and co-operatives were now turned suddenly into provincial politics; their new provincial parties were soon to be combined in an effective single national organization. All during 1919, the United Farmers of Ontario were energetically preparing to contest the approaching provincial election, which they won decisively in October of that year; and out west the farmers' organizations of the three prairie provinces were in the throes of active preparation for the better political world of the future. Already, as early as November, 1918, the Canadian Council of Agriculture — the national union of all these provincial farmers' organizations — had issued a new agrarian political platform under the disturbing, the challenging title of a 'New National Policy'; and in January, 1920, a new federal party, the National Progressive party, with Thomas A. Crerar as leader, was formed to bring this programme of drastically lowered tariffs and publicly owned utilities into realization.

Faced by this alarming agitation, what were the old federal parties to do? In the past their success had been largely based upon their ability to reconcile the various groups and sectional interests of the country in a common national policy. But now this hoary technique of bargaining and compromise was suddenly denounced as fraudulent and inequitable; and a new political movement, founded frankly on occupational interests and strongly moved by class feelings, had arisen to challenge the old composite national interest of the past, and the old national policies by which Macdonald and Laurier had tried to advance it. The future, for the Liberal and Conservative parties, looked highly dubious. The whole organization of Canadian politics seemed to be breaking up under the disintegrating influence of post-war social unrest. The Liberal party had been divided and apparently ruined during the war; and now the Unionist party — the supreme example of the national unity of the war — was exposed to all the disagreements of the peace. Its wartime friends began to leave it for the Liberal party, the new Progressive party, and for private life. It began to lose bye-election after bye-election. Was its defeat inescapably approaching? Was it destined to be overwhelmed by the Progressive party, just as it had overwhelmed the Liberal party a few short years before?

There was no doubt about it — the challenge of the farmer-progressive parties was the great disturbing, disconcerting factor in post-war politics. Confronted by the possibility of their own extinction in the collapse of the old political order, the Conservative and Liberal parties began hurriedly to reorganize and reform themselves; and for a few years the Canadian electorate was entertained by a most bewildering succession of new party names, new party programmes, new political leaders, and new political earnestness. The 'New National Policy' of the farmers had been published in November, 1918. It was followed, in August, 1919, by the elaborate programme of the rejuvenated Liberal party, and, in July, 1920, by the equally formidable platform of the National Liberal and Conservative party. Thomas A. Crerar was made leader of the Progressive party in January, 1920; but less than six months before William Lyon Mackenzie King had assumed the mantle of the departed Sir Wilfrid Laurier, and less than six months later Arthur Meighen took over the post of the retiring Sir Robert Borden. All these men were still on the right side of fifty. By a stretch of the imagination which was pardonable in view of the endless succession of aged Canadian statesmen, they could even be considered young. One of them might conceivably dominate the future of Canadian politics in much the same way as Laurier and Macdonald had dominated the past. There might be a Meighen age, or a Crerar epoch, or a King era. Which would it be?

On the whole, it looked at first as if the Liberals had found the most effective answer to the challenge of Progressivism. The Liberal convention, which met in August, 1919, to elect a new leader and to draft a new programme, was almost painfully aware that reform was in the air, that the electorate was full of vague, imperious demands, that political survival could perhaps be purchased only by such wild extremities as youthful leadership and political daring. The new Liberal platform, which was long and extremely detailed, discreetly omitted the Progressive demand for public ownership of public utilities. But it included the Progressive plank of drastically reduced tariffs, as well as the Progressive plank of taxes on business profits and personal incomes; and in the controversial new matters of labour and social security, where the agrarian Progressives had been rather brief and niggardly, the Liberals suggested a new principle for the management of factories and a new system of insurance for unemployment, sickness, and old age. A programme so resolutely forward-looking as this demanded — and received — a new type of leader. The convention — though by a curiously narrow majority — rejected the time-worn veteran W. S. Fielding, and elected W. L. Mackenzie King. He seemed to have all the qualifications. He talked the fashionable new language of social reform with practised oratorical fluency. A university man, a social theorist who had embodied his reflections on the labour problem in a book entitled *Industry and Humanity,* he had enjoyed, in addition, years of practical experience as Deputy-Minister, and then Minister of Labour under Sir Wilfrid Laurier. And finally, was he not descended, on his mother's side, from William Lyon Mackenzie, the irascible social and political revolutionary of the 1830's, upon whom the sedate and conservative Liberals of 1919 looked back with an odd mixture of affection, misunderstanding, and embarrassment?

The prospects of the Conservative party appeared to be in sharp contrast with all this. If political defeat had roused the Liberals to a spirited recovery, political victory had apparently depressed the Conservatives into a discouraged decline. While Sir Robert Borden was absent from Ottawa for long intervals in a vain endeavour to recover his health, the Unionist government went slowly and inexorably to pieces: but it was not until the summer of 1920 that the wartime Canadian prime minister finally resigned his office and Arthur Meighen was chosen to lead a new and reorganized Liberal-Conservative government. Meighen had been a contemporary of Mackenzie King at the University of Toronto. A serious, reserved, almost austere man, his strength seemed to lie particularly in his mastery of debating technique, in his sure knowledge of parliamentary strategy. He could be aggressive, trenchant, sardonically witty. But was he the man to re-educate the Conservative party in the new doctrines of social democracy and international co-operation? It seemed highly doubtful. In fact, it began to look more and more as if the Conservatives would take up the official defence of those historic national policies against which the Progressives had first launched their attack.

At first this was by no means clear, for everybody, including the Conservatives, was talking the language of the fight for democracy. It was, indeed, out of this general democratic enthusiasm that there arose the curious excitement over titles which swept through Canada in 1918-19. The proposal to abolish titles, non-hereditary as well as hereditary, for residents of the Dominion was not, of course, a measure of the Unionist government; but Conservatives supported, or did not oppose, it; and it was sponsored, with crusading ardour, by W. F. Nickle, the Conservative member for Kingston, Ontario. There had been a good deal of criticism of some of the honours which were distributed during, and immediately after, the war; and, in the circumstances of the moment, these objections to particular titles were soon combined in a general disapproval of the institution of honours as a whole. On his part, Nickle was convinced that the inequity of titles was one of the major causes of the industrial and rural unrest which agitated the country. The agricultural and urban workers might imagine that they were distressed by long hours, high prices, and insufficient income; but to W. F. Nickle it seemed obvious that they were really labouring under a profound dissatisfaction with their status. As he saw it, the fight against titles was simply part of the great struggle for democracy against German autocracy. He discoursed volubly on the Browningesque theme of 'all service ranks the same with God'; and he reminded his audience of the Widow's Mite. Arguments such as these could scarcely fail of their effect; and, in due course, Parliament accepted a resolution requesting the crown to grant no more titles to residents of Canada.

This sounded like the trumpet blast announcing a new and better era. But the new era showed few signs of appear-

ing: and the Conservatives gave even fewer indications of
wishing to legislate it into existence. It was true that the
government made special grants-in-aid to the provinces in
support of public health and technical education; it was also
true that the government reduced the tariff on agricultural
machinery to the benefit of the farmer. But of all the novel
proposals which were contained in the Progressive Manifesto
and which in 1919 constituted radicalism for the ordinary
Canadian, the Conservatives took up only one — the idea of
public ownership — on a really large scale: and even here
the nationalization of the Canadian Northern Railway and
the Grand Trunk Railway System was a solution imposed
on them by force of circumstances and accepted without
much enthusiasm or conviction. As early as the first years
of the war it had become clear that the ambitious scheme of
railway building, which had been sponsored with such confidence and high hopes by the Laurier government, was tottering on the edge of complete failure. Years before the
railways were effectively finished, the stream of capital available for their support began to dwindle alarmingly; and,
with the outbreak of war, it completely stopped. The Canadian Northern and the Grand Trunk could get no more
funds from London or New York; the Canadian government
hesitated to go on feeding the bottomless maw of their deficiencies. And yet for the public credit, as well as for the
public service, the railways could not be permitted to fail.
In 1916, the Conservative government appointed a royal
commission to investigate the railway problem; and the
majority report of the Commission, the so-called Drayton-
Acworth Report, recommended that the two railway systems
should 'be assumed by the people of Canada.' In 1917 the
Canadian government acquired the Canadian Northern; two
years later it took over the Grand Trunk Pacific, and the
original Grand Trunk Railway with all its subsidiaries. The
long process of consolidating these new acquisitions with the
older government lines in a great state transport system

called the Canadian National Railways was to be spread over the next few years.

This enormous adventure in public ownership was, on the whole, an exceptional incident in the last years of a Conservative administration. Far from accepting new public responsibilities, far from pressing eagerly into the new fields of social betterment and economic regulation, the Conservatives seemed almost anxious to get rid of the duties which the war had imposed upon the state. The state, it was true, could not escape quite so quickly as its leaders desired, for the disturbances of the post-war period required some regulation. The continuance of inflationary prices, the clamour against the post-war high cost of living compelled the government to pass the Combines and Fair Prices Act in 1919 and to empower the Board of Commerce to administer it. The post-war chaos which reigned in the international wheat markets persuaded the administration to continue the war-time supervision of the grain trade by appointing a Wheat Board to purchase and market the entire crop of 1919. But these were the last important concessions. The Board of Commerce ceased to function early in 1920, unlamented by the government; and, in the summer of the same year, it was announced that the work of the Wheat Board would be wound up after the disposal of the 1919 crop. Government was returning to its traditional sphere; and the Conservative party, as the new party platform of 1920 clearly showed, was going back thankfully to its traditional philosophy. The tariff was perhaps the most prominent plank in this rather uninspiring programme; and it was the tariff which the newly elected leader, Arthur Meighen, began to emphasize more and more in his speeches as the time of the general election drew gradually closer.

In external, as well as in domestic affairs, the government also seemed disposed to stand by the traditions of the past. It showed a greater satisfaction with the form of imperial co-operation which had been worked out during the war than it did with the new system of collective security which had been set up at the Peace of Versailles. At the first meeting of the League of Nations Assembly, in November, 1920, C. J. Doherty, who was the principal Canadian delegate, moved that Article X be deleted from the Covenant; and at the next Assembly, when this extreme proposal had been rejected, Doherty again voiced Canada's strong objections to the clause. To a certain extent, the wartime system of imperial co-operation also suffered in the early post-war period, as Great Britain and the Dominions each became intensely preoccupied with domestic affairs. But the Borden conception of a British Commonwealth of six nation-states, equal in status, pursuing a common foreign policy through continuous consultation, had not yet been abandoned. And, as a matter of fact, Arthur Meighen, the successor of Borden, gave a convincing demonstration of its possibilities in peacetime in the Imperial Conference of 1921. Here, in the Conference of the Prime Ministers, he vigorously opposed the renewal of the Anglo-Japanese Alliance; and he was to a considerable extent responsible for the decision against renewal which was the effective prelude to the Washington Conference on the limitation of armaments. It was a striking illustration of the working of the new system; but the United States, whose friendship and goodwill Meighen had stressed so strongly at the Imperial Conference, appeared to be unaware that the new system existed at all. Her invitation to the Washington Conference was sent to Great Britain alone. Far from welcoming the new status of the Dominions which the other powers had accepted at Versailles, she chose studiously to ignore it.

By this time the decade of Conservative-Unionist rule was obviously drawing to a close. The Progressive movement reached the climax of its success; Mackenzie King redoubled his attacks against the government; and, in the general elections of December, 1921, the Conservative administration of Arthur Meighen was completely beaten at the polls. There were one hundred and seventeen Liberals in the new House; there were sixty-five Progressives; and there were only fifty Conservatives. The old order had fallen. The hour of the 'New National Policies' had struck; and perhaps most people believed — or feared — that soon those confused hopes and aspirations which had been born of the war and the peace would be realized at last. The decision seemed so positive. And yet, as time went on, people began to wonder whether it had been so unequivocal after all. The new Liberal government made no radical changes in the tariff; it did not sponsor a great programme of social-security legislation. Under the Liberals, as under the Conservatives, the state seemed almost to draw back in embarrassment, if not in fear, from those new responsibilities, both domestic and foreign, which the war had first revealed.

There were reasons, of course, for the rather negative and inconclusive attitude which the new government adopted. Politically, the Liberal administration was none too strong, for the Progressives virtually held the balance of power in the House; financially, the Liberal administration was extremely weak, for it laboured under both the wartime debt and the peacetime demand for retrenchment. In the period from 1913 to 1921, the national debt increased sevenfold — from five hundred million to three and a half billion dollars. Part of this increase was accounted for by the nationalization of the two transcontinental railways, and part by the enormous expenditures of the war, for which, of course, there were no productive assets at all; and, as a result, nearly half of the current annual expenditure in the early 1920's was paid out to service the debt and to discharge other current obligations which the war had created. Under such cautious Liberal ministers of finance as W. S. Fielding and James Robb, the government gave up the thought of new, adventurous, and expensive projects, and sought merely by strict economy to reduce controllable expenditures and to balance the budget.

There was, however, a far more serious barrier to the enlargement of the federal government's tasks in the field of economic regulation and social welfare. The inhibitions which resulted from the Dominion's sense of weakness no doubt played their part; but the prohibitions of the constitution were final. Ever since the opening of the war, the federal government, by virtue of its residuary power to legislate for 'the peace, order, and good government of Canada,' had done a great many important things which incidentally affected the powers of the provinces. For years this wartime federal authority went unchallenged; it might almost have seemed as if the reaction against Lord Watson's decisions of the 1890's was to be permanent. But such was not the case. In a series of crucial decisions in the early 1920's, the Judicial Committee of the Privy Council unequivocally declared that the recent extension of federal powers could be justified only by the emergency of the war and must cease with the ending of that emergency. The Combines and Fair Prices Act of 1919, which had set up the Board of Commerce, and the older Industrial Disputes Act, were now declared to be *ultra vires* of the Dominion. This, to a large extent, was the work of Viscount Haldane, who delivered judgment in the important post-war cases and who was an uncritical admirer of his predecessor Lord Watson. It was Haldane who completed the work of providing Canada with two constitutions, one for peace and one for war; and since peace had now come, the federal government found itself surrounded by all the forbidding limitations of the provincial power to legislate in relation to property and civil rights.

There was only one great case which stood in the way of Haldane's interpretation. This was, of course, the case of *Russell* vs. *The Queen* (1882), which had declared the Canada Temperance Act of 1878 to be *intra vires* of the Dominion on the ground that the promotion of public order and morals was a legitimate exercise of the federal residuary authority, even though such promotion might incidentally affect property and civil rights. *Russell* vs. *The Queen* was the ghost that stalked through the Canadian constitution — the phantom of the residuary clause as the Fathers of Confederation had designed it; and Haldane determined to lay this wraith of the past once and for all. His method was absurdly simple. Since the Judicial Committee had declared that the federal government could only 'trench upon' property and civil rights in times of peril, then obviously it must be assumed that the Canada Temperance Act had been enacted during a crisis of this kind. In actual fact the Canada Temperance Act was a perfectly ordinary law passed in a time of profound peace, both domestic and foreign. The task of converting it into a desperate measure of public safety might therefore seem a little difficult to the uninitiated; but it was a task before which the ingenious Haldane did not quail. By a great effort of pure reason, entirely unhampered by even the thought of historical research, he announced that the Canada Temperance Act must have been passed in a period of transcontinental intoxication, of acute, all-Canadian alcoholism, of Dominion-wide moral collapse through drink. 'Their Lordships think,' he declared gravely, 'that the decision in *Russell* vs. *The Queen* can only be supported today . . . on the assumption . . . that the evil of intemperance at that time amounted in Canada to one so great and so general that at least for the period it was a menace to the national life of Canada so serious and pressing that the National Parliament was called on to intervene to protect the nation from disaster. An epidemic of pestilence might conceivably have been regarded as analogous.'

Because of these constitutional impediments as well as because of its own political and financial weaknesses, the new Liberal government seemed loath to undertake the duties of economic regulation and social welfare. In addition it appeared even more unwilling to accept the commitments of international co-operation; and in this respect its insularity was even more pronounced than that of the Meighen government. The Conservatives had questioned collective security, but welcomed imperial partnership; the Liberals appeared to be doubtful of both. They kept up the campaign of criticism against Article X of the League of Nations Covenant; but, at the same time, they seemed almost equally restive under the obligations of a collective imperial foreign policy. In this, of course, they simply followed the lead of Sir Wilfrid, just as the Conservatives had followed the tradition of Sir Robert. Borden had been willing to accept responsibility in return for a share in the determination of policy; Laurier had refused a share in the determination of policy precisely because he wished to escape responsibility. And for the Liberals, the so-called Chanak incident of 1922 seemed to demonstrate the wisdom of Laurier's view. In this sudden quarrel with Turkey which blew up over the peace settlement in the Dardanelles, Great Britain was obliged to take a stand without previous consultation with the Dominions; and then, again without warning, she invited their military support. It was an unfortunate episode, for inevitably it raised doubts about the feasibility of 'continuous consultation' in the sudden crises of peace; and from that time forward the foreign policies of Great Britain and Canada showed a slight, but significant, tendency to diverge. In 1923, Canada insisted that her representative alone should sign the Halibut Treaty with the United States; and in 1925 the Dominions were specifically excepted from all obligations incurred by Great Britain in virtue of the Locarno Agreements. Imperial co-operation for particular ends in foreign affairs was by no means over; but a single, collective imperial foreign policy, worked out through continuous consultation, had been tacitly abandoned as a workable plan in times of peace.

Thus the Dominion, which appeared in 1919 to face a new national future and a new world order, had sunk back comfortably into the habits of the past. It had chosen the safe, the middle, way; and it had seemingly accepted Mackenzie King as the appropriate personification of the new political age. For some years the outcome of the contest between King and Crerar and Meighen had been uncertain. Crerar, it was true, had fairly early resigned the leadership of the Progressives, and, in the election of 1925, the party's following had been reduced from sixty-five to twenty-eight; but, at the same time, the Conservatives had made a strong recovery, and with one hundred and sixteen members to the one hundred and one for the Liberals, they constituted the largest single group in the new House. King, however, continued to govern with the assistance of the Progressives; but his hold upon office was precarious; and in June, 1926, when a report on the scandals in the Department of Customs and Excise was presented to the Commons, his government was obviously in grave difficulties. At this point, while a Conservative motion censuring the administration of the Customs Department was still being debated, King took the unusual step of asking the Governor-General for a dissolution. To this he believed that he was 'entitled' under British practice. Since the beginning of the session, he argued, he had demonstrated his ability to govern. Meighen, with equal chances or better, had not been able to win the confidence of the House and prove that he could provide an alternative government; and therefore 'the public interest demands a dissolution of this House of Commons'. Lord Byng was unable to agree. He declined to grant King's request on the ground that all reasonable expedients should be tried before resorting so quickly to another election and that Meighen had not yet been given a chance of trying to govern. On June 28, refusing to hold office until their successors had been appointed, King and his colleagues resigned.

At Lord Byng's request, Meighen agreed to form a government and — with the help which he expected to receive from the Progressives — to conclude the business of the session as promptly as possible. His position was one of great difficulty. By the law as it then stood, every Member of the Commons on accepting office under the Crown was obliged to vacate his seat and seek re-election; and this requirement would obviously have affected some fifteen or sixteen Conservatives and necessitated the delay of an adjournment or a prorogation. In these circumstances — and for the duration of the session only — Meighen decided to constitute a small 'temporary Ministry'. He himself accepted office and vacated his seat; but the other six members of the government were appointed without portfolio, accepted responsibility for the different Departments as 'acting Ministers' only, and were not therefore affected by the law. For two days the temporary Ministry was sustained by majorities rather better, on the average, than those which the previous administration had enjoyed; but its constitutionality was then vigorously and successfully challenged by the Liberals and, on July 1, it was defeated by a single vote. Meighen requested a dissolution; and — 'all reasonable expedients' having been tried — he was granted it.

In the event, the electorate was persuaded to reject the temporary Ministry more emphatically than the Commons had already done. Meighen attempted to make the maladministration of his predecessor the main issue of the campaign; but King succeeded in convincing the voters of the transcendent importance of the 'constitutional crisis' of the last days of June. In King's version of these events, Lord Byng's refusal of a dissolution was made to appear as an imperial affront to Canadian national autonomy, and Meighen's temporary Ministry was darkly portrayed as an autocratic subversion of responsible parliamentary rule. Thus the recent Liberal government, which had been so embarrassed and vulnerable at the time of the customs scandal, presented itself to the public as the innocent victim of repeated constitutional injuries; and, on this highly questionable interpretation of a complex constitutional issue, King won the general election of 1926. The Conservatives, who had made such an impressive recovery in 1925, declined again, though not so seriously as in 1921; and the Progressives, whose inward divisions had been growing in seriousness during the past few years, virtually ceased to exist as a distinct political party. Stable government had at last returned. The post-war period of political turmoil was surely over. For a few years it almost seemed so. And yet, at the same time, new forces, beyond the control of Ottawa, were already beginning to have their first disturbing effects upon Canada and the other nations of the western world.

[*II*]

In some important ways, the half-dozen years which elapsed from 1923 to 1929 resembled the first far-off railway-building age which had ended for the old Province of Canada in the depression of 1857. It was true that the 1920's, which inherited the tragic legacy of the first World War, were troubled by underlying disturbances far more complex and serious than those of the 1850's; but in both periods Canada responded impressively to the brisk foreign demand for her export staples, as well as to the lavish expenditure of capital in her new export trades; and in both periods also — which was far more important — the country passed through a major revolution in basic economic technique. The railway boom of the 1850's had brought the age of steam, steel, and rail to British North America; the post-war prosperity of the 1920's ushered in the new era of oil and electricity, of base metals and alloys, of automobiles, aeroplanes, and motor-boats. The first economic unity of Canada, based on the export of wheat and promoted by transcontinental railways, had been achieved during the iron age; but the age of oil and electricity, with its new methods of transport and its new areas of exploitation, was to make drastic changes in this first simple integration.

The prairies, which had, of course, been the centre of expansion in the pre-war wheat boom, were by no means overshadowed in the post-war prosperity. In fact, they continued to advance on much the same lines as before. Encouraged by the building of northern branch railways and by the breeding of new, early-maturing brands of wheat such as Garnet and Reward, a last contingent of migrants moved into northern Saskatchewan and Alberta; and the Peace River district was brought into life as the final agricultural frontier in North America. After 1923, wheat prices picked up again. Freights were lower, agricultural machinery was cheaper; and the farmers, disappointed when the government declined to continue the Wheat Board, proceeded in 1923 and 1924 to organize voluntary contract Wheat Pools on a co-operative basis in the three prairie provinces and to establish a Central Selling Agency which was intended to market all pool wheat in an orderly and unspeculative fashion. The Wheat Pool was the pinnacle of co-operative enterprise and community planning in the new prairie west. Like the reduced tariff on agricultural implements, the lowered railway rates on western traffic, the farmers' governments in Manitoba and Alberta, and the Progressive party at Ottawa, it represented the organizing, constructive influence of the prairie farmers at the height of their power. The great plan of Confederation had at length been realized. The west was occupied. It stood, active, aggressive, confident, and buoyant. But, to a great extent, the basis of its life was wheat; and wheat was a vulnerable commodity, exposed both to the treachery of nature and the rivalries of sovereign states.

Yet perhaps, after all, it was not in the west that the new energy of the 1920's was most clearly to be seen. The post-war regions of exploitation were scattered all over transcontinental Canada; but if there was any general direction, any main goal, in this fresh expansion, it was north. The oil fields of the Turner Valley lay in southern Alberta, the complex silver-lead-zinc mines of the Kootenay region in British Columbia were situated close to the international boundary; but, at the same time, it was extraordinary how many of the new enterprises carried men into the Appalachian Highlands and back again to the Precambrian Shield. The Shield, the enormous irregular triangle of rocky, ravaged upland, had been both a barrier to economic progress and a bulwark of economic development. These ancient, worn-down rocks, with their vast stretches of towering conifers, their elaborate mazes of lakes, lakelets, rivers, falls, rapids, and spillways, had been the basis of both the fur trade and the timber trade. There had been two great 'crops' in the Precambrian Shield. Men had exploited its animals and forests; but now they were to tear out wealth and power from its soils, and rocks, and waters. The north became the great new impulse of Canadian life. It filled men's pockets and fired their imaginations. Its massive forms, its simple, sweeping rhythms, its glittering and sombre colours, inspired in Tom Thomson and the members of the Group of Seven the most distinctive group of painters which the country had yet produced.

The new north was enormous in extent and endlessly varied in character. It reached to the pole; in Ontario and Quebec it extended far below the forty-ninth parallel of latitude. Part of it formed the northern hinterland of the central and western provinces; great masses of it, lying north of the sixtieth parallel, had been divided politically into the Yukon, and the North-West Territories, with their three divisions, Keewatin, Mackenzie, and Franklin. This vast empire — the North-West Territories alone were equal in area to the three provinces of Quebec, Ontario, and Manitoba — was thinly populated by a curiously mixed assortment of races and classes; and their occupations varied all the way from trapping and subsistence farming on the one hand to the big enterprises of mining, paper-making, and hydro-electric development on the other. Pushing far into the Arctic Circle, the Hudson's Bay Company extended the fur trade to King William Land and Somerset Island and made contact with the last northern bands of Eskimo. Restless pioneers, with the old urge for space, free land, and independence, were encouraged by the colonization policies of the two central provinces to move into the Lake St. John

region of northern Quebec and the Clay Belts, within the
Precambrian Shield, in northern Ontario. Here the progress
of farming was hard and slow; the whole future of agriculture in these northern latitudes was the subject of anxious
debate. But in mining, pulp-and-paper, hydro-electric power,
the developments were immediate and spectacular. It
was through these industries that the revolution in technology entered the north. It was by these industries that
the north won its new fame. Its typical, not its exceptional, features — its rocks, its falls and rapids, its forests of
spruce and balsam — were the source of this new wealth.
The last northern boom was achieved, not in despite of the
Shield, but because of it.

The production of wood-pulp and newsprint was simply a
new phase in the history of those forest industries which
had reached a large-scale output in the days of the Napoleonic blockade with the carriage of huge square-timbers to
Great Britain. In the period which followed the War of
1914-18, the increasing demands of the press of the United
States, and the exhaustion of the chief American supplies of
wood-pulp, transferred the industry to Canada; and the attack on the northern spruce forests of Canada began on a
huge scale. Lumbering had always been linked with the
rivers for transport; but the pulp-and-paper industry was
also dependent upon their falls and rapids for hydro-electric
power. The new paper mills were scattered all the way from
the south shore of Nova Scotia to the British-Columbian coast.
They used the wood of both the Appalachian Highlands and
the Precambrian Shield, the water-powers of the youthful
rivers that flowed into the Atlantic, the St. Lawrence, Hudson Bay, and Lake Winnipeg. But it was on the tributaries
of the lower St. Lawrence, the Saguenay, the St. Maurice,
and the Ottawa that the biggest enterprises were based.

The rise of mining was only less spectacular than the
growth of the newsprint industry. As far back as the 1850's,
gold mining had begun on both sides of the continent, in

Nova Scotia and British Columbia; and the search for gold which had begun on the Fraser and Thompson Rivers, on the Pacific slope, far back in 1858, continued slowly up the coast until the final amazing discovery was made in the Klondike in 1896. Precious metals had now done their work for the Pacific province, leaving behind them, as a permanent bequest, the base metal mines in the Kootenay; and the intense interest which before had been focussed on the Appalachian Highlands and the Cordillera was now shifted to the Precambrian Shield. Here the new technology of the post-war period brought to its peak a development which had started more than a decade before. It was the construction of the Temiskaming and Northern Ontario Railway which led to the discovery of silver at Cobalt in 1903; and Cobalt became the inspiration, and the source of technical skill, for a series of mining ventures which shifted from silver to gold, and then to gold in conjunction with base metals. In 1909, the three famous gold mines, Hollinger, McIntyre, and Dome, were staked in the Porcupine region in northern Ontario; and in 1911-12, the Wright-Hargreaves properties and Lake Shore mines were discovered in the Kirkland Lake district. The enormous nickel deposits at Sudbury were rapidly exploited during the War of 1914-18. The post-war age, with its many sources of hydro-electric power, its new mining machinery and chemical processes, its aeroplanes and tractors, carried Canadian mining into new and more remote regions and vastly increased production. Work was pushed rapidly forward in the gold and copper deposits at Rouyn in northern Quebec and on the complex gold, copper, and zinc of Flin Flon in northern Manitoba.

The post-war industrial system, which had whipped up the development of the north, also brought into existence new methods of transport, new trade routes, and new markets. The western prairies, which had been the centre of economic expansion and the basis of economic unity in the pre-war era, had relied on a great east-west system of steam railways; but now the rise of the north and of the other new centres of development, with their reliance on new ocean ports and routes, their heavy dependence on motor traffic by road, river, and airway, cut across this old trunk-line of the steam age, at least to a considerable extent. Far to the south, the Panama Canal was about to provide a successful new link between the Atlantic and Pacific for water-borne traffic; and to the north, the Hudson Bay Railway was soon to reopen the old northern outlet for the transport of western produce to Great Britain. The motor-boat and the tractor helped to speed expansion in the Hudson Bay and Mackenzie River drainage basins; Canadian airways were making records in the carriage of freight in the north; a great new system of paved highways served the country's rapidly growing motor traffic. It was not without significance that, in the first post-war years, the state was obliged to take over the two trans-continentals of a previous generation, the Canadian Northern and the Grand Trunk, with their terminals at Montreal and Halifax. Ever since the 1890's Great Britain had been the chief market for Canadian exports; the flow of goods from Canada to the United Kingdom had been exceptionally high during the War of 1914-18; but in 1921, by a slight margin, the United States regained its old position as Canada's best customer. The Fordney-McCumber tariff of 1922, the most exclusive tariff which the United States had enacted up to that time, seriously interfered with several valuable Canadian trades with the Republic; but a number of important staple products — newsprint, base metals, gold — continued to enter in large and increasing quantities. The United States became the principal purchaser of the new staples of the post-war period, while Great Britain remained the chief customer of the traditional agricultural products of the past.

The effects of these changes on the Canadian economy as a whole — on the economic integration and political unity which had been achieved in the war and the pre-war periods — were varied and somewhat contradictory. Without any question, Canada was in many ways a more favoured and stronger country in an age of electricity, alloys, and airways than she had been in the era of steam, steel, and rail. And yet, though the economic life of the whole country unquestionably grew richer and more varied, the bounty of the post-war period seemed unequal in its distribution, partial in its rewards, disintegrating in some of its consequences. Wheat had proved itself to be a force in favour of national unity; but the new staples almost seemed to encourage the unfortunate process of regional division. In the pre-war age, wheat had been the one great export staple, round which the whole economic life of the country had centred; but now there were half a dozen distinct staple-producing regions, each with its own important export specialty or specialties, each with its regional interests in markets outside Canada, each with its individual successes and misfortunes. While some provinces, such as Ontario, Quebec, and British Columbia, profited superlatively from the new enterprises, others, like Manitoba and Alberta, benefited only moderately, and still others, like Saskatchewan and the Maritime Provinces, gained little advantage at all. Saskatchewan depended largely on the old staple, wheat; Nova Scotia's coal and steel industry was linked with the bygone railway-building age and her fisheries with the ancient sugar-producing markets of the West Indies. These regions were relatively untouched by the new industries and trades; but there were other, lucky places upon which the post-war economic energies seemed almost to converge. The development of northern Ontario strengthened Toronto as a financial centre of central Canada. The opening of the Panama Canal helped to make Vancouver a great ocean port, with a hinterland stretching far back into the prairies.

One of the most important effects of the post-war age and its regional tendencies lay in the rapidly changing relations of the Dominion and the provinces. In every federal state the balance of power will tend to oscillate between the cen-

tral and local governments. For a whole generation — even
despite the decisions of the Judicial Committee of the Privy
Council — the influence and authority of the federal power
in Canada had risen steadily toward its pinnacle in the War
of 1914-18. Now the movement was halted, then reversed;
and the importance of the provinces began unmistakably to
ascend. There were a number of reasons for this; but prominent among them was the close association of the provincial
governments — an association partly accidental and partly
deliberate — with the new sources of economic power and the
new problems of social welfare. The very fields which, in
the early 1920's, the federal government had felt itself both
inhibited and prohibited from entering were now claimed
and occupied by the provinces as their private property.
During the age of western development and European war,
the Dominion had retained its leadership; but, amid the
post-war problems of regional expansion and social security,
its pre-eminence began to decline.

At Confederation, the ownership and control of natural
resources had been vested in the provinces. It was true, of
course, that there had always been an important exception
to this generalization, for, when the North-West Territories
were transferred to Canada, she assumed control of the public domain in the west as a necessary basis for her land, settlement, and railway policies. But now the west was occupied, the goals of the settlement policies had been attained;
and, significantly enough, as if in acknowledgment of the
fulfilment of its trust, the federal government transferred the
public domain back to the western provinces in this period.
Once again the provincial control of natural resources was
complete. It lay with the provinces to promote and develop
and control the new regional frontiers based on oil and electricity, forests and minerals. The provinces, which were
obliged by the constitution to superintend roads and local
public works, now undertook a great programme of paved
highways and sponsored such enormous public utilities as

the Ontario Hydro-Electric Power Commission. Empowered by the constitution to levy 'Shop, Saloon, Tavern, Auctioneer, and other Licences,' they took over the complete control of the sale and distribution of liquor, as well as the regulation of automobiles and motor traffic. Money poured into the provincial treasuries from liquor sales, motor licences, gasoline taxes, and public domain, as well as from the more familiar direct taxes of the past. Money poured out again lavishly in highways, public utilities, and the promotion of natural resources. In the decade from 1921 to 1930, the expenditures of all provincial governments rose from ninety million to one hundred and eighty-three million dollars. Measured at least by the outlay required, the work of the provinces had exactly doubled in the first post-war decade.

But it was through their social responsibilities, as well as through their economic interests, that the provinces gained in importance during the 1920's. At Confederation they had been given a number of duties — duties which were supposedly small, which were given to them precisely because they were small, and which now, in a new and changing age, grew suddenly to an inordinate importance. It had always been the business of the provinces, with the help of the municipalities, to maintain education; but education in pre-war times was a vastly different thing from education in a post-war world, which was vitally dependent on scientific knowledge, and technical instruction. At Confederation, also, the provinces had been obliged to shoulder the burden of 'Hospitals, Asylums, Charities and Eleemosynary Institutions'; but the 'poor relief' which did duty in the old days of individualism and free land, of family support and private charity, differed almost in kind from the mass assistance which the slumps of industrial capitalism might require. The great programme of social security, which had been dimly glimpsed at the end of the war, which the Liberal party had outlined in its 1919 manifesto, was never put com-

pletely into effect by any government during this period; but
in so far as it was realized at all, the task fell to the provinces
rather than to the federal government. No general scheme
for federal grants-in-aid of provincial social services was ever
worked out during this period. The Dominion, to be sure,
initiated a provincially operated plan of old-age pensions
and contributed substantially to its support; but earlier
grants-in-aid for public health, agricultural instruction, and
technical education, which had been introduced by the Conservative government, were allowed to lapse in the later
1920's, on the somewhat curious ground that any effort on
the part of the federal government to ensure economy in the
expenditure of its funds would constitute a dangerous interference with the autonomy of the provinces. At all costs —
including, apparently, the public interest — the prestige of
the provincial cabinets must not be wounded. Left thus
severely to their own resources, the provinces went confidently ahead with enlarged programmes of education and
social services — programmes which varied greatly from government to government according to the financial state, the
religious beliefs, and the social philosophy of each.

Along with the rise of the provinces went inevitably the
relative decline of the federal government. There could be
little doubt about it — the federal government had lost its
old place of leadership. Even the end of the political insecurity and unsettlement of the early post-war era did not
encourage it to resume its old place. The Progressive movement visibly declined; and even though the election of 1925
left Mackenzie King in a more precarious position than ever,
the election of the following year gave him, for the first time
in the 1920's, a comfortable working majority. The return
of stable government did not prompt the Dominion to set out
on new ventures. It had finished its old tasks; it assumed no
new responsibilities of comparable magnitude. The strange
fact seemed to be that the Dominion had played its most
effective part in the early, formative period of nation-build-

ing, and that it was unfitted, by its very nature, powers, and inclinations, for the novel, complex problems of maturity. It pursued a cautious, negative, defensive rôle, while the vigorous provinces pressed it for concessions. It handed back what remained of the public domain in the west to quiet the agitation for the return of the prairie natural resources; it granted new and additional subsidies to the Maritime Provinces to satisfy the clamour for 'Maritime Rights.' Surprisingly enough, the internal problem of the post-war Canadian nationality seemed largely to have fallen to the provinces. Even more surprisingly, it appeared that they might have their say in its external problems as well.

The achievement of Dominion status, the public recognition of the principle of equality within the British Commonwealth of Nations, was a final important goal of Canadian external policy which had yet to be formally attained. For generations, against all kinds of opposition both positive and negative, Canada had pursued this goal. To a very large extent, the principle of Dominion status was her own creation — her main contribution to the science of world politics. Slowly and by traditional British empirical methods, Macdonald, Laurier, and Borden had helped to work out the various principles of the new relationship; and the war and the post-war period served to bring the system they had devised into a working reality. All that remained to do was to give formal acknowledgment to the new imperial association; and in the Imperial Conference of 1926, and chiefly at the instance of Eire, South Africa, and Canada, the formal political theory of the British Empire eventually overtook its empirical political practice. The position and mutual relation of the self-governing Dominions were defined in the fluent and graceful sentences of the *Report*. 'They,' read the *Report*, 'are autonomous Communities within the British Empire, equal in status, in no way subordinate one to another in any aspect of their domestic or external affairs, though united by a common allegiance to the Crown, and freely asso-

ciated as members of the British Commonwealth of Nations.
. . . Every self-governing member of the Empire is now the
master of its destiny. In fact, if not always in form, it is subject to no compulsion whatever. . . . The British Empire is
not founded upon negations. It depends essentially, if not
formally, on positive ideals. Free institutions are its life-
blood. Free co-operation is its instrument. Peace, security,
and progress are among its objects.'

The next few years were spent in working out the implications of this general declaration. The Imperial Conference of 1926 itself made a big start. Among other things,
it clarified the position of the Governor-General in the Dominions by declaring that he was to be considered in future
as 'the representative of the Crown . . . and not the representative or agent of His Majesty's Government in Great
Britain or of any Department of that Government.' The arrangements for imperial representation at international conferences as well as for the drafting and signing of treaties affecting the Empire were laid down and described in considerable detail; and it became perfectly clear henceforth that
any self-governing Dominion which did not participate in
the making of a treaty would not be bound by its provisions.
Only one major problem remained — the complex problem
of the relation between Dominion laws and imperial legislation; and in 1929 a committee of experts and civil servants
from the different governments of the Commonwealth met
to frame specific recommendations for the extinction of the
remaining legal inferiority of the Dominions. The main
job of the committee was to deal with the so-called Colonial
Laws Validity Act of 1865. This statute embodied the old
principle that a colonial legislature was inferior to the British Parliament and repeated the old maxim that a colonial
statute which conflicted with a British Act of Parliament ex-
tending to the colony in question was void to the extent of
the conflict. Actually, this 'restriction' had long ago ceased
to cause the Dominions anything more than an occasional

temporary inconvenience. But obviously it was inconsistent with their new acknowledged status; and the committee of 1929 included a recommendation for its removal which was to be submitted to a new Imperial Conference in the following year.

At this point G. Howard Ferguson, the Conservative Prime Minister of the Province of Ontario, suddenly intervened. In a memorandum to the Prime Minister of Canada which was made public in September, 1930, Ferguson declared that the repeal of the Colonial Laws Validity Act was in effect an amendment to the British North America Act, and that, since the British North America Act was a compact or treaty among the provinces, it could not be altered without their previous consent. It was a vigorous, confident gesture, characteristic of a period of rising provincial power and assurance; and in the end it did not seem to matter very much that its basic assumptions were highly questionable, if not unsound. Actually no binding compact had been made, nor could have been made, by the provinces at Confederation; and the necessity of prior provincial consent to the amendment or alteration of the 'treaty,' far from having been recognized by the Parliament of Canada, had in fact been expressly repudiated on several occasions in the early days of union. According to the procedure which was carefully worked out and followed in all the early cases of amendment, it had become established that the Canadian parliament, by a joint resolution of its two houses, would request the Imperial Parliament to make whatever changes were desired in the British North America Act, and that the Imperial Parliament would then act in accordance with the joint resolution. All this was certainly true; and yet it did not completely settle the matter, for the early amendments had dealt, on the whole, with relatively unimportant affairs. The historical and legal case of the provinces might be weak; but their political position, in the post-war era, was extremely strong. The federal government had tacitly ad-

mitted this. In the Dominion-Provincial Conference of
1927, it had itself raised the whole problem of constitutional
amendment. It had pointed out that Canada, as a result of
the declaration of the Imperial Conference of 1926, should
now be logically empowered to alter its own constitution;
and it recommended that the provinces should be consulted
in all cases of amendment, that their majority consent would
be sufficient in all ordinary matters, but that in a certain
number of matters deemed fundamental their unanimous
agreement would be required. It was, therefore, extremely
difficult for the federal government to disregard Ferguson's
argument; and thus before the recommendations of the Imperial Committee of 1929 and the Imperial Conference of
1930 could be translated into a final statute of the Imperial
Parliament, Canada sought and secured the approval of the
provinces to the changes proposed.

The Statute of Westminster — the statute by which the
goal of self-government within the Empire was finally attained — was enacted by the Imperial Parliament in 1931.
The Act summed up in final legal form the changes which
had accumulated in the past few years; it translated into
statute law the conventions which had already become firmly
established in the imperial constitution. On the one hand,
Great Britain renounced her legal right to legislate for the
Dominions; and, on the other, the Dominions were freed
from the last legal limitations on their legislative power. In
future no statute of the Imperial Parliament could extend to
a Dominion except at its request and with its consent. The
extra-territorial restrictions on Dominion legislation were
removed; the Colonial Laws Validity Act was repealed; and
henceforth the statutes of the Dominions could no longer be
subjected, even in theory, to the test of their repugnancy to
English law. There was only one limitation on the new legislative sovereignty of the Parliament of Canada — a limitation imposed of necessity in virtue of the federal nature of the
Canadian Union. It was not intended that the Statute of

Westminster should disturb the existing process of constitutional amendment in the different Dominions, or enlarge the constituent powers of the federal parliaments at the expense of the provincial legislatures; and therefore, by Clause 7 of the statute, it was carefully stipulated that 'nothing in this Act shall be deemed to apply to the repeal, amendment, or alteration of the British North America Acts . . .'

The *Reports* of the Imperial Conferences of 1926, 1929, and 1930, together with the Statute of Westminster of 1931, gave final form to the political and legal theory of the new Commonwealth. The *Report* of 1926 cautiously observed that 'the principles of equality and similarity, appropriate to *status,* do not universally extend to function,' but obviously a certain amount of fresh machinery was necessary through which the different members of the Commonwealth could work out their new relations with each other, as well as with the rest of the world. As far back as 1920, it had been decided, by the then Conservative government, to establish a Canadian diplomatic representative in Washington; but, though provision for this legation had been regularly included in the estimates since that time, no appointment to the office had ever been made. In 1926, the first Canadian envoy extraordinary and minister plenipotentiary to the United States was finally appointed; and in the next three years similar legations were set up in Paris and Tokyo. As for Great Britain, Canada had had its representative there, in the person of the High Commissioner for Canada in London ever since 1880. And now that the Governor-General had ceased to be an agent of the imperial government, Great Britain found it advisable to have similar officers to urge her interests and explain her views in Ottawa, Capetown, and Canberra. In 1928 she began to send high commissioners to the various Dominions.

[*III*]

It was at this moment that the problems of national social security and international political stability began once more to grow acute. In 1919, Canada, like other powers far more important than herself, had appeared to face a novel and uncertain future. On the one hand was a new world order, maintained by the method of collective security; on the other was a new national state, supposedly devoted to the principles of social security and economic justice. At first it almost seemed as if the demands and requirements of these new ideals would cause a revolution in Canadian policies, both internal and external. But the lurid appearances of 1919 were highly deceptive. Far from departing on new adventures, Canada had returned slowly but persistently to the traditions of the past. She had practised, in the League of Nations, the same policy of no commitments that she had developed in the British Empire. She had pursued, in the post-war era, the same domestic national policies that she had worked out in the pre-war age. In all this she had acted in much the same way as other countries, both smaller and vastly larger than herself; and the results of this conduct now began to grow rather ominous. Abroad, where Canada's influence was very small, the position of world trade and international finance had become extremely precarious; at home, where Canada's responsibility was final, the division of duties between Dominion and provinces had reached a state of obvious unbalance. It was at this crucial moment that the depression descended. It was the first of the great catastrophes, economic and political, of the post-war age. And in Canada it at once raised problems of all orders, economic, social, political, and constitutional.

The depression was bound to have very serious effects for Canada. Despite the increasing diversity of the Canadian economy, despite the growing maturity of its various industries and trades, the country was still dependent, to a large extent, upon the sale of a few export specialties, chiefly primary staple commodities, to more mature industrial nations.   Canada obtained over one-third of its national income from the sale of its products abroad, and two-thirds of these exports consisted of raw materials.   The depression undermined the very foundations upon which this vital part of Canada's economic life depended.   Between 1929 and 1933 the value of world trade fell by nearly fifty per cent and the prices of all Canada's staple commodities declined drastically.   Newsprint, base metals, lumber — they were all down; but agricultural prices — thanks to the enormous world surplus of wheat and the new prohibitive tariffs against farm produce in Europe and the United States — rushed downward even more steeply.   In December, 1932, the price of a bushel of wheat in Winnipeg fell to thirty-eight cents — the all-time low in recorded history.

The depression lay over the entire country; but its weight was very unevenly distributed.   In sharp contrast with the depressions of the late nineteenth century, when the terms of trade had not been bad for agricultural Canada, this was a slump in which the prices of manufactured goods declined much less seriously than those of raw materials.   Tariffs, monopolies, fixed interest charges, and rigid wages kept up the prices of consumers' goods; the costs of services, including professional services, were similarly unyielding; and in the industrial centres the real victims of the depression were the unemployed, who were laid off in hundreds of thousands in an effort to reduce output rather than to lower prices. The heavy burden of the depression was borne largely by these people and by the fishermen, lumbermen, and farmers, whose products were left unprotected before the disastrous influences of the slump.   The Precambrian Shield and the Appalachian Highland both suffered; but the worst evil of all fell on the wheatlands of the west.   The prairies lost not only their markets, but also their crops.   They were beaten down both by the blows of the depression and the calamities of nature — by drought, soil-drifting, and rust. For days, for long weeks, the sky maintained its unrelenting and pitiless serenity; and the winds that blew over the high, arid plains of Palliser's Triangle were laden with a cloudy accumulation of dust. From 1929 to 1933, the national income of Canada declined by nearly fifty per cent; but, while the loss was serious enough in the central provinces of Ontario and Quebec, it was catastrophic in the Province of Saskatchewan. Under the weight of these disasters the ambitious western Wheat Pool collapsed. In 1931, the farmers were released from their contracts, the minimum price system was abandoned, and the Central Selling Agency ceased to market pool wheat.

But the consequences of the depression were political and constitutional, as well as social and economic. Unquestionably the slump exposed the basic weaknesses in the Canadian economy; but it also revealed, with equal clarity, the fundamental deficiencies in the national policies of Canada and in the Canadian federal system. Ever since the war, the national policies had remained relatively unchanged; ever since the war, the federal system had grown more and more ominously lop-sided. The federal government, with potentially far greater tax and credit power, had decided, for a variety of reasons, not to increase its duties and functions materially. The provinces, with far weaker resources, had accepted commitments and responsibilities which now threatened to become unendurable. To a large extent, the new social services and, to a lesser extent, the new economic controls, seemed to have fallen into the hands of the provinces and their subordinate governments, the municipalities. And now the depression, with its prostrate farming class and its hundreds of thousands of unemployed industrial workers, glaringly revealed the inadequacy of this division of power. A great many of the municipalities buckled in under the strain; the finances of a province like Saskatchewan were overwhelmed in the disaster; and even the wealthier central provinces would not have been able to meet their obligations by themselves. It was obvious that a major crisis in the relations of Canada and its provinces was at hand.

The ground-swell of that long series of political earthquakes which were spread over the next half-dozen years began in 1930, in the first year of the depression. In the general election of 1930, Mackenzie King, who in the troubled 1920's had shown a talent for political longevity equal to that of his departed leader, was at length defeated; and the Conservatives were returned to power on the strength of their confident promises to end the depression. They had a new leader now, Richard Bedford Bennett, who had been elected to succeed Arthur Meighen in the Conservative Convention of 1927 in Winnipeg. Richard Bennett was a New Brunswicker, a descendant of an old Loyalist family established for many generations in the new world, an easterner who like so many other Canadians had gone west in the early years of the Laurier boom to settle in the future Province of Alberta. He was a tall, robust man, vigorous, vital, dynamic, with an instinct for command, a monopolizing capacity for work, and an annihilating talent for political attack. He seemed, from the first, to overshadow his cabinet; he could make the House of Commons quail before him. And his 'reign' — for it almost deserves to be called such — was full of political commotion and excitement which contrasted oddly with the placidity of the previous few years.

Once again, Canada undertook some large enterprises comparable to those of the great days of western expansion. Some of these enterprises had no direct relation to the politico-economic challenge of the depression; but they were major national undertakings conceived in terms of the new post-war world; and though several of them had been initiated earlier, under the Liberal administration, they seemed to mark off the 1930's from the previous and less adventurous decade. The long negotiations with the United States for the St. Lawrence Waterway were at length completed and the treaty — which was subsequently rejected by the American Senate — was signed in 1932. The preparations for an all-Canadian transcontinental air service were pushed ahead, in part as a relief work, though it was not until 1937 that the new corporation, the Trans-Canada Air Lines, was finally created by Act of Parliament. In 1932, Canada decided in principle for the public ownership and control of radio broadcasting and established the Canadian Radio Broadcasting Commission — later renamed the Canadian Broadcasting Corporation. Trans-Canada Air Lines and the Canadian Broadcasting Corporation were typical Canadian national enterprises — characteristic Canadian efforts to promote national unity and to preserve national independence through twentieth-century modes of transport and communications; and perhaps the most remarkable feature about them was that they were undertaken by the federal government as a result of two crucial decisions of the Judicial Committee of the Privy Council in favour of the Dominion. In Canada, the federal government was to control both the air and the airways. After the paralyzing decisions of the 1920's, it was a most amazing development. Apparently the Watson-Haldane constitutional trend had been stopped — at least momentarily. Perhaps it had even been reversed. Who could tell?

These enterprises, however, did not constitute the main task of the government. The main task of the government was the depression, which it had sworn to end; and the first efforts to make good these confident promises were, in the main, traditional and cautious. When Great Britain went off the gold standard in September, 1931, and when the Canadian dollar began to appreciate in terms of the British pound, a number of western members of Parliament urged that Canada should deliberately depreciate in order to ease the difficulties which her wheat exporters now experienced in their important British market. But, of course, Canada had important dealings with two major countries, with the United States as well as Great Britain; and therefore the government continued to permit the Canadian dollar to find its own level, which, until the United States' devaluation of 1933, hovered about halfway between the American dollar and the British pound. Deliberate inflation or currency depreciation was regarded as an unsound and perilous expedient. But, on the other hand, there was the tariff, which seemed safe and was certainly in the best Conservative tradition. It was around the tariff, and the commercial policy generally, that the main initial recovery programme of the Conservatives was to turn.

In all this, of course, Canada simply followed the lead which other and more important powers set for her. The new German and Italian tariffs against Canadian wheat, the new Smoot-Hawley tariff of the United States against Canadian lumber, cattle, and agricultural products, were all examples of the panic rush for self-protection which the depression had unloosed; and even Great Britain, the home of free trade, went back in her emergency tariff of 1931 to a system of protective duties which included foodstuffs and raw materials. Inspired in part by these examples and in part by its own conviction in the necessity of protection for Canada, the Conservative government proceeded to raise the tariff steeply, and to increase its height still further by a number of administrative devices for the prevention of dumping. On the whole, these measures brought no comfort to the staple-producing regions of the country and simply tended to transfer a larger slice of a diminished national income to the manufacturing provinces of central Canada. The tariff, however, was only one part, though by far the most important part, of the Conservative fiscal programme; and it was supposedly balanced by the agreement reached in the Imperial Economic Conference held at Ottawa in 1932. By the Ottawa Agreements, Great Britain agreed to grant Canada preferential duties on a number of commodities, including wheat, lumber, apples, and bacon, in return for an extension of the list of goods included in the Canadian preferential tariff and for a possible reduction of its rates. In the main, Bennett had relied on the old Conservative policy of protection and the still older Tory policy of imperial preference.

But these modifications of the traditional policies were obviously insufficient as a cure for the depression. Other remedies had to be sought and immediately applied, even if they were only mere palliatives. The provincial governments, even the richest of them, simply could not supply relief to the hundreds of thousands of unemployed and impoverished victims of the depression; and the federal government, which had been warned off the field of social services by the courts and shouldered out of it by the provinces, was now obliged to rush to the rescue of governments which had taken on rather more than they could manage. In the first place, the Dominion assumed part of the burden of unemployment relief, according to proportions which were occasionally revised, but which, for the entire period from 1930 to 1937 amounted to about forty per cent of the total. In the second place, it lent over a hundred million dollars to the impecunious western provinces, which had rapidly come to the end of their tax and credit powers and which would otherwise have been unable even to meet their own portion of unemployment relief. Even in this extremity, however, the federal government made no attempt to interfere in what was still regarded as constitutionally the affair of the provinces; it simply gave these emergency unconditional subsidies — these enormous grants-in-aid — without any effort to supervise or control the expenditure of its money. Financially, the federal system had broken down completely; but no new machinery had been devised.

In the main, this unemployment relief, these changes in fiscal and commercial policy, were the chief measures by which, at first, the government sought to relieve the depression. Obviously they failed to satisfy great masses of the people; and a wave of discontent, of resentful protest, of confused, ill-formed aspiration, which was like a revival, on a grander scale, of the post-war unsettlement of 1919, began to move swiftly through the country. This movement, which grew steadily larger and more rapid in 1932-33, was able to make use of two chief channels of development. On the one hand, it could take a national course and assume the shape of a radical federal party, with a new and radical national policy; or, on the other hand, it could go off in a regional direction and take the form of a new provincial recovery administration or a new local co-operative enterprise. Its expressions were varied in the extreme; but they had one important feature in common, which was their enthusiasm for the community, their belief in co-operation, their reliance upon planning.

The new radical party in the federal field was the first to appear. The Progressive party, with its increasingly mild reformist Liberalism, had grown steadily weaker in the 1920's — had, indeed, reached the nadir of political fortune in the general election of 1930. But, in 1932, the cause it represented began suddenly to show unmistakable signs of lusty life. In August, 1932, after some preliminary conferences, a meeting of farmer and labour representatives from the four western provinces and Ontario was held in Calgary, Alberta; and it was at this meeting that the new national party, the socialist Co-Operative Commonwealth Federation, was established, officers elected, and a provisional platform adopted. Nearly a year later, in July, 1933, the C. C. F. (the abbreviated form into which the party's cumbrous name was at once translated) met at Regina, Saskatchewan, and adopted the basic party platform, known as the Regina Manifesto. In origin, the C. C. F. stemmed from both the agrarian radicalism of the North American west and from the socialist philosophy of the labour movement of Great Britain; and it grew up amid all the favourable influences of the New Deal in the United States.

The rise of the new national party was followed by the

sudden appearance of the new provincial governments. The policies of the Bennett administration, far from reducing the differences of economic good fortune which existed between the provinces, probably accentuated them. The drift towards regionalism, which had begun during the post-war boom, set in even more strongly during the depression; and a new set of provincial governments openly identified themselves with the interests peculiar to their own areas and confidently announced that they alone could cure the various grievances of their citizens. In 1930, six of the nine provincial governments were controlled by the Conservatives; but in the exciting years from 1933 to 1936 these traditional administrations were buried under a series of political 'landslides' which thundered down from one end of the country to the other. The new cabinets, though most of them bore the old party names, zealously took up new programmes of social betterment which varied all the way from a mild reformism to a rather nebulous radicalism. The new provincial leaders, though several of them stood true to the old Canadian type of sober local politician, revealed, as a group, a new talent for the extravagant, the eccentric, and the picturesque. Down in the Maritime Provinces, Messrs. Macdonald and Dysart stuck to the traditional and highly respectable business of 'Maritime Rights.' In Quebec, Maurice Duplessis, the leader of *Union Nationale,* the new French-Canadian nationalist party, united the racial feelings and the economic grievances of French Canadians in his attack on 'alien' industrial and financial control; and out in British Columbia Pattullo sponsored a vaguely energetic programme of 'Work and Wages.' But the most peculiar philosophy, as well as the most picturesque personality, were united in the new prime minister of Alberta, William Aberhart. A native of Ontario, of German extraction, Aberhart was a Calgary schoolmaster who had, in recent years, become the leading spirit of an institution described as the Prophetic Bible Institute. In Aberhart's case the road from Biblical prophecy to economic revelation was apparently an easy one; and he became a convert to the Social Credit theories of Major Douglas. In 1935, when the Social Credit party overwhelmed the Farmers' government, Aberhart set out to solve the problem of frontier, debtor Alberta with the A + B theorem.

Unfortunately it soon became obvious that the provinces would find it very difficult to solve the recovery problem by themselves. Some of them made no very strenuous efforts to do so; and even those governments which were anxious to adopt novel policies and methods soon found out that their work was likely to be seriously restricted by financial weakness and constitutional limitations. As for the heterodox Social Credit government in Alberta, it discovered in short order that it was simply not going to be permitted to carry out the monetary changes it had in mind. Undoubtedly the federal government had not disallowed a provincial statute for years; the federal Minister of Justice, Ernest Lapointe, even went so far as to make an official pronouncement against the use of disallowance. 'I do not think,' he declared, 'that in a federation such as this the power of disallowance could easily be exercised by the central government.' It was a rather curious doctrine for a Liberal minister of justice to profess, for the Liberals had disallowed a larger number of provincial statutes than the Conservatives; and it was a doctrine which had to be hurriedly revised when the new Alberta legislature began passing highly unorthodox statutes relating to banks and banking. In August, 1937, the Dominion government disallowed three Alberta acts; in October of the same year, the Lieutenant-Governor reserved three Alberta bills for the signification of the Governor-General's pleasure; and finally in June, 1938, the federal government disallowed two more Alberta statutes. Evidently the business of making Alberta a Social Credit paradise was going to be beset with difficulties.

In the meantime, however, attention had long ago shifted back to the federal government once more. As the bad times continued, as the failure of the early half-measures and palliatives became more and more apparent, the general public pressure in favour of some kind of positive national attack upon the depression grew almost irresistible. In Canada, J. S. Woodsworth and his followers in the Co-Operative Commonwealth Federation had first voiced this demand; in the United States it had just won a great popularity and an enormous prestige through the election of President Roosevelt and the inauguration of the National Recovery Administration. Surrounded by these potent influences, urged on by this rising clamour, Bennett decided abruptly to break with the past. At almost the eleventh hour, for a general election was due in 1935, he took up the long delayed and heroic task of reshaping and restating the ancient Conservative national policies in response to the new economic and social demands. Early in 1934, in a preliminary move of some significance, he supported the appointment of a special parliamentary committee to inquire into price spreads and the effects of mass buying. In January, 1935, in a series of five radio broadcasts to the nation, he outlined an extensive reform programme; and the parliamentary sessions of 1934 and 1935 were crowded with the passage of a long series of social-security laws, labour statutes, and economic-control measures. Obviously this was not merely a national attack on the depression; it was a frontal onslaught on the constitution as well.

The results of this belated piece of political daring were significant. For a moment, Bennett actually seemed to have recovered the initiative and to have regained political strength. But his abrupt political conversion had been too much for both his friends and his foes. It strained the credulity of the electorate in general and the loyalty of the Conservatives in particular; and in the general election of 1935 the Bennett government was decisively beaten. This complete defeat of the Conservatives and the triumphant return of the Liberals under Mackenzie King was obviously the most striking retort to the Bennett 'New Deal'; but it was not the only retort, nor ultimately the most important. In 1935 the Canadian electorate politically rejected the Bennett plan to cope with the depression; but in 1937 the Judicial Committee of the Privy Council judicially condemned virtually any national plan to cope with any Canadian depression. Five of the major statutes of the Bennett New Deal — the Minimum Wages Act, the Limitation of Hours of Work Act, the Weekly Rest in Industrial Undertakings Act, the Unemployment and Social Insurance Act, and the Natural Products Marketing Act — were all declared to be *ultra vires* of the federal Parliament.

The principal reason for the rejection of these statutes was, of course, that they affected 'Property and Civil Rights in the Province.' The Dominion sought to justify this alleged interference by various arguments; but these were uniformly turned down. It was useless, for example, for the central government to rely upon its residuary power to legislate for the peace, order, and good government of Canada. The Judicial Committee had already decided that any exercise of this power which even indirectly affected 'property and civil rights' could be justified only on two grounds — war or the transcontinental intoxication of 1878; and thus it only remained now to declare that a mere depression, which threw five hundred thousand people out of work, could obviously not be regarded as on a level with these great national calamities. The residuary power availed nothing; the enumerated powers were equally ineffective. According to the Judicial Committee, the phrase 'the regulation of trade and commerce' meant international and interprovincial, but not provincial, trade; and since the Natural Products Marketing Act had not completely solved the superhuman task of separating the former from the latter, then obviously it was *ultra vires* as well.

When the federal government, having apparently exhausted the powers granted to it in section 91 of the British

North America Act, turned to other parts of the statute for support, it came under equally categorical rebuke. Section 132 of the Act empowered the Dominion to implement 'the obligations of Canada or of any Province thereof, as part of the British Empire, towards Foreign Countries, arising under Treaties between the Empire and such Foreign Countries.' It was this clause which had been the main basis of the federal Parliament's victory in the Aeronautics Case of 1932; it had apparently been of some help also in the Radio Case of the same year; and accordingly Bennett based the validity of his labour statutes on certain draft conventions of the International Labour Organization which the federal Parliament proceeded to ratify. Perhaps the argument seemed more promising than all the others; but it was, none the less, decisively rejected. The Judicial Committee decided that Section 132 applied only to 'British Empire Treaties' and not to treaties which Canada had negotiated 'by virtue of her new status as an international person.' If an imperial executive signed a treaty, then presumably the Parliament of Canada could carry out its obligations; but if a Canadian executive signed a treaty, then it could only be implemented by both Dominion and provinces acting in accordance with the division of powers in sections 91 and 92. The decision, coming so soon after the passage of the Statute of Westminster, had about it a certain air of mockery. Canada had hoped, as a result of the achievement of Dominion status, to gain a new autonomy and strength in the conduct of her foreign affairs. But what precisely had she gained after all? In effect, as a result of the decisions of 1937, the grant of Dominion status had enlarged her powers to negotiate treaties and restricted her ability to carry them out. Ten governments were apparently now necessary to implement treaties in Canada where one had sufficed before; and it almost seemed as if the country had been better off as a colony than it was going to be as a Dominion. Perhaps, indeed, this was the lesson of the decision. And, if so, there was a peculiar appropriateness in the fact that it had been delivered by Lord Atkin, who had openly criticized the Statute of Westminster in 1931.

Long before this Mackenzie King was back in office once again. Fifteen years before it had been uncertain which of the three new Canadian political leaders would stamp the post-war period with his name and character; but after the smashing Liberal electoral victory of 1935, all uncertainty was ended for ever. In Canada, the post-war era would go down in history as the Mackenzie King era. This short, thick-set man, with his air of mild and diffident benevolence, was a statesman of extraordinary astuteness and of uncommon good fortune. With infinite and imperturbable patience, he had watched the rise and fall of rival political parties, and of rival political leaders, both Conservative and radical. Under his bland and unexcited gaze, the Progressives were gradually reduced in the prosperity of the 1920's and the Conservatives exhausted themselves in the depression of the 1930's; and now, with the first breath of better times, he was back in power once more. He could take his time. The most pressing problems, the desperate urgencies, of the depression were over. Once again he could practise those strategic delays, those statesmanlike postponements, those salutary procrastinations which he had used so well, and so often, in the past.

The problem of the division of powers and revenues between the Dominion and the provinces, which R. B. Bennett had tried to solve by a frontal attack on the constitution, seemed admirably suited to Mackenzie King's more deliberate treatment. The new Prime Minister announced that his government would attempt to act only after a thorough and impartial survey of the question had been made; and in 1937 a Royal Commission on Dominion-Provincial Relations was appointed to investigate the original settlement of Confederation in the light of the economic and social changes of the past seventy-five years, and to suggest ways and means by which a more satisfactory balance of functions and revenues might be achieved. It was nearly three years later, in May, 1940, that the Commission finally presented its *Report* to the government; and both as a comprehensive, factual survey and as a balanced programme of reform, few state papers in the history of British North America have equalled this monumental document. In general, the Commissioners recommended that certain crucial economic controls and certain costly social services, such as unemployment relief and unemployment insurance, should be transferred to the Dominion, while the provinces were to remain in possession of the residual social and developmental services. In addition, the federal government was to take over all existing provincial debt; it was to pay all the needy provinces a so-called National Adjustment Grant by which they would be enabled to maintain their various services at the average Canadian standard without exceeding the average Canadian rate of taxation; and finally, in order to bear these heavy financial burdens, it was to be granted the exclusive power to take income, corporation, and inheritance taxes. This was a formidable programme. Even in times of peace it might have been carried through only in part and with very great difficulty. But this final chance was denied it; and like every other domestic problem, big or little, it was gradually overshadowed by the sinister peril from abroad.

For, in the end, it was not the collapse of domestic social security but the failure of international political stability which broke up the post-war world. Mackenzie King had been able to avoid the problems of the Canadian depression; he had postponed the reorganization of the Canadian constitution; but, at the last, like so many other statesmen, he was swept irresistibly into the vortex of world affairs. The Japanese invasion of Manchuria, the Italian conquest of Abyssinia, the outbreak of the Spanish Civil War, were simply the most notorious episodes in a long and increasingly sombre history of force, and fraud, and intimidation;

and gradually, inexorably, however much the Prime Minister and his cabinet might struggle to escape it, they were pinned down by the insoluble problem of external affairs. Mackenzie King used all his acts of delay and postponement, for he was well aware that the issues of foreign affairs might crack the national unity which had already been strained by both prosperity and the depression. English Canada was concerned, and French Canada uninterested, in the fate of Abyssinia; French Canada tended to sympathize with General Franco, while large sections of English Canada favoured the Spanish Republic. Within the country there were people who believed fervently in the collective system as embodied in the League of Nations, other people who relied implicitly upon a policy of North American isolation, and still other people who trusted instinctively to co-operation and mutual defence within the British Commonwealth. All the Prime Minister's experience and address were called into play to reconcile these differences, and head off these impending conflicts. Invariably he declared that no prior binding commitments to action would be made; repeatedly he insisted that, when the moment of crisis came, the Canadian Parliament would decide its course in the light of all the circumstances of the moment, both domestic and foreign. 'One thing I will not do and cannot be persuaded to do,' said Mackenzie King as late as the summer of 1939, 'is to say what Canada will do in regard to a situation that may arise at some future time and under circumstances of which we now know nothing.'

And yet, though the decision might be put off, and off, and off, the time was coming swiftly when it could be postponed no longer. The last defences of tranquillity were toppling quickly now, and the League of Nations, the embodiment of the idealism of the war and early post-war period, declined into a state of moral insignificance. From the first Canada had been restless under the political commitments of the League; she had questioned the various attempts, such as the Geneva Protocol of 1924, to find a satisfactory basis for mutual assistance; and when, in the autumn of 1935, Doctor Riddell, Canada's permanent representative at Geneva, appeared to sponsor the imposition of oil sanctions against Italy in her quarrel with Abyssinia, the Canadian government hastened to explain publicly that this was merely the personal opinion of the minister and not the view of the Canadian administration. Canada, of course, had already imposed the original economic sanctions and maintained them until the end; but once the capture of Addis Ababa in 1936 had revealed the futility of these efforts to embarrass imperialist Italy, Mackenzie King was quick to put forward a new and somewhat more limited interpretation of Canada's obligations under the Covenant of the League. Like other smaller powers, Canada now made it quite plain that her dislike of automatic economic commitments was as great as her suspicion of automatic political commitments; and indeed, for all powers, big and small, the Italo-Abyssinian quarrel was a blow from which the League never really recovered.

Inevitably this bankruptcy of the collective system limited still further the possible courses of action which Canada might follow in the tragic days to come. On the one hand, she could seek safety in the isolation of the North American continent and in the protection of the United States; or on the other hand, she could pursue a policy of co-operation and mutual assistance in the British Commonwealth. There were a number of French-Canadian nationalists and English-Canadian isolationists who preferred to rely on the security of North America; and in so far as this meant the increase of the country's defences and the improvement of its relations with the United States, the Mackenzie King government was heartily ready to agree. In 1935, the long tariff war with the United States which had begun with the American Smoot-Hawley Tariff of 1930 came unregretted to an end; and the two countries signed a trade agreement by which Canada granted its intermediate or treaty rates to the United States, and the United States gave reduced duties on cattle, dairy products, potatoes, fish, and lumber to Canada. In 1938, after elaborate triangular negotiations which resulted in trade agreements between the United Kingdom and the United States, and the United States and Canada, the scope of the earlier treaty was widened further; and Canada not only reduced her own duties, but also surrendered some of the preferences she had secured in Great Britain by the Ottawa Agreements of 1932 in return for a freer entry into the American market. This was a contribution to the good relations of the English-speaking peoples in general; and, as President Roosevelt's statement at Kingston, Ontario, in August, 1938, had already indicated, this growing friendship pervaded the political as well as the economic sphere. 'The Dominion of Canada,' declared the President, 'is part of the sisterhood of the British Empire. I give to you assurance that the people of the United States will not stand idly by if domination of Canadian soil is threatened by any other Empire.'

Two days later, in his speech at Woodbridge, Mackenzie King hastened to welcome this spontaneous and generous assurance. But, at the same time, he took care to point out that the promise of the President in no way reduced Canada's responsibility for her own defence and in no way affected Canada's relations with Great Britain and the other members of the Commonwealth. In fact, by this time, it was perfectly obvious that reliance upon the supposed isolation and security of North America was a policy which would never satisfy the great majority of Canadians. By the whole nature of her being and the entire course of her history, Canada was identified with the British Empire and the values for which it stood. In large measure, the modern Commonwealth was her own creation; and all her capital, both moral and material, had been put into its free institutions, its ordered liberties, its open seaways and its transoceanic trade.

As the sky over Europe darkened with menace, as the very safety of the motherland itself became imperilled, the Canadian consciousness of the reality — and the vitality — of this ancient tie steadily strengthened; and the visit of King George and Queen Elizabeth, in the early summer of 1939, confirmed, though it had no need to inspire, this realization of the values and vital interests which were bound up in the old partnership of the British peoples. The King was simply a long absent prince who had come back to a homeland where every administrative act, and every judicial decision, and every legislative measure was done in his name and by his authority. 'We would have Your Majesties feel,' said the Prime Minister at the first official luncheon which was given to the King and Queen, 'that in coming from the old land to the new you have but left one home to come to another; that we are all of one household. Free institutions and democratic ideals are as dear to the hearts of your people in Canada as to the people in any other part of the Empire. We regard their preservation as the common concern of all.'

In the first ten days of September, 1939 — the first ten days which followed the German invasion of Poland — the British Commonwealth took its stand and prepared to fight. This time the imperial declaration of war on September 3 was not regarded as a formal commitment for the entire Empire. Australia and New Zealand immediately associated themselves with Great Britain; Eire decided to remain neutral; and the Union of South Africa delayed its final decision for three days and Canada for a week. On September 7 the special Parliament which the Canadian Prime Minister had always promised to convene assembled at Ottawa to determine Canada's course; and three days later, with the unanimous approval of the Senate and the virtually unanimous consent of the House of Commons, the King declared a state of war to exist between Canada and the German Reich. It was a brief, simple, sober session of Parliament, without bravado, or hysteria, or declamation; and perhaps its most moving incident was the solemn appeal uttered by the Minister of Justice, Ernest Lapointe, the old French-Canadian colleague of Mackenzie King, who had stood by him in much the same way as Georges Cartier had stood by Sir John Macdonald in the past. Once again, the two races, whose association had given Canada its distinctive character and history, were jointly committed to an enormous and dangerous task. They were well aware that latent differences of opinion lurked between them. The whole course of the War of 1914-18 had taught them the gravity of the difficulties and possible disagreements which lay ahead. But they went forward together to meet them.

CHAPTER TEN

MODERN CANADA
IN A GREAT-POWER WORLD

[*1*]

O N MONDAY morning, September 10, 1939, the Canadian people awoke to the realization that once again, for the second time in a single generation, it was formally and irrevocably at war with Germany. The decisive vote had been taken in the Canadian Parliament on Saturday; on Sunday, a proclamation in the King's name had announced the fateful news in the *Canada Gazette.* 'Now therefore We do hereby declare and proclaim,' ran the solemn and traditional words of the proclamation, 'that a State of War with the German Reich exists and has existed in Our Dominion of Canada as and from the tenth day of September, 1939. Of all which Our Loving Subjects and all others whom these presents may concern are hereby required to take notice and to govern themselves accordingly.' There were about twelve million Canadian subjects of the Crown for whom 'these presents' were to be a matter of terrible concern for the next six years; and on that first Monday of the first week of the war they began the difficult and dangerous business of 'governing themselves accordingly'.

There was a tremendous, a staggering amount of work to do. For, once again, Canada, even more than the other nations of the English-speaking world, was lamentably unprepared for war. The Canadians remained, what they had been in 1914, a profoundly unmilitary people. The War of 1914-18, which had given the country its national status and won for the Canadian army an international reputation, had had curiously little permanent effect upon the military policy of the Dominion. During the 1920's, the peace-time establishment of the Army, Navy, and Air Force, remained strangely at variance with the country's valiant pretensions of national autonomy; and, with the onset of the depression, the state of the armed services sank to a level which seemed almost to imply a relapse into colonial irresponsibility. In the fiscal year 1932-33, the total expenditure for national defence was reduced to a little over fourteen million dollars, which was the lowest annual outlay since 1913, exactly twenty years before.

This was the nadir. But, despite the rapidly increasing gravity of the international situation, the ascent from it was very slow. The appropriations for defence for the fiscal year 1935-36 — the last year for which the Conservative government was responsible — amounted to thirty million dollars. Three years later, under the watchful eye of Mackenzie King, the budget for the armed services had risen by only six additional millions. On the eve of war, the total strength of the Army, Navy and Air Force was less than ten thousand men; there were slightly over fifty thousand enrolled in the Non-Permanent Active Militia; and all branches of each service were badly armed and equipped. Down until the summer of 1939, the Canadian Army possessed only two tanks; there were only a few Hurricane fighter planes in the Royal Canadian Air Force; there were thirteen ships of all classes in the Royal Canadian Navy. The most significant step towards the building up of an armament industry in Canada had been the belated signing of the Bren gun contract in 1938.

Thus, for the second time in its history, Canada was compelled to prepare for war, after war had actually begun. It had to repair the neglect of the past. It had also to unlearn the past's mistaken assumptions and prepossessions. Even during the past few years the authorities at Ottawa had indulged all too frequently in the delusion that the next war would be a 'limited-liability' war, a war in which economic and technical assistance would be generously granted to Great Britain but in which 'great, expeditionary forces of infantry' crossing the Atlantic would be most unlikely. All these naïve strategical preconceptions had to be laid aside; and in the false, sinister calm of the early months of the 'phony' war, they were not perhaps forgotten as quickly and completely as they might have been. Even so, the known and probable circumstances of the conflict and, above all else, the Canadian response to them, quickly forced a revision of the unrealistic plans of the past. It began to be appreciated that, although the character of the new war might be different, its dimensions and gravity would certainly be comparable to those of the War of 1914-18. It began to be realized also that it would probably require similar efforts and similar sacrifices.

It was with the guidance of these rough and ready conclusions, that the Canadian government plunged ahead through the mazes of improvisation and uncertainty. This, like the conflict of 1914-18, was going to be a total war; and the total effort of 1914-18 had established, beyond any serious question, the war-time pre-eminence of the Dominion and had given it both confidence and experience in the control of a great national effort. In the economic sphere, the government could draw upon the lessons provided by the planned economy which had taken shape in the years from 1917 to 1919. It could also, of course, rely upon a vastly stronger and more varied industrial machine than had existed in 1914. The War Supply Board, which was the precursor of the new Ministry, the Department of Munitions and Supply, began the vast and exciting business of organizing the nation's powers of destruction; and the Foreign Exchange Control Board and the Wartime Prices and Trade Board, the latter of whose sway gradually extended over every department of Canadian economic life, were set up to undertake the super-intendence of the national economy as a whole.

Here, in the realm of economic organization, the past provided precept and example. But, in the desperately important sphere of military policy, its counsels were less authoritative and more uncertain. It seemed obvious, on the face of it, that in the new war the Air Force and the Navy were likely to play a relatively much more important rôle than they had played in the previous conflict. In the years from 1936 to 1939, the government had decided, in principle, to give first priority to 'air development', to put the expansion of the small Canadian Navy next in order, so far as this was possible, and to give third place to the land forces. It was true that at first these theoretical priorities were not carried out very emphatically in practice. The improvement of the Navy proceeded in a steady but unspectacular fashion, and the greatly increased consequence of the air arm did not begin to show up markedly in the defence estimates until the very eve of war. In the fiscal year 1939-40, the appropriations for air services exceeded those for land forces by over eight millions. And then, when war actually broke out in the autumn of 1939, the pre-eminence of the Air Force seemed for a while assured. Mastery of the air, Canada and the other Commonwealth countries agreed, could only be achieved by the training of aircrew on a large and increasing scale over the next few years; and in December, 1939, Great Britain, Canada, Australia and New Zealand agreed to co-operate in an extensive Commonwealth Air Training Plan. Canada, with the safety of its space and peace, was to become a great Commonwealth trackway to the skies; and the Air Training Plan, to which the Dominion agreed to contribute four-fifths of the trainees, was probably expected to be the nation's most substantial contribution to the war.

The Air Force was the design of the future. The Army — Canada's senior service, for the 'militia' was the oldest armed force in the country — was the tradition of the past. In the minds of the military planners and the North American isolationists of 1939, the Army was one thing; it was something quite different and infinitely more important in Canadian military history and in the actual circumstances of the new conflict. On September 1, ten days before the country declared war, orders were given for the immediate mobilization of a force of two divisions; and on September 28 it was publicly announced that a decision had already been taken to send the first division overseas. Early in October, Major-General A. G. L. McNaughton, a former Chief of General Staff who had for some time been seconded to the presidency of the National Research Council and who thus represented the modern conception of scientific and mechanized warfare, was appointed the First Division's Commander; and during the autumn months, a typically Canadian citizen and volunteer army, drawn mainly from the willing ranks of the Non-Permanent Active Militia, was being quickly organized. On December 10, the troops of the 'First Flight' marched up the long gang-planks of the waiting ships of the convoy in Halifax harbour. Seven days later, the *Aquitania*, the *Empress of Britain*, the *Empress of Australia*, the *Duchess of Bedford*, and the *Monarch of Bermuda*, with their seven thousand five hundred Canadian soldiers safely aboard, were steaming slowly up the River Clyde while the watching Scots waved and shouted their welcome. The second and third 'flights' followed at shorter or longer intervals through the winter; and before the end of February, the entire First Division, nearly twenty-five thousand strong, was completely established in barracks at Aldershot.

By the end of September, the main lines of Canadian policy, for the first phase of the war at least, were clearly apparent. The government, after repeated delays and postponements and infinite circumspection, had finally taken its stand. It had adopted a moderate but realistic programme which, it hoped, would win wide acceptance from an aroused

and determined public opinion, but which also, and inevitably, would invite attack from the extremists on either side.
The country was irrevocably committed. War, in Canada's
own right, had been declared. The half-declared, tentatively
held pre-war scheme of limited, 'practical' participation, with
emphasis upon North American defence and production of
munitions and raw materials for overseas, had been tacitly
abandoned in favour of a much more positively belligerent
rôle. Canada, the Canadian government had decided, was
to make an important military contribution, through both
the old and the new armed services; but — and this was an
equally important decision — it was to be a characteristic
Canadian contribution, a voluntary effort of free Canadian
citizens, in sharp contrast with the conscript military service
beloved of many twentieth-century states. Before the war,
both major Canadian political parties had declared themselves opposed to conscription for overseas service; and from
the moment that Parliament met on September 7, the Prime
Minister and his principal colleagues had repeatedly confirmed their promise not to resort to conscription in the
most solemn and unequivocal terms.

Such was the policy — cautious, guarded, but solid and
definite. What support would it secure from the anxious
Canadian people? In the past, every Canadian government,
with one calamitous exception, had tried to cling to moderate
military measures. Every Canadian government, with no
exceptions, had been attacked by a larger or smaller body
of voters on the far left or the distant right. And now, as
though Canadian politics were a science which had been
reduced, through frequent experimentation, to a series of
precise and invariable laws, there arose exactly the same old
opposition from exactly the same two traditional sources of
discontent. On the one hand was Maurice Duplessis, the
leader of the *Union Nationale* party, which had won power
in Quebec three years before; on the other was Mitchell
Hepburn, the Premier of Ontario, a cocksure, tempera-

mental politician with a puffy, petulant face, who pointedly insisted that he was a Liberal, but not 'a Mackenzie King Liberal'. For the past few years, these two had been linked in a fraternal union of resistance to the Dominion government; and now, though they differed markedly in their attitudes to the war, they found it equally easy to transfer the focus of their opposition from federal domestic policies to federal military plans.

Duplessis began the attack. His professional business was defence of the cultural and political autonomy of the Province of Quebec against the encroachments of the Dominion and the clutches of foreign imperialists; and he thought he saw in the Canadian declaration of war a handsome opportunity which could be irresistibly exploited to his own profit and to the prejudice of his enemies at Ottawa. A fortnight after war had been declared, he pulled down Quebec's political heavens on top of the Dominion. A provincial election, he announced, would be held immediately. Its issue would be nothing more or less than the preservation of Quebec's identity against the hideous perils of 'participation, assimilation, and centralization', which had been unloosed by the new war.

King, Ernest Lapointe, the other French-Canadian ministers, and the Cabinet as a whole looked apprehensively at this gauntlet of defiance which had been thrown with such confident violence. They decided that they could not afford to leave it lying on the ground. It was impossible to ignore, at the very beginning of a great conflict, such a direct, deliberate threat to national unity and the national war effort. The issue must be joined, and at once; and the only possible way in which Duplessis' daring raid against Ottawa and its policies could be answered was by an equally downright federal intervention in Quebec provincial politics. Lapointe, who was King's closest French-Canadian colleague and the leader of the Quebec contingent in the Cabinet, came forward courageously as the portly embodiment of the government's purpose and moral indignation. 'This electoral adventure,' he declared roundly, 'is an act of national sabotage.' He and other French-Canadian ministers announced that, if the *Union Nationale* were returned to power, they would all resign their posts and that French Canada would consequently lose all representation in the federal government. Duplessis' boast, that a vote in his favour was the only valid vote against conscription, was denounced as a piece of arrant misrepresentation; and Lapointe and his colleagues solemnly confirmed their previous solemn promises that, so long as they remained in the Cabinet, there would be no conscription for overseas service.

The instant acceptance of Duplessis' challenge was a daring, and, in the eyes of many, an almost foolhardy act. But, at the same time, the forces arrayed on the side of the Liberals, federal and provincial, were very substantial; and Duplessis, by his sudden and violent foray, had sinned against the reasoned French-Canadian conviction that, in the long run, the way of moderation was probably the best way to protect French Canada's distinctive mode of life. Adélard Godbout and the provincial Liberals were carried into power at Quebec by a reversal of political fortune almost as dramatic as that which had lifted Duplessis himself into the seats of the mighty three years earlier. It was, for a nation which had just entered the first stages of the greatest common endeavour in its history, a good, a comforting, result; and Mackenzie King, with a pardonable resort to hyperbole, gravely assured his compatriots that 'nothing since Confederation has contributed more to national unity'. English-speaking Canadians were perhaps inclined to read a deeper meaning in the defeat of Duplessis than were their French-speaking fellow-citizens. Yet these, after all, were minor differences of interpretation. Despite all qualification, the election had revealed a large measure of national agreement about the war.

This unity was even more strikingly and conclusively

revealed a few months later. In the meantime, the post of chief critic and detractor of the Dominion — left vacant by the defeat of Duplessis — had been confidently taken over by Mitchell Hepburn. During the late autumn and early winter, Hepburn began, with increasing vehemence, to denounce the inadequacy and inefficiency of the federal government's war effort; and, early in the new year, a resolution of censure was passed in the Ontario Legislative Assembly, deploring the fact 'that the Federal Government at Ottawa has made so little effort to prosecute Canada's duty in the war in the vigorous manner the people of Canada desire to see'. It was January 18, 1940. In a week, on January 25, Parliament was to open. And in the near proximity of these two dates, the calculating eye of Mackenzie King discerned a delectable opportunity. Parliament, which had been elected in 1935, was nearing its legal term; but it still had over six months to run, and everybody, including King himself, had assumed that another session would be held. Obviously the opposition was looking forward with eager expectation to the account which the Prime Minister would be obliged to render of the stewardship of his government during the first five months of a great war. Obviously also King regarded this prolonged bout of interrogation, explanation, and argument as a highly unwelcome prelude to the approaching general election.

But did he need to go through with it? Had not Mitchell Hepburn, at the penultimate hour, unwittingly provided him with a convenient way out? Could he not dissolve Parliament, shortly after the session began, on the plea that Hepburn's unprovoked political attack required an immediate appeal to the country? This, to be sure, would be a very curious interpretation of the law and custom of the Parliament of Canada. The notion that the federal government had the right, or the duty, to appeal to the national electorate from a vote of censure in a provincial legislature, was a strangely novel one. But King, who was in general of a deliberate habit of mind, took advantage of this convenient excuse with lightning speed and blunt conclusiveness. 'My advisers . . .,' said the Governor-General, reading the Speech from the Throne on the afternoon of January 25, 'have decided upon an immediate appeal to the country.' 'Do we sit tonight?' inquired one member with interest towards the close of the brief debate of that first afternoon. King decided that they would not. The members of Canada's Parliament, who had come from the length and breadth of a transcontinental country to deal with the public business, found that the dinner recess had terminated their proceedings.

The general election was held on March 26, and the Liberals won a victory more sweeping and conclusive than almost anybody had expected. The voters were not greatly interested in the unceremonious dismissal of the last session of Parliament. They were not greatly interested in the details of the conduct of the war, of which, indeed, they had been kept largely in the dark. What concerned them most were the general lines of the government's war policy; and these, in the last complacent, deceptive weeks of the 'phony' war, they had what seemed to be the best of reasons for approving. They liked the Liberal programme for its moderation, its unhurried good sense, its respectable sufficiency and its reassuring absence of excess; and they flocked to the polls in quietly determined numbers to say so. The Liberals won every seat but four in the Province of Quebec; they won fifty-five out of eighty-two seats in the Province of Ontario; and in the new House of Commons Mackenzie King was actually to have a slightly larger following than he had had in the old. The people of Canada were more closely united, and more conscious of their union, than they had been seven months before, at the beginning of the war. Only, unfortunately, September, 1939, had seen only the official beginning of the war. The real war was yet to come.

On April 9 — exactly a fortnight after the Canadian general election — it began. The successful invasion of Denmark and Norway was the first calamity in what became, in a few weeks, an unbroken and appalling train of disaster. On May 10, Germany attacked the Netherlands and Belgium with efficient and terrific violence. On June 17, the French Republic, its defences overwhelmed and its government divided and demoralized, sued for an armistice. In those five short, hectic weeks, the armies of the greatest powers of Western Europe were out-manoeuvred, out-fought, and either compelled to retreat or shattered into dissolution. Only a handful of reserves, of which the First Canadian Division was a highly important part, remained in Great Britain; and as first one and then another front collapsed, as the retreat of the British Expeditionary Force was followed by the disintegration of the French armies, McNaughton's men were inevitably involved in all the plans which were made and reversed with frantic haste, in a final effort to avert the complete breakdown of western power. On May 23, it seemed almost certain that at least a portion of the Canadian Division would be sent to France as part of an attempt to strengthen the threatened communications of Lord Gort's retreating force. On June 12, the First Canadian Brigade Group actually began to land in Brest with the forlorn hope of holding a part of Brittany against the advancing German armies. All these vain schemes were abandoned, though barely, in time. The defeats and retreats were absolute and unqualified. The continent had been swept swiftly and completely into German control.

'We are now squarely set,' General McNaughton wrote to General Dill, the new Chief of the Imperial General Staff, 'for what I have long thought was the important task, the defence of these islands.' The defence of these islands! Who could help with it now? Denmark and Norway had been knocked out. Belgium and the Netherlands were occupied and disarmed. France, the proudest and greatest of them all, had abjectly capitulated. And no new nations, great or small, had come forward with their forces to make good in part the losses and defections of those ruinous two months. The whole world looked on with hostility, or indifference, or polite concern, slightly sharpened by apprehension; and nobody apparently wished or dared to join the conflict in this black depth of its fortunes. The nations of the Commonwealth — Great Britain, Canada, Australia, New Zealand, and South Africa — stood alone. Upon them, and them only, rested the entire burden of the great cause. Where all the rest of the world had defaulted, they had come forward to save civilization from the bankruptcy of submission and defeat. 'Let us therefore brace ourselves to our duties,' Prime Minister Churchill declared on the morrow of the capitulation of France, 'and so bear ourselves that, if the British Empire and its Commonwealth last for a thousand years, men will still say, "this was their finest hour".'

It was, at any rate, an hour of the deepest urgency and the greatest conceivable effort. All through the spring and summer, Canada, like the other nations of the Commonwealth, was rapidly overhauling its governmental machine, augmenting its armed services, and quickening its war-time production. In Great Britain, political leadership had already been altered, on the eve of the catastrophe; and although the changes in Canada were far less dramatic and significant and though the new ministers were all unimpeachably orthodox Liberals, a definite effort was made during the summer to build up a vigorously effective war-time cabinet. The old Defence Ministry, now in the throes of an enormous expansion, was divided into three Departments, with C. G. Power as Minister of Defence for Air, Angus L. Macdonald as Minister for Naval Affairs, and J. L. Ralston, the acknowledged senior of the triumvirate, still retaining the old title of Minister of National Defence. The newly created portfolio of Munitions and Supply was given to C. D. Howe; and J. L. Ilsley took Ralston's old place at the Ministry of Finance. These five men, with Mackenzie King himself and his principal French-Canadian colleague, Ernest

Lapointe, made up the group of senior ministers who were largely responsible for the war effort.

Their first and basic requirement was obvious. They had to conduct a great war. They must speedily find the means to do it. And the means, in sufficient quantity, could only be found in a systematic and vigorous employment of federal taxing powers. Obviously the sweeping exercise of this unlimited financial authority would have serious effects on the relations of the Dominion and the provinces. A conference on the subject was clearly advisable; and the occasion for it had already been provided by the publication in 1940 of the *Report of the Royal Commission on Dominion-Provincial Relations,* or *Rowell-Sirois Report.* If the federal ministers hoped that the patriotic fervour of the moment would ensure provincial acceptance of the far-reaching recommendations of the *Report,* they were soon undeceived. But, on the other hand, if the provincial premiers fondly imagined that their successful opposition to the *Report* would prevent the Dominion from proceeding with its expansive financial plans, they also were quickly made aware of their mistake. Shortly after the conference opened on January 14, 1941, it became perfectly clear that three provinces, Ontario, Alberta, and British Columbia, refused even to consider the *Report* as a basis for discussion. Nothing could overcome this intransigent opposition; and the conference was over in less than forty-eight hours.

Before it broke up, however, the Minister of Finance, J. L. Ilsley, delivered a plain lecture on the future to the provincial premiers. He described the drastic nature of his proposed new taxes and he warned the conference that if the provinces did not come to an agreement with the Dominion, they would soon find their finances in a grave embarrassment. In April, three months later, without the formality of a new conference, he proposed a way out of these ominously approaching difficulties. The provinces were to surrender their personal income and corporation taxes for a year beyond the duration of the war; and in return they could take their choice of two forms of annual compensation offered by the federal government. Either they would receive the amount of revenue which they had actually collected from personal income and corporation taxes during the previous fiscal year; or they would be paid the net cost of the service of their debt in 1940 (less the revenue from succession duties) and, in addition, a special subsidy if the fiscal need for it could be shown. The federal government disclaimed the very idea of coercion; but the obvious requirements of the war, together with their own financial weakness, left most of the provinces with little real option. In short order all the provincial governments signed the tax suspension agreements; and the Dominion was left free and unhampered in its employment of the greatest fiscal devices of modern times.

The sinews of war had been secured. The team that was to direct the war-time effort had been brought together. And under its inspiration and control, the vast buzzing commotion that had reigned in Ottawa during the summer of 1940 became by degrees an orderly hum of productive activity. The Second Division was gradually dispatched to England. Orders for the mobilization of the Third Division had already been given; and plans for still another division had been begun. The systematic progress of the Commonwealth Air Training Plan was at first thrown into the greatest confusion by the inability of Great Britain to send its expected contribution of equipment and training planes. The dangerous and vital business of convoy escort into which the small fleet of Canadian destroyers had plunged in September, 1939, had already resulted in the loss of the *Margaree* and the crippling of the *Saguenay*. There were dangers, deficiencies, and difficulties on every hand. But the Canadian government rapidly pushed the Air Training Plan forward, and vastly increased the immediate and prospective output of aircrew. And in the last months of 1940, a dozen or more small steel warships — the first corvettes produced by the ambitious Canadian shipbuilding programme — slipped down the St. Lawrence and into the sea.

The ships and planes, the tanks, and trucks and armoured cars, the guns, and explosives, and chemicals, which began to pour out of the nation's factories in ever-increasing volume from then on, were a formidable sign that the Canadian economy had definitely passed into a new and important stage in its development. The war was a war characterized by the speed and strength and deadliness of machines. Hitler's armies had just demonstrated the terrible striking power of mechanization; and the equipment and supply of the Canadian forces for such armoured conflicts placed a new and strange burden on Canadian industry. In the War of 1914-18, Canadian factories had been busy enough; but their chief task then had been the manufacture of enormous quantities of shells; and when war began again in 1939, the nation had scarcely the vestige of an armament industry. Now, in the desperate circumstances of the autumn and winter of 1940-41, with Great Britain obsessed with its own necessities and the United States still neutral, the Dominion was compelled to begin the production of most of the materials of modern war on a grand scale. A quarter-century before, the task would have been too much for her. Now it was within the nation's power to carry the undertaking through. In the inter-war period, Canada had ceased to be an essentially agricultural, and had become an essentially manufacturing, country. By the middle of the war she was to be ranked as the fourth industrial power on the side of the allied nations.

The object of all this stupendous activity was one — the 'defence of these islands' and the defiance of Hitler's continent. It was a terrible enterprise for a small group of powers to undertake. It was also a co-operative enterprise in the most real and intimate sense of the term, for the nations of the Commonwealth had similar traditions, similar political institutions, and were bound together by their common allegiance to the same Crown. In the War of 1914-18, this easy, natural feeling of brotherhood had found institutional expression in the Imperial War Cabinet and the Imperial War Conference; and through her membership in these bodies Canada had taken a not unimportant part in the conduct of the war and in the making of the peace. In the vastly changed circumstances of 1940-41, the Dominion obviously deserved a position of much greater influence and authority; and a council or similar co-operative institution, in which the free realms of the Commonwealth could direct their effort together, would have been far more appropriate than it had been a quarter-century before. If King had wished to do so, he might have insisted upon the establishment of a Commonwealth Council. But, in fact, he repudiated the very idea of such a body. He had a deep dislike of what used to be referred to, in a previous generation, as 'imperial centralization'; and his obsession with the controversies of his youth blinded him to the realities of the present situation. Canada in 1940-41 was not a colonial dependency, but Great Britain's principal ally. She was the second greatest power then engaged in the war with Germany; and to her, all plans and policies for attack and defence in the United Kingdom and the North Atlantic were of supreme importance. Yet King preferred to deal with the conduct of the war in an aloof and gingerly fashion, as if any formal association with Great Britain were derogation of Canadian autonomy. In effect, he was prepared to let Great Britain direct the war in Europe. He wanted to do his own negotiating in North America.

In the meantime, the defence of North America and the North Atlantic had become a matter of the greatest consequence. The fall of France had sent a shiver of apprehension through the whole English-speaking world; and the United States began to take a number of energetic and far-reaching measures for the security of the Western Hemisphere. King was perfectly prepared to fall in with these plans. He was ready to co-operate with a neutral in a way in which he refused to co-operate with an ally. On August 17, 1940, at Roosevelt's invitation, the American President and the Canadian Prime Minister met at Ogdensburg, on the American side of the St. Lawrence; and next day, after a night's discussion, the two statesmen issued a press release announcing the formation of a Permanent Joint Board on Defence. The Board, which was to be composed of an equal number of Canadian and American representatives, was to consider, in an advisory capacity, 'the defence of the north half of the western hemisphere' and was to commence 'immediate studies relating to sea, land, and air problems'. The arrangement was evidently the President's suggestion; and King accepted it on his own responsibility and after only a single night's reflection. In the past, he had repeatedly, and with the utmost solemnity, assured the Canadian people that his government would make no commitments — above all, no permanent commitments — without the concurrence of Parliament. Yet now, within a fortnight of the prorogation of Parliament and without any consultation of his colleagues, he had made an important, long-term engagement.

This, however, was not the only important decision respecting the defence of the Western Hemisphere which was reached during the troubled summer of 1940. At the same time the United States was quietly concluding another, equally significant unilateral bargain with the United Kingdom. On August 20, two days after the Ogdensburg declaration, it was announced that Great Britain, in exchange for fifty over-age destroyers, had agreed to lease bases in the British West Indies, Bermuda, and Newfoundland to the United States. This cession of the keys of the old island British Empire for some obsolescent ships was full of sinister significance for the completion of the Canadian union. Ever since a united British North America had first been planned, Canada had hoped and believed that Newfoundland would eventually become a province of the federation. Since the beginning of the war, Canadian statesmen had spoken and acted on the assumption that the defence of Labrador and Newfoundland was vitally necessary to the defence of Canada. Yet now King seemed to regard this ninety-nine-year American lodgement in Canada's strategic outpost with virtual equanimity. Possibly he expected that the Dominion would be represented as a principal in the subsequent negotiation of the formal agreement respecting Newfoundland. But when, in March, 1941, the arrangements for the transfer of the bases were completed, Canada was invited to participate merely as an observer. Her interest in Newfoundland was completely ignored in the formal agreement. And it was only as an afterthought, and at Canada's insistence, that a protocol was added, somewhat lamely asserting that 'the defence of Newfoundland is an integral feature of the Canadian scheme of defence' and that throughout the American use of the bases 'Canadian interests in regard to defence will be fully respected'.

The 'destroyers for bases' deal and the Ogdensburg agreement were both significant indications of a very gradual but very important change in the American attitude to the war. The rigid and complacent policy of neutrality was being slowly undermined by a mounting sense of national insecurity, as well as by a growing concern for the tribulations of others. The United States still confidently hoped to escape 'involvement' in the sorry mess of European affairs; and most of the actions which she took in 1940-41 — including the agreements with Great Britain and Canada and the military occupations of Iceland and Greenland — were inspired by a very realistically self-interested design for the defence of North America. There were other measures, however, of which the Lend-Lease Act of March, 1941, was the most important, which expressed more fittingly the sympathetic wish for 'all aid short of war'. Throughout the conflict, Canada did not request and did not accept any direct lend-lease aid; the Canadian government disliked, among other things, the complex conditions and restrictive commitments with which the lend-lease agreements were fettered. But it was obvious that the crisis of the spring of 1940 and the concentration of British industry upon Great Britain's own requirements had vastly increased Canada's economic dependence on the United States; and it was plain that the Dominion must quickly find some means of lessening the serious drain upon her precious American dollar reserves. On April 20, 1941, a partial solution to this urgent problem was embodied in the Hyde Park declaration — a declaration which was the economic counterpart of the Ogdensburg agreement. Its declared principle was that each country was to provide the other 'with the defence articles which it is best able to produce'; and it provided in detail that American purchases of Canadian metals and strategic materials were to be increased, and that Canadian imports from the United States, used in the filling of armament orders from the United Kingdom, were to be charged to the British lend-lease account.

The extent to which the United States, though still obstinately neutral, had become a preponderant influence in a distracted world was dramatically illustrated in the meeting of Churchill and Roosevelt on the *Prince of Wales* off Newfoundland in August, 1941. In this conference, Great Britain had hoped, above all else, to enlist the support of the United States in a common policy of resistance to the ominously expanding threat of Japanese aggression. Roosevelt, despite the sinister portents of what was to occur less than four months later, did not believe that the American people would accept such an emphatic stand; and the meeting on the *Prince of Wales*, which might have had a practical result, ended instead in the resounding generalities of the Atlantic Charter. The original British draft, which Roosevelt and Hopkins regarded condescendingly as a mere 'publicity handout', was subjected to the magic ministrations of American advertising technique; and, doubtless undergoing a marked moral elevation in the process, it emerged in glossy splendour as a 'charter' of freedoms.

Canada, still Great Britain's senior English-speaking ally

in the struggle, had not been present at the meeting. The two great powers had apparently been perfectly capable of talking to each other, and to some purpose, without the good offices of their self-styled 'interpreter' and 'mediator'. The Canadians, who had good reason to be conscious of the fact that they were the sole belligerents in the Western Hemisphere, and who had almost come to believe themselves the indispensable instruments of Anglo-American co-operation, were understandably hurt by this pointed exclusion; and only a few days after the announcement of the Atlantic Charter Mackenzie King posted off in a great hurry to London in an aeroplane. It was his first visit to England since the war had begun two years before. And even now he made no effort to alter the determination of Commonwealth high policy in the struggle. It was probably too late for such efforts in any case. The war and its conduct were already changing. They were to change infinitely more in the next few months.

[*II*]

By the end of the year, the entrance of the Soviet Union and the United States had profoundly altered the whole character of the conflict. The war had become, in truth, a world war. But this vast and terrifying extension of its boundaries was not the only index of its changed character. The perils and difficulties confronting the allied powers had enormously increased; but so also had their chances of ultimate success. The entrance of the United States and the Soviet Union into the conflict was certain to be infinitely more important in the long run than the sudden intervention of Japan. The Soviet Union and the United States were great powers, capable of deploying immense and probably decisive forces; and they were certain to demand, and to exercise, a correspondingly large authority in the grand strategy of the war. Great Britain they would be obliged to regard as roughly on their own level; but the rest of the

British Commonwealth, except in so far as it was politically associated with Great Britain, they could afford politely to ignore. Canada, which for a year had been the principal ally in a Commonwealth resistance, discovered that she had suddenly become a submissive satellite of the Big Three.

Even the Big Three, however, could not in a short time repair the disastrous results of unpreparedness and appeasement. The long train of calamities which had begun in April, 1940, had so far had only one interruption — the great defensive success of the Battle of Britain; and now, with the eastern onslaught of Germany and the intervention of Japan, losses, withdrawals, and defeats began to be heaped on each other in a huge accumulation of misfortune.

The great German advances in Russia and Africa, the Japanese capture of Malaya and the Philippines were disasters which were borne chiefly by the great powers; but Canada, though the bulk of her forces was not engaged in these encounters, had her own small but bitter share of the humiliation of defeat. At the request of the British, two Canadian regiments, the Royal Rifles and the Winnipeg Grenadiers, were sent across the Pacific at the eleventh hour to reinforce the garrison of Hong Kong. Only a little over a month after their arrival, on the most terrible Christmas Day of the war, the little defending force laid down its arms and Hong Kong was lost to the successful Japanese.

It was only one disaster among many. And Canada, like all the other anti-Axis powers, could but endure and prepare in patience and resolution for a better day. The first months of 1942 were months of defeat, disappointment, and frustration. But 1942 as a whole was a year of great achievement in the recovery of both striking power and strategic initiative; and in Canada, as throughout the Grand Alliance, the times were tense with effort and endeavour. The country laboured to arm itself, to realize its maximum military power, to defend its own shores, and to make sure of the routes between itself and the more certain theatres of conflict. On the Atlantic coast, the great air base at Goose Bay, near the Northwest River, in Labrador, which was to play such a vital part in the northern air route to Europe, had been constructed. On the Pacific side of the continent, the north-west staging route, with its string of air bases from Edmonton to Whitehorse, was now enlarged for the greatly increased traffic which the war with Japan might necessitate; and, on the recommendation of the Permanent Joint Board on Defence, it was agreed that the United States should undertake the construction of a highway linking the bases and running into Alaska.

Some of the Canadian members of the Permanent Joint Board doubted the necessity of the Alaska highway. They looked even more sceptically upon the north-east staging route, another and still more grandiose American project, with two strings of enormous air bases converging in a second, far northerly transatlantic route. Their doubts were silenced under American insistence. Under American pressure, the Canadian government gave way. The American Army, with its technicians and engineers, arrived triumphantly and in force. 'If the Canadian public had been aware of the extent of United States undertakings in the North, a Canadian geographer wrote later, 'there might have been alarm at their magnitude and distribution.' Even as it was, there was a sufficient amount of disquiet and irritation. And the deeds and legends of the 'American Army of Occupation' lived long and died very hard.

The economy, and the political state, of total war had arrived. The Dominion, having abruptly solved the problem of its financial relations with the provinces, was using its taxing powers to the limit. The whole business of supply and distribution of materials was under governmental control; and in October, 1941, the Wartime Prices and Trade Board had imposed a general price ceiling on all goods and services. In January, 1942, the Prime Minister announced an ambitious project — which the military authorities had been discussing for some months — the creation overseas of a Canadian Army of two army corps, one of which was to be armoured. The British Commonwealth Air Training Plan, with its one hundred and forty training schools and centres scattered across the country, had already attracted over one hundred thousand recruits to the Royal Canadian Air Force; and the Royal Canadian Navy, now equipped with a rapidly increasing fleet of destroyers, corvettes, mine sweepers, frigates, and motor torpedo boats, had taken over much of the dangerous labour of protecting the precious convoys against the perils of the intensified German submarine campaign. The search for manpower was growing rapidly in intensity. Army, Air Force, Navy, industry — all were deeply and passionately involved in it.

The old familiar problem was back again. The old, disturbingly familiar controversy broke out once more. The government had solemnly pledged its word — and had given its promise statutory form in Clause Three of the National Resources Mobilization Act of 1940 — that there would be no conscription for overseas service. The pledge was now well over two years old; and, in the meantime, everything had gone from bad to worse. The government was pressed and embarrassed, not only by the opposition's shrill demands for conscription, but also, as might have been expected, by the inexorably exacting circumstances of total war; and in the end the Cabinet decided to seek a release, through the unparliamentary form of a plebiscite, from the restrictions of its incautiously given promise. 'Are you in favour,' the voters were asked in a national inquiry on April 27, 'of releasing the government from any obligations arising out of any past commitments restricting the methods of raising men for military service?' The nation as a whole voted 64 per cent to 36 per cent in favour of removing the pledged restrictions. There was a 72 to 28 per cent negative vote in the Province of Quebec; and an 80 to 20 per cent affirmative vote in the other eight provinces. The government, reassured by these results, proceeded to introduce a bill removing the limitations on conscription from the National Resources Mobilization Act. But this action was purely to prepare in advance for the possible contingencies of the future. At the moment no change was made in the methods of mobilization. In the famous phrase of Mackenzie King, the policy of the government was 'not necessarily conscription, but conscription if necessary.'

The sense of postponement, inactivity and frustration, which weighed so heavily during 1942 on the Canadian Army and the Canadian civilian population, was varied only by the horrified realization of the tragic defeat and losses of the Dieppe raid. For a year now, the clamour for a second front in aid of the savagely pressed Russians had been steadily growing. Churchill and Roosevelt who, with their service chiefs, had taken over exclusive control of the grand strategy of the war, had come to the conclusion that a full-scale invasion of north-western Europe would have to be postponed until 1943 at least; and during the summer of 1942 they reached a second decision, of fundamental importance for the future, to land a considerable force in French North Africa before the year was out. Any serious effort in Western Europe, even of the subordinate nature of a diversion, was clearly impossible for some time. But raids, it was thought, could and should be undertaken; and, at the end of April, 1942, an outline plan for an attack on Dieppe, which no Canadian political or military authority had ever heard of before, was presented verbally to General McNaughton. Nearly four months later, in the early hours of August 19, 4,963 Canadians and 1,075 British soldiers launched a gallant but vain frontal assault upon the well fortified town of Dieppe and its immediate surroundings. By nine o'clock the last reserves of the expedition had been committed, without effect. In the early afternoon, the attack was abandoned, an almost complete and terrible failure.

Canadian losses in this brave, tragic enterprise were unexampled in their heaviness. Nine hundred and seven officers and men were killed or died of wounds: nineteen hundred and forty-six were left behind as prisoners of war. The Canadian people, when they knew the full horror of the event, felt shattered with grief and shock; and the tumult of their feelings was only increased by the initial and flagrant misrepresentations of the news reports. North American newspapers in general, fed with dispatches from the great American press associations, represented the Dieppe operation as largely an American raid. The British newspapers, which likewise stressed the importance of the part played by their forces, had vastly more justification for their emphasis, for British Commandos had taken part in the assault on the beaches and Great Britain had contributed the great majority of the supporting ships and planes. On the other hand, only seven of the seventy-four attacking aircraft squadrons were American; and only fifty American Rangers, distributed among the various Canadian and British units as observers, actually took part in the raid. It was true that the first false reports were fairly quickly corrected; but, as is usual in such matters, the corrections never quite caught up with the errors. The huge propaganda machines of the two great powers now in exclusive control of the western war had effectively concealed the gravity of Canada's bloody sacrifice.

The Dieppe raid was the last great calamity that the allied powers sustained. The war, in fact, had reached its turning-point. In the summer of 1942, the storm of adversity and frustration ended at last; and by the close of the year the winds of good fortune were blowing again with steady force. The armies of the Soviet Union, fortified with their stupendous defence of Stalingrad, were driving the enemy back along the whole long line of the invasion front. In the South Pacific, as early as May and June, the American Navy had won the decisive victories of the Coral Sea and Midway. The battle of El Alamein was a brilliant victory which set the British Eighth Army off in eager pursuit of Rommel's retreating corps westward across North Africa; and early in November, only a fortnight later, British and American forces made their successful landings in French North Africa.

By the middle of May, 1943, the power of the Axis in North Africa had been overthrown. Canada contributed little to this achievement, though a small number of Canadian officers and men gained valuable experience with the First British Army in Tunisia. But in the campaign which opened immediately afterwards, the forces of the Dominion were to play a different and vastly more important rôle. In January, at the Casablanca Conference, the decision had been taken to attack Sicily; and at the meeting in Washington in the spring this plan was confirmed and enlarged with the idea of knocking Italy completely out of the war. A very large enterprise — though an enterprise still definitely subordinate to the main invasion of northern Europe which was now set for the spring of 1944 — was about to get under way in the immediate future. Who was to undertake it? Would all — or part — of the Canadian Army have its share of the assault?

The Army stood at the peak of its efficiency and striking power. Composed of two armoured divisions, three infantry divisions, and two army tank brigades, it was a formidable instrument of warfare; and now, after the disappointments, reverses, and frustrations of nearly four years, the question of its use had become, for the Canadian government and the Canadian people, the most anxious and absorbing problem of the day. General McNaughton, the field commander, had always believed that, as far as possible, the Army should operate as an undivided national force; and he had looked forward to the invasion of northern Europe as the preferred strategic enterprise in which the united Canadians would play a most important part. The invasion of northern Europe was, however, still a year away; and in the meantime the Canadian government was being pressed on all sides to end an inactivity which was fretting both its soldiers and its civilians, and to put at least a part of the splendid Canadian force into action. In the original plan for the invasion of Sicily, the Canadians had been given no place. But now the Canadian government suggested that some of its troops might be included; and in April it was decided that the First Division and the First Tank Brigade would be sent to the the Mediterranean to take part in the assault.

Before dawn on July 10, while the Mediterranean rolled forward in a heavy swell towards the coast of southern Sicily, the Canadians went ashore at Pachino and into their first major battles of the war. On August 17, after only a little over a month of stiff fighting in tropical heat over the island's rugged hills and dusty tortuous roads, the allied forces made good their conquest of Sicily; and less than three weeks later, on September 3, the fourth anniversary of Great Britain's declaration of war, the spearhead of the Eighth Army, consisting of the Canadians and a British division, crossed the straits successfully and made the first lodgment on the mainland of Europe. At first, in the early official announcements about the fighting in Sicily, no mention whatever was made of the part which the Canadians were playing; the communiqués from General Eisenhower's Supreme Headquarters had referred merely to 'allied forces' or 'Anglo-American forces'. It was only after a protest to London and an appeal to Roosevelt, that Mackenzie King succeeded in securing a belated admission of the presence of the Canadians; and thereafter the American High Command, in both the Mediterranean and the Pacific, began slightly to alter its Olympian attitude to the forces of the Dominions.

By the end of September the Eighth Army had cleared the whole of the 'toe' and 'heel' of the boot of the Italian peninsula; and, with the Fifth American-British Army to the left, it held the north-eastern sector of the line from Naples on the Tyrrhenian Sea to the Adriatic. A month later, after bursts of harder fighting through olive groves and high

Italian hill towns, the Canadians were solidly established along the Sangro River, which the enemy had determined to make his winter line of defence. In the meantime, the major change in Canadian army policy, which had been impending now for some months, was finally decided upon. The First Canadian Division and the First Canadian Tank Brigade had not been recalled to England after the Sicilian campaign, as it was first assumed they might be; and in November, after two months' further campaigning in the peninsula, they were greatly reinforced by the transference of the Headquarters of the First Canadian Corps and the Fifth Canadian Armoured Division to Italy. The Canadian forces, hitherto concentrated in England, were divided; the policy of maintaining the Army's identity, through its unity, had been abandoned; and with its abandonment came General McNaughton's retirement and General H. D. G. Crerar's succession to the chief command.

During December, 1943, the allied efforts to break the Winter Line and to capture Rome were vigorously continued. The furious series of battles by which the Canadians crossed the River Moro, captured Ortona, and drove a salient up the coast of the Adriatic were as violent and exhausting as any in the war. Then, when this offensive was grinding to a slow stop in the appalling weather of winter, the First Canadian Corps, with its two Canadian divisions, took the field for the first time. Its appearance as a unit in active operations coincided with the awakening of a new and sharper sense of urgency in the Italian struggle. The vast enterprise of the invasion of northern Europe was looming up. Its requirements were to weaken the Italian effort still further; but its imminence convinced the allied high command that a more emphatic decision must be sought in Italy without delay. A great new offensive, west of the Apennines, was to be launched when the spring came. The First Canadian Corps, and the bulk of the Eighth Army, was transferred from the Adriatic across the mountains. They faced the long, flat valley of the Liri and Sacco Rivers which stretched, like an easy, natural boulevard, north-westward towards Rome. And in May the Eighth Army stormed up the valley through the triple line of formidable defences which the Germans had created. The Canadians broke the Adolf Hitler Line in a frontal attack; and the advance which followed rapidly became a pursuit. The Germans abandoned their imperilled defence of Rome; but it was the Americans of the Fifth Army, and not the Canadians, who entered the Italian capital in triumph.

Rome fell on June 4. It was an end gained only two days before the beginning of a greater endeavour. During the winter and spring of 1944, the final touches had been made on the giant plan 'Overlord' for an assault of the Normandy coastline along a five-division front, and its naval counterpart, the plan 'Neptune'. Gradually Canadian minesweepers, motor torpedo boats, corvettes, frigates, landing ships and destroyers, to the number of one hundred and ten, had moved forward to join the great armada of the invasion fleet which was gathering in the Channel. The men of the Royal Canadian Air Force, in either their own or British squadrons, had played their part, through strategic bombing operations and great air battles, in establishing that overwhelming mastery of the skies which was the vitally essential condition of the success of 'Neptune' and 'Overlord'. One Canadian Division — the Third Infantry Division — was to take part in the assault on the beaches. The First Canadian Army, which, like other British and American forces, was to be committed later, was intended to exploit the initial gains and to break out from the established bridgehead into the surrounding territory.

It was the morning of June 5. The whole gigantic attack — men, ships, planes, tanks, guns, and bombs — stood poised, like an avalanche, trembling upon the brink of its inevitable descent. The luck of the glorious weather of May had vanished. The south-west wind freshened in violent gusts.

Already the huge operation had been postponed a day; but at the last moment, and after hours of debate and agonizing uncertainty, the high command decided to risk everything upon the promise of a brief interval of better weather that even then was hastening across the Atlantic. The final, fatal orders were given. The first and slowest ships of the invasion fleet slipped their lines from Southampton docks. A little after ten o'clock on that unquiet night of early summer, when dusk closed in at last over the Channel, the long, dark, crowded columns of the armada were pressing steadily south. Low, ragged, threatening clouds scudded across the sky. The full moon, which had climbed above the horizon by midnight, shone only fitfully; and the hard wind drove the sea into a bursting swell and sent the spray flying in stinging showers over the decks. It was the taut, final moment of suspense before total action. The paratroopers had swept into the dark sky; the airborne divisions were on their perilous way; at half-past eleven the great aerial bombardment of the assault area began.

At a few minutes before eight o'clock on the morning of June 6 the Canadians were borne in through the last creaming breakers to their section of the long crescent of the assault. Here, over these beaches, the weather was, if anything, worse than on any other part of the front. The tumbling sea and the treacherous off-shore reefs delayed the run-in; the armour, which could not be put down as early as the plan required, failed in places to lead the troops in; and the infantry, racing across sand and shingle, found German gun emplacements, which ought to have been silenced, blazing instead with fire. Even so, this first Canadian assault wave — Royal Winnipeg Rifles, Regina Rifles, Queen's Own Rifles, and North Shore (New Brunswick) Regiment — carried everything before them in the superb dash of their attack. The delays, the German defences, the losses, the hideous congestion of men, armour, and transport on the beaches and the first villages, could not prevent their advance. When the first day ended, the Third Canadian Division had pushed six to seven miles inland. It had gone farther, in fact, than any other division of the assault, and when night fell its advance battalions had dug in only three miles from the north-western outskirts of the city of Caen.

The ambitious objective of D-Day had nearly been attained. A half a dozen miles in a single day! The little distance into Caen and the modest twenty-one miles of the road that ran south-eastward through the wheatfields to Falaise, must have seemed, in that first flush of triumph, such easily obtainable objectives. But, for whole weeks that followed, the Canadians were to expend their strength and exhaust their ingenuity in the desperate struggle for that short stretch of town and industrial suburb and pleasant countryside. Caen and the area about it had become, in fact, the focal point of the entire struggle. Both sides, allied and German, regarded it, for different but equally compelling reasons, as the key to the position. On their part, the Germans continued to fear a second and greater allied invasion to the east in the region of the Straits of Dover. They persistently underestimated the possibility of a serious attack by the Americans on their western flank; and they confidently expected that the main allied effort at a break-out would be made at the eastern end of the bridgehead, in the closest proximity to Paris. The great bulk of their forces, therefore, including the overwhelming majority of their armoured divisions, was massed in the Caen region. Caen was the anchor of their defence. And nothing could have suited Montgomery better. For him the Caen region was the solid hinge upon which his right wing was to swing forward through the German defences in a wide encircling sweep to the south and east. The break-through was to be made on his right, in the west, where it was not expected. And, in the meantime, the most, and the best, of the German forces were to be pinned down at Caen.

It was this task that the Canadians, and the Second British

Army as a whole, were expected to carry out. All during June and July they fought their difficult way slowly through Caen and its suburbs and up the long white road towards Falaise. In the meantime, at the end of July, the Americans, with their now vastly superior numbers, broke through the thinning German defences, rushed south and east, and began to execute the long 'right hook' which Montgomery had designed. The Germans were now in serious trouble; but it was Hitler, not his generals, von Rundstedt and Rommel, who changed this real danger into a deadly peril. In one of the most infatuated of his dramatic interventions, he ordered a massive counter-offensive westward which was intended to sever the communications of Patton's advancing columns and to cut the American forces in two. The last disposable German armoured divisions plunged to the west in blind obedience. But this vain, gambling counter-stroke only increased the danger of their encirclement and magnified the catastrophe which was to overtake them. The ring of steel round the German divisions had become a cauldron in which a hundred thousand men faced extermination. Only one gap — the Falaise gap — remained open for retreat to the east. The allied armies struggled to close it. Elements of Patton's Army hastened up from the south. On the north, the Canadians took Falaise. They pressed forward to the south-east; and on August 18, a small detachment of the Fourth Canadian Armoured Division, composed of men of the South Alberta Regiment and the Argyll and Sutherland Highlanders, and commanded by Major D. V. Currie, fought their way into the village of St. Lambert close to one of the last roads of escape which lay open to the frantically retreating Germans. The gap was not completely closed in time. There were thousands of trapped Germans who managed to crash their way through to safety. But in the cauldron of Falaise the Wehrmacht had suffered its greatest disaster after Stalingrad.

For an incredible fortnight, the pursued and the pursuers

raced through north-western France across territory over
which the contending armies in the First World War had
fought a savage stalemate for four long years. The Americans
entered Paris. The British took Brussels and Antwerp. And
then, as the German line began to straighten out, and fill in,
and stiffen in resistance, the allied high command began a
great debate over the nature of the next operation, the operation which might complete the rout of the German defences
and win the war. In the north, Montgomery was eager to
direct a great, concentrated single thrust towards the Ruhr;
the American Patton, in the south, was equally determined
not to let anybody 'steal the show' from him. And while the
principals argued with an emotional tenacity appropriate to
ageing opera stars, Crerar's First Canadian Army, 'the
Cinderella of Eisenhower's forces', was attempting to carry
out the hard, bloody, necessary, but unspectacular tasks
which everybody wanted done, but which nobody else was
particularly anxious to undertake. The British and American
Armies now pressing forward towards the Rhine had so far
outrun their distant base in the Bay of the Seine that the
problem of supply had become acute. Nearby ports were
vitally necessary to arm and power the new offensive; and it
was essential that the Channel ports be captured, the estuary
of the Scheldt River occupied, and the great city of Antwerp
freed and open for allied traffic from the sea. During September and October, the Canadians struggled to complete these
tasks. In the estuary of the Scheldt, they found the Germans
well protected, formidably powerful, and savagely resisting.
And from allied generals, whose eyes were fixed upon their
own triumphant entry into Berlin, they got little consideration and less help, until almost the end of the long campaign.
The freeing of Antwerp, despite the obstacles of nature and
the resistance of the enemy, was very largely the triumph of
the courage, determination, and endurance of the Canadian
Army.

The Army had given of its best. It had paid dearly for the

right to its subordinate position beside the armies of the great powers. The losses at Caen and Falaise, the losses on the canals and over the flooded ground of the Scheldt estuary would have been serious enough, even if they had stood alone. But, of course, they were only a part, though a very considerable part, of the total casualties of the Canadian Army. The campaign in Italy was stubbornly continued, though with steadily diminishing resources. A number of divisions were transferred from the allied forces in the peninsula in aid of that doubtfully useful enterprise, upon which the United States insisted, the invasion of southern France; and the priority which the great powers had given the campaigns in north-west Europe and the Pacific could be plainly read in the declining volume of equipment and material which reached the Eighth and Fifth Armies in Italy. Despite these obvious evidences of depreciation and neglect, the 'forgotten men' of the First Canadian Corps, and their comrades-in-arms in the famous Eighth Army, fought their way up the peninsula on the strength of their own courage and perseverance. During the late summer and autumn, the Canadians, transferred once again to the Adriatic sector, broke through the enemy's Gothic Line, captured the fortified eminences of the last spurs of the Apennines and began the struggle northward through the mud and swollen rivers of the Lombard plain. September, 1944, was the deadliest month of the entire Italian campaign for the Canadian Corps.

It was these tragic losses which gave a new and desperate urgency to the problem of reinforcement. It was the problem of reinforcement which suddenly thrust Canada into the gravest political crisis of the entire war. The submerged but irrepressible dispute over conscription, which had caused a frightening tremor to run through the whole land two years before, now broke out openly in a great upheaval. The casualties of the last few months had been heavier than the planners of the great powers had predicted; recent voluntary enlistments in Canada had been far lower than the authorities had ventured to hope; and it was obvious that the war was going to last a good deal longer than people had fondly expected in the flush of the great victories of August and the great advance of September. What was to be done? The one great remaining source of reserves lay in the over sixty thousand men, still serving in Canada, who had been called up for compulsory service under the National Resources Mobilization Act. Ever since this statute had been amended in 1942, the government had possessed the power to employ these men anywhere for general service. But it had carefully held this formidable authority in reserve. The N.R.M.A. men who had not volunteered for the Army or the other armed services had been used for home defence. Should they be kept at this increasingly perfunctory duty any longer? Or, at this crisis, should not a considerable detachment of them be sent at once to reinforce the brave but battered Canadian forces in Europe?

Colonel J. L. Ralston, the old soldier who had become Canada's Minister of Defence, determined that an answer to this imperative question must be sought at once. He wanted to know the truth about the problem of reinforcements. He decided that the only way in which he could discover the real truth was by a personal visit to the Canadian Armies in the field. And on September 23, after the second allied conference at Quebec had ended, he flew to London. He visited headquarters in Italy. He went to Brussels. It was a shattering revelation. His old geniality vanished. He was a man preoccupied, disquieted, almost obsessed. He could think and talk about nothing but the need of reinforcements. He was haunted by the anxious voices of commanders, the beseeching eyes of officers, the mute, exhausted faces of the other ranks. And he knew now, without the slightest shadow of doubt, what he and the Canadian government must do. The Prime Minister had formally promised, in a public statement of policy, that full conscription would be introduced, 'if necessary'. He himself had become convinced, by a searching and distressing personal investigation, that full conscription was necessary. The pledge had been given. The pledge must now be kept. He hoped and believed that, in the light of the facts, it would be kept. He knew also that, if it were not, his own course was clear. He would resign.

He reached Ottawa on October 18. That afternoon he saw the Prime Minister. The next day he took his place in a meeting of the War Committee of the Cabinet. He told his colleagues of his visit and its findings. He proposed that conscription for overseas service should now be enforced and that fifteen thousand N.R.M.A. men should be dispatched without delay for the reinforcement of the Canadian Armies in Europe. The War Committee listened to him in portentous silence. As soon as he had finished, King solemnly warned the little group that conscription would break the country apart in a savage, irreconcilable, and unforgettable conflict. It was obvious, as he spoke the words, that a political crisis of the highest order was at hand. For ten anxious and exasperating days, the War Committee and the Cabinet as a whole sought to avoid it. They argued over the manpower figures. They debated all possible alternative courses to conscription. They were driven irresistibly back to the solution which was dividing them and which threatened fatally to divide the nation. A majority of the Cabinet, led by the Prime Minister and including all the ministers from Quebec, were opposed to conscription. A small but very powerful minority, composed of Ilsley, Crerar, Macdonald, and possibly Howe, gave support to Ralston's views. Between these two groups there was no discoverable compromise. The fruitless frustrating debate continued. But now it was clear that it could not go on much longer. The nation, at last beginning to get some inkling of the deep division in its government, was obviously uneasy, suspicious, passionately concerned. The affair, at any moment, might get completely out of hand. And if any solution existed, it must be found, not in days, but in hours.

It was the supreme moment of King's life. His whole long career had been devoted, as he truthfully claimed, to the reconciliation of French-speaking and English-speaking Canadians. And now, at the very moment when the nation had reached the pinnacle of its material achievement, this spiritual concord was threatened as it had never been before in all his long years of power. A catastrophic national division was imminent. It seemed utterly unavoidable. And then, on October 31, at what was literally the last possible moment, King discovered what seemed to be a way out. He remembered General McNaughton. It was ten months since McNaughton had retired from his position of Commander-in-Chief of the Canadian Army and had returned to Canada. He had been opposed to the policy of the division of the Canadian Army. He had been, to some extent, at outs with the high command in the United Kingdom, and with the civil and military authorities in Canada. But he was a soldier who had created the modern Canadian Army, and in the popular mind, he was the very personification of the Army's fighting strength. He had always been a firm believer in the principle of voluntary recruitment. And it was here of course that, in King's eyes, the inestimable political value of the General lay. Would McNaughton, at this crisis in the Army's history, consent to act as Minister of Defence and give the strength and prestige of his name to the continuance of the policy of no conscription for overseas service?

King saw the General at once. McNaughton agreed to enter the Ministry on the desired terms; and, on November 1, the Prime Minister met his unsuspecting Cabinet with the name of a new Defence Minister concealed, like a conjurer's property, on his person. Ralston restated his position. The dreary, hopeless discussion was resumed once more. There was talk of a compromise — the last of a long line of meaningless compromises. And then, after the fatigued, desultory conversation had lasted an appropriate time, King suddenly intervened. Two years ago, he intimated, Colonel Ralston had submitted his resignation. That resignation, he implied, might now be accepted, for the Cabinet was not prepared to accept the Colonel's recommendation and Ralston himself was unwilling to make a final effort to secure volunteers. General McNaughton, on the other hand, believed that voluntary recruitment could still yield the desired results, and McNaughton therefore should be invited to assume the post of Minister of Defence.

The Cabinet received this announcement in stunned surprise. The nation heard the news with a curious and troubled mixture of relief, hope, anxiety, impatience, and angry resentment. The last chance had arrived. The last, desperate effort must now be made. And for three weeks, from November 2 to November 22, the government frantically attempted to secure volunteers for general service from the remaining sixty thousand men called up under the National Resources Mobilization Act. The country waited breathlessly; but it had not long to wait. The period of reprieve and uncertainty would have its inevitable term in the opening of Parliament; and on November 22 Parliament met. Within forty-eight hours, almost certainly, it would have to pronounce judgment upon the government and its policy. How could that judgment be anything but adverse? It was obvious now, beyond any qualification, extenuation, or concealment, that the last attempt to obtain volunteers had been a failure. Colonel Ralston had been completely vindicated. The resignation of half a dozen of the conscriptionist ministers seemed imminent. Mackenzie King and Mackenzie King's government would surely fall.

And yet they did not fall. For once again, and again at the last possible moment, King had discovered a way out of the hideous tangle of his perplexities. Conscription, as a general principle with general application, would not be adopted; but sixteen thousand N.R.M.A. would be sent overseas immediately as an emergency reinforcement for the Canadian army. This was the solution which King presented to his astonished Cabinet colleagues on November 22. St. Laurent, the leading minister from Quebec and obviously at this moment a figure of commanding importance, accepted the proposal. The conscriptionist ministers decided to remain at their posts. Colonel Ralston, the selfless patriot whose devotion was given solely to his country and its Army, declared that he would vote in support of the government's resolution. And, as the debate went on, and the sinister atmosphere of impending cloudburst changed gradually into the common light of an ordinary parliamentary day, it became clear that the government and its new policy were through in safety. Two sacrifices had ensured their survival. King had ruined Ralston; the country was to reject McNaughton. But once French-speaking and English-speaking public opinion had been to some extent propitiated by these human burnt offerings, the policy, for all its contradictions, could be accepted, and the government, despite — or because of — its divisions and inconsistencies, could be given a grudging support.

Most important of all, the reinforcement crisis was declining in intensity for the simplest and most fundamental of all reasons. The war, despite a last, vain, gigantic offensive inspired by Hitler, was drawing to a close; and the final successful battles were preceded by a fairly lengthy period in which the bulk of the Canadian forces had relatively little to do. In Italy, it was true that winter brought little lull in the fighting about Ravenna; but in north-west Europe the First Canadian Army continued its uneventful watch on the Maas River for nearly three months; and it was against the Americans, in the Ardennes, that Hitler directed his last, great, gambling counterstroke. Late in February, when the allied offensive recommenced in the north, the Canadians played their part in the bitterly contested battles which ended in the clearing of the Rhineland; and the First Canadian Corps, newly arrived from Italy, took its place beside the other divisions of the Canadian Army just in time for the crossing of the Rhine and the final advance to victory. The enemy's defences, so long and tenaciously maintained, cracked, broke, and fell apart in disintegration; and the Canadian pursuit streamed north-east across Germany and the Netherlands.

[*III*]

In August, 1945, when the capitulation of Japan brought the conflict to a close, the vague outlines of the post-war world could already be perceived dimly through the mists of uncertainty and anxious speculation. Already it was perfectly evident that Canada, along with the rest of long-suffering humanity, was not going to enter at once into the possession of a new heaven and a new earth. A large part of the world had been sacked and ravaged by the contending armed forces; an immense and painful task of reconstruction lay ahead. Even in Canada, which had not suffered the losses or felt the exhaustion of the countries of western Europe, there was no great sense of elation or confidence at the coming of peace. The ending of the First World War of the twentieth century, the War of 1914-18, was barely more than a quarter-century away. It was impossible to recapture the joyful hope of 1918-19. It was impossible to banish completely the oppressive sense of repetition, the feeling of having been through all this once before. Everybody knew now that 'the world that was fit for heroes to live in' did not lie immediately beyond the capitulation of Germany and Japan. Everybody knew that peace and prosperity could be won, and kept, only by effort and with difficulty.

Obviously the question of the international organization of the future was one of the greatest which confronted the world. It was attacked in a spirit of practical, realistic purposefulness which contrasted curiously with the mingled idealism and disbelief of 1919. In November, 1943, at Moscow, the great powers had issued a joint declaration affirming the necessity of a general international organization; and nearly a year later, in the early autumn of 1944, a draft plan of the proposed world institution was prepared at a conference held at Dumbarton Oaks and attended only by representatives of the United States, Great Britain, Russia, and China. These 'sponsoring powers' then issued a general invitation to the allied nations to meet and discuss their proposals at a conference which was to be held at San Francisco in the spring of the following year. Canada accepted this invitation with the readiness of sober conviction. She had been excluded from the direction of the war; she was determined to use what influence she possessed for the maintenance of peace; and it was already plain that, in the view of the Canadian government, a workable international organization offered Canada her best chance of playing an effective part.

As early as January, 1944, Mackenzie King had been at some pains to make the Canadian position perfectly clear. His explanation of the hopes and intentions of his government was prompted by an address delivered to the Toronto Board of Trade in which Lord Halifax, then British ambassador to the United States, had foretold with astonishing accuracy the probable state of post-war international politics. The future peace of the world, Lord Halifax had implied, would depend upon the maintenance of a balance of power among the 'big four' of the war; and he had appealed to Canada to join with Great Britain in making the Commonwealth the fourth power, a power of wisdom and moderation, which could venture to claim equal partnership with the 'titans', Russia, the United States, and China. This was too much for Mackenzie King. He hastened publicly, and within a week of Lord Halifax's utterance, to express his complete disagreement. He not only rejected the conception of the Commonwealth as a diplomatic and military bloc — that was to be expected in view of his long-continued insistence on a separate foreign policy for Canada: he also refused to accept the assumption of the inevitable post-war rivalry of the great powers. 'Could Canada, situated as she is geographically between the United States and the Soviet Union, and at the same time a member of the British Commonwealth, for one moment give support to such an idea?' he inquired rhetorically. The best way of attaining peace was not by a balance of strength among a few great powers; peace, on the contrary, must be preserved by a system of 'firm commitments' in which all peace-loving states would join. 'We look forward therefore,' the Prime Minister concluded, 'to close collaboration in the interests of peace not only inside the British Commonwealth but with all friendly nations small as well as great.'

The old phrases 'no commitments' and 'Parliament will decide', the old attitude of cautious and complacent detachment, had evidently vanished. The cordial reception with which Canada greeted the United Nations could hardly have differed more from the half-hearted valedictory with which she had ushered the League of Nations into oblivion in the dark days before the war. A whole lifetime of bitter experience had been packed into those six terrible intervening years. Beyond all doubt or question, the war had proved the desirability of a general security system. The concord of the great powers, born of the war-time grand alliance, seemed to make a general security system perfectly possible. All the greatest powers — the powers, as it happened, with which Canada had close relations or common frontiers — were united in sponsoring the scheme of a new international organization. Was not this act of joint sponsorship the best guarantee that could be found of their continued collaboration in the cause of peace? Here surely was a broad solid foundation upon which one could base one's hopes for the future.

The decision was firm and unhesitating. The nation and its government were perfectly agreed. A new general security system could be accepted cordially in principle. But the details of its organization were another and more debatable matter; and here the Canadian government had some very definite views of its own. It was perfectly evident, of course, that the great powers were determined to exercise a far greater authority in the United Nations than they had done in the old League. The Dumbarton Oaks proposals and, above all, the Yalta voting formula, which required the unanimity of the permanent members of the Security Council, were harshly candid reminders of the domination which the great powers proposed to share exclusively among themselves. This was the price which the world would have to pay for the great powers' support of the new organization; and the Canadian government was willing to pay it. The great powers would have to be granted their pre-eminence. But did it follow, as a necessary consequence, that the rest of the nations of the world must be relegated to a common level of inferiority?

The Canadian government emphatically rejected this assumption. In its view, there were a few countries — Canada certainly was one — which, though they made no claim to be regarded as great powers, were to be sharply distinguished from the large group of lesser powers at the bottom of the hierarchy. These 'middle powers' had already proved their capacity in international affairs by their performance. It was their readiness and ability to accept responsibility — to perform the functions of maturity — which justified their claim to a place of special prominence. 'Representation,' Mackenzie King declared as early as July, 1943, in a general discussion of the international organization of the future, 'should be determined on a functional basis which will admit to full membership those countries, large or small, which have the greatest contribution to make to the particular object in question.' Canada was becoming the principal theorist of the rôle of the middle powers; and the 'functional principle', as it came to be called, was the principle by which she sought to claim a useful and significant part in the work of the United Nations.

The Canadian delegation to the San Francisco Conference

in the spring of 1945 was a varied one which included representatives of the principal opposition parties. The group
spoke with a united, though not a particularly forceful or
distinguished voice; and though it took part in a large
number of activities in a way which had been utterly impossible for the Canadians at the Paris Peace Conference in
1919, the delegation at San Francisco concentrated its best
efforts on three subjects of major importance. The Dumbarton Oaks proposals respecting future economic and social
co-operation had been peculiarly meagre and perfunctory;
and the Canadians, because of the relative importance of
their country's external relations of all kinds, busied themselves zealously with the expansion and the clarification of
this chapter of the United Nations' work. It was, however,
the composition and powers of the Security Council and the
provisions for the enforcement of peace which concerned
Canada — and, for that matter, the entire conference — more
than anything else. Mackenzie King and his colleagues obviously disliked and feared the preponderant authority which
the great powers had arrogated to themselves as permanent
members of the Security Council. The veto which, if irre-
sponsibly used, might paralyse the work of the organization,
was a particularly objectionable feature of that authority;
and the Canadians, like other delegates, sought to limit its
exercise. They did not prolong their efforts as brilliantly and
tenaciously as the Australians. They tried by different and
somewhat more indirect means to attain the same object.

The principal amendments which the Canadian delegation
had in mind were two. Both were designed to extend the
influence and safeguard the interests of what Mackenzie
King described as 'secondary powers with world-wide interests'. In the first place, the Canadians argued, suitable
conditions of eligibility should be laid down which would
ensure the frequent election of the 'middle powers' to the
non-permanent seats in the Security Council; and, in the
second place, some limitation must be placed upon the

Security Council's power to order states not among its members to contribute armed contingents to the enforcement of peace. In the eyes of the Canadians, these proposals were obvious corollaries of the 'functional principle'. After the great powers themselves, the secondary powers would most likely be called upon to undertake the duties of enforcement; and it followed reasonably that states which could make a real contribution to the work of the organization, had a preferred claim on the non-permanent seats in the Council.

In the end, Canada succeeded in obtaining an amendment which declared that the Assembly, in electing the non-permanent members, would have due regard, 'in the first instance', to the capacity of the candidates to perform the duties of the post. But, at the same time, 'equitable geographical distribution' was also declared to be a factor which deserved consideration. Plainly the Canadians did not get all they wanted here. They failed similarly to gain the full protection they desired for the middle and smaller powers against the arbitrary use of their armed forces. It was agreed that a state, not a member of the Security Council, could 'participate' in the Council's decisions respecting the employment of its contingents; and with that the Canadian delegation had to be content. On the whole, Canada's campaign for the public recognition of the importance of the 'middle powers' had been only a qualified success. The great powers had continued to hold, and to impose on others, their conception of the state system of the world. In their view, international society was composed, in an unreformed feudal fashion, of a very small group of great barons and a very large group of biddable peasants. If an aspiring member of a new middle class hoped to rise out of this undifferentiated feudal residue, it could only do so very slowly and by dint of its own exertions.

There was little inspiration or enchantment in the postwar world. Abroad, the realities of international politics were harsh. At home, domestic affairs had an appearance of uninspiring familiarity. In Canada, there was evidently to be no repetition of that period of social unsettlement and political agitation which had followed the War of 1914-18. The new parties, the radical political manifestoes, the crusading zeal for political reform and social betterment, which had been so characteristic of so much of the inter-war period, made no dramatic reappearance on the stage of the post-war world. There were no new 'third' parties. The 'third' parties of the period of the depression and the early war years were getting older without becoming noticeably more robust. The influence of Social Credit had not extended much beyond Alberta. In Quebec, the power of the extreme nationalist groups was evidently declining. The Co-operative Commonwealth Federation (C.C.F.), which, during the war, had captured power in Saskatchewan and had been recognized as the official opposition in Ontario and British Columbia, failed, in the immediate post-war years, to hold its hardly-won gains.

The best proof, however, that there was to be no dramatic interruption in the familiar course of Canadian politics lay in the return of the ageing Mackenzie King and his veteran government in the federal general election of June, 1945. The old Liberal leader had entered the ultimate phase of his long career. A year hence his tenure of office as Prime Minister of the Dominion would exceed in length that of Sir John A. Macdonald; and in the end he was to beat even Sir Robert Walpole's record as First Minister of the British Crown. Unloved, not even, perhaps, very widely or deeply respected, and without any of that fanatically adoring loyalty which Laurier or Macdonald could always command, he had been proved, by the mere march of events, to be the necessary, the indispensable, Canadian. The war had given him an opportunity of crowning his own peculiar contribution to Canadian political life. By methods which were undeniably contradictory and yet curiously effective, he had prevented a great national explosion over the conscription issue.

Almost unconsciously the country was aware of this; and it prepared to pay the grudging reward of its recognition. Only a few months before, on the morrow of the reinforcement crisis, it might have seemed that everything was against him. His old enemy, Maurice Duplessis, was back in power in Quebec. His new rival, the Conservative leader George Drew, had successfully clinched his hold on the government of Ontario in a provincial general election which took place immediately before the national poll was held. The omens were sinister to the last degree. A catastrophe was feared, was confidently predicted. Yet it did not occur. The Progressive-Conservatives, under their new leader, John Bracken, improved their position considerably in the House of Commons; but that was all. The C.C.F., though it gained in strength, did not repeat the sudden rise of the Progressive party in 1921. And Mackenzie King, with the swollen following of wartime not too seriously reduced, was given a final lease of authority on comfortable terms.

The middle-of-the-road party was back in office again. The sedate, unhurried journey down the middle of the road was resumed once more. There was little disposition, in that first summer of the peace, to wander off up inviting by-paths or, in a moment of abandon, to leave the highway for the freedom of the woods and pastures on either side. The country hoped for prosperity and feared a depression; but it was very far from being socialist-minded. The Liberal party had gradually appropriated much of the social service programmes of successive third parties, and had, in fact, provided Canada with an acceptable variant of the welfare state. In 1941, after a necessary amendment to the British North America Act, the National Unemployment Insurance Act came into operation; and three years later, the federal Parliament adopted a comprehensive and expensive scheme of Family Allowances for all children under sixteen. Now, at the close of the war, and moved, no doubt, by a determination to prepare in advance for the expected post-war slump, the federal government proposed a more ambitious and integrated plan of social security and public investment. There was an obvious occasion for it. The war-time tax agreements between the federal and provincial governments would be running out within another year; and Mackenzie King and his colleagues took advantage of the need for new financial arrangements to return to the unsolved and contentious problem of the division of functions and revenues between the provinces and the Dominion. The politically objectionable proposals of the Royal Commission on Dominion-Provincial Relations, and in particular, the scheme of National Adjustment Grants based on fiscal need, were quietly dropped; but it was quite plain, at the same time, that the federal government clung with determination to the real substance of the famous *Report* of 1940. It still aspired to maintain a position of acknowledged pre-eminence and leadership in the modern Canadian state. It proposed, as the Royal Commission had already proposed and as had been accepted during the war, that the great productive modern taxes — income tax, personal and corporation, and succession duties — should be kept by the Dominion; and it obviously intended to standardize social services, and to time and control public investment, in accordance with a great national plan of its own devising. The provinces, in return for their surrender of revenues and their acceptance of federal leadership, were to be associated with, and assisted in, an elaborate governmental programme for the promotion of social welfare and full employment.

In August, 1945, a Dominion-Provincial Conference, the first since the abortive session of January, 1941, met in Ottawa. The federal government presented its proposals; but it soon became clear that this fresh instalment of the planned economy and the welfare state would encounter the traditional opposition of the powerful central provinces. Quebec and Ontario objected. Ontario presented a detailed counter-proposal. The conference, reconvened in April, 1946, when the Dominion proposed still more generous per capita subsidies, still failed to reach a general agreement. The federal government, in despair, gave up its comprehensive social security plan; and over the next year it proceeded to negotiate a series of more limited agreements by which seven of the provinces transferred a large part of their tax revenues to the Dominion in return for considerably increased subsidies. Once again, the strength of provincial interests and the weaknesses of a constitution, which had been strangely perverted, by judicial decision, from the character which its authors had intended, had sufficed to cripple an important national plan at its inception. The central provinces had triumphed; but they had perhaps not triumphed solely by virtue of their own strength. The Dominion's programme had been designed, in large measure, to meet the onset of an expected post-war depression. But there were few signs of an approaching post-war depression. And the urgency which all the provinces might have felt to make a quick financial settlement with the Dominion was forgotten in the ever-brightening prospect of a post-war boom.

Yet domestic prosperity, by itself, was not enough. Better Dominion-Provincial relations were only one important item in the Canadian government's recovery programme. The proposals for social welfare and public investment constituted the domestic part of the plan; but, for an exporting nation of such relative importance, the other, the external, aspects of reconstruction were perhaps equally significant. Canada had the strongest interest in the restoration of the normal courses of world trade; she had a special and compelling concern in the recovery of Europe. Her overseas markets, particularly the markets in Great Britain and western Europe, had traditionally strengthened the east-west axis of the Canadian economy and protected it against the pressures of North American continentalism. During the war, through loans, outright gifts, and Mutual Aid legislation, Canada had given financial help to the United Kingdom and Europe on a scale which was proportionately larger than that of the

United States; and when peace came, the Canadian government had the best of reasons for deciding that the country's interests could not be better served than by the rehabilitation of Europe and the freeing of international trade.

Canada's efforts were made in ways both general and particular. As one of the world's greatest trading nations, she took a prominent part in the complex negotiations at Geneva which in 1947 resulted in the General Agreement on Tariffs and Trade and its related treaties. Canadian funds, in generous quantities, were put into military relief and into the work of the United Nations Relief and Rehabilitation Administration; and through the Exports Credit Insurance Act, passed in 1944, the Canadian government provided loans for its principal allies in Europe and Asia which by the end of 1947 totalled over half a billion dollars. The greatest loan of all, the $1,250,000,000 loan to Canada's best overseas customer, the United Kingdom, was made in 1946; and in the same year Canada negotiated the controversial Anglo-Canadian Wheat Agreement which for four years gave the United Kingdom a very substantial part of the Canadian crop at prices which, as it turned out, were substantially below those prevailing in the world market.

Yet despite this help and the far greater assistance of the United States, the work of international post-war reconstruction went forward slowly and with great difficulty. The impressively swift recovery of the United States and Canada was exceptional, if not unique. The discrepancy between the buoyant strength of North America and the inert distress of an exhausted Europe became a disturbingly important factor in world affairs. During the first post-war years, Canada's exports to her principal overseas markets remained large; but these big sales were mainly financed by Canadian loans which, as a result of the desperate state of the borrowers, were used up much more quickly than had been anticipated. The economic connection with Europe was by credit; but, as soon as the war was over, the cash nexus ruled once more on the North American continent. The continued high level of prosperity in Canada, which confounded all the experts, led inevitably to large imports from the United States, at steeply rising prices, and payable of course, in cash. The old problem of squaring Canada's accounts with the republic, which had been solved with relative ease in the days of free convertibility, had now become infinitely more difficult; and the large reserves of gold and American dollars which had been accumulated during the war drained rapidly away.

During 1947, the situation went from bad to worse. In the previous summer, the Canadian dollar had been restored to parity with the American dollar; and despite the growing number of critics who now attacked the unwisdom of this step, the government declined to adopt the policy of devaluation as a way out of the country's growing exchange difficulties. Finally, in November, 1947, when the financial drain had become really alarming, the new Finance Minister, Douglas Abbott, announced a variety of restrictions designed to reduce imports from the United States and to limit pleasure travel in the republic. Rapidly the strain grew easier. The reserves began to accumulate again during the next two years. But the experience was an extremely disturbing one. It brought home to Canada the difficulties, present and prospective, which were likely to confront a country with a small population and a large export trade, in an economically divided and unequal world.

It would have been bad enough if these intractable economic disparities had been the one great disappointment of the post-war world. But they were not. The unfulfilled hopes of a workable political organization which would comprehend all nations brought an even more profoundly gloomy disillusionment. The exchange crises, the end of free convertibility, the embarrassments of multilateral trade were misfortunes matched and exceeded by the calamities which overtook the great post-war effort to establish a new general security system. Everything depended upon the concord of the great powers; and the hopes of the world were soon blackened by their strife. The discouraging disagreements reappeared in situation after situation; they were repeated in meeting after meeting and conference after conference. For the most part, the Canadian government merely looked on, a dismayed observer, at the disputes and obstruction in the Council of Foreign Ministers and the Security Council of the United Nations; but in the matter of the future use and regulation of atomic energy, it had its own part to play in the elaborate game of postponement and futility. The contribution which Canada had made to the war-time development of this terrible form of power enabled her to join with Great Britain and the United States in a joint declaration on the subject in November, 1945; and as a result she became a member of the Atomic Energy Commission of the United Nations. There the Canadian delegates were to have ample opportunity for observing how irreconcilable differences of opinion could lead, through repeated disagreements and endless delays, to a feeling of complete and hopeless frustration.

The disenchantment had begun. The Canadian government and its servants grew wearily accustomed to the acrimony and purposelessness of international politics. The Canadian people had already received its first sharp lesson in the bad faith and hostility which still seemed to govern world affairs. On September 5, 1945, Igor Gouzenko, an obscure cipher clerk in the Soviet Embassy in Ottawa, left his job for ever, carrying with him a mass of documents which proved, beyond any question, that Russian agents had been for years directing a fairly extensive spy ring in Canada. Early in February, 1946, after much hesitation and preliminary inquiry, the Canadian government appointed a Royal Commission to investigate the matter; and on February 15, a number of suspected persons were rounded up and held — for some time without communication with the outside world — in the Royal Canadian Mounted Police Barracks in Ottawa. These and other witnesses were carefully examined *in camera* by the Royal Commission; and in the end, on the basis of the information collected, eighteen persons were brought to trial, of whom eight were found guilty and imprisoned.

The Canadian people watched these unexpected and dramatic events with very mixed feelings. Regret and some incredulity were expressed as well as shocked surprise and indignation. The arbitrary methods which the government had resorted to in order to obtain evidence aroused deep concern in the minds of many Canadians; and the great capital of good will which the U.S.S.R. had accumulated during the war was not easily exhausted by a single deception. The scales of judgment seemed to hang evenly for a while. Then they tilted slowly against the kind of treachery which the investigation had revealed and the nation which had inspired it. Throughout the whole of West Europe and North America, the attitude of peoples and governments to the U.S.S.R. began to change. Disputes and obstruction had been the first ominous signs of Russian ill will and aggressive purpose; and these were succeeded, during 1946-48, by still more disturbing evidences of the expansive and dictatorial nature of revolutionary communism. The establishment of the Cominform, the tightened Communist control of the satellite countries in Eastern Europe, and, above all, the terrifying swiftness and completeness of the *coup d'état* in Czechoslovakia in the winter of 1948, all combined to drive home the fear of a vast Russian imperialist design. A different, militant, and threatening way of life was suddenly revealed. A vast part of the world was evidently organized as an armed and hostile camp. And under the leadership of the United States, which moved forward vigorously to assume the direction and main burden of defence, the nations of West Europe and North America began to draw together for protection.

The 'age of the titans' had arrived. The truth of 'the inevitable rivalry between the great powers', which Mackenzie King had complacently denied, had apparently been proved once more. Lord Halifax had been right; but the power politics which were to rule the world henceforth were of an even starker simplicity than he had predicted. The peace of the world did not depend upon a balance of strength among four great powers. There were not four great powers. There were two super-powers, and two super-powers only; and the independent and sufficient support which Great Britain had given Canada in the nineteenth century was no longer available, even if the Dominion had wanted it. By the force of circumstance, as well as by her own choice, Canada was 'on her own' as a middle power; and it became quickly clear that both strategically and politically, being in the middle was in fact a highly uncomfortable and exposed position. Between the two great continental empires of North America and Eurasia, Canada had become, in fact, a potential Belgium. And in an age of atom bombs and aerial attack, the North Polar Sea was a quick and obvious invasion route, and the Canadian northland an open and undefended frontier.

There was only one choice; and Canada accepted what was forced upon her by ineluctable circumstances. In February, 1947, a month before the Truman doctrine of aid to Greece and Turkey was made public, a joint statement, issued at Ottawa and Washington, announced the resumption of Canadian-American collaboration in the defence of North America. The Permanent Joint Board on Defence was to be continued; the main principles on which it was to carry on its work were carefully laid down. It was the first important military commitment undertaken in the light of the Soviet threat; it had been preceded by a good deal of excited and grandiose talk in Washington about the requirements of northern defence; and the knowledge that Canada had been fitted with such astonishing speed and lack of ceremony into a continental system dominated by the United States filled a great many Canadians with resentment and misgivings. A few months later in the summer of 1947, when a bill was presented empowering American military authorities to maintain discipline over their forces in Canada, this angry fear of Canada's degradation to the level of an American military satellite found vigorous expression in Parliament. The government sought to convince Canadians that the scope of the joint military undertakings would be limited and that within it Canadian sovereignty had been carefully preserved. By the terms of the new agreement, concessions were, at least in principle, to be reciprocal, and Canada was to maintain control over all operations in her own territory. There were to be no American bases on Canadian soil; but the two governments undertook certain joint military exercises under Arctic conditions, set up a series of northern weather stations, and, later on, began to lay down radar defence lines.

Yet, if the hope of a new general security system was to be realized, continental defence was clearly not enough. If the United Nations were to fail to maintain world order, then, both for its own sake as well as that of others, Canada was not prepared to rest its defence within the fortress of North America. To accept a position as a solitary northern protectorate of one of the super-powers would be humiliating enough; but it would be infinitely more mortifying, in times of possible crisis, to surrender the historic connections with Great Britain and Western Europe. A satisfactory response to the threat of Soviet aggression — the Canadians instinctively reasoned — would have to be a transatlantic response, made by a union of nations on both sides of the ocean. It was not, of course, a peculiarly or uniquely Canadian solution of the difficulty of the moment; but it was a solution which satisfied Canada's historic interests and existing position very nicely. Some of the earliest expressions of the basic ideas behind the future North Atlantic Treaty

Organization came from Canadian statesmen. There were plain hints of it in the summer and autumn of 1947. In April, 1948, after the formation of the Brussels Pact in Europe, Louis St. Laurent, the Secretary for State for External Affairs, announced Canada's readiness 'to associate ourselves with other free states in any appropriate collective security arrangement'. In June, following the passage of the Vandenberg resolution in the American Senate, he defined much more precisely the composition and geographical limits of the western union which he had in mind. Less than a month later, Canada joined with the Brussels Treaty powers and the United States in exploratory discussions at Washington. The formal negotiations began in December. On April 4, 1949, L. B. Pearson, the new Minister of External Affairs, signed the North Atlantic Treaty for Canada; and on April 29 it was ratified by the Canadian Parliament.

Outwardly, at least, the signing of the North Atlantic Treaty marked a radical, an unprecedented, change in the nature of Canadian foreign policy. The contractual obligations which Canada had already assumed through membership in the League of Nations and the United Nations were onerous enough; but the new Treaty imposed the precise and binding commitments of a military alliance. It was true, of course, that these commitments were a good deal less automatic than those already accepted by members of the Brussels Pact, for Canada, as well as the United States, was anxious to preserve a certain discretionary freedom of action and her own right to declare war. But, however they were qualified, the obligations were clear and inescapable. Canada had taken a leading part in the advocacy and negotiation of the Treaty. Was not this a revolutionary departure from the cautious and complacent detachment of the 1930's?

And yet, despite this apparently decisive break with the past, the historic continuity of Canadian external relations had been maintained. A treaty which included both Great Britain and the United States, which linked Western Europe and North America, obviously served Canada's traditional general interest; and the particular claims which she had made, as a middle power and as a principal exporting nation, each found recognition in different parts of the document. Article II, which concerned economic collaboration and for which the Canadians were largely responsible, expressed their instinctive belief that the North Atlantic region should be regarded as a social and cultural community as well as a military organization, and that exchange difficulties and tariff barriers should not be permitted to divide and weaken it. Article IX established a council on which all the parties to the Treaty were to be represented. It gave Canada a voice in the determination of policy as well as a share in the burden of carrying it out; and it therefore went far to satisfy the claim which successive generations of Canadian states- men had been making in respect of co-operative undertak- ings inside and outside the Commonwealth. 'That is one reason,' L. B. Pearson told the House of Commons, 'why I attach so much importance to the Council which will be set up under the proposed treaty and which is a genuine agency for collective consultation and collective decisions . . .'

In April, 1949, when the North Atlantic Treaty was rati- fied, it was nearly four years since the San Francisco Con- ference had met — nearly four years since the war with Germany had ended. For Canada, as for the rest of the world, they had been years of bitter experience and painful readjustment. The nation had certainly not entered the post- war world with the blind eyes of over-confidence. It had realized that the task of repairing the material destruction of the war and of building a new international order would be long and difficult. Complete or instant success had never been assumed; but four years had proved to the Canadian people that even so they had expected too much and allowed too little time. The post-war world was a harsh world in which a nation could learn to live only by experience and realistic effort. A process of education had been required, and now it was nearly complete. The Canadians had succeeded in coming to terms with their new existence. The country was reasonably prosperous. The first, most obvious economic difficulties of the peace were now in the way of being overcome. And an effective response, mainly satisfying so far as Canada was concerned, had been found to the threat of Soviet aggression. In all these affairs, the nation had played a fairly active part. Without any question it had gained in stature and prestige during the process.

The entrance of Newfoundland into Confederation — the completion of the plan for a united British North America which had been conceived over eighty years before — summed up this new sense of national maturity as nothing else could possibly have done. The war, of course, had vastly increased Canada's contacts with the island and revived her old interest in its ultimate political destiny. The war had also completed Newfoundland's recovery from the financial collapse into which it had fallen during the depression, and brought within sight the term of the Commission government which had been administering its affairs ever since 1934. In September, 1946, a popularly elected Convention met in St. John's to make recommendations for the constitutional future of the oldest dominion. A proposal, made by Joseph Smallwood, one of the members, that a mission of inquiry should be sent to Ottawa, was at first rejected and then, at a later day, accepted by the Convention; and during the summer of 1947 a delegation arrived from Newfoundland and discussed with Canadian ministers and civil servants a possible basis for the island's entrance into Confederation.

There were other possible destinies, however. In the end, after the Convention had disbanded, the British government decided to put the issue squarely before the people in a referendum. The electorate was invited to make a choice among the three possibilities: Commission government for another five years, responsible government as it had existed in 1933, and Confederation with Canada. The first referendum, held in June, 1948, decided nothing but the rejection of Commission government. The second vote, which took place over a month later, gave Confederation a close majority, with the outposts voting strongly in its favour and St. John's and the Avalon peninsula supporting responsible government and a separate provincial existence. The second vote settled the issue. By December the terms of union had been arranged. It was no easy matter to fit a relatively simple, economically undeveloped and politically immature colony such as Newfoundland into the much more complex Canadian system. But it was done and done generously. And on March 31, 1949, with its own provincial legislature, six Senators and seven members of Parliament, the island began its course as the tenth province of the Canadian union.

Months before this occurred, Mackenzie King was out of office. But before he resigned the leadership of the Liberal party and the office of Prime Minister, his government had, in effect, completed Canadian Confederation. Macdonald had largely created the original union, and had brought in the three additional provinces of Manitoba, British Columbia, and Prince Edward Island. Laurier, his great successor, had added Alberta and Saskatchewan. And it was perhaps not inappropriate that, after an interval of over forty years, the honour of accepting the tenth and last province and thus finishing the original design of a united British North America had been reserved for William Lyon Mackenzie King. There was, to be sure, a grave defect in the achievement. Newfoundland entered Confederation encumbered by the ninety-nine-year American military leaseholds; and the base, a primitive form of military imperalism, grimly questioned Canada's claim to control her own affairs. Yet military leases, King may have reasoned, were not everlasting. Time had always been on his side. Time was on Canada's side. He had tried to maintain the nation's unity, to preserve its identity, to guard the infinite possibilities of its future.

[*IV*]

The mid-point of the century rapidly approached. The war was nearly five years away. The dangers, disappointments, and difficulties of the first agitated post-war years had been met and solved in some fashion or other. There were signs everywhere that the country was entering a new, different, and probably very important phase in its development. A new generation was assuming control of the nation's affairs; and its arrival was symbolized by the appearance of two new political leaders on the national scene. George Drew, the highly successful Conservative Premier of the Province of Ontario, replaced John Bracken as leader of the Progressive-Conservative party; and Louis St. Laurent, who had been elected to the leadership of the Liberal party at its convention in the summer of 1948, succeeded King as Prime Minister in the following November.

St. Laurent's rise to prominence and power had been extraordinarily rapid. It was only six years before, on the death of Ernest Lapointe, that he had joined the Cabinet as Minister of Justice. Fluent in both languages, half French and half Irish by birth, he certainly possessed some important basic assets for a useful and successful career in Canadian politics. But in 1941, when he first accepted office, he had no political experience whatever. His manner seemed a little stiffly formal, his voice somewhat harsh. Yet the proofs of his ability were quickly furnished. The conscription crisis of 1944 gave him an influence in the Cabinet which certainly equalled that of the departed Lapointe. The constructive part which he played as Secretary of State for External Affairs suggested that here was a statesman who might well stand in the great tradition of Laurier. He had demonstrated his courage and self-reliance while King was still in the Cabinet; and, once established as Prime Minister, he soon proved how great was the prestige and the following which he had acquired in his own right. In the golden June of 1949, only a few months after Newfoundland had entered Confederation and the North Atlantic Treaty had been signed, the Canadians flocked to the polls again in a new general election. It was the first encounter between the new Liberal and Conservative leaders; and, under St. Laurent, the Liberals emerged victorious with the stupendous total of one hundred and eighty-nine seats in the House of Commons. Not even King in the war-time election of 1941 had done as well.

A French-speaking Canadian again at the helm of national affairs! The omens were auspicious. Laurier had brought national expansion, national integration, and national prosperity to Canada. Could St. Laurent do the same? Laurier had said — it was perhaps the most famous of his sayings — that 'the twentieth century belongs to Canada'. The aphorism, repeated by countless after-dinner speakers and hopefully taught to millions of school children, had been only partly realized in the first half of the century. Would the second half see it really come true? Fifty years ago, a fortunate, an almost magical, combination of favourable circumstances had completed the settlement of the Canadian West and brought it rapidly into full-scale production. In those days the tide of grain pouring out of the western wheatlands had been like the golden river in the fairy story which enriched and fructified all the barren, lifeless country through which it passed. The whole national economy, so long and tragically dormant during the depression of the last quarter of the nineteenth century, responded eagerly to this new stimulus. The rapid expansion of eastern industry matched the headlong progress of the agricultural West. And, for the first time, Sir John Macdonald's conception of a settled, prosperous, transcontinental country, solidly based on an east-west economic axis, had come to be a reality. The West had made a nation. Wheat was the solid foundation and the golden crown of Canada's success.

In this triumphant fashion, the first half of the century had opened. Would the commencement of the second half see a repetition of the same inspiring prosperity? Would St.

Laurent preside over the same kind of success as had Laurier? This time, it was obvious, the prime physical sources of good fortune would not be exactly the same. During the past fifty years, the material conditions of national prosperity and national power had unmistakably changed. In the nineteenth century coal and iron had always been acknowledged as the strongest sinews of a diversified and mature economy; and in respect of these basic requirements Canada had seemed notably ill-equipped. The country's main coal deposits were situated in Nova Scotia, Alberta, and British Columbia, far away from the industrial concentration of the central provinces; and, east or west, few important quantities of iron ore had been discovered. In 1945, at the end of the war, these serious deficiencies still existed. But by this time the relative strength or weakness of a country was not being measured in exactly the same way as it would have been a few generations before. There were new factors — metals, fuels, sources of energy — which emphatically had to be taken into account. In the past half-century, oil, natural gas, hydro-electric power, and uranium had all acquired a tremendous importance.

How would the Canada of the second half of the twentieth century meet these requirements? Where would she be ranked in an age of new sources of power? Favourable answers to these questions were not likely to be found in the original Maritime Provinces, which had long been settled and exploited. The southern lowlands of Ontario and Quebec would probably have something of great importance to contribute, for the projected St. Lawrence seaway would vastly enlarge the supplies of hydro-electric power, as well as the volume of traffic on the great river and its lakes. The west and the north, however, would in all likelihood settle the question of Canadian development for the next fifty years. The western prairies, an extension of the great plains which stretched northward from the Gulf of Mexico to the Arctic Ocean, were obviously a known or potential source of other forms of wealth and power; and north of the prairies and the lowlands of the St. Lawrence lay the enormous complicated riddle of the Precambrian Shield. Long before 1939, uranium had been added to the impressive list of precious and base metals which were extracted from the Shield; and by the time the war ended, it was perfectly evident that in respect of the newest and most terrible of all sources of energy, atomic power, Canada was strong enough to be associated with the greatest nations. Eldorado Mining and Refining Limited, the company which had been founded to exploit the first great uranium discovery on Great Bear Lake, was expropriated by the federal government in 1944; and at the end of the war, the atomic pile at Chalk River near Ottawa, like the similar greater enterprises in the United Kingdom and the United States, was producing energy by nuclear fission.

The work of prospecting these immense regions of the west and north was laborious, expensive, and frustrating. But as soon as peace came, it was resumed with the old pertinacity and enthusiasm; and there followed a series of exciting mineral discoveries which equalled or surpassed in value those of the inter-war years. A number of fresh deposits of uranium was found; new base-metal mining enterprises were begun; and in 1947 came two other discoveries of perhaps even greater fundamental importance. In that year systematic surveys began to reveal the full possibilities of the enormous body of iron ore whose existence, close to the boundary of northern Quebec and Labrador, had been known since before the war; and, far away to the west, the long, dogged search for petroleum on the Canadian plains led, on February 13, to the discovery of the Leduc oil field, some sixteen miles south-west of Edmonton. This, which was the first important find since that of the Turner Valley field over thirty years before, might have been an isolated stroke of good luck; but Woodbend, some four miles north of Leduc, and the still more important Redwater, thirty-five miles north-east of

Edmonton, which were both discovered in the following year, proved conclusively that it was not. In the next few years, with the discovery of other though less important wells in Alberta, and a few finds in Saskatchewan and Manitoba, the growth of the western Canadian oil industry became the most spectacular economic development in Canada. The number and capacity of the refineries in western Canada were greatly increased. The domestic needs of the three prairie provinces were soon met, and the search for more remote markets began. A pipe-line was constructed from Edmonton to the head of the Great Lakes, and then to Sarnia, in southern Ontario; another pipe-line soon bore western crude oil across the Rocky Mountains to the refineries of Vancouver and the adjacent United States. In the six years from 1947 to 1952, the production of oil in the Province of Alberta rose from less than seven million barrels to sixty million barrels a year; and although consumption for all purposes increased very rapidly in Canada during the same period, Canadian wells were producing over forty per cent of the nation's requirements by 1952.

Yet the promise of the second half of the century did not lie simply in material things — in western fuels, northern metals, hydro-electric power and atomic energy. It lay also, and above all, in the people. And once again, after an interval of nearly thirty years, the rate of Canada's population growth was swinging upwards with confident vigour. In the past, the years from 1901 to 1921 had been the two proudest decades in the rise of the nation's human resources. In 1901-11, the period of the Laurier boom, Canada's relative rate of increase was the highest in the world; in 1911-21, Australia alone had narrowly succeeded in recording a higher gain. And now, as the second half of the century opened, the new census revealed the fact that in the turbulent decade of the 1940's the rate of increase had fairly closely approached that of 1911-21. Immigration, which had almost entirely ceased during the war, recommenced with the peace, but not

yet in numbers which were likely to make it as important
a factor in population growth as it had been in the early
decades of the century. Emigration abroad, particularly to
the United States, was also evidently declining in importance.
The increased population with which the Canadians entered
the second half of the century was very largely the result of
a growth of the native stock. The marriage rate had abruptly
advanced in the last years of the war; the birth rate was up.
And in 1951, when the decennial census revealed a population for the ten provinces of slightly over fourteen million
people, the nation felt confident that it stood simply at the
beginning of a very great and sustained increase in its human
resources.

It was certain also, as the first years of the second half of
the century went quickly past, that there was little chance
of these new Canadian resources, both human and material,
lying idle for some time to come. Massive supplies of capital
were necessary to develop the new metals and fuels and to
supply industry with its new equipment. A great and continued demand, both at home and abroad, for Canada's raw
materials and manufactured products was required to maintain a high level of domestic prosperity. World circumstances might have been unfavourable, as almost everybody
had feared and predicted at the end of the war; but instead,
as everybody was now driven to recognize, world circumstances, for better or worse, could hardly have been more
advantageous. The expected post-war depression had never
arrived. The demand, long pent-up during the war, for con-
sumer goods continued to sustain a high level of employment; and now, as the hopes for the swift success of the
United Nations faded, a new and powerful impetus was given
to the onward movement of the industrial machine. The
days of post-war retrenchment and disarmament were over.
The formation of NATO was, in fact, an emphatic formal
announcement that a period of active rearmament was in
full swing. Peace still lasted; but it was an uncertain and

precarious peace. And a little over a year after the signing of the North Atlantic Treaty it suddenly ended. In June, 1950, just as Canada was preparing to enter the second half of 'its' century, the war in Korea began.

The Korean War was a characteristic episode in the new age of great-power politics which Canada, like all other nations, had just been obliged to enter. The world was divided into two great political camps, which had become, or were becoming, armed camps; and into these two battlemented enclosures most of the states of the world had crowded, either eagerly or reluctantly, but in all cases with fearful appreciation of the realities of isolation. Over these two vast, frightened divisions of the human race, the two super-powers, Russia and the United States, had assumed a large measure of direction and control. Both the United States and Russia possessed enormous areas for expansion. They were separated from each other by enormous distances. But the new methods of aerial and atomic attack had brought them within point-blank range. And during the last few years their growing rivalry had been characterized by a feverish search for allies and a frantic pursuit of strategic advantages.

At the mid-point of the twentieth century, the fortunes of each side in this game of global strategy were not unevenly balanced. The year 1949, which saw the creation of NATO, had brought the Atlantic powers and their great leader an important diplomatic victory in Western Europe. But in the Far East, on the other hand, the same twelve months had witnessed a signal victory for Communism in the defeat of the Kuomintang and the triumph of the Chinese People's Republic. For a time it looked as though the United States was prepared to accept this new state of affairs and its probable consequences. General Chiang-Kai-Shek, who had latterly received no additional American aid, was compelled to retire to the island of Formosa. Korea remained arbitrarily divided at the thirty-eighth parallel in accordance with the arrangement which Russia and the United States had determined on after the surrender of the peninsula by the Japanese. The southern Republic of Korea was as obviously a client of the United States as the northern Democratic People's Republic of Korea was a client of the U.S.S.R. But both great powers had withdrawn their forces from the region.

The North Korean attack on the South Korean Republic, which took place on June 25, 1950, provoked a swift change in the policy of the United States. At its request, the Security Council of the United Nations met on the same afternoon; and, in the absence of the Soviet representative, passed a resolution demanding an immediate cessation of hostilities and the withdrawal of the North Korean forces to their own side of the thirty-eighth parallel. Two days later, on the strength of this resolution alone, and before the Security Council had decided directly to request the assistance of the United Nations in repelling the armed attack on South Korea, President Truman ordered American naval and air forces to give cover and support to the South Korean troops. He did more than this; at the same time he also directed the Seventh Fleet of the American navy to insulate by force the island of Formosa from the Chinese, Communist-controlled mainland. Thus, from the very beginning, the United Nations' policy concerning Korea was complicated by the private decision of the United States regarding Formosa. The intervention of the Security Council in Korea had as its sole legitimate purpose the stopping of armed aggression; but the insulation of Formosa could only too easily be regarded as an important strategic move in the American programme for the military containment of Communism.

The double purpose which was implicit in these initial actions of the United States also seemed to find expression, as time went on, in the words and actions of American political and military leaders and in the American conduct of the Korean War. The brilliant offensive which General Mac-Arthur launched was continued past the thirty-eighth parallel and up to the very borders of China, in the face of the evidently growing doubt and apprehension of the principal allies of the United States. Communist China, who had promised that she would not stand idly by if the thirty-eighth parallel were crossed, intervened at this point, with great strength and very successfully; and when the first effort to compose this more serious conflict by a cease-fire proved not completely successful, the United States sought at once to have China declared an aggressor by the United Nations. Finally, it was not until April, 1951, after he had again threatened to broaden the scope of the conflict by attacking China, that General MacArthur was dismissed from his post as United Nations commander by President Truman.

In this troubled and ambiguous war, which was confused by cross-purposes and insufficiently regulated by the United Nations, Canada pursued, on the whole, a fairly consistent course. On the one hand, the Canadian government was prepared to honour its pledges to the United Nations and to assist in stopping armed aggression; but, on the other hand, it was equally anxious to keep the war focused on its original purpose, to prevent any enlargement of its scope or change in its character, and to bring it to a conclusion as quickly as possible. Units of the Canadian Navy and the Royal Canadian Air Force gave support to the United Nations' cause in the early weeks of the war. In November, 1950, a battalion of Princess Patricia's Canadian Light Infantry, the first detachment of a brigade which was being organized as the Canadian contribution to the war, sailed for Korea. It was joined, in the following spring, by other battalions of the Royal Canadian Regiment and the Royal Twenty-second Regiment. The completed Canadian brigade became an important unit of the Commonwealth Division and continued in service throughout the duration of the war.

In these important ways, Canada espoused the cause of the United Nations and accepted the direction of the military authority which the United Nations had appointed. Collective resistance to aggression was a principle which the Canadian government was prepared to act upon; but it was not ready to accept the view that the principle justified a war against Communist China or a serious division between West Europe-America on the one hand and Asia on the other. Like Great Britain, the senior partner in the Commonwealth, Canada was inclined to sympathize with India's concern for Asian nationalism and to assist India's efforts to limit and terminate the war. Canada was represented on the original Cease-Fire Group appointed in December, 1950, at the instance of a number of Asian and Middle Eastern powers. Canada regarded the American resolution naming China as an aggressor in Korea as 'premature and unwise' and voted for it reluctantly. In the autumn of 1952, when the second prolonged attempt at a cease-fire broke down completely over the problem of the repatriation of prisoners, the Canadian delegation at the United Nations warmly supported the solution proposed by India; and in the late summer of 1953, after the armistice had been finally concluded, Canada, Great Britain, Australia and New Zealand proposed that India should send a delegate to the political conference which was to be called to settle the terms of a permanent peace.

On the whole, throughout the war, Canada had urged counsels of moderation and conciliation. Her position had been her own. The persistence with which she had held to it was an indication of her new-found sense of strength and maturity. The nation's new responsibilities as a member of the United Nations, as a signatory of the North Atlantic Treaty, and as an associate of the United States in the defence of North America were all seriously regarded; but in addition the struggle in the Far East had taught Canada to see a new value and usefulness in the historic Commonwealth connection. In the past few years, this old association had been radically altered by the granting of independence to India, Pakistan, and Ceylon, and by the free decision of these realms or republics to remain within the Commonwealth. The self-assertive days of 'Dominion status' were over; and Canada herself had just put the last finishing touches on this completed chapter in her history. The Canadian Citizenship Act of 1947 had established the dual loyalty of the Canadian citizen who is also a British subject. Appeals from the Supreme Court of Canada to the Judicial Committee of the Privy Council were finally abolished in 1949; in 1950 the Parliament of Canada took power to amend the substantial part of the British North America Act relating to federal powers; and early in 1952, to the great satisfaction of many Canadians, Mr. Vincent Massey, the first native-born Canadian to hold the office, was appointed Governor-General of Canada. The problem of status, the concern for equality were no longer important. The Commonwealth had become a collective association which was valuable for the world as a whole as well as for the free and equal nations which comprised it. It had been the oldest, the most deeply felt expression of Canada's concern for the strength and welfare of Western Europe. It had now become a means of intimate and informal communication — 'a genuine bridge of understanding', as Mr. St. Laurent called it — between the West and the East.

The same robust feeling of confidence in the future found expression in Canada's words and deeds as a North American power. Nobody troubled any longer to give serious consideration to the old fear of annexation to the United States. The idea of an alternative political destiny for the northern half of the North American continent seemed preposterous and incredible. In the early post-war years, a popular American periodical incautiously attempted to revive the venerable project of a North American commercial union; but Canadian public opinion, in slightly varying tones of boredom, impatience, or anger, showed itself unanimously opposed. The United States was Canada's best customer, her senior partner in the business of North American defence, and the principal external source of the capital which was developing her new resources. A multitude of associations, which were the result of friendly propinquity and similar ways of life, bound the two countries together at all levels of human experience and activity. These relationships were close and important; but they did not weaken Canada's consciousness of her own identity or her belief in her own standards and values. They did not qualify her determination to safeguard her own political and economic future and to express her own independent view of world affairs.

Canadians made their position clear to their American neighbours with careful moderation — a moderation which befitted the citizens of a responsible 'middle power'. But, in these early years of the second half of the century, a questioning and critical note became more sharply evident in their speech. The implications of the Canadian-American defence programme — and particularly of the American-built and -manned radar installations in the far north — were obviously causing the nation a good deal of concern. The long delay of the United States in ratifying the St. Lawrence Seaway Agreement and the bargain terms on which the republic subsequently entered the project at the eleventh hour, were both exasperating to Canadians; and they were astonished and angered to discover that Canada's proposals for the development of the Columbia River had been held up in the International Joint Commission by the protests of hydro-electric power interests on the American side of the line. There were signs of growing perturbation over the possible consequences of large-scale American investment in Canadian mining, manufacturing, and petroleum industries. The commercial war of nerves against importers, carried on under the generous sanction of the American tariff, baffled Canadian manufacturers. The American government subsidies, lavishly granted in aid of the export of American wheat abroad, hurt and angered the primary producers of the Canadian prairies. McCarthyism, with its sinister mixture of informers, slander, and intimidation, genuinely shocked Canadians; and over many aspects of international affairs, including the Far East in general and the Korean War in particular, they were often in sharp disagreement with their neighbours to the south.

Unquestionably the nation was more conscious than ever before of its corporate identity, its separate interests, its distinctive point-of-view. It was making a far more vigorous and serious effort than it had ever done to free itself and find itself. Material success, as great as that of Laurier's day or greater, seemed assured. But would this be accompanied by any corresponding achievement in the things of the mind and the spirit? Canada had known to the full the bitter experience of every small country which attempts vainly to find an outlet or a hearing for its ideas, its scholarship, its letters, and its artistic impulses. English-speaking Canada had been a cultural colony of two nations, the United Kingdom and the United States; French-speaking Canada, though its different language afforded some protection for its spiritual independence, was only slightly less vulnerable to external influences. Most Canadians spoke the same language as the citizens of the two nations which had dominated the English-speaking world during the nineteenth century and would continue to dominate it through the twentieth. All Canadians had the best of reasons for knowing that a great art and a great literature are normally the possession of great powers. In Great Britain and the United States were established the universities, libraries, art galleries, museums, learned societies, publishing houses, newspapers, periodicals, broadcasting and television systems which were, or had been, the pride of the English-speaking world. It was from these centres, in the past, that Canadians had got much of their intellectual stimulus and aesthetic satisfaction. It was to these centres that Canadians had been accustomed for a long time to go for advanced education, special training, artistic careers, literary publication, and recognition of all kinds.

It was impossible for a Canadian to become a part of one of these cultural empires except on its own terms. It was difficult for him to gain admittance at all except by abandoning a part, or the whole, of his own tradition or special point-of-view. The mere possession of talent was clearly not enough; the favourable circumstances upon which talent depended for its development were the exclusive monopoly of the great powers. The artistic and literary achievement of one of these great powers might be very fine or extremely feeble; but fine or feeble, it was glorified by political prestige. It was supported and maintained by the elaborate communication system which invariably accompanied political and economic preponderance. At the metropolitan centre of each one of these great-power artistic monopolies there was established a relatively small group of artists, musicians, poets, novelists, journalists, critics, and scholars, most of whom were friends and acquaintances, who reviewed each other's works, interpreted and evaluated each other's achievements, composed each other's biographies, and endeavoured to ensure each other's immortality. A Canadian artist or writer who wished to be accepted in this company, could either leave Canada for the metropolitan centre of his choice, or he could give up Canadian themes, except those which were regarded as quaint or barbaric, and therefore interesting, in the artistic and literary capitals of Western Europe and America.

This old state of affairs, like so much else in Canadian life, was gradually but perceptibly changing. In the first years of the second half of the century, the signs of the approach of a new and rather different order grew more numerous; and perhaps one of the most important pieces of evidence was the fact that that typical Canadian institution, the Royal Commission of inquiry, was used to survey the country's cultural possibilities and needs. In the past, the support of the state had been constantly required to promote Canadian social growth and economic well-being; and the appointment, in April, 1949, of a Royal Commission on National

Development in the Arts, Letters, and Sciences, implied that the preservation of Canada's intellectual and spiritual independence was now recognized as an urgent matter of both public and private concern. '. . . It is in the national interest,' declared the Order-in-Council which established the Commission, 'to give encouragement to institutions which express national feeling, promote common understanding, and add to the variety and richness of Canadian life'; and it was in the light of this injunction that the Commissioners plunged into a thorough review of Canadian achievement in scholarship, letters, and the arts, as well as into a careful investigation of the operation of the voluntary associations and federal agencies which sought to encourage these activities. The Commission's *Report*, which was published in 1951, included a number of particular recommendations concerning the Canadian Broadcasting Corporation, the National Film Board, and other federal institutions, such as galleries, museums, libraries, and archives. But unquestionably the Commissioners' most important proposal was the establishment by government of a Canada Council, which would give generous encouragement and support to arts, letters, humane studies, and social sciences in Canada.

In the meantime, through the talents and efforts of individual Canadians, the country was slowly ceasing to be a submissive province of a larger cultural empire. On the one hand, the prestige of the great-power literary and artistic monopolies was mysteriously but definitely declining; on the other, the popularity of everything produced in Canada, about Canada, by Canadians, was just as obviously on the increase. It was, no doubt, an excessive preoccupation; but there were signs that the new-found and independent critical spirit had sharpened the Canadians' attitude to their own productions as well as their reception of imports from abroad. The communication systems of the great metropolitan centres did not carry quite the same authority and conviction as before. The circuits around which plays and concerts used to travel out from New York no longer operated with nearly their old regularity; and the long procession of English lecturers, which had paraded so confidently through Canada in the 1920's and 1930's, had dwindled away to occasional appearances of not very impressive celebrities, including a few bores or boors. The best-selling books of the United Kingdom and the United States could no longer be certain of either acclaim or a reasonably cordial reception in the Dominion. Canadian novels were beginning to outsell American and British novels three or four times over; the circulation of a Canadian periodical, dealing exclusively in Canadian material by Canadian authors, was twice as great as that of its nearest glossy American competitor. In a few of the principal cities, dramatic repertory companies or symphony orchestras succeeded in establishing themselves; and now a Canadian theatrical production could find it possible to go on a short tour of its own native 'provinces'.

There were still not enough Canadians, of course, to support a prosperously flourishing Canadian literature and art. The Canadian artist or writer who wished to make a reasonable living by his craft would have to consider other markets and other audiences; but at home he would find far more opportunities and far more encouragement than he had ever found before. An intense national curiosity, an awakening national interest, awaited him; and in these first brave years of the second half of the century he was responding to it, in all fields of literary and artistic creation, with a vigour and a competence that he had never yet achieved. In the past, it had usually been a group of artists in one particular craft, such as the poets born in the 1880's or the painters of the Group of Seven, who had captured the country's imagination and won recognition abroad. But now creative energy and artistic talent were far more widely diffused and generously recognized than they had been in the past. The poets, the prose writers, the painters, the composers seemed all to be caught up in a sustained burst of activity such as the nation had never before experienced. Even in the arts of the theatre, drama, ballet, and opera, where almost no native tradition existed, the achievements of the new age were spectacularly sudden. The little theatres, the Dominion Drama Festival, and the Canadian Broadcasting Corporation had helped to train a large company of youthful and energetic talent. It would not be long before the National Ballet Company would be successfully touring a string of cities in Canada and the United States; and in the summer of 1953, one of the greatest of the new enterprises, the Stratford Shakespearean Festival, opened for its first season.

Only a few weeks earlier a new Queen had ascended the throne of Canada and the second Elizabethan age had begun. 'Elizabeth the Second, by the Grace of God of the United Kingdom, Canada and her other Realms and Territories Queen, Head of the Commonwealth, Defender of the Faith' would rule over a strangely varied but mainly youthful group of states. The Realms of the Commonwealth were new to their sovereignty; their great achievements and tribulations lay ahead of them; but not one of the Queen's peoples looked forward to the promise of her reign with more curious interest and eager anticipation than the Canadians. They had survived the perils of the nineteenth century. The ordeals of the first half of the twentieth had toughened them. And they now expectantly faced the most exciting, rewarding, and dangerous period in their collective existence.

BOOKS FOR FURTHER READING

THE following is not meant to be a systematic or comprehensive list of the principal works on Canadian history. It is rather a brief selective reading list, chosen chiefly from the publications of the last twenty-five years, and intended simply for those readers who may wish to pursue the study of Canadian history further. The first section of the list includes books on Canadian history as a whole, or on one of its general themes; the three following sections, which correspond with the three main divisions of Canadian history, include studies of a somewhat more specialized character.

I

GENERAL WORKS

Brebner, J. B. *The Explorers of North America, 1492-1806*. London, 1933.

Brebner, J. B. *North Atlantic Triangle, the Interplay of Canada, the United States, and Great Britain*. New Haven, 1945.

Buchanan, D. W. *The Growth of Canadian Painting*. London, 1950.

Cambridge History of the British Empire. Vol. VI, *Canada and Newfoundland*. Cambridge, 1930.

Clark, S. D. *The Social Development of Canada*. Toronto, 1942.

Clark, S. D. *Church and Sect in Canada*. Toronto, 1948.

Dawson, R. M. *The Government of Canada*. Toronto, 1952.

Easterbrook, W. T., and Aitken, H. G. J. *Canadian Economic History*. Toronto, 1956.

Glazebrook, G. P. de T. *A History of Transportation in Canada* (The Relations of Canada and the United States). Toronto, 1938.

Glazebrook, G. P. de T. *A History of Canadian External Relations*. Toronto, 1950.

Innis, M. Q. *An Economic History of Canada*. Ed. 2. Toronto, 1943.

Kennedy, W. P. M. *The Constitution of Canada, 1534-1937, an Introduction to its Development, Law, and Custom*. Ed. 2. London, 1938.

McInnis, E. W. *The Unguarded Frontier, a History of American-Canadian Relations.* New York, 1942.

Massey, Vincent, *On Being Canadian.* London, 1948.

Pacey, Desmond. *Creative Writing in Canada, a Short History of English-Canadian Literature.* Toronto, 1952.

Putnam, D. F. *Canadian Regions, a Geography of Canada.* Toronto, 1952.

Ross, M. M. *Our Sense of Identity, a Book of Canadian Essays.* Toronto, 1954.

Shortt, A., and Doughty, A. G. (eds.). *Canada and Its Provinces.* 23 vols. Toronto, 1913-17.

Smith, A. J. M. (ed.). *The Book of Canadian Poetry, a Critical and Historical Anthology.* Chicago, 1943.

Stanley, G. F. G. in collaboration with Jackson, H. M. *Canada's Soldiers, 1604-1954, the Military History of an Unmilitary People.* Toronto, 1954.

Wade, Mason, *The French Canadians, 1760-1945.* Toronto, 1955.

II

New France

(Chapters I-III)

Bishop, M. G. *Champlain, the Life of Fortitude.* New York, 1948.

Brebner, J. B. *New England's Outpost, Acadia before the Conquest of Canada.* New York, 1927.

Chapais, T. *The Great Intendant, a Chronicle of Jean Talon in Canada, 1665-1672.* Toronto, 1921.

Colby, C. W. *The Fighting Governor, a Chronicle of Frontenac.* Toronto, 1915.

Crouse, N. M. *Lemoyne d'Iberville: Soldier of New France.* Ithaca, 1954.

Eastman, M. *Church and State in Early Canada.* Edinburgh, 1915.

Fauteux, J. N. *Essai sur l'Industrie au Canada sous le Régime Français.* 2 vols. Quebec, 1927.

Filteau, G. *La Naissance d'une Nation, Tableau du Canada en 1755.* 2 vols. Montreal, 1937.

Graham, G. S. *Empire of the North Atlantic, the Maritime Struggle for North America.* Toronto, 1950.

Harvey, D. C. *The French Régime in Prince Edward Island.* New Haven, 1926.

Innis, H. A. *The Cod Fisheries, the History of an International Economy.* Revised edition. Toronto, 1954.

Innis, H. A. *The Fur Trade in Canada, an Introduction to Canadian Economic History.* Revised edition. Toronto, 1956.

Jenness, D. *The Indians of Canada.* Ottawa, 1932.

Kellogg, L. P. *The French Régime in Wisconsin and the Northwest.* Madison, 1925.

Long, M. H. *A History of the Canadian People.* Vol. I, *New France.* Toronto, 1942.

MacKay, D. *The Honourable Company, a History of the Hudson's Bay Company.* Revised to 1949 by Alice MacKay. Toronto, 1949.

McLennan, J. S. *Louisbourg from Its Foundation to Its Fall, 1713-1758.* London, 1918.

Munro, W. B. *The Seigniorial System in Canada.* New York, 1907.

Newbigin, M. C. *Canada, the Great River, the Lands, and the Men.* London, 1926.

Salone, E. *La Colonisation de la Nouvelle-France.* Paris, 1906.

Waugh, W. T. *James Wolfe, Man and Soldier.* Montreal, 1928.

Wrong, G. M. *The Rise and Fall of New France.* 2 vols. Toronto, 1928.

III

British North America

(Chapters IV-VI)

Brebner, J. B. *The Neutral Yankees of Nova Scotia, a Marginal Colony During the Revolutionary Years.* New York, 1937.

Burt, A. L. *The Old Province of Quebec.* Toronto, 1933.

Burt, A. L. *The United States, Great Britain, and British North America* (The Relations of Canada and the United States). New Haven, 1940.

Chittick, V. L. O. *Thomas Chandler Haliburton ('Sam Slick'), a Study in Provincial Toryism.* New York, 1924.

Cowan, H. I. *British Immigration to British North America, 1783-1837* (University of Toronto Studies). Toronto, 1928.

Creighton, Donald. *John A. Macdonald, the Young Politician.* Toronto, 1956.

Creighton, Donald. *The Empire of the St. Lawrence.* Toronto, 1956.

Filteau, G. *Histoire des Patriotes.* 3 vols. Montreal, 1938-39.

Graham, G. S. *Sea Power and British North America, 1783-1820, a Study in British Colonial Policy* (Harvard Historical Studies). Cambridge, Mass., 1941.

Grant, W. L. *The Tribune of Nova Scotia, a Chronicle of Joseph Howe.* Toronto, 1920.

Kerr, D. G. G. with the assistance of Gibson, J. A. *Sir Edmund Head, a Scholarly Governor.* Toronto, 1954.

Kilbourn, William. *The Firebrand, William Lyon Mackenzie and the Rebellion in Upper Canada.* Toronto, 1956.

Landon, F. *Western Ontario and the American Frontier* (The Relations of Canada and the United States). Toronto, 1941.

Longley, R. S. *Sir Francis Hincks, a Study of Canadian Politics, Railways, and Finance in the Nineteenth Century.* Toronto, 1943.

Martin, C. *Empire and Commonwealth, Studies in Governance and Self-Government in Canada.* Oxford, 1929.

Masters, D. C. *The Reciprocity Treaty of 1854, Its History, Its Relation to British Colonial and Foreign Policy, and to the Development of Canadian Fiscal Autonomy.* London, 1936.

Morton, A. S. *A History of the Canadian West to 1870-71.* London, n. d.

New, C. W. *Lord Durham, a Biography of John George Lambton, first Earl of Durham.* Oxford, 1929.

Shippee, L. B. *Canadian-American Relations, 1849-1874* (The Relations of Canada and the United States). New Haven, 1939.

Sissons, C. B. *Egerton Ryerson, his Life and Letters.* 2 vols. Toronto, 1937-47.

Skelton, O. D. *The Life and Times of Sir Alexander Tilloch Galt.* Toronto, 1920.

Stacey, C. P. *Canada and the British Army, 1846-1871, a Study in the Practice of Responsible Government.* London, 1936.

Trotter, R. G. *Canadian Confederation, Its Origins and Achievement, a Study in Nation Building.* Toronto, 1924.

Tucker, G. N. *The Canadian Commercial Revolution, 1845-1851.* New Haven, 1936.

Whitelaw, W. M. *The Maritimes and Canada before Confederation.* Toronto, 1934.

Wilson, G. E. *The Life of Robert Baldwin, a Study in the Struggle for Responsible Government.* Toronto, 1933.

Wrong, G. M. *Canada and the American Revolution, the Disruption of the First British Empire.* Toronto, 1935.

IV

CANADA SINCE CONFEDERATION

(Chapters VII-X)

Armstrong, E. H. *The Crisis of Quebec, 1914-18.* New York, 1937.

Borden, H. (ed.). *Robert Laird Borden: His Memoirs.* 2 vols. Toronto, 1938.

Canada. *Report of the Royal Commission on Dominion-Provincial Relations.* Book I, *Canada, 1867-1939.* Ottawa, 1940.

Canada. *Report, Royal Commission on National Development in the Arts, Letters, and Sciences, 1949-1951.* Ottawa, 1951.

Creighton, Donald. *John A. Macdonald, the Old Chieftain.* Toronto, 1955.

Dafoe, J. W. *Clifford Sifton in Relation to His Times.* Toronto, 1931.

Dafoe, J. W. *Laurier, a Study in Canadian Politics.* Toronto, 1922.

Dawson, R. M. *Constitutional Issues in Canada, 1900-1931.* London, 1933.

Dawson, R. M. *The Development of Dominion Status, 1900-1936.* London, 1937.

Dawson, R. M. *Canada in World Affairs, Two Years of War.* Toronto, 1943.

Farr, D. M. L. *The Colonial Office and Canada, 1867-1887.* Toronto, 1955.

Forsey, E. A. *The Royal Power of Dissolution of Parliament in the British Commonwealth.* Toronto, 1943.

Gelber, L. M. *The Rise of Anglo-American Friendship, a Study in World Politics, 1898-1906.* London, 1938.

Glazebrook, G. P. de T. *Canada at the Paris Peace Conference.* Toronto, 1942.

Harrison, W. E. C. *Canada in World Affairs, 1949-1950.* Toronto, 1956.

Hedges, J. B. *Building the Canadian West, the Land and Coloniza-tion Policies of the Canadian Pacific Railway.* New York, 1939.

Hughes, E. C. *French Canada in Transition.* Chicago, 1943.

Hutchison, Bruce. *The Incredible Canadian, a Candid Portrait of Mackenzie King: his Works, his Times, and his Nation.* Toronto, 1952.

Keirstead, B. S. *Canada in World Affairs, September 1951 to October 1953.* Toronto, 1956.

Lingard, C. C. and Trotter, R. G. *Canada in World Affairs, September 1941 to May 1944.* Toronto, 1950.

Logan, H. A. *The History of Trade-Union Organization in Canada.* Chicago, 1928.

Lower, A. R. M. *The North American Assault on the Canadian Forest, a History of the Lumber Trade Between Canada and the United States.* With Studies of the Forest Industries of British Columbia by W. A. Carrothers and of the Forest Industries in the Maritime Provinces by S. A. Saunders (The Relations of Canada and the United States). Toronto, 1938.

Lower, A. R. M., and Innis, H. A. *Settlement and the Forest and Mining Frontiers* (Canadian Frontiers of Settlement, vol. 9). Toronto, 1936.

McDiarmid, O. J. *Commercial Policy in the Canadian Economy.* Cambridge, 1946.

MacGibbon, D. A. *The Canadian Grain Trade.* Toronto, 1932.

MacGibbon, D. A. *The Canadian Grain Trade, 1931-51.* Toronto, 1952.

MacKay, R. A., and Rogers, E. B. *Canada Looks Abroad.* Toronto, 1938.

Mackintosh, W. A. *Prairie Settlement, the Geographical Setting* (Canadian Frontiers of Settlement, vol. 1). Toronto, 1938.

Mackintosh, W. A. *The Economic Background of Dominion-Provincial Relations* (Report of the Royal Commission on Dominion-Provincial Relations, Appendix 3). Ottawa, 1940.

MacNutt, W. S. *Days of Lorne, From the Private Papers of the Marquis of Lorne 1878-1883 in the Possession of the Duke of Argyll at Inverary Castle, Scotland.* Fredericton, 1955.

Morton, A. S., and Martin, C. *History of Prairie Settlement and 'Dominion Lands' Policy* (Canadian Frontiers of Settlement, vol. 2). Toronto, 1938.

Morton, W. L. *The Progressive Party in Canada*. Toronto, 1950.

Parker, J. *Newfoundland, 10th Province of Canada*. London, 1950.

Patton, H. S. *Grain Growers' Co-operation in Western Canada* (Harvard Economic Studies). Cambridge, Mass., 1928.

Pope, J. *Memoirs of the Right Honourable Sir John Alexander Macdonald*. 2 vols. Ottawa, n.d.

Schull, Joseph. *The Far Distant Ships, an Official Account of Canadian Naval Operations in the Second World War*. Ottawa, 1950.

Sharp, P. F. *The Agrarian Revolt in Western Canada, a Survey Showing American Parallels*. Minneapolis, 1948.

Skelton, O. D. *Life and Letters of Sir Wilfrid Laurier*. 2 vols. Toronto, 1921.

Soward, F. H., *et al. Canada in World Affairs, the Pre-War Years*. Toronto, 1941.

Soward, F. H. *Canada in World Affairs, from Normandy to Paris, 1944-1946*. Toronto, 1950.

Stacey, C. P. *The Canadian Army, 1939-1945, an Official Historical Summary*. Ottawa, 1948.

Stanley, G. F. G. *The Birth of Western Canada, A History of the Riel Rebellions*. London, 1936.

Index